I0802531

absolute newness
chaos theory
collaborative malleability
configurational irreducibility
dispositional intelligence
double-edged individualism
irreversible temporality
latent arrangements
local nonreplaceability
multivalent force
noncausal adjacency
noncompositional totalities
nonlinear sequence
ontological reversal
patterned idiosyncrasy
positional intelligibility
processual aesthetics
programmatic linkages
quasiperiodic crystals
quintuplet assembly
radical anamnesis
requirement graph
soft zoning
sonic structures
spatial reciprocity
stylistic nonreferentiality
subversive disciplinarity
topological distinctness
transition regions
translation unit

José Aragüez

# Dispositional Intelligence in Architecture

# Dispositional Intelligence in Architecture

# Introduction

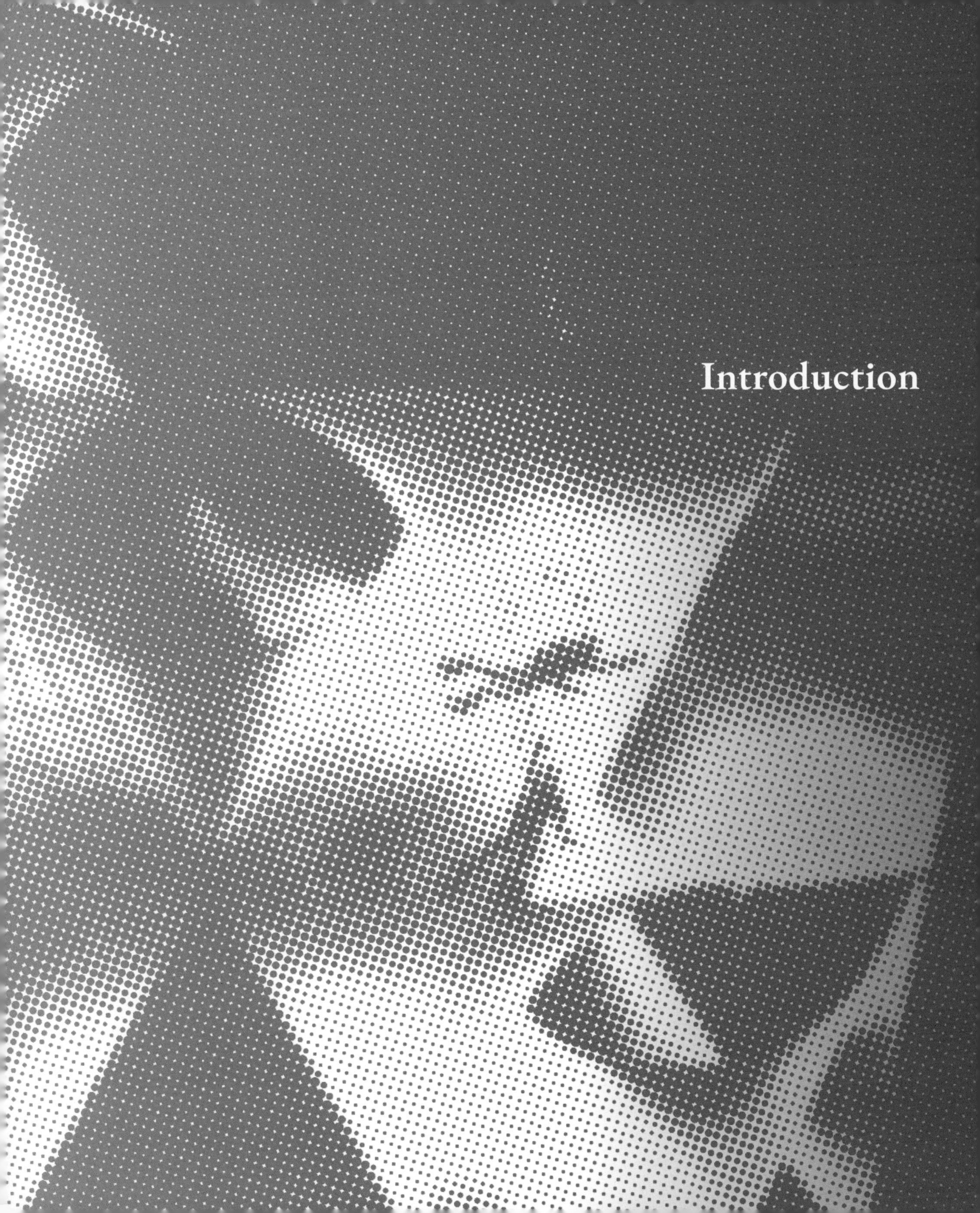

As social, environmental, and political concerns became increasingly pressing over the course of the twentieth century, the question of form in architecture was a constant and was forever evolving. The understanding of form in nature, form as the reification of power structures, the psychology of formal perception, the probing of form's "interiority," form as the catalyst of participatory processes, the phenomenology of form, the relationship between form and formalism—the ubiquity of form in our field can only be taken as a marker of its significance. As Adrian Forty put it, form is perhaps "the most important, but also the most difficult concept within the architecture of this [twentieth] century."[1] Though everywhere, however, the domain of form proper is rarely addressed as a problem in its own right. It has turned into a theoretical black hole in current architectural discourse. With an understanding of it presupposed, it tends to remain in the background of other narratives and discursive formations.

For all its complexity, discussions around form in architecture have too often been grouped around a dualism of supporters of "autonomy" versus factions championing "engagement." This dualism is rather misleading, since, insofar as form is a medium for engagement, a committed attitude is only possible when a deeply informed knowledge of form is available to begin with.[2] It is to the quest for this knowledge that the present work is devoted. While the medium itself and its capacity for engaging with issues pertaining to fields other than architecture (e.g., theology, ethics, or politics) are two sides of a single construct called "form," this book focuses more on the former than on the latter—that is, it focuses on addressing the constituencies of the form-medium, and it does so primarily within the field of architecture. For the goal is to contribute to architectural thinking, understood here as a domain of discursive knowledge both connected to and distinct from the other domains making up the map of the humanities and the social sciences, such as the sociological, the philosophical, and the literary, to mention a few.[3]

Given these premises, the investigation that follows is an attempt to extend the bounds of possibility of the concept of architectural form, where form is understood as a constitutive category for architecture to take place. In contrast to formal epistemologies defined around external envelope, volumetric outline, or "mass," the grounds for this study are established around the notion of spatial organization and related terms such as configuration, arrangement, and disposition—which will be construed as determining a potential for a set of human activities to be housed within a delimited region of three-dimensional space at the

1 Adrian Forty, "Form," in *Words and Buildings: A Vocabulary of Modern Architecture* (New York, NY: Thames & Hudson, 2000), 149.

2 The dualism of "autonomy" and "engagement" has been fueled over the past couple of decades by the common belief that two different approaches to architectural form were mutually exclusive: on the one hand, that of figures like Peter Eisenman and Aldo Rossi, who sought to theorize the architectural form-object as largely cut off from other discursive regimes; on the other, that of authors such as Manfredo Tafuri and, more recently, Pier Vittorio Aureli, for whom the form-object can only be at stake insofar as it is a vehicle for cultural and political participation in general and an instrument to render legible the dominant socio-political forces of late capitalism in particular. For an enlightening way out of this dualism see K. Michael Hays, "Critical Architecture: Between Culture and Form," *Perspecta* 21 (January 1, 1984): 15–29. A similar alternative is addressed by the curatorial premises behind *Small Scale, Big Change*, a show held at the Museum of Modern Art in New York from October 3, 2010 to January 3, 2011. See Hashim Sarkis's "Autonomy as Engagement," in http://www.moma.org/explore/inside_out/2010/10/26/autonomy-as-engagement/. Accessed November 30, 2013.

3 For a more elaborate discussion of this distinction, see José Aragüez, ed., *The Building* (Zürich, Switzerland: Lars Müller Publishers, 2016), 14.

scale of a building. In the context of this book, epistemologies of the first kind will be made to correspond to "shape" and those around spatial organization to form proper.

The platform from which to craft this formal domain is a historically situated discussion of the work of three figures who operated at the margins of architecture: Vittorio Giorgini (1926–2010), Michaël Burt (b. 1937), and Cecil Balmond (b. 1943). Although their bodies of work fell mostly within the purview and scale of architecture, the design thinking of Burt, Giorgini, and Balmond was strongly driven by science and therefore determined to a large degree by aspects historically associated with engineering. Thus, this book suggests that the status of a particular kind of production within architecture (on the edge, simultaneously inside and outside) enables such production to offer a frame for a new conceptualization of form. As will be shown, despite the obvious differences between their design procedures, their work can be read together as featuring a self-defined rigor which, rooted in science, underlies what might appear capricious. Whether through geometrically controlled, topologically sound transformations (Giorgini), the periodical continuity of certain complex geometric structures (Burt), or sequences of numerical templates (Balmond), all three established a relatively consistent set of principles capable of generating what might otherwise come across as whimsical, arbitrary, or just plain weird. It is in the negotiation of these two aspects—and therefore as an index of what sets the production of each author apart in terms of such a negotiation—that this book captures *form's patterned idiosyncrasy*: a qualitative domain of form set within the threshold between that which is rule-governed and that which falls outside received ways of grouping resemblances and differences.

## POST-WAR DEEP SCIENTIZATION OF DESIGN

If aesthetics, style, intuition, and psychology of perception *à la Gestalt* were central to the modern architecture of the first half of the twentieth century, the second half witnessed a shift toward what might be regarded as a deep scientization of the sphere of design that, in Joan Ockman's words, caused "a transition of architecture from a soft to a hard discipline."[4] A sizeable sector of the disciplines around the built environment—with MIT functioning as a node within a network of geographically scattered transatlantic locales—developed an enormous interest in

4 Arindam Dutta et al., eds., *A Second Modernism: MIT, Architecture, and the "Techno-Social" Moment* (Cambridge, MA: The MIT Press, 2013), back cover.

the possibility of establishing scientific grounds on which to base design practice and research. Primarily through the harnessing of systems, the implementation of more and more sophisticated analytical models, and an emphasis on rule-based judgments rooted in logic and mathematics, this epistemology channeled an understanding of the new technologies emerging in the post-war decades—such as those involving information, computers, and artificial intelligence—no longer with a view to problem-solving alone but also with respect to their synthetic, projective capabilities. As a salient consequence of this shift, breaking down formal processes into their smallest sets of constituents gained tremendous precision, which in turn allowed such processes to incorporate a much greater degree of complexity in terms of the relationships between those constituents.

Some commentators have gone so far as to characterize this shift as one giving rise to "a second modernism." While the term may be far-fetched, it does suggest the need to differentiate between the rationalism behind early twentieth-century modernism and that underpinning the shift described above. The former focused primarily on outcome and had to do with functionalism. A consistent emphasis was placed on reasoning through the components of a building in relation to their function, whether a construction detail, a particular room, an assemblage of spaces, or the perceived image of the artifact as a whole. The latter, on the other hand, sought to reason through questions of system and method as relevant to process, with far less regard for function, representation, or even the final outcome itself.

To be sure, early modernism manifested a certain degree of empiricism, systematicity, and positivism relative to the Beaux-Arts tradition. (Some Bauhaus practices claimed to model design methods on scientific procedure, although they did so primarily at an associative or inspirational level.) But early modern architecture also maintained a considerable dose of humanism, spiritualism, and aestheticism that was mostly absent in the rationalism undergirding the shift toward an acute scientization of design, grounded rather in a marked pragmatism. Whereas, formerly, aesthetic volition played an essential role in rational decision-making, this shift left aesthetics behind and, through a heavy reliance on mathematically deduced geometric techniques, algorithms, numerical data, and set theory—as opposed to mere associative or inspirational links to any such domains—it honed in on the deep logic of organizational structures.

In addition to a particular type of rationalism and the grounding of analysis and design methods in actual sciences—in the case of the figures studied here: topology for Giorgini,[5] morphology for Burt, and chaos theory for Balmond—the third aspect that defines the term "deep scientization" as employed here involves an externalization of those analyses and design methods. Their formalization into self-consistent, rigorous procedures enables their use and implementation by anyone

5 As a preliminary definition, it should be indicated that topology refers to the study of spatial relations and geometric properties that remain unaffected by continuous deformations of figures and volumes—deformations including bending, twisting, crumpling, or stretching, but not gluing and tearing.

beyond the person or team that developed them. In a sense, therefore, the process of deep scientization has gone hand in hand with a challenging of authorship as it is traditionally understood.

The overarching paradigm triggered by the intense scientization of design created the conditions which allowed the design approaches of Giorgini, Burt, and Balmond to emerge. Their three bodies of work share strong links to that paradigm, while the attributes differentiating each of them were determined partly by the diverse contexts in which they originated, and partly by the particular characteristics of each designer as a creative individual. As will be shown, Giorgini's topological approach cannot be understood outside the critique of modern architecture in Italy and elsewhere embodied in a number of organicist tendencies; Burt's morphology was directly inspired by that of his teacher Alfred Neumann, which in turn stemmed from—and in some cases turned against—a few of the most conspicuous modernist tropes, notably in regard to theories of proportion and the role of nature; Balmond's philosophy of design was largely ignited by the Frei Otto legacy within ARUP, pointing in a very different direction to Ove Arup's own modernist credo.

## Biological Structuralism

One key modality that shall be seen to underlie all three reactions to earlier forms of modern architecture is a veiled, if complex, biological structuralism. This particular approach to nature—focusing more on deciphering its patterns, structures, and laws than on seeking to imitate its imagery—is also central to the larger shift toward a deep scientization of design. As is well known, the very domain of systems theory (systemic thinking being at the core of that larger shift) was born within biology in the immediate post-war years in an attempt to derive laws applying to relationships between interdependent parts within an organized whole out of the dynamic complexity of organic patterns.[6] Indeed, during the 1950s and 1960s the advancement of science in general, and biological research in particular, along with the availability of more and more powerful visualization technologies, began to uncover a whole new range of previously unseen patterns pertaining to natural life—from bones, plants, material textures, and animal species and habitats, to cosmic rays, viruses, supersonic waves, and atoms. A renewed interest in D'Arcy Thompson's *On Growth and Form* (republished in 1947) and articles such as C. H. Waddington's "Biological Form and Pattern" (published in 1958 in the *Architectural Association Journal*) helped those patterns to be understood both as types of forms and in terms of their structural constitution, revealing the central role of geometry and mathematics in grasping their transformational and relational properties, such as rhythms, symmetries, and divisibility. The theme of biological

6 Ludwig von Bertalanffy, generally considered the father of systems theory, was originally a biologist.

structuralism will therefore be central here in a twofold sense: it encapsulates the role of nature vis-à-vis the general shift toward an intense scientization of design during the second half of the twentieth century, and at the same time connects elements of the coming-into-being of the design ideologies of Giorgini, Burt, and Balmond within their specific contexts to the operative and epistemological milieus to which that shift gave rise.

György Kepes stands out as an essential name in the trajectory of twentieth-century biological structuralism. Composed of images collected largely from various laboratories at MIT between 1947 and 1952—and inspired by the role of scientific imagery in the work of his mentor László Moholy-Nagy—his *The New Landscape in Art and Science* of 1956 became one of the most influential early documents disclosing the spatial appeal of the patterns behind certain natural phenomena and organisms. Kepes can be seen as a hinge figure between pre-war modernism and post-war radical scientization of design. His oeuvre bridged the two kinds of rationalism discussed above, and it did so through some of the tenets of biological structuralism. In an attempt to synthesize art and technology via nature's expressive logic, his project capitalized on the new imaging techniques available at the time, rather substantially engaged a number of scientific domains—such as the behavioral and the physiological—and helped unearth a hidden language directly relevant to questions concerning organizational structure.

The purpose of Kepes's whole enterprise, however, was centered squarely round aesthetics and the psychology of visual perception, which kept it tied to the ethos of the first half of the twentieth century. As this book shows, the production of Giorgini, Burt, and Balmond shared a number of elements pertaining to pre-WWII modern architecture with that of Kepes—such as a particular use of intuition and spontaneity as well as a number of aesthetic biases—while also exhibiting a strong interest in the logics of spatial organization partially driven by biological structuralism. In this regard, it is no wonder that Kepes was first introduced to the intriguing images of the scientific world by a metal-expert friend in the 1930s in much the same way as Giorgini was by physician and natural scientist Hans Jenny some twenty years later; that Kepes emphasized the importance of accepting randomness and even invoking chance events as central to a design process much like Balmond did in his time; and that Burt explicitly acknowledged the influence of Kepes's *The New Landscape*. However, other than these overlaps, the humanism driving Kepes's project, as well as his interest in perception, Gestalt psychology, and visual properties, stood completely at odds in relation to the design frameworks engendered by the three case studies explored here.

## Twofold Idiosyncrasy

While these design frameworks arose in the context of a larger shift toward an acute scientization of the sphere of design and were further determined by conditions relating to the specific locales in which each emerged, it will be shown that they evolved in ways that proved to be idiosyncratic in relation to both levels of contextual influence. Upon looking closely at the most significant applications of the organizational and logical thinking of the designers and researchers partaking in and effecting that larger shift, it becomes clear that they mostly fell outside of architecture. Buckminster Fuller's production is best characterized as pertaining primarily to engineering and industrial design; György Kepes's as art; Christopher Alexander's as mathematical and intellectual; Nicholas Negroponte's as computer science; William Mitchell's as urban theory; Lionel March and Philip Steadman's as building science; the list goes on (environmental design, computer graphics, graphic design, etc.). In still other cases, such as those involving deans and institution directors, the newly acquired sensibility was directed toward managerial, administrative, and financial goals.

In contrast to these alternate applications, Giorgini, Burt, and Balmond belong to a small group of individuals who made use of an intense scientific basis—as opposed to the light scientism of Cedric Price or the Archigram group—to produce a substantial amount of spatial organizations that were directly wired into architectural thinking. As shall be seen, their work also singled itself out with respect to their specific contexts in a number of significant ways: by endowing organicism with a topological basis (Giorgini); by depriving morphology of its humanist and contextualist underpinnings in order to go hardcore scientific (Burt); by interpreting chaos theory in terms of architectural space (Balmond).

When compared to practices centered round a strong scientization of design after the war, Giorgini, Burt, and Balmond's body of work appears idiosyncratic in that it intensely engaged with the production of spatial organizations within architecture. At the same time, such a heightened scientization of design carried with it a shift from an emphasis on aesthetics to questions concerning logic and organizational structures. Consequently, it can be said that it is the very idiosyncratic character of their body of work that facilitates the study of those questions as they relate to architectural form.

The main historical argument of this book can therefore be phrased thus: the architectural thinking embedded in the idiosyncratic character of the oeuvres of Giorgini, Burt, and Balmond—in the context of both the general and the specific conditions which nurtured their emergence—gives rise to a domain of design that constitutes a distinctly appropriate medium to craft a new conceptualization of form in architecture.

## THE HYBRID CONDITION OF THE WORK OF GIORGINI, BURT, AND BALMOND VIS-À-VIS THE FORMAL DOMAIN

The deep engagement of designers and researchers with scientific methods during the immediate post-war decades went hand in hand with the engagement of engineers with these methods. Some commentators argued that such a deep engagement with science early on in that period "began not with architects but with engineers," specifically "at the Ulm Hochschule für Gestaltung in the 1950s."[7] Indeed, the engineering theme appears as a matter of course as soon as the scientization of design being relevant to the production of physical form becomes a topic of discussion. The operational use of aspects pertaining to science and the enactment of a scientific frame of mind with a view to form-making is exactly what some forms of engineering are and have historically been about. It follows that the work of Giorgini, Burt, and Balmond must be understood in relation to engineering on some fundamental level. Yet since the forms they developed fell mostly within the ambit of architecture rather than engineering, it will be necessary to frame their domains of design, more specifically, within the tradition of what might be called *the architecture-engineering hybrid*,[8] devoting much attention to the role of the scientific elements within it.

Trained as architects, Giorgini and Burt dealt with design scenarios that were mostly architectural in nature throughout their careers. In both cases their approaches to those scenarios were deeply influenced by science, Giorgini being closer to the figure of the artist and Burt to that of the geometer. Balmond, on the other hand, is an engineer who grew into a polymath of sorts and ended up developing a design ideology whose ethos was determined by the specificities of architecture. None of them were an architect-engineer in any customary sense, but the work of all three reveals a hybrid condition between engineering and design problems in architecture.

The engineering side of this hybrid condition is based on a number of attributes historically connected with its scientific character. For one thing, Giorgini, Burt, and Balmond sought to rely on an objective basis of knowledge. The central role that pure math and geometry played for them and a marked physical empiricism—particularly present in Burt's and Giorgini's work—signal their need for scientific rigor, which engineers have traditionally pursued with a view to testing

7 As Mary Louise Lobsinger pointed out. See Marie Louise Lobsinger, "Two Cambridges: Models, Methods, Systems, and Expertise," in *A Second Modernism: MIT, Architecture, and the "Techno-Social" Moment* (Cambridge, MA: MIT Press, 2013), 668.

8 The term "architecture-engineering hybrid" relates to Antoine Picon's "hybrid architect engineer." See Antoine Picon, *Marc Mimram: Hybride Architecte Ingénieur = Hybrid Architect Engineer* (Gollion: In folio, 2007). While Picon referred to the figure of one particular hybrid architect-engineer, here a different term is used to more generally allude to a design domain at the intersection of the two disciplines and to suggest implications at an epistemological level.

solutions on solid grounds. Two salient aspects stemming from these inclinations are the rational geometrism at the core of the design principles of Giorgini, Burt, and Balmond, and their recurrent attempts to synthesize structure and form.[9]

Secondly, their production features a reduction of the contextual sphere to that of the object itself. In contrast to what is usually the case for architects—and even though they may begin with a site—culture, history, and memory, as well as the consideration of a broad range of scales, fall outside the main set of concerns for the individuals studied here. The engineer tends to believe that science is what allows for a unique, justifiable structural solution, with questions of tradition and place in the wider sense becoming nearly or completely irrelevant.

Thirdly, Giorgini, Burt, and Balmond shared a strong drive to transpose the teachings of nature to human construction, rather than interpret it as a source of mimicry. Seeking laws from which inspiration can be drawn, their biological structuralism gave great intellectual consideration to the organizational principles of the living world, especially the structure of natural forms, the laws of gravity, inertia and moment diagrams, and the path of light. Nature was for them simultaneously the locus of creative intuition and of reason.

Fourthly, all three relied heavily on procedural thinking, something in which engineering historically specialized well before design turned to science during the second half of the twentieth century. Whether within a sequence defined by origination, construction, and implementation, or at the level of conception alone, their design processes were deeply rooted in the step-by-step nature of such procedural thinking, with consistency and smoothness being qualities often pursued within it. Lastly, Giorgini, Burt, and Balmond displayed a general lack of interest in the experiential dimension, which is connected to the fact that, unlike architecture, engineering design rarely has to cater for the individual needs, tastes, and feelings of its users.

## Architectural versus Engineering Form

As defined here, their hybrid territory of action is further determined by the ways in which these engineering inclinations beget architectural configurations. The complexity of functions and activities to be housed in a building (say, a museum or a school, as compared to a bridge or a dam) gives rise to the characteristic intricacy and relational properties of architectural form in contrast to those of engineering form. With the exception of a building's load-bearing structure—an engineering form to be sure, but one featuring a distinctive internal three-dimensionality determined by architecture's habitability—engineering forms such as roads, shells, and roof structures lack the same degree of intricacy in their unfolding, even when they do so three-dimensionally. Frei Otto's membranes and Heinz Isler's sheds come to mind

9 Such a synthesis fulfills the need to describe form in terms of the scientific parameters typically linked to the genesis of structure. In the work examined below, one of the main manifestations of this drive involves rendering the flow of forces evident in physical realizations.

as relevant examples: their organizational intricacy is practically negligible even when compared to that embodied in a simple single-family house. Fundamental differences in the degree and kind of organizational intricacy distinguish architectural form from engineering form. In this regard, what distinguishes the production of Giorgini, Burt, and Balmond from that of other engineers who also ventured into architecture is that, while both embodied engineering attributes of the kind enumerated above, the former tackles the kinds of spatial organizations that are typically architectural—i.e., those possessing the distinctive intricacy and relational properties derived from being necessarily inflected with a programmatic potential—and the latter does not.

## THE TRADITION OF THE ARCHITECTURE-ENGINEERING HYBRID

Permanent professional hierarchies between architects and engineers only began to articulate themselves fully in the France of the *grand siècle*. A marked hybridity nonetheless remained, for the two professions stayed very much in flux well into the nineteenth century. Architecture—and more generally, design—was crucial to the concerns of engineers during the Enlightenment, as buildings continued to be central to their activities. But a gradual course of change came into being whereby they sought to rationalize the way in which works were conceived and put into practice, relative to the art of the traditional architect. Their goal became to develop an exhaustive definition of the project, from the moment of conception to its materialization, including not only design documents but also the technologies involved and the quantities and prices of materials. Engineers strove for strong, self-consistent continuity within the design process, and this pursuit led to the increasing autonomy of their field of operation, in contrast to the tendency of architects to base their vocabulary upon the imitation of nature. Technological and scientific shortcomings in the eighteenth century only allowed for that rationalization process to be empirical and descriptive, rather than accurately scientific and analytical.[10] But the way was being paved for a novel engineering sensibility to be consolidated. This would only occur after the real split between the disciplines originated in the years between 1794 and 1798.

The troublesome but constituent tension between the engineer and the architect is too well known to be described in full here. However, there is one

10 For example, eighteenth-century engineers did not yet count on accurate stress calculations, which would only become available with the appearance of Claude Louis Marie Henri Navier and Augustin-Louis Cauchy's theories in the nineteenth century.

specific aspect of this long history that is important for the concerns of this book. The split played itself out differently in contexts other than France, but one of the most salient trends was common to all: a mathematic-scientific or rational strain in engineering skills that was becoming more and more pronounced. Since a number of the engineering attributes enumerated above emerged hand in hand with this strain, it can be said that the seed for the hybrid condition of the work of Giorgini, Burt, and Balmond—otherwise a twentieth-century phenomenon, as shall be argued further on—was already written into the highly disciplinary differentiation that occurred gradually from the end of the eighteenth century. For example, the birth of descriptive geometry in the 1760s had as significant an impact then on design and visualization as it would two centuries later in the production of Giorgini, Burt, and Balmond, to mention one of the shared dimensions.

## After the Disciplinary Split

The seed leading to the hybrid quality of these designers' work can be traced to the origin of the disciplinary separation, which in turn makes it possible to assess the consequences of the split in terms of engineering-inflected attitudes toward form in architecture. Indeed, the application of certain aspects of the new engineering sensibility that emerged at the end of the eighteenth century engendered a novel disciplinary hybridity. But while some significant common ground can still be found, this hybridity is largely different from that underwriting the design ideology of the figures examined here. The doctrine that Jean-Nicolas-Louis Durand taught at the École Polytechnique between 1797 and 1833 is a particularly revealing example. To be sure, Durand's view of architecture—expounded in his *Préçis des leçons d'architecture données à l'École Polytechnic* of 1813—moved away from an emphasis on questions of construction that had been so essential to the architecture-engineering hybrid prior to the disciplinary split and focused instead on problems that were predominantly spatial. In addition, like the design ideologies of Giorgini, Burt and Balmond, Durand's also incorporated a number of aspects of the kind associated with an engineering attitude, such as an interest in looking at nature with a view to learning from its principles of organization; a lack of concern with context and the experiential dimension; and a marked scientific bent.

Durand's teachings were based on turning classical architecture into a system that could be manipulated by engineers. This system combined the use of elementary geometrical outlines with serial models of composition. Over and above the design of decoration, Durand based his method on the combination and assembly of the various parts of a building, which he determined with regard to the function they served (vestibules, rooms, porches, courtyards, staircases, etc.). He then supplied indications as to how these could be arranged as regards general organizational axes, with the placement of secondary elements, such as columns and walls, following almost automatically. The character of an edifice was determined entirely from within, with no reference to setting, only to its own type and plan-form. Inspired by the deductive spirit at the core of the exact sciences, architecture was for Durand the result of a combinatory logic that was to govern a set of rigorously predefined components. His production displayed no trace of the handsome renderings, washes, and shadings so dear to the students of Jean-Rodolphe Perronet at the École des Ponts et Chaussées during the eighteenth century. Only the depersonalized space of grid layouts—which, not unlike the connecting marks and guiding lines of Gaspard Monge's geometry, served as references for the development and analysis of typological combinations.

Despite this shared engineering attitude towards form *qua* arrangement, the differences between Durand's approach and the approaches of Giorgini, Burt, and Balmond are relatively clear cut. In most cases, the problem of spatial organization in their work is treated three-dimensionally from the outset, while Durand operated sequentially and mainly in two dimensions, defining plan configuration first and then section. Another fundamental dissimilarity lies in Durand's use of fragments of ordinance or parts of buildings wrenched from history. For the individuals studied here, history did not act as a repository of architectural components from which to borrow—or play any part at all, for that matter. On the contrary, they sought to expand the formal domain by elaborating reference systems that fell outside received formats. Other differences include geometrical economy versus geometrical sophistication; reduction and simplification versus expansion; and a quest for standardization versus a striving for singularity, with the former aspects being present in Durand's doctrine and the latter in the methods of Giorgini, Burt, and Balmond.

Not unlike a cupola in the Renaissance, the buildings resulting from Durand's doctrine could equally be arrived at via his engineering-inflected methodology or by means of the architect's more traditional approach. What was distinct, therefore, was not the outcome, but the process leading up to it. As Antoine Picon put it, "[t]he difference discernible between the two professions [architecture and engineering] were in reality more concerned with the status of the production of space than with its concrete modalities."[11] The same had been the case prior to Durand's teachings, during the eighteenth century, when the architectural renderings done by the students at the École des Ponts et Chaussées under Perronet showed essentially the same language and architectural configurations as those coming out of the Académie Royale d'Architecture. In this particular sense, the origin of the disciplinary separation at the end of the eighteenth century made little difference in the decades that followed.

11 Antoine Picon, *French Architects and Engineers in the Age of Enlightenment*, Cambridge Studies in the History of Architecture (Cambridge, England; New York, USA: Cambridge University Press, 1992), 119.

Indeed, this book poses the question of to what extent, up until the second half of the twentieth century, a substantially engineering-informed approach to form produced three-dimensional configurations in architecture that were indissolubly tied to it. During the period after Durand's teachings and all through the nineteenth century, much of what Sigfried Giedion famously termed "new" architecture (that triggered by the industrial revolution) came about due to some form of architecture-engineering hybrid. Joseph Paxton's Crystal Palace of 1850 and William Henry Barlow's St Pancras Station of 1868, both in London; Ferdinand Dutert's Gallerie des Machines in Paris of 1889; Tony Garnier's *La Mouche* in Lyon of 1914; Eugène Freyssinet's hangar in Orly of 1923; or the factories designed by engineers such as Owen Williams, Giacomo Mattè-Trucco, or Marco Zanuso can be cited here as representative examples of that "new" architecture.[12] Yet, the advances brought about by the coming together of architecture and engineering in these and similar instances primarily translated into a fascination with either large spans or the new constructional possibilities enabled first by iron and glass and later by concrete: for example, new kinds of beams and support elements, construction details, modes of ornament, enclosures, modularity, and prefabrication. One would be hard pressed to find contributions to the realm of form as defined here—that is, radical alternatives to received models of intricate spatial organizations for accommodating human activities. Indeed, the nature of the spaces that those architects and engineers conceived was essentially reducible to some version of the old basilica (i.e., configurations structured in parallel naves); to the single, shed-like space; and more generally, to open layouts punctuated by columns.

## A Specific Segment within the Architecture-Engineering Hybrid

The figure characterized by a certain hybridity between architecture and engineering is thus rather old. In fact, it predates the figure that falls unambiguously into either of the two domains. Fast-forward to the twentieth century, and it becomes evident that, upon examining the cross-pollination between architecture and engineering, Giorgini, Burt, and Balmond belong to a very specific segment of design thinking and research within the historical tradition of the hybrid mindset. On one side are engineers whose architectural production limited itself to two fundamentally engineering themes: the shed and some version of the large-span roof (pleated surfaces, shells, etc.). Heinz Isler, Félix Candela, and Pier Luigi Nervi, for example, would fall into this category. There are others whose approach may be defined as both/and but not as *hybrid*. They certainly operated in both architecture and engineering, but they tackled architectural scenarios with the conventional design approach of an architect, and engineering scenarios with the approach of an engineer. As a result, their architectural work did not differ substantially from that

12 Giedion dated the birth of a "new" kind of industrial architecture to around the year 1830. See S. Giedion, *Building in France, Building in Iron, Building in Ferroconcrete*, Texts & Documents (Santa Monica, CA: Getty Center for the History of Art and the Humanities, 1995), 86.

which could have been conceived by an architect, just as discussed above concerning Durand. This category includes names like Marc Mimram, whose residential projects on the Barbès and Jaurès boulevards, for instance, cannot be judged but as rather commonplace buildings from an architectural standpoint. A third group comprises names like Eladio Dieste and Santiago Calatrava. Their architecture features clear traces of an engineering attitude towards design. But these traces do not appear to have any significant impact on the internal arrangement of space; only at the level of sculptural gesture or external envelope.

Unlike that of Isler, Candela, and Nervi, the production of Giorgini, Burt, and Balmond transcends the typically engineering typologies; unlike Mimram's, its outcomes are indissolubly linked to the engineering-inflected design attributes through which they were begotten; unlike that of Dieste and Calatrava, their design thinking tackled the internal spatial intricacy characteristic of architectural form, beyond questions concerning the envelope. One other important distinction with respect to all these twentieth-century architects and engineers is the fact that Giorgini, Burt, and Balmond constructed relatively self-consistent theoretical frameworks registering their design ideology.

## PROBLEMS INHERITED WITHIN THE FORMAL DOMAIN IN ARCHITECTURE

Surprising though it may seem, extensive theoretical frameworks around the concept of architectural form produced through in-depth discursive procedures are and have been quite rare historically. (The term *discursive* is used here and throughout in its classical sense, which alludes to the kind of knowledge that involves premises, narratives, judgments, inferences, concepts, ideas, conclusions, etc., as channeled through thought and expressed through language. In the context of architecture, it is important to distinguish *discursive* from *representational* knowledge, which instead proceeds through images, drawings, models, etc., and is associated with design and related practices, such as graphic analysis. Though different in principle, these types of knowledge can be related and in fact representational knowledge is often used as a vehicle to produce discursive knowledge.) If, additionally, traces are sought of a realm of signification involving internal three-dimensional arrangement, spatial organization, or disposition in their inseparability from a programmatic potential—the term "program" is here used in its contemporary sense to refer to the collection of human or human-related activities housed within a building—then the precedents are even scarcer.

Theoretical elaborations of form in architecture first appeared only as a minor component within a more general *theory of architecture* in which most of the writing was devoted to the description of architectonic "elements" (columns, walls, roofs, etc.), construction materials, building restoration, ornament, and proportions. Indeed, up to the nineteenth century, sustained theoretical reflections on architectural form had hardly been conceived.

As mentioned above, in his *Précis* of 1813 Durand emphasized the importance of "composition"—a term nearly coextensive here with *disposition* ("disposition")—as "the architect's sole concern."[13] Two decades later, Quatremère de Quincy's *Dictionnaire Historique de l'Architecture* constituted the first architectural treatise offering a more thorough theoretical development of the different aspects of form. Quatremère's somewhat lengthy discussion of concepts such as "disposition," *ordonnance*, and "system" vis-à-vis architecture helped expand the organizational aspect of form merely introduced in Palladio's notion of *struttura*, even if the concept of form as such was absent from his compendium of terms.

Many previous treatises were dedicated to typological taxonomies—whether as a recording (Vitruvius) or as an attempt to establish the principles for a future architecture (Alberti)—and those taxonomies were a way to grapple with the problem of form *qua* spatial organization. However, such taxonomies involved only drawing and descriptive narratives, and barely any discursive thinking addressing the inner workings of architectural form. The slightly more theoretical meditations appear as rather vague definitions and are at best limited to a few paragraphs.

## Semper's "Law of Configuration"

Gottfried Semper's 1860 *Style in the Technical and Tectonic Arts or Practical Aesthetics; A Handbook for Technicians, Artists, and Patrons of Art* is one of the rare examples in which form was an important concept. In the prolegomenon to this book, Semper introduced what he termed *Gestaltungsgesetz*, or "law of configuration."[14] He proceeded, in the manner of a brief theory of form, to describe a number of principles of configuration that art ought to seek in nature in order to attain beauty, for he believed, in the tradition of early modern aesthetics, that "[a]rt, like nature, displays a similar variety of combinations but cannot exceed nature's bounds by an inch; *its principles of formal configuration must be in strict accordance with the laws of nature.*"[15]

The significance of Semper's account of form is twofold. On the one hand, his thinking showed a clear inclination to grapple with the problem of form as spatial organization. This is apparent both in his terminology and his argumentation,

13 Jean-Nicolas-Louis Durand, *Précis of the Lectures on Architecture; with, Graphic Portion of the Lectures on Architecture*, Texts (Los Angeles, CA: Getty Research Institute, 2000), 88.

14 It is worth recalling here that the German *Gestaltung* alludes to a laying out or arrangement. Its root being *Gestalt*–which is usually rendered in English as "form"–the German terminology paves the way for an understanding of the concept of form that implies a sense of configuration and arrangement.

15 Gottfried Semper, *The Four Elements of Architecture and Other Writings* (Cambridge, MA: Cambridge University Press, 2010), 209.

which resulted in a rather elaborate conceptual framework around the question of form in that particular sense. Second, he built a *dynamic* understanding of form into his theory, whereby, echoing Goethe's genetic view of organic nature, processes of coming-to-be emerged that were as substantial as structures in their stasis. Semper did not, however, target architectural form as such, but rather form in nature, whose principles were to be found—or read into—architectural creations only *a posteriori*. Furthermore, these architectural creations were not buildings embodying spatial organizations, but rather ornamental motifs, architectural elements (architraves, columns, etc.), and buildings considered as envelopes or sculptures (e.g., the pyramids).[16]

## Manifestos, History, and the Formalist Lineage

In the twentieth century, theoretical elaborations on architectural form took on more diverse formats. For one thing, positions articulated in a marked dogmatic, manifesto-like fashion became rather common. In his *Vers une Architecture* of 1923, for example, Le Corbusier wrote:

> [C]ubes, cones, spheres, cylinders, and pyramids are the great primary forms that light reveals well; the image is clear and tangible for us, without ambiguity. That is why these are beautiful forms, the most beautiful forms. Everyone is in agreement *about this: children, savages, and metaphysicians. It is the very condition of* the plastic arts. ... A cathedral interests us as an ingenious solution to a difficult problem, but one whose givens were badly formulated because they do not proceed from the great primary forms.[17]

A year later (1924), Ludwig Hilberseimer posited the identity of construction and form as an "indispensable prerequisite of all architecture."[18]

At the same time, there was a proliferation of theoretical reworkings of formal codes that were intrinsic to styles of earlier times. Emil Kaufman's reflections on the relationship between "forms" and system through Ledoux's work in his 1943 essay "Claude-Nicolas Ledoux, Inaugurator of a New Architectural System" is a case in point. Another relevant instance is Rudolf Wittkower's rereading of Renaissance architecture via Alberti and Palladio in his influential *Architectural Principles in the Age of Humanism*, first published in 1949.

Wittkower's legacy lay behind so-called "formalist" readings in architecture throughout the second half of the twentieth century, as evident in the work of both his disciple Colin Rowe and that of Rowe's disciple, Peter Eisenman. Two years after completing his MA thesis under Wittkower in 1947, Colin Rowe published his celebrated article "The Mathematics of the Ideal Villa." The British

16 Given his interest in extrapolating from nature, Semper may well be considered a proto-organicist, one not so far removed from his contemporary, the American writer and sculptor Horatio Greenough. A precursor to organic functionalism, in his 1852 essay "Structure and Organization" Greenough espoused a similar drive to find purposiveness in the organic teleology of the forms of nature as well as inspiration in its organizational models. "Organization is the primal law of structure," he stated aphoristically. In Horatio Greenough, *Form and Function: Remarks on Art, Design, and Architecture* (Berkeley: University of California Press, 1947), 118.

17 Le Corbusier, *Toward an Architecture*, Texts & Documents (Los Angeles, CA: Getty Research Institute, 2007), 103–5. There he was referring specifically to Gothic cathedrals, which he did not regard as a plastic work, yet "a drama: the fight against gravity."

18 Ludwig Hilberseimer, "Construction and Form," in *The Tradition of Constructivism* (New York, NY: Da Capo Press, 1974), 122. Published originally in G (Berlin), no. 3, June 1924. For Hilberseimer, both organization of space and resulting external appearance ought to be inextricably connected with the possibilities of the structural system employed, whether this be in iron or reinforced concrete. New forms, which he encouraged to be sought, could only be derived from the exploitation of this bond.

author attempted to show that there were compositional rules in Palladio's Villa Malcontenta that loosely corresponded to those underlying Le Corbusier's Villa Stein at Garches. This parallelism, Rowe maintained, was applicable to other Palladian and Corbusian villas as well. While being careful to demonstrate the differences and dissonances between the two pieces, his argument staged the existence of a transcendental composition from which both derived:

> Geometrically, both architects may be said to have approached something of the Platonic archetype of the ideal villa to which the fantasy of the Virgilian dream might be supposed to relate. ... For here is set up the conflict between the absolute and the contingent, the abstract and the natural; and the gap between the ideal world and the too human exigencies of realization here receives its most pathetic representation.[19]

Rowe never set out to construct a self-consistent theoretical apparatus beyond the analysis of specific examples, but his allusion to the dialogue between "the absolute" and "the contingent" became central to subsequent conceptualizations of architectural form.

Peter Eisenman undertook that project in his 1963 PhD thesis at Cambridge University. *The Formal Basis of Modern Architecture* remains to date one of the few thoroughgoing attempts to grapple with the conceptual grounds of architectural form in a markedly theoretical manner. There are, however, a number of points in Eisenman's theory that invite reconsideration. First, he sought to infer several principles which, while specific to the language of modern architecture, would illuminate the formal reading of any building regardless of style. This is hardly possible, for principles derived in that fashion tend to end up inflected by the contingencies of the style from which they evolved. The resulting piece of theory becomes a means to promote, however implicitly, some reworked version of the style that served as a starting point. Much of Eisenman's own architectural work is a case in point.

Second, there is a distinction that appears central to Eisenman's theoretical construct, one that echoes Rowe's allusion to "the absolute" and "the contingent." It is the distinction between "generic form" and "specific form," the former being "form thought of in a Platonic sense, as a definable entity with its own inherent laws," the latter designating "the actual physical configuration realized in response to a specific intent and function."[20] Throughout his dissertation, Eisenman argued—and tried to illustrate by means of drawings, both diagrammatic and of actual buildings—that generic forms always stand as references for specific forms, in such a way that for every form considered in a specific sense it would be possible to show that it refers to, or is derived from, a generic one. Further, he held that

19 Colin Rowe, "The Mathematics of the Ideal Villa," in *The Mathematics of the Ideal Villa and Other Essays* (Cambridge, MA: MIT Press, 1982), 14.

20 Peter Eisenman, *The Formal Basis of Modern Architecture* (Baden, Switzerland: L. Müller, 2006), 33–35.

all generic forms may be reducible to two categories only: the centroidal (cube and sphere) and the linear (double cube and cylinder). On the assumption of a duality of worlds, ideal and empirical, Eisenman believed that all the ways in which architectural space may be bounded and articulated are exhausted by two originary models. The study of space via geometry, however, has made much progress since the times of Plato and Euclid. The discipline of morphology, which underwent particularly intense development starting in the mid-1960s, has shown infinite ways in which space can be structured—from models in non-Euclidean geometry involving saddle polyhedra and minimal surfaces, to configurations stemming from studies of crystallography, to name just a couple of pointers here.[21] Thus, a project attempting to reduce all possible architectural configurations to an *a priori* closed set of ideal forms is doomed from the start.

Lastly, Eisenman uncritically associated notions such as configuration and part-to-whole relations *with* Gestalt psychology and, based on this assumption, he regarded these notions as inadequate in relation to architecture, since they would strike the "visual or pictorial in [their] suggested emphasis."[22] To be sure, *the configurational* belongs in the visual or perceptual inasmuch as that to which it gives rise can be apprehended as a separate entity within the continuum of the perceptual field. But this is just an entirely *a posteriori* approach to the understanding of configurational, and certainly not the only one. Indeed, formal configurations can also be described, and independently so, by means of *a priori* relational properties alone. Identifying a cube inside an empty room is very different from describing its inherent properties as a geometric figure. Furthermore, syntheses between *a priori* and *a posteriori* considerations, as performed in this book, are not only possible but might be seen as desirable.

## Norberg-Schulz's "Elements" and "Relations"

The same year Eisenman submitted his dissertation at Cambridge University (1963), Norwegian architect, theorist, and historian Christian Norberg-Schulz published *Intentions in Architecture*.[23] One of the chapters in *Intentions*, significantly influenced by Gestalt psychology, deals extensively with the question of form. Norberg-Schulz's point of departure was to establish that formal analysis in architecture ought to account for "elements" and "relations," stressing the importance of moving back and forth between "whole" and "parts." An element is "a characteristic unit which is a part of an architectural form," one distinguished "by being *bounded* and *articulated*,"[24] while "the term 'relation' denotes a lawful way of distributing elements," one that, in the case of architecture, is necessarily "three-dimensional or 'spatial'."[25] Norberg-Schulz divided elements into three types, "mass," "space," and "surface," and relations into two, "topological" and

21 The phrase "saddle polyhedra" refers to the space packing of polyhedra with double-curved surfaces, whereas the term "minimal surface" designates a double-curved surface across which load transmission runs solely through tensile and compressive membrane stresses. In other words, it is a surface in which flexure has been reduced to zero.

22 Eisenman, *The Formal Basis of Modern Architecture*, 57.

23 The book came out first in Oslo and did not become known in English-speaking circles until two years later, when published by MIT Press in 1965. Hence Eisenman in his afterword of 2006 claimed that his dissertation had been finished two years before Norberg-Schulz's *Intentions*, which is not the case. See Eisenman, *The Formal Basis of Modern Architecture*, 381.

24 Christian Norberg-Schulz, *Intentions in Architecture* (Cambridge, MA: MIT Press, 1968), 133, 139.

25 Ibid, 140.

"geometrical." Instances of topological relations are "proximity," "closure," "fusion," "division," "succession," and "continuity," whereas "centralization," "axiality," "direction," "parallelism," and "perspective" stand for geometrical ones. Lastly, elements governed by relations—as opposed to "an accidental 'aggregate' of independent units"—give rise to "formal structures," examples of which are "group," "row," and "cluster."[26]

Rather than conceptually developing the character of these three subcategories *qua* spatial units so as to determine the possible distinctive nature of any given formal arrangement, Norberg-Schulz rendered them either indexes of a set of contingent gestures (leaving corners in a mass-element intact or not, piercing a surface-element with more or fewer windows, etc.), or heuristic devices to characterize the perceptive quality of a piece of architecture (e.g., skeleton-like, massive, etc.). Norberg-Schulz did something that Eisenman did not in terms of the question of form as spatial organization, for he deliberately and systematically tackled the problem of the configurational—the notion of "relations"—as a separate issue. But his taxonomy of "relations" fell on the unspecific side, proving inadequate to characterize spatial types at some fundamental level. The formal structures resulting from his elements and relations come across as generic and vague; it is difficult to determine whether the configurational nature of a "group" and a "row" would be essentially different if they were to be taken beyond a certain level of abstraction. In other words, the conceptual tools that Norberg-Schulz offered vis-à-vis "relations" lacked specificity and were unable to identify the distinctive nature of different formal configurations.

## The Appearance of Topology and the Distinction between Form and Shape

However, what remains of great value is his in-depth dealing with the problem of form as spatial organization, as well as the comprehensiveness of his conceptual framework, especially when compared to the previous literature on architectural form. Also of notable interest is his use of topology, a term whose first two appearances in writings about architecture only date back to 1955, eight years before *Intentions*.

Engineer Robert Le Ricolais opened his scientistic piece "Topology and Architecture" by quoting Cyril Stanley Smith (then director of the Chicago Institute of Metals): "How could Architecture, which deals with connections, ignore Topology, which by itself is the science of connectivity?"[27] As Maurizio Sabini pointed out, Le Ricolais did not address this question very deeply in the piece, and when he returned to it in a later text titled "Introduction to the Notion of Form" (1966), he did so from a mathematical rather than architectural standpoint.[28] The second instance is Reyner Banham's celebrated article "The New Brutalism," but his use of topology here bordered on the strictly metaphorical.[29] Norberg-

26 Ibid, 146.

27 Robert Le Ricolais, "Topology and Architecture," *Student Publications of the School of Design, North Carolina State College* 5, no. 2 (Spring 1955), 10.

28 See Maurizio Sabini, "Between Order and Form. Fragments of an Idea of Architecture," *Rassegna*, no. 21 (March 1985), 24.

29 See Reyner Banham, "The New Brutalism," *Architectural Review*, no. 118 (December 1955), 354–61.

Schulz utilized the term profusely in the adjectival form ("topological") and in a conceptual fashion that differed from both that of Le Ricolais and of Banham. In *Intentions,* "topological" becomes almost a synonym for "loose" when referring to "relations": it designates an organizational pattern that is to be contrasted with the "geometrical" one, which would allow the nature of a given formal arrangement to be related to a point, an axis, or a co-ordinate system.

In addition to Eisenman and Norberg-Schulz, a third individual who stood out in discussions around form in the 1960s was Christopher Alexander, especially owing to the 1964 publication of his doctoral thesis, *Notes on the Synthesis of Form*. Alexander's text, however, does not on any account constitute a theory of architectural form, as the absence of the word "architecture" in the title already seems to suggest. Rather, it is a reflection on the generic process of design. Alexander attempted to diagram the ways in which "programmatic clarity" could be achieved in the designer's mind in relation to the problem being tackled, whether the object of design be a house or a vacuum-cleaner, an entire city or a stove, a piece of engineering or a small tribal settlement. Heavily influenced by set theory, Alexander put forward a number of analytical and mathematical methods that were to aid decision-making when confronting the functional problems posed by a design context. He never focused on architectural form *per se* in order to scrutinize it.

What was of greater interest here was his qualification of the terms "shape" and "form." "The crucial quality of shape, no matter of what kind, lies in its organization, and when we think of it this way we call it form," he stated.[30] A similar distinction in the field of architecture had already been made by Louis Kahn in his essay "Form and Design" of 1960—that is, three years before *The Formal Basis*, and four before Alexander's book. For Kahn "form" constituted the most basic organizing principle in the structuring of space, whereas "shape," which he associated with "design," represented a specific configuration of a form.[31] Through design the architect *shapes* form; "[f]orm has no shape or dimension. ... Form has nothing to do with circumstantial conditions," he wrote.[32] The resonance of this duality with "generic form" and "specific form" is obvious enough. However, within "specific form" Eisenman included other properties besides "shape," such as color, texture, size, scale, and proportion, while for Kahn the interplay between form and shape involved a certain conceptual charge that was partially marked by fitness for purpose and some kind of spiritual fulfillment.

The thread relating to the distinction between form and shape advanced by Kahn and Alexander is particularly pertinent to the aims of this book. In 1986, Kent Bloomer pointed out that, if shape has a "sculptural" or, at least, "outline" character, then form possesses a "topological" or "spatial" one.[33] Along the same lines, Antonio Juárez suggested in 2000 that Kahn's designs

30 Christopher Alexander, *Notes on the Synthesis of Form* (Cambridge: Harvard University Press, 1964), 134.

31 Plato's distinction between "eidos" and "morphe" certainly appears relevant to Kahn's.

32 Louis Kahn, "Form and Design," in *Louis Kahn: Essential Texts* (New York, NY: W. W. Norton, 2003), 64.

33 Kent Bloomer, "Form, Shape, and Order in the Work of Charles Moore," in *Charles Moore: Buildings and Projects 1949-1986* (New York, NY: Rizzoli, 1986), 21.

in general (although he was specifically thinking of the several iterations of the City Tower project for Philadelphia, produced between 1952 and 1957, which was largely an invention of Anne Tyng) ought to be thought of in relation to Le Ricolais's fundamental dictum: namely, that what really constitutes a material configuration is its internal "topological arrangement," not the external "form." In Juárez's reading—significantly influenced by that of Sabini—the basis of poetics and load-bearing structures for Le Ricolais was likewise topological organization. While "composition" would be driven by visual considerations, "disposition" would release "arrangement," that is, an open order of sorts. By way of synthesizing these thoughts with respect to Kahn, Juárez wrote that:

> what Kahn understood as form—'conceptual patterns without dimensions'—was very close to some kind of "topological order" in the project. ... Kahn's desire seems to lie in seeking out the formal structure of the project. This means that the origin of the project can be traced beyond any specific formal solution. What Kahn means by "Form" can be understood as a flexible disposition or arrangement, an open form organizing space. The nature of the building, what the space "wants to be," is rooted in the relationship between spaces, in their internal connections or disconnections, and in their proximities and separation, but not in the concrete form.[34]

In addition to Kahn, Alexander, Bloomer, and Juárez, Sabini and Forty also identified a distinction between form and shape. For reasons yet to be explored, such a distinction never caught on in architectural discourse. But the intuitions of these writers, even if only at the level of suggestion and brief commentary, remain of great interest with regard to the objectives established here, as does the notion of topology which, reformulated on architectural grounds, will become central to overcoming some of the inherited limitations around the question of form outlined below.

### Generic Form/Specific Form versus Form/Shape

Formal domains in architecture structured around binaries such as generic form/specific form or absolute/contingent—i.e., those based on positing a realm of ideal "forms" from which particular manifestations derive in the empirical world—have proven only relatively productive. The main problem is that they presuppose a fixed set of so-called "generic forms" which, typically coextensive with Platonic solids, is considerably limited. As a result, the variability characterizing the regime of "specific forms" is only apparent, since it gets restricted to gestures affecting questions of volume and surface.

34 Antonio Juárez, "Topology and Organicism in the Work of Louis I. Kahn. Notes on the City Tower," *Perspecta* 31 (January 1, 2000), 77.

Scrutinizing the organizational nature of such specific forms in depth reveals that the laws defining their capacity to structure a bounded section of space are by and large traceable to a few originary models: primarily, the container and some version of the floor-upon-floor arrangement. By this reasoning, a neoclassical building and one by Zaha Hadid Architects might very well be formally identical when the concept of form as spatial organization is invoked as a mode of inquiry. In other words, a framework constructed around the generic form/specific form binary is unable to account for an expanding field of possible three-dimensional configurations far exceeding the reduced group of Platonic solids and its derivatives. In this respect, the bodies of work studied in this book have been deliberately selected to illustrate, in contrast, such an expanding field.

As will be shown, the point of entry to the problem of architectural form, once established as grounded in spatial organization, ought to be shifted to a thoroughgoing discussion of the distinction between the domains of form and shape, which has so far merely been sketched out by a few authors. Indeed, form is one of those architectural aspects that seemingly gets rearticulated by the substitution of one label after another: deconstructivist, biological, land-form, etc. It remains to be seen whether these rearticulations have mostly been specious or limited, since they may have concerned questions of shape but not those of spatial organization in any fundamental fashion.

## Stylistic Nonreferentiality

Previous theories of architectural form were often built around a direct link to a style, the consequence of which was the promotion of a particular kind of architectural expression. Eisenman and his championing of a revised version of certain languages of modern architecture—from Le Corbusier to Terragni—is a case in point. Here, by focusing on the domain of form as spatial organization, a style-specific theoretical framework will be avoided. In fact, in delineating that domain without relying on any specific representational references or set of aesthetic codes, this book questions the validity of the notion of style when the problem of architectural form is at stake. Discussing the determination of the fundamental structure of architectural space, beyond an immediate referent based on appearance, requires us to set aside concerns about style and instead appeal to the ultimate organizational capacity of architectural form, regardless of how it is aesthetically rendered.

For one thing, this priority addresses the necessity of preventing the abovementioned problem of apparent reformulations. For another, it sets this book's approach apart from one which might have stemmed from Gestalt principles. As is well known, these principles gave rise to a kind of phenomenology of form rooted in the psychology of sensorial perception. This being the case, the study of form undertaken by Gestalt theories favored an entirely *a posteriori* analysis aligned with Lockean or Humean empiricisms. If Rudolf Arnheim designated the whole as a structure that "can be explained neither by the qualities of its single elements, nor by the relations between these elements," here the exact opposite will be pursued, namely a delineation of the domain of formal wholes by way of an inquiry into their internal spatial organization.[35] In other words, the present work is concerned with the basis of that which ought to be there first for it to be perceived; that which occurs prior to perception—indeed, that which allows it to occur.

### Form vis-à-vis Formation

Theories of formation—that is, those taking questions of form-thinking and form-making as their primary objects—constitute something of a gap in architectural theory, for they have been even rarer than theories of form *per se*, especially if in-depth discursive thinking is sought in them. As a result, the problem of form as potential (its built-in generative capacity) appears to have been little studied. Considered historically, this occurrence is somewhat paradoxical, since the notions that were closer to featuring something of an organizational valance in the earliest architecture treatises—"ordination" and "disposition" (Vitruvius), "lineamenta" (Alberti), and "disegno" (a Renaissance term)—referred not so much to form as such, as to processes of formal conception through drawings and models, from intuitions in thinking to materialization. Mies van der Rohe's comment on the title of the journal *Die Form* encapsulated succinctly the difference between the two realms:

> Do you not think that the title Die Form makes too great a claim? ... Do we not guide the attention away from the essential? Is form really an aim? Is it not rather the result of the form-giving process? Is it not the process that is essential?[36]

Of the writings mentioned above, neither that of Rowe nor of Eisenman reflected on the making of form. The former utilized already existing objects to extract a number of formal rules; the latter rehearsed his previously formulated principles through a few *given* buildings. Norberg-Schulz did not account for the processual aspects of form-making either. Among more recent texts grappling with the problem of form-thinking and form-making at length, Greg Lynn's *Animate Form* (1999) deserves a mention. The omission here, however, is the reverse, since, while challenging traditional conceptions of design thinking, Lynn does so without

35 Rudolf Arnheim, "Gestalt and Art," *The Journal of Aesthetics and Art Criticism* 2, no. 8 (October 1, 1943): 71–72.

36 Mies Van Der Rohe, "Regarding the New Volume," in *The Artless Word* (Cambridge, MA: MIT Press, 1991), 257.

addressing the implications of alternative models for the ontology of the forms they yield—that is, once they are there, finalized, frozen in time.

In the context of these reflections, a distinction made by Sanford Kwinter between "poor formalism" and "true formalism" in his 2004 "Who's Afraid of Formalism?" is most pertinent. The former would be a kind of "unextended formalism," one which, in mistaking the notion of "form" for that of "object"—the "end-product"—leaves the process of "formation" unaccounted for. He posits this process as "ordering action," a "logic deployed" whereby discernible patterns become recognizable entities within their physical milieu. For Kwinter, those patterns of formation are modeled on embedded forces that are internal and pre-concrete, and it is only true, extended formalism which, rather than stopping at the level of "the shell of the object-form," targets the dynamic resonances between those patterns. The origin of Kwinter's form is not static, but a formative principle, which he associates with the Goethean notion of "type": an abstract origin or "deep structural element" that is always already active, in the sense of generative. He thus illustrated in rather a nuanced fashion that the study of any formal structure in architecture cannot be disengaged from the dynamics of form-thinking and form-making leading to its realization, and therefore that discussions of formation and outcome in architecture are inextricably bound together.

Within this general precept in the tradition linking together Goethe, Semper, and Kwinter, this book attempts a critical dialecticization of the formation-outcome pairing, dissociating the two terms from one another yet keeping them in tension. Every element of a spatial configuration's make-up stands in relation to the generative potential driving the process of its formal emergence, whether that relation be consequential or antagonistic. Therefore, though primarily targeting the study of form as organization, this domain will be partly delineated on the basis of how a spatial configuration conforms, clashes, or relates in any way to the critical framework established by the formation process leading up to it.

## Beyond the Duality of Form and Program

The study of form, whether in architecture or in other fields such as art and literary theory, has often been associated with the term "formalism." In architecture in particular, formalism has generally been applied to projects privileging the object as a thing: its form, rather than its content, with form and content being regarded as two separable aspects. The term "content" in relation to architecture mainly encompasses two realms of meaning. On the one hand, it alludes to the iconographic, cultural, sociological, or political metanarratives that may be embodied in an architectural object. On the other hand, content may also refer to issues involving function, technique, construction, materiality, and beauty as they relate to the object itself. The first sense invokes domains other than architecture proper and therefore its relevance will be considered negligible here as regards the main goal established at the outset: to contribute to knowledge in architectural thinking. By the same token, the second sense will be wholly pertinent. Within it, a distinction needs to be made between architectural aspects that are primordially constitutive and therefore *a priori* (i.e., form and *program*, the term that will mostly be used here instead of function for reasons that will be explained in the last chapter); secondarily so, insofar as they merely make up architecture's *medium* (technique, construction, materiality); and *a posteriori*, owing to complete dependence on perception (beauty).

Consequently, this study revolves around the premise that a combination of form and program on some fundamental level constitutes the necessary basis for any architectural work. More precisely, form will be here posited as *three-dimensional organization inflected with a programmatic potential*. Thus, program will not be understood as an aspect to be attached to form, but rather as one inhering in form.[37] In other words, form—insofar as an architectural category—will be described as always already programmatic. These propositions will fundamentally distinguish the present investigation from one falling into the realm of morphology—where formal principles are discussed without regard to any content-related aspects—and will seek to overcome the limitations associated with formalism.

## SPLIT UNDONE

There are a number of reasons as to why a particular kind of design work poised between architecture and engineering constitutes an especially fruitful medium for constructing an alternate epistemology around the concept of architectural form. On one hand, as a result of the experiential dimension of such work being discounted and the contextual sphere being reduced to that of the object itself, engineering thinking addresses form with a much greater degree of concentration than architectural thinking. This narrowness of focus facilitates contributions specific to the question at hand, with an emphasis on science only further catalyzing them. It is no wonder that engineering designers have proven especially prolific at coming up with novel, unconventional ways of form finding (e.g., Frei Otto). On the other hand, the architectural sensibility embedded in the design methods studied here prevents their outcomes from falling outside of what is realistic at the scale and

37 Different versions of the impossibility of a separation between form and content have been articulated in disciplines such as literary theory, film theory, and art theory and criticism. See, for instance, Bois, "Introduction: Resisting Blackmail," xvii–xxiv.

within the purview of a building. In this sense, the formal experimentations of Giorgini, Burt, and Balmond pertain to what might be regarded as the realm of the architecturally possible.

## Subversive Disciplinarity

The chapters presented here define and capitalize on a subversive disciplinarity which, determined by the ways in which certain design approaches pertaining to the architecture-engineering hybrid translate aspects from engineering thinking into architectural terms, is essential to rethinking the formal domain in architecture. These design approaches prove capable of displacing architectural conventions in a manner that would be difficult for architects, given their far less sophisticated understanding of the constituencies of the structural dimension and their relationship with the organizational aspects of form. This distinction lurks behind one of the central questions posed by this book, namely, whether, despite the apparent expansion of formal vocabularies, architects' contributions over the past few decades have been by and large more substantial at the level of shape than of form proper. A second noteworthy attribute of the individuals analyzed here is their tendency to define the starting points of design and research procedures as abstract situations. This tendency will be particularly germane to the possibility of stylistic nonreferentiality, as it does away with typological and representational references at the outset of form-generation processes.

Giorgini, Burt, and Balmond were selected because the defining features of their work make them specially attuned to constituting the substrate through which to produce the conceptual framework here pursued. Those features were enumerated and defined above vis-à-vis the formal realm: the capacity of their design thinking to yield intricate three-dimensional configurations that are characteristically architectural; the distinctness resulting from the condition that such configurations could only have been generated via an engineering-inflected approach to design; and the fact that whether in graphic production, in writing, or in both, all three put together theoretical frameworks registering the elements of their design thinking in relation to the spatial organizations they conceived.

Notwithstanding this common ground, some may be uncomfortable with how Giorgini, Burt, and Balmond fit together given the disparate nature of their bodies of work. However, it is the very dissimilarities of their individual design and research approaches that constituted the second reason for choosing them vis-à-vis the question of form. Giorgini's approach primarily involved the potential of surface topology, Burt's the periodical continuity of models for the subdivision of space, and Balmond's nonlinear sequences of relational templates. The combined discussion of the work and design mindset of the three figures offers a broad and sufficiently differentiated range of aspects that are amenable to being turned into discursive components relevant to the problem of architectural form, such as the characteristic relationality of minimal surfaces, or the aggregational logic derived from saddle polyhedra. In other words, the grounds and breadth of this range of aspects are such as to allow for a substantial extension in the bounds of possibility of the formal domain in architecture. In addition, the dissimilarities between the three designers are precisely what allow for a uniquely productive reading of each one: the study of one body of work shifts the reader's perspective with regards to the next, thereby enabling a different understanding thereof.

## A Novel Hybrid Mindset

Picon identified a number of recent developments influencing the disciplinary relationship between architecture and engineering: namely, the increasing significance of environmentalism requiring a rapport to be established between local, national, and transnational interests when undertaking a large infrastructural project; novel approaches to design based on hypotheses of a "techno-nature" that promote a symbiotic relationship between human work and nature, as opposed to the former aspiring to dominate the latter; and a decrease in the importance of composition in architectural design that has occurred in parallel with a discovery of the potential of infrastructures for the conception of buildings, the work of Renzo Piano and Norman Foster being cases in point.[38]

Other dynamics specific to our time that signal the need to address the problem of the architecture-engineering hybrid include the advances and popularization of ever more sophisticated pieces of design software, scripting languages, and BIM technologies. Significant progress in these industries has brought about new workflow and communication possibilities among the different parties involved in the design and construction of built structures. Consequently, common languages have emerged for information exchange that have triggered closer-than-ever collaborations between architects and engineers. At the same time, advances in design software have expanded the territory of what is conceivable in terms of the complexity of artificially shaped spaces as well as the efficiency with which they can be erected. Within the resultant, ever more scientifically driven sphere of design, engineers are seeing their role increasing exponentially.

Some of the consequences of these rapid developments can be read into the specific kind of creative mindset that has emerged in collaborative enterprises between architects and engineers over the past few decades. A few commentators have gone so far as to refer to a "structural turn" in architecture culture occurring during the early part of the twenty-first century as a result of a renewed interest in the structural logic of buildings.[39] As Nina Rappaport noted, the 1950s also

38 See Picon, *Marc Mimram*, 148.

39 See introduction in Neil Leach, David Turnbull, and Chris Williams, eds., *Digital Tectonics* (Chichester, West Sussex, UK; Hoboken, NJ: Academy Press, 2004), 4.

constituted an especially prolific decade in terms of these collaborations. The buildings of Tecton, Louis Kahn, Mies, and Adalberto Libera would not have been possible without Ove Arup, August Komendant, Myron Goldsmith, and Sergio Musmeci respectively, to cite a few examples. But these and similar collaborations between architects and engineers still fell under a paradigm wherein architects maintained ultimate creative control over the fundamentals of the articulation of space relative to programmatic requirements, however substantially their decisions may have benefited from the technical contributions of engineers.

In contrast, alliances have cropped up in recent years, like those of Mutsuro Sasaki and Toyo Ito, or Balmond himself with Koolhaas, Libeskind, and also Ito, where the technician is virtually as responsible for some of the central features defining a building—including the spatial intricacies of form—as is the architect. The latter starts by considering program; then the engineer joins in and together they discuss the kinds of spaces and structure they would like to design; decisions concerning materials are typically made at the end. Given their increased role in this sequence, it is no wonder that another telling difference vis-à-vis their predecessors is that the writings of this new breed of engineers tend to read as design theories in their own right—as opposed to a collection of biographical, poetic, and ethical statements, as in the case of Peter Rice's *The Engineer Imagines* and much of Ove Arup's musings.

When read together, all these aspects suggest that the distinction between architecture and engineering is again becoming blurred, with the limits of the engineering profession stretching. Thus, somewhat following a tendency in the opposite direction from that triggered by the split at the end of the eighteenth century, this hybrid design mindset may be gaining greater and greater relevance—yet another reason to turn it into an object of discussion here, and through it explore the possibility of a new hybrid, discursive subdiscipline that breaks down received oppositions between architecture and engineering.

## An Alternative to Post-Modernism

The three individuals explored here occupy a distinctive position within the different lineages to which they belong. Namely, aside from a few isolated gestures in some of Antoni Gaudí's buildings, and unlike other designers whose work has been signaled as a referent (e.g., Frederick Kiesler), Giorgini was a pioneer in instrumentalizing surface topology for the purpose of architectural design with a marked level of scientific self-consciousness. Within the sphere of morphology, Burt's body of work represents one of the earliest, most thoroughgoing investigations into three-dimensional models for the subdivision of space based on patterns of configurational continuity. Balmond was a trailblazer in theorizing the question of nonlinearity at the core of the digital turn and interpreting it as a design basis for architecture.

The decision to study Giorgini, Burt, and Balmond also rests upon the fact that a historically situated discussion of their work becomes a contribution within a larger narrative concerning the possibility of bypassing post-modernism in architecture. As this book points out, between the late 1950s and the early 1970s (with some remote precedents in the 1920s), while the foundations of post-modernism were being laid elsewhere, a group of (mostly) non-mainstream architects, artists, and engineers developed various research projects involving architectural form in a number of significant ways. Forming part of the larger interdisciplinary transformation outlined above—one where new models in linguistics, computation, behaviorism, and cybernetics originated a distinctive resolve to turn architecture into a scientifically verifiable field of knowledge—this non-self-constituted group included architects and engineers like Sergio Musmeci, Moshe Safdie, Robert Le Ricolais, Keith Critchlow, Anne Tyng, and Peter Pierce in addition to the figures examined below. The avoidance of previously coded formal vocabularies, an intense organizational approach to structure, and a synthesis underwriting the dispositional properties of form can be cited as shared motivations. When understood in relation to the time period in which they arose, this set of concerns suggests that an alternative chapter to post-modernism in architecture dealing with the intersection of experimental geometry, biological structuralism, and architectural form is yet to be written. The language resulting from those somewhat marginalized practices has been assumed to have emerged only during the 1990s and 2000s, owing to the explosion of digital design. Retrospectively, the following chapters construct the story of the progressive development of these apparently recent kinds of formal explorations as they took place in the shadow of the tale of post-modernist architecture.

## NAVIGATING *DISPOSITIONAL INTELLIGENCE*

There is no architectural history of twentieth-century engineering—just as there is no history of twentieth-century architecture written from the engineer's point of view. A number of solid writings concerning the history and theory of structural engineering can certainly be found, yet they remain very few and far between.[40] Indeed, the discipline of engineering at large lacks a properly developed humanistic

40 Those scarce historians have dealt primarily with the history of engineering as history of structures and construction technologies (Sigfried Giedion, Roberto Gargiani, Robert Carvais, André Guillerme, Valérie Nègre, Robin Middleton, and Andrew Saint), addressed the history of materials and the history of the disciplinary constitution of engineering and the engineer (Antoine Picon, Ulrich Pfammatter), and studied the social meaning underpinning German engineering theory (Katherine Romba).

discipline of its own.[41] This book is to be regarded as a contribution towards filling those inexplicable gaps. With respect to those writings, the present work launches an alternate historiography concerning the scientization of conceptions of architectural form—in the specific sense in which this notion is defined here—grounded in engineering thinking.

Despite their radical importance, Giorgini, Burt, and Balmond have so far been neglected by the architectural mainstream, to the extent that the first scholarly account of their bodies of work will be provided here. This account, corresponding to chapters one through three, will induce a theoretical framework (chapter four) whose basis will be constructed entirely on the grounds of architectural thinking. This is intended as an alternative to importing the foundations of a theoretical framework from a field other than architecture (linguistics, literary criticism, film theory, etc.) and then translating it into architectural terms. As philosopher Andrew Benjamin put it with respect to design being the locus of architectural theory, "it is not the application of philosophical or theoretical propositions, which in being external to architecture can then be applied. Rather, both the philosophical and the theoretical are deployed within and as part of a range of practices that constitute architecture."[42]

The idiosyncratic character of Giorgini, Burt, and Balmond's formal production is essential to the objectives of this book, for it allows received limitations to be overcome around the question of form, postulations of which have revolved mainly around canonical architecture. In-depth examination of their projects will supply the launching platform from which to reconsider the conceptual grounds of form in architecture.

More specifically, a number of theoretical propositions tied to the discussion of each body of work are offered in chapters one through three. In chapter four, those propositions are collected—their importance and impact elaborated upon—and assembled into a coherent framework, a task for which a number of additional theoretical propositions proved necessary. Capitalizing, to continue with Benjamin's words, on "the differing ways in which the relationship between history, theory, and the practice of design allows for a configuring and reconfirming of the project of architecture," a new vocabulary will emerge that comprises an ensemble of redescriptions and concepts capable of assimilating into literature a set of distinct discoveries made within the realm of design.[43] In proceeding thus, the goal for the resulting piece of theory is to extend the bounds of possibility for discursively understanding form in architecture.

The first chapter looks at the branch of research concerning shell structures and surface topology on which Vittorio Giorgini worked between the late 1950s and the late 70s, partly in Italy, partly at the Pratt Institute in New York City. This

41 The best indication of this is the absence of PhD programs specifically devoted to the history and theory of engineering (topics in this domain tend to be addressed from within architectural studies, history of science, or even art history).

42 Andrew Benjamin, *Architectural Projections* (Melbourne: RMIT University Press, 2012), 6.

43 Ibid.

chapter argues that the idiosyncratic character of Giorgini's approach to design may only have emerged as a combination of the anti-rationalist organicist tendencies of post-war Italian architecture and the rationalist basis it acquired upon his move to the US in the late 1960s. In other words, the contention is that the distinctiveness of Giorgini's line of work is indissolubly tied to the fact that it came about as a result of a process of rationalizing an originally anti-rational reaction against pre-war modern architecture.

The second chapter deals with Michaël Burt's research into systems of space subdivision that achieve continuity through periodicity. By examining Burt's work in the context of the morphology of his teacher, Alfred Neumann, and the wider Israeli scene, this chapter shows that, if Burt departed from the aspects of morphology most closely linked to architectural thinking by depriving Neumann's architectural morphology of its humanism and contextualism via an extreme scientization of its basic tenets, a considerable segment of his production nevertheless turned out to be architectural in nature, despite his own near-total lack of awareness of this. Indeed, the chapter suggests that, though embarking in a direction dismissive of any engagement with architectural conditions or discourses, Burt's body of work ultimately carried the central elements of morphology's critique of modernism—notably the challenges to functionalism, the modernist language, and the condition of building-as-object—to their logical conclusions.

The third chapter investigates Cecil Balmond's formal ideology, focusing on how he interpreted chaos theory as a design basis for architecture. It argues that the origins of that ideology can be decisively traced to Frei Otto's legacy at ARUP, as a result of which the anti-modernist tenets of Otto's schemes and research approach became written into Balmond's own and inspired the development of other anti-modernist attitudes. The chapter also highlights the limitations, contradictions, and incompleteness of Balmond's design theory and production, and reveals the degree of inevitability of those weaknesses insofar as they resulted partly from the very same ambitions conducive to his subversive disciplinarity, and partly from discursively enacting the same attributes he sought to implement in his design procedures.

The fourth and final chapter is primarily a self-contained piece of theory dealing with the concept of architectural form. Some of the central issues structuring this piece of theory include the fundamental link between form and program; an understanding of the notion of topology architecturally (not merely geometrically) and its utilization for determining formal sameness and formal singularity; the role of three-dimensional networks to interpret and generate programmatic regimes; the possibility of discursively construing an expanding field of configurational patterns in architecture that exceeds the reduced group of Platonic solids; the identification of special organizational constructs; and the problems of formation and style vis-à-vis the conceptual basis of architectural form.

There is a substantial overlap in terms of the time period in which all three individuals were operating: Burt and Giorgini had greatly developed their research practices by the early 1970s, and continued to do so thereafter; Balmond started to work at ARUP in 1968. As a result, the first three chapters chart the conditions for the unfolding of a historically determined disciplinary event: the emergence of a particular kind of hybrid design work straddling architecture and engineering.

In contrast to the historical temporality of chapters one through three, the fourth chapter is built around one of a conceptual nature. If, as John Summerson once claimed, architecture theory is "a historical process with a life of its own in its own medium or words," one partly operating through abstraction of principles from practice, conceptual temporality may be understood here as that encompassing a past through which the realm of possibility delineated by previous formulations around the concept of form has progressively come into being.[44] This book pursues the extension of the bounds of this realm by replacing some traditional questions and presenting a variety of aspects in a different way, up to the point where a novel, self-consistent understanding springs forth.

By combining history and theory, this book proposes an alternative to the norm in terms of methodology—theory being understood here, not as referring to the theoretical registers that are typically employed in history writing, but rather as a self-contained, if porous, scheme of ideas and concepts which, rendered consistent through logic and exemplification, aims to explain underlying, generalizable patterns found in facts and events. On one hand, theory is necessary because it is an extremely powerful mechanism through which to develop original ideas, arguments, and concepts in discursive domains. On the other, the activity of theory has historically been adept at systematically revising guiding assumptions. A pressing need for theory can therefore also be justified on the grounds that a number of traditional beliefs and principles have been discredited by some significant changes originating since the mid-1990s at the intersection of architectural design and technology, and the sphere of the built environment at large.

As regards methodological experimentation, the marriage of history and theory in this book ought to be seen as a plea against their all-too-common mutual exclusion—one affecting humanistic studies more generally, as evident in the painful alienation between history and philosophy—and for the possibilities of benefiting from the complementarity of each epistemological register. For, as Foucault masterfully demonstrated, rather than hardening the separation of the project of the contingent and that of the general, new levels of reality, as well as

44 John Summerson, "The Case for a Theory of Modern Architecture (1957)," in *Architecture Culture 1943-1968: A Documentary Anthology* (New York, NY: Rizzoli, 1993), 228.

accuracy and understanding with respect to facts and events, can be reached by turning such complementarity into an analytical tool.

.....................................

A good number of received disciplinary systems of thought tied to the self-serving dichotomy of modernism/post-modernism and its derived beliefs and principles remain unrevised, due to the decline in weight of architectural thinking and theory. If these two modalities converged at their peak for the last time in the 1990s and early 2000s—and specifically around themes pertaining to the formal domain—the present work retrieves them and attempts to endow them with a renewed importance. To complete a full exercise in what Sanford Kwinter would call *radical anamnesis*, this book also recovers some of those themes in the belief that, by historicizing them, the past that did not get to happen—the incomplete developments, the promising statements of intent that never progressed beyond infancy, the concepts and frames of understanding that showed much potential but were never fully worked out in regard to architectural thinking—can be isolated and productively projected into a novel territory. The following pages have been written in the hope that such historicization and the subsequent theorization taking on some of those semi-formed, unevolved propositions will help supersede the dichotomy of modernism versus post-modernism, which, in 2024, continues to be as active as ever.

CHAPTER 1

# Vittorio Giorgini: Surface Topology and the Rationalization of Organicism

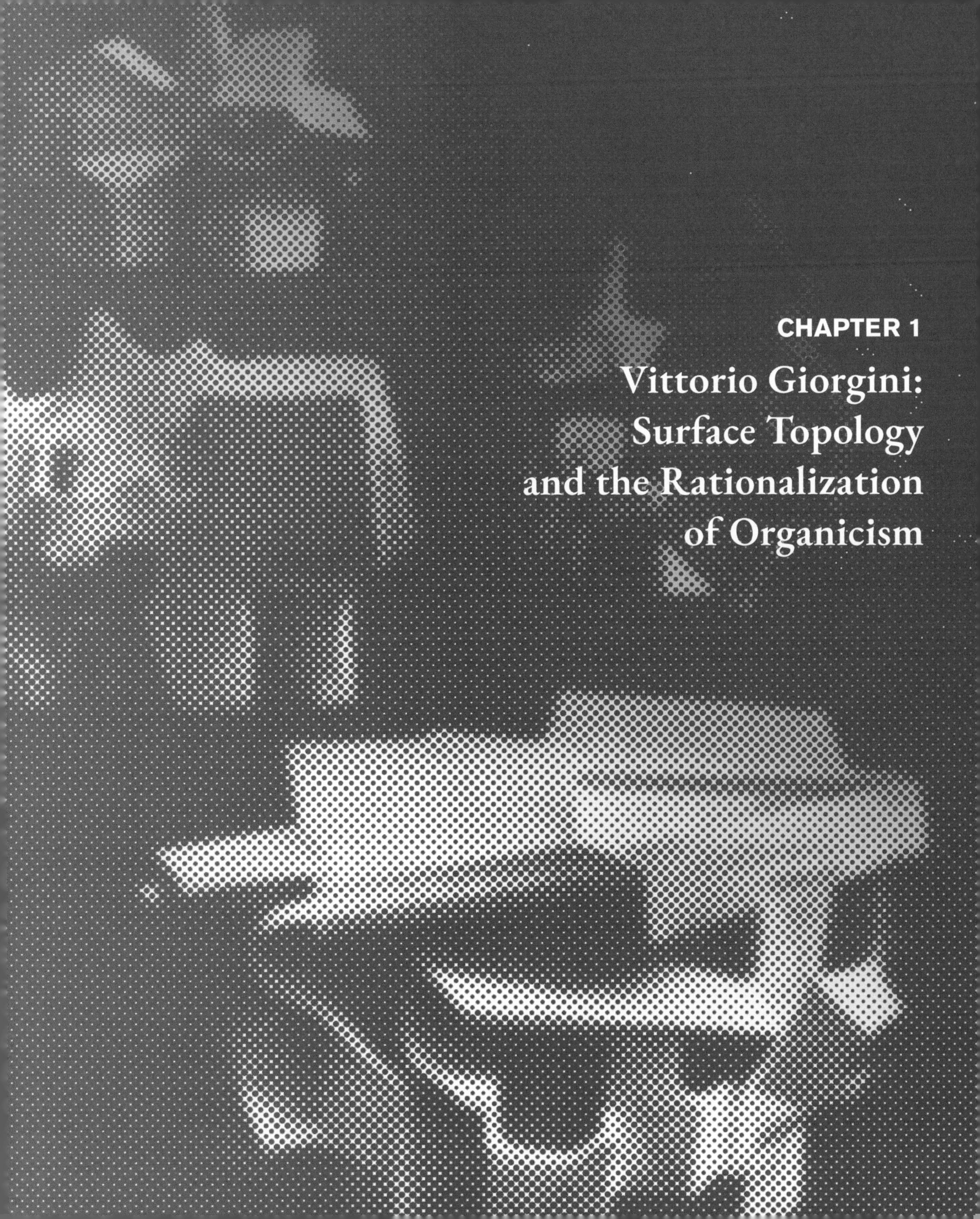

## GIORGINI'S ITALIAN PHASE: ORGANICIST CONTEXT, REFERENTS, AND FORCED ESCAPE

The academic training and formative years of Florentine architect, artist, and educator Vittorio Giorgini (1926–2010) took place at a moment in Italian culture when Frank Lloyd Wright's writings and design ideology had gained a strong popularity. In 1945, having just returned from finishing his architectural studies in the United States, Bruno Zevi published Verso un'architettura organica (Towards an Organic Architecture) and founded the review Metron and the Association for Organic Architecture (APAO). He sought to supersede European functionalism and Italian rationalism by championing Wright's "organic" ideals "as something equally opposed to the theoretic and the geometrical, to the artificial standards, the white boxes and the cylinders which distinguish so much of the first modern architecture and to its general nudism."[1] His agenda resonated with a need for liberation and freshness that many Italian architects felt on confronting the period of reconstruction after the war. As a result of this resonance, a sizeable group of these established and emerging architects adopted Wright as their main referent and began to explore forms of organic expression. In some cases, such as Ludovico Quaroni's project for the church in Rome's Prenestino neighborhood (1949), old ties with German expressionists such as Max Taut, Otto Bartning, and Hans Poelzig were reinvigorated, as Vittorio Gregotti observed.[2]

While the renewed force of organicism originated in Rome—where both Quaroni and Zevi were based—its impact reached many other cities, including Florence. In fact, it was at the Palazzo Strozzi in Florence that the world tour of the exhibition *Frank Lloyd Wright: 60 Years of Living Architecture*—conceived, in Maristella Casciato's words, "as the largest one-man show ever realized for an architect"—opened in 1951.[3] Giovanni Michelucci offered a medium for ongoing appraisal of Wright's architectural theory between 1945 and 1954 with his magazine *La Nuova Città*. The first years coinciding with his brief tenure as dean of the Facoltà di Architettura in Florence (1944–48), he favored organicist views and formal gestures within the Facoltà and continued to implement them through his late period as an architect. The building that epitomized this phase in his body of work was the Autostrada church, which, erected in Florence at the same time as Giorgini's most important built work, the Saldarini House on the Gulf of Baratti (1960–62) **(fig. 1.1–4)**,

1 Bruno Zevi, *Towards an Organic Architecture*, 1st ed. (London, UK: Faber & Faber, 1950), 72. For an examination of the philosophical implications of the term "organic" and its intersection with twentieth-century architecture, as well as a discussion of the relationship between "organic" and "organicist," see José Aragüez, "Towards a Critique of 'The Organic' in *Architectural Thinking*," Pidgin, no. 12 (2011): 246–63.

2 Vittorio Gregotti, *New Directions in Italian Architecture*, 1st ed. (New York: George Braziller, 1968), 43.

3 See Maristella Casciato, "The Promise of Organic Architecture," in *Frank Lloyd Wright: Europe and Beyond* (Berkeley, CA: University of California Press, 1999), 84–87.

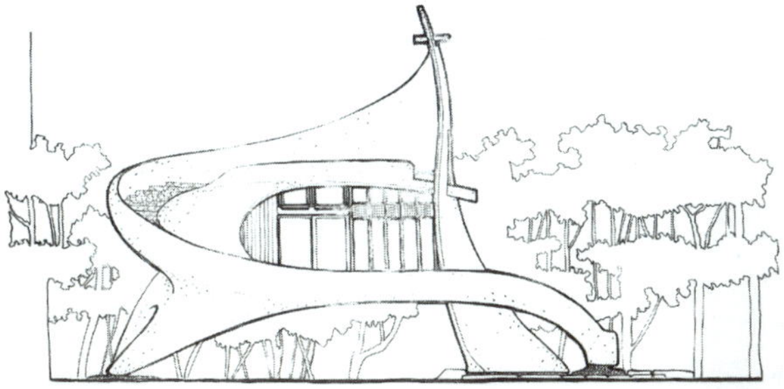

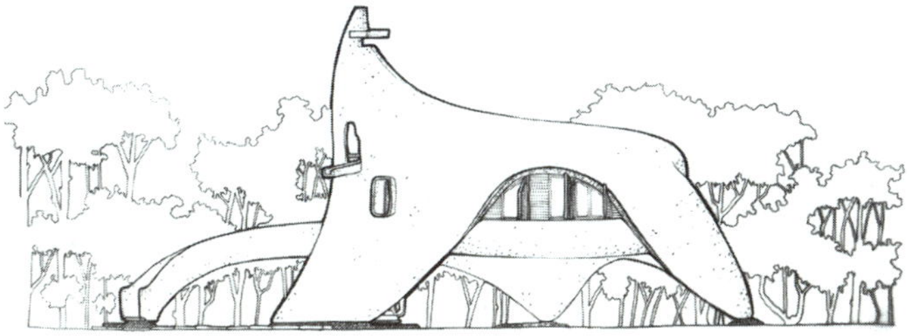

**1.1–2** Saldarini House on the Gulf of Baratti, 1960–62. West elevation (left) and east elevation (right).

**1.3** Saldarini House on the Gulf of Baratti, 1960–62. Main entrance.

**1.4** Left: Saldarini House on the Gulf of Baratti, 1960–62.

**1.6** Below: Leonardo Ricci. Villa in Monte degli Ulivi near Riesi, Italy (1963).

Opposite page:
**1.5** Giovanni Michelucci. Borgo Maggiore church, San Marino (1966).

**72**

● *Eglise de San Marino.*

*Photos F. Barsotti.*

**1.7** Vittorio Giorgini as a student in Florence c. 1946.

Opposite page:
**1.8** Personal postcard from Ludovico Quaroni, 1962

combined Tuscan craftsmanship with influences from Le Corbusier to Hans Scharoun **(fig. 1.5)**. The Sicilian work of Leonardo Ricci—who graduated from the Facoltà in 1941 and remained a presence in Florence afterwards—is also pertinent here in its regional interpretation of the spatial continuity of Wright's late designs, as exemplified in his 1961 scheme for the village of Monte degli Ulivi, near Riesi **(fig. 1.6)**.

## The Florentine School

This shift on the part of Italian architects in general, and Florentine architects in particular, is to be seen in the context of a more general "rejection of the first highly technological 'Great War' via an embrace of the biomorphic and irrational" that "evolved in the 1950s to widespread anti-technological practices in Europe," as expressed by Caroline Jones.[4] From a strictly architectural standpoint, owing to the indiscriminate use of references, the partial and idiosyncratic application of elements taken from the organicist imaginary, and the strength of the various regionalisms, their series of experiments never amounted to anything like a recognizable Italian organic style. Overall, a marked eclecticism of dubious success resulted. Yet, as regards the genesis of Giorgini's design inclinations, their influence cannot be overstated. Far from constituting an isolated phenomenon in the Italian scene, the architectural language and motivations of his formal explorations were very much present in his environment, to the point that the words "Florentine School" have occasionally been used to implicitly emphasize the common ground shared by a

4 Caroline A. Jones, "Artist/System," in *A Second Modernism: MIT, Architecture, and the "Techno-Social" Moment* (Cambridge, MA: MIT Press, 2013), 508.

group of architects operating around the Facoltà di Architettura in Florence from the late 1940s through the early 1960s. As critic Marco Dezzi Bardeschi stated, this common ground involved making "the praise of nature, the critique of all stereotypes of abstract form and the exaltation of fluid, vibrant, indescribable space ... the constant points of reference for the development of new experimentation."[5]

Giorgini trained at the Facoltà in Florence, which he entered in 1945 **(fig. 1.7)**. At the time, the Facoltà was undergoing a major change in its pedagogical philosophy, galvanized by the appointment of Michelucci as dean in 1944. In light of the shift discussed above, Dezzi Bardeschi noted that this transitional period around the mid-1940s was in fact the second renewal process within the then young Facoltà, its academic atmosphere described thus:

> [D]etectable in the enthusiastic aspirations of the architects who came out of the heavy and depressing war interlude, [was] a will to become promoters of a "new civil order" born "out of a concordance of interests." In their pursuit of a theory of the environment, these architects advocated for a process of renovation—one rooted in the rediscovery of reality by involving nature and spontaneity.[6]

This milieu played a crucial role in shaping Giorgini's ensuing vocation, especially in regard to his fascination with nature. Michelucci became the most inspirational figure for the young student—indeed somebody close to a master, who triggered the imagery and design thinking Giorgini would pursue thereafter. They overlapped in Florence until 1948, when Michelucci stepped down as dean and transferred to the Facoltà di Ingegneria at Bologna. Having befriended him, Giorgini tried to stay in touch despite his departure.[7]

5 "… dell'elogio della Natura, della critica a tutti gli stereotipi della Forma astratta e dell'esaltazione di spazi tanto fluidi, pulsanti, indescrivibili . . . il proprio costante punto di riferimento per proiettarsi in sempre nuove sperimentazioni," in Marco Dezzi Bardeschi, "Kiesler, La Scuola Fiorentina e La Curvatura Del Mondo," *ANATKH*, no. 14 (June 1996), 74. Dezzi Bardeschi himself and Leonardo Savioli were also part of the Florentine School in those years. Despite favoring a certain stylistic freedom and primacy of the imagination, their architectural work did not display the same degree of formal experimentation as that of Michelucci, Ricci, and Giorgini.

6 "…individuabile nell'aspirazione entusiastica degli architetti, usciti dalla pesante ed avvilente parentesi della Guerra, a rendersi promotori di un 'ordine civile nuovo,' nato 'dalla concordanza degli interessi,' facendosi interpreti di un rinnovamento che si fondava sulla riscoperta della realtà e si radicava nel culto della natura e dello spontaneo facendo leva sulla teorica dell'ambientamento," in Marco Dezzi Bardeschi, "L'influenza Della Personalità Nell'insegnamento Dell'architettura," *Casabella*, no. 287 (May 1964), 18. The Facoltà di Architettura in Florence was founded in 1926. According to Dezzi Bardeschi the first renewal came about with the conversion of the school to "rationalism," in 1931. For further insight into the history of the Facoltà up to the mid-1960s, see Dezzi Bardeschi, "L'influenza della personalità," *Casabella*, 16–18.

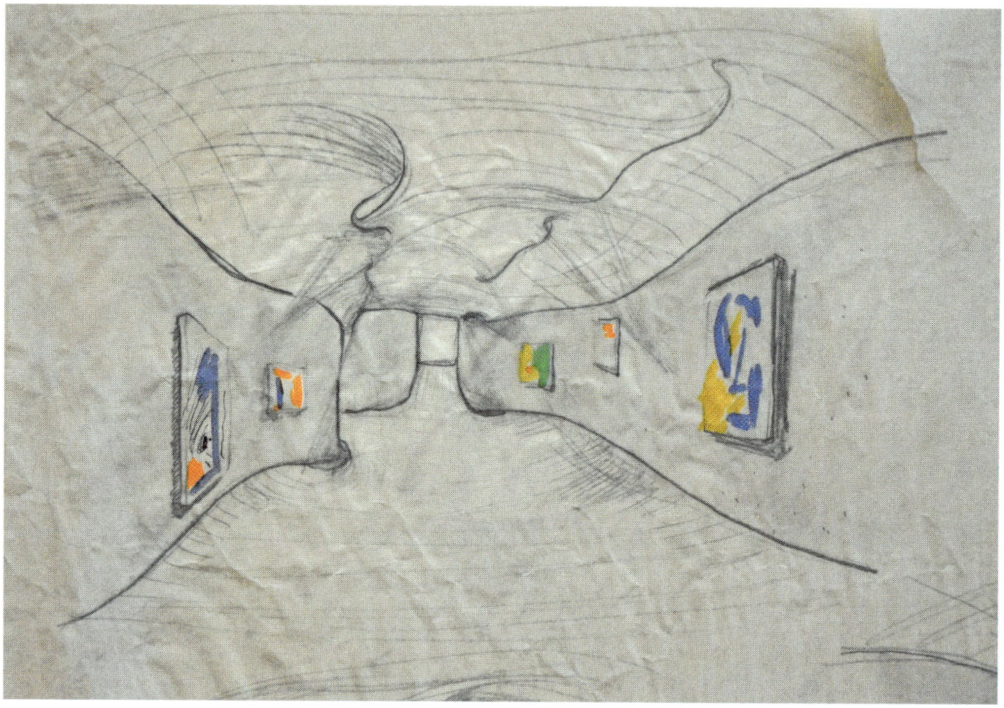

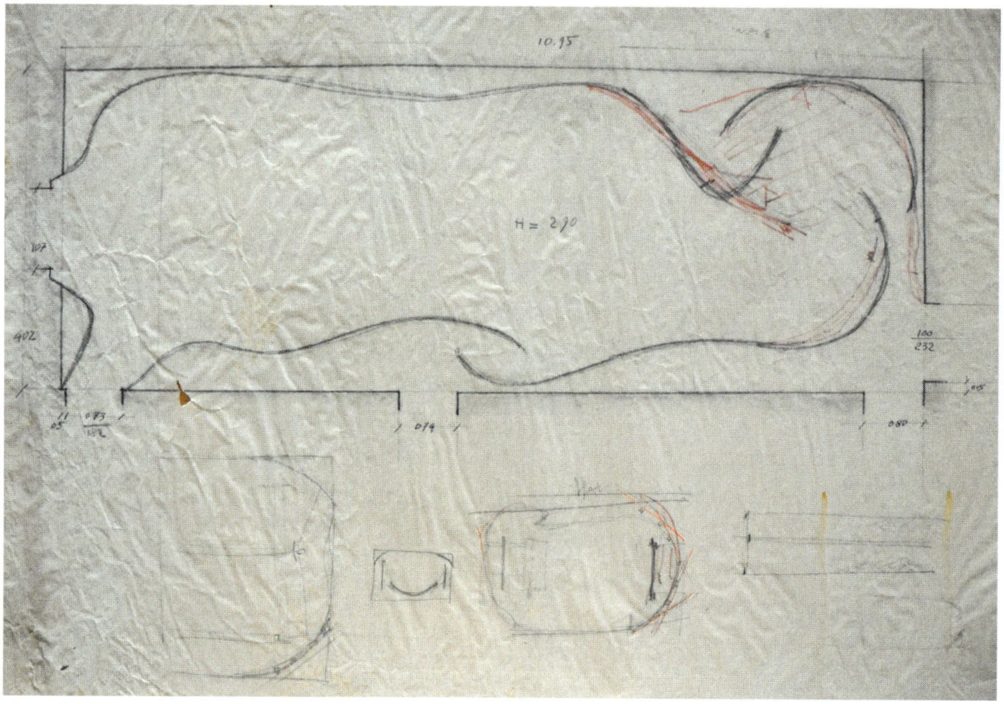

**1.9–12** Quadrante gallery in Florence, 1959. Sketches and interiors (opposite page).

## First Involvement with the Art World

After graduating, Giorgini worked for Quaroni (fig. 1.8) as well as for Edoardo Detti and Leonardo Savioli, both of whom had been his professors and former students of Michelucci. Between 1957 and 1969 he served at the Facoltà di Architettura in Florence as an assistant, first to Savioli (1957–66) and subsequently to architect Giuseppe Gori in Interior Design (1967–69). Giorgini's early professional activity was marked by obvious references to the language of modernism, from Le Corbusier to Savioli himself. But in the mid-1950s some of the organicist views to which he had been exposed started to turn into personal interests—primarily the observation of natural structures as sources of inspiration, which ignited his first experiments with an incipient surface topology. It was, in fact, following these initial inklings that two of Giorgini's most successful built works came into being: the Quadrante art gallery in Florence (1959) (fig. 1.9–12) and the aforementioned Saldarini House.

In 1962, through author and curator Lara Vinca Masini, Giorgini met André Bloc at the Quadrante gallery, where the French painter, sculptor, architect, and founder of the journals *Architecture d'Aujourd'hui* and *Aujourd'hui* was exhibiting his "mixed media" work (fig. 1.13).[8] This encounter, which evolved into a four-year friendship that ended with the untimely death of the French artist in 1966 (fig. 1.14), had a significant impact on Giorgini's career. Bloc, attracted by what he found in Giorgini's work—namely, a formal affinity with his own as well as with that of the other artists and architects he was promoting at the time (fig. 1.15)—offered Giorgini the chance to publish some of his designs for the first time outside of Italy.[9] Along with some of the acquaintances he had made through Quadrante, such as Bloc himself, Giorgini frequented the valley area of Querceta, where the Henraux quarry offered residency to artists in exchange for pieces made out of their marble. It was there that he mingled with prominent artists such as Henry Moore, Isamo Noguchi, Jean Arp, and Max Bill.

7 When he was only in his first year of study at Florence, Giorgini attended the fourth-year courses taught by Michelucci. Once the master left, Giorgini and a group of friends from the Facoltà took the train to Bologna regularly to continue attending Michelucci's classes there.

8 Quadrante was commissioned and run by Giorgini's sister, Matilde, who in turn was aided by Lara Vinca Masini. It was open until 1965, when Vittorio's father, Giovanni Battista Giorgini, who had been supporting the project all along, could no longer provide substantial funding. That same year Masini included Giorgini's work at the Prima Triennale Itinerante d'Architettura Italiana Contemporanea, and later on in "Topology and Morphogenesis," one of the sections of the collateral architecture show titled *Utopia e Crisi dell'antinatura – Intenzioni architettoniche in Italia* (Utopia and Crisis of Anti-Nature – Architectural Intentions in Italy) that she curated, along with Enrico Crispolti, at the 1978 Venice Biennale. Masini was always particularly fond of Vittorio Giorgini.

9 In *Aujourd'hui* no. 41, May 1963; no. 45, April 1964; and no. 53, May–June 1966.

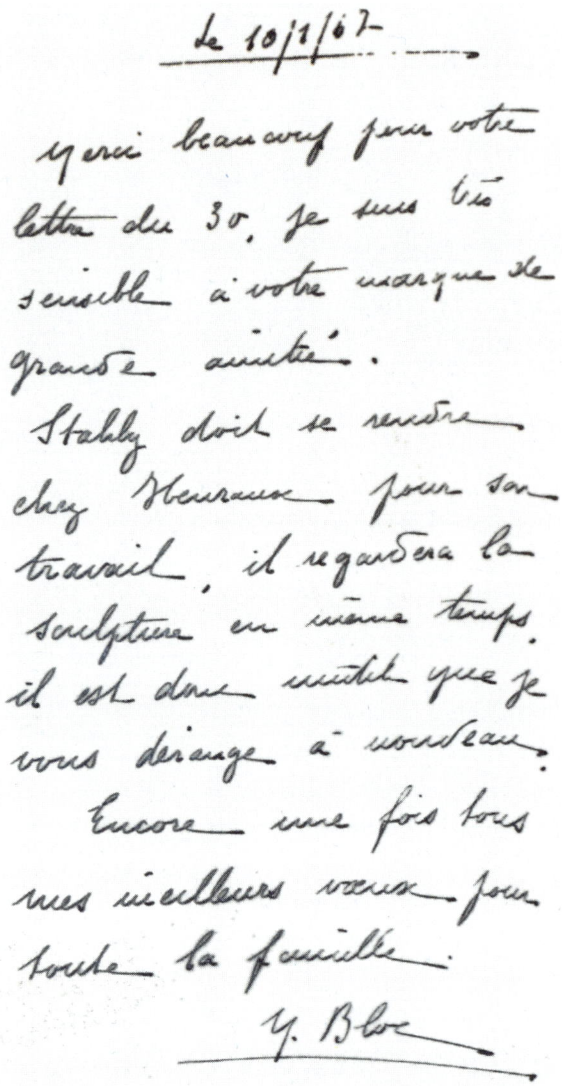
Le 10/1/67

Merci beaucoup pour votre lettre du 30, je suis très sensible à votre marque de grande amitié.

Stably doit se rendre chez Heureux pour son travail, il regardera la sculpture en même temps. Il est donc inutile que je vous dérange à nouveau.

Encore une fois tous mes meilleurs vœux pour toute la famille.

Y. Bloc

**1.14** Personal postcard from a member of the Bloc family, 1967.

Opposite page:
**1.13** Above, left: André Bloc speaking at the Quadrante gallery, with Giorgini changing the slides.
**1.15** Above, right: André Bloc. Studies for Individual Habitation, 1964–65.

## Kiesler

The references with which Giorgini was already familiar in the 1950s included Gaudí's structures, Le Corbusier's Ronchamp, Saarinen's TWA terminal, and Rudolf Steiner's Goetheanum. However, it was only after designing Quadrante and Baratti, and thanks to Bloc's journal too, that he encountered the work of Hermann Finsterlin **(fig. 1.16)**, and more importantly, that of Frederick Kiesler.[10] Kiesler's work offered the closest precedent to Giorgini's topological designs. Through his notion of "endlessness," the Austrian-American designer pursued an architecture of continuity and shell structures that he often equated with sculpture.[11] He started his search for "endlessness" as far back as 1924, in his "Endless Theater" project, although it would not be until his series of "Endless Houses"—the first sketches appearing in 1947 and the last versions in 1959, the same year Giorgini opened Quadrante—that the formal language of his designs reached a distinct complexity similar to that of Giorgini **(fig. 1.17)**. In the 1960s Kiesler began to arouse a great deal of interest among the Italians.[12] In Giorgini's case in particular, Kiesler was referred to as his "prophet and guru"—even though he had already started his experiments with surface topology and built the Saldarini House before he knew anything about the Austrian-American artist **(fig. 1.18–19)**.[13] The similarities between the architectural languages deployed in the Saldarini House and in Kiesler's Sisler House, to take one of his most representative schemes, are indeed apparent enough—not only in terms of the use of folded envelopes, but also in regard to the handling of the inside, both featuring an alternation between elements that adjust to the curvature of the enclosure and those perpendicular to it, with this enclosure brought to an extreme thinness.

10 See Marco Del Francia and Anna Guerriero, *Vittorio Giorgini: La Natura Come Modello* (Florence: A. Pontecorboli, 2000), 131–33.

11 See "Notes on Architecture as Sculpture," in *Art in America* (May 1966); quoted in "Frederick Kiesler 1923–1964," *Zodiac*, no. 19 (1969), 21.

12 According to Dezzi Bardeschi, a momentous gathering was to bring together Bloc and Kiesler in Michelucci's studio in Fiesole, in 1966. But this meeting was prevented by Kiesler's death in December 1965, and then Bloc's in 1966, meaning that Michelucci was unable to learn more about the former's artistic ideology. See Dezzi Bardeschi, "Kiesler, La Scuola Fiorentina e La Curvatura Del Mondo," 74.

13 See ibid., 72.

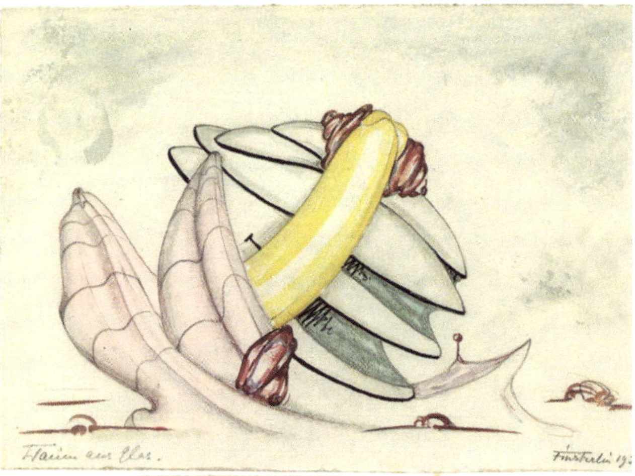

Opposite page:
**1.16** Above: Sketch by Vittorio Giorgini dedicated to Haresh Lalvani, 1980.
Below: Finsterlin. Traum aus Glas (left) and Casa Nova (right), 1920.

**1.17** Above: Frederick Kiesler. Sisler House, 1961.

**1.19** Right: Saldarini House on the Gulf of Baratti, 1960–62.

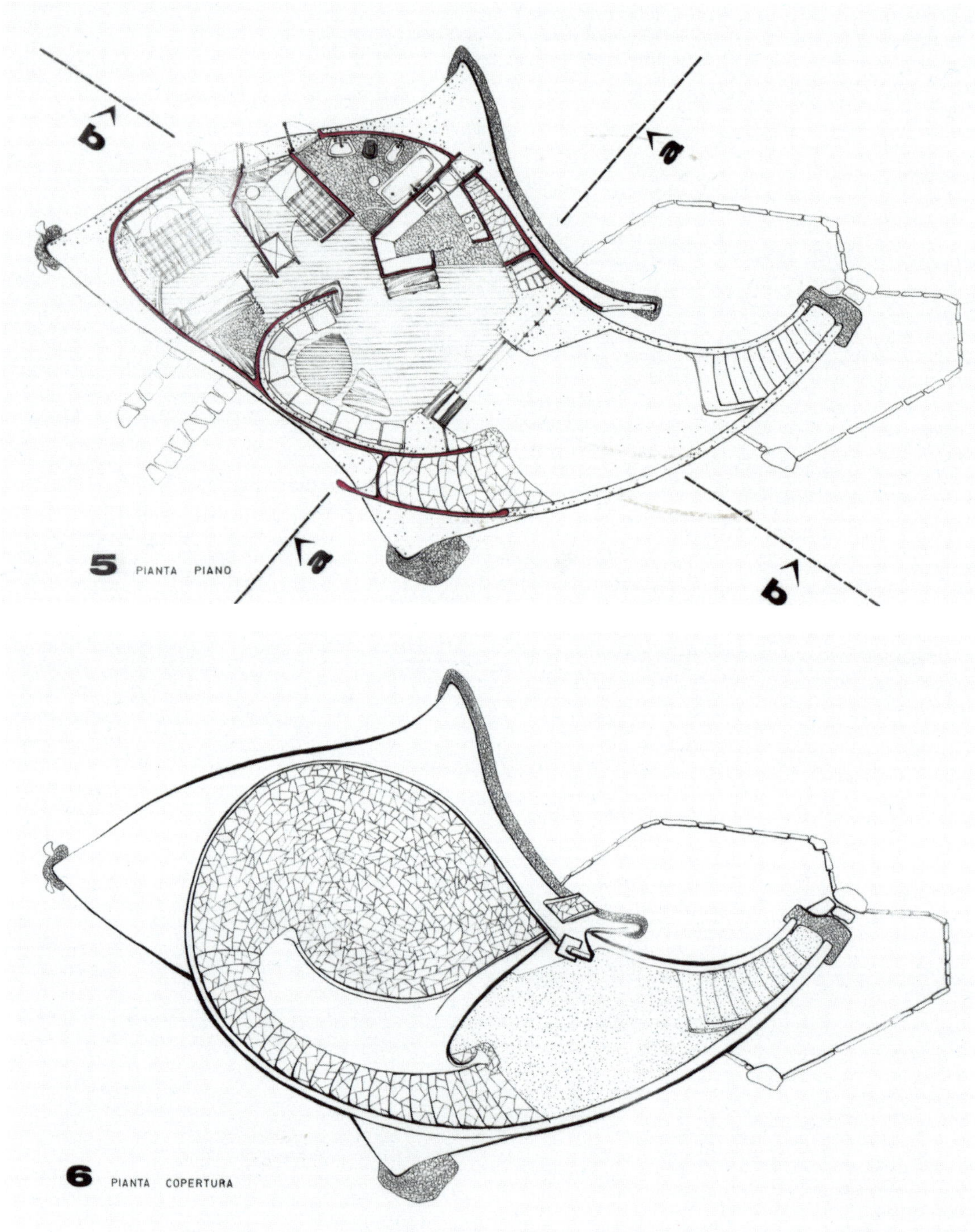


**1.18** Saldarini House on the Gulf of Baratti, 1960–62. First level and roof plans

The parallels between the two architects, however, are not to be discussed only on the basis of language and form, but also with respect to the deeper motivations behind their architectural ideologies. For Kiesler, architecture, art, and stage design offered ways to explore his conceptions of time, space, and motion. In doing so he was seeking to exert an emotional impact on the user's life so as to make it "freer" and more "exuberant" in the context of daily routine.[14] Similarly, Giorgini advocated for moving away from conventional orthogonal homes—which he considered "cages"—and toward the predominance of mobility and flexibility in living situations where physical space would not condition function. Giorgini believed that, to restore man's biological and psychological balance, the interior habitat ought to be in tune with the exterior world. That being the goal, a "geometry of a superior order" like the one found in nature ought to determine the space in which human beings were to live.[15] More self-conscious about architectural discourses than Kiesler, Giorgini expressed his intent early on as follows: "[w]ith these experiences I also tend to refuse adhesion to any artificial and false mode of expression derived from a formalism and culturalism devoid of any real and necessary meaning."[16]

Giorgini never showed any impulse to hide his referents. In 1966 he acknowledged Kiesler himself and other architects as particularly inspirational: "[s]ome historical studies of the baroque, of the experiments of Gaudí and Van de Velde, the rediscovery of Kiesler and Saarinen's attempts at models of free organizations, all the way to the Sydney Opera, have awakened my interest in this type of research."[17] In 1968, the Florentine architect discussed the importance of these models further in the catalog of his first solo exhibition in 1968, held at the Palazzo dei Diamanti in Ferrara: "the consequences of my interest in the work of Moore, Mendelsohn, Klee, Kandinsky, Kiesler, and others, in the proliferation of utopian proposals of fantastic architecture, and the reevaluation of Gaudí, aroused a nagging curiosity."[18]

## Uneasy Fit

Shortly beforehand, in 1965, Giorgini had been invited to the Prima Triennale Itinerante d'Architettura Italiana Contemporanea along with other relevant members of the Italian design scene, such as Achille Castiglioni, Vittorio Gregotti, and Paolo Portoghesi. Though produced one year earlier, it was at this Triennale that he delivered his first "Spaziologia" Manifesto. Giorgini intended this neologism to characterize the study of space in architecture as driven by investigations into natural structures—investigations which, in his view, would be termed "morphology" when undertaken for purely scientific purposes, as he stated towards the end of his life.[19] On the occasion of his Ferrara show in 1968, he presented his second "Spaziologia" Manifesto, along with the results of his research in architectural design.[20]

14 For a recent in-depth study of Kiesler's contribution to architecture and the visual arts see Stephen John Phillips, *Elastic Architecture: Frederick Kiesler and His Research Practice – A Study of Continuity in the Age of Modern Production* (PhD Dissertation, Princeton School of Architecture, 2008).

15 See Vittorio Giorgini, "Comunicazione Personale," in *Utopia E Crisi Dell'antinatura: Momenti Delle Intenzioni Architettoniche in Italia: Topologia E Morfogenesi* (Venice: La Biennale di Venezia, 1978), 130–31.

16 "Con queste esperienze tendo anche a rifiutare ogni adesione ad artificiali e false espressioni, sorrette su formalismi e culturalismi vuoti di significato reale e necessario," Marco Dezzi Bardeschi and Lara Vinca Masini, *Prima Triennale Itinerante d'Architettura Italiana Contemporanea* (Edizioni Centro Proposte, 1965), 103.

17 "Quelques vérifications historiques sur le baroque, sur certaines expériences de Gaudi et de Van de Velde, la redécouverte de certain essais d'organisations libres comme les expériences de Kiesler et de Saarinen, jusqu'à l'Opéra de Sydney, ont réveillé mon intérêt pour ce type de recherche," in "Les Architectes de Florence," *Aujourd'hui*, no. 53 (June 1966), 69.

18 "Le conseguenze degli interessi di lavoro sollevati da Moore, Mendelsohn, Klee, Kandinski, Kiesler, e gli altri, le proposte utopistiche di architetture fantastiche che andavano moltiplicandosi, la rivalutazione di Gaudi, ponevano assillanti curiosità," in Paolo Riani, "Case immaginarie: Vittorio Giorgini, lo spazio dell'anima," *Ville giardini*, no. 257 (March 1991), 38–41. The quote was originally taken from Giorgini, *Strutture Soniche – Ipotesi per Un Habitat Più Naturale, Catalogo Della Personale Tenuta a Ferrara Nel Palazzo Dei Diamanti* (Comune di Ferrara, 1968).

19 In an autobiography he recorded on tape in 2005.

20 See Giorgini, *Strutture Soniche – Ipotesi per Un Habitat Più Naturale.*

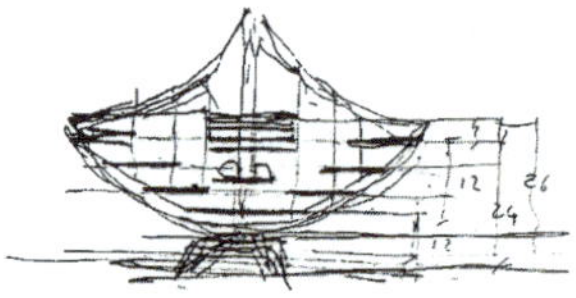

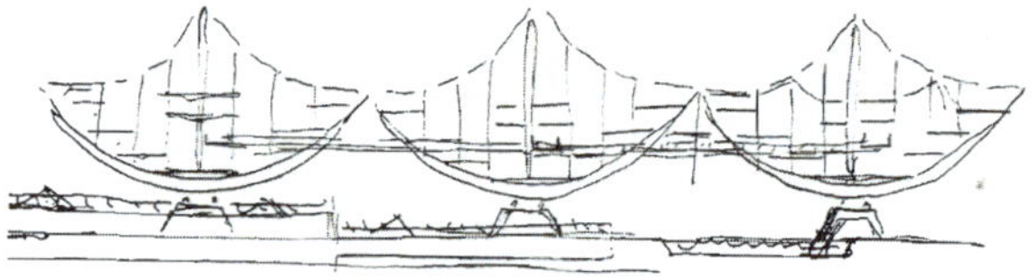

**1.20** Left: "Hydropolis" project (1981–82)

**1.21** Below: Vittorio Giorgini in collaboration with Claudio Cantella. Entry for the European Patent Office competition in The Hague (1989).

Slowly but surely, Giorgini built something of a reputation in the Italian architecture scene of the 1960s. But the last push never occurred—mainly due to his somewhat difficult character, but also to the fact that he wished to keep pursuing the design approach he had been nurturing since the mid-1950s, despite the changes that were beginning to take place in Italian architectural culture. Firstly, during the second half of the 1960s, he had some serious fallings-out both with Savioli and Ricci, then one of the most prominent figures in the Florentine academic scene. Secondly, the Facoltà refused to create a laboratory for his topological investigations. Thirdly, the growth of the so-called "radicals" in Florence (*Superstudio* and *Archizoom* appeared in 1966, *UFO* and *i 9999* in 1967), which marked the start of the third renewal process at the Facoltà, did not help, as Giorgini found himself in deep conflict with their anti-architectural stance. A divorce from his wife at the time only made matters worse. Having all the odds stacked against him and hoping to find a more open-minded setting in which to undertake his experiments, Giorgini moved to New York City in 1969.

By the summer of 1971, he was teaching at the Pratt Institute School of Architecture, where he remained for twenty-five years. He combined his lecturing with his research involving geometry, morphology, and construction, often with the aid of his students.[21] It was in this period that Giorgini began conversations with a group of other architects and artists, including John Johansen, William Katavolos, and Haresh Lalvani, regarding the idea of founding a Center for Experimental Structures at Pratt. The enterprise, however, remained a proposal at that time, with the Center not being formally established until the year 2000, after Giorgini had left the school.[22]

Following pages:
**1.22** Letter from the chairman of Columbia University's School of Architecture, 1972 (p. 60).
**1.23** Letter from a research assistant at the Museum of Modern Art, 1968 (p. 61).

21 In addition to his work involving surface topology, Giorgini embarked on a related yet different research path in 1979, one concerning the development of urban megastructures based on geometric spatial patterns. Hydropolis (1981–82), Walking Tall (1982–83), Genesis (1984), Patenport (1989), and River Crane (1993) were projects that resulted from this alternative line of inquiry **(fig. 1.20–21)**. Giorgini's megastructure projects will not be considered for the purposes of this book; only his designs featuring shell structures.

22 Among other venues, a number of his projects were displayed at Columbia University (1970) **(fig. 1.22)**; Syracuse University, as a participant in the *Enviro Vision* show (1971); in the *Making Megalopolis Matter* exhibit at the Cultural Center of New York in 1972; at the 1978 Venice Biennale, within the section on architecture titled "Topology and Morphogenesis;" and at MoMA in 1979, partaking in the *Transformations in Modern Architecture* show curated by Arthur Drexler **(fig. 1.23–24)**. In 1996, due to a degenerative eye disease that led to him going blind a few years later, he returned to his native Florence. There he continued his personal research in a more casual manner, until he died on February 18, 2010. Currently, Giorgini's work is part of the permanent collections at the Pompidou Center and the FRAC, both in France. For a comprehensive biographical account of Vittorio Giorgini's life and work, see the only monograph published to date: Marco Del Francia and Anna Guerriero, *Vittorio Giorgini: La Natura Come Modello* (Florence: A. Pontecorboli, 2000).

**Columbia University** in the City of New York | *New York, N. Y. 10027*

SCHOOL OF ARCHITECTURE

Chairman, Division of Architecture

Avery Hall

17 May 1972

Mr. Vittorio Giorgini
620 Greenwich Street
New York, New York 10014

Dear Vittorio:

I wish very much to express my sincere appreciation for your contribution to the "Italian Architects" exhibit. It was very successfully executed.

We would like to invite you to participate in our platform reviews on either Tuesday or Wednesday, May 23rd or 24th, whichever day is most convenient for you. Please call Bernadette (280-3504) and let her know your preference.

Once again, many thanks and I hope you will be able to join us for a review.

My best,

Alexander Kouzmanoff
Chairman

AK/bd

**The Museum of Modern Art**

245-3200

11 West 53 Street, New York, N.Y. 10019 ~~Circle 5-8900~~ Cable: Modernart

August 5, 1968

Signore Vittorio Giorgini
Lungarno Acciaioli 18
Firenze
Italy

Dear Mr. Giorgini,

The Department of Architecture and Design at the Museum of Modern Art maintains an extensive photographic collection of buildings and projects by 20th century architects. It is used by visiting scholars and by museum personnel for research and exhibition purposes.

This summer I am preparing for this collection (and eventually for an exhibition) a file dealing with the subject of "architecture as sculpture". Naturally your house in Populonia, Italy is of great interest to me. It is certainly an exciting free form house. We would much appreciate photographs of its interior as well as exterior such as those which appear in <u>Aujourd'hui</u> in May-June, 1966. If you have done similar work elsewhere, please include photos of it, as well. A statement of your aims would be very helpful.

I want to thank you for your cooperation, in advance. I'm certainly looking forward to hearing from you soon.

Sincerely yours,

Peter S. Kaufman

Peter S. Kaufman
Research Assistant

P.S. For our purposes, the best size for the photos is 8" X 10". Enclosed with this letter you will also find a data sheet, if you would please complete it.

Miss Mary Jane LIGHTBOWN
384

Mr. Graham

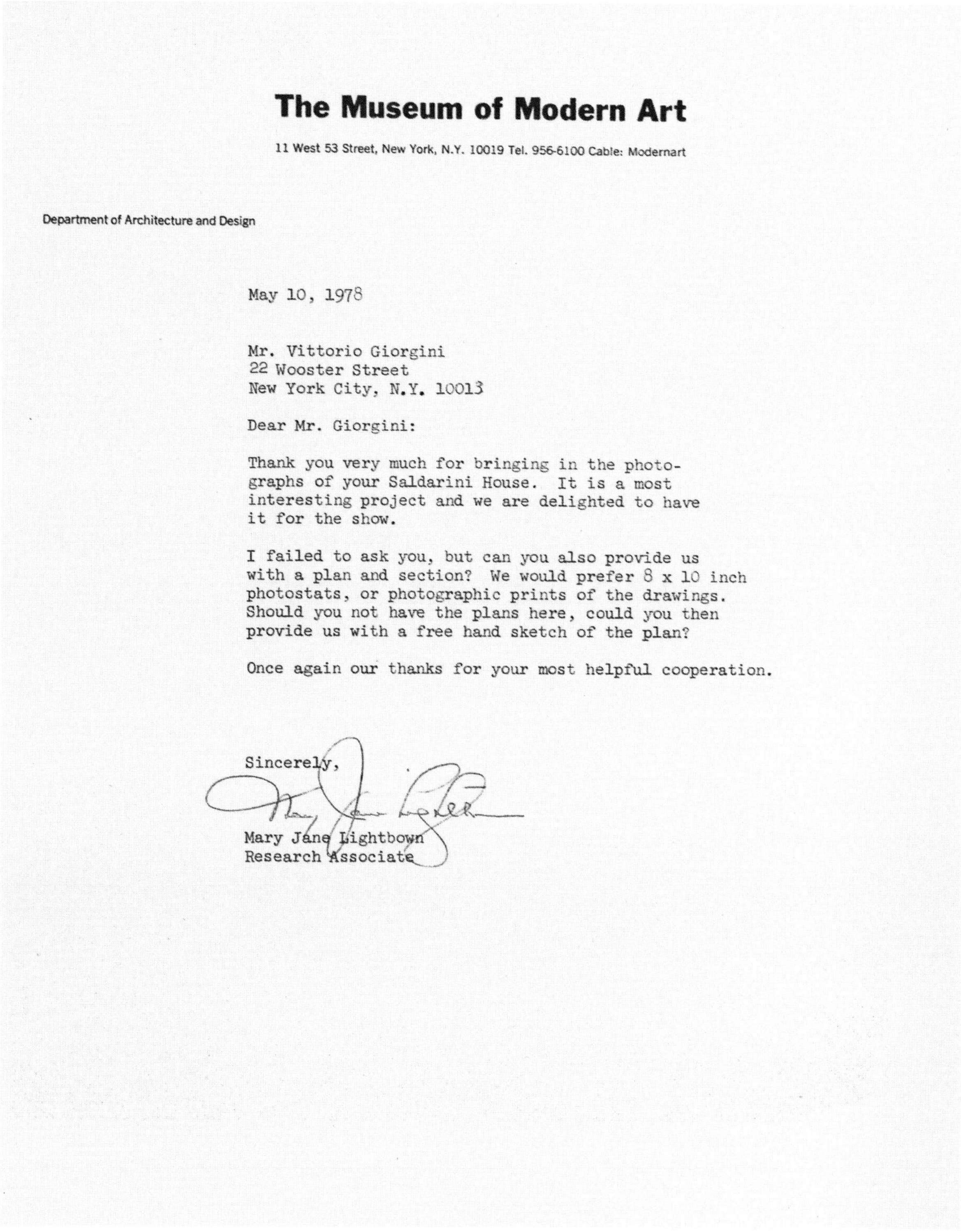

The Museum of Modern Art

11 West 53 Street, New York, N.Y. 10019 Tel. 956-6100 Cable: Modernart

Department of Architecture and Design

May 10, 1978

Mr. Vittorio Giorgini
22 Wooster Street
New York City, N.Y. 10013

Dear Mr. Giorgini:

Thank you very much for bringing in the photographs of your Saldarini House. It is a most interesting project and we are delighted to have it for the show.

I failed to ask you, but can you also provide us with a plan and section? We would prefer 8 x 10 inch photostats, or photographic prints of the drawings. Should you not have the plans here, could you then provide us with a free hand sketch of the plan?

Once again our thanks for your most helpful cooperation.

Sincerely,

Mary Jane Lightbown
Research Associate

Precedent page:
**1.24** Letter from a research associate at the Museum of Modern Art, 1978.

# GRADUAL SCIENTIZATION OF GIORGINI'S ARCHITECTURAL THINKING IN AMERICA: TOWARD A THEORY OF DESIGN

Unlike other Italian architects employing organicist motifs in their design—most of whom stopped doing so in the early 1960s—Giorgini continued on the same track throughout his entire life. Contrasting with the production of Burt and Balmond, however, his investigations did not start off on a strong scientific foundation. Rather, the basis of his design methods remained one of intuition, analogy, and a certain aesthetic resemblance to elements of the natural world during his first fifteen years of experimentation with architectural form. The initial phase of his design thinking, therefore, had more to do with typical modernist modalities—albeit with a view to devising a different range of forms—than with the paradigm of the intense scientization of design that unfolded across the West over the course of the second half of the twentieth century, with which his work ultimately resonated powerfully.

## Cymatics

And yet his interest in the sciences was awakened early on. Giorgini's curiosity about the principles of nature, eventually leading to his explorations in geometry, was piqued by his acquaintance with the research of Swiss physician and natural scientist Hans Jenny. The father of *cymatics*—a term designating the study of methods to render sound and vibration visible—had been visiting Florence regularly since before World War II and was an old friend of Giorgini's family **(fig. 1.25)**. One of those visits, in 1950, proved to be of particular significance for the young Florentine architect. Jenny had brought along a number of intriguing photographs. During his investigations into how to better understand and improve electrocardiograms for making diagnoses, Jenny had developed a technique to shape fluids and powder through vibration by means of piezoelectric valves.[23] Vibration, so the scientist predicted, could reveal a greater degree of resolution and complexity upon examining the brain and heart than was obtained at the time from electrocardiograms. Giorgini was thrilled by the results of the new vibration processes shown in Jenny's photographs **(fig. 1.26)**.

23 Jenny's starting point were the sonorous figures discovered by Ernst Chladni in the late eighteenth and early nineteenth century. Jenny used electric impulses to visualize in three dimensions what his predecessor had managed to do only on a plane surface. See Hans Jenny, *Cymatics: A Study of Wave Phenomena and Vibration* (Newmarket, NH: MACROmedia, 2001), 21ff.

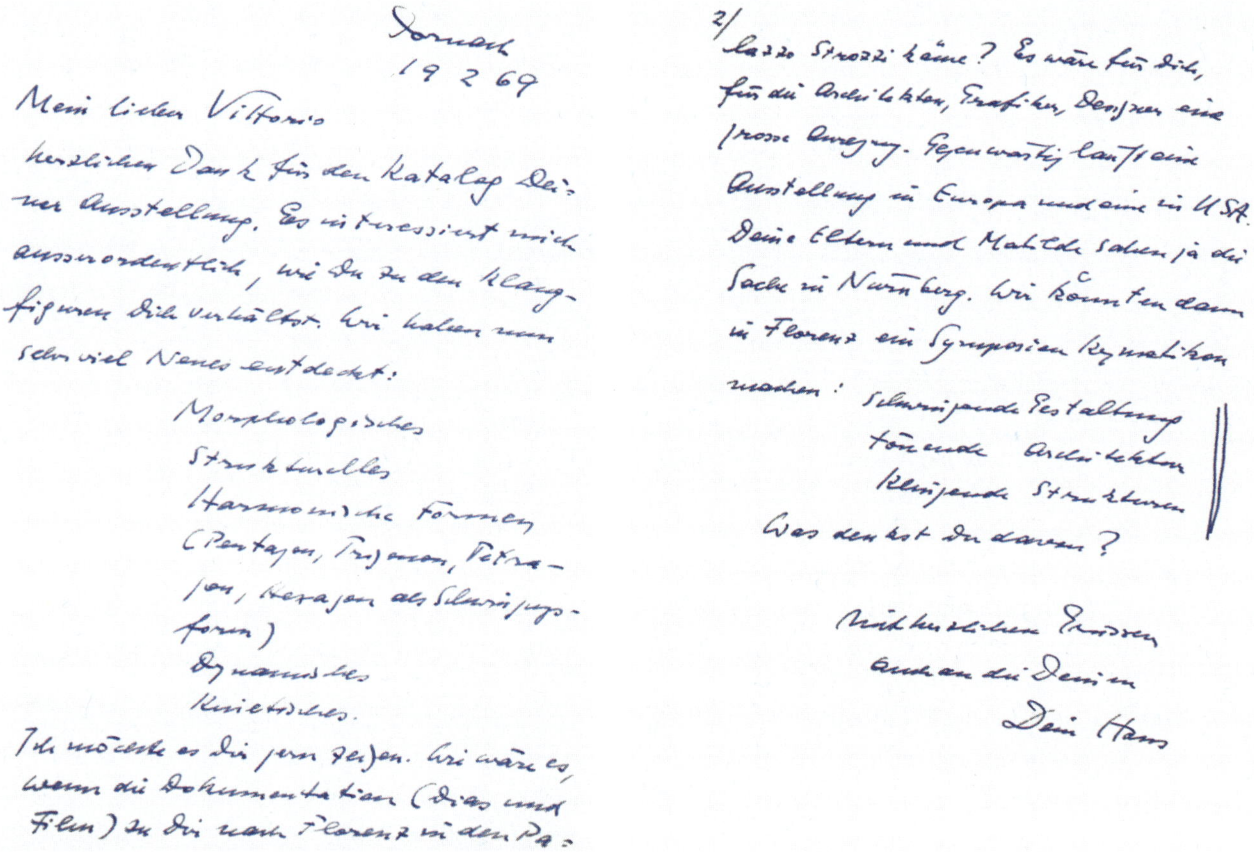

Dornach
19 2 69

Mein lieber Vittorio
herzlichen Dank für den Katalog Deiner Ausstellung. Es interessiert mich ausserordentlich, wie Du zu den Klangfiguren Dich verhältst. Wir haben nun sehr viel Neues entdeckt:

Morphologisches
Strukturelles
Harmonische Formen
(Pentagon, Trigonon, Tetragon, Hexagon als Schwingungsform)
Dynamisches
Kinetisches.

Ich möchte es Dir gern zeigen. Wie wäre es, wenn die Dokumentation (Dias und Film) zu Dir nach Florenz in den Pa-

2/
lazzo Strozzi käme? Es wäre für Dich, für die Architekten, Grafiker, Designer eine grosse Anregung. Gegenwärtig läuft eine Ausstellung in Europa und eine in USA. Deine Eltern und Mathilde sahen ja die Sache in Nürnberg. Wir könnten dann in Florenz ein Symposion Kymatikon machen:

Schwingende Gestaltung
tönende Architektur
klingende Strukturen

Was denkst du davon?

Mit herzlichen Grüssen
auch an die Deinen
Dein Hans

1.25 Above: Personal letter from Hans Jenny, 1969.

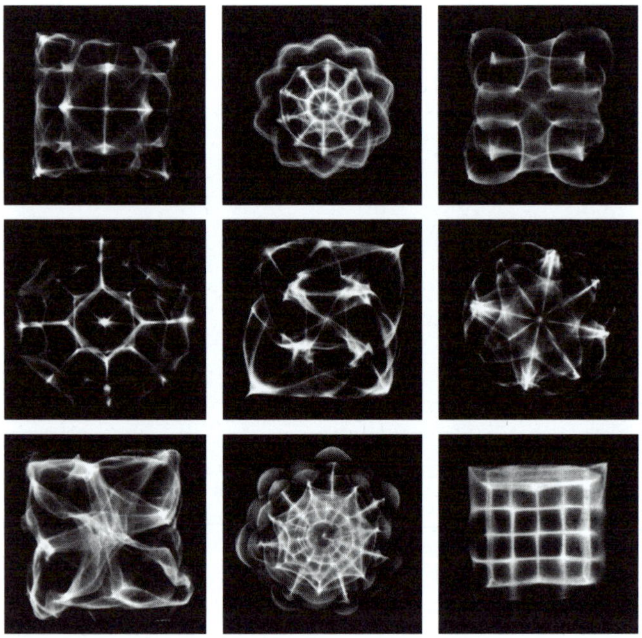

1.26 Left: Hans Jenny. Three-dimensional geometric wave patterns caused by sound vibrations in water, 1967.

They enabled him to envision how, with the aid of a then incipient computer, a new design procedure would be able to generate forms resembling the deep structures of nature. Such was Jenny's influence over Giorgini that the Italian architect entitled his Ferrara exhibit of 1968 "Sonic Structures" in reference to the scientist's experiments. In a passage written a few decades later, Giorgini described his new design hypothesis:

> In the forms he [Jenny] produced this way, geometric structures and figures of extraordinary resemblance to natural ones could be recognized, especially in the microstructure. . . . Scientific development and observation of nature had already prepared the road. The computer was still in its infancy, but already showed a capacity for memory and complex operation. I imagined that a catalog of shapes obtained by vibrations could be stored in the memory of a computer. This would enable you to design a model, and have the computer "scan" the model and compare its shape to those in the catalog. The computer could then define the parameters of the vibratory types and sources within the model's form, and trigger the system. Then we would produce a form by vibrating a light material, for example "ionic dust," that would "freeze" over the virtual surface of the vibration—in a manner similar to electrolytic processes.[24]

This encounter with Jenny brought biological structuralism into Giorgini's picture, and by extension it catalyzed the eventual rapport of his design thinking to the larger paradigm shift involving an intense scientization of design. Indeed, encounters in which a scientist inspired a designer became something of a pattern at the time, this being one central engine for that shift. For example, Kepes first encountered the hidden images of the natural world through the photomicrographs a metallurgist friend showed him in Weimar-era Berlin. Similarly, Frei Otto was introduced to a number of key microscopic images of living organisms, like the skeletons of radiolarians and the shells of diatoms, by German biologist Johann-Gerhard Helmcke. The difference here, however—as with many other figures partaking in that paradigm shift—is that Giorgini put scientization processes specifically to the service of architectural thinking, as opposed to that of other disciplines, such as art (Kepes), membrane-based engineering structures (Otto), or in yet other cases, industrial design, building science, and managerial enterprises.

Deeply moved by the structures of nature he had been able to visualize through Jenny's technology, Giorgini began to turn those structures into full-scale, three-dimensional designs just a few years later, in the mid-1950s. Yet the scientization of his design thinking was not consolidated until he arrived in New York. It was

24 Vittorio Giorgini, "Early Experiments in Design Derived from Study of Nature's Morphologies," *International Journal of Space Structures* 11, no. 1 & 2 (1996), 58.

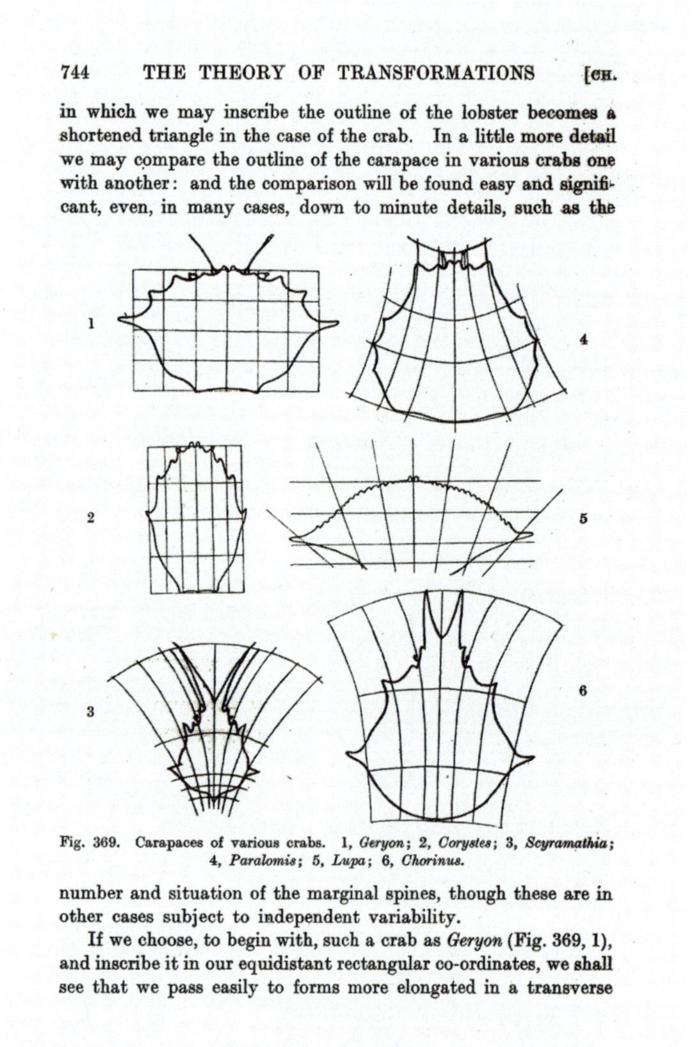

744 THE THEORY OF TRANSFORMATIONS [CH.

in which we may inscribe the outline of the lobster becomes a shortened triangle in the case of the crab. In a little more detail we may compare the outline of the carapace in various crabs one with another: and the comparison will be found easy and significant, even, in many cases, down to minute details, such as the

Fig. 369. Carapaces of various crabs. 1, *Geryon*; 2, *Corystes*; 3, *Scyramathia*; 4, *Paralomis*; 5, *Lupa*; 6, *Chorinus*.

number and situation of the marginal spines, though these are in other cases subject to independent variability.

If we choose, to begin with, such a crab as *Geryon* (Fig. 369, 1), and inscribe it in our equidistant rectangular co-ordinates, we shall see that we pass easily to forms more elongated in a transverse

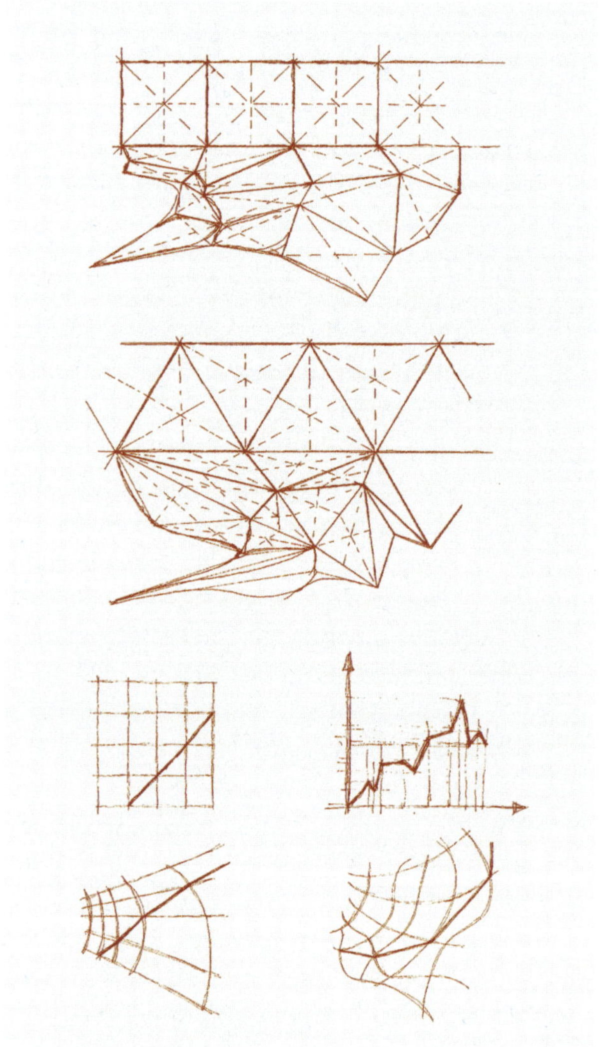

**1.27** Left: D'Arcy Wentworth Thompson, the comparison of related forms in On Growth and Form.

Right: Sketches in Vittorio Giorgini's Spatiology: The Morphology of the Natural Sciences in Architecture and Design.

at the beginning of his American period, in 1969, that he came across the work of D'Arcy Thompson. This finding was crucial. It triggered a ten-year period in which Giorgini undertook substantial research in the sciences—research that proved to be essential to rationalizing the curved components of his design processes. The Thompsonian paradigm, as expounded in his well-known *On Growth and Form* of 1917 (republished in 1942, and then again in an abridged version in 1961), established that forms found in nature are but a reflection of those registered by geometry; in other words, that there exist sequences of mathematical logic behind the morphology of living species—say, a fish or a shell **(fig. 1.27)**. This is the kind of biological structuralism where Giorgini's focus on nature in the interest of grasping its organizational structures—rather than seeking formal imitation of external appearance—is to be located. Notably, through D'Arcy Thompson's theories, he also deepened his understanding of how forces can shape formal configurations.

## Missing Connections

Before moving to the US there is no indication that Giorgini may have been attracted to the work of Rome-based architect Luigi Moretti, despite the close rapport between the architectural scenes of Rome and Florence during the 1950s and 1960s, as well as Giorgini's direct connections to the former, primarily via Quaroni. From the 1960s onward, some of Moretti's work presented an obvious organicist character, yet no evidence is found of Giorgini's reference either to Moretti's Stadium N exhibited at the 1960 Parametric Architecture show as part of the 12th Milan Triennial, or to schemes such as the sanctuary of the Primato di San Pietro (1965–68) and the church of the Concilio Sancta Maria Mater Ecclesiae (1965–70), to cite a few of Moretti's most overtly organicist projects.

Other than the work of Frank Lloyd Wright (which he came across in the late 1940s) and Eero Saarinen (in the 1950s), there is also no evidence that Giorgini was influenced by—or even aware of—the production of any American architects typically associated with twentieth-century organicism, such as John Lautner and Bruce Goff. This ignorance continued during the first decade after relocating to New York City—when he devoted most of his efforts to advancing his design language with organicist overtones—and, indeed, throughout his entire American period. Therefore, it cannot be said that Giorgini's line of development, while rooted in the Wright-influenced Italian scene, ultimately led back to the American trajectory of the master's protégés. Nevertheless, this makes perfect sense, since, apart from the organicist overtones, the architectural languages of Lautner and Goff and that of Giorgini have little in common.

More surprising is the lack of evidence that the Florentine architect may have known of David Jacob's "Simulated House for a Family of Five" from 1970, as the

10. WESTON, Edward American, 1886-1958.

6 Nudes, 1933-5, from a group of 12. Gift of Willard Van Dyke, 1971.

11. WILLOUGHBY, Bob American, born 1927.

5 Film Stills from The Cowboys, 1971. Acquired by the Department of Film for its Film Stills Archive.

12. JACOB, David, architect. American, born 1928.

Model: Simulated Dwelling for a Family of Five. 1970. Fiberglas and polyester resin. Scale: 3/8" = 1'.

The conventional scheme presents a sequence of entry, living, dining and individual spaces ascending helically around a central stair and elevator. This model is one of a series made to study the effect and usefulness of the unified shell principle applied to problems in architectural design.

13. JENSEN, Jakob Danish.

Beogram 4000. Tangential arm record player. Designed 1972, production scheduled 1973. Manufacturer: Bang and Olufsen, Denmark. Gift of the manufacturer.

Servo-driven pick-up arm and guide arm with photocell. Tangential pick-up arm tracks the record in a straight line toward the centre, tangential to the groove, eliminating skating effects and tracking errors. Pressure operated control panel for manual selection of speed, pause, stop and lowering of pick-up arm at any point on the record.

14. OLIVIER French?

Hand Mirror. c. 1915? Silver frame; beveled mirror. Gift of Mrs. Douglas Auchincloss.

15. SAPPER, Richard Italian, born Germany.

Rocket. Electronic digital clock; designed and produced 1972. Manufacturer: Ritz-Italora, Italy. Gift of the manufacturer.

Transparent acrylic casing; transistors and electronic digital vacuum lamps (110/220 volts 50/60 cycle AC); 33 degree plane angle.

16. WEINSTEIN, Berel American, born 1946.

Disposable Thermometer. 1972. Manufacturer: Bio-Medical Sciences, Inc. Gift of the manufacturer.

1.31 Left: "Twenty-Five New Acquisitions on View at Museum," p. 3. Museum of Modern Art press release from January 20, 1973.

1.32 Below: Installation view of the exhibition 25 Recent Acquisitions (XII), January 17, 1973 – March 18, 1973. Photographic Archive. The Museum of Modern Art Archives, New York. Photograph by Kate Keller.

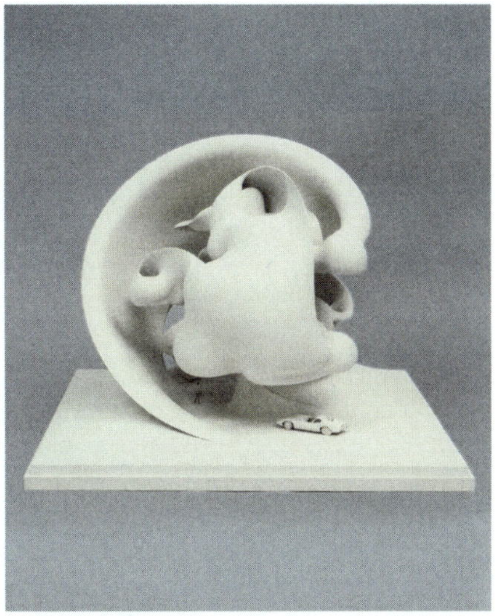

**1.28–30** David Jacob (b. 1928). Simulated Dwelling for a Family of Five Project, 1970. Fiberglass, polyester resin, metal, paper, plastic, and synthetic polymer paint. 28 x 34 3/8 x 34 3/8" (71.1 x 87.3 x 87.3 cm). Estée and Joseph Lauder Design Fund.

expressive and spatial similarities with his own designs are nothing short of striking. In a series of fiberglass models, Jacob explored the possibilities of the continuous shell principle on the scale of domestic architecture. The columnless structure was intended to suggest a sequence of living functions, such as entry, living, dining, and a series of individual spaces, that bleed into one another in a fluid procession without partitions, so as not to isolate the occupants and their activities **(fig. 1.28–30)**. General inspiration for the scheme ought to be traced back to Jacob's work for Saarinen on the main terminal at Dulles International Airport (1958–63), while the particular language was informed by taking a mollusk as a referent. Although one of the models for this project was acquired by the Museum of Modern Art in New York shortly after it was made—and exhibited in this venue three times during the 1970s (1973, 1974, 1979) **(fig. 1.31–32)**—Jacob was not particularly well-known at the time, which would largely explain the fact that Giorgini may not have encountered it. In fact, Jacob's career as an architect remains virtually unknown to this day.

One possible Italo-American connection to consider involving organicism is Paolo Soleri, who was apprenticed to Frank Lloyd Wright in the 1940s, returned to his native Turin in 1950, and moved back to the States in 1954 to stay there for good. There was a mere seven-year age gap between Soleri and Giorgini, but they each came from a different part of Italy, and Soleri left for America over a decade earlier, settling far from New York City, in Arizona. All these misalignments in time and space may justify the lack of evidence of Giorgini's interest in or indeed knowledge of Soleri's work.

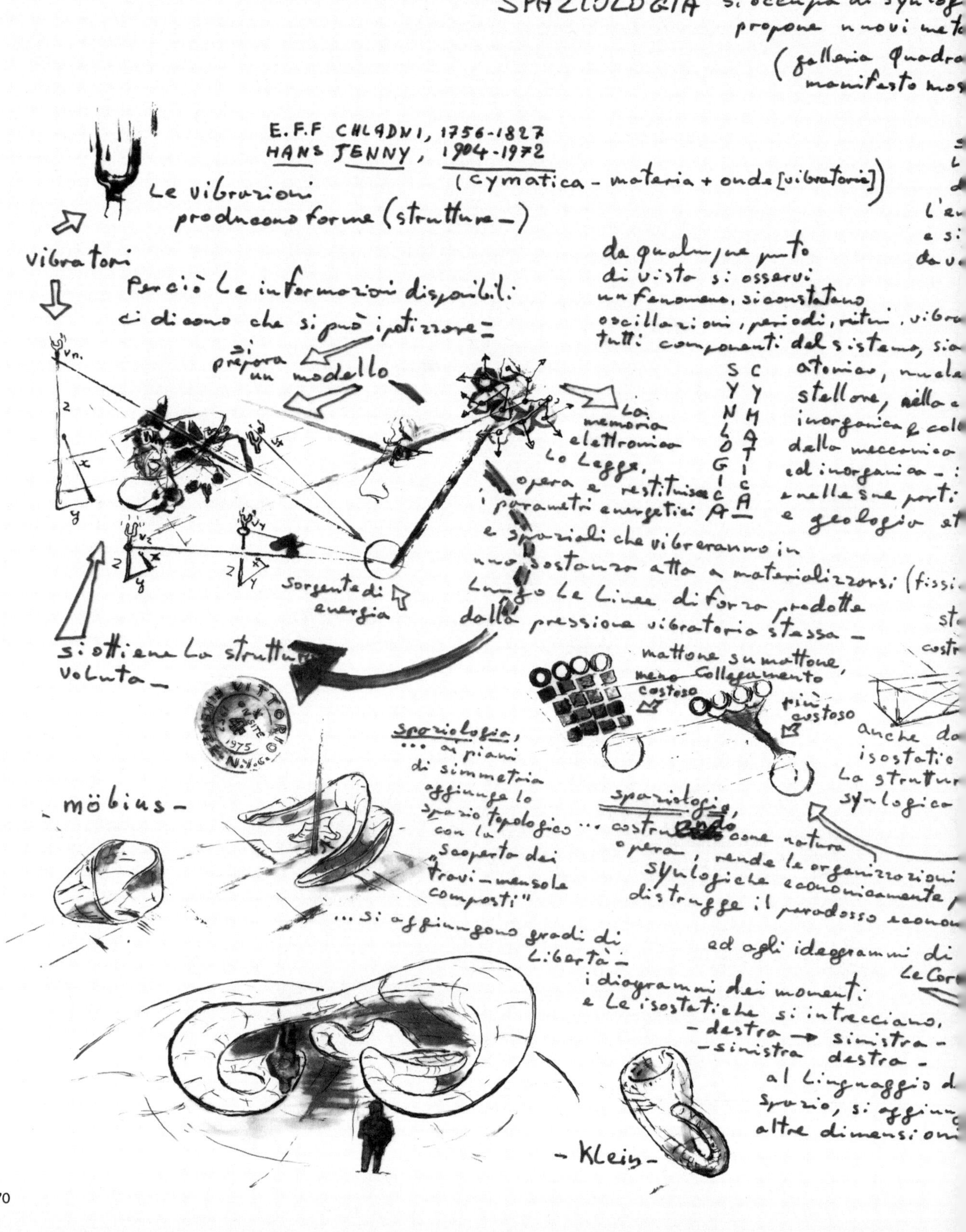
SPAZIOLOGIA
E.F.F CHLADNI, 1756-1827
HANS JENNY, 1904-1972
(cymatica - materia + onde [vibratorie])
Le vibrazioni producono forme (strutture -)
vibratori
Perciò le informazioni disponibili ci dicono che si può ipotizzare =
si prepara un modello
da qualunque punto di vista si osservi un fenomeno, si constatano oscillazioni, periodi, ritmi,
la memoria elettronica la legge, opera e restituisce i parametri energetici e spaziali che vibreranno in una sostanza atta a materializzarsi
lungo le linee di forza prodotte dalla pressione vibratoria stessa -
SYNLOGICA
SCYMATICA
sorgente di energia
si ottiene la struttura voluta -
mattone su mattone,
costoso
più costoso
spaziologia, ... ai piani di simmetria aggiunge lo spazio topologico con la scoperta dei "travi-mensole composti"
möbius -
spaziologia, ... costruendo come natura opera, rende le organizzazioni synlogiche economicamente, distrugge il paradosso econom
... si aggiungono gradi di libertà -
ed agli ideogrammi di Le Cor
i diagrammi dei momenti e le isostatiche si intrecciano,
- destra → sinistra -
- sinistra destra -
al linguaggio d spazio, si aggiun altre dimensioni
- Klein -

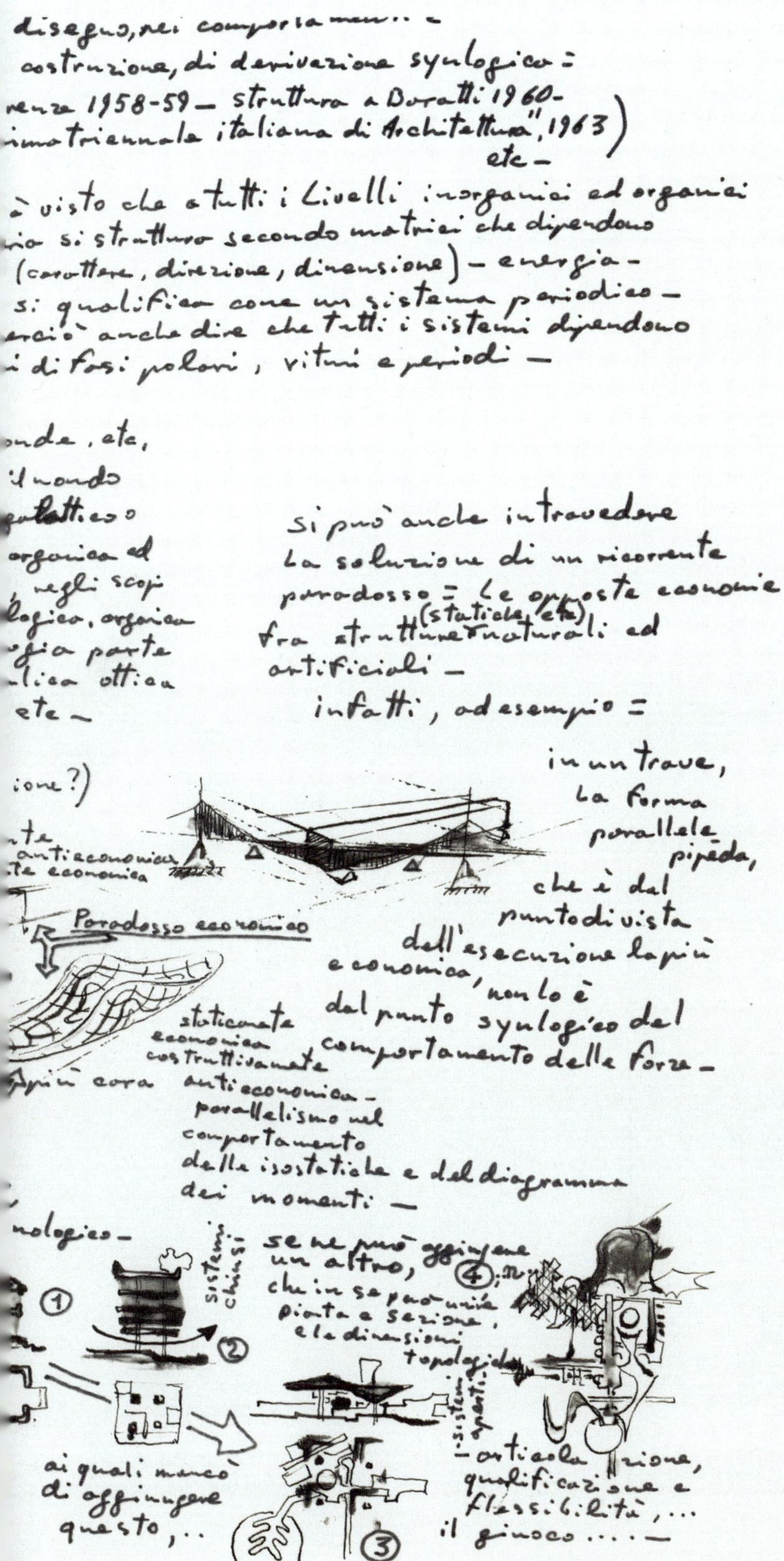


**1.33** Giorgini's sketches for the 1975 "On Site" conference in New York City.

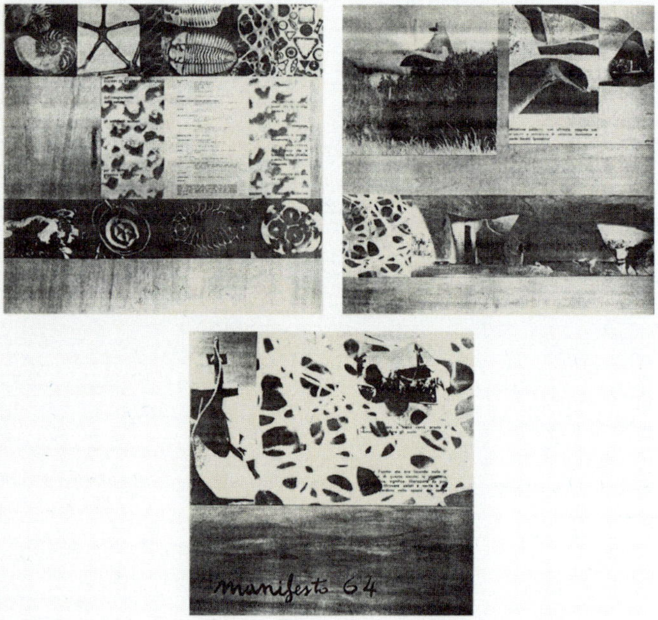


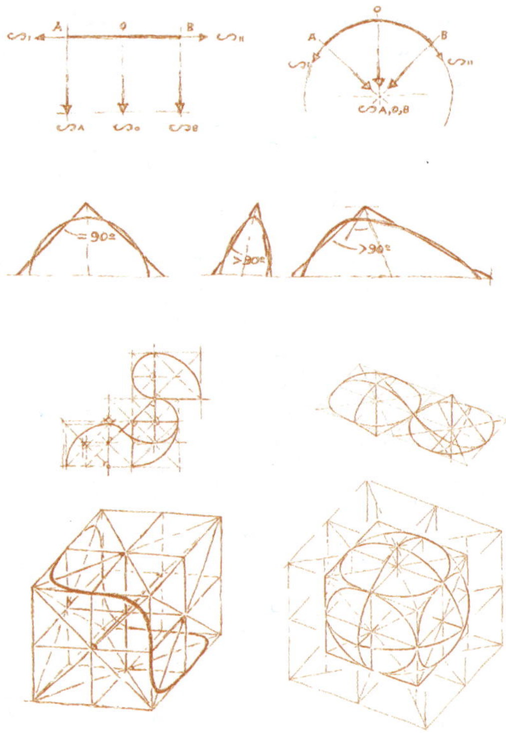

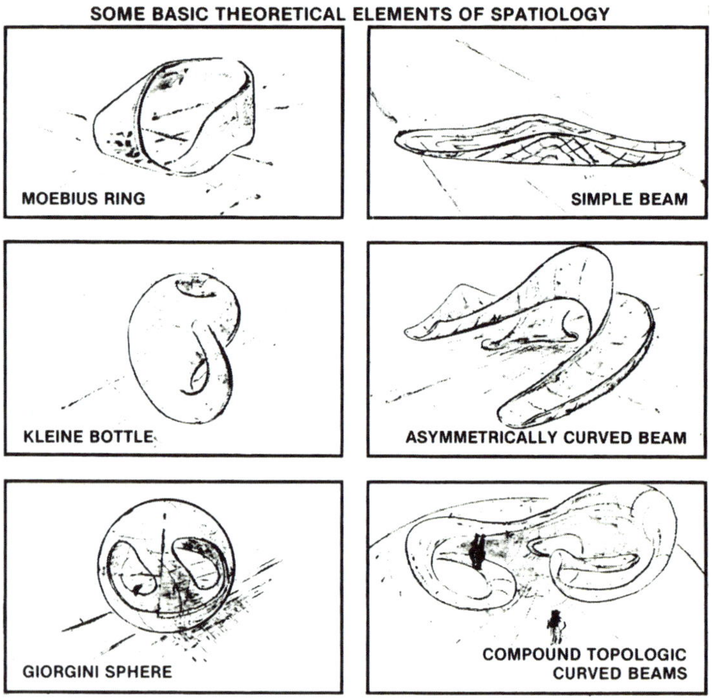


**1.34** Above, left: Giorgini's 1st "Spatiology" manifesto, 1964.

**1.35** Left: Basic theoretical elements of "Spatiology."

**1.36** Above, right: Sketches in the "Geometry" section of *Spatiology: The Morphology of the Natural Sciences in Architecture and Design.*

## Consolidation of Scientific References

References in the sciences and science-driven practices became increasingly inspirational for Giorgini's architectural investigations in the decade between the late 1960s and the late 70s, as anticipated above. After D'Arcy Thompson, the contributions of August Möbius and Felix Klein in the domain of topology, in addition to the work of M. C. Escher, proved to be of particular importance. Giorgini was fascinated by the sophistication and efficiency he found in the structures of the living world, as well as in the possibility of accounting for their morphology by means of geometry. But his visionary structures did not yet possess the level of logic and consistency with which a set of geometric procedures could endow them. The School of Architecture at the Pratt Institute and his loft on Wooster Street, in Manhattan's SoHo, became the milieu in which he perfected the scientific foundations of his design methods—the former as the locus of his teachings, the latter as his design atelier.

The first abstract sketches concerning his study of surface topology in non-Euclidean space appeared as part of his fifth and final *spatiology* manifesto, which Giorgini delivered at the 1975 "On Site" international conference in New York City **(fig. 1.33)**. It was not until November of 1979, however—in a letter to an advisee of his at the University of Florence by the name of Nicola Barrachia—that Giorgini developed the first full-fledged manuscript of his design theory. It included a set of annotated drawings illustrating his advances in surface topology. By this stage, the term *spatiology* had acquired a different meaning than that of his first Manifesto of 1964 **(fig. 1.34)**. Then it was used to advocate for a "liberated" project methodology that would reject formal restrictions and move towards the efficiency of natural structures. This position represented the defining trait of Giorgini's Florentine phase. But by the mid-1970s, he had come to define *spatiology* as a research project concerning the study of systems of double-curved structures, foreshadowing the construction of a geometric theory of design **(fig. 1.35)**.[25]

He first observed and attempted to prove geometrically that in nature there were only curved lines and surfaces, and that asymmetry was the rule rather than the exception. Symmetry, straight lines, flat planar surfaces, and the resultant volumes defined by polyhedra were simply conventions created by humans that had helped them abstract, visualize, and build artificial structures in accordance with their limitations—namely, their own perceptual system and representational capabilities, as well as more general economic and technological constraints. But according to Giorgini's interpretation, volumes typical of natural morphology were usually the resulting compounds of curved lines and surfaces: "those figures we call free-forms do not exist but are complex combinations of different sets of asymmetrical curves lying on curved, non-planar surfaces."[26] **(Fig. 1.36)** The work of Gaudí, Finsterlin,

25 See Vittorio Giorgini, "Spatiology and Thin Shell Structures," in *LSA86: Proceedings of the First International Conference on Lightweight Structures in Architecture, Sydney, Australia, 24–29 August 1986.* (Kensington, NSW, Australia: Unisearch Limited, University of New South Wales, 1986), 224.

26 Giorgini, *Spatiology: The Morphology of the Natural Sciences in Architecture and Design.*

**1.37** Sketches in the "Statics" section of *Spatiology: The Morphology of the Natural Sciences in Architecture and Design.*

and Kiesler was originally inspiring for Giorgini since it reflected some of the formal aspects of the living world. Now the experiences of such engineers as Pier Luigi Nervi, Eugène Freyssinet, Konrad Wachsmann, Félix Candela, Riccardo Morandi, Frei Otto, and, above all, Robert Maillart became central to understanding that, were complex forms to be built, then the static diagram ought to play a fundamental role throughout the design process.[27] In some cases it was about forms of objects being construed as diagrams of forces—that is, as the more or less literal translation of the static diagram into form, *à la* Nervi or Otto **(fig. 1.37)**. But in most cases, it was about deriving form from a dynamic process of transformation triggered by one or several forces. This is the type of design thinking at the core of Giorgini's contribution—one which, in his mind, required "adding to the three dimensions of geometry (space), the force (potential energy) as a fourth physical dimension."[28]

## Geometry, Systems, Statics

The two most comprehensive texts Giorgini ever composed were the 1979 manuscript and its book form, published in 1995 as *Spatiology: The Morphology of the Natural Sciences in Architecture and Design* and launched in New York City in February 1996 at an event where the speakers included Kenneth Frampton and engineer Guy Nordenson **(fig. 1.38)**. Both texts can be seen as a generative design theory registering in the abstract the basis of the organizational patterns he had found in nature. Giorgini divided this theory into three sections: geometry, systems, and statics.

"Geometry" was for him a tool for understanding and handling networks of connections between elements, as well as the structure of the organization of those networks. In addition, he elaborated on what he termed "implied" forces in geometry. Rather than static geometric forms, Giorgini presented geometric forms resulting from dynamic processes driven by internal forces. The triangle, the sphere, the torus, the half-cylinder, and several volumes featuring synclastic and anticlastic curvature can be described as the outcome of simple rotations or translations—for him the two main categories of force behavior—applied to basic elements, such as points, segments, and curves and planar surfaces, depending on the case. He also illustrated how, within a given piece of geometry (e.g., a rectangle), regular grids along with their multiples and submultiples can easily be derived. The resultant lattices enable force behavior to be tracked within the original figures, thereby unveiling the potential of these to be submitted to a series of controlled transformations **(fig. 1.39)**.

27 See Vittorio Giorgini, "Early Experiments in Design Derived from Study of Nature's Morphologies," *International Journal of Space Structures* 11, nos. 1 & 2 (1996): 57. Giorgini had been familiar with the works of some of these engineers since the 1950s. It was not, however, until 1969 that he started studying them from a scientific point of view and began to consider the role of forces in the generation processes of his shell structure designs.

28 Giorgini, *Spatiology*, 29.

**ISTITUTO ITALIANO DI CULTURA**
**NEW YORK**

Istituto Italiano di Cultura

cordially invites you to

Morphology as a Turning Point in Architecture and Urban Research
*An architectural forum on the efficiency rapports in architecture between morphological characteristics and their functions*

**Panelists:** Barry Commoner - *Queens College, CUNY*
Kenneth Frampton - *Columbia University*
Vittorio Giorgini - *Pratt Institute*
Guy Nordenson - *Princeton University, Hove, Arup & Partners*

**Moderator:** Paolo Spedicato - *Brooklyn College, CUNY*

The volume ***Spatiology: The Morphology of the Natural Sciences in Architecture and Design*** by Vittorio Giorgini (Milan, L'Arcaedizioni, 1995) will be presented

Wednesday, February 7, 1996
6:00 p.m.
reception to follow

Istituto Italiano di Cultura
686 Park Ave., NY City

**R.S.V.P. only**
**879-4242 ext. 66**

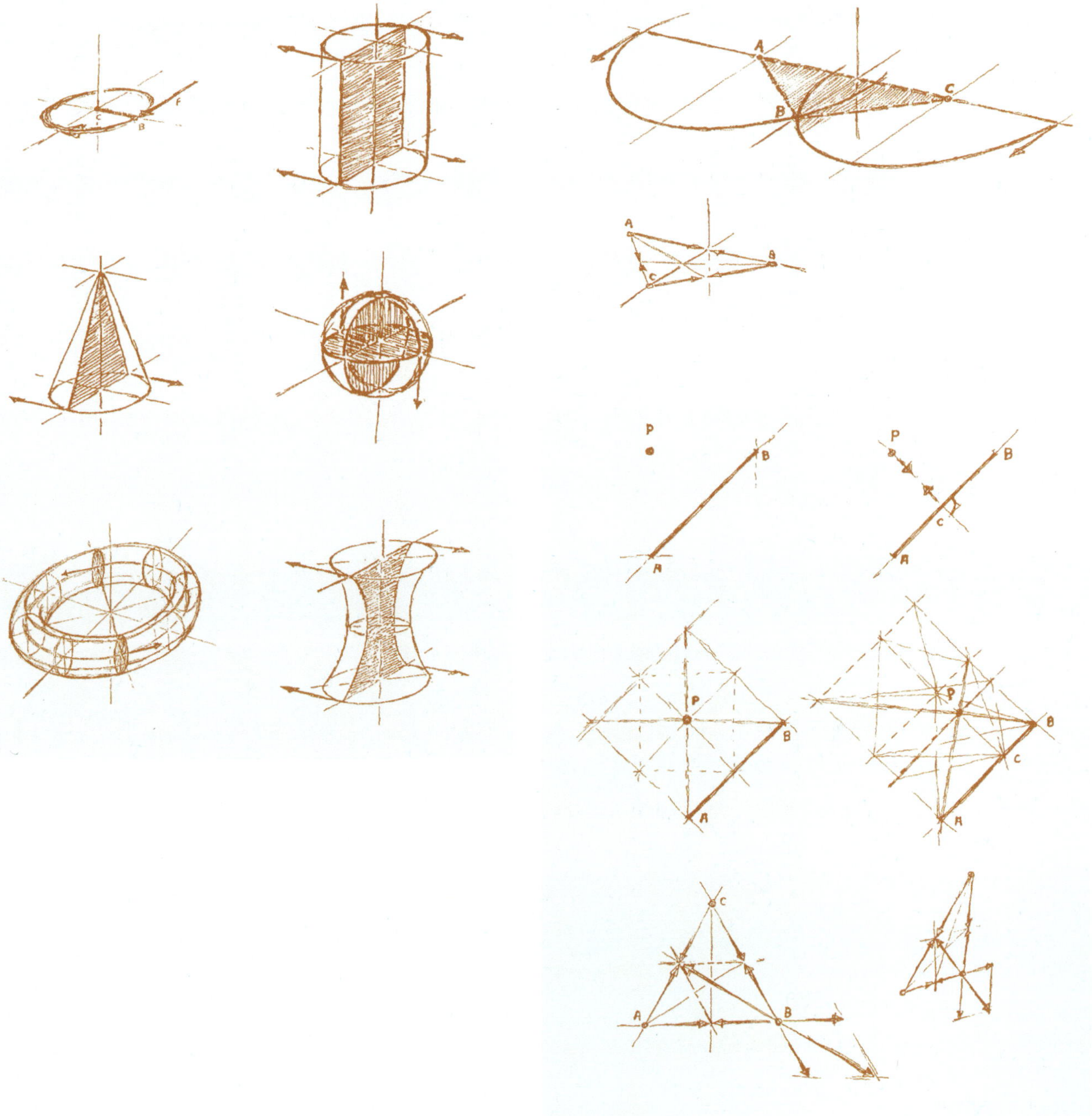

Precedent page:
**1.38** Invitation to panel discussion on the presentation of Giorgini's *Spatiology: The Morphology of the Natural Sciences in Architecture and Design* at the Italian Institute of Culture in New York, 1996.

**1.39** Sketches in the "Geometry" section of *Spatiology: The Morphology of the Natural Sciences in Architecture and Design.*

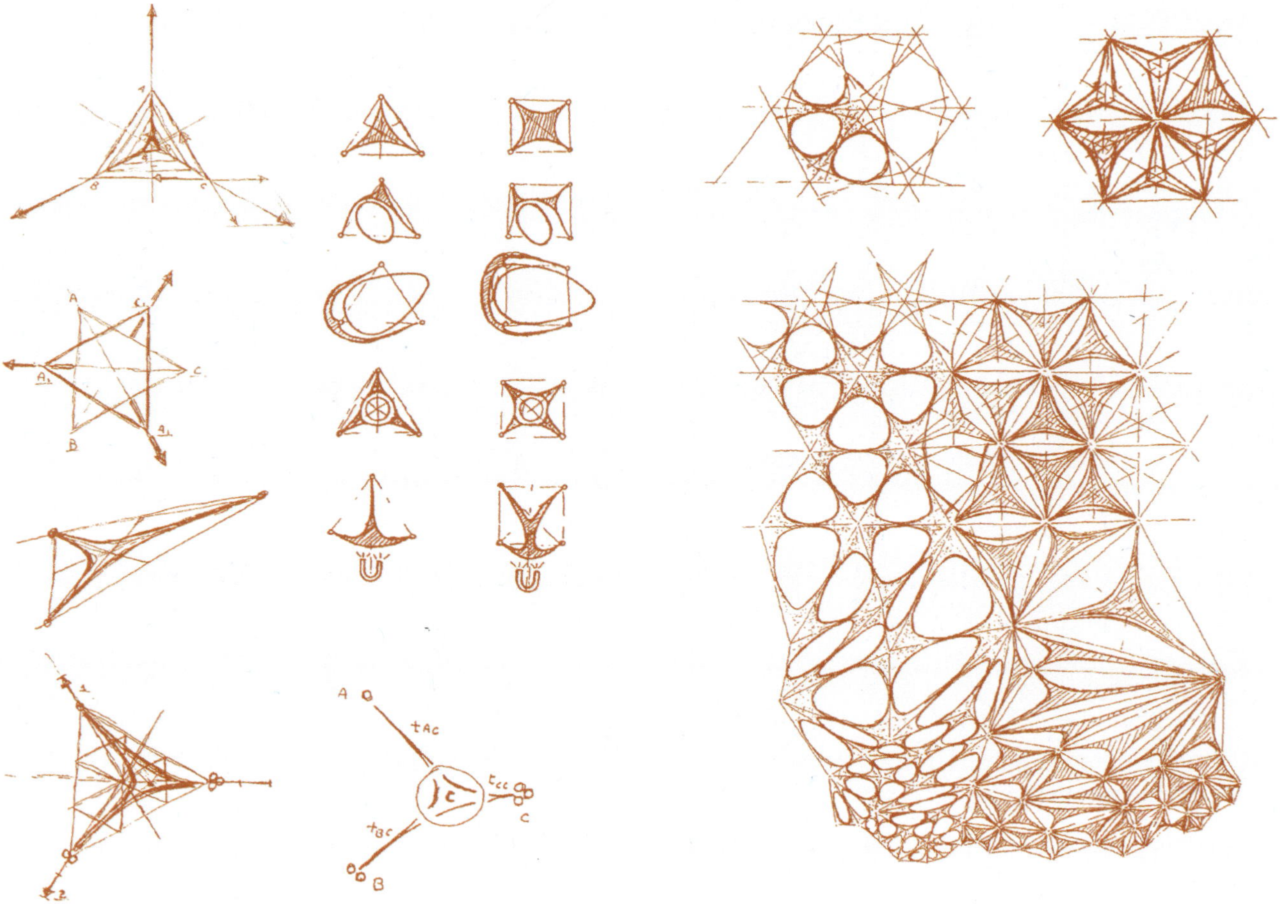

**1.40** Sketches in the "Systems" section of *Spatiology: The Morphology of the Natural Sciences in Architecture and Design.*

In "systems" Giorgini discussed ways in which diagrams can be employed to represent part-to-whole relationships in an abstract fashion, and how these, which may serve the purpose of decoding natural principles, can in turn be interpreted in geometric terms. The part is that which cannot be subdivided in accordance with certain established criteria. They do not relate to each other directly, but rather by means of what he called "transitional elements." For example, in a diagram representing triangular relationships, the transitional elements may be the vertexes, the sides being the parts; or vice versa, the sides may be the transitional elements, the vertexes being the parts. All the parts and transitional elements together form the whole of the system, which may be open or closed, and whose structure Giorgini defined as the order in which parts and elements organize themselves. He stressed that the definition of the connective structure—formed by all the transitional elements—relative to the main parts depends upon the geometric and dynamic characteristics of the system, with the former alluding to the specific structure of spatial relations, the latter to the behavior of forces. These forces, Giorgini explained, are not only internal to the system but may also be applied to it externally—that is, those resulting from the system conforming to external factors such as site conditions, programmatic components, etc. **(fig. 1.40)**

In "statics" Giorgini studied the behavior of structural forces. In the 1995 book, he examined them in relation to rigid and elastic joints and in their application to common situations in building construction: cantilevers, columns, beams, tension cables, and space frames. These models were often tested vis-à-vis their performance within a given polygonal or polyhedral figure, with the goal being to provide static organizations based on geometric criteria. Giorgini's focus on recognizable models was driven by his belief that it was only by mastering those first that more complex, asymmetrical structures might ultimately be understood and realized. He nonetheless regarded the former merely as conventions and the latter as real, arguing that it had historically been the rule for models to be mistakenly regarded as actual **(fig. 1.41)**.

In the 1979 manuscript, the section on statics was longer and more thorough, featuring different examples from those in the 1995 publication. Firstly, Giorgini introduced the so-called "beam shell" as an elementary unit. This beam shell is a thin piece of surface whose longitudinal dimension is greater than its transversal one, being thereby assimilable to a structural beam. It has only one curvature in its basic definition, as a result of being symmetrically bent around the long axis. He then went on to give a detailed explanation of the elastic and static behaviors of such a basic beam shell in a cantilever scenario, addressing both concave and convex relative to the ground, and elaborating on how curvature contributes to the overall stiffness of the piece **(fig. 1.42)**. A simple transformation of this unit resulted in what he

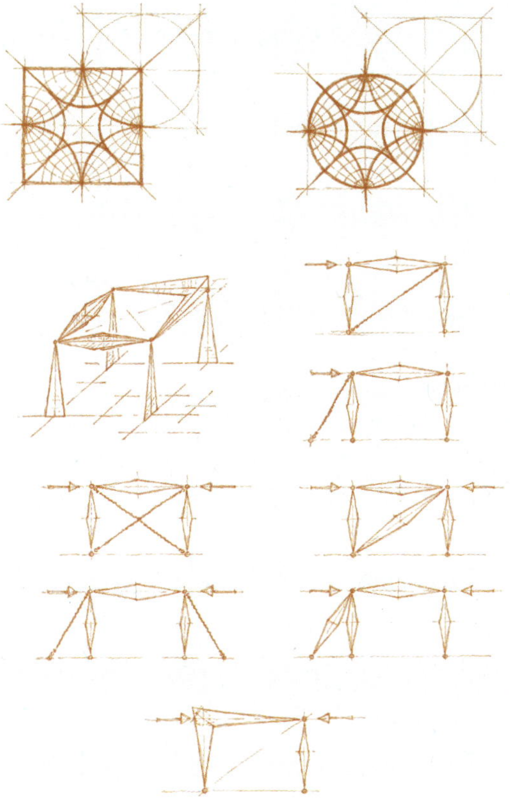

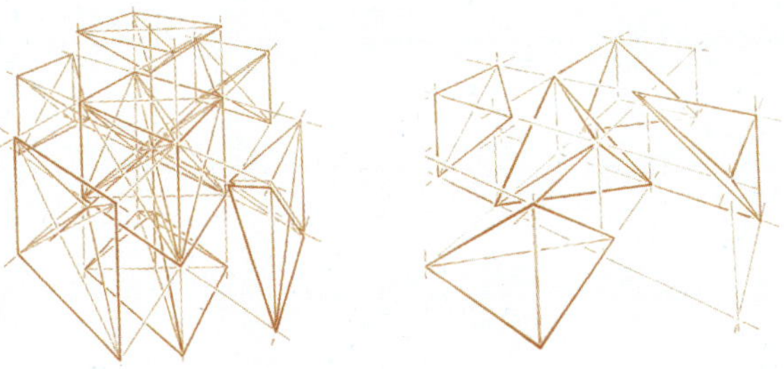

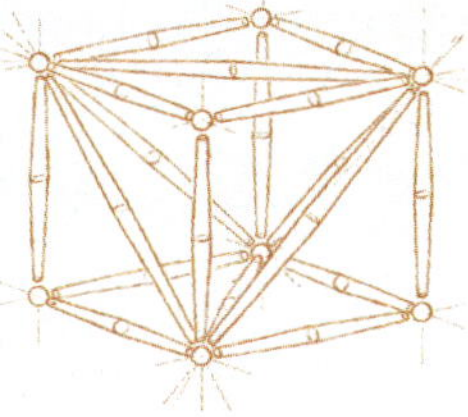

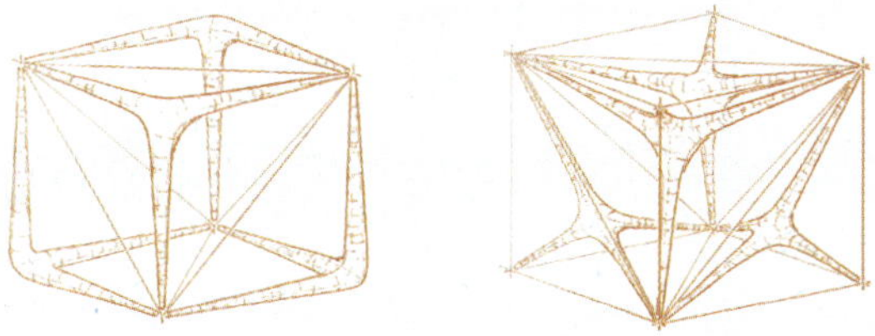

**1.41** (all three images)**; 1.48** (left)**; 1.49** (above, left) Sketches in the "Statics" section of Spatiology: The Morphology of the Natural Sciences in Architecture and Design.

termed "cantilever-base compound" [mensola composta base], the first elementary compound model for all systems of double- and triple-curved membranes. As its name indicates, it is an element comprised of a beam shell on the ground (base) that folds upon itself to become a cantilever. Further analysis follows to determine the structural properties of this cantilever-base compound **(fig. 1.43)**.[29]

This sequence of studies leads naturally to the illustration of a series of topological transformations, chiefly based on rotation, bending forces, and triangular symmetry, which ended up constituting Giorgini's idiosyncratic design vocabulary. First, he went back to the basic beam shell, if now simply resting on two points on the ground, rather than cantilevering out **(fig. 1.44)**. A third point added off the main axis turns the original beam shell into a triangular one **(fig. 1.45)**. Thus emerges the second elementary compound model in Giorgini's conception of membranes as sets of beams in equilibrium. A string of alterations may then be applied to this triangular module for it to accommodate functions and adjust to other external factors. It might be extended in one direction; one of its "legs" might be lifted off the ground and become a cantilever; an opening might appear in the middle of the triangular membrane, above or through which an extension of one of the original legs might connect to a point external to the unit **(fig. 1.46)**; it might close upon itself in different ways so as to generate a number of diversely complex enclosed spaces; etc. **(Fig. 1.47)** Most often related to three axes (minimum two) and comprised of ever more elaborate "beam shells," the resulting asymmetrical structures were intended to be analogous to those existing in nature. More generally, these dynamic procedures of transformation were successful for him, insofar as they constituted methods for constructing complex systems outside Euclidean geometry (which he considered "classical") and within non-Euclidean space instead—where, he believed, the structures of nature belonged.

The 1995 book contains an equivalent section describing a series of topological transformations which, though not linked to the one on statics, nevertheless unfolds along the same lines **(fig. 1.48)**. Only a few additions stand out, such as the inclusion of the topological development of the torus and the sphere, and the study of the topological analogies that may be found between the two figures **(fig. 1.49)**. Mention is also made of similar kinds of successive modifications being applied to two- and three-dimensional networks, polyhedra, and larger space frames, one of which resulted in the so-called "bubble package"—the only instance of Giorgini's involvement with a configuration assimilable to a grouping of minimal surfaces **(fig. 1.50)**.

Following pages:
**1.42** (p. 82, above), **1.43** (p. 82, below), **1.44** (p. 83; above, left), **1.45** (p. 83; above, right), **1.46** (p. 83; below) Sketches in the "Statics" section, 1979 manuscript.

29 Giorgini's exploitation of Cartesian axes in order to define a range of curved configurations links his method directly to that of Gaspard Monge and drives it away from the limitations of Durand's. Cf. Robin Evans, *The Projective Cast: Architecture and Its Three Geometries* (Cambridge, MA: The MIT Press, 2000), 327.

21
è estremamente complicato - inoltre si parla qui di mensole curve in tre direzioni e con collegamenti (composte) continui -
Tensione
compressione
asse neutro
compressione
tensione
A
B
D
F1
F2
come sai il diagramma della sezione dipende appunto dalla sezione ove le distanze dall'asse neutro di A e B sono inversamente proporzionali alle forze - F1 x AD = M
se si riduce A o F1 deve aumentare per ottenere lo stesso momento.
se A diminuisce in A1, B1 aumenta rispetto a B -
date queste premesse, vediamo come una mensola semplice, curva si comporta
si hanno, diciamo così, due bordi di tensione ed una superficie che nel punto d'incontro fra i due bordi diviene compressa con un passaggio uniforme -
e viceversa - per il comportamento di sezione data un'uguale situazione statica si opera sulle dimensioni come si usa in altri sistemi -
A : B = D : C il rapporto non credo sia proporzionale, però.

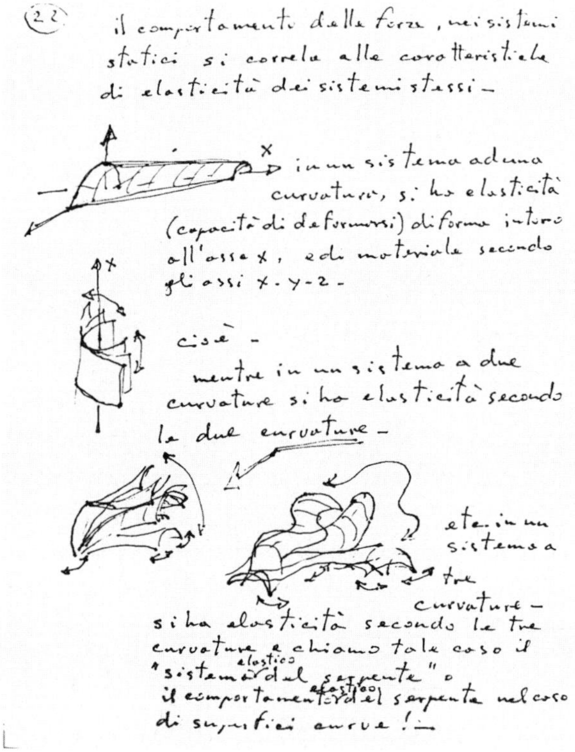
22
il comportamento delle forze, nei sistemi statici si correla alle caratteristiche di elasticità dei sistemi stessi -
X
in un sistema ad una curvatura, si ha elasticità (capacità di deformarsi) di forma intorno all'asse x, ed di materiale secondo gli assi x-y-z -
cioè -
mentre in un sistema a due curvature si ha elasticità secondo le due curvature -
etc. in un sistema a tre curvature -
si ha elasticità secondo le tre curvature e chiamo tale caso il "sistema elastico del serpente" o il comportamento elastico del serpente nel caso di superfici curve !-

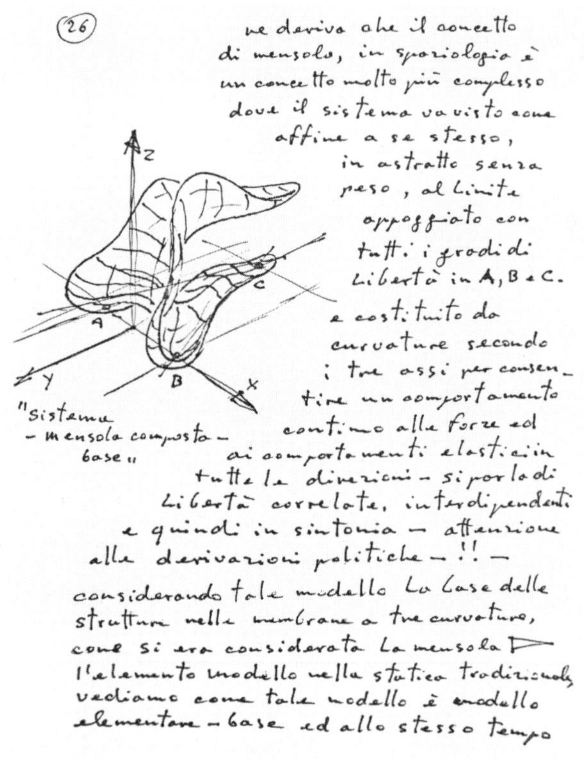
26
ne deriva che il concetto di mensola, in spaziologia è un concetto molto più complesso dove il sistema va visto come affine a se stesso, in astratto senza peso, al limite appoggiato con tutti i gradi di libertà in A, B e C.
Z
A
B
C
Y
X
"Sistema - mensola composta - base"
è costituito da curvature secondo i tre assi per consentire un comportamento continuo alle forze ed ai comportamenti elastici in tutte le direzioni - si parla di libertà correlate, interdipendenti e quindi in sintonia - attenzione alle derivazioni politiche - !! -
considerando tale modello la base delle strutture nelle membrane a tre curvature, come si era considerata la mensola l'elemento modello nella statica tradizionale vediamo come tale modello è modello elementare - base ed allo stesso tempo

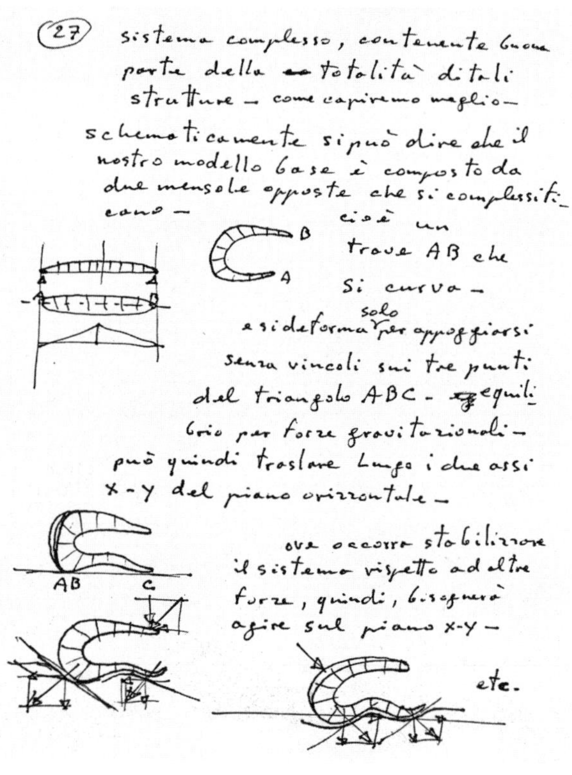
27
sistema complesso, contenente buona parte della totalità di tali strutture - come capiremo meglio -
schematicamente si può dire che il nostro modello base è composto da due mensole opposte che si complessificano -
cioè una trave AB che si curva - e si deforma solo per appoggiarsi senza vincoli sui tre punti del triangolo ABC - equilibrio per forze gravitazionali - può quindi traslare lungo i due assi x-y del piano orizzontale -
A
B
AB
C
ove occorra stabilizzare il sistema rispetto ad altre forze, quindi, bisognerà agire sul piano x-y -
etc.

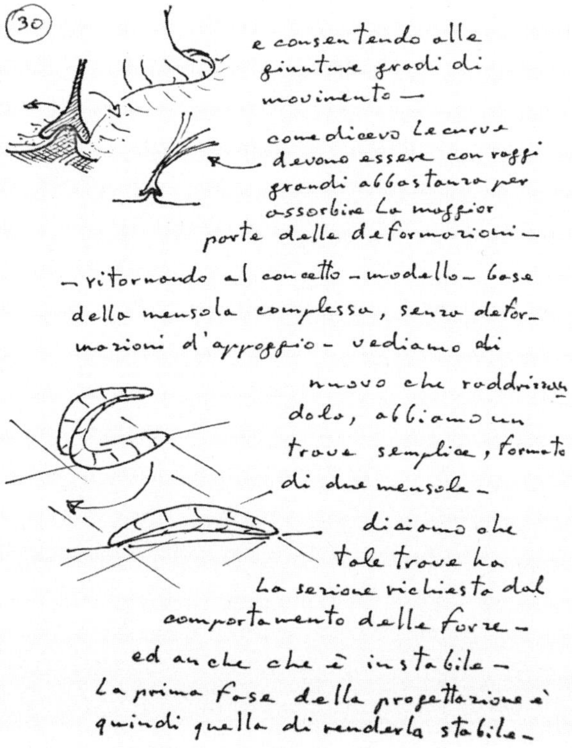
30
e consentendo alle giunture gradi di movimento —
come dicevo le curve devono essere con raggi grandi abbastanza per assorbire la maggior parte delle deformazioni —
— ritornando al concetto-modello-base della mensola complessa, senza deformazioni d'appoggio — vediamo di nuovo che raddrizzandolo, abbiamo un trave semplice, formato di due mensole —
diciamo che tale trave ha la sezione richiesta dal comportamento delle forze —
ed anche che è instabile —
La prima fase della progettazione è quindi quella di renderla stabile —

31
perciò la trave va appoggiata su tre "punti di appoggio"
produciamo la deformazione di tali due "punti superficie" A-B
e decidiamo di deformarne uno, ad es. A nella direzione trasversa ad AB — ricavando il triangolo A-A1-B.
riconducendoci al comportamento dei sistemi nel collegarsi di tre parti, vediamo che il trave si deforma nel trave a Y che è la base (modello) progettuale delle membrane come travi composti in equilibrio — confronta con il modello della mensola — Le successive deformazioni seguono le fasi del programma, ma prima vediamo una precisazione di carattere statico
B
A
sezione
A
B
A1
B
A
C

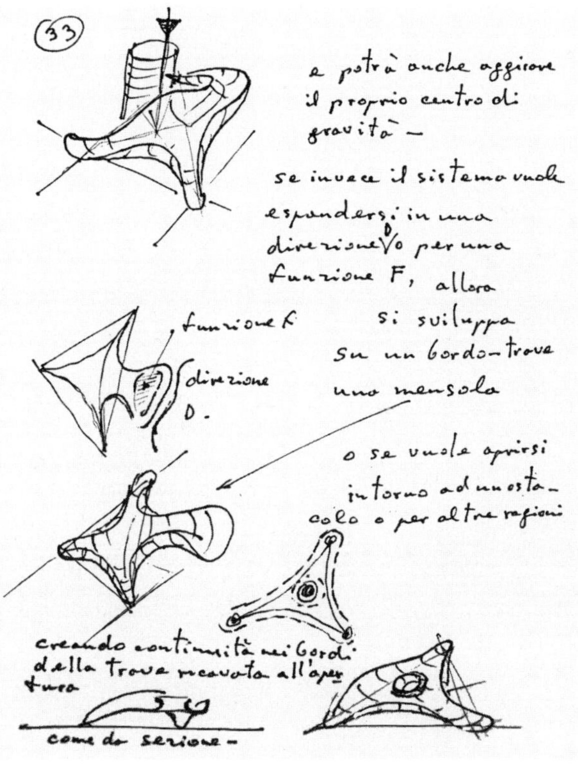
33
e potrà anche aggiorne il proprio centro di gravità —
se invece il sistema vuole espandersi in una direzione D per una funzione F, allora si sviluppa su un bordo-trave una mensola
funzione F
direzione D.
o se vuole aprirsi intorno ad un ostacolo o per altre ragioni
creando continuità nei bordi della trave ricavata all'apertura
come da sezione —

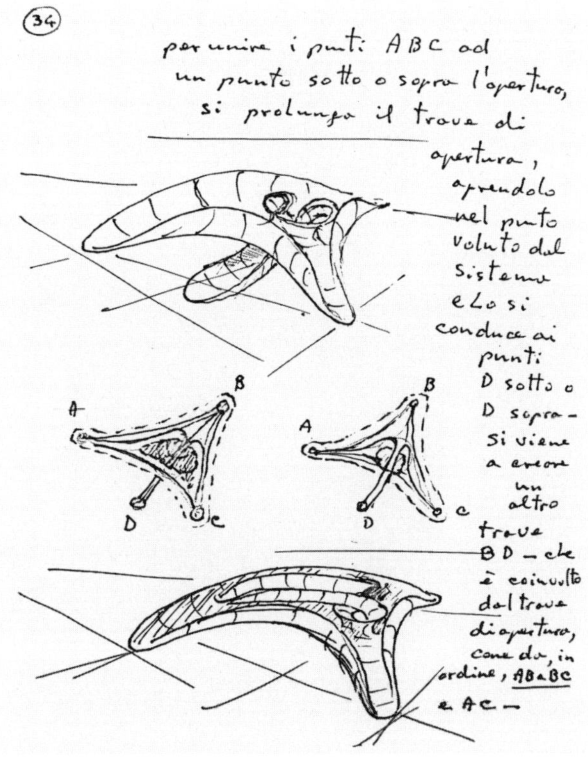
34
per unire i punti ABC ad un punto sotto o sopra l'apertura, si prolunga il trave di apertura, aprendolo nel punto voluto dal sistema e lo si conduce ai punti D sotto o D sopra — si viene a creare un altro trave BD — che è coinvolto dal trave di apertura, come da, in ordine, AB a BC e AC —
A
B
D
C
A
B
D
C

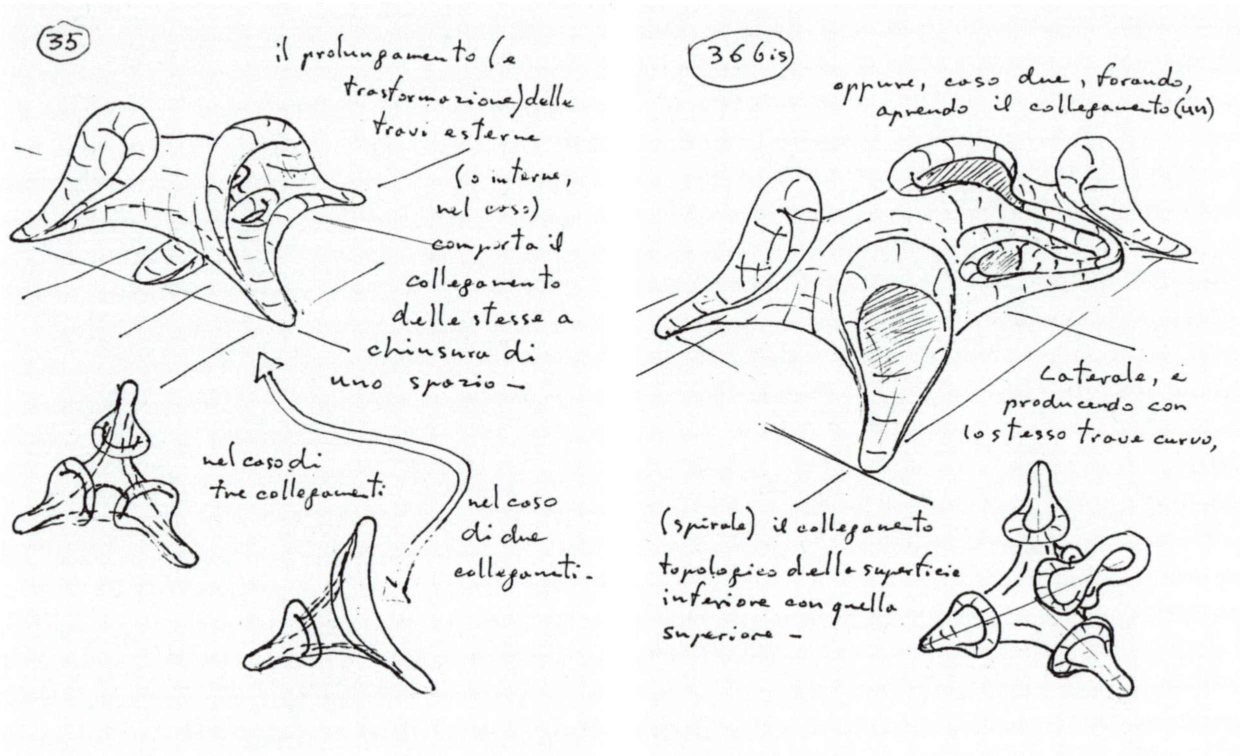


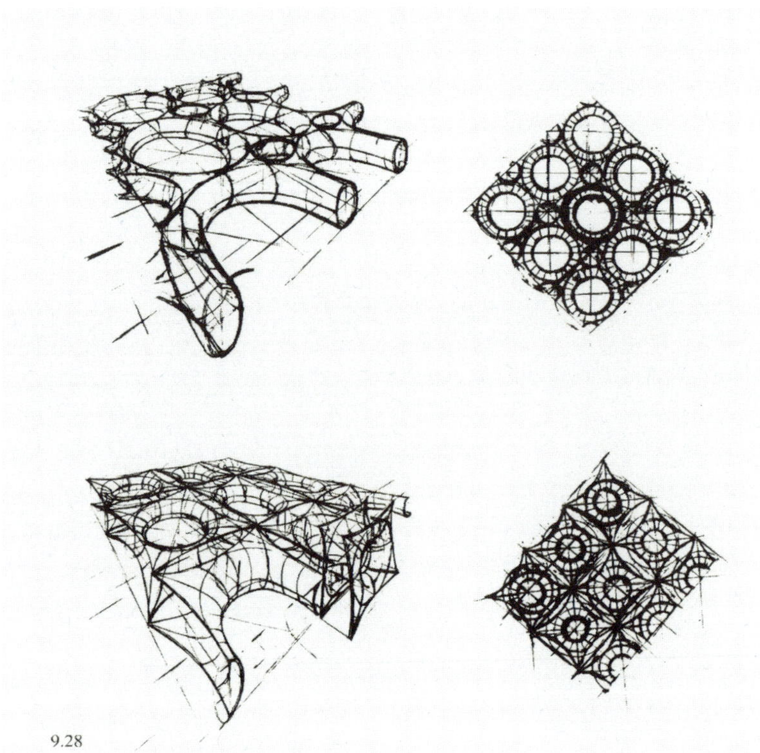


**1.47** Above: Sketches in the "Statics" section, 1979 manuscript.

**1.50** Left: Geometric configurations assimilable to groupings of minimal surfaces in Giorgini's *Spatiology: The Morphology of the Natural Sciences in Architecture and Design.*

# EXPRESSION, LATENCY, AND PROGRAM: A TOPOLOGICAL APPROACH TO THE ARTICULATION OF SPACE

In terms of a seeming arbitrariness that in fact rests on a logical basis, one of the closest precedents to Giorgini's shell structures is Ronchamp. Shortly after its completion in 1954, Nikolaus Pevsner and James Stirling labeled Le Corbusier's church irrational, expressing a view shared by many commentators.[30] As Robin Evans masterfully showed, however, the design process was grounded in a strong geometric rationale, despite the outcome's apparently whimsical appearance. Rectilinear generators and curved directrices define the major volumes, the south wall being the result of the manipulation of two opposing ruled surfaces, and the roof shell of two reversed conoids parallel to one another.[31] While Le Corbusier was indeed one of Giorgini's most admired figures, there is no evidence that Giorgini knew of Ronchamp's geometric basis. Nevertheless, the architecture of Notre Dame du Haut and the curved structures designed by the Florentine architect share the same design attitude, described by Evans as follows:

> When architects attempt to escape from the tyranny of geometry, meaning by that the tyranny of the box, where can they escape to? Either they must give up geometry altogether (which would be exceptionally difficult), or they can escape to another, always more complex and demanding geometry, or they do the last while giving the impression of having done the first, as at Ronchamp, which is why Le Corbusier's attitude to Gaudí's architecture during his last years is so revealing.[32]

However, two fundamental features differentiate Ronchamp and Giorgini's structures. In the former, geometry only entered the picture, via engineering technique, after specific shapes had already been imagined by Le Corbusier. In other words, it was a rationalization *a posteriori*. In Giorgini's works, on the other hand, there is a tendency for geometry and shapes to be indissolubly connected from the beginning of the process, especially as he became more knowledgeable about the workings of topology. The second dissimilarity concerns Le Corbusier's use of stereotypical pieces of geometry—ruled surfaces, conoids, etc.—as opposed to Giorgini's method

30 See Nikolaus Pevsner, *An Outline of European Architecture*, 7th ed. (Harmondsworth, Middlesex: Penguin Books, 1963), 429, and James Stirling, "Ronchamp: Le Corbusier's Chapel and the Crisis of Rationalism," *Architectural Review*, no. 119 (March 1956): 155–61.

31 See Evans, *The Projective Cast*, 302–3.

32 Ibid., 331. As Evans explains, Le Corbusier was aware of and influenced by the geometric prescience behind many of Gaudí's seemingly free-flowing forms. It was only during his last years that he became interested in applying such a design pattern to his own designs, even though the only sketch he ever made of a work by the Catalan dates from much earlier, in 1928. The sketch shows a ruled surface representing the warped roof of the parish school built in 1909–10 next to the Sagrada Familia.

of generating iterations of novel geometric patterns. This particular drive ought to be seen within a larger set of attributes determining the latter's procedures for the production of form. As evident in the section above, those attributes reflect a desire for the objectivity associated with scientific knowledge, the reduction of the sphere of design to that of the object itself, a strong interest in procedural thinking, a lack of attention to the experiential dimension, and inspiration drawn from the hidden structures of nature. An engineering approach of this kind characterized Giorgini's design framework, yet its outcome was a range of spatial articulations whose intricacy is characteristic of architectural rather than of engineering form.

## The Curve as Aesthetic Drive

The role of "nature" in relation to this architecture-engineering hybrid condition deserves a closer reading. Marco del Francia, the author of the only monograph on Giorgini's work thus far, endorsed the latter's own description of his design ideology—namely, as one fundamentally grounded in nature as a model. But beyond a mere endorsement, Giorgini never offered any in-depth account of it. Nowhere in his production do we find pictures of organisms or hidden structures of the living world and a detailed explanation of how those might correspond to specific pieces of geometry. Likewise, he never provided any step-by-step interpretation of natural processes with a view to clarifying their translation into his procedural thinking, nor did he explain how his design framework might be ascribed back to the living world. It is therefore no wonder that his geometric theory of design can be construed as entirely disengaged from the deep structures of nature: it developed an autonomy of its own.

However, it can be argued that those natural structures inspired him on two levels. Firstly, Giorgini identified a number of principles that he believed to be intrinsic to their biological and physical mechanisms: namely, efficiency, sophistication in relational properties, and statics. He then abstracted them away in the form of laws of physics and geometry, which became the basis of his design approach. As a result, he ended up operating within the generalization of such laws, not within the specificities of particular natural structures—in contradistinction to Burt and his soap bubbles, as shall be discussed in the next chapter. Secondly, while not a source of mimicry, natural imagery played an aesthetic role in Giorgini's work, however objectionable he found this idea.[33] Despite his focus on underlying principles, his claim that in nature "there are only curves" was a judgment based on appearance—one that became central to his topological designs, all of which featured curved shapes. In other words, if his shell structures were to be related back to nature, it would be impossible not to point out the apparent resemblances, which was precisely what Giorgini wished to avoid.

33 In an interview with the author conducted on June 9, 2013, his long-time friend and colleague at Pratt, Giuliano Fiorenzoli, claimed that Giorgini was constantly critical of anyone concerned with "aesthetics." Also, in the autobiography he himself recorded on tape in 2005, he emphasized several times that his work was never about "copying" the forms of nature or about "sculpture" for that matter.

Therefore, the curve in his projects was largely fulfilling an aesthetic drive, something to which he would never have admitted. For the curve is certainly not a necessary option when the main interest lies in structures of organization, or when the notion of topology is accurately observed. A cube and a sphere are topologically tantamount to each other because it is possible to distort one into the other through a continuous transformation not involving cuts or holes on the surface. In turn, this *homeomorphism* can be interpreted in terms of both cube and sphere articulating a bounded section of space identically at some fundamental level, with the specific shape of either being irrelevant in that respect. To take the simplest scenario, let us recall that, in topology, as Stephen Barr didactically put it, "a straight line doesn't have to remain straight" as long as "it retains the quality of being continuously connected along itself, and with its ends disconnected—or not, as the case may be."[34] By analogy, all of Giorgini's curved designs can be imagined turned into equivalent versions made up of straight lines only—"equivalent" here meaning that the structures of the spatial organizations in the former and the latter would correspond to one another. Designers versed in topology know that they do not need to resort to curves of necessity, as they would be well aware that the curved or straight condition of a surface is in itself inconsequential in topological terms. Giorgini qualifying as such a designer, his fixation with the curve may therefore not have been determined but by choice—an understanding of topology and personal aesthetic inclinations being perfectly compatible.

## Topology Renders "Shape" Irrelevant

Despite Giorgini's geometric literacy, the sequences of transformations he so painstakingly described were not always topologically consistent. For example, holes sometimes appeared in the middle of the process. This flaw, however, is not to be construed as something of which he was unaware, but rather as an action that may be interpreted as topologically permitted when developing a piece of architecture—in a way it may not when within the boundaries of geometry proper. Otherwise Giorgini's topological manipulations were fairly sound concerning the general properties of connectedness, both in his abstract studies and in his finalized designs. For instance, we see a general effort to conceive the larger openings in the Saldarini House (i.e., the main entrance and the rear windows) as gaps resulting in between folds, rather than holes punched randomly in the surface **(fig. 1.51)**.

Qualities concerning shape, such as volumetric outline or figural conditions, are therefore rendered irrelevant by topology. By extension it could be argued that the specificities of style, *qua* format of architectural expression that unfolds at the level of shape, are equally of no importance when topological characterization is at stake. That said, the question of the irrelevance of style does, in a different

34 See Stephen Barr, *Experiments in Topology* (New York, NY: Crowell, 1964), 4.

**1.51** Saldarini House on the Gulf of Baratti, 1960–62.

sense, prove profitable to further discussion of Giorgini's shell structure projects. There are no traces of specific stylistic elements being used at the beginnings of the design processes leading up to them. Rather, these starting points are defined as abstract scenarios: diagrams of forces, networks, structural elements, nonfigurative dispositions in space, etc. As a result of ignoring stylistic references and relying on the evolution of those scenarios according to laws made immanent to them—those of physics, topology, geometry, etc.—an expressive singularity emerges, that is, an overall absence of codified linguistic elements. Which is to say, the singularity of Giorgini's shell schemes is tied to the search for processual self-consistency through the application of scientific laws. Generalizing, it could be said that an initial *stylistic nonreferentiality* along with the design process triggered by it are central to the possibility of engendering a self-referential style, that is, one that refers to no pre-given format of architectural expression, only to itself. While topology is essential to the analysis of form *qua* three-dimensional configuration, the possibility of self-referentiality, which instead belongs in the realm of shape, is of no consequence within it. Yet, it is of great significance to the general stylistic domain in architecture, with respect to which it enables a contribution. For a self-determined vocabulary characterized by a marked singularity falls outside received linguistic frameworks, and this outsideness constitutes an expansion of the expressive imaginary of architecture offering new possibilities.

The paradox of the simultaneous relevance and irrelevance of style as embodied in Giorgini's work is thus unveiled: irrelevant with regard to form *qua* three-dimensional configuration and its topological reading; relevant as its singularity allows for an extension of the stylistic domain of architecture. His 1963 *Casa Topologica* (Topological House) exemplifies this point quite clearly **(fig. 1.52–53)**. Its simplicity enables us to easily imagine an analogous version of the exact same house yet featuring straight lines and angles. From a configurational point of view, stylistic preferences regarding shape would be inconsequential, for both houses would exhibit an identical articulation of space, one comprised of two levels, the top one shifted to one side, the bottom one wider, the same height variations, a matching staircase, similar volumetric proportions, etc. If assessed according to a different value system, however, the stylistic singularity of the *Casa Topologica* as conceived by Giorgini is rather consequential in itself. Its characteristics—the protrusion upwards on the top; the opaque, curved envelopes; the lack of allusions to conventional elements associated with a house such as "door," "window," "roof," etc.—single out the building conspicuously within the tradition of residential architecture, thereby expanding the bounds of such tradition.

### Topological Invariants and Formal Consequences

Many of Giorgini's sketches illustrate clearly the difference invoked throughout this book between form as spatial organization and shape as specific figural condition. In one of the sketches a symmetrical, curved surface divides its surrounding area into three regions, one beneath a concave spine separating two other convex sides, and two above these. Next to this surface is another that, though made up of planes, articulates space in an identical way, with the three resulting regions having a corresponding set of relations to one another **(fig. 1.54)**. The shapes of the two surfaces are different, the first curved, the second featuring only straight outlines and sharp edges. However, the three regions into which the surfaces arrange space may be described along the same lines. Therefore, the two surfaces possess the same form. This conclusion is tantamount to saying that the two are topologically equivalent; in other words, that there is no topological alteration involved in transforming one into the other. Neither surface features holes (i.e., they are simply connected); both can be oriented (i.e., they have two clearly identifiable sides); both can be mapped flat (which would not be possible if they were cylindrical or toroidal, for example). These are a few of the so-called "topological invariants," which determine the quality of connectedness of a given surface, that is, the way in which it is internally connected. Different sets of topological invariants define different primitive surfaces (e.g., the rectangular plane, the sphere, the Möbius strip, the torus, etc.), and each of these may be said to articulate a bounded region of space in a fundamentally distinct fashion.

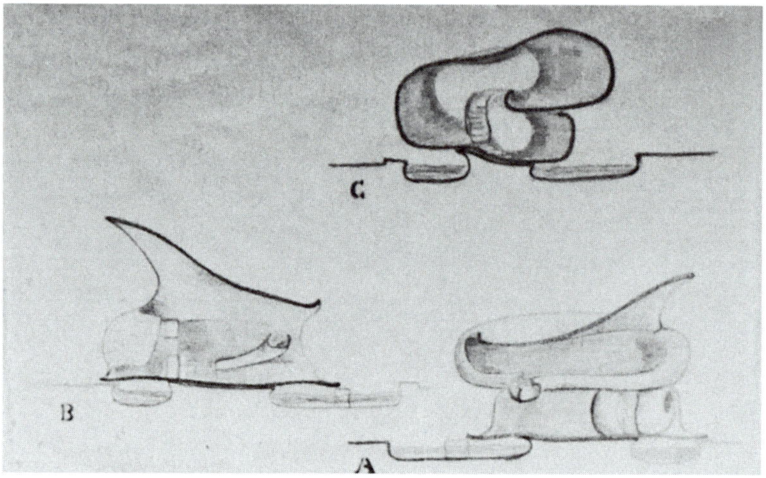


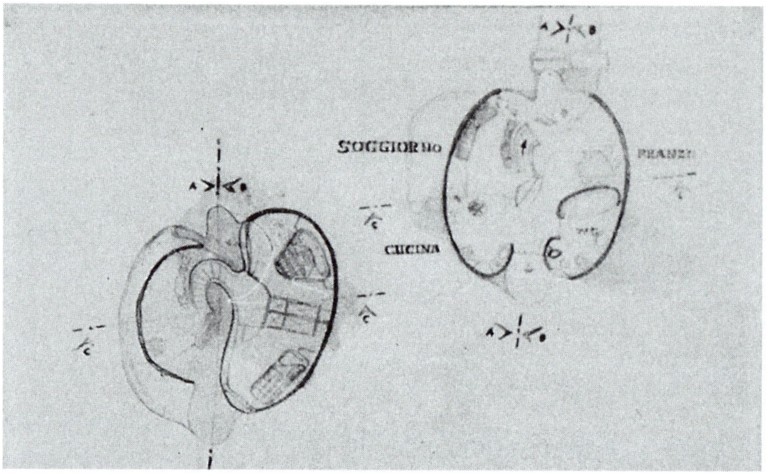

**1.52–1.53** Casa *Topologica* project, 1963.

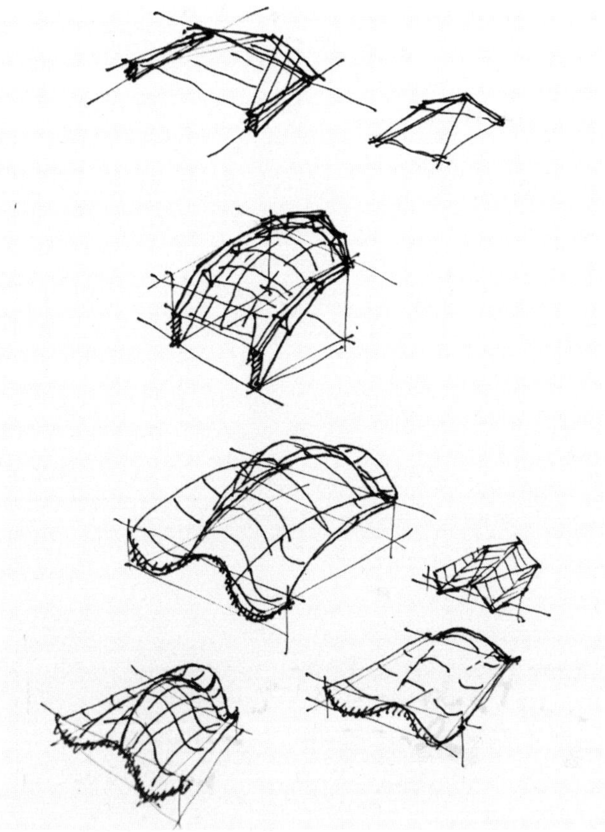

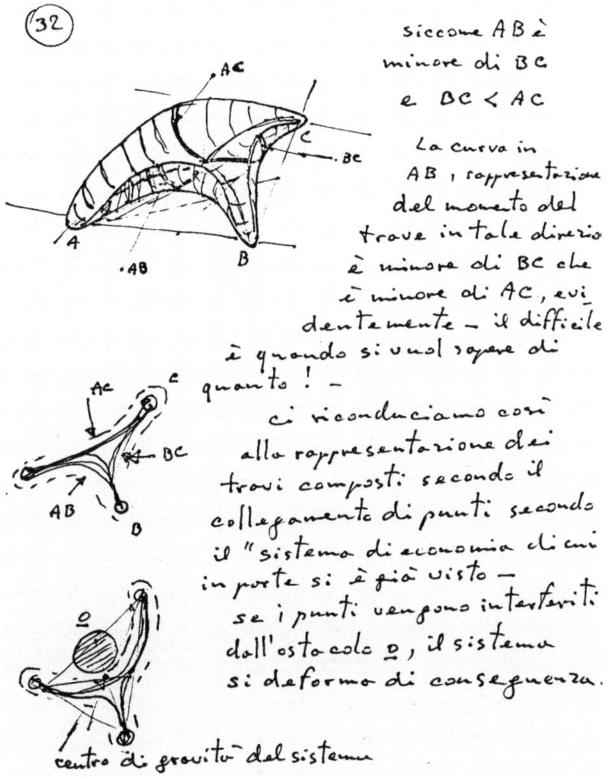


**1.54** Above, left: Undated sketch by Giorgini.

**1.55** Above, right: Sketches in the "Statics" section, 1979 manuscript.

That is to say, each of them may be regarded as *formally singular*. If the topological invariants are observed throughout sequences of transformation, then the surfaces involved in such sequences will not feature any topological alteration and will therefore be equivalent in topological terms, even if the shape of every single one of them is different. In other words, they will arrange a section of space in the same way at a fundamental level, which would make them *formally similar*. Giorgini's design thinking as rendered in drawing lends itself to being a medium for introducing how topological analysis may be made instrumental to determining formal qualities, that is, to delineating what it is for a piece of architecture to articulate space differently in essence, rather than for it to embody a distinct shape (i.e., a figure, outline, or envelope).[35]

35 In chapter four, where this issue will be explored extensively, it shall be seen that one of the chief challenges is to define these topological invariants *architecturally*, not just geometrically. The latter criterion, though valid for this introduction of topology's relevance to the basis of architectural form, nevertheless yields too general a domain a possibility where architectural scenarios are at stake, and does not address, by definition, the grounds of these scenarios.

## A Configurational Field

The general study of spatial configurations and their lawfulness, regardless of content, is the object of the science of morphology. Of all the configurations unveiled and analyzed by morphology, only a relatively small percentage are realistically capable of accommodating a set of human activities. Since the idea of a "program" is written into Giorgini's series of topological transformations, they cannot be interpreted solely in morphological terms. For one thing, every iteration within those series features a spatial articulation whose proportions and relational properties—i.e., the way in which the different regions are connected to one another—make it readily available to house a program. In other words, the defining traits of the spatial organizations Giorgini devised never prevent them from falling directly in the domain of potential programmatic configurations in architecture. Those organizations are never impossibly slender, outrageously complicated, or illusorily intricate, to mention a few of the possible restraining attributes. Secondly, Giorgini showed how certain regions might be extended or distorted in size in relation to the rest of the system, in such a way that those deformations appeared to be built into the overall articulation itself. He did not point to programmatic components explicitly as causes of such deformations, but, almost in the manner of mathematical variables, he did divide such causes into "O" (i.e., "obstacle"), whenever external to the spatial system, and "F" (i.e., "function"), whenever internal to it **(fig. 1.55)**.[36]

These two conditions confer the quality of being always already programmatic on Giorgini's spatial organizations: program becomes immanent to form, rather than merely a category attached to form *a posteriori*. Looking at specific examples, the sketches for his Toshiko House of 1972—an unbuilt project for a sculptor friend of Isamo Noguchi in New Jersey—provide a precise illustration of such immanence.[37] Labels for the different functions are placed within the regions comprising an unfolding spatial arrangement when still in its very early stages. Thus, on the basis of their becoming, Giorgini's spatial organizations—in all their idiosyncratic character—ought to be understood as form-program constructs, with the two abovementioned conditions enabling this **(fig. 1.56–58)**.

There are two other concepts he introduced in his theory that can be interpreted as further grounding this principle of program inhering in form: on the one hand, what he called "zones of influence," and, on the other, the transitional elements briefly touched on earlier. The former designated the areas resulting from "the implicit subdivision and distribution of space" relative to individual geometric elements brought into proximity. For instance, a segment and a point can be disposed close to each other on a plane in such a way as to give rise to a division of the surrounding space into a number of areas whose range varies vis-à-vis the position of either element. Analogously, three planes placed in space may

36 The terms "program" and "function" do, however, crop up in Giorgini's writings. While here they are used in a traditional architectural sense—that is to say, alluding to a set of activities being housed in a piece of architecture—Giorgini had a different meaning in mind. An example of "program" for him was, for example, "an elementary system composed of three positive forces which alternate with three negative forces according to the three axes at a distance x and height y from the point 0" (on page 4 of a manuscript for a presentation at the World Congress for Non-Typical Structures convened in Buenos Aires by the International Association for Shell and Spatial Structures from November 7 to 13, 1982). The term's domain was therefore that of physics or, inasmuch as related to form, that of engineering. "Function" seemed more ambivalent. Sometimes it referred to the program's underlying structure, thus also falling into the domains of physics and engineering. At other times, it did seem to designate a particular human activity, though never explicitly, only by invoking the abstract label "F" (on p. 33 of the abovementioned 1979 manuscript).

37 Giorgini received the commission to design a house with atelier for American sculptor Toshiko Takaezu through Frederick Kiesler's widow, Lilian. Isamo Noguchi had introduced his Italian friend to the artistic circles of Manhattan upon his arrival, and it was there that he met Lilian Kiesler. In 1970 she organized a show of her husband's work at the Howard Wise Gallery in Manhattan, where she also had some of Giorgini's experiments on display. It was the first chance he had to exhibit his work in the US. According to historian and architect Marco del Francia—the closest of Giorgini's confidants during the last thirteen years of his life—Lilian Kiesler had sentimental feelings for the Florentine architect, which seems to be confirmed by some of the post-

engender a set of zones of influence around them comprising what Giorgini termed "three-dimensional zonal manifestation" of the planes.[38] Extrapolating from abstract individual geometric units, Giorgini's zones of influence offer an alternative to more or less rigid programmatic partitioning. Rather than the various components of an architectural configuration defining specific compartmentalizations univocally, they can be conceived so that they yield *latent arrangements*. None of these arrangements are really privileged over the rest, and within any given one its different areas can be reorganized and redimensioned in such a way that a new arrangement emerges.

The transitional elements, on the other hand, are the connecting components between two parts in a system of relationships. They may have a certain dispositional charge of their own, thus not being necessarily limited to a point, boundary, or plane.[39] In an architectural scenario, the system of relationships cannot be interpreted but as a sequence of programmatic regions immanent to a particular spatial configuration. This configuration may, in turn, be read as comprised of "parts" *qua* regions corresponding to distinctive areas within it and elements of transition that can also themselves take on the character of programmatic regions. As a result, a spatial arrangement in architecture can be construed on the basis of its various constituents giving rise to a series of program areas whose differentiation is not dependent upon elements that dissociate themselves distinctly from the surrounding field (e.g., a wall), but rather upon other areas that act as a threshold and whose definition is itself contingent on the totality of relations conforming the whole of the arrangement. Since, as is apparent in Giorgini's sketches, a capacity for fluctuation in size might be granted to the elements of transition, the connective structure linking all such elements together could virtually take over the entirety of the arrangement, thereby shifting in character to becoming the parts. This possibility is, in turn, consistent with the fact that Giorgini's transitional elements are not grounded in a fixed ontology, as was evident in the example of the triangle, where sides and vertexes can be made into either parts and transitional elements, respectively, or vice versa, depending on the way the system of relationships is described. Other than in his abstract sketches, transitional elements can easily be read into his Liberty structure—half built between 1977 and 1979, and the only project of whose topological development Giorgini was fully in control **(fig. 1.61–66)**. Looking at the plans of this building, such elements appear as occasional narrowings segmenting an otherwise completely fluid interior, thereby loosely articulating it into a number of recognizable zones. In other situations, the structure deploys the abovementioned ontological reversal. The transitional elements take on a stronger identity of their own by becoming extremely elongated regions, a process through which they co-opt the entirety of the spatial arrangement and relegate what were main areas to a secondary status.

cards that she wrote to him **(fig. 1.59)**. This might have been one the reasons why she promoted his work and endorsed his residency in the US **(fig. 1.60)**, although he never reciprocated such feelings. Marco del Francia, in conversation with the author in Follonica (Italy), September 19, 2013.

38 See Giorgini, *Spatiology*, 37–38.

39 See ibid., 57–59.

**1.56–57** Sketches for the Toshiko House project, 1972.

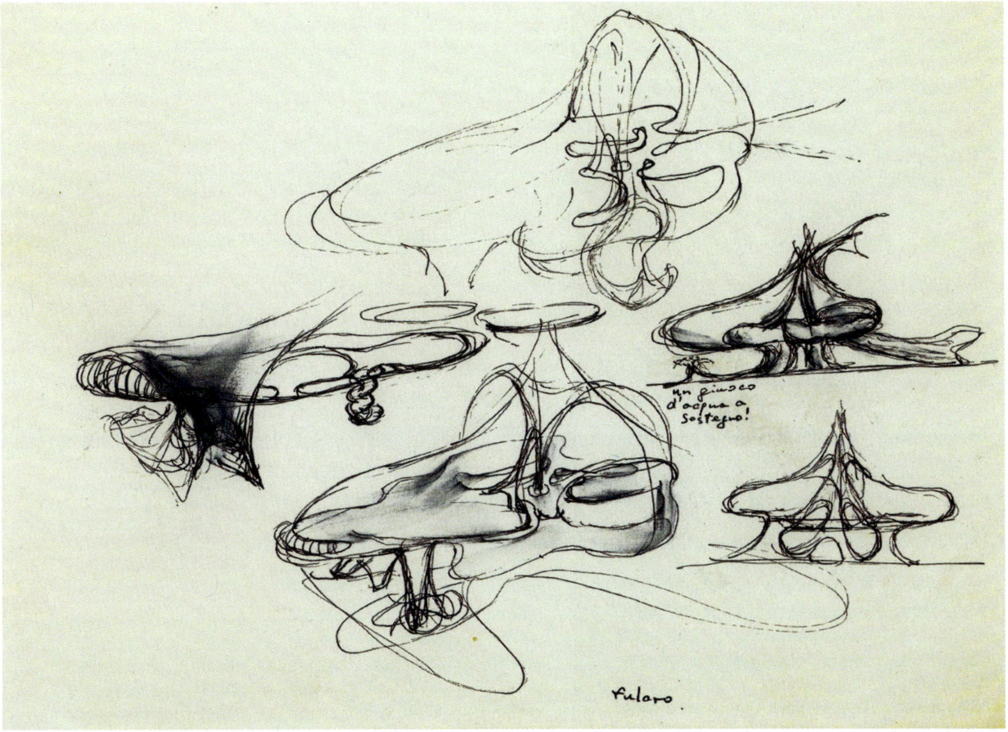
un giuoco d'acqua a sostegno!
Futuro.

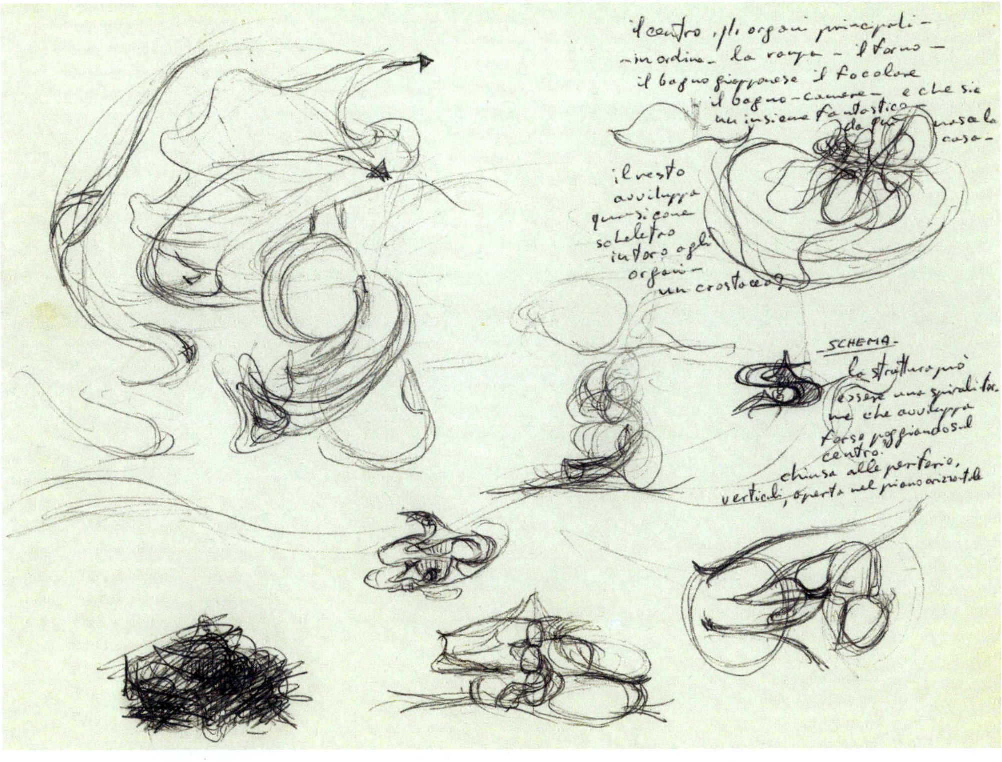
il resto avviluppa quasi come scheletro intorno agli organi – un crostaceo?
SCHEMA

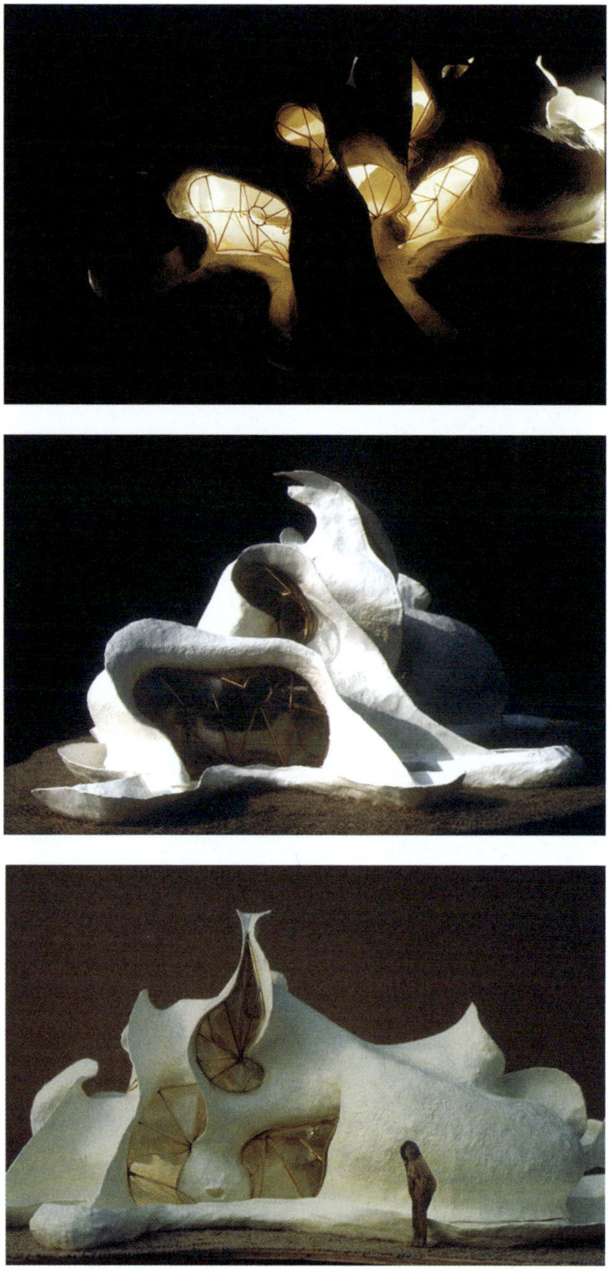

1.58 Toshiko House project. Fiberglass model, 1972.

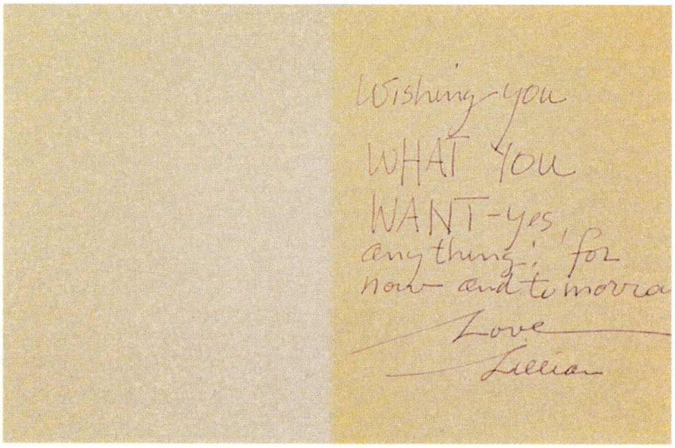

Wishing you
WHAT YOU
WANT-yes,
anything! for
now and tomorro
Love
Lillian

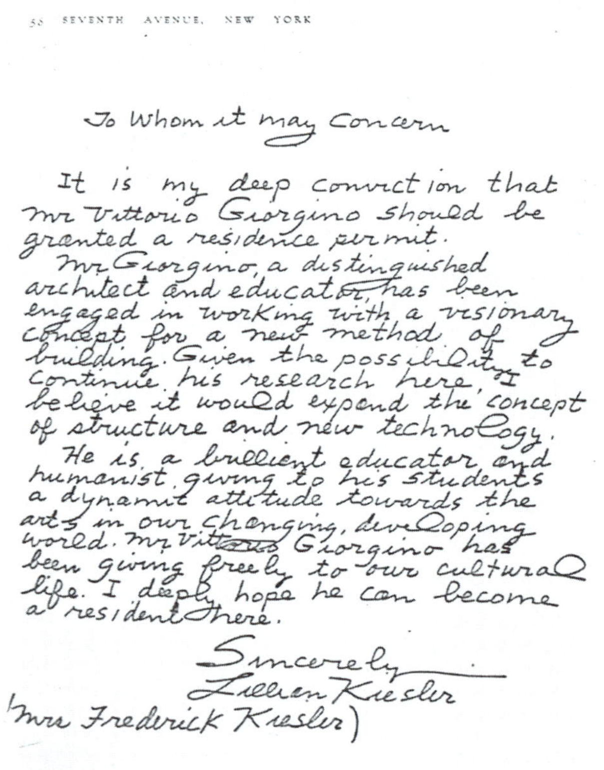

56 SEVENTH AVENUE, NEW YORK

To Whom it may Concern

It is my deep conviction that Mr Vittorio Giorgino should be granted a residence permit.

Mr Giorgino, a distinguished architect and educator, has been engaged in working with a visionary concept for a new method of building. Given the possibility to continue his research here, I believe it would expand the concept of structure and new technology.

He is a brilliant educator and humanist, giving to his students a dynamic attitude towards the arts in our changing, developing world. Mr Vittorio Giorgino has been giving freely to our cultural life. I deeply hope he can become a resident here.

Sincerely
Lillian Kiesler
(Mrs Frederick Kiesler)

1.59 Above: Personal postcard from Lilian Kiesler, undated.

1.60 Below: Letter from Lilian Kiesler in support of Giorgini's application for a residence permit in the US, undated.

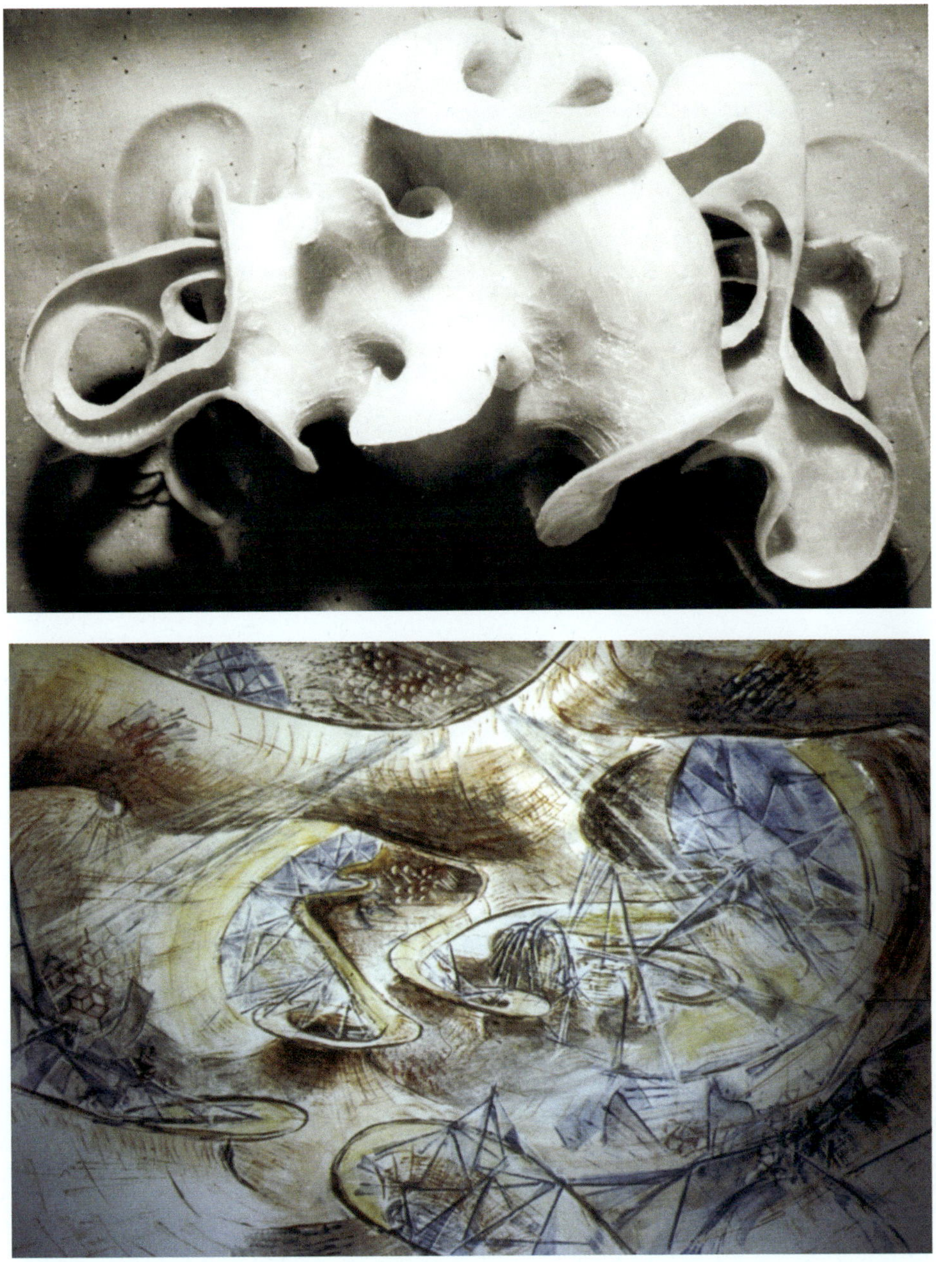

**1.61** Model and sketch for the Liberty House project, late 1970s.

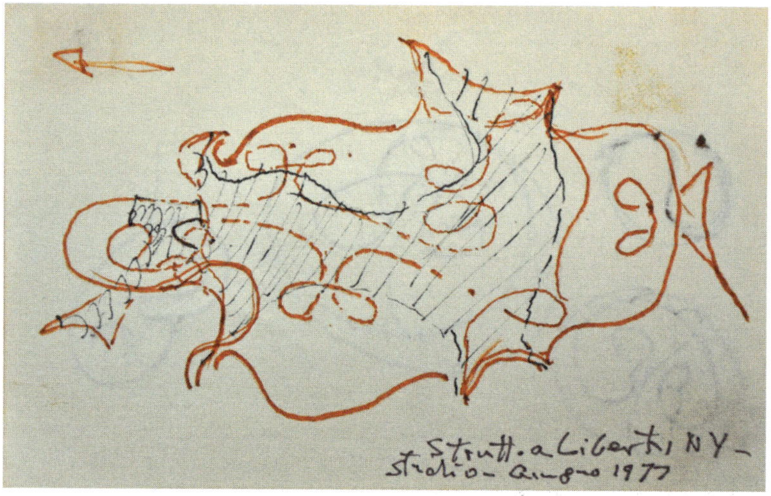


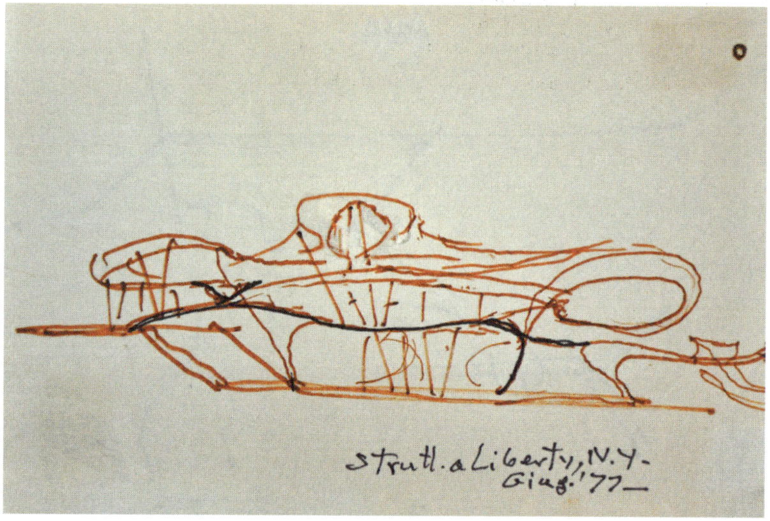


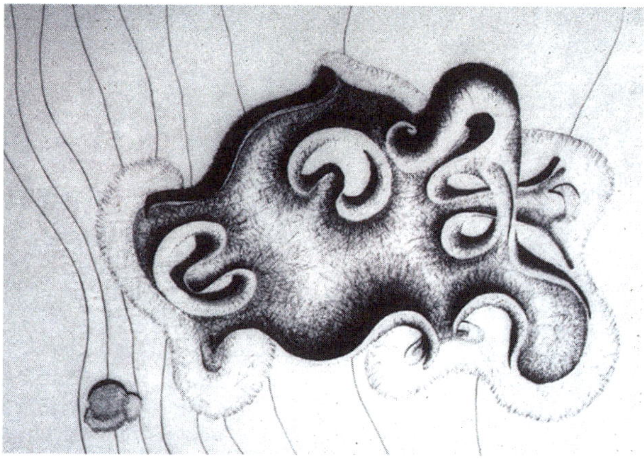

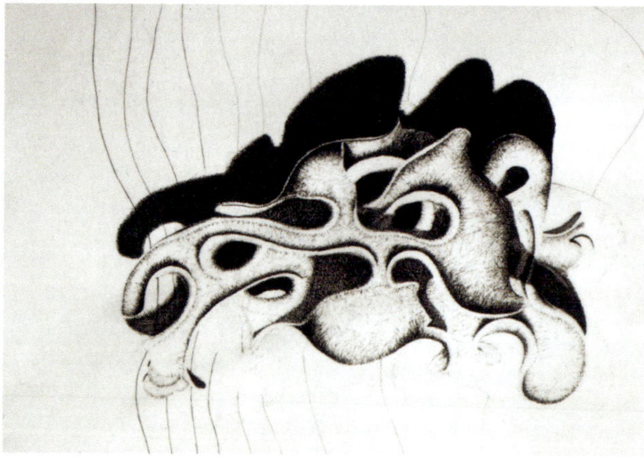

**1.62** Left: Sketches for the Liberty House project, 1977.

**1.63** Below: Ground level and roof plans for the Liberty House project, late 1970s.

Opposite and following page:
**1.64–66** Liberty House in New York City under construction, 1978–79 (pp. 99–100).

## Multivalent Force

The notion of "force" determines the dynamic character of Giorgini's design theory, within which it plays four different (if related) roles. Firstly, it is a vehicle to show how generic pieces of geometry may be described as nascent constructs—something on which Balmond capitalized, as shall be discussed in chapter three. Secondly, it prompts the introduction of the concept of "inherent grids." These grids or lattices embody patterns according to which structural performance in figures like triangles and parallelograms may be registered. Thirdly, Giorgini used his grasp of force behavior in linear structural elements (e.g., beams) to produce variations of compounds of these within a given geometric outline. In this way a number of symmetric isostatic models are unveiled that apply to the same shape and divide up the region within it accordingly. Fourthly, he analyzed the forces affecting a number of given structural units, be they typical ones (e.g., cantilever, column) or the ones he created through topological transformations (e.g., the cantilever-base compound).

Despite this multiplicity of purposes, however, Giorgini did not employ sets of forces directly as instruments to develop his distinctive configurations. Rather, these configurations resulted from specific topological manipulations that were inflected by certain aesthetic inclinations, as argued above. That said, his deep understanding of the structural performance of the basic components making up those configurations suggests not only a built-in awareness of their feasibility, but also an active role, however implicit, for the sets of forces in inducing their emergence. This process differs from that of form finding in that it is not deterministic, that is, it is not one whereby form is surrendered to the specificities of a given surface stress and its boundary conditions. Rather, the force in Giorgini acts as a veiled drive; it underlies the design process but is not explicitly shaped into a particular surface language, as was the case in Frei Otto's work, for instance. Giorgini's gesture is idiosyncratic—ultimately, it is artistic impulse defining a vocabulary of expression. No biunivocal determination can be found between gesture and force, and yet they follow parallel paths, the latter written into the former. The evolution of his sculptures illustrates this description. The first ones, dating back to 1957, were produced intuitively. They arose as an attempt to convert his incipient interest in curved surfaces into a specific material language **(fig. 1.67–68)**. It was not until 1969, in his drawings for a piece in Cento, that he made use of the diagram of forces for the first time **(fig. 1.69)**. Those forces manifest themselves as coextensive with the particularities of the sculptural language—a language whose defining traits had nonetheless appeared over a decade earlier, when no knowledge of forces was mobilized.

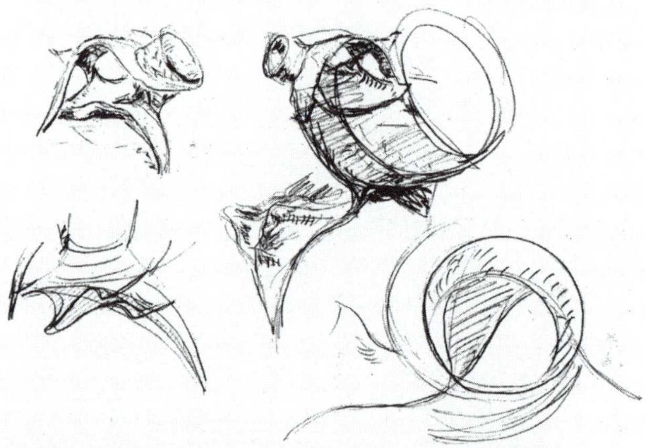

**1.67–68** Sketches and shell surface sculpture, late 1950s.

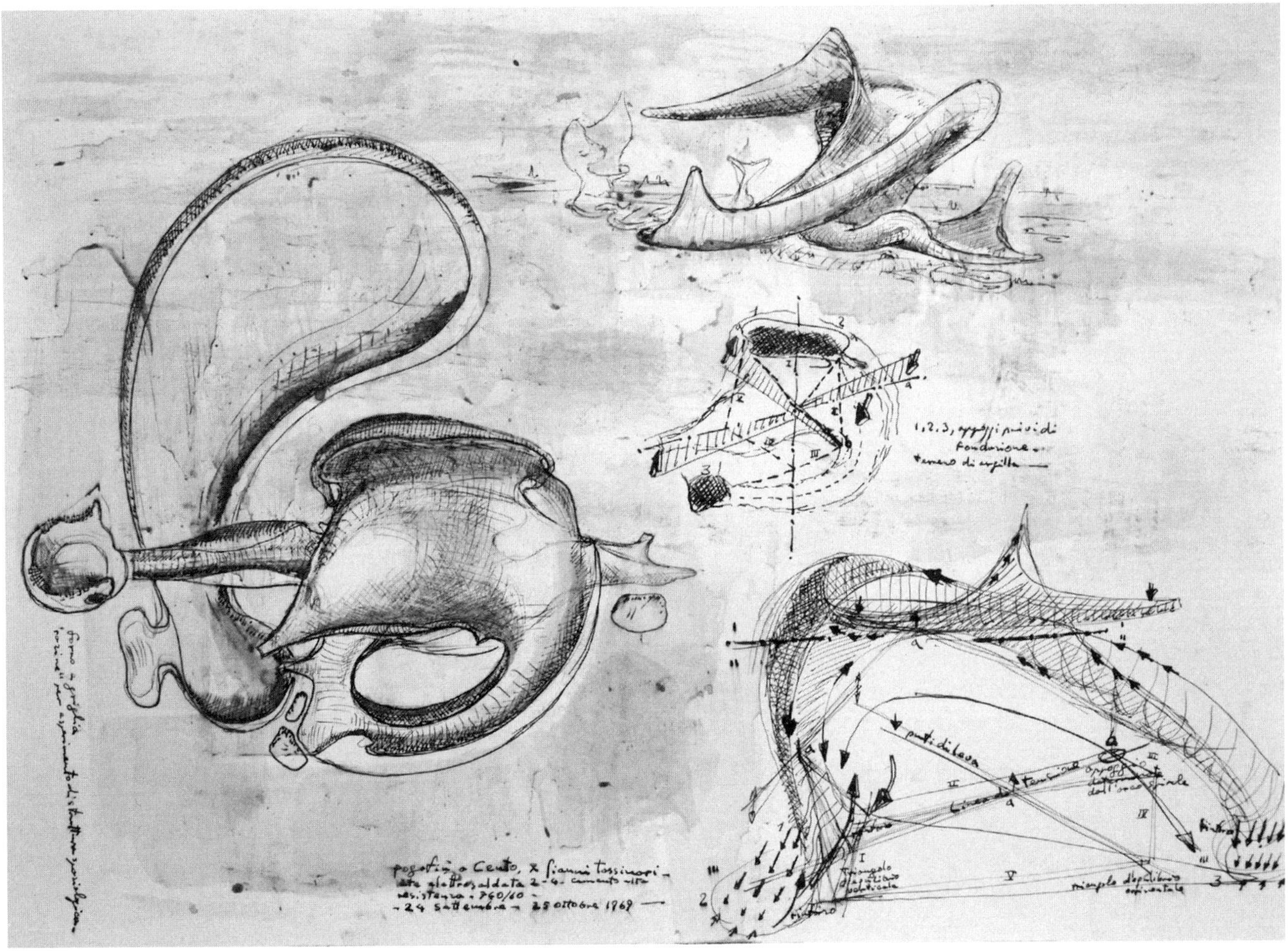

**1.69** Drawings for a piece in Cento, 1969.

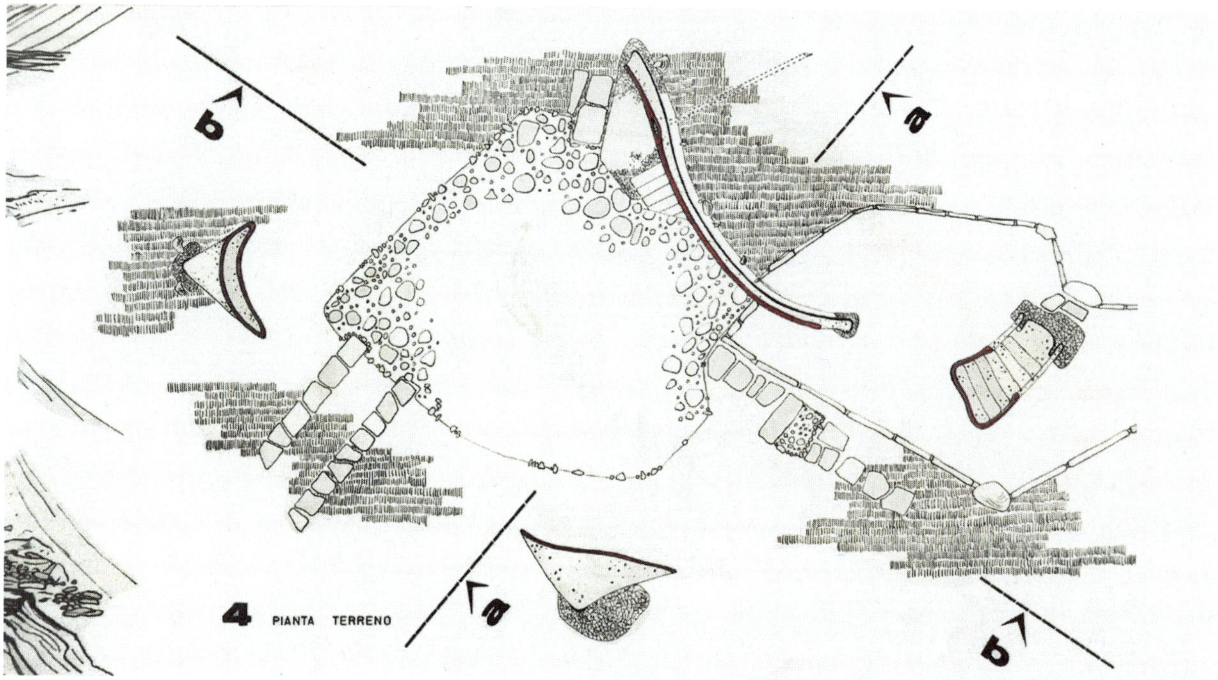


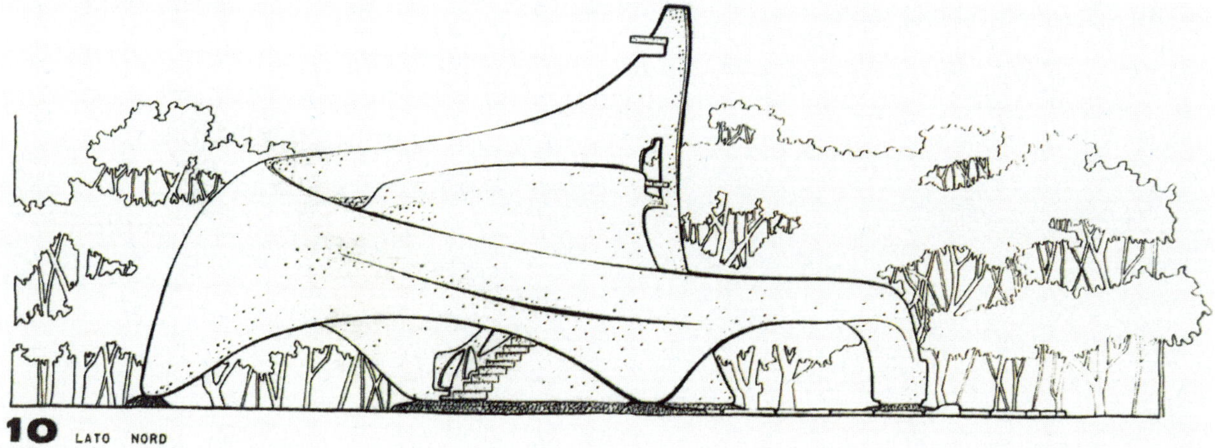


**1.70** Saldarini House on the Gulf of Baratti, 1960–62. Ground level and north elevation.

**1.71** Saldarini House on the Gulf of Baratti, 1960–62. Current state.

## Low-Tech Sophistication

A similar coextension of force and form is perceived in another project where that knowledge was also not yet instrumentalized for design purposes: the Saldarini House. The smooth continuity of the surfaces (never impossibly complicated, always gently curved) and the strategic way in which they touch the ground (in four loosely equidistant regions placed along a rhomboidal outline) **(fig. 1.70–72)** suggest that the building embodies the forces at play—even if it was conceived and erected merely on an empirical basis, since Giorgini had not yet mastered the behavior of forces in built form. The Saldarini House was built in so-called "ferrocement," a construction technique previously used in boatbuilding. It consisted of an overlay of welded wire meshes freely sculpted on site to the desired curvature, and then thinly coated with mortar. No heavy steel rods or coarse aggregate of conventional concrete work was employed. Supported with temporary wooden props where necessary, the mesh layers being overlaid ranged from two across the top of the structure to four near the ground, the thickness including the mortar averaging three inches **(fig. 1.73–74)**. The result is a continuously curved, asymmetric, extremely light membrane that may have cost about a third of the budget for a house with comparable floor area at the time.[40] Stanley Abercrombie explained the empirical character of Giorgini's construction method quite accurately:

> The irregularities [of the structure] are based on reason, intuition, and experience of the material's structural behavior. The design is thus founded on the idea that increasing degrees of strengthening curvature (rather than, as in conventional structures, increasing thicknesses) can be provided where the greatest stresses are expected. . . . Its shapes are based . . . on an empirical knowledge of where strengthening is required and of how it can be supplied by means of compound curvature and contiguity of adjacent sections of construction.[41]

This construction method had already been rehearsed by Giorgini both in his large-scale sculptures and in Quadrante **(fig. 1.75)**. It was also employed in Liberty, the difference being that by then, 1977, intuition had given way to an informed *a priori* knowledge of what the structural performance of the building would be, relative to the design specificities **(fig. 1.76–79)**. This connection between performance and expression, whether via intuition or *a priori* knowledge, was precisely Giorgini's argument against those who defined his work with labels such as "organic," "informal," and "sculptural." He bitterly disapproved of such labels, since for him they carried an association with aesthetic choice, as opposed to technique and method. He never ceased to insist that his interest did not lie in copying the

40 As Giorgini seems to have claimed in an interview in 2001. See Valentina Sonzogni, "Casa Saldarini, Baratti, Italie: Vittorio Giorgini Architecte = Vittorio Giorgini: Casa Saldarini, Baratti, Italy," *Architecture d'Aujourd'hui* 2003, no. 349 (2003), 67.

41 Stanley Abercrombie, *Ferrocement: Building with Cement, Sand, and Wire Mesh* (New York, NY: Schocken Books, 1977), 134, 140.

appearance of nature but in studying its structures so as to achieve more complex and efficient ways to build architecture. As argued above, however, the expressive vocabulary of his structures was certainly fulfilling an aesthetic drive, for it would not be possible to justify the overall assembly of curvatures purely on technical grounds. The need to respond to structural stresses surely determined those curves to a great degree, but their specific manifestation may only be fully described on the basis of a certain set of aesthetic preferences. The fact that, in the Saldarini House, handfuls of moist fine gravel and cement were thrown against the still-damp ferrocement walls in order to obtain a random textured effect further confirms that aesthetics was by no means out of the equation for Giorgini—very deliberately not so in this particular case **(fig. 1.80)**.

**1.72** Saldarini House on the Gulf of Baratti, 1960–62.

One last consideration regarding construction-related aspects involves the unorthodox character of Giorgini's *oeuvre* being conducive to the belief that his was a fundamentally utopian drive, as a consequence of which he was a "theoretical" architect. Though not utopian, at least in one sense he was theoretical, having striven to become something of a thinker during the latter part of his life. After he moved to the United States, his range of interests grew exponentially, from classical philosophy (Socrates, Plato, Aristotle, Epicurus) to the philosophy of science (Popper); from the social sciences and critical theory (Max Weber, Hans Albert, Jürgen Habermas) to psychoanalysis and psychiatry (Wilhelm Reich, Elisabeth Kübler-Ross). But while he reflected extensively on the basis of all this knowledge—he wrote constantly about questions concerning design as well as existential and political issues—from a different perspective Giorgini was the opposite of a "theoretical" architect. He enjoyed the actual construction of his structures **(fig. 1.81)** and was very much a hands-on designer; a maker whose priority was to build. In contrast to Burt—who, as shall be seen, was particularly interested in finding elemental order via speculative means—Giorgini was application-driven.

**1.73–74** Saldarini House on the Gulf of Baratti under construction, 1961–62.

**1.75** Giorgini's sculptures under construction, late 1950s.

**1.76–79** Liberty House in New York City under construction, 1978–79.

**1.80** Saldarini House on the Gulf of Baratti, 1960–62. Current state.

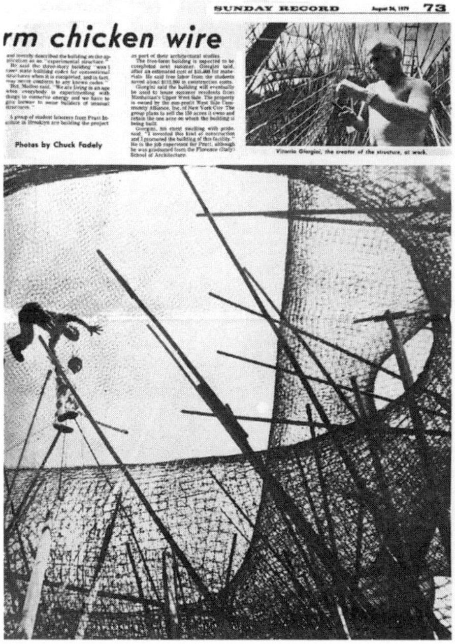


**1.81** Left: Giorgini working on one of his sculptures, late1950s.

Right: Sunday Record feature of Giorgini at the Liberty House site in New York City. Dated August 26, 1979.

## DOUBLE-EDGED INDIVIDUALISM

Reacting against the rationalism of the Modern Movement—notably with respect to its ideals about the prominent role of technology, abstraction, and geometric purity, deemed alienating for the human condition—the organicist views arising in Italy over the course of the two decades after the war articulated a political and cultural agenda of great scope that was to be architecturally implemented through a particular expressive language. Giorgini fully embraced the anti-rationalist value of these aspirations, even if he did not have nearly as much ideological ambition. Within the prospects of organicism as a whole, his project concentrated on just two axes that ultimately reveal his artistic motivations. For one thing, he capitalized on organicism's advocacy of a rapport with nature of a different kind than that propounded by modernism. Out of this position he favored the study and observation of living structures with a view to developing tools and building models related to nature itself. For another, he adhered to elements of the format of expression that was intended to elicit the unfolding of organicism's existential dimension. Just like other organicist designers at the time, Giorgini found in that format of expression the possibility of engendering a "freer" architectural language, one liberated from the geometric "restrictions" imposed by the right angles of modernism.

A good number of Italian architects during the post-war years shared some of these and other organicist values and design tendencies. However, the vast majority of those who employed organicist elements in their architectural languages—whether in Florence or elsewhere—did not continue to do so after the early 1960s. By contrast, Giorgini consistently explored the path initiated by the Florentine School for the duration of his entire career. This is a first level of distinction with respect to the context that shaped the origins of his design thinking. A second factor that sets his work apart not only from the architects of the Florentine School, but also from artists like Kiesler and Bloc, was the fact that Giorgini proceeded toward the construction of a geometric logic that ended up underlying the seemingly arbitrary appearance of his designs. This chapter has shown that the second level of idiosyncrasy was a result of the first. For it was the resolution to keep delving into the same project—indeed, a kind of individualistic perseverance—that enabled its development in the American context, thereby making it possible for its scientization to occur. In other words, a zeal to continue growing a framework for design thinking originally born out of the prospects of doing away with any rationalism is what allowed rationalism back into the picture, albeit in a different guise. If geometric rigor was a main target for the criticism of modernism put forward by organicist positions, Giorgini turned such criticism into an opportunity for cultivating a project that synthesized the anti-rational spatial language of organicism with a different kind of geometric rigor: that dictated by topology.

In short, Giorgini's project centered round an approach to architectural design wherein nature became an inspiration for conducting in-depth research in surface topology. Although the scientization of his design thinking took place mostly in America, the origins of the biological structuralism eventually leading to that rationalization are traceable to his encounter with Hans Jenny in Florence in 1950. Certainly, had Giorgini's interest in nature not already been elicited by the organicist views circulating around Italy, he might very well not have been drawn to Jenny's images. Consequently, since there was a pattern of encounters where the biological structuralism embedded in a scientist's images proved to be inspirational for a designer during the paradigm shift toward efforts to make design scientific in the second half of the twentieth century, it can be said that such a theme of biological structuralism connected Giorgini's local context of influence with that larger shift. This connection is therefore to be seen both in the design scientization processes ultimately catalyzed by such biological rationalization and in the exact way in which those processes were first inspired.

All things considered, it is because of a biological structuralism thus ignited that Giorgini's work emerged as pioneering in terms of knowingly and consistently employing surface topology as the basis of design of fully fledged buildings—introducing, more specifically, the possibility of instrumentalizing non-orientability in design. His contribution to architecture is to be acknowledged on two fronts: first, owing to the development of a geometric theory of design which, based on the study of topology, lends itself to the generation of a diverse range of spatial articulations; second, at the level of aesthetics, for developing an expressive language which, resulting from such a geometric theory, fell outside received formats of architectural expression.

Yet the same individualism that drove the singularity of his production, both within the context in which his design ideas originated and beyond, did not help in his career overall. Giorgini's impulse to rationalize the complexity of natural structures by rendering them comprehensible, legible, and ultimately buildable was driven by the belief that such a translation would make it possible to achieve a certain economy of construction methods, which were ideally more efficient and better suited to the potentialities of technological performance. But if his investigations on shell structures were to be judged on the basis of his built work, then their impact would have to be regarded as minimal. Aside from the Quadrante gallery, the Saldarini House, and his various sculptures—all of which were erected at the beginning of his career—Giorgini did not see any of his shell designs completed. Even today, the technology involved in the construction of double-curved structures in architecture is rather expensive and far from standardized. Giorgini acknowledged his frustration toward the end of his career:

> The research [on shell structures] is still in its infancy, and due to the complexity of asymmetrical topological double curved surfaces, it is difficult; this curvilinear system is limited due to the lack of economical constructive techniques.[42]

He never seriously questioned whether it was feasible to realize his structures, but simply kept pursuing them, holding on to his motivations wholeheartedly and steadfastly. Although he was unyielding, he failed to convince most of his peers, their sensibilities differing substantially. Both in his public appearances and at Pratt he often came across as being out of sync with what everybody else was doing, which resulted in progressive isolation. This is the price he had to pay for being categorical about his architectural approach. If he was capable of producing difference in the sense of engendering a design ideology that was in many ways alien to established patterns of understanding, he was also all too adamant about making everyone see that his views were the way to go. His was an individual search and it might be argued that this was necessarily so as a condition for his contribution, yet frustratingly so at the same time.[43]

42 Giorgini, "Early Experiments in Design Derived from Study of Nature's Morphologies," 63.

43 His laments were recurrent towards the end of his life, this being one of the most telling: "because I have always been left pretty much alone, nobody has ever taken a great interest in me, hence your interest [that of the interviewer] matters to me and makes me feel I am not alone, and this is an important thing." (*"[P]erché sono sempre stato lasciato molto solo, non ho mai avuto grandi interessi da parte di nessuno e quindi questo vostro interesse mi preme e mi fa sentire che non sono solo, e questa è una cosa importante"*). In an unpublished interview that took place at his Florence home on September 11, 2009.

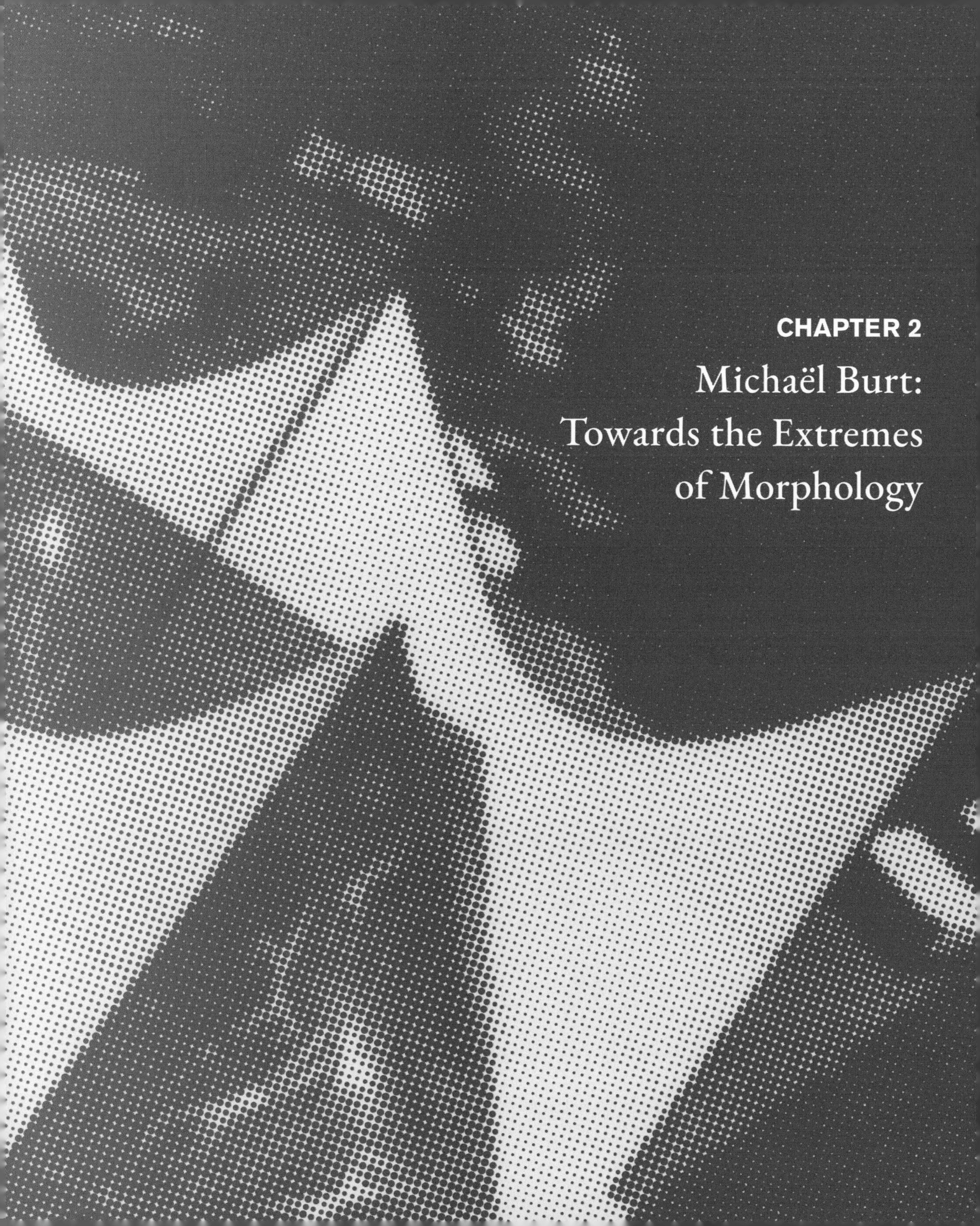

CHAPTER 2

# Michaël Burt: Towards the Extremes of Morphology

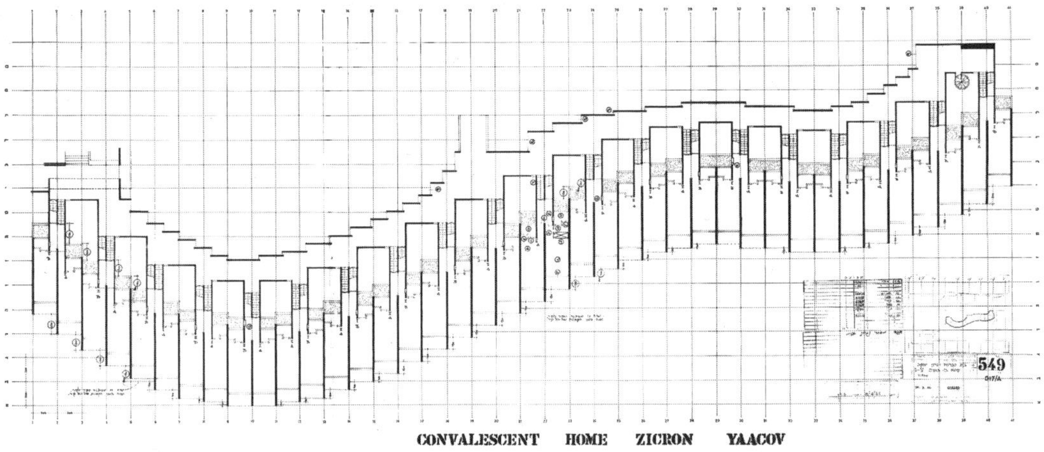

**2.1** Yacov Rechter. Mivtachim sanatorium, Zichron Yaakov, Israel (1968).

# CONDITIONS UNDER WHICH BURT'S APPROACH COULD ORIGINATE: PROGRESSIVE GEOMETRIC SINGULARITY AND ALFRED NEUMANN'S ARCHITECTURAL MORPHOLOGY[1]

Modern architecture was introduced in Israel in the 1920s and 1930s by a number of immigrant architects and engineers who had trained in Europe, with Arieh Sharon, Zeev Rechter, and Dov Karmi being the most representative names. As a result of this wave, a style generally identified as "Jewish Bauhaus" developed that coexisted with the British colonial architecture then being implemented in Palestine.[2]

The establishment of the state of Israel in 1948 brought about a drastic change. In a small country with a rapidly growing population, demands for new construction soared. Bauhaus style gave way to a broader Israeli modernism, itself also the outcome of looking to the West as a model, even if now to a wider array of styles (e.g., those of Aalto, Kahn, Stirling, Corbusier, and the Smithsons). Much of this modernism displayed an inclination toward strong, abstract geometric expression and exposed concrete, which has led some commentators to characterize it under the label of "brutalism."[3]

Rising to prominence during the late 1950s, a second generation of architects, mostly born in Israel and trained at the Technion, found themselves building projects on all scales, despite their youth and lack of experience. By the 1960s they had begun to replace their predecessors—as in the case of Dov Karmi's son, Ram. Much of the production of these younger architects was distinguished by a desire to singularize the different building components and emphasize their elementary and reproducible nature. Some of the work by another "son," Yaakov Rechter, as well as that by Al Mansfeld (a figure in between the two cohorts) reflected such a tendency, often associated with structuralism and systems theory **(fig. 2.1–2)**.[4] Within it, a group of designers inspired by Alfred Neumann—himself belonging to the old generation due to his age, though he only arrived in Israel in 1949—became interested in evolving a more idiosyncratic architecture specifically grounded in morphology. Prominent among these designers were Zvi Hecker, Israel Goodovitch, David Yanai, and yet another "son," Eldar Sharon **(fig. 2.3–4)**. Ukrainian-born Israeli Michaël Burt (b. 1937) was part of this second generation **(fig. 2.5)**.

1 Architectural morphology restricts itself to the individual building and therefore is to be distinguished from both *urban* morphology and *geographical* morphology. The former was led by the Italian school of figures like Saverio Muratori and Gianfranco Caniggia during the second half of the twentieth century, whereas Günter Conzen was perhaps the most visible head in geographical morphology.

2 "Jewish Bauhaus" was primarily about simple geometric volumes, white stucco facades, and other distinctive design features–such as frames, *brise-soleils*, and screens–that appeared out of the necessity to adjust what otherwise would have been the language of the Modern Movement at its purest to local climate conditions and the building technology available in the region. Prominent until well into the 1940s, this Bauhaus style gave rise, as is well known, to the legend of Tel Aviv as the "White City."

3 Zvi Efrat, "The Object of Zionism: Architecture and Statehood in Israel 1948–73" (Basel, Swiss Architecture Museum, 2012), 9.

4 Architectural structuralism, however, came about primarily through the production of a Dutch collective led by Aldo van Eyck (the "FORUM group") and secondarily via other architects designing buildings on similar principles in Europe, Japan, and North America, including Mohse Safdie. See for instance Wim J. van Heuvel, *Structuralism in Dutch Architecture* (Rotterdam: Uitgeverij 010 Publishers, 1992), and Arnul Lüchinger, *Structuralism in Architecture and Urban Planning*, Dokumente Der Modernen Architekt (Stuttgart: K. Krämer, 1981).

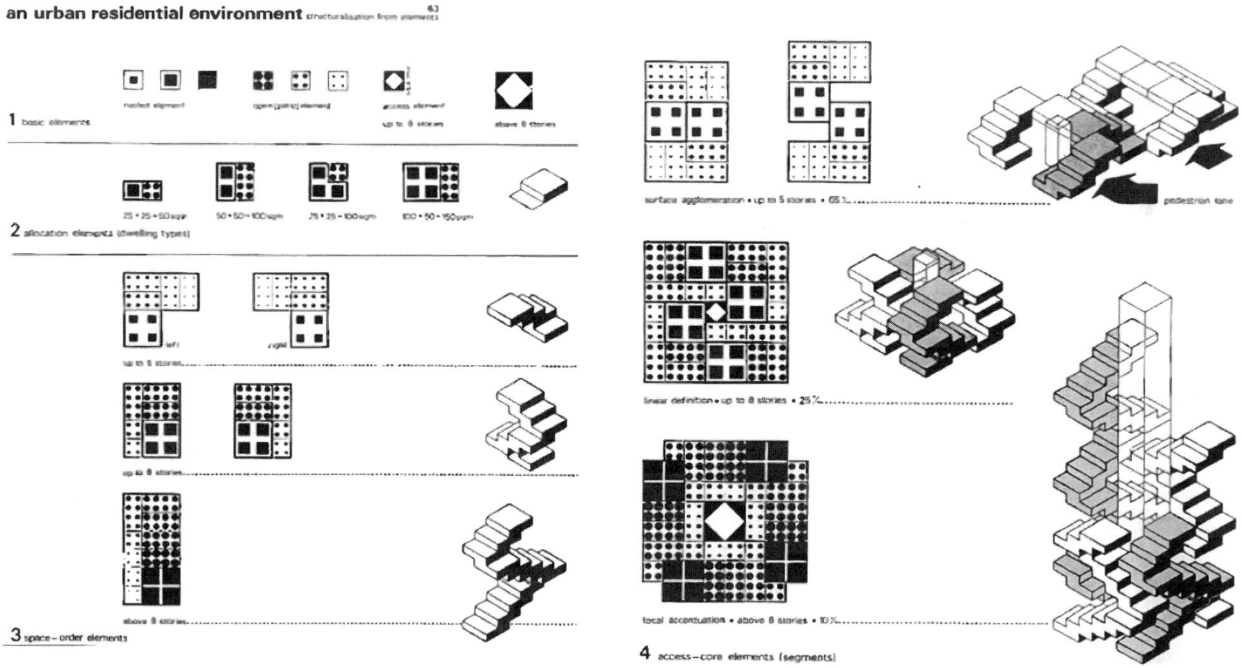
an urban residential environment
1 basic elements
up to 8 stories
above 8 stories
2 allocation elements (dwelling types)
3 space-order elements
up to 8 stories
above 8 stories
surface agglomeration • up to 5 stories • 65%
pedestrian lane
linear definition • up to 8 stories • 25%
focal accentuation • above 8 stories • 10%
4 access-core elements (segments)

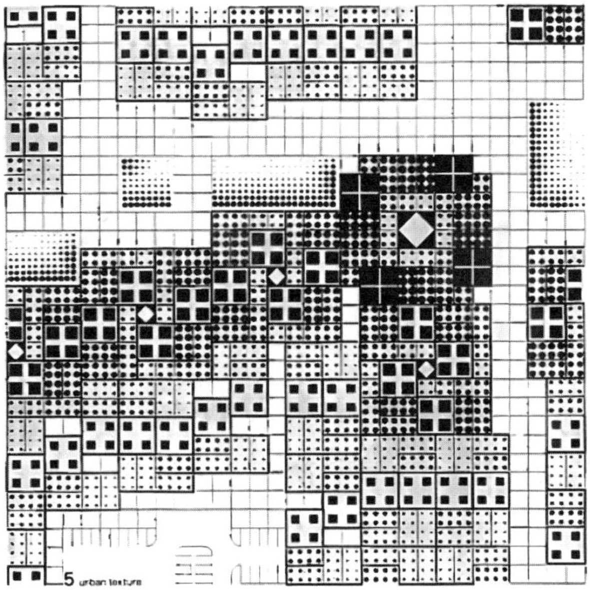
5 urban texture

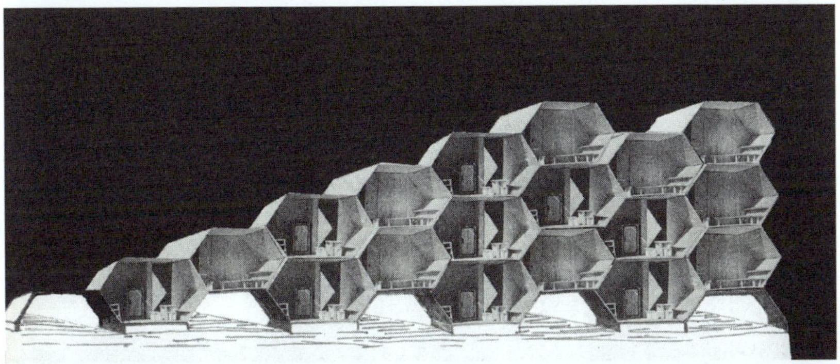

Opposite page:
**2.2** Above and below, left: Al Mansfeld's architectural structuralism.
**2.3** Below, right: Zvi Hecker. Ramot Polin in Haroe, Jerusalem (1977).

**2.4** Above: Israel Goodovitch. Housing building prototype, 1957.

**2.5** Right: Michaël Burt aged 33.

He entered the Faculty of Architecture of Planning at the Technion Institute of Technology in 1959, obtaining his bachelor's degree in 1963. In 1960, during his second year of study, he completed a mandatory course titled "Architectural Morphology," taught by Alfred Neumann. It was this encounter with the research interests of the Czech architect that triggered Burt's life-long commitment to morphology.

## Alfred Neumann's Morphology

Neumann advanced the domain of morphology with a view to constructing a scientific approach to the study and production of architecture. "Morphology" as such, as a scientific domain, was initiated by Goethe as an alternative to the Linnaean tradition, dominant throughout the second half of the eighteenth century in zoology and botany. While the Linnaean approach was based on fundamentally descriptive taxonomies of the natural world, Goethe proposed an analytical study of "the principles of structured form and the formation and transformation of organic bodies." Insofar as Neumann conceived morphology as an independent field of study, disengaged from the object's function or use, his approach echoed Goethe's original idea that his was a "a theory in and of itself" yielding "a specialized set of principles." It was meant to be a "new science," drawing "as little as possible on the other sciences ancillary to biology," in the service of which it nevertheless ought to define its purpose.[5] Analogously, the science of morphology in architecture concerned itself with the general study of forms and their lawfulness, regardless of content.

In his first published article, "Morphologic Architecture" (1963), Neumann explained the principles defining his theory, stating that:

> The possibility exists to conceive the whole man-made human environment from a unifying point of view by applying morphological criteria. . . . A science of architecture, like any other science, should describe the different phenomena by a common lawfulness.[6]

Such "common lawfulness" alluded to the morphological rules according to which a section of space can be bounded and articulated. He identified these as embodied in material reality by studying, on the one hand, the formal evolution of a number of historical archetypes—ranging from domestic architecture and cupolas all the way through to igloos and other vernacular constructions—and certain structures of the living world, such as those built by wasps and bees, on the other. After scrutinizing these instances and further extracting their formal logic, Neumann observed that "one could follow the way from cell to cell (aggregate), the transformation of shape and dimension which the element undergoes, the laws and symmetries

5 Johann Wolfgang von Goethe, "Morphology," in *Scientific Studies*, ed. Douglas Miller (1790–1808; Princeton, NJ: Princeton University Press, 1995), 57.

6 Alfred Neumann, "Morphologic Architecture," *Zodiac*, no. 16 (1966), 136–39. First published in *RAIC Journal* 40, May 1963.

determining the shape of the aggregations."[7] During his teachings on morphology in the School of Architecture at Laval University (between 1965 and 1968) he extended this research to animal houses: the efficiency—both material and in terms of the use/floor area ratio—with which these structures were constructed proved to be an invaluable lesson for Neumann's understanding of form.[8] In addition, being so invested in spatial groupings, it was natural for crystallography to become relevant to his explorations. The examination of crystal structures reveals highly ordered subdivision patterns that follow rules known as "space packing" or "close packing." These rules give rise to unbounded arrays of elementary periodic units or *unit cells* placed together in such a way that no spaces are unaccounted for and no intersections between contiguous cells exist. Such unit cells are usually polyhedra of various kinds whose complexity itself is also the object of space packing.

Neumann's theoretical and design production exhibited a marked humanism that sheds light on the intentions behind his architectural thinking, leading to his operative interpretation of morphology. In 1956, he published his only book, *L'Humanisation de L'Espace: Le Système M Ph*, where he discussed his idea of "humanized space" and advocated the need to pursue it in society. This humanized space would be particularly suitable for appropriation by the human body, accomplished through an abstract system of proportion grounded purely in geometry and mathematics.[9] Although Neumann did not advance any strategies in his book for turning this system of proportion into an operative design tool, applications of the system can be found embodied in his buildings of the 1960s. The breaking down of space into small units achieved through space packing constituted Neumann's strategy for making architecture relate to the scale of the human body.

Neumann's book ought to be seen in the context of postwar attempts to address concerns with humanism in architecture through the role that can be played by systems of proportions in the conception of built space. As Rafi Segal convincingly suggested, the two contributions that set the tone in the early 1950s in terms of these attempts were Rudolph Wittkower's *Architectural Principles in the Age of Humanism* (1949) and Le Corbusier's *Modulor* (1950).[10] These contributions tackled the introduction of the human figure as a standard of proportions and dimensions, and by doing so within the framework of a system, they provided a number of aesthetic formats with a basis that was better attuned to the demands of scientific reasoning than that of other such formats in the past. Employing features inherent to the meter itself, rather than the human figure, and being fundamentally spatial rather than planar, Neumann's system differed methodologically from both Wittkower's and Le Corbusier's.[11] But it shared similar motivations and kept building on the possibility of a rationalized approach to the "humanizing" of space through proportions, accomplishing a more scientific iteration than its predecessors.

7 Ibid., 136.

8 See Rafael Segal, *Unit, Pattern, Site: The Space Packed Architecture of Alfred Neumann 1949-1968* (PhD Dissertation, Princeton School of Architecture, 2011), 102.

9 See Alfred Neumann, *L'humanisation de L'espace: Le Système M Ph.* (Boulogne-sur-Seine: Éditions A.A., 1956).

10 See Segal, *Unit, Pattern, Site: The Space Packed Architecture of Alfred Neumann 1949-1968*, 28–48.

11 Ibid., 45–47.

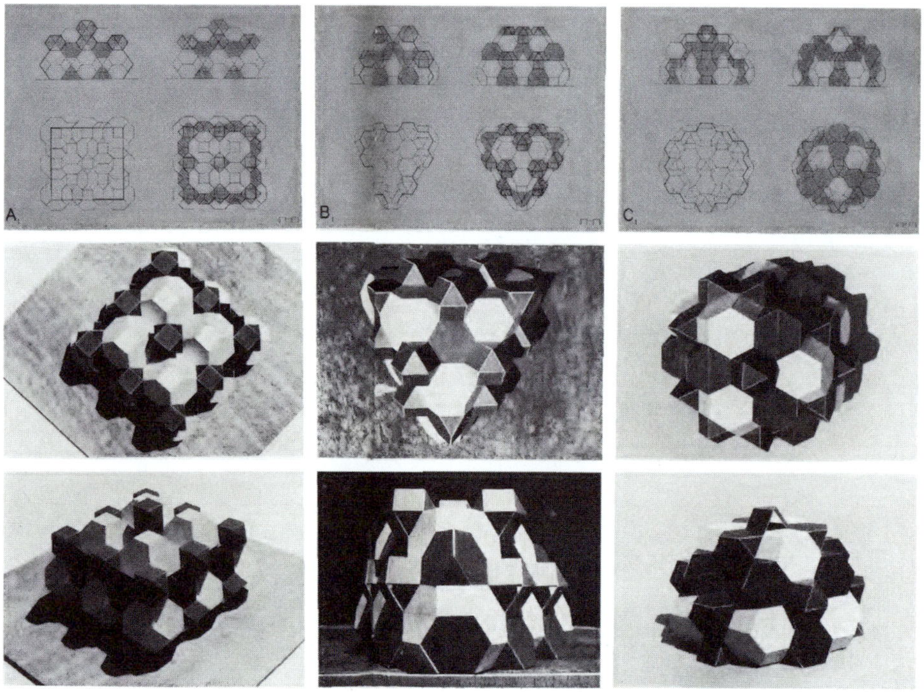


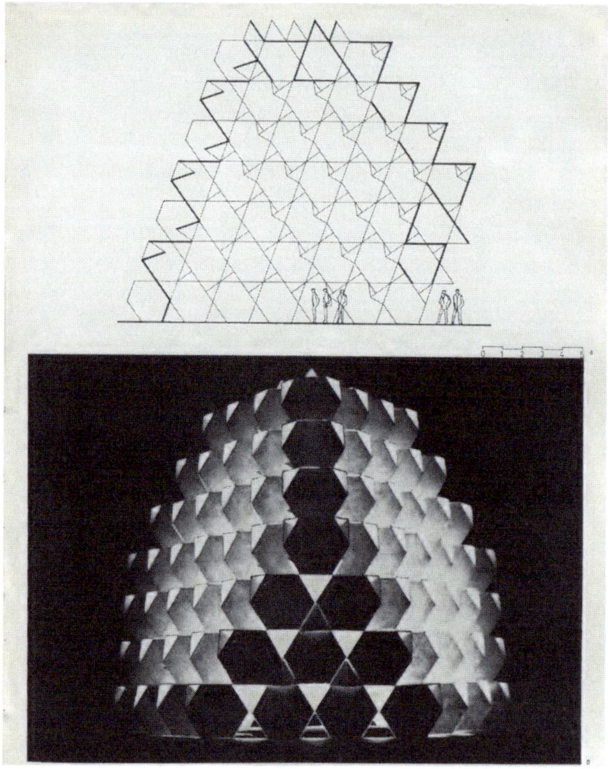

**2.6–7** Alfred Neumann. Studies in Polyhedric Architecture, 1967.

As Segal went on to recount, the other international discourses with respect to which Neumann's development of his conception of space toward morphology and space packing ought to be understood were those involving the use of patterns as templates to generate architectural and urban form. From some of the members of Team X and the architects of the Dutch Forum group (notably Aldo Van Eyck and Herman Hertzberger), to Japanese Metabolists like Fumihiko Maki, Masato Ōtaka, and Kenzo Tange, all the way through to SOM's Walter Netsch in America, a sizeable sector of international production during the 1950s and 1960s shifted toward the genesis of spatial systems which, proceeding mostly along a horizontal plane, served as frameworks for visual connections and physically interdependent parts to unfold.[12] The integrity of the overall structure was meant to hold together clusters of identifiable units that appeared otherwise separate. While Neumann's harnessing of patterns somewhat distinguished itself from appropriations elsewhere (for example, by being three-dimensional in nature rather than planar, and by maintaining the legibility of the object intact, as opposed to dissolving it into its surroundings), his design approach substantially shared the same pattern-driven paradigm.[13]

## Fourfold Critique of Modernism

Although Neumann's morphology arose as the result of a series of transitional moments in Israeli architectural production stemming from modernism, it ultimately posited a critique of its original source. Theories of proportion and pattern thinking in the postwar decades provided the conditions for such a critique of modernism, which can be outlined along the following four axes.

First, there is the question of nature. In classicism, nature was regarded as a source of imitation, whereas for the masters of the Modern Movement it was the idyllic background with which the new machine society ought to be in harmony. Alternatively, by undertaking to scientifically explore the laws underlying the forms of the living world so as to determine their spatial possibilities, Neumann pursued an experimental rapport with nature.[14] This approach belongs squarely in the tradition of biological structuralism defined earlier by authors and scientists such as D'Arcy Thompson.[15] Via nature, Neumann's goal was to define what he termed "a grammar of space," that is, a set of criteria that would enable him to explore the limits of Euclidean geometry—which he considered "far from being fully exploited"—beyond rectangular prismatic patterns.[16] This research path led him to turn a series of geometric and morphological principles—among which the relationship between cell and aggregate and the operativity of three-dimensional space packing became central—into directives for architectural design **(fig. 2.6–10)**.

12 Ibid., 75–86.

13 Ibid., 91–96.

14 Cf. Maria Bottero, "Technological Research and Architecture," *Zodiac*, no. 21 (1971), 229–32.

15 As already mentioned, biological structuralism can generally be related to the search for structures underlying the forms of the living world, in contrast to mimicry of their external appearance.

16 Neumann, "Morphologic Architecture," 139.

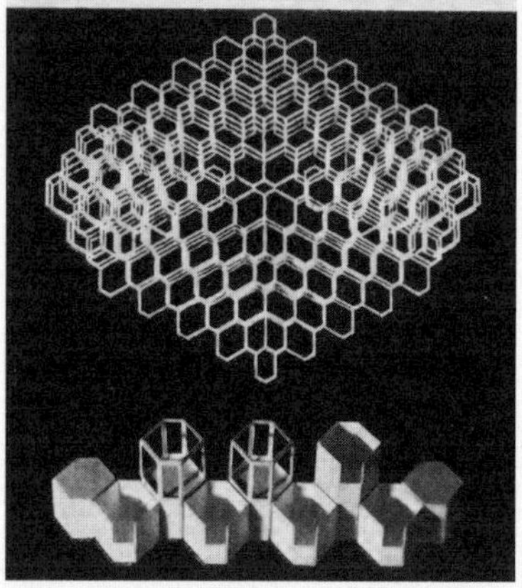

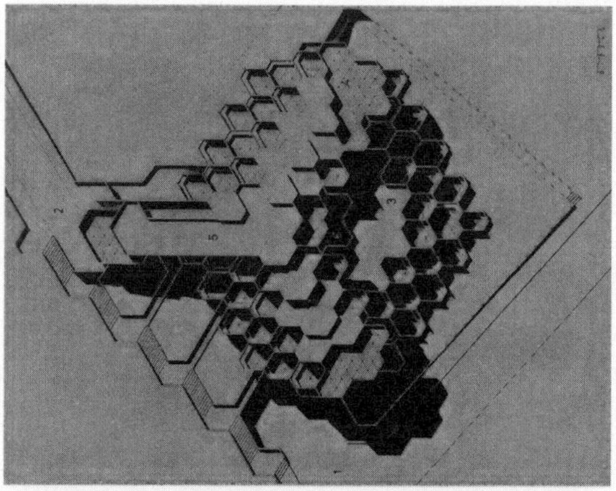

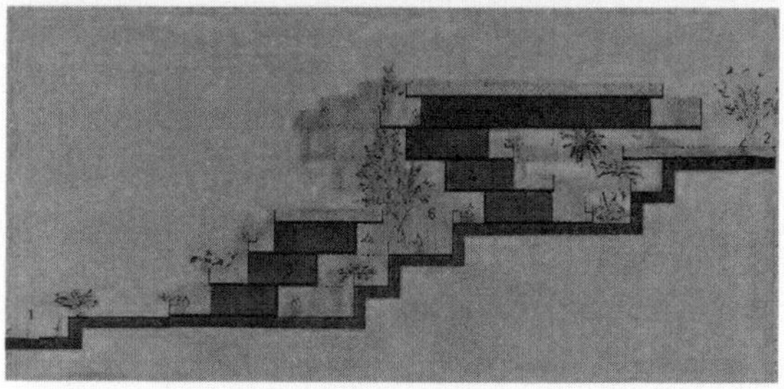

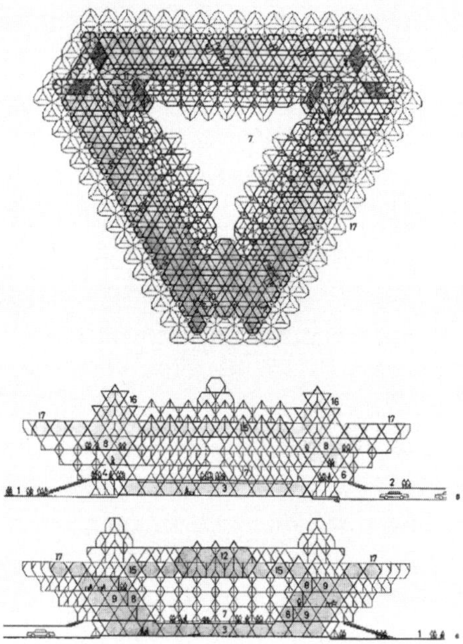

*4. Third floor plan; 5. Section through the main and side entrance; 6. Section through the council chamber and offices area. Key to the plans and sections: 1. Lower piazza - 2. Upper piazza (Covering the parking area) - 3. General service and mechanical equipment area - 4. The main entrance from the lower piazza - 5. Side entrance from the parking - 6. Side entrance from the upper piazza - 7. The triangular certral court - 8. Interior galleries - 9. Offices - 10. Major's office - 11. Stairs to the council chamber - 12. Triangular council chamber - 13. Entrance to the council chamber - 14. Roof garden - 15. Truncated*

Second, Neumann's morphology can be construed as a challenge to the functionalism of the Modern Movement. Rather than the form of a building being predetermined or substantially conditioned by function, the morphological arrangements at the heart of Neumann's projects are self-reliant: they arise on the basis of their own rule system. By extension, the ensuing aesthetics are a by-product of those rules, as opposed to being the expression of a link between form and function. The building envelope encapsulates this difference quite clearly. If Neumann's envelopes are but the result of a three-dimensional pattern unfolding outward—one subsequently adjusted in relation to its context by responding to site, climate, and light—those of modernism were made up of carefully composed, minimal planar surfaces conceived as membranes expressive of function.

Opposite page:
**2.8** Above: Alfred Neumann with Zvi Hecker and Eldar Sharon. Dubiner Apartment House in Ramat-Gan, Israel (1961–64).
**2.9–10** Below: Alfred Neumann with Zvi Hecker. Netanya City Hall Competition in Netanya, Israel (1964)

As a mode of thought built around the notion that signs are arbitrary entities that only convey meaning through a structure of internal relations within a particular system—rather than that meaning being independently fixed with regard to an outside reality—structuralism provided a useful reference for further grounding the kinds of challenges to functionalism found in the practice of architectural morphology. As Alan Colquhoun argued, structuralism helps us understand that function cannot constitute the only valid set of culturally predefined values through which a building acquires meaning.[17]

If structuralism provided a framework through which to expose a core weakness of functionalism, it also bolstered the reexamination of another of the traits central to modernism that was countered by morphology: the quality of the building as object. Although Neumann's buildings did retain a certain condition of objecthood, the notion of the building as a pattern, as suggested by morphology, channels a conception of the built artifact as an open organizational system made up of repetitive elements: a field, rather than an unmistakably defined figure featuring clearly set boundaries. Ostensibly resonating with structuralism's emphasis on systems of relations rather than individual constructs, the design strategies triggered by the employment of spatial patterns were thus to contest the object-oriented approach prevalent in modernism.

Morphology's fourth point of entry into a critique of modernism has to do with a building's language of expression. Neumann moved away from the formal vocabulary of the modern masters by advancing a novel format of architectural language. In this regard his approach echoed that of a number of other designers elsewhere who, in pursuit of alternative languages during the 1960s and 1970s, relied heavily on experimental geometry and biological structuralism as well as on certain aspects of morphology. Names such as Anne Tyng, Moshe Safdie, Robert Le Ricolais, Rinaldo Semino, Frei Otto, and Félix Candela can be mentioned here, although they engaged with the technological

17 See Alan Colquhoun, "Post-modernism and Structuralism: A Retrospective Glance," *Assemblage*, no. 5 (February 1988), 9.

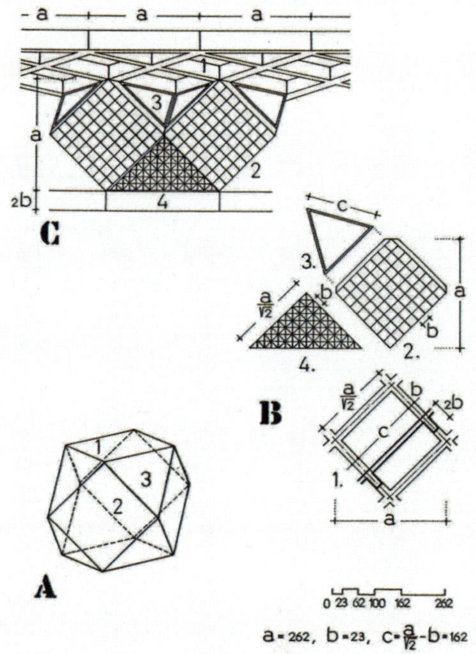

**2.11** Left: Basic geometric unit; cubucahedron. Fit to dimensions from Alfred Neumann's MΦ system. Studies for the Bat-Yam Town Hall and Civic Center in Bat-Yam, Israel (1959–63) by Alfred Neumann with Zvi Hecker and Eldar Sharon.

**2.12** Above: Basic geometric volumes used in the overall structure and roof elements of the Bat-Yam Town Hall and Civic Center in Bat-Yam, Israel (1959–63) by Alfred Neumann with Zvi Hecker and Eldar Sharon.

**2.13** Below, left: Top: Model without roof showing central interior public space. Bottom: Model view; early scheme for roof elements. Alfred Neumann with Zvi Hecker and Eldar Sharon. Bat-Yam Town Hall and Civic Center in Bat-Yam, Israel (1959–63).

**2.14** Below: Alfred Neumann with Zvi Hecker and Eldar Sharon. Bat-Yam Town Hall and Civic Center in Bat-Yam, Israel (1959–63).

advances of their time and the world of engineering far more substantially than Neumann ever did. Being particularly sensitive about the prospects of this design research and related practices, Maria Bottero turned the journal *Zodiac*, which she edited between 1963 and 1973, into a platform for extensively showcasing their work—an architectural counterculture of sorts, it might be added, as distinguished from, though definitely related to, the social and political ones.[18]

What emerges from the sequence of historical developments sketched above and from the various defining traits of morphology as an approach to formal analysis and design is that Burt's production ought to be seen in the context of the progressive distilling of a particular bent of Israeli architectural thinking in which geometry played an ever more singular role. From the abstract, yet marked and nuanced, geometric expression of the Israeli modernism being practiced between 1948 and the late 1950s, to the second generation's emphasis on and experimentation with the individuality of a building's spatial sectors vis-à-vis their elementary nature and degree of reproducibility, to the increasing linguistic specificity of Neumann's morphology, this gradual process of geometric specialization in architectural thinking—both derived from and ultimately critical of modernism—constituted the domain of design that enabled Burt's approach to emerge.

## CURBED INTERNATIONAL PROJECTION

Burt had been interested in problems of space for a few years before taking Neumann's course, but not in any systematic way. It was only after completing Neumann's morphology in 1960 that he envisioned how those initial concerns could amount to a project of its own. During the 1950s Neumann had been working on his theory of proportion and had begun his morphological analysis both of historical archetypes in architecture and of a host of structures of the living world. By 1960 he had already derived an abstract geometric basis from these studies, as clearly embodied in the projects he designed at the time along with Zvi Hecker and Eldar Sharon **(fig. 2.11–14)**. What Burt first encountered was therefore this relatively incipient geometric basis, one primarily constituted by simple polygonal and polyhedral configurations. Neumann's morphological approach was still to develop much further.

Polish-born researcher Avraham Wachman (subsequently dean of the Technion, from 1986 to 1989, and six years Burt's senior) was then one of Neumann's

18 Caroline Maniaque also used the term "counterculture" to refer to a number of related practices, focusing on the French-American context. See Caroline Maniaque-Benton, *French Encounters with the American Counterculture 1960–1980* (Burlington, Vt: Routledge, 2011).

REGULAR CONTINUOUS PERIODIC SURFACE (SPATIAL INDEX OF 300°).

30

משטח מחזורי נמשך רגולרי (אינדכס מרחבית 300°).

6

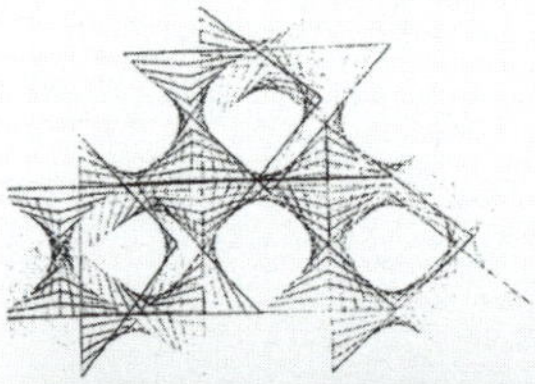

5

4

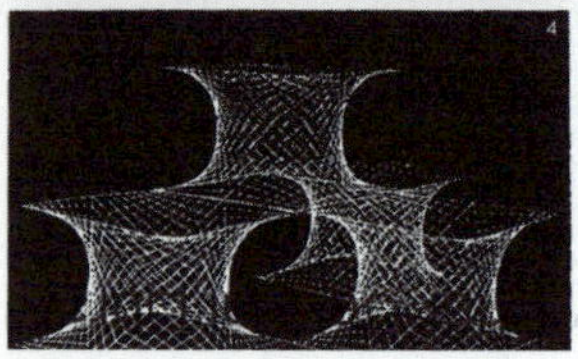

1.* סקיו פוליהדרון בעל פאות רבו-עיות ( $4^6$ ) זהה בסימטריה של ל"משטח 300°".

2. צרוף היפארים ל"משטח 300°".

3. "יחידה חוזרת מורכבת" של "משטח - 300°". בנוייה מ-12 יחידות חוזרות אלמנטאריות".

4. "משטח 300°" בנוי "מיחידות חוזרות מורכבות" (שתוארו ב-3).

5. קטע של "משטח-300°", בנוי ממשושים מרחביים של 60°.

6. "יחידה חוזרת מורכבת" של "משטח 300°". המתומן מורכב מ-4 יחידות חוזרות אלמנטאריות של "משטח 300°".

*1. Skew polyhedron with square, faces ($4^6$), with symmetry properties identical to those of "300° surface".

2. Sets of hyperbolic-paraboloids forming continuous "300° surface".

3. "Combined repetitive unit" of "300° surface", composed of 12 "elementary repetitive units".

4. "300°-surface" composed of "combined repetitive units" (as described in No. 3).

5. Part of "300°-Surface", composed of spatial hexagons of 60°.

6. "Combined repetitive unit of "300° surface". The octagon in itself is composed of 4 "elementary repetitive units of the surface".

* פורסם ע"י : Coxeter

* Published by Coxeter

1

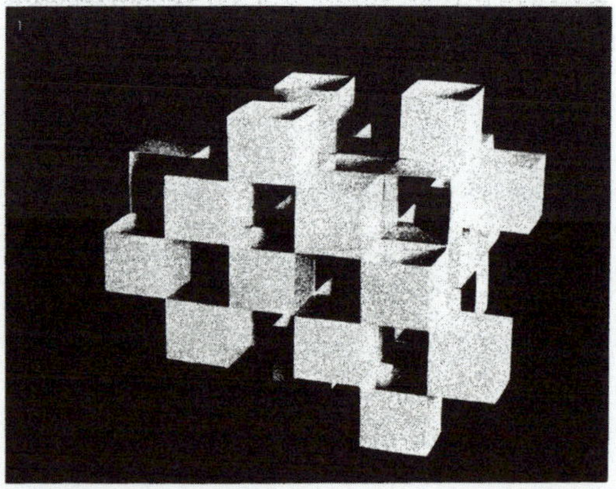

3

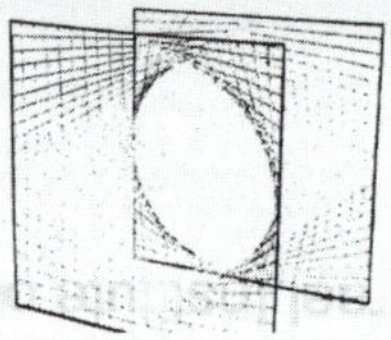

2

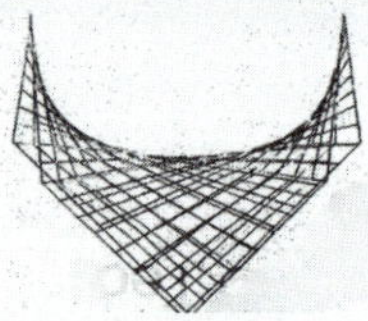

REGULAR CONTINUOUS PERIODIC SURFACES.

23

משטחים מחזוריים נמשכים רגולריים.

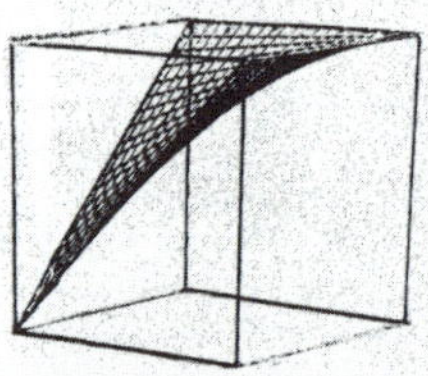

אינדכס מרחבית 330°

SPATIAL INDEX OF 330°

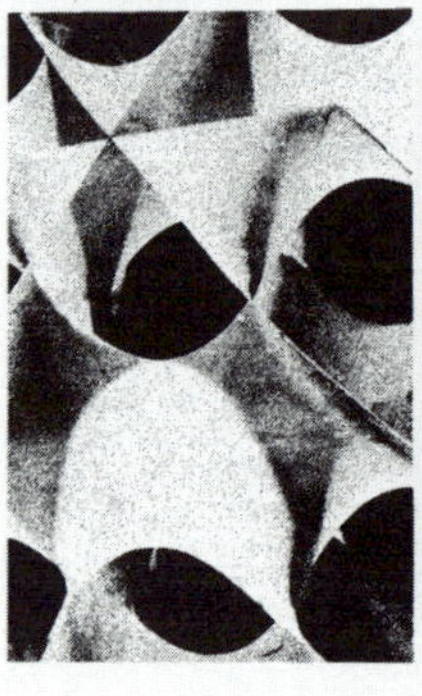

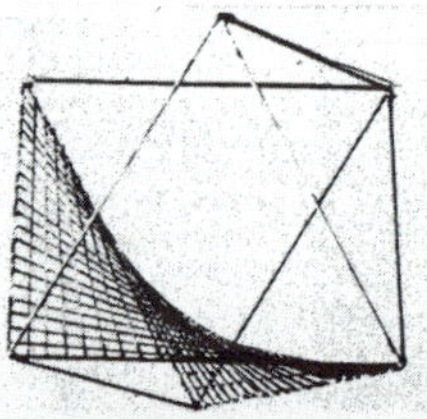

אינדכס מרחבית 300°

SPATIAL INDEX OF 300°

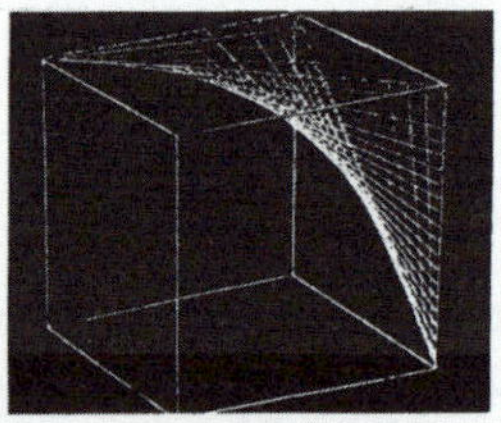

אינדכס מרחבית 270°

SPATIAL INDEX OF 270°

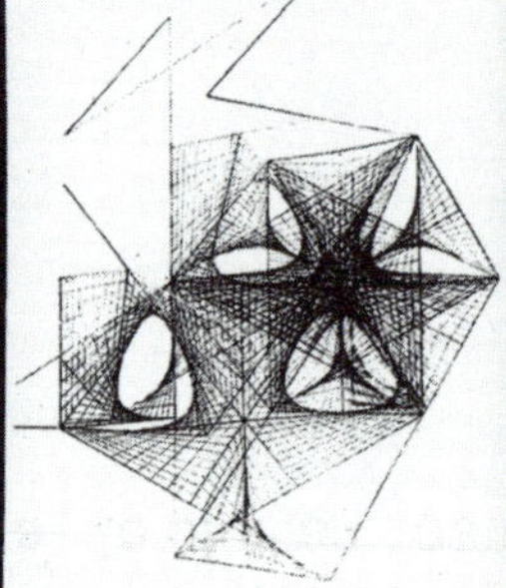

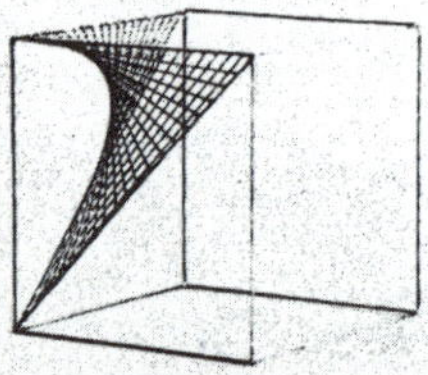

אינדכס מרחבית 240°

SPATIAL INDEX OF 240°

**2.15** Various kinds of infinite polyhedra featuring planar and double-curved faces.

assistants. Burt admitted to interacting mainly with Wachman, as Neumann was quite "unapproachable" for a twenty-three-year-old. Stimulated by Neumann's teachings, the two young men became close and started to delve deeper into the master's geometric framework. It was out of these early conversations with Wachman that the focal point of Burt's interests began to take shape and move away from that of his morphology teacher. In 1962 Burt asked Wachman whether he thought it possible to do close packing with identical, double-curved surfaces—as opposed to just polyhedra with planar surfaces, to which Neumann's research was limited. Wachman replied that it was impossible. It was a trick question, claimed Burt, because by the time he inquired he had already found four solutions.[19] This particular geometric problem became the focus of Burt's research through his graduate studies and ultimately the trigger that caused his work to depart significantly from that of Neumann's.

Burt's body of work as relevant to architectural form within the framework of this book will be carefully examined below. By way of a brief introduction, the core of his field of inquiry can be best summarized as the study of systems of space subdivision, both open and closed, that achieve continuity through periodicity. Most of these systems are generated through space packing.[20] More specifically, Burt's work dealt with polyhedra featuring double-curved surfaces (so-called "saddle polyhedra") with incidental reference to analogous cases with planar surfaces **(fig. 2.15)**. His project retained Neumann's engagement with crystallography (contradicting some recent claims that this domain of experimental science has only lately become a source of inspiration for designers).[21] But in taking the scientific character of his teacher's approach to form to the extreme, Burt's undertaking ended up taking a completely different path, one that disregarded both Neumann's humanism and the contextualist drive that led him to attentively consider the climate and site conditions for which his geometric configurations were intended. Indeed, dismissive of architectural function, and unwittingly continuing to build on morphology's anti-modernist language and anti-object stance, Burt's investigations were guided by an unremitting scientific vector that, from the very outset, resonated with the intense scientization of design unfolding across the West during the second half of the twentieth century.

Given the many opportunities to build in Israel in the 1950s and 1960s, most of the architects who, inspired by Neumann, began to utilize certain aspects of morphology for design purposes devoted themselves to practice, just like the other second-generation architects. Burt, however, engaged throughout his career far more in research and teaching than in practice. The only other figure who followed a similar trajectory within the Israeli scene of architectural morphology was Wachman, whose overall contribution was not comparable to Burt's on the grounds of inventiveness, variety, and density of production.

19 In an interview with the author conducted in Haifa, Israel, on October 18, 2013.

20 Beginning in the 1980s, Burt developed another line of inquiry concerning what he termed "alternative urban design paradigms." These were fundamentally utopian visions that Burt devised to respond to what he saw as a need for urban density. "Bridge Avenues," "The Strata City," and "Urban Development in the Marine Environment" were among the conceptual schemes that resulted from this parallel research path, with specific instances tested in cities like Haifa, Paris, Istanbul, Zurich, and Messina. For the purposes of this book, these projects will not be considered **(fig. 2.16–17)**.

21 "More recently, holistic structures in particular, such as crystals, have begun to interest designers." Nina Rappaport, *Support and Resist: Structural Engineers and Design Innovation* (New York, NY: Monacelli Press, 2007), 10.

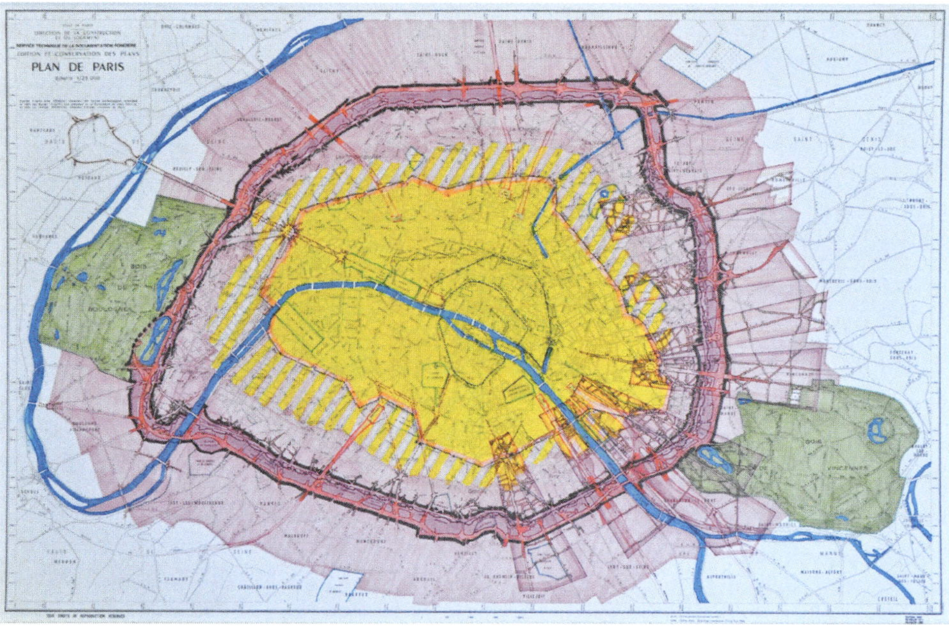


**2.16** Left: Michaël Burt, urban scheme for Paris. 1990s.

**2.17** Below: Michaël Burt, Bridge Avenues project. Early 2000s.

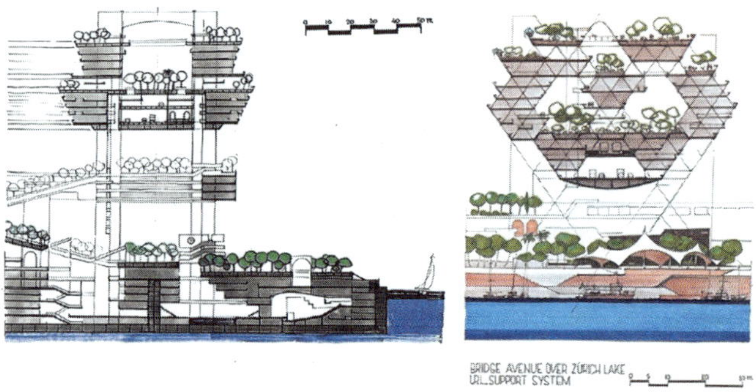

## Early Breakthrough

The course of Burt's career was defined early on. Right after graduating in 1963, he started to work toward his master's degree. While busy on that front, he was chosen by Wachman in 1965 as his assistant for the morphology course, which the latter had inherited from Neumann upon his departure from Israel.[22] Ten years later it was Burt himself who took over the course, even if only for a short time, as his preference was always studio pedagogy.[23] He also served as the dean of the Faculty at Technion during two different periods, 1977–79 and 1989–93.[24]

Burt submitted his thesis on November 1966 and the outcome put him on the map. The young student's contribution was deemed above master's level and, after two committee meetings, the examiners concluded it qualified for the rank of Doctor of Science in Technology. Burt became the first person to get a doctoral degree in architecture in the history of the Technion. In an unprecedented move, the Technion translated the thesis into English, published it in November 1967, made 200 copies, and sent them out, without letting Burt know, to world-renowned figures and institutions in the fields of both architecture and engineering.

The excitement was, however, halted by the tension building up in Israel with the neighboring Arab states (Egypt, Jordan, and Syria)—tension that led to the Six-Day War (June 5 to 10, 1967). Burt's graduation ceremony, originally scheduled for May 28, 1967, was eventually cancelled, that year being quite unproductive in terms of research and other academic work. But in 1968, when Burt was thirty-one, his thesis started to gather national as well as international attention **(fig. 2.18)**. Between 1968 and 1972, at first to his utter surprise, he received congratulatory letters from the likes of Frei Otto, Conrad Roland, Walter Gropius, and I. M. Pei; requests to publish and acknowledgement messages from *Progressive Architecture*, *Israel Magazine*, *Casabella*, and *Zodiac*; and an invitation from Renzo Piano to exhibit his work in the "Changing Form in Architecture" pavilion that the Italian architect was curating for the 14th Milan Triennale.[25]

22 By that time Burt already had some experience as a teaching assistant. In his third year of undergraduate study, artist Paul Konrad Hoenich–who introduced the Technion students to Hans Jenny's cymatics, so important to Giorgini–noticed Burt's painting and drawing skills and chose him as an assistant for his *2-dimensional design* course, wherein he was evolving a pedagogy around color theory à la Bauhaus. Having graduated first in his class in 1963, it was then Al Mansfeld who offered Burt a position as his studio assistant.

23 By the late 1960s Burt's popularity within the school was already strong, largely due to the success of his thesis, which will be discussed further on. Paradoxically, however, Zvi Hecker–Neumann's partner during the 1960s, occasional professor at Technion, and by then a well-known figure in Israel–claimed that he did not know Professor Burt "personally." From Zvi Hecker, interview with the author, May 2, 2011. Burt continued to teach uninterruptedly at Technion, until his retirement as a Professor Emeritus in 2006.

24 During his first deanship–a position for which, aged thirty-nine, he retrospectively felt himself to be "much too young"–there was a debate at the school over whether or not the faculty should be moved from where it was located at the time, in downtown Haifa, to the main Technion campus. Burt was in favor of doing so, whereas his former instructor and later collaborator, Avraham Wachman, led those who held the opposite opinion. As the decision went against him, Burt stepped down from his deanship, which should have ended in 1980. Ironically, the faculty was eventually transferred to the main campus under Wachman's deanship, in the late 1980s. From an interview with Burt conducted by the author in Haifa on October 20, 2013.

25 In addition to this Triennale (1967), Burt had his work exhibited at the Noguchi Museum in New York in 2005, among other venues. He also represented Israel at the 1969 Paris Biennial for young artists, and had a few solo shows, notably at the Ha'aretz museum in Tel Aviv (1968), the Haifa Art Museum (1997), and the National Architecture Museum in Moscow (2003).

Continuous roofing from shell-elements (or stretched membranes) composing regular "plane" networks.

## Sagorsky Architecture Prize Awarded

The Abraham and Deborah Sagorsky Prize in Architecture and Town Planning in the amount of IL. 5,000, awarded bi-annually to a graduate of the Faculty of Architecture and Town Planning at the Technion, was won this year by Dr. Michael Burt, for his thesis on "Spatial Arrangements and Polyhedra with Curved Surfaces and their Architectural Applications". The prize is intended to enable the winner to advance his academic education through travel and research.

In a search for minimalistic solutions in structural design, the author of the thesis resorted to highly unconventional sources of inspiration : crystal lattices and soap-solution films. Through analysis of their structural qualities, and exhaustive exploitation of their continuity and periodicity characteristics, the thesis arrives at shell configurations and surfaces applicable in building practice.

The potentialities of the study lie in the field of industrial building, especially with regard to prefabricated hall-roof systems with large and medium spans.

The thesis was initially submitted for the degree of Master of Architecture. However, the committee of examiners decided that the work was of such a high standard that it qualified for the degree of Doctor of Science in Technology.

R. Buckminster Fuller, the well-known American architect, was so impressed with Dr. Burt's work, that he is including a chapter of it, together with chapters from the works of seven other famous architects and scientists, in his forthcoming book "Synergeticts", to be published by the MacMillan Press.

Dr. Michael Burt. He also received a citation for valour during the Six Day War.

The Abraham and Deborah Sagorsky Prize was established by the will of the late Mr. Abraham Sagorsky of Capetown, South Africa, in the framework of a bequest, the interest of which is also devoted towards the award of annual scholarships to students of architecture and town planning at the Technion, and to medical students at the Hebrew University.

The jury was composed of Professor A. Mansfeld, Professor A. Kashtan, Professor S. Gil'ad of the Technion, and Dr. A. Shachar of the Hebrew University.

Technion Magazine — October 1968

2.18 Feature on Burt as the Sagorsky Prize winner in the October 1968 issue of Technion Magazine.

## Buckminster Fuller and the American Lineage

In late 1967 Burt met Buckminster Fuller at an architecture congress in Tel Aviv. During this encounter Fuller asked Burt to include a section of his research production (thirty to fifty pages) in the book *Synergetics*, which the former was preparing at the time. The chapter was to be part of an appendix titled "Neighboring Disclosures," the other confirmed contributors to which were notable researchers in the domain of morphology, such as Keith Critchlow, Peter Pearce, and Anne Tyng. Initially expected to be ready by early 1968, the book suffered several delays and the appendix never made it into the published version, which came out in 1975. In a personal letter with apologetic overtones, Fuller attempted to assuage Burt's disappointment, by writing: "[y]our mind has been the most lively and perceptive one I have as yet encountered in respect to the polyhedral hierarchy and its energy intertransforming accommodations. I am confident that I will find my publisher friends eager to publish you."[26] Correspondence shows that Fuller was indeed quite fond of Burt, to the extent of making repeated attempts to get him to move to the US.[27] In May 1968 he offered him support to teach at UCLA, Berkeley, or the University of Illinois, and in December that year, he urged William Perk, then head of the design science department at Carbondale, to hire Burt for a one-year term, arguing that "[i]f you can get Mr. Burt and Ed Schlossberg on your staff, you will have established potentially the greatest design science school in the world."[28] All of this interest was, however, to no avail, as Burt always declined any teaching engagements that would entail too long a stay abroad. His decision to remain based in Haifa was grounded in a very strong sense of responsibility toward serving his country and his culture.[29] He would not meet Fuller again until 1976, when Otto invited both men to Germany to discuss space structures along with Félix Candela, Ove Arup, and Edmund Happold.[30]

While working on his thesis, Burt became aware of the work of some of these colleagues—notably that of Otto—as well as that of György Kepes, engineers Eduardo Torroja and Robert Le Ricolais, and mathematician David Hilbert. None of these figures, however, operated in the domain of theoretical morphology vis-à-vis architecture. In this regard, his thesis bibliography featured barely any references to publications on morphology proper, the main exception

26 Letter signed by Buckminster Fuller and dated April 30, 1974. Personal archive of Michaël Burt.

27 Burt fought in both the Six-Day and the Yom Kippur Wars and received the highest honor for service after both for "exemplary behavior under fire." On October 27, 1973, during the Yom Kippur War, he was severely wounded. Upon learning about this, Fuller wrote him a personal letter in which he said "[y]our friends are shocked at the news that you have been a casualty. We hope the further news that you are hospitalized and that you are getting better is really true. Your beautiful mind is one of humanity's important resources." Letter dated February 2, 1974 and found in Michaël Burt's personal archive.

28 In a personal letter addressed to William Perk and dated December 27, 1968. Personal archive of Michaël Burt. Fuller was a University Professor at SIU Carbondale from 1959 to 1972.

29 Over the years Burt did accept a number of occasional, short-term teaching- and research-related positions in Europe, the US and Canada: namely, as a visiting professor at Waterloo University (1970–71); at Southern Illinois University Carbondale (summer of 1971); as a visiting critic in 1981 at University of Oregon, University of British Columbia and Carleton University; and as a visiting scholar at Otto's Institute for Lightweight Structures in Stuttgart (1985–86), School of Architecture Paris–La Villette (1994–96), and several schools in Australia (2004). In 1982, Burt was even nominated for the position of director of the architecture school at Carleton.

30 It was at this event that Burt's friendship with Otto was consolidated and a new one with Candela started, lasting until the latter's death. According to Burt, Fuller asked him to breakfast together the morning after the discussion event. In a conversation with the author conducted in Haifa on October 18, 2013.

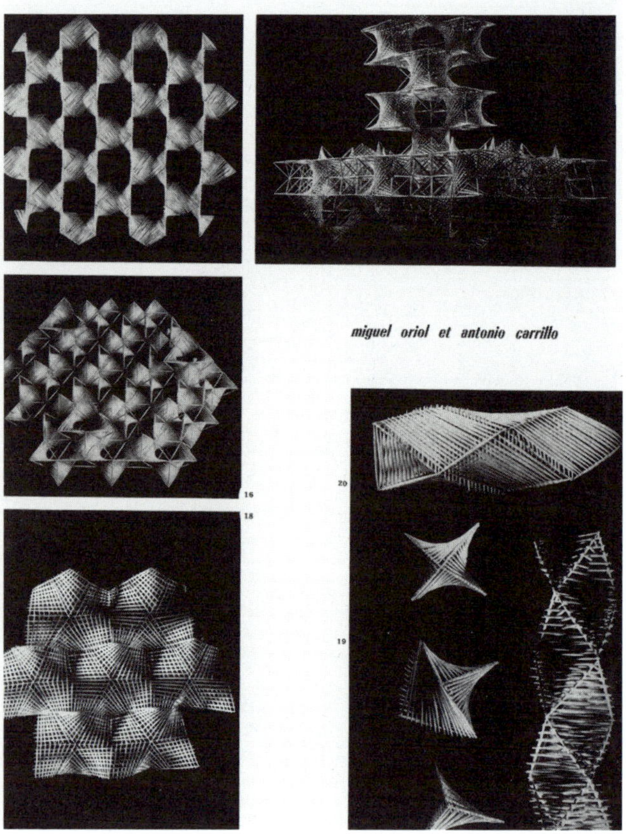


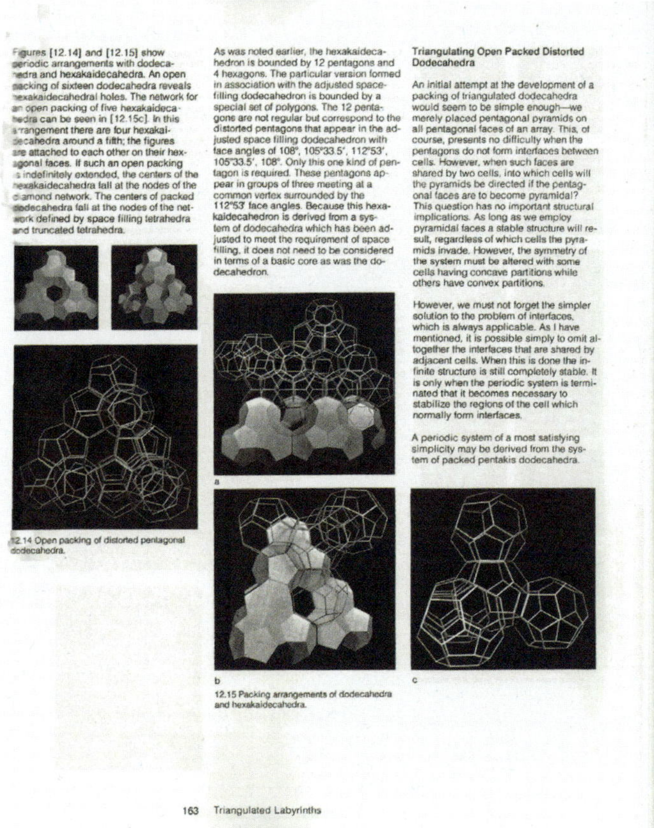

Figures [12.14] and [12.15] show periodic arrangements with dodecahedra and hexakaidecahedra. An open packing of sixteen dodecahedra reveals hexakaidecahedral holes. The network for an open packing of five hexakaidecahedra can be seen in [12.15c]. In this arrangement there are four hexakaidecahedra around a fifth; the figures are attached to each other on their hexagonal faces. If such an open packing is indefinitely extended, the centers of the hexakaidecahedra fall at the nodes of the diamond network. The centers of packed dodecahedra fall at the nodes of the network defined by space filling tetrahedra and truncated tetrahedra.

12.14 Open packing of distorted pentagonal dodecahedra.

As was noted earlier, the hexakaidecahedron is bounded by 12 pentagons and 4 hexagons. The particular version formed in association with the adjusted space-filling dodecahedron is bounded by a special set of polygons. The 12 pentagons are not regular but correspond to the distorted pentagons that appear in the adjusted space filling dodecahedron with face angles of 108°, 105°33.5', 112°53', 105°33.5', 108°. Only this one kind of pentagon is required. These pentagons appear in groups of three meeting at a common vertex surrounded by the 112°53' face angles. Because this hexakaidecahedron is derived from a system of dodecahedra which has been adjusted to meet the requirement of space filling, it does not need to be considered in terms of a basic core as was the dodecahedron.

**Triangulating Open Packed Distorted Dodecahedra**

An initial attempt at the development of a packing of triangulated dodecahedra would seem to be simple enough—we merely placed pentagonal pyramids on all pentagonal faces of an array. This, of course, presents no difficulty when the pentagons do not form interfaces between cells. However, when such faces are shared by two cells, into which cells will the pyramids be directed if the pentagonal faces are to become pyramidal? This question has no important structural implications. As long as we employ pyramidal faces a stable structure will result, regardless of which cells the pyramids invade. However, the symmetry of the system must be altered with some cells having concave partitions while others have convex partitions.

However, we must not forget the simpler solution to the problem of interfaces, which is always applicable. As I have mentioned, it is possible simply to omit altogether the interfaces that are shared by adjacent cells. When this is done the infinite structure is still completely stable. It is only when the periodic system is terminated that it becomes necessary to stabilize the regions of the cell which normally form interfaces.

A periodic system of a most satisfying simplicity may be derived from the system of packed pentakis dodecahedra.

a

b

12.15 Packing arrangements of dodecahedra and hexakaidecahedra.

c

163 Triangulated Labyrinths

**2.19** Above, left: Miguel Oriol and Antonio Carrillo, "Recherches Pour La Compréhension et l'Ordonnancement de l'Espace."

**2.20** Above, right: Peter Pearce, triangulated labyrinths.

being that of the Spaniards Antonio Carrillo and Manuel Oriol, upon the discovery of which Burt acknowledged being "knocked over" **(fig. 2.19)**.[31]

Indeed, there may not have been many relevant sources at the time. Burt was a pioneer in the discovery and especially the visualization of complex, three-dimensional configurations based on periodic geometry. In terms of earliness, rigor, scientific basis, and number of patterns found, the other comparable lineage was the American one, whose most representative figures were the abovementioned Pearce and geometer Alan Schoen **(fig. 2.20–25)**. It was only in 1965 (four years after Burt first began looking at the space packing of double-curved surfaces) that Pearce initiated his research project in the realm of polyhedra, crystal structures, and related topics, supported by a one-year grant from the Graham Foundation.[32] By 1966 he had come up with a way to generate periodic structures by means of space packing minimal surfaces.[33] Schoen, for his part, started to work in a similar direction upon meeting Pearce that same year. Burt and the Pearce-Schoen duo developed their respective investigations independently. They did not find out about one another's projects until 1968.[34]

31 Their work happened to constitute one of the most direct precedents to Burt's research into the articulation of space using periodic geometry. See Miguel Oriol and Antonio Carrillo, "Investigaciones Sobre Ordenacion Del Espacio," *Revista Nacional de Arquitectura*, no. 55 (July 1963), 28–38. Oriol and Carrillo's investigations gained some international recognition, especially after being published in *L'Architecture d'Aujourd'hui*. See Miguel Oriol and Antonio Carrillo, "Recherches Pour La Comprehension et l'Ordonnancement de l'Espace," *L'Architecture d'Aujourd'hui* 34, no. 117 (November 1964), 102–105.

32 Pearce was one of Fuller's editorial assistants at the time and had worked for the Eames between 1958 and 1961. Being interested in the physical performance of spatial systems, his profile as a researcher is quite similar to Burt's, both operating in the realm of structural morphology. Pearce's production, however, epitomized in his 1975 book *Structure in Nature is a Strategy for Design*, was not nearly as sophisticated and prolific as Burt's, albeit certainly more didactic in its presentation. Schoen, on the other hand, was not a designer but someone working exclusively in the domains of mathematics and geometry. He came up with a large number of two-dimensional tiling patterns, although his main contribution–the core of which he developed while a senior scientist at NASA Electronics Research Center between 1967 and 1970–concerned minimal surfaces; infinite, triply periodic ones, in particular.

33 The term "minimal surface" designates a particular kind of double-curved surface, the properties of which will be discussed further on.

34 Burt and Pearce were never close. Their first contact–by correspondence, in early 1968–was not particularly smooth, establishing a distance that would persist for good. Pearce was then an editor for *Synergetics*, Buckminster Fuller's magnum opus and the result of forty-seven years of work, as he told Burt in writing. After receiving the piece by Burt to be included in the book–at Fuller's personal request–Pearce sent a letter back warning him about the need to add a footnote to his text. He demanded an acknowledgment that the term "saddle polyhedra," used by Burt, had first been proposed by himself in a report to the Graham Foundation. Burt replied apologizing but insisting that he had not even been aware of Pearce's work while carrying out the thesis. This offended Pearce, but in May 1968 Fuller reassured Burt by letting him know that he very much approved of his response. The Israeli designer, rather indifferently, admitted to his American peer having been the one who invented the term. In actuality they had both come up with it, independently, and almost simultaneously. For Pearce submitted his report in October 1966, whereas Burt handed in his thesis in November of that same year, which means that by then he must have been using it for a certain period of time.

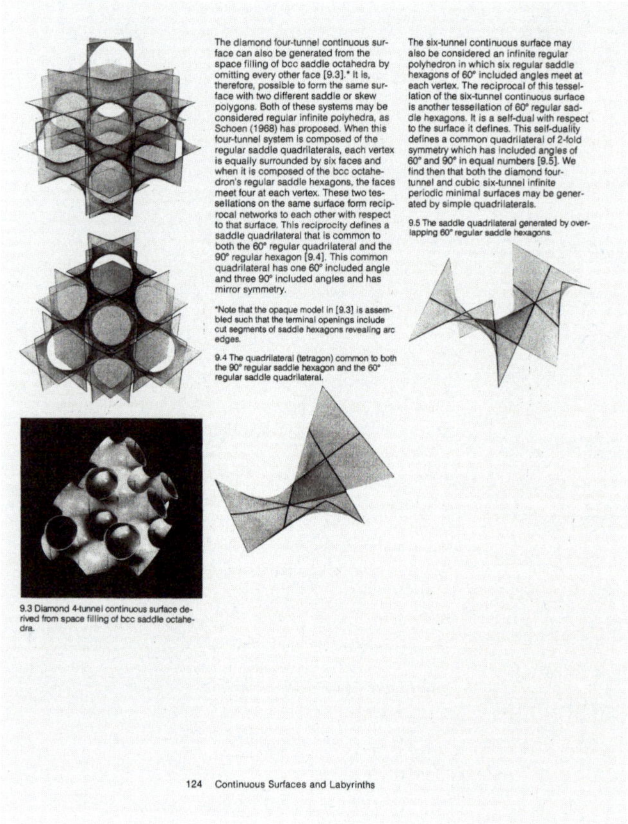

The diamond four-tunnel continuous surface can also be generated from the space filling of bcc saddle octahedra by omitting every other face [9.3].* It is, therefore, possible to form the same surface with two different saddle or skew polygons. Both of these systems may be considered regular infinite polyhedra, as Schoen (1968) has proposed. When this four-tunnel system is composed of the regular saddle quadrilaterals, each vertex is equally surrounded by six faces and when it is composed of the bcc octahedron's regular saddle hexagons, the faces meet four at each vertex. These two tessellations on the same surface form reciprocal networks to each other with respect to that surface. This reciprocity defines a saddle quadrilateral that is common to both the 60° regular quadrilateral and the 90° regular hexagon [9.4]. This common quadrilateral has one 60° included angle and three 90° included angles and has mirror symmetry.

*Note that the opaque model in [9.3] is assembled such that the terminal openings include cut segments of saddle hexagons revealing arc edges.

9.4 The quadrilateral (tetragon) common to both the 90° regular saddle hexagon and the 60° regular saddle quadrilateral.

The six-tunnel continuous surface may also be considered an infinite regular polyhedron in which six regular saddle hexagons of 60° included angles meet at each vertex. The reciprocal of this tessellation of the six-tunnel continuous surface is another tessellation of 60° regular saddle hexagons. It is a self-dual with respect to the surface it defines. This self-duality defines a common quadrilateral of 2-fold symmetry which has included angles of 60° and 90° in equal numbers [9.5]. We find then that both the diamond four-tunnel and cubic six-tunnel infinite periodic minimal surfaces may be generated by simple quadrilaterals.

9.5 The saddle quadrilateral generated by overlapping 60° regular saddle hexagons.

9.3 Diamond 4-tunnel continuous surface derived from space filling of bcc saddle octahedra.

124 Continuous Surfaces and Labyrinths

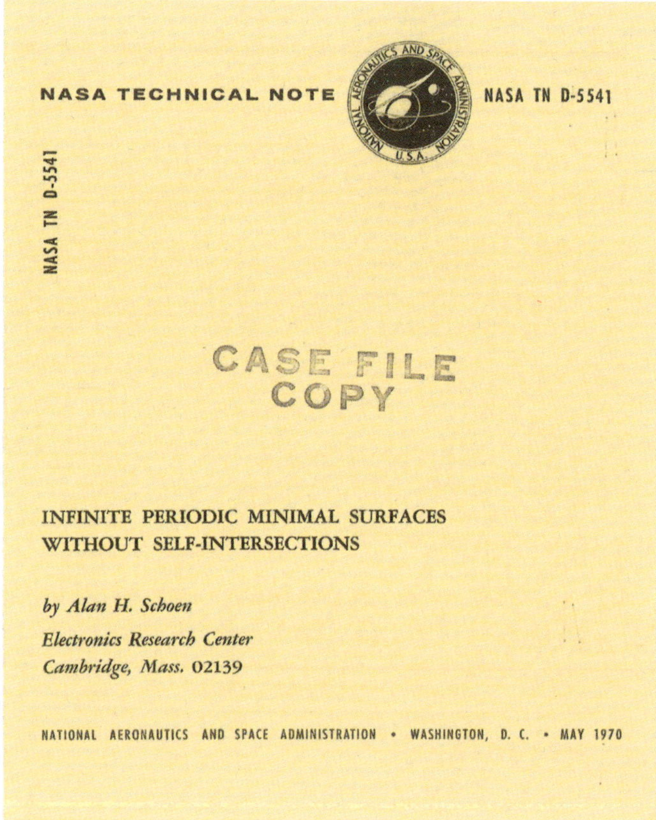

NASA TECHNICAL NOTE NASA TN D-5541

NASA TN D-5541

CASE FILE COPY

INFINITE PERIODIC MINIMAL SURFACES WITHOUT SELF-INTERSECTIONS

*by Alan H. Schoen*

*Electronics Research Center*
*Cambridge, Mass.* 02139

NATIONAL AERONAUTICS AND SPACE ADMINISTRATION • WASHINGTON, D. C. • MAY 1970

**2.21** Above, left: Peter Pearce, continuous surfaces and labyrinths.

**2.22** Above, right: Cover of Alan H. Schoen, *Infinite Periodic Minimal Surfaces Without Self-Intersections*

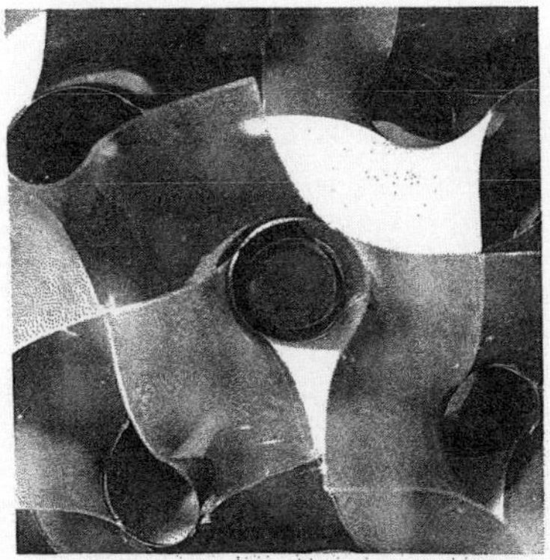

f. Close-up view of the approximately helical tunnel in one labyrinth of G. View is along (100) axis.

g. View of G along (110) axis.

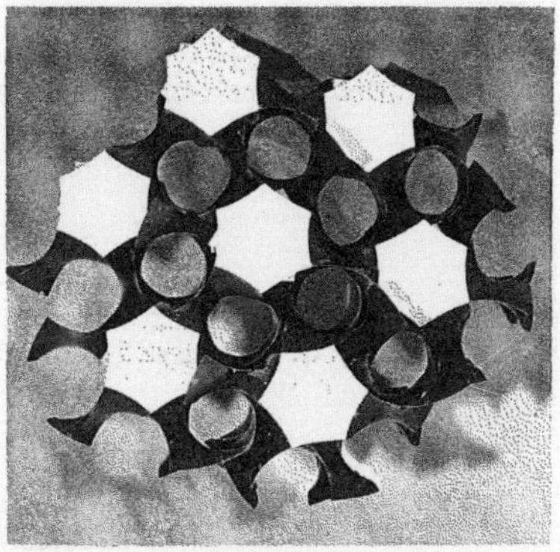

h. View of G along (111) axis.

Figure 7.- Concluded.

a. C(P) (from a photograph of Neovius' model, shown in his Ph.D. thesis, 1883, ref. 4).

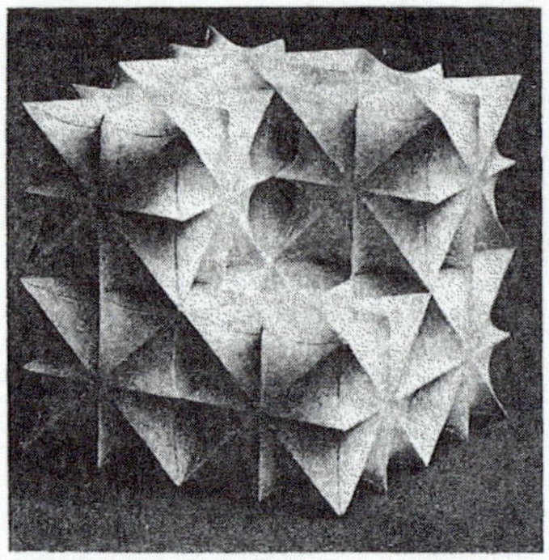

b. The surface adjoint to C(P) (ref. 4).

Figure 3.- The two surfaces analyzed by Neovius: C(P) (the complement of P) and the surface adjoint to C(P).

7

Precedent and present page:
**2.23–24** Alan H. Schoen, *Infinite Periodic Minimal Surfaces Without Self-Intersections*

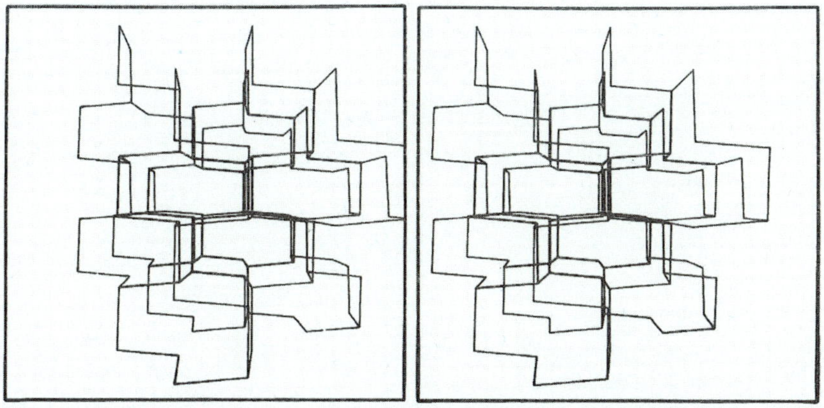

Figure II-1b.- Partially collapsed Laves graph (stage 2).

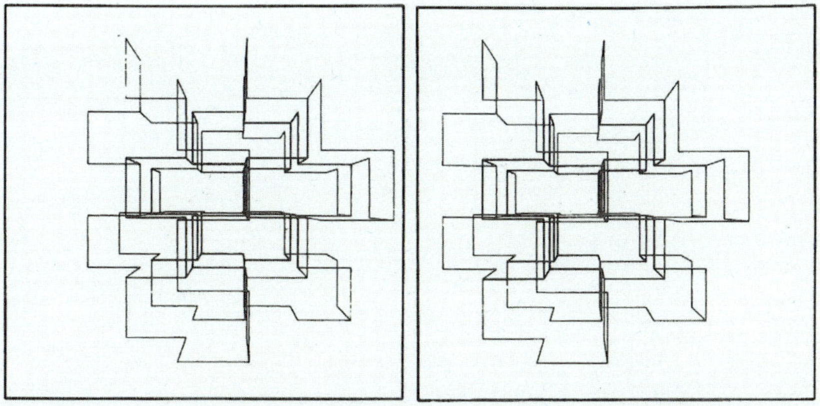

Figure II-1c.- Partially collapsed Laves graph (stage 3); the graph has become transformed into the "defective" simple cubic graph (cf. discussion on p. 83).

87

PERIODICITY OF MINIMAL SURFACES

Assume that a minimal surface defined by a closed spatial perimeter, contains two straight lines, a and b. These provide information on the surface itself (reflection of segments of the perimeter) and on its extension outside the perimeter). By repeating the surface segments bounded by a and b, so that each straight line is an axis of rotational symmetry for the surface, we generally obtain an infinite periodical sequence.

The surface segment bounded by a, b and the extended perimeter is the periodic unit of the surface. This part of the infinite periodic surface bounded by the extended perimeter comprises a number of periodic units. The perimeter of the periodic unit must contain at least two segments belonging to more than one straight line.

Three relationships between a and b are possible:

(I) Skew (rotation & translation).

(II) Intersecting (rotation)

(III) Parallel.

These generalizations enable us to understand, and in many cases to predict the shape of a minimal surface as function of a given perimeter. Straight lines on the surface subdivide it into smaller and simpler surface - elements; conversely smooth continuous surfaces can be constructed from elementary units provided straight-line segments are contained in this perimeter.

The relationship between the minimal surface and the straight lines in it is of considerable practical significance, as will be shown later.

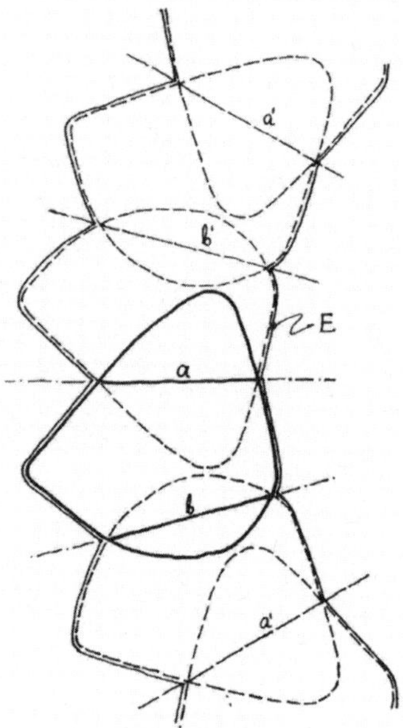


Fig. 13. Infinite periodic minimal surface. The "whole" surface is formed by multiplication of the repetitive unit.

Corollary A: A plane perpendicular to an axis a at any point O will intersect the minimal surface along AOB, bisected by the straight line a at point O. Point O will also be the inflection point of curve AOB. Points O, A and B are collinear. AO ≡ OB.

Corollary B: Consider two identical spatial surfaces S and P which have a straight a as part of their perimeter. If we join the surfaces along a, maintaining rotational symmetry about this straight line (the corresponding points of the two surfaces being coplanar, perpendicular to a), the junction of the two surfaces along the above straight line will be smooth and continuous.

At every point of a there will be only one plane tangent to the two surfaces.

3. If a minimal surface S for a closed spatial perimeter P contains a straight line intersecting the perimeter at two points (Fig. 12), at least part of this surface is bisected by the straight line.*

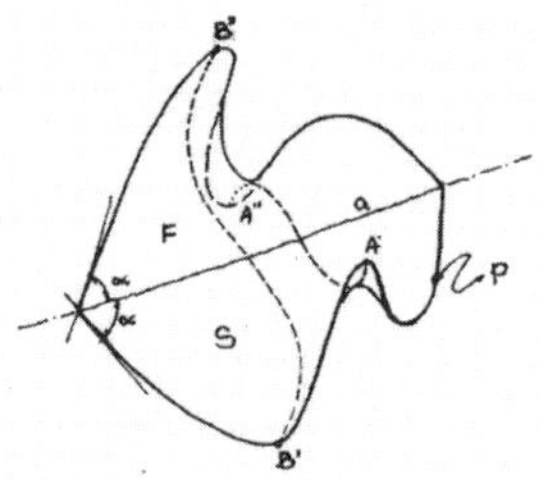


Fig. 11. Two identical curved surfaces combining into one continuous smooth surface.

EXTENSION OF MINIMAL SURFACES OUTSIDE THE PERIMETER

In the foregoing generalizations, we discussed minimal surfaces defined by a closed spatial perimeter and containing a straight line. This straight line is an axis of rotational symmetry for the whole surface (if it bisects the perimeter), or for part of it. It may be said that if the straight line forms part of the spatial perimeter, it may still be regarded as an axis of rotational symmetry for the surface defined by the perimeter and its extension outside the latter.

Assuming that a minimal surface defined by a given perimeter extends beyond the latter to infinity, this straight line, which is part of the perimeter, may provide information on this extension or at least a part of it.

Example: Assume a minimal surface S defined by a closed spatial perimeter P (Fig. 11) with the straight line a as part of it. By the existence of a it is possible to describe the extension of the surface outside the perimeter within a limited domain F, identical to S.

Definition: "Extended perimeter" - a perimeter defining the domain of the minimal surface derivable from the existence of the straight lines on it.

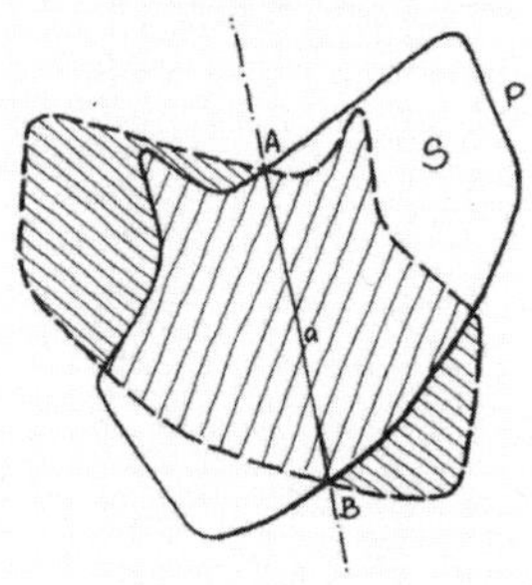


Fig. 12. Extension of minimal surface beyond its perimeter:
part of the surface bisected by a into two identical and symmetric parts.
Extension of the surface S beyond the perimeter P, determined by the straight line a.

* Whenever symmetry is discussed hereafter, it refers to rotational symmetry of $180^{\circ}$, unless otherwise specified.

## THE SPECIFICITIES OF BURT'S MORPHOLOGY AND ENGINEERING INCLINATIONS

Throughout his career Burt devoted most of his energies as a researcher to sponge surfaces and polyhedra, in the belief that these "seemed to be divorced from classical morphology which is mostly dominated by finite topological cylindrical or dome-like surfaces and plane-faceted polyhedra."[35] He presented the bulk of his production across three publications. The first one, his aforementioned 1966 thesis titled *Spatial Arrangement and Polyhedra with Curved Surfaces and their Architectural Applications*, established the basis of his life-long project. In it he explored sponge surfaces with a focus on the special cases of continuous periodic minimal surfaces **(fig. 2.26)** and hyperbolic paraboloids ("hypars"), sometimes alongside their related skew polyhedral **(fig. 2.27)**; introduced and analyzed a number of regular and semi-regular nonplanar polyhedra together with their compact packing **(fig. 2.28)**; developed several patterns of curved surfaces forming regular two-dimensional lattices (in a manner analogous to plane tessellations) **(fig. 2.29)**; studied so-called "stellated solids" and their close packing **(fig. 2.30)**; and speculated on the architectural applications of some of the figures described **(fig. 2.31)**.[36] The book features a large number of definitions, numerical descriptions, scattered mathematical formulae, multiple annotated illustrations of geometrical figures, extended sections on the configurational properties of those, and numerous polyester models of the spatial patterns described.

Precedent page:
**2.26** Continuous periodic minimal surfaces.

Following pages:
**2.27** Skew polyhedra (p. 144)
**2.28** Regular and semi-regular nonplanar polyhedra (p. 145)
**2.29** Two-dimensional lattices of curved surfaces (p. 146)
**2.30** Stellated solids (p. 147)

35 Michaël Burt, "New Forms and Conceptual Architecture," in *Conceptual Architecture*, exhibition catalog (Haifa, Israel: Haifa Museum, Museum of Art, 1998), 43. Continuous, unbounded hyperbolic surfaces have the property of subdividing space into two complementary, reciprocal subspaces that can be represented by means of two dual networks. First studied by German mathematician Hermann Schwartz in his 1890 *Gesammelte mathematische Abhandlungen*, the sponge-like appearance they take on when extended in space is the reason for their being named "sponge surfaces." Sponge polyhedra, on the other hand, are an extension of the idea of a polyhedron. Unlike a commonplace one, which is generally defined as a surface made up of a set of polygons that bounds a spatial region, sponge polyhedra extend indefinitely in space without forming a closed surface. Also termed "infinite skew," they have regular polygon faces but in some of them these are planar whereas others feature nonplanar vertex figures. This geometric domain originated in 1926, when John Flinders Petrie generalized the existing notion of regular skew polygon to that of regular skew polyhedron (a particular case of sponge polyhedron) by discovering two instances. Given their capacity to explain and visualize structures and relationships of solid-state materials, sponge polyhedra started to feature also in chemistry books, most notably in Alexander Frank Wells's *Structural Inorganic Chemistry*, first published in 1945. A periodic crystal is a structure that can be modeled abstractly by means of a lattice, with the point array representing atoms or molecules. Hence chemists' interest in investigating the expanding domain of spatial lattices and networks.

36 Three-dimensional repeating modules or unit cells, particularly when they are invoked as point arrays only, are referred to as "lattices," which are typically polyhedra of various kinds. The term "tessellation" alludes to a set of polygons fitting together to cover a plane in such a way that every side of each one of them belongs at the same time to one other polygon. Also referred to as *tiling* or *packing*, and first documented by mathematician and astronomer Johannes Kepler in his 1619 *Harmonices Mundi*, it results in the subdivision of a surface by means of an *elementary periodic unit*, namely, a basic unit that repeats itself. A "stellated solid" is a polyhedron or a composite of polyhedra whose appearance loosely resembles that of a star.

SEMI-REGULAR CONTINUOUS PERIODIC SURFACE (SPATIAL INDEX OF 210°). **34** משטח מחזורי נמשך סמי-רגולרי (אינדכס מרחביות 210°).

2

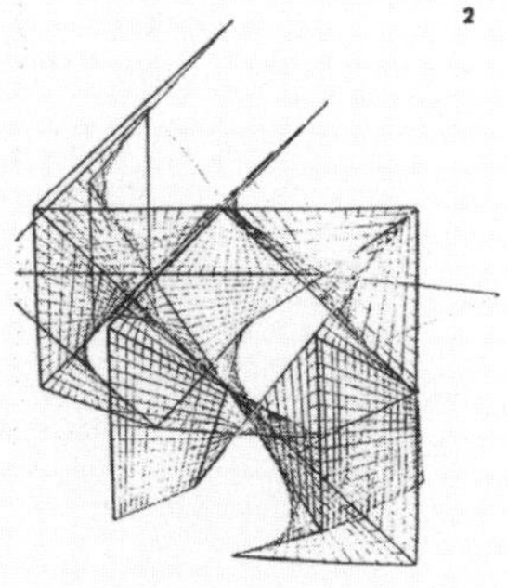

3

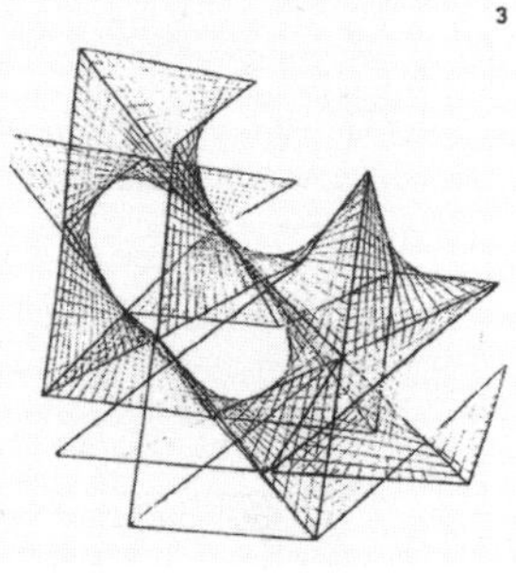

המשטח מגיע לחתוך עצמי במרחב לאורך קוים ישרים ועקומים באופן רגולרי. כל הקדקדים כשייכים למערכת רגולרית אחת - המערכת הקובית.

1,2,3. צרוף מרובעים היפאריים לאורך קוי הרשה של "משטח המינימום 210°" (מודל מחוטי מתכת).

A surface with regular self-intersection in space along straight and curved lines.

All vertices are arranged according to the cubic system.

1, 2, 3. Quadrant hyperbolic-paraboloids connected along the network lines of the "210° minimal surface" (wire model).

1

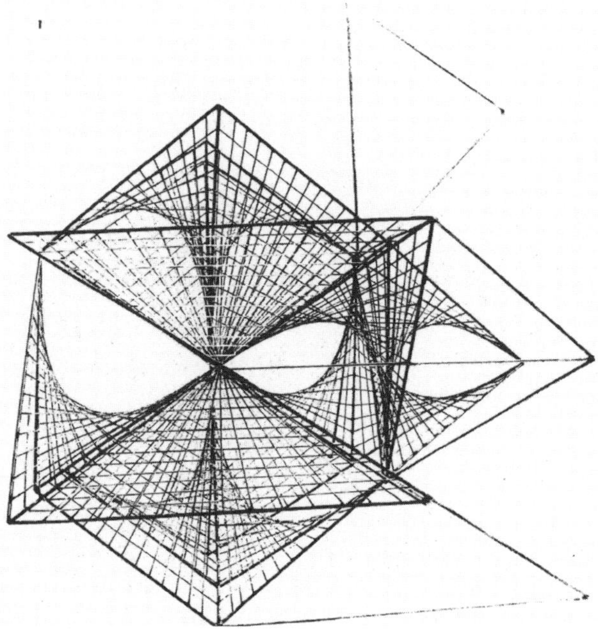

REGULAR CONTINUOUS PERIODIC SURFACE (SPATIAL INDEX OF 330°). **27** משטח מחזורי נמשך רגולרי (אינדכס מרחביות 330°).

1

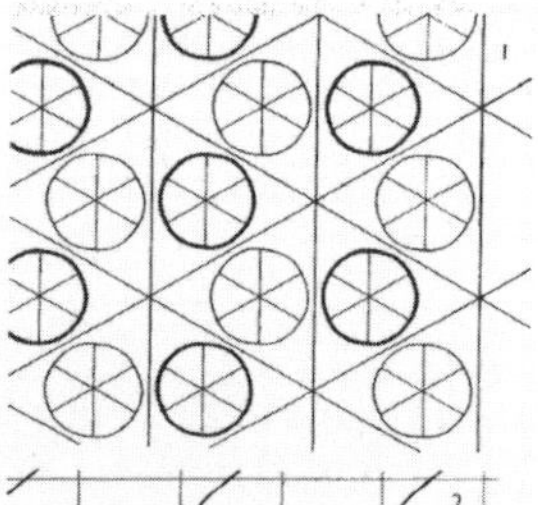

2

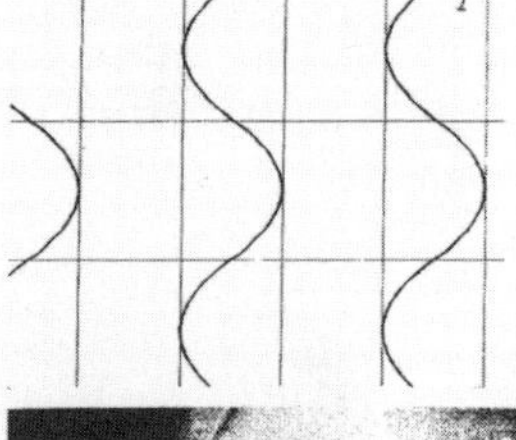

1-2. חתכים אופייניים של "משטח 330°" נמשך.
1. חתך המראה את המשכיות החלל הפנימי.
2. חתך לרוחב "המנהרות".
3. צלום של החלל הפנימי.
4. צרוף היפארים למשטח נמשך של 330°.
5-6. קטעים של "משטח 330°".
7. סקיו-פוליהדרון בעל פאות מעויינות מישוריות בעל אותן הסימטריות של "משטח 330°".

1-2. Typical sections of continuous "330° Surface".

1. Section showing continuity of interior space.
2. Section across "Tunnels."
3. Close-up photo of interior space.
4. Series of hyperbolic-paraboloids forming continuous "330° Surface".

5-6. Parts of "330° surface".

7. Skew polyhedron with rhombic faces, having the same symmetries as "330°surface".

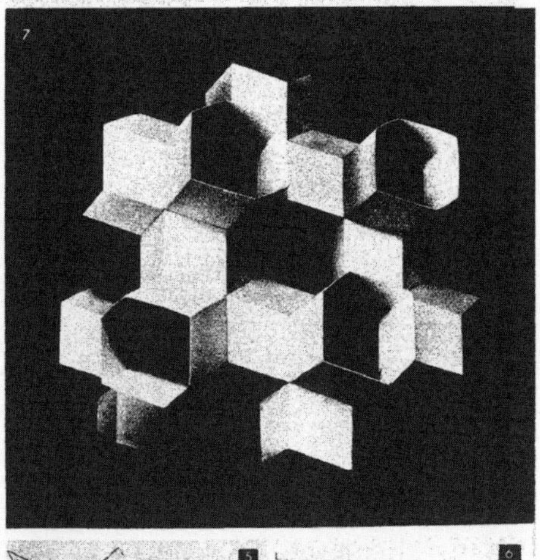

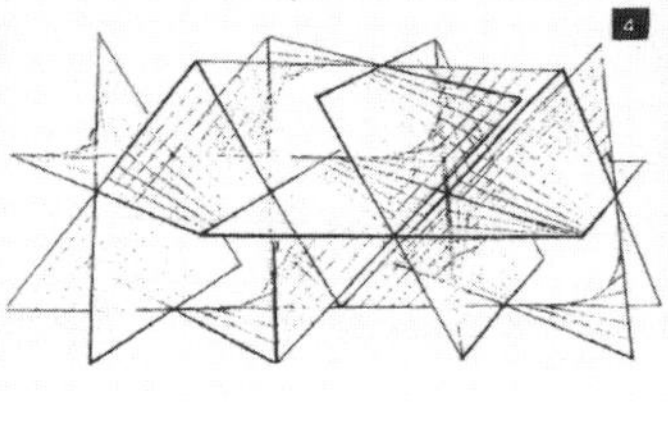

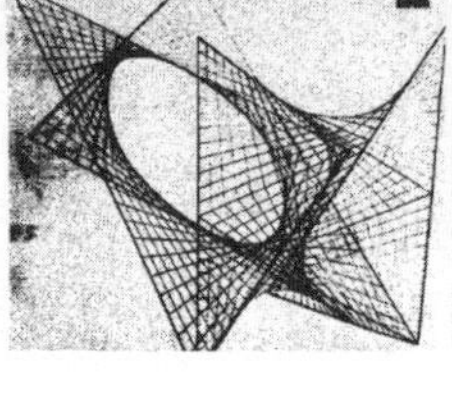

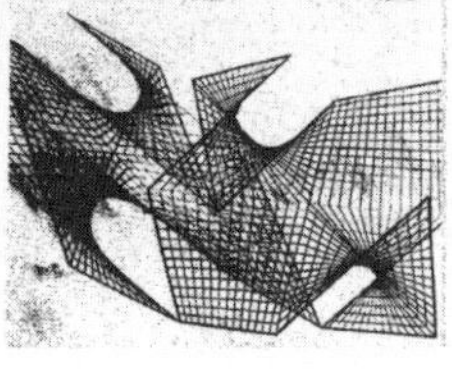

question is formulated as follows: What is the most regular elementary ial unit cell defined by the lattic lines and angles alone, which, through pact space-packing, yields the diamond lattice?

attempt to answer this by means of a body defined by plane faces, ›ssitates edges not forming part of the network, and the result is far ı regular. The answer is a regular body composed of four spatial ıgons (fig. 6), with the symmetries of tetrahedron. Each hexagon ompletely regular, with equal edges and angles (109°28'). As for the ›s, there are numerous possibilitties. If we continue to report to mini- istic structural principles the answer is simple a minimal surface, ›oth and curved in all cases, (in fact, double-curved, as we have al- ıdy seen in the preceding chapter) and subdivided into six identical units ›ded by spatial quadrilaterals of 60°, 90°, 90° and 109°28'. This is iously a circumferential periodic surface above a centre of periodicity ›oincident with the centre of the face and with the point of intersection traight lines bisecting (on the surface itself) the opposite edges.

s surface is characterised by its special rotational symmetries about ›e axes on the surface. While the sides of the polygons are straight- › segments without continuous extension beyond the centres of the ice, the faces contain straight lines bisecting the edges and combining › infinite regular netwroks of triangles.

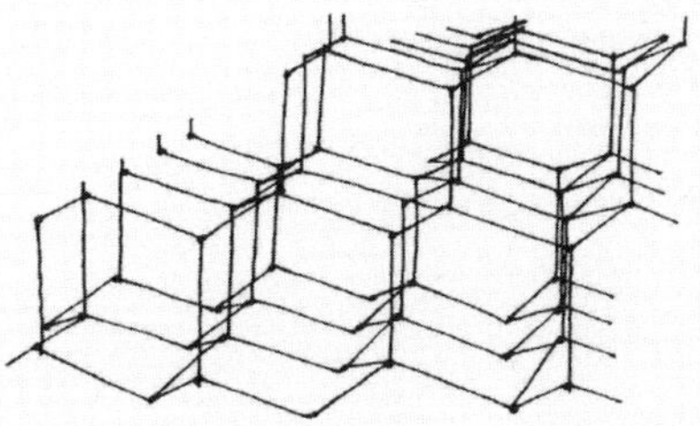

Fig. 5. Layer structure of spatial hexagons as in diamond lattice.

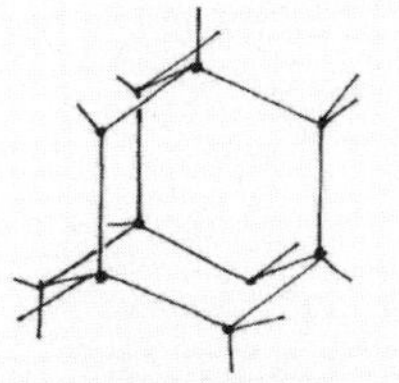

Fig. 6. Edges of volumetric unit-cell compactly space-packed in the diamond lattice.

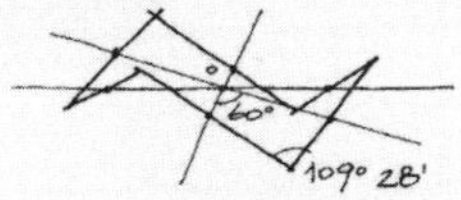


Fig. 7. Six-membered ring from the diamond lattice.

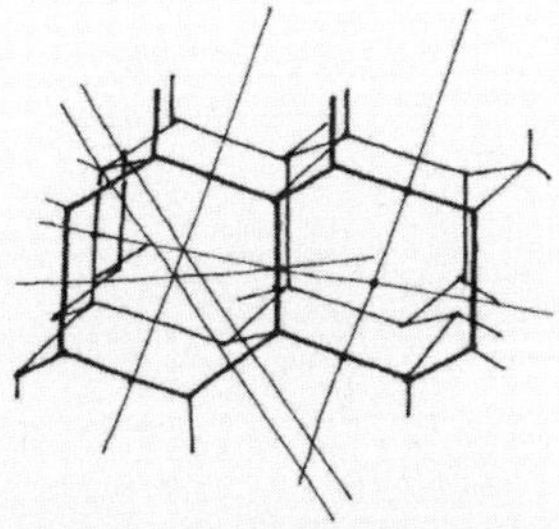

Fig. 8. Continuous two-dimensional grids developing inside the doub layers. The straight lines of these grids bisect the counter edges of each hexagonal ring.

The crux of the problem is that when one atom layer of the close-packed type overlies another at a suitable distance an atom of layer $\overline{A}$ may be closer to three atoms of layer $\overline{B}$ than to its own. The bonds between the two layers are stronger than those within either of them, so that the con- cept of the plane layer loses its significance and is justifiably by that of the double non-plane layer, consisting of spatial hexagons.

The problem is illustrated by the diamond lattice, in which each atom forms bonds with the four nearest atoms constituting a tetrahedron, i.e., each atom is the centre of a tetrahedron relative to its four nearest neighbours. The characteristic angle of the lattice (the angle of any pair of intersecting edges) is the Maraldi angle of 109°28'.

The double layers, composed of regular spatial hexagons, are clearly seen as they develop parallel to four sets of planes in space (the faces of the tetrahedra).

From here, it is a short step to considering the spatial hexagon as the faces of a physical solid- a polyhedron. In fact, this example and the en- suing question were a starting point for the present study. The lattice may be regarded as compact space packing of uniform bodies.

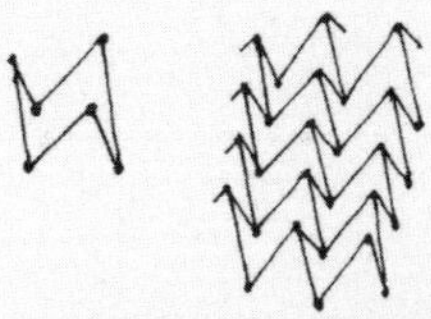

Fig. 1. Corrugated double layer of atoms as found in the structure of Bismuth. On the left an isolated hexagonal ring from the structure.

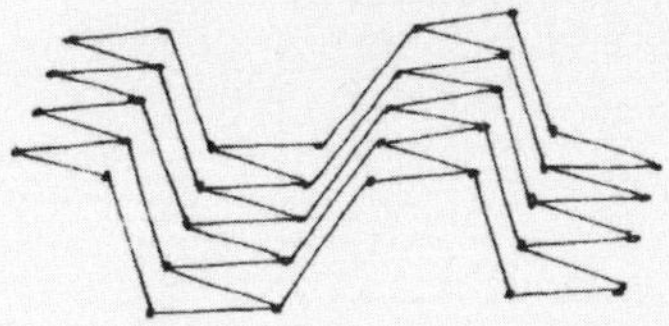

Fig. 2. Corrugated double layer as found in the structure of black Phosphor.

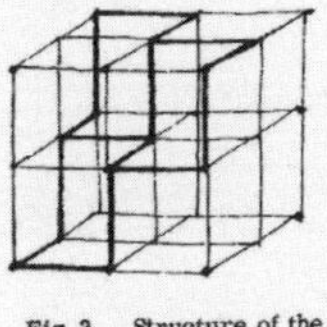

Fig. 3. Structure of the layers of Sodium-Chloride.

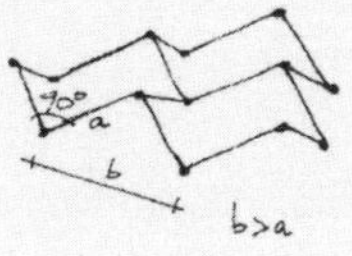


Fig. 4. β Polonium structure.

* The sketches are taken from "The Allotropy of the Elements" by W. E. Addison.

:RIES OF CURVED SURFACES FORMING REGULAR
:WO DIMENSIONAL" LATTICE. (ANALOGOUS TO
REGULAR PLANE TESSELATIONS").

40

pposed to two-dimensional (one-layered) networks, regular le-layered * networks cannot contain polygons with an odd ber of edges, except to the detriment of the regularity of the aces and to their internal periodicity. The even number of es is dictated by the nature of the periodicity, i.e. by the requirets of the symmetry in question.

e circumstances a number of regular planar networks (in fact, networks based partially or wholly on triangles) are not repreed in this category.

straight lines contained by these surfaces, which in fact are of rotational symmetry, intersect at the centres of periodicity tres of the surfaces), bisect the opposite edges of the polygon are perpendicular to them. All these straight lines combine a single continuous planar system parallel to the planes of the layers of vertices at equal distances from both. This is a fact th bearing in mind in practical applications.

"Double-layered" refers to the vertices of the spatial polygons.

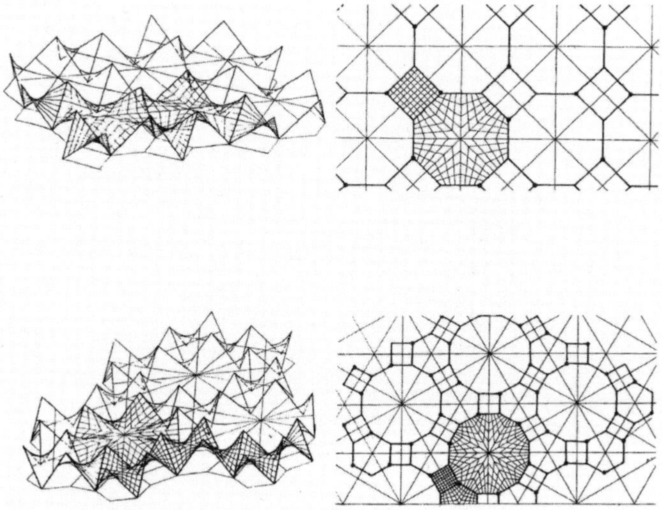

1. 2. Lattice of regular spatial quadrants and octagons. Plan and axonometric drawing.

3. 4. Lattice of regular spatial quadrants, hexagons and dodecagons. Plan and axonometric drawing.

1,2. רשת של מרובעים ומתומנים מרחביים רגולריים. תכנית ואקסונומטריה.

3,4. רשת של דודקגונים+ משושים + מרובעים מרחביים רגולריים. תכנית ואקסונומטריה.

SERIES OF CURVED SURFACES FORMING REGULAR "TWO DIMENSIONAL" LATTICES. (ANALOGOUS TO "REGULAR PLANE TESSELATIONS").

39

When discussing corrugated double layers it should be borne in mind spatial six-membered rings are not the only alternative for arranging spatial polygonsin two-dimensional space. To the same four and eight-membered rings, etc. are similarly feasible, combining to yield two-dimensional compact packings or what might (rather paradoxically) be termed "spatial two-dimensional lattices" or regular two-dimensional curved networks.

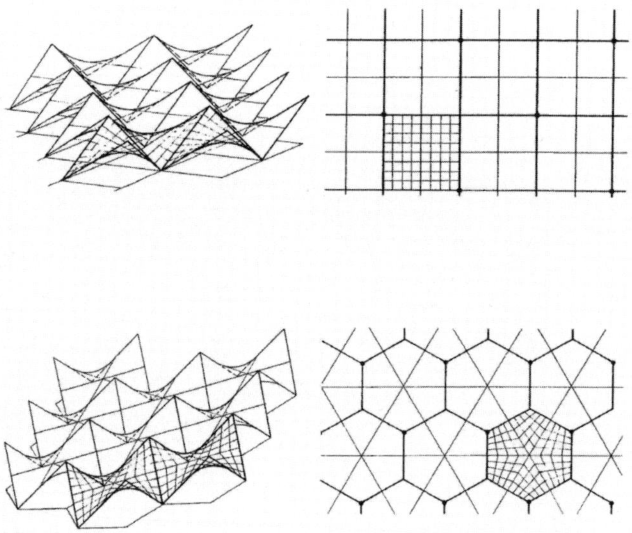

Series of curved surfaces whose vertices are in two parallel planes. The normal projection of the surfaces form a "regular tesselation".

1. 2. Lattice of spatial quadrants. Plan and axonometric drawing.

3. 4 Lattice of spatial hexagons. Plan and axonometric drawing.

מערכים של משחים עקומים אשר קדקדיהם מסודרים בשני מישורים מקבילים. היטל ניצב של המשטחים נותן רשת מישורית רגולרית.

1.2. רשת של מרובעים מרחביים. תכנית ואקסונומטריה.

3.4. רשת של משושים מרחביים. תכנית ואקסונומטריה.

**SEMI-REGULAR STELLATED SOLIDS WITH CURVED SURFACES.** 42

Subject to the above restrictions, a number of sets of solids may be distinguished:

I. BI-PYRAMIDAL * ($P^f_n = 4^n_n$) **

All polygons are regular and spatial, and the normals through the centres of the faces pass through the centre of the solid. In addition, these solids have on principal axis of symmetry different from the rest, namely the one through the two principal vertices (at which more than two edges meet).

The set is infinite. The number of faces $\bar{n}$ ranges from 3 to infinity.

There is a principal plane of symmetry normal to the principal axis of symmetry and containing all secondary vertices (other than the two principal vertices).

All faces are regular spatial quadrilaterals with two of their vertices on the principal axis of symmetry.

As $\bar{n}$ increases, so does the length of the edges relative to that of the central axis. With a fixed distance $\bar{a}$ between the principal vertices, the perimeter increases with the number of faces.

---

* The termins are derived from geometric phenomena within the area of the "planar polyhedra" identical from the aspect of spatial arrangement of the symmetries.

** In ($P^f_n$) P - number of sides of polygon,
n - number of faces of polyhedron,
f - number of faces meeting at each principal vertex

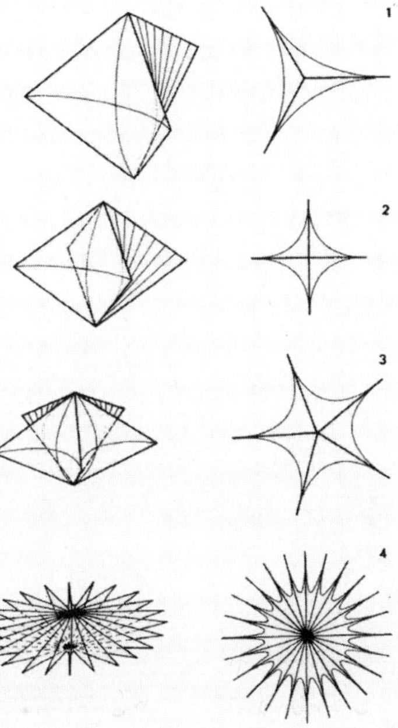

"Bi-pyramidical" bodies with curved surfaces.

1. $4^3_3$. A body with three quadrant faces.
2. $4^4_4$
3. $4^5_5$
4. $4^n_n$

78

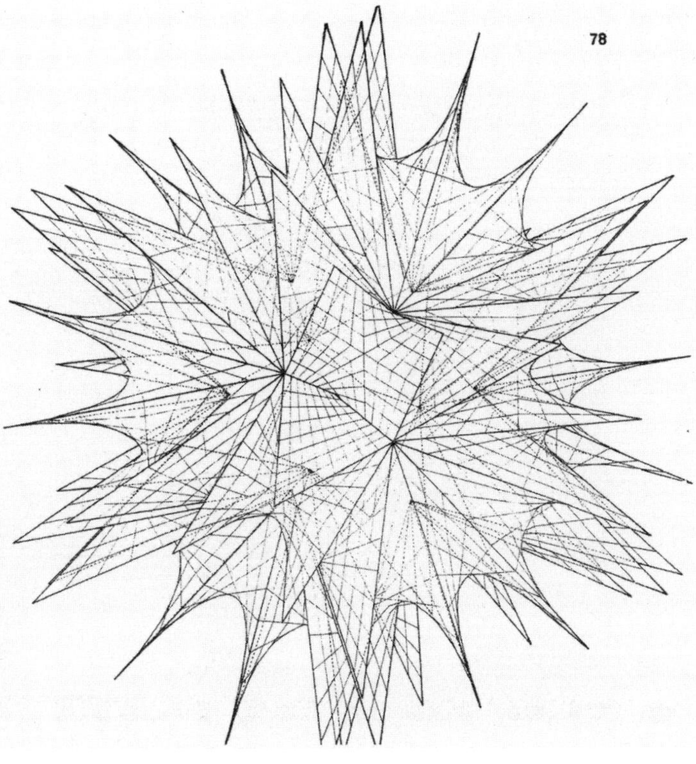

CONTINUOUS ROOFING FROM SHELL-ELEMENTS (OR STRETCHED MEMBRANES) COMPOSING REGULAR "PLANE" NETWORKS.

123

קרוי נמשך מאלמנטים קליפתיים (או ממברנות מתוחות המצטרפים למערכים "מישוריים" רגולריים.

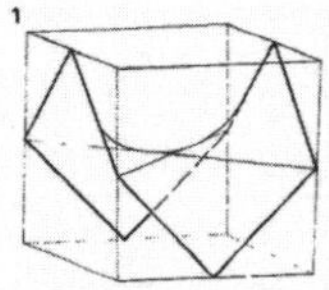

.1.2.3 קרוי נמשך המבוסס על צרוף של משטחים מתומנים (בהשלכה רבוע).

.4.5.6 קרוי נמשך המבוסס על צרוף של קליפות דודקגוניות (קטע של "משטח $240^{\circ}$").

1.2.3. Continuous roofing based on combination of octagonal surfaces.

4.5.6. Continuous roofing based on combination of dodecagonal surfaces (part of "$240^{\circ}$ surface").

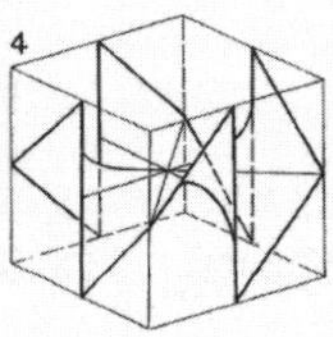

CONTINUOUS ROOFING BASED ON REGULAR COMBINATIONS OF SHELL-ELEMENTS (OR STRETCHED MEMBRANES).

125

קרוי נמשך מבוסס על קומבינציות רגולריות של אלמנטים קליפתיים ( או ממברנות מתוחות ).

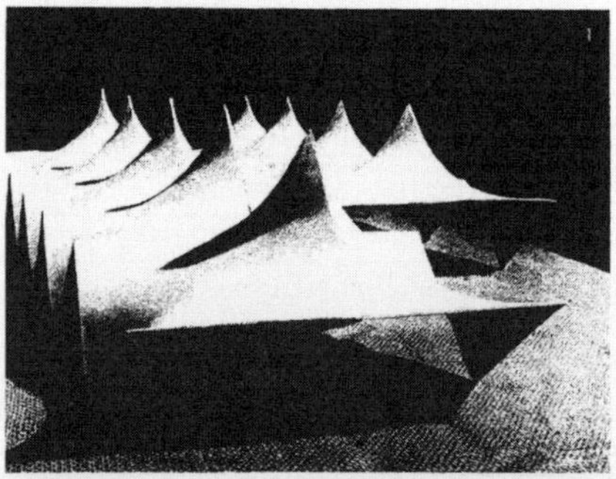

.1-4 קרוי נמשך המהווה צרוף של משט-חים משושים רגולריים.

מבוסס על קטעי האריזה המרחבית הקומפקטית של גופי $6^4_8$.

1-4. Continuous roofing consisting of combination of regular hexagonal surfaces.

Based on parts of the compact space-packing of $6^4_8$ solids.

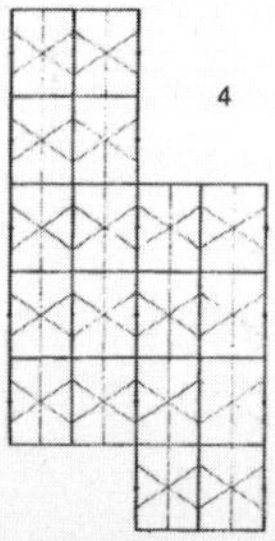

4

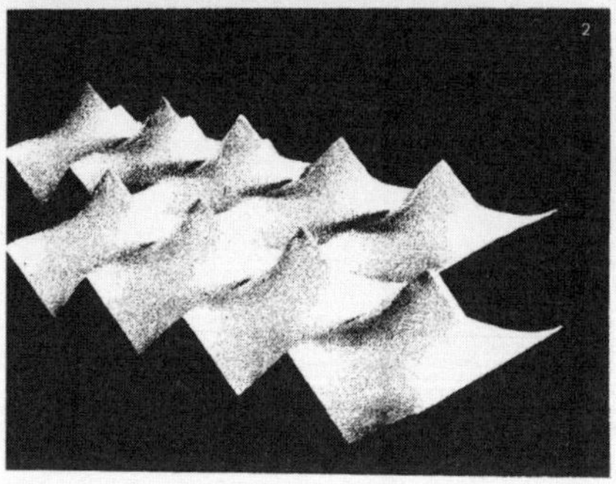

## Minimal Surfaces

A few years after being published, Burt's research was labeled "essentially theoretical" by a number of architectural theorists, most notably Maria Bottero.[37] Indeed, the work of the Ukrainian-Israeli architect appeared to be solely geometric in nature. But the Italian critic missed Burt's drive to show the relevance of his formal speculations to practical architectural matters. Not unlike some his fellow Israeli architects at the time, he believed that periodicity was a central economic factor when envisioning spatial configurations in architecture. Rooted in a high degree of symmetry and regularity, periodicity enabled the repetition of spatial units, thereby facilitating standardization and industrialization as means to drop production costs and speed up construction processes **(fig. 2.32–33)**.[38] Furthermore, in the pursuit of structural efficiency, Burt studied the relations between the static and material properties of minimal surfaces within a given boundary **(fig. 2.34–36)**. As empirical models for these, he looked at the membranes formed by soap-solution films in foams **(fig. 2.37–38)**.[39] A minimal surface turns out to be a special kind of sponge surface, with a homogeneous mean curvature equal to zero. Because of this singularity, load transmission across it runs solely through tensile and compressive membrane stresses; in other words, it is a surface in which flexure is reduced to zero. For this reason, Burt stressed that in minimal surfaces the material achieves its "moment of truth" vis-à-vis its structural properties—they allow for an optimal input/output ratio in terms of amount of material invested relative to the size and stability of resulting surface, since such a material will only have to resist tension and compression forces. He put it thus: "[a] film stretched over a closed spatial perimeter represents the 'ideal configuration' as regards the ratio of material input to resulting surface area, with minimum numbers of points of support."[40] Aside from their structural efficiency and their lending themselves to standardization, continuous periodic surfaces feature two other attributes insistently highlighted by Burt. For one thing, the structural capacity of the system as a whole exceeds that of the sum of the units comprising it, due to the geometric principles governing the combination of periodicity and continuity within a single surface (what might be referred to as *organic performance*); secondly, these surfaces possess a two-way structural nature—with both their positive and negative sides exhibiting the same static behavior when submitted

Precedent page:
**2.31** Architectural applications of Burt's geometric configurations

37 See Maria Bottero, "Editorial," *Zodiac*, no. 22 (1972), 238–39.

38 Notably Moshe Safdie shared those preoccupations at the time: "I believe that the immediate step is to put the construction industry in the factory. Building must be subdivided into 'space cells,' each space cell must be capable of complete factory production, of transporting from central plants to construction sites, and of assembly with minimum labor." Moshe Safdie, "New Environmental Requirements for Urban Building," *Zodiac*, no. 19 (1969), 180–82.no. 19 (1969 What made Burt uncomfortable about Safdie, however, was that, despite claims about standardization lowering costs, economy of materials, etc., apartments in projects like Habitat 67–which was conceived as an urban prototype to be replicated–were eventually rather pricey. This being the case, Burt felt that Safdie was privileging his own artistic impulse and desire to experiment over the pressing need to provide affordable housing solutions at the time.

39 This approach was first considered extensively by Belgian physicist Joseph Plateau in his 1873 *Statique Expérimentale et Théorique des Liquides Soumis aux Seules Forces Moléculaires* ("Experimental and Theoretical Statics of Liquids Subject to Molecular Forces Only").

40 Michaël Burt, *Spatial Arrangement and Polyhedra with Curved Surfaces and Their Architectural Applications - Doctoral Thesis* (Haifa, Israel: Technion, Israel Institute of Technology, 1966), I.

# ГHE APLICATIVE MEANING OF DOUBLE CURVED ЗURFACES.



## :NTRODUCTION

Ѕuch structures as have survived from ancient times mostly serve as nonuments to their parent cultures. Some of them were expressly set-ıp for this purpose. Government buildings and temples, as well as civil ɜngineering projects such as dams, towers, walls of forts, bridges and ıqueducts served as evidence not only of a ruler 's might, and of the ɔrevailing economy and social order, but also of the state of technology ınd science and of the mentality of their era.

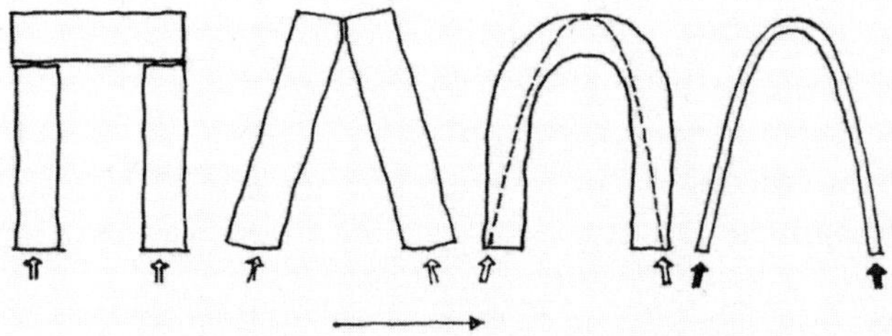

Fig. 1. Development of sections of pressure - structure towards decrease of bending forces.

Гhe desire and need for higher, stronger and larger buildings provided ı major challenge to the human intellect, inventiveness and capacity for ɔrganisation.

Want, that basic fact of human existence led to the study of material and ɜnergy minima, and led to the creation of the concepts of economy and ɜfficiency. Trends of development of artificial and natural structures ıre dictated by the last-named criterion, i.e. by the input-output ratio. (Maximum efficiency means minimum input in realising a given project). Morphologically, progress in the field of structures is reflected in ever-closer intuitive approximation (controlled by experience) of sections determining "lines ɔf support" in relation to given loads; gradual transition to more economical, structural shapes, such as the catenary, the spherical dome, the parabolas ınd the truss; development of space structure circumventing (or completely eliminating) bending stresses and confined to pure compression and tension.

Гhe idea of efficiency analysis with regard to structures is relatively new. It permits comparison of different structural principles with energy input as ɜriterion. Clearly for a specific project to be realised at minimum input, a specific structural principle, combined with a specific material must be applied.

Гhe reluctance to extend the term "minimum energy input" to such factors as labour, time, financing and know-how is understandable. These factors, in spite of their occasionally decisive influence on the input-output ratio, cannot be treated as absolute, in view of their continual variability. This is the main drawback in attempting to formulate a basic "minimum theory" for solving design problems.

## ɪMAL-SURFACE SHELL OR MEMBRANE

already noted a minimal surface is one whose mean curvature at all points is zero.

· all non-plane minimal surfaces in three-dimensional space, this implies double curvature sitive and negative) at every point of the surface, with the resulting resemblance to a saddle. ı liquid membrane is subjected to membrane tension only (pure tensile stresses) due to the sur-ɜ tension of the liquid, and but for its weight would constitute a physical realisation of the mini-l surface (see p. 1, on soap bubbles). Actually it is the very deformation due to this weight which bles the liquid membranes to be used as an ideal model for a suspended structure subjected to a form load over its entire area.

ː liquid membrane is thus an ideal "support surface" for a uniformly loaded tensile or suspended ucture. Reversed it will play the same role with regard to a structure under pure axial compression.

ɜ minimal surface is an ideal support surface a) for a theoretically-weightless stretched mem-ne (or shell) not subjected to external forces, b) for a structure in simultaneous and equivalent tes of compression and tension, as in reinforced concrete and reinforced plastics (capable of both sion and compression).

## GREE OF PERIODICITY AS CRITERION IN SELECTING SHAPES FOR BUILDING PURPOSES

noted in the introduction, one of the most marked drawbacks of curved surfaces (in contrast to ne surfaces) is their "individuality", reflected in the difficulty in combining and packing them ɔ compact systems in two-and three-dimensional space. This difficulty, or rather the impossibility e to their low periodicity) of resolving the curved surfaces into identical elements, hinders the ustrialisation of their production and considerably increases their cost. By the present trend in development of membrane structures, the degree of periodicity is likely to become the decisive terion in their selection for building purposes.

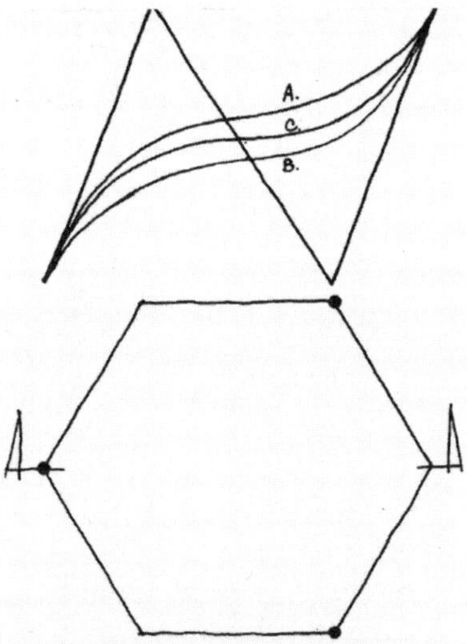


Fig. 4. Surface with perimeter of regular spatial hexagon:
A. Section representing "supporting line" of a shell receiving its load by axial pressure stresses inside the surface.
B. Section representing "Supporting line" of suspended stretched membrane.
C. Section through the minimal surface.
1. Representing "Supporting line" of structure without any load (not even its own weight) or-
2. Structure combining simultaneously systems of pressure and tension (identical in their impact).

to a given scenario—which is linked to their quality of dividing space into two identical halves (or "subspaces") that never meet **(fig. 2.39–40)**.[41] Encapsulating the rationale behind minimal surfaces, Burt argued for curved structures in a way Giorgini himself might have, in a passage written some thirty years after the publication of his thesis: "[c]urvature is one of the most effective design strategies of nature by which to reduce stresses in surface structures and to achieve far-reaching material reduction."[42]

41 See ibid., 128. Later in his career Burt emphasized the fact that, even though the spaces confined by two-manifold envelopes were commonly referred to as interior and exterior, "telling which is which is a relativistic notion." In Michaël Burt, *The Periodic Table of The Polyhedral Universe* (Haifa, Israel: Technion, Israel Institute of Technology, 1996), 8.

42 See Burt, "New Forms and Conceptual Architecture," 42.

Precedent page:
**2.32** "Applicative meaning" of double-curved surfaces, and role of periodicity

**2.33** Below: Examples of roof structures made out of "plane" networks

Following pages:
**2.34–35** Static and material properties of minimal surfaces (pp. 152–53).

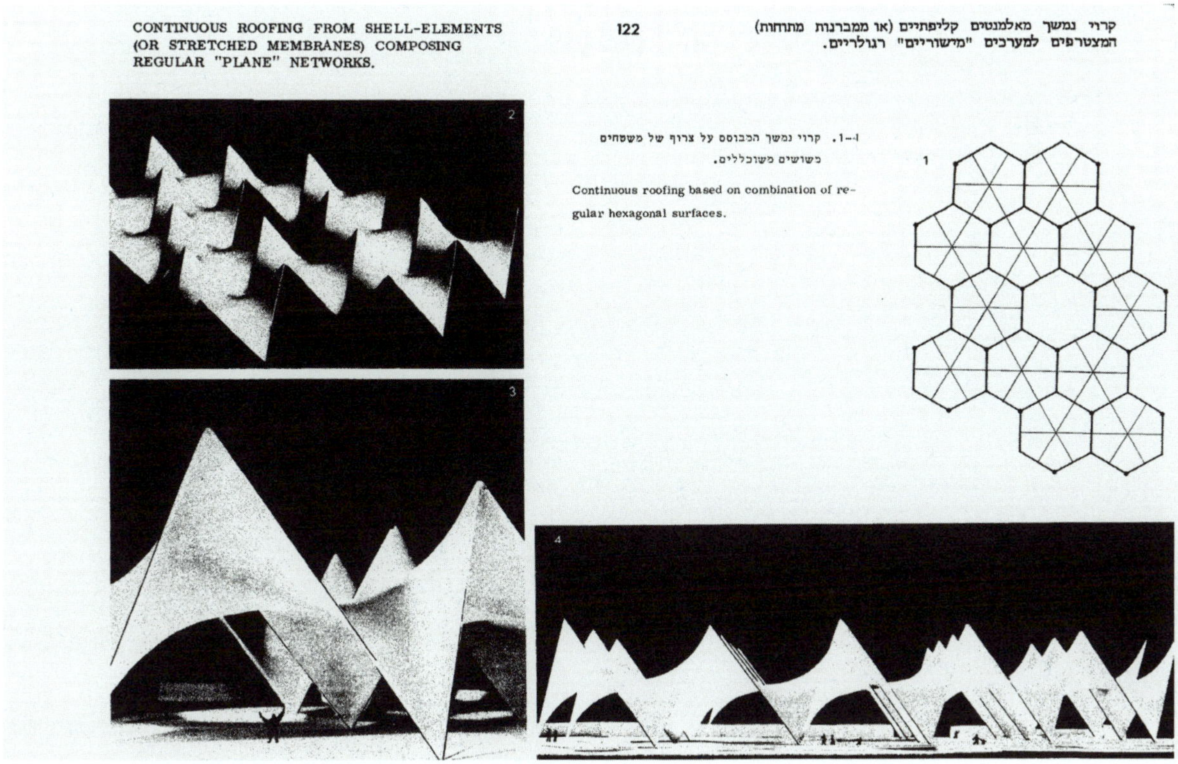

## FREELY-STRETCHED FILMS ON A SIMPLE, CLOSED SPATIAL PERIMETER

The shape assumed by the surface following immersion of any spatial perimeter in a soap solution, is always a function of the shape of the perimeter and forces acting upon, and within, the membrane.

Let us take a general case: given a perimeter K (rigid) and a membrane M stretched over it under a load q per unit area , as illustrated.

The tension inside the film (which is a result of surface tension specific to the solution in which the perimeter is immersed) is identical at all its points. Therefore the perimeter is uniformly loaded at every point. The tension within the surface is balanced by external forces induced within the perimeter. External forces applied to the surface can only be balanced by a suitable curvature, for the surface cannot resist bending forces. Let us examine what happens at point O within the surface and in close proximity to it, M, bounded by the perimeter C. The surface at O is subjected to force P, which can be balanced only by a mean positive curvature giving rise to a vector D equal to P.

Assuming that the radius of maximal (positive) curvature is $R_1$ and the radius of minimal (negative) curvature is $R_2$. In this case - $R_1 < R_2$.

$K_1 > K_2$ (principal curvature). Hence the mean curvature $H = [\frac{k_1 + k_2}{2}] > 0$. D balances the vectors induced by $K_1$ and $K_2$.

How will the surface react if we remove the load P at point O? As a result of removal of the load at O, static equilibrium will be upset. Structures in stable equilibrium are those associated with minimal general potential energy. Owing to the tendency of the membrane to attain stable equilibrium, the vector D will act to eliminate the cause of formation by shifting the surface in a positive direction until $K_1$ and $K_2$ are equalized (i.e., $R_1 = R_2$).

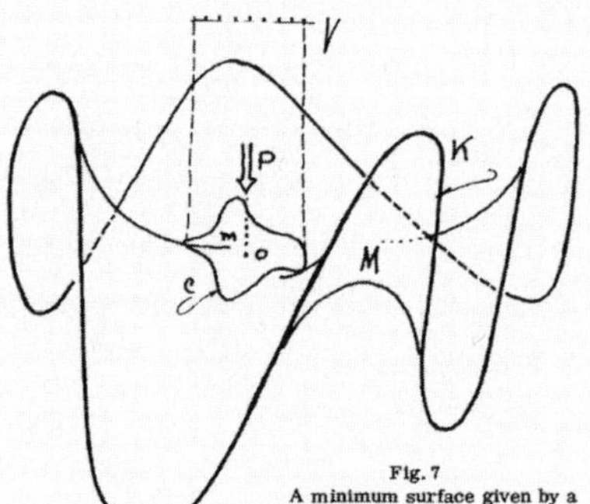

Fig. 7
A minimum surface given by a spatial perimeter.

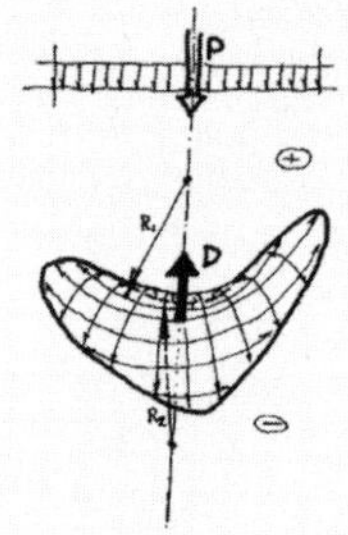

Fig. 8

In the latter case, where the number of axes of symmetry is odd (2 n + 1) the section will have an inflection point at its centre.

It is possible to describe periodic minimal surfaces with a centre of rotational periodicity and an unlimited number of axes of symmetry intersecting at this centre. Fig. 19 shows this type of surface, in which the unit is a surface segment bounded as a , b and the line m.

The spatial line m , part of the extended perimeter, can assume any shape without affecting the periodicity of the surface due to the existence of a and b and the angle between them. Hence a surface with a centre of circumferential periodicity undergoes torsional deformation about an axis perpendicular to the periodicity plane at O, without loss of periodicity.

Affine transformation destroys the periodicity.

Another popular example of a periodic minimal surface with a centre of circumferential periodicity is the spatial hexagon (Fig. 21). Segment m of the extended perimeter appears here as two combined straight lines segment AC and CB. The axes of symmetry of the surface divide it into six identical spatial quadrilaterals of the type OACB. Each vertex of the quadrilateral is the intersection point of two straight lines, and hence a centre of circumferential periodicity of the surface extends in all directions outside the perimeter and filling the three-dimensional space to infinity. Generally such a surface is self-intersecting but judicious choice of suitable angles and proportions yields infinite periodic minimal surfaces without self-intersections or singularities. The straight lines, or axes of symmetry combines into regular spatial networks, and the centres of periodicity into regular spatial point systems. This will be treated in more detail further on.

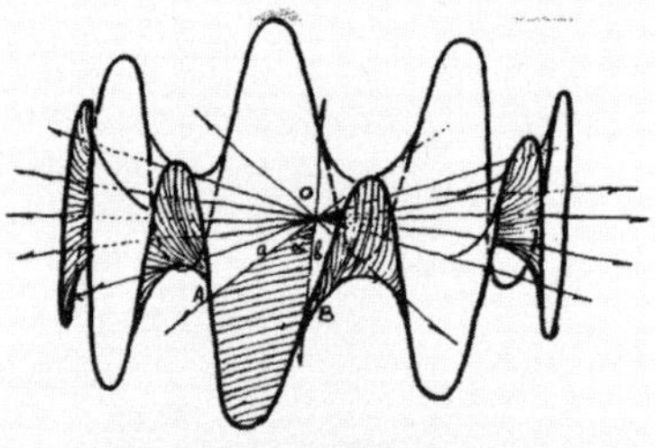

Fig. 19. Periodic minimal surface with periodicity focus 0.

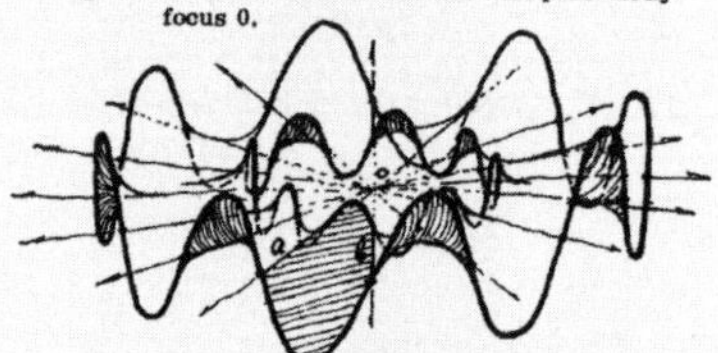

Fig. 20. Periodic minimal surface stretched between two concentric spatial "rings", forming the "extended perimeter", with circumferential periodicity focus outside the surface.

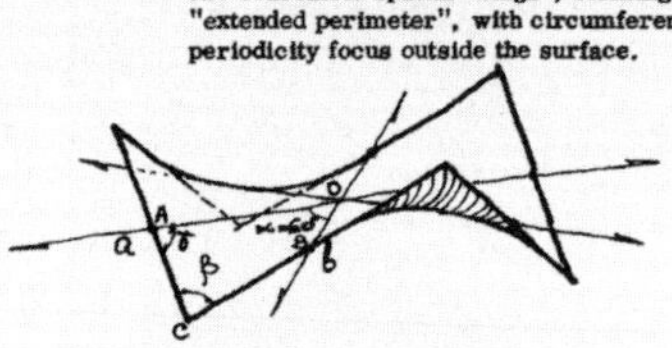

Fig. 21. A perimeter of a periodic minimal surface constructed of straight line segments with three axes of symmetry.

## II. INTERSECTING STRAIGHT LINES

A minimal surface S defined by a perimeter p contains two intersecting straight lines a and b. All straight lines on the infinite periodic surface are clearly coplanar and concurrent at a point O within or outside the surface. About this point, circumferential periodicity will develop. Point O, as the centre of this circumferential periodicity must be at the centre of the extended perimeter of the surface.

If the extended perimeter defines a simple periodic minimal surface (non-self-intersecting in space) the simple relationship is: $2\pi/\alpha\ p = 2n$, where n is the number of straight lines concurrent at O, or the number of axes of symmetry of the extended perimeter and the periodic minimal surface, and $\alpha$ p - the period angle of the surface.

"Periodicity plane" - a plane containing the straight lines and the "centre of rotational periodicity" of the surface.*

Two very popular examples of periodic minimal surfaces with a centre of circumferential periodicity are the saddle-shaped minimal surface (Fig. 17) and the monkey saddle (Fig. 18). In the first case we have two axes of rotational symmetry on the surface and the period angle is 90°; in the second case the surface contains three axes of symmetry and the angle is 60°.

In the former case where the number of axes of symmetry is even (2 n), a normal section of the surface through O, bisecting the angle, will yield a line with one-way curvature (positive or negative). (See Fig. 17).

* Centre of rotational periodicity the point of intersection of the axis of rotational periodicity and the surface.

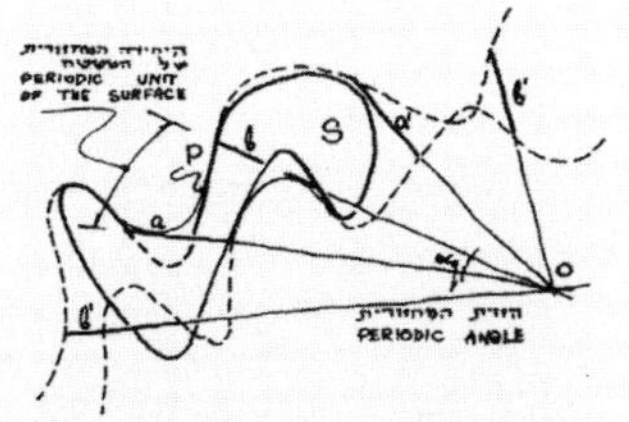


Fig. 16. Periodic minimal surface. All the straight lines of the surface are on one plane and meet in the "focus of the circumferential periodicity" O.

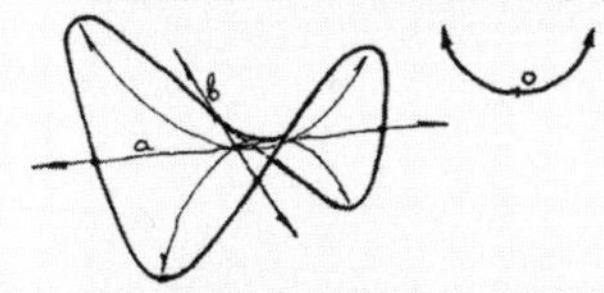

Fig. 17. Saddle shaped periodic minimal surface with two axes of symmetry intersecting at O (with periodic angles of 90°).

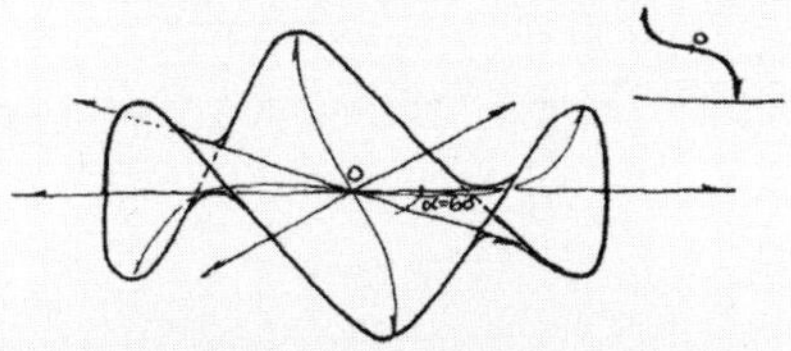

Fig. 18. Saddle shaped periodic surface (monkey saddle) with three axes of symmetry intersecting at 0 (with periodic angle of 60°).

## III. PARALLEL STRAIGHT LINES

A minimal surface S defined by a spatial perimeter P contains two parallel straight lines, a and b. As in case II, there is a periodicity plane containing all axes of symmetry. The spread of the surface, based on parallelism of axes of symmetry, is one-directional.

Fig. 23 and 24 show infinite periodic minimal surfaces based on a network of parallels. The two parts of the perimeter (sine-wave-shaped) are identical but differently interrelated. While in Fig. 23, the first part is a mirror image of the second, in the second example, as a result of translation along the axis of spread, the parts are rotationally symmetrical. The axis of this symmetry appears as a straight line on the surface coincident with the axis of spread. The unit is bounded by three straight lines and a curve as shown.

The perimeters described in Fig. 26, consisting of straight segments only (right angles), define minimal surfaces forming units of infinite periodic surfaces, without self-intersections or singularities.

It is seen that the dominant factors determining the topological nature of the surface are the angles and number of sides of the elementary unit in their specific spatial combination. By contrast, the proportions of the segments are immaterial in this respect.

By altering the proportions of the perimeter segments, additional symmetries can be created. This will be represented by straight lines on the minimal surface and result in further subdivision. Hence it is desirable as a matter of principle to distinguish between elementary units, incapable of acquiring a

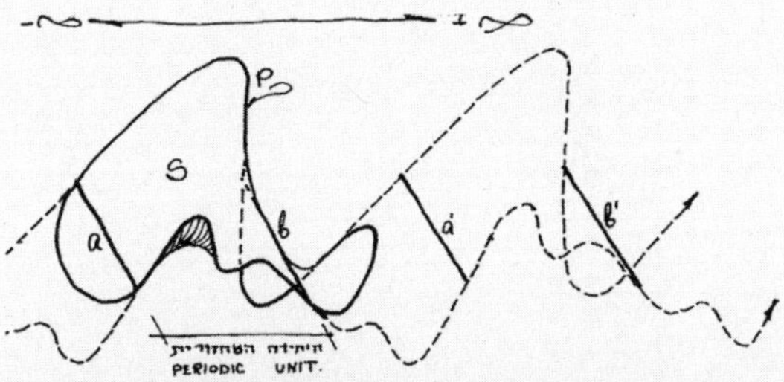


Fig. 22. Infinite periodic minimal surface with parallel axes of symmetry.

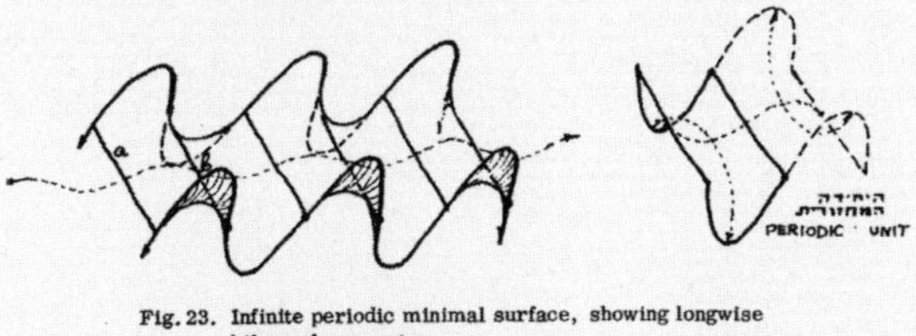


Fig. 23. Infinite periodic minimal surface, showing longwise bilateral symmetry.

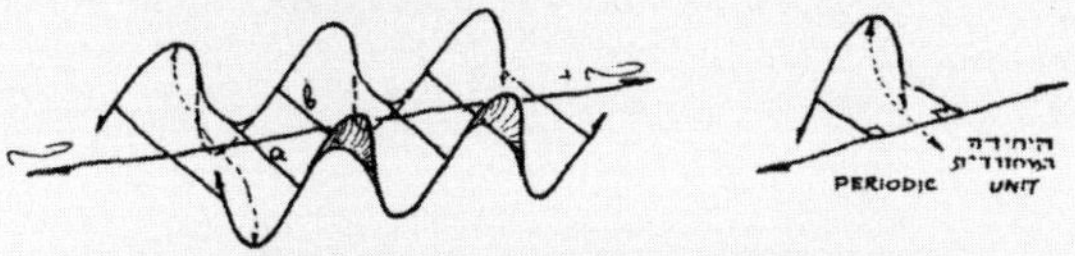


Fig. 24. Infinite periodic minimal surface with longwise rotational symmetry: (containing a straight line perpendicular to all the parallel lines).

higher degree of rotational symmetry by changing their proportions, and ordinary units, capable of subdivion under certain conditions.

In the two examples of continuous periodic surfaces, the unit of the first is elementary, while that of the second can acquire a higher degree of symmetry eventually subdividing into identical spatial quadrilaterals with angles $60^{\circ} - 90^{\circ} - 90^{\circ} - 90^{\circ}$ (Fig. 26).

Two additional examples of subdivisible units are shown in Fig. 27. In these interesting examples, the minimal surface is defined by two plane polygons acting as a split perimeter *. In both cases the continuous periodic surface has no singularities or self-intersections and is characterised by stratified array of plane networks of straight lines. No additional straight lines are found between these regular straight-line networks. Given certain proportions of the periodic unit (Fig. 27), the surface attains a superior degree of symmetry, and the unit subdivides into spatial quadrilaterals.

These two surfaces are dealt in more detail in the chapter dealing with regular continuous periodic surfaces.

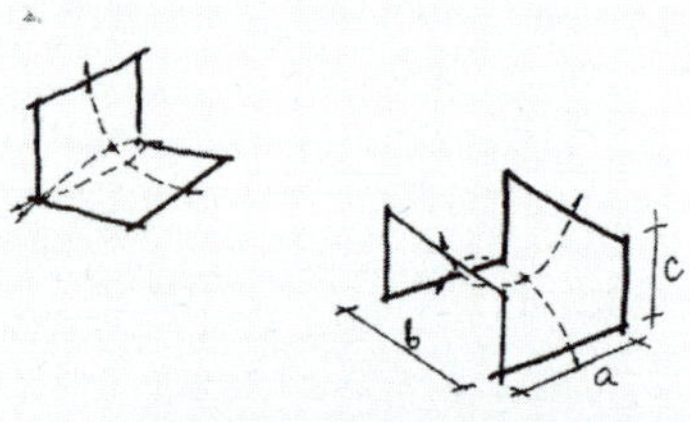


Fig. 25. Repetitive units of infinite periodic minimal surface (extending over the entire three dimensional space).

Fig. 26. Any increase in the degree of symmetry results in the division of repetitive unit into more and more elementary units.

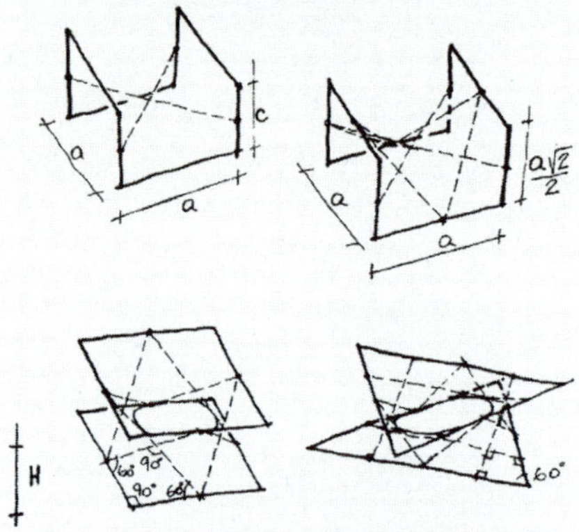


Fig. 27. Repetitive units of infinite minimal surfaces which can be split into more elementary repetitive units taking the form of spatial quadrilateral.

* This type of perimeter falls outside the scope of the present work.

**2.36** Static and material properties of minimal surfaces

Opposite page:
**2.37** Burt's soap-solution films.

Following pages:
**2.38** Burt's soap-solution films. (p. 156)
**2.39** Continuous periodic surfaces dividing space into two identical halves (p. 157)

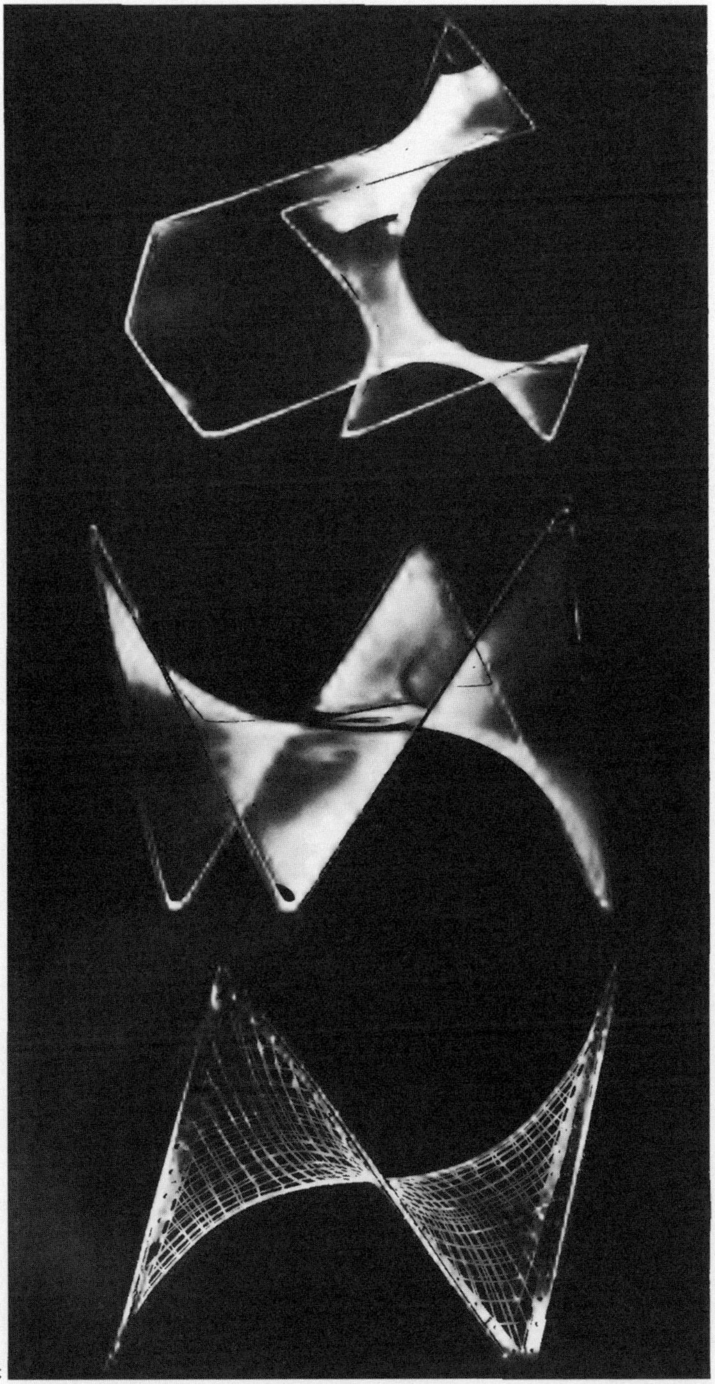

A

B

C

define the polyhedra which are the periodic unit cells of volume in the diamond lattice (*fig. 5*). The qualititative definition of the curved faces is arbitrary in as far as it does not violate the properties of symmetry of the spatial perimeter of the face.

In the case of the diamond lattice the spatial hexagon contains three two-fold rotation axes of symmetry, which pass through the mid-points of the opposite edges (*see fig. 4*). These axes are con-

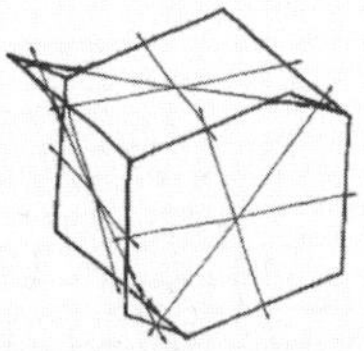

5

tinuous (beyond the boundaries of the hexagon) and form an element of the symmetry group of the diamond lattice. They have to be contained in every surface bounded by such a hexagonal perimeter, with the result that the positive and negative sides of the surface are identical.

The characterization of the face, bounded by the hexagonal perimeter, as minimal surface is justified, being mathematically definite, and it holds true for all types of simple spatial perimeters, with either straight or curved edges. (A plane surface is a special case of a minimal surface).

The inclusion of minimal surfaces in the subject of close-packing is not new. A classic example is the Kelvin solid, which is a model of an elementary unit cell of an ideal conglomeration of uniform soap-bubbles with minimal interface area (*see fig. 6*).

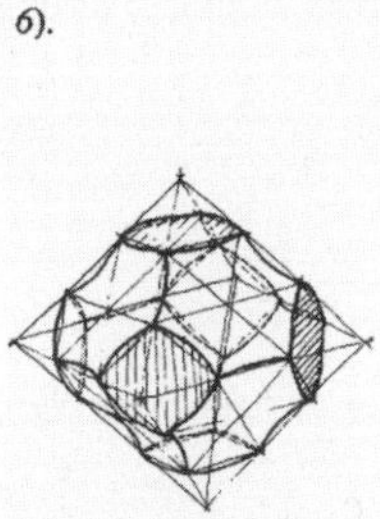

6

Robert Williams presented an alternative periodic unit-cell (*see fig. 7*), developed on the basis of speculations of Lord Kelvin. He arrived at the same number of edges — $5\frac{1}{7}$ — per face of the conglo-

PERIODIC MINIMAL SURFACES. 18 .משטחים מינימאליים מחזוריים

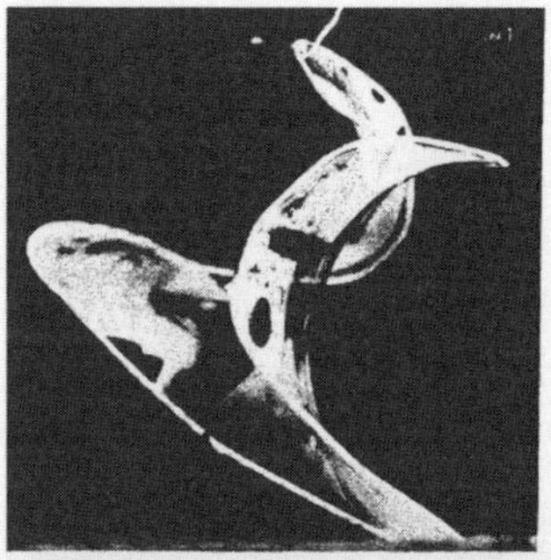

1א. משטח מינימאלי נתון ע"י פרימטר מרחבי סגור ומכיל ציר סימטריה סיבובית.

1ב. צלום לאורך ציר הסימטריה של המשטח. ציר הסימטריה נמצא במקום בו השלכת המשטח מצטמצמת לנקודה.

2. משטח מינימאלי מחזורי נתון ע"י פרימטר מרחבי סגור ומכיל מספר צירי סימטריה מקבילים הנח- תכים ע"י ציר הניצב לאורך המשטח.

3. צלום לאורך ציר הסימטריה הראשי (מופיע בהשלכה כנקודה).

4. צלום לאורך אחד מצירי הסימטריה המקבילים.

$1_A$. A minimal surface, defined by a closed spatial perimeter and includes a rotational symmetry axis.

$1_B$. A view along the symmetry axis for the surface. The symmetry axis is located where the projection of the surface reduces to a point.

2. A minimal surface, defined by a closed spatial perimeter, including a set of parallel symmetry - axes and an axis perpendicular to them.

3. A view along the main symmetry axis.

4. A view along one of the parallel axes.

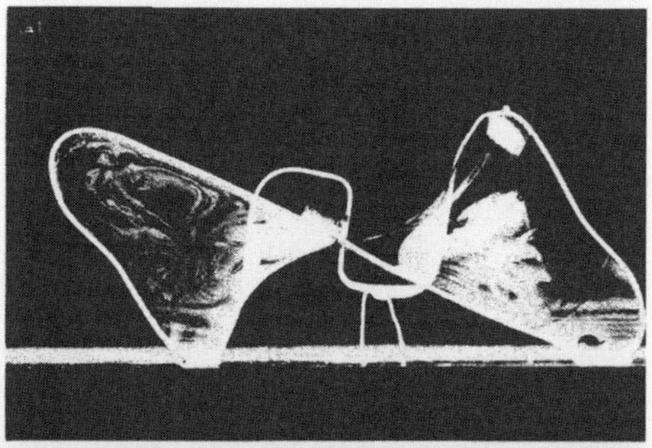

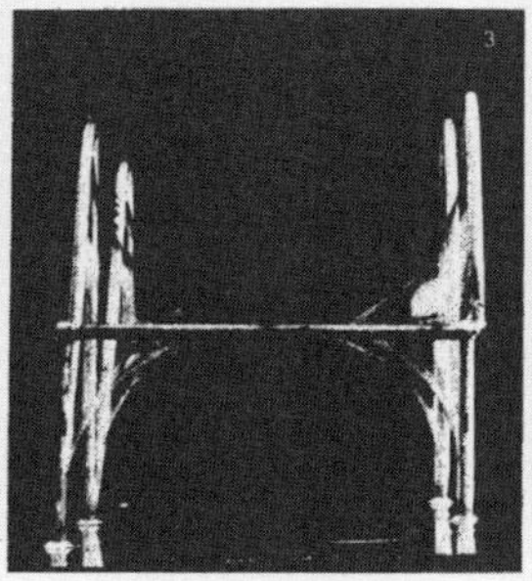

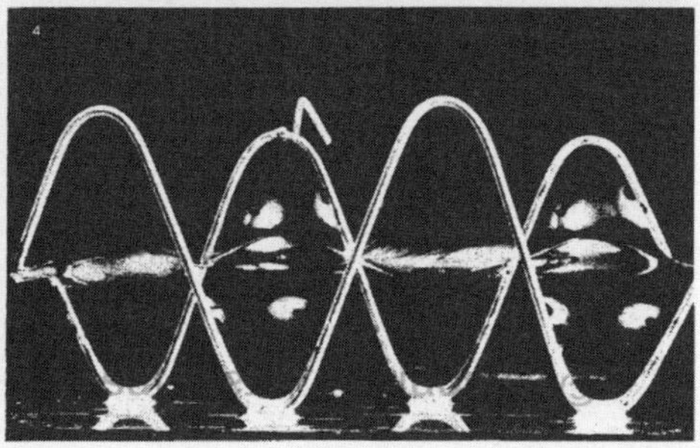

PERIODIC MINIMAL SURFACES. 19 .משטחים מינימאליים מחזוריים

Periodic minimal surface defined by hexagonal spatial perimeter, including a "focus of rotational periodicity" O and three symmetry axes intersecting at $60^0$ angles.

A view along one of these axes. The axes divide the surface into 6 "elementary repetitive units".

Periodic minimal surface defined by a spatial octagon, including a "focus of rotational periodicity" O and 4 symmetry axes intersecting at $45^0$ angles.

A view along one of these axes. The axes divide the surface into 8 "elementary repetitive units".

1. משטח מינימאלי מחזורי הנתון ע"י פרימטר משושה מרחבי. מכיל מוקד מחזוריות היקפית O ושלשה צירי סימטריה הנחתכים בו בזוית של $60^0$.

2. צלום לאורך אחד מצירי סימטריה אלה. הצירים מחלקים את המשטח ל-6 "יחידות חוזרות אלמנ- טאריות".

3.4. משטח מינימאלי מחזורי הנתון ע"י פרימטר מתומן ע"י פרימטר מתומן מרחבי. מכיל מוקד.מחזוריות היקפית O ו- 4 צירי סימטריה הנחתכים בו בזוית של $45^0$.

5. צלום לאורך אחד מצירי סימטריה אלה. הצירים מחלקים את המשטח לשמונה "יחידות חוזרות אלמנטאריות".

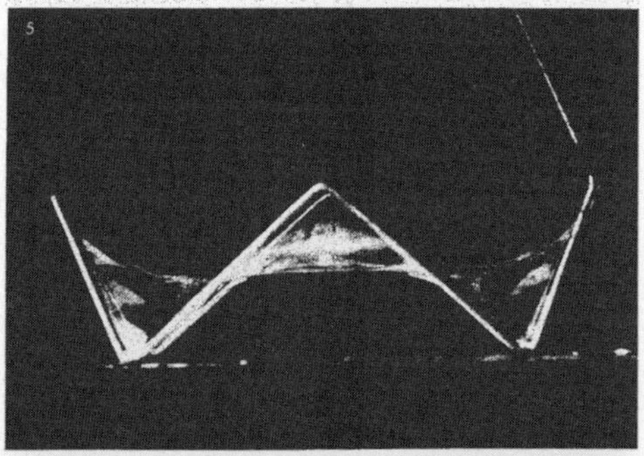

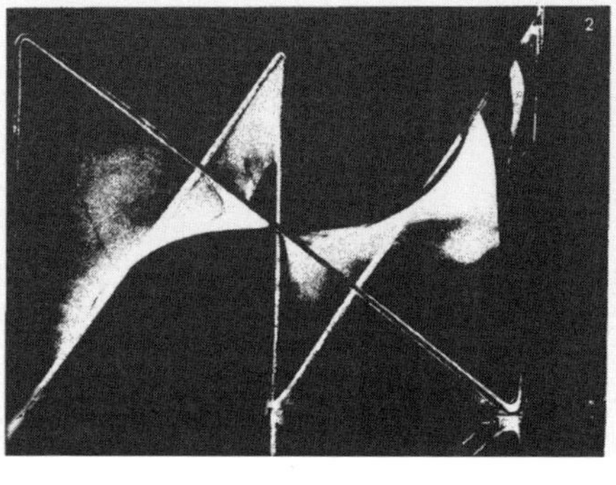

1

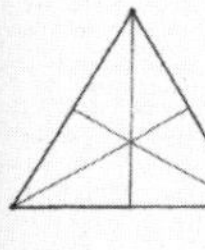

3

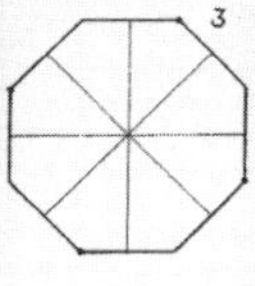

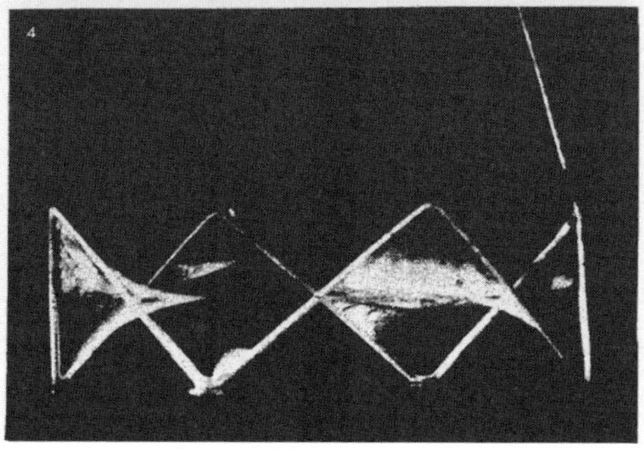

CONTINUOUS PERIODIC MINIMAL SURFACES. **15** .משטחים מינימאליים מחזוריים נמשכים

1

1. A continuous periodic minimal surface without singularity and self-intersection, constructed of 90° spatial *hexagons as its* elementary repetitive units.

2-3. Typical sections of the surface.

4. Symmetry axes of the interior space. The principal axes are emphasized.

1. משטח מינימאלי מחזורי-נמשך, ללא נקודות סינגו-לריות וללא חתוך עצמי. את היחידה החוזרת האל-מנטאריות של המשטח מהוה משושה מרחבי בעל זויות של 90°.

2-3. חתכים אופייניים של המשטח.

4. צירי הסימטריה של החלל הפנימי. הצירים הפרינ-ציפאליים מודגשים.

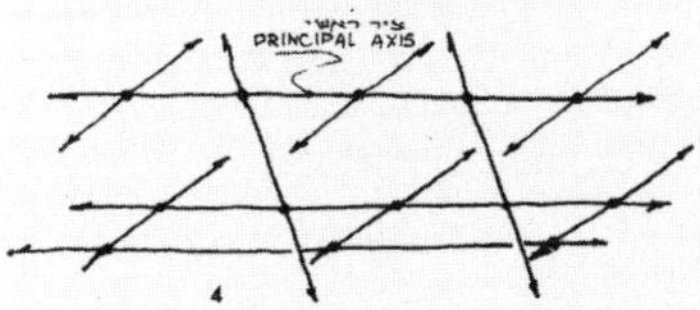


4

2

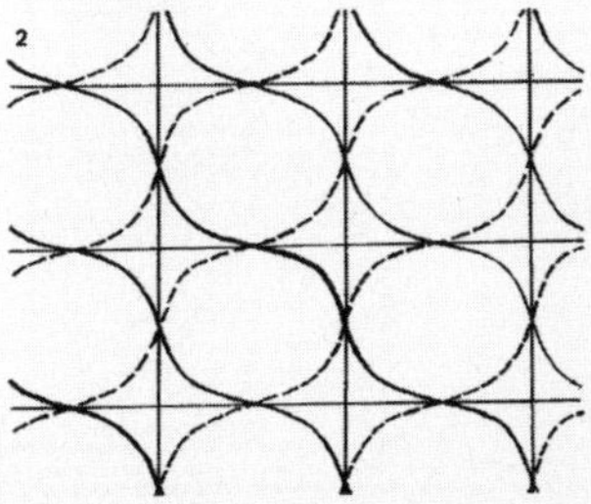

3

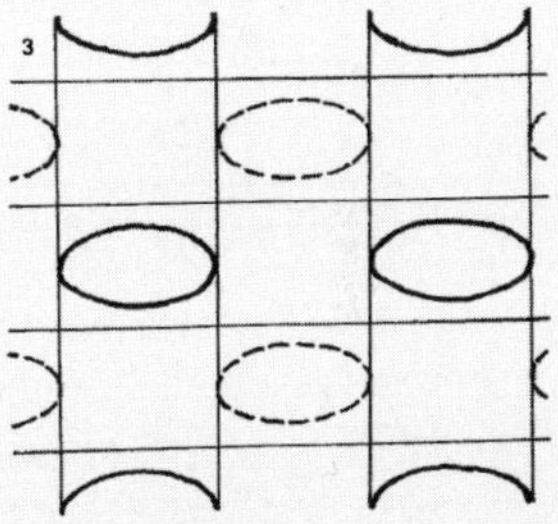

CONTINUOUS PERIODIC MINIMAL SURFACES. **16** .משטחים מינימאליים מחזוריים נמשכים

1

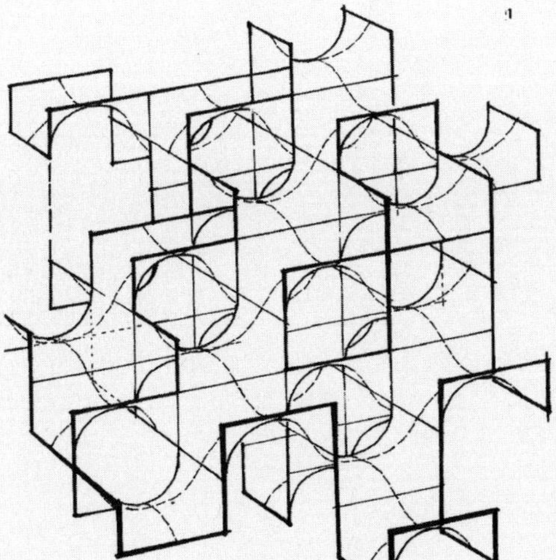

1. A continuous periodic minimal surface without singularity and self-intersection, consisting of 90° spatial octagons as its periodic units.

2-3. Typical sections.

4. Symmetry axes of the interior space. For definite proportions of the repetitive unit the axes of the interior space will describe the diamond lattice.

1. משטח מינימאלי מחזורי נמשך, ללא נקודות סינגולריות וללא חתוך עצמי. את היחידה החוזרת של המשטח מהווה מתומן מרחבי בעל זויות של 90°.

2-3. חתכים אופייניים.

4. צירי הסימטריה של החלל הפנימי. עם התאמת הפרופורציות של היחידה החוזרת $(a; a; \frac{a\sqrt{2}}{2})$ יתארו צירי החלל הפנימי את שריג היהלום.

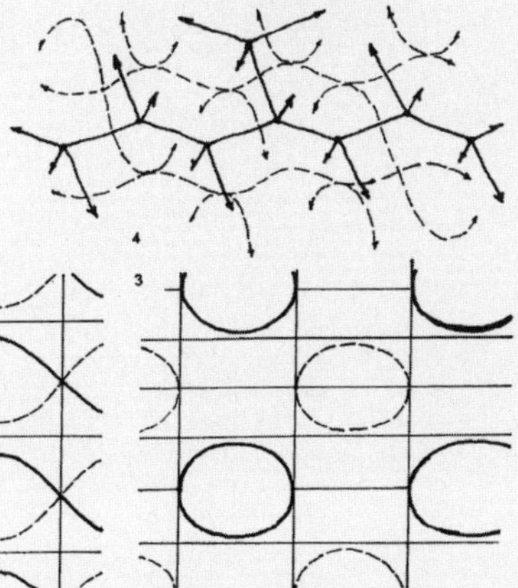

4

2



3

polyhedra. The number of such solids that result from one saddle polyhedron is the same as the number of possible transformations of one elementary periodic surface unit that exists within the face of that saddle polyhedron.
*Fig. 16* illustrates four possible types of

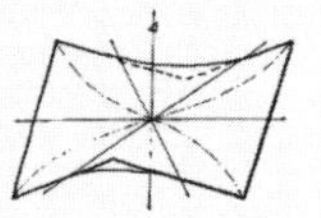

16

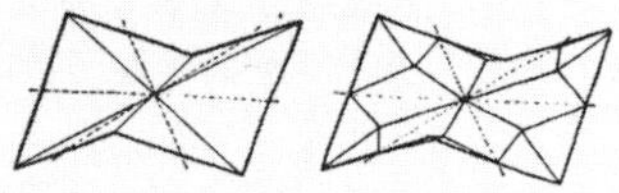

16a 16c

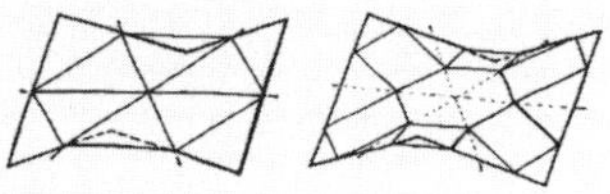

16b 16d

segmentation of a saddle surface on a regular hexagonal perimeter. *Fig. 17* illustrates four possible variations of solids with plane segments based on the saddle polyhedron of the diamond lattice $(\underset{\sim}{6}{}^3_2)$ (4).

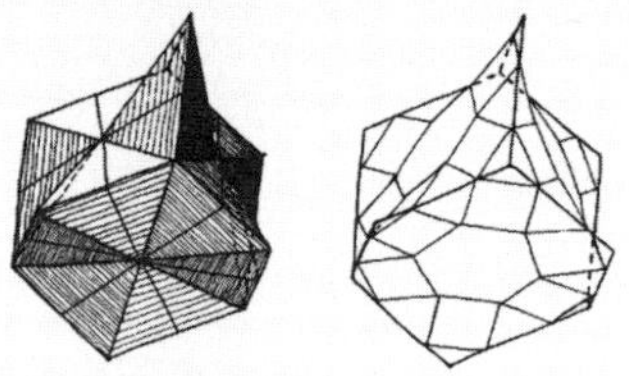

17a 17c

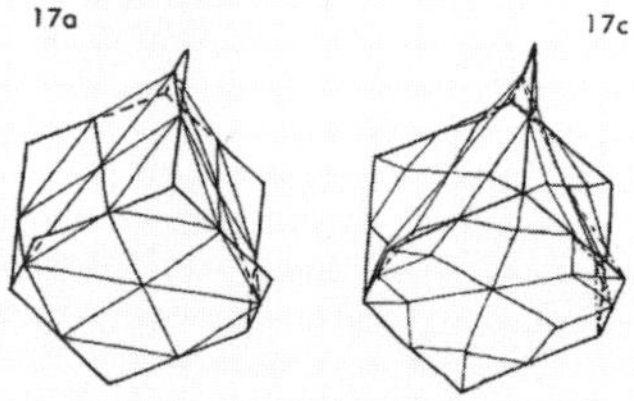

17b 17d

The potographs $H_5$-$H_7$ illustrate self-packing solids with plane surface segments based on the saddle polyhedra $\underset{\sim}{6}{}^3_2$ $\underset{\sim}{6}{}^4_2$ $(\underset{\sim}{4.6})^3_1$ $\underset{\sim}{4}{}^4_2$ according to the segmentation shown in *fig. 16a.*
The relationship between continuous minimal (or polyhyparic) surfaces and the respective configurations with plane surface segments is analogous to the relationship between the sphere with its various geodesic subdivisions and the respective convex polyhedra.

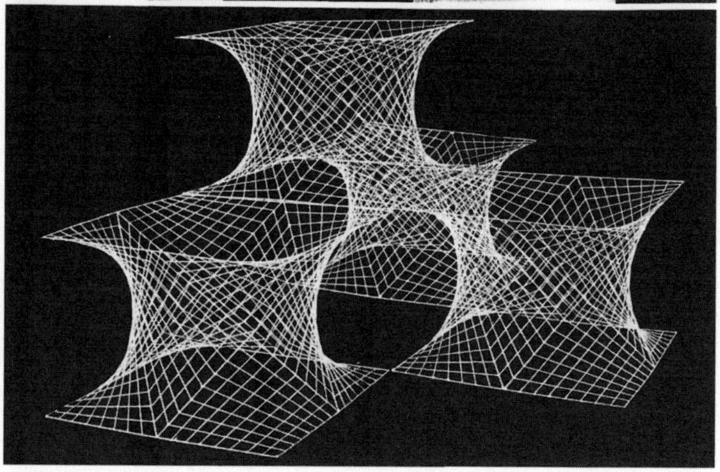

169

## Composite Patterns of Configurational Continuity

Burt distinguished his composite patterns of configurational continuity from what he considered a "static approach" to the structuration of space, one based on "isolated forms." As opposed to the latter, he was convinced that his investigation was able to offer "an inexhaustible source of forms and designs," relevant to architecture as well as to other fields such as art, chemistry, biology, engineering, computer graphics, and mathematics.[43] In a later statement, it became apparent that his position was based upon a resistance to what he viewed as the stagnant formal vocabulary commonly handled by architects:

> The number of forms which had acquired a name or a specific notation through the ages is amounting to infinity, although the number of those which comprise our day-to-day formal vocabulary is extremely (and regretfully) limited, by comparison, even amongst designers and architects, whose profession, by definition, compels them to manipulate and articulate forms and space.[44]

Burt's second important publication was his 1974 *Infinite Polyhedra*, co-authored with Avraham Wachman and architect Menachem Kleinman. John Flinders Petrie and H.S.M. Coxeter described three infinite skew polyhedra that were labeled "regular" because they displayed similar properties to those of convex or planar Platonic ones **(fig. 2.41)**.[45] Building on this, *Infinite Polyhedra* catalogued a large number of sponge polyhedra discovered by Burt, Kleinman, and Wachman which, without showing the same level of regularity as the three precedents, nevertheless possessed comparable symmetry and periodicity. They called them "semi-regular" and divided them into three categories on the basis of their configurational nature: namely, *cylindrical*, when developing vertically along an axis **(fig. 2.42)**; *corrugated* and *mono-layered*, both unfolding two-dimensionally on a plane, the former simply a conveniently creased plane tessellation **(fig. 2.43)**, the latter comprised of two layers of a plane tessellation connected by squares or triangles **(fig. 2.44)**; and *multilayered* and *multidirectional*, both unfolding three-dimensionally, the former featuring a clear division into layers perpendicular to the main symmetry axes **(fig. 2.45)**, the latter without a main direction of

Precedent page:
**2.40** Continuous periodic surfaces dividing space into two identical halves

Following pages:
**2.41** Regular skew polyhedra (p. 160, above).
**2.42** Cylindrical infinite polyhedra (p. 160, below).
**2.43** Corrugated and mono-layered infinite polyhedra (p. 161).

43 Ibid., II.

44 Burt, *The Periodic Table of The Polyhedral Universe*, 8.

45 Their "faces are equal regular planar polygons; exactly two faces meet at every edge, and no faces have a common segment which is not an edge; the vertex figure is a regular polygon, though a skew one; all the vertices are equivalent (brought into each other by a symmetry operation belonging to the polyhedron); all the edges are equivalent; all the faces are equivalent." Michaël Burt, Menachem Kleinmann, and Avraham Wachman, *Infinite Polyhedra*, 2nd ed. (1974; Haifa, Israel: Faculty of Architecture and Town Planning of the Technion, Israel Institute of Technology, 2005), III.

## INFINITE POLYHEDRA

## פוליהדרה אינסופיים

H.S.M. Coxeter described in 1937 three Platonic polyhedra [1] additional to those known till then. The first, denoted $4^6$, consists of squares, six of which meet at every vertex, the second, denoted $6^4$, consists of regular hexagons, four at every vertex, the third, denoted $6^6$, consists of regular hexagons as well, six at every one of its vertices, (see ill.1). Each of these three polyhedra has many properties similar to those of a convex or a planar Platonic polyhedron: the faces are equal regular planar polygons; exactly two faces meet at every edge, and no faces have a common segment which is not an edge; the vertex figure is a regular polygon, though a skew one; all the vertices are equivalent (brought into each other by symmetry operation belonging to the polyhedron); all the edges are equivalent; all the faces are equivalent. The $6^4$ is dual to the $4^6$ in the manner the octahedron is dual to the cube, the $6^6$ is self-dual like the tetrahedron.

בשנת 1937 פרסם ה. ס. מ. קוקסטר מאמר [1] בו הוא תאר שלושה פוליהדרה פלטוניים אינסופיים הנוספים על אלה הידועים עד אז (ראה תמונה 1): האחד (1.a - סימנו $4^6$) בנוי מריבועים, ששישה מהם נפגשים בכל אחד מקודקודיו. השני (1.b - סימנו $6^4$) בנוי ממשושים משוכללים, כך שבכל קודקוד נפגשים ארבעה. השלישי (1.c - סימנו $6^6$) בנוי אף הוא ממשושים משוכללים, ובכל אחד מקודקודיו נפגשים שישה מהם.
לכל אחד משלושת הפוליהדרה האלה מספר תכונות הזהות לאלו של הפוליהדרה הפלטוניים הקמורים או המישוריים. הפאות הן מצולעים מישוריים משוכללים וזהים; בכל אחד מהמקצועות בפוליהדרה אלו נפגשות רק שתי פאות, ואין לפאות קטעים משותפים חוץ מצלעותיהן; תצורת הקודקוד (Vertex Figure) היא מצולע משוכלל, אם כי מרחבי; כל הקודקודים הם אקויולנטיים (כלומר ניתן להביאם לחפיפה ע"י פעולת סימטריה השייכת לפוליהדרון); כל המקצועות אקויולנטיים; כל הפאות אקויולנטיות. ה $6^4$ דואלי ל $4^6$ באותו המובן שהאוקטהדרון דואלי לקוביה, ה $6^6$ דואלי לעצמו באותו המובן שהטטרהדרון דואלי לעצמו.

(1) The three Infinite Platonic Polyhedra.

1.a - $4^6$. Six squares at every vertex (see also p. 67).
1.b - $6^4$. Four regular hexagons at every vertex (see also p. 68).
1.c - $6^6$. Six regular hexagons at every vertex (see also p. 76).

(1) שלושת הפוליהדרה הפלטוניים האינסופיים.

1.a - $4^6$. בכל קודקוד שישה רבועים (ראה גם עמ' 67).
1.b - $6^4$. בכל קודקוד ארבעה משושים משוכללים (ראה גם עמ' 68).
1.c - $6^6$. בכל קודקוד שישה משושים משוכללים (ראה גם עמ' 76).

## INFINITE POLYHEDRA

## פוליהדרה אינסופיים

A. The Cylindrical Infinite Polyhedra .

.A הפוליהדרה הגליליים האינסופיים .

(4) קבוצת הפוליהדרה הגליליים האינסופיים.

4.1 - $4^4$ מרכבים מטבעות פריסמטיות.
4.2 - $3^6$ מרכבים מטבעות אנטיפריסמטיות.
4.3 - $3^3.4^2$ מרכבים מטבעות פריסמטיות ומטבעות אנטיפרסימטיות לסרוגין.
4.4 - $3^6$ מרכבים מרצועות מישוריות של משולשים שוי צלעות.
4.5 - $3^3.4^2$ מרכבים מרצועות מישוריות של רבועים ורצועות מישוריות של משולשים שוי צלעות לסרוגין .
4.6 - $3^6$ מרכבים מרצועות הליקואידליות של משולשים שוי צלעות.

(4) The Cylindrical Infinite Polyhedra.

4.1 - $4^4$. Composed of prismatic rings.
4.2 - $3^6$. Composed of antiprismatic rings.
4.3 - $3^3 \cdot 4^2$. Composed of alternating prismatic and antiprismatic rings.
4.4 - $3^6$. Composed of planar strips of equilateral triangles.
4.5 - $3^3 \cdot 4^2$. Composed of alternating strips of squares and strips of equilateral triangles.
4.6 - $3^6$. Composed of helicoidal strips of equilateral triangles.

symmetry that can be singled out **(fig. 2.46)**. Every multilayered and multidirectional polyhedron divides space into two halves, which only in certain cases are congruent (i.e., exactly alike yet three-dimensionally shifted with respect to one another). *Infinite Polyhedra* includes a brief section on "nets" or "networks,"[46] **(fig. 2.47)** and many of the latter two kinds of polyhedra feature specific nets as part of their graphic description. These are generated by placing a point in each of the nodes constituting the two subspaces to which the polyhedron gives rise, and then connecting them with edges through the tunnels in between. For every semi-regular skew polyhedron there are two dual nets that are only identical (i.e., self-dual) when the subspaces they represent are congruent **(fig. 2.48)**.[47] In addition, every such net of tunnels happens to constitute a close packing of polyhedra, even when the two subspaces are not congruent. A page is devoted to each semi-regular infinite polyhedron, described graphically by way of two photographs of a physical model, a drawing of the vertices of its elementary periodic unit, and a drawing of its net of tunnels.

Following pages:
**2.44** Monolayered infinite polyhedra (p. 162).
**2.45** Multilayered infinite polyhedra (p. 163).
**2.46** Multidirectional infinite polyhedra. (p. 164).
**2.47** Nets (p. 165).

46 A "net" or "network" is a three-dimensional form of tessellation, namely, a set of straight-line segments connected to each other at their ends, its effect being the articulation of a spatial region.

47 *Dual* nets or networks are formed by joining the center of each unit cell in a space-packing array to all neighboring cells with which it shares a common face.

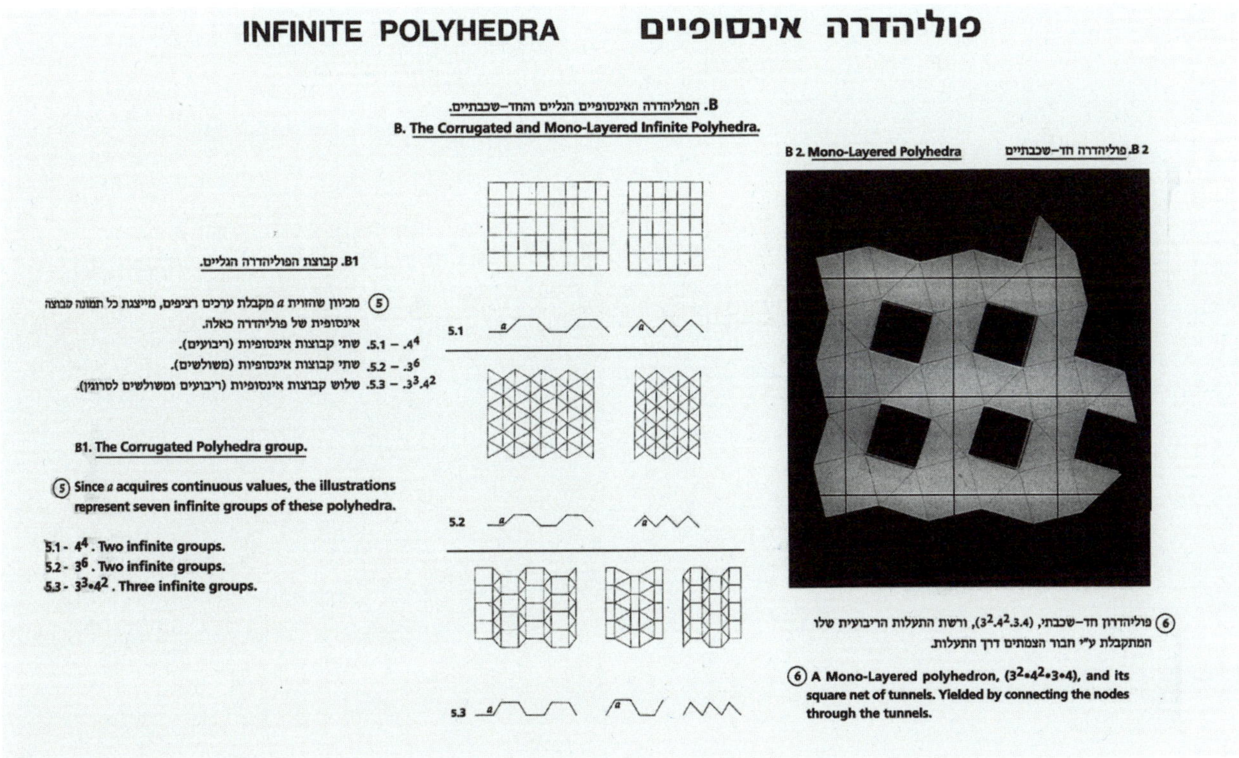

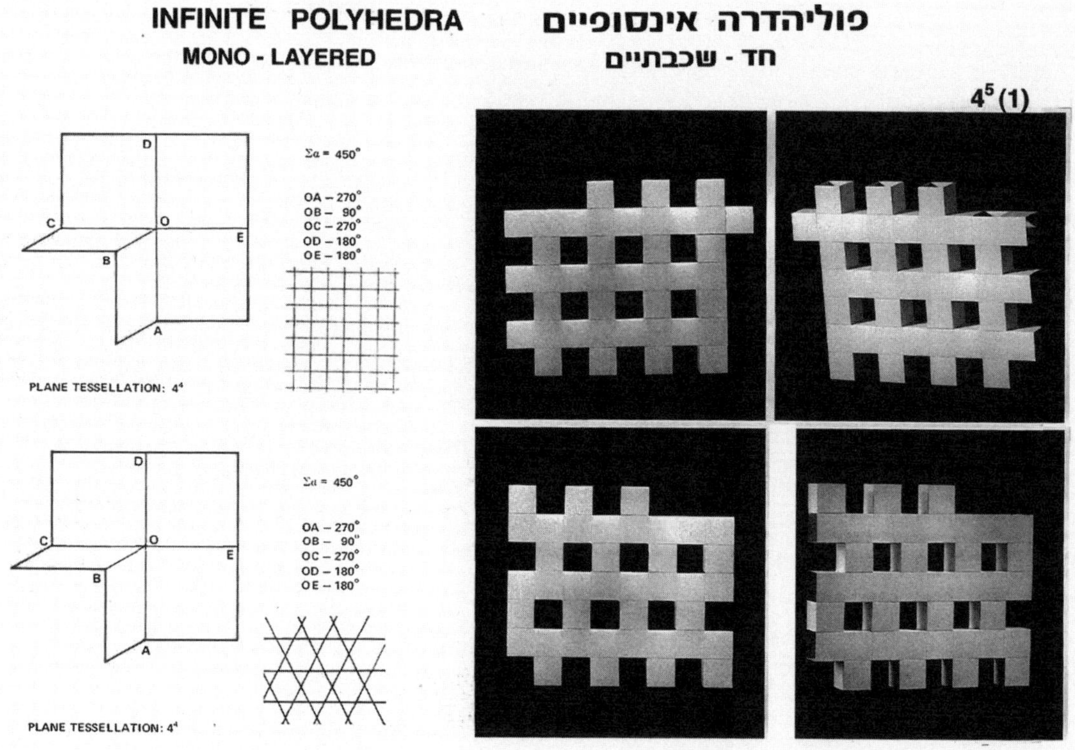
INFINITE POLYHEDRA
MONO - LAYERED
פוליהדרה אינסופיים
חד - שכבתיים
4⁵ (1)
D
C
O
E
B
A
Σa = 450°
OA – 270°
OB – 90°
OC – 270°
OD – 180°
OE – 180°
PLANE TESSELLATION: 4⁴
D
C
O
E
B
A
Σa = 450°
OA – 270°
OB – 90°
OC – 270°
OD – 180°
OE – 180°
PLANE TESSELLATION: 4⁴

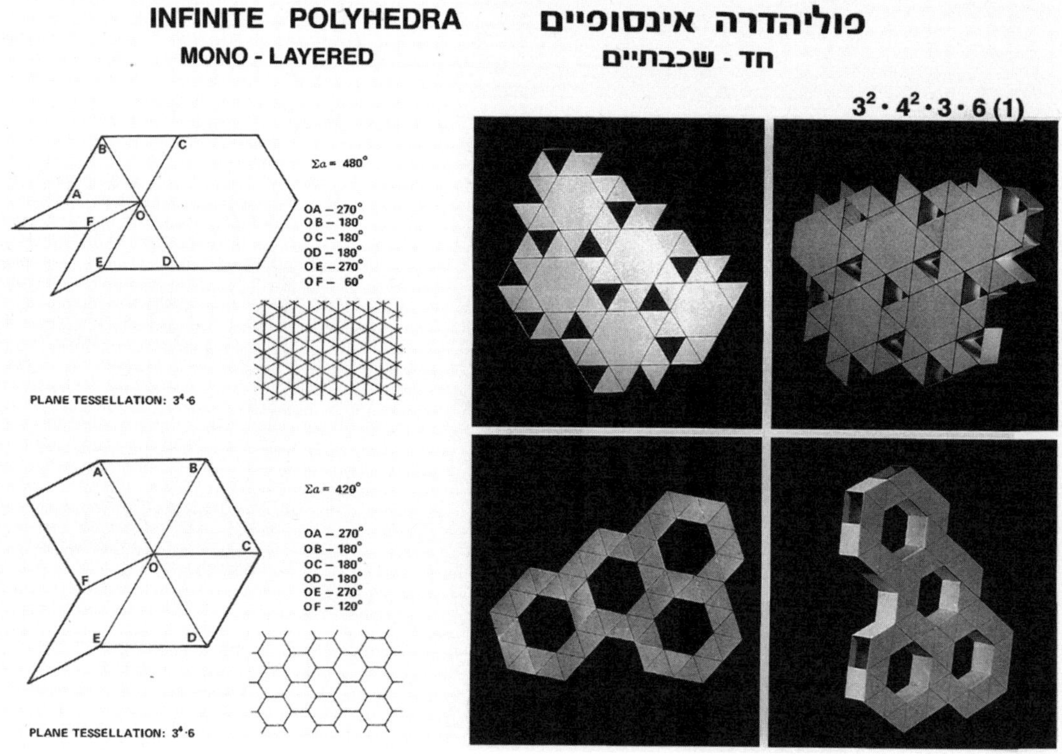
INFINITE POLYHEDRA
MONO - LAYERED
פוליהדרה אינסופיים
חד - שכבתיים
3² · 4² · 3 · 6 (1)
B
C
A
F
O
E
D
Σa = 480°
OA – 270°
OB – 180°
OC – 180°
OD – 180°
OE – 270°
OF – 60°
PLANE TESSELLATION: 3⁴·6
A
B
C
O
F
E
D
Σa = 420°
OA – 270°
OB – 180°
OC – 180°
OD – 180°
OE – 270°
OF – 120°
PLANE TESSELLATION: 3⁴·6

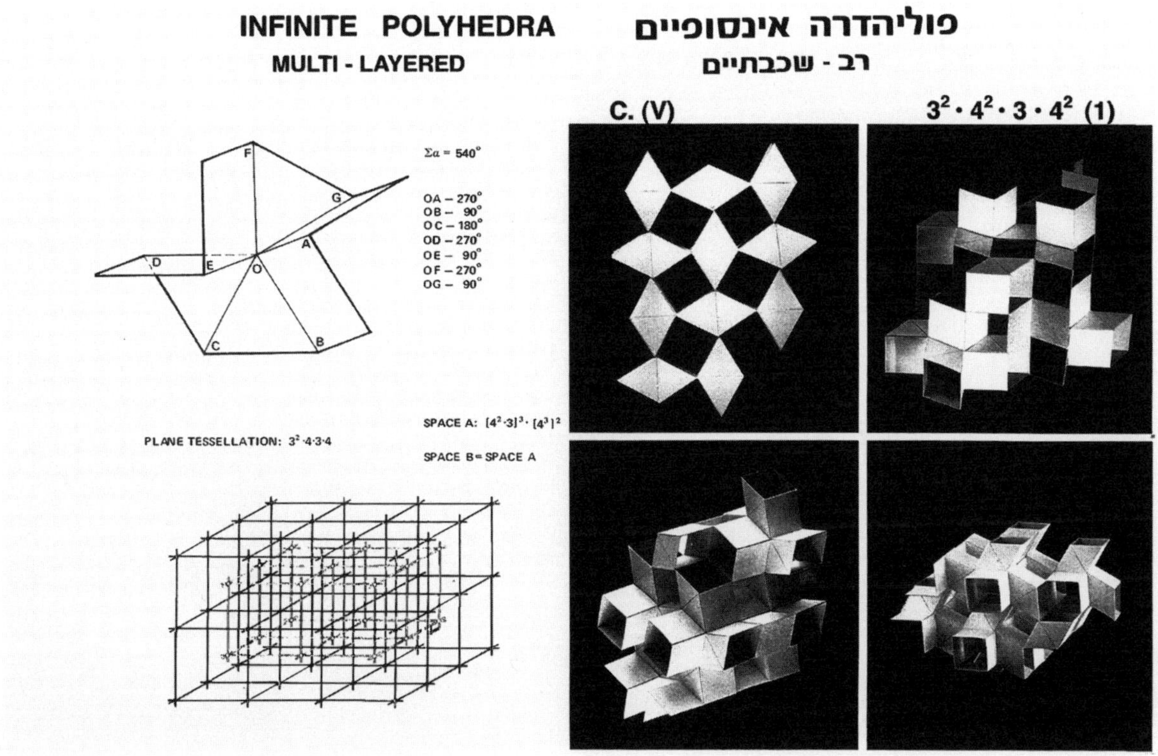
INFINITE POLYHEDRA
MULTI - LAYERED
פוליהדרה אינסופיים
רב - שכבתיים
C. (V)
3² · 4² · 3 · 4² (1)
Σα = 540°
OA – 270°
OB – 90°
OC – 180°
OD – 270°
OE – 90°
OF – 270°
OG – 90°
PLANE TESSELLATION: 3²·4·3·4
SPACE A: [4²·3]³ · [4³]²
SPACE B = SPACE A

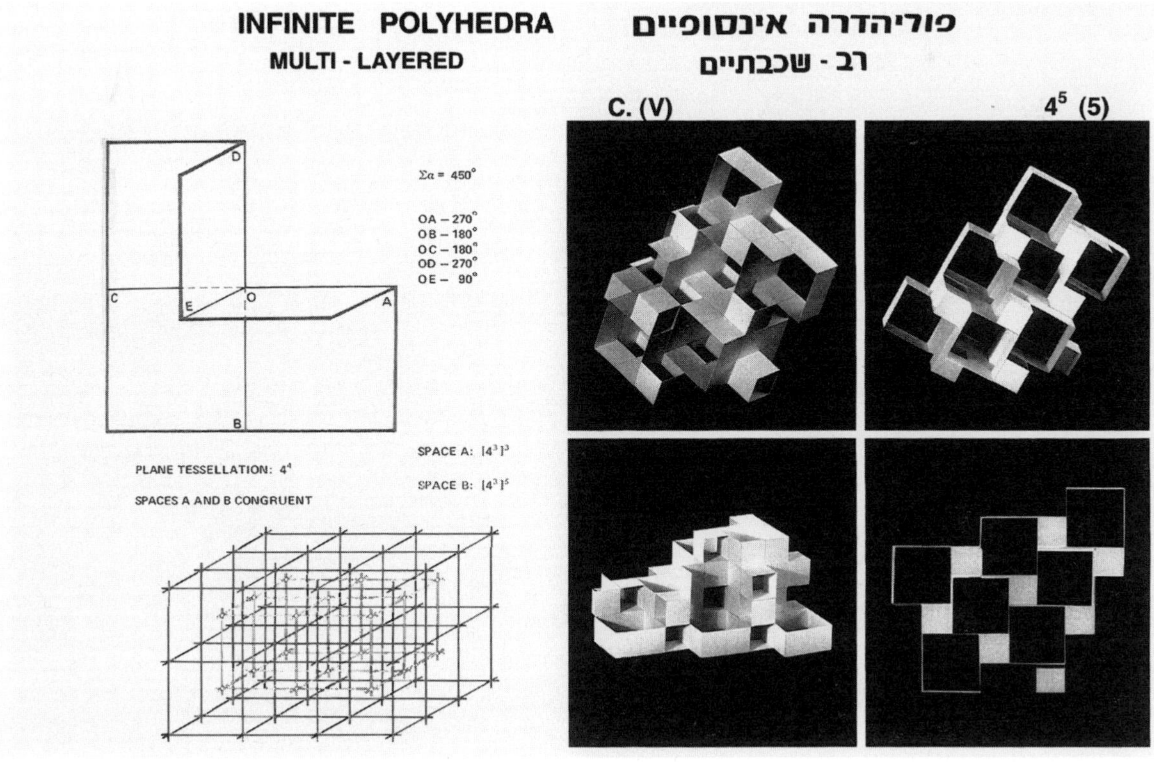
INFINITE POLYHEDRA
MULTI - LAYERED
פוליהדרה אינסופיים
רב - שכבתיים
C. (V)
4⁵ (5)
Σα = 450°
OA – 270°
OB – 180°
OC – 180°
OD – 270°
OE – 90°
SPACE A: [4³]³
SPACE B: [4³]⁵
PLANE TESSELLATION: 4⁴
SPACES A AND B CONGRUENT

## INFINITE POLYHEDRA — פוליהדרה אינסופיים

**MULTI - DIRECTIONAL — רב - כיווניים**

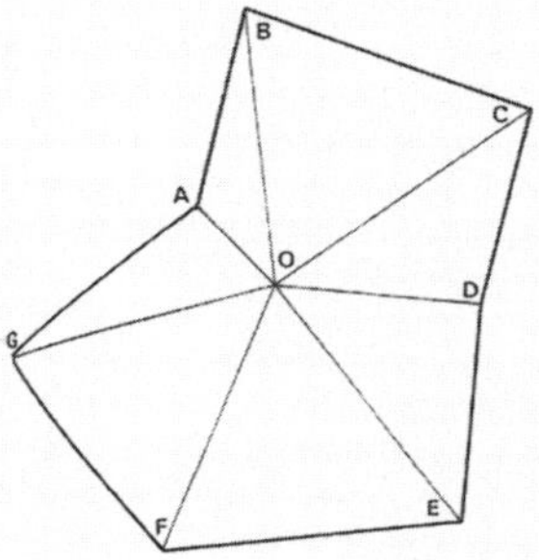


$\Sigma a = 420°$

OA – 247°39′
OB – 109°28′
OC – 109°28′
OD – 247°39′
OE – 138°11′
OF – 138°11′
OG – 138°11′

SPACE A: $[3^4] \cdot [3^5]$

SPACE B: AMORPHOUS

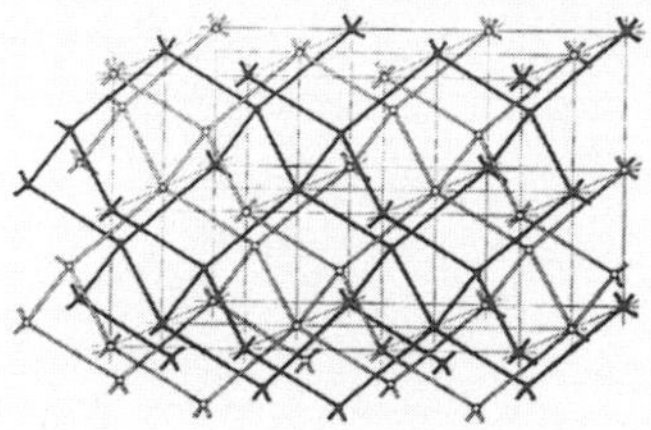

**D.** **$3^7$**

## INFINITE POLYHEDRA — פוליהדרה אינסופיים

**MULTI - DIRECTIONAL — רב - כיווניים**

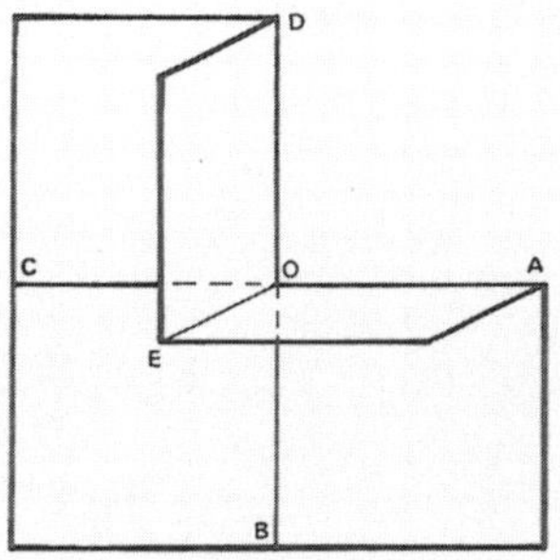


$\Sigma a = 450°$

OA – 270°
OB – 180°
OC – 180°
OD – 270°
OE – 90°

PLANE TESSELLATION: $4^4$

SPACE A: $[4^3]^3$

SPACE B: $[4^3]^5$

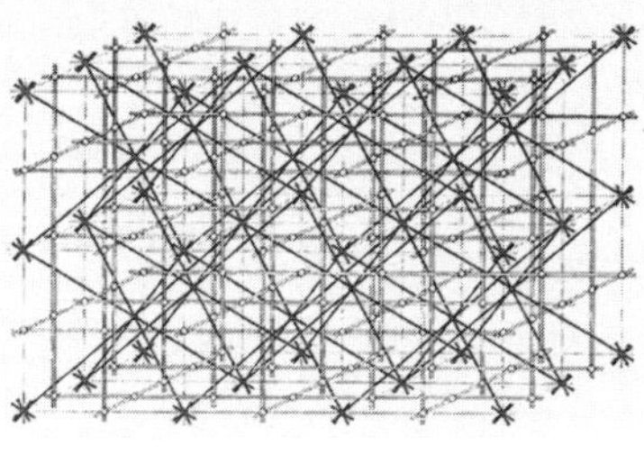

**C. C.** **$4^5(10)$**

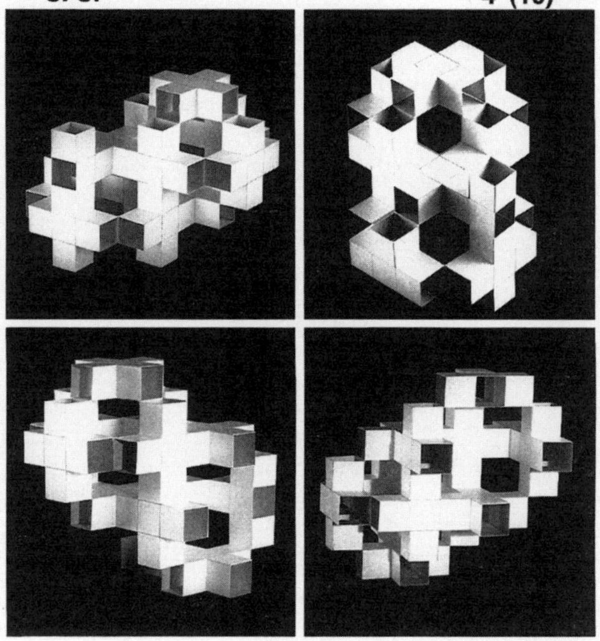

## INFINITE POLYHEDRA פוליהדרה אינסופיים

(13) שתי רשתות "גרפיט" דואליות (.G).
הקודקודים של רשת ה"גרפיט" מתייחסים זה לזה כמו אטומי הפחמן בגרפיט. בכל קודקוד של הרשת ארבעה מקצועות: שלושה במישור אחד, כשהזוית בין כל שניים °120, והרביעי ניצב להם. יחס האורכים של שני סוגי המקצועות אינו משפיע על הסימטריה של הרשת. הפאות הנוצרות הן משושים, חלקם מישוריים וחלקם מרחביים, הפוליהדרה – טטרהדרה, שכל אחד מהם מרכב ממשושה מישורי ושלושה משושים מרחביים. רשת ה"גרפיט" איזומורפית לרשת ה"יהלום". אחת מתקבלת מהשניה ע"י שינוי הזוויות בין המקצועות.

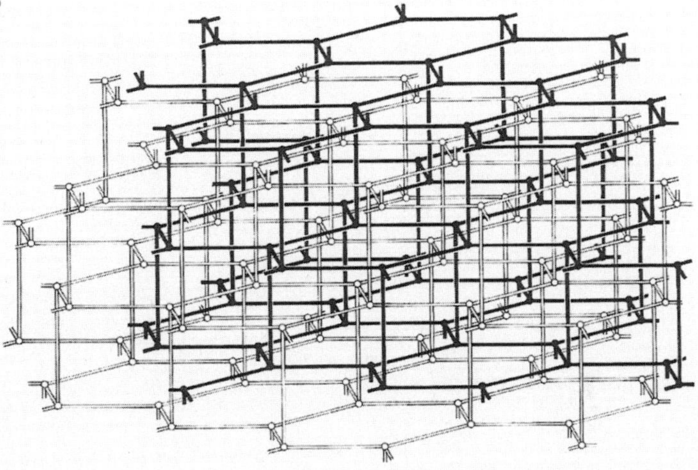

(13) Two dual "graphite" nets (G.).
The relative position of a "graphite" net's vertices is like that of carbon atoms in graphite. There are four edges meeting at every vertex of the net: three coplanar, every pair subtending an angle of 120°, and the fourth perpendicular to their plane.
The ratio of the lengths of the two kinds of edges has no bearing upon the net's symmetry. The resultant faces are hexagons, planar and skew, the "graphite" net is isomorphic to the "diamond" net. They are transformed into each other by changing the angles between their edges.

XIX

## INFINITE POLYHEDRA פוליהדרה אינסופיים

(9) שתי רשתות קוביות דואליות (.C).
הרשת הקובית היא הרשת הנוצרת ע"י מקצועות הקוביות באריזה קומפקטית. הרשת הדואלית לרשת קובית אף היא קובית. כל קודקוד של רשת אחת נמצא במרכז קוביה של הרשת השניה. ששת המקצועות היוצאים מקודקוד דוקרים את שש הפאות של הקוביה העוטפת אותו. כל פאה ברשת אחת היא ריבוע והיא נדקרת ע"י מקצוע של הרשת השנייה, אשר סביבו ערוכות ארבע קוביות. כל פוליהדרון של רשת אחת הוא קוביה, ושמונת הקודקודים שלו נמצאים במרכזי שמונה הקוביות הערוכות סביב קודקוד אחד של הרשת השניה. מכאן אפשר להבין כי הרשת דואלית לעצמה (אפשר לומר: לרשת הזהה לה), כאשר: א). מספר המקצועות בקודקוד שוה למספר הפאות של הפוליהדרון הנוצר ע"י הרשת. ב). מספר המקצועות בפאה שוה למספר הפוליהדרה הערוכים סביב מקצוע. ג). מספר הקודקודים בפוליהדרון שווה למספר הפוליהדרה הערוכים סביב קודקוד. ד) מספר מקצועות בפוליהדרון שווה למספר הפאות הנפגשות בקודקוד. דבר זה נכון גם במקרים שיש ברשת יותר מסוג אחד שלקודקוד..

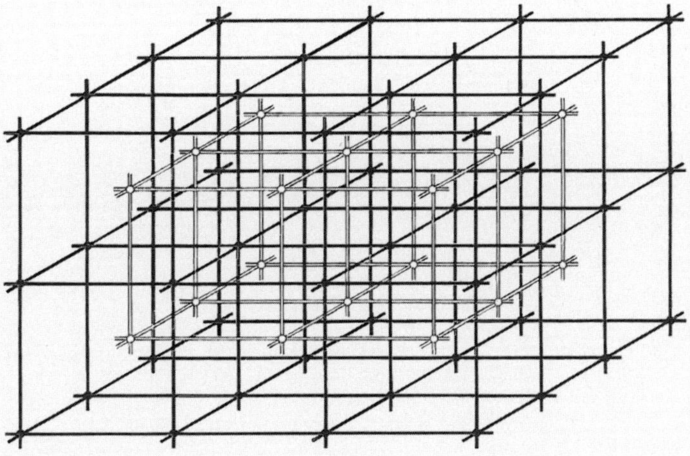

(9) Two dual Cubic nets (C .).
The cubic net is created by the close packing of cubes. The dual to the cubic net is a cubic net as well. Every vertex of one net lies in the center of cube of the other net. The six edges originating at the vertex pass through the centers of the faces of the enveloping cube. Every face of one net is a square and it is transfixed by one of the other net's edges in which four cubes meet. Every polyhedron of one net is a cube, and its eight vertices lie in the centers of the eight cubes which meet in the other net's vertex.
It follows that a net is self-dual (or dual to an identical net) if: A. the number of the edges meeting at a vertex is equal to the number of the faces of the polyhedron created by the net; B. the number of the edges of a face is equal to the number of the polyhedra meeting at an edge; C. the number of the vertices of a polyhedron is equal to the number of the polyhedra meeting at a vertex; D. the number of the edges of a polyhedron is equal to the number of the faces meeting at a vertex. This is true of nets with more than one kind of vertices as well.

XV

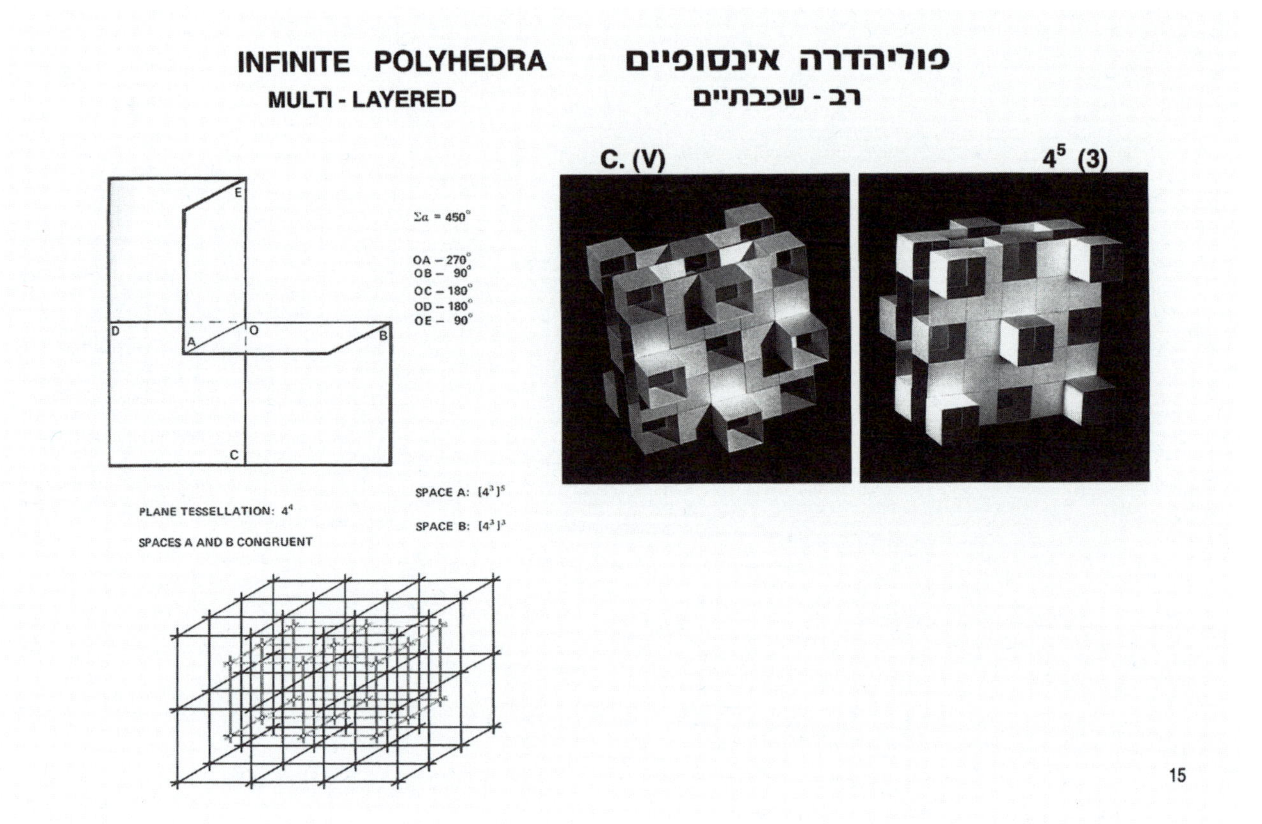


**2.48** Congruent nets in multi-layered polyhedra.

## Mapping the Polyhedral Universe

*The Periodic Table of the Polyhedral Universe* of 1996, a project Burt started to work on during his time at Carbondale, was his third main published contribution. Here he attempted to construct a theoretical umbrella for the entire polyhedral domain in three-dimensional space—that is, a general framework accounting for all theoretically possible polyhedra (whether defined to this day or not) conforming with Euler's theorem: Vertices - Edges + Faces = 2(1-Genus). Modeled on Mendeleev's 1869 *Periodic Table of the Elements*, Burt aimed to provide insight into the extent of the polyhedral universe and a path for its comprehensive exploration. He held that Euler's formula captured like any other the mathematical-topological essence of polyhedral structures; hence his table, he suggested, may be seen as a metastructure of that law, a visual animation displaying both its apparent and hidden meanings. The table is assembled on the basis of three primary parameters: namely, *valency* (which, borrowed from Mendeleev, indicates the number of edges connected to a vertex, being thus an index for density); *sum of angles* in a vertex (taken from Descartes' *Theorem of Angular Deficiency*; it determines curvature) or—when the faces are nonplanar—the total surface curvature of a vertex region; and *genus* (defined in terms of the Euler characteristic, one of the chief topological invariants), with the former two expressed in average terms for all the vertices involved **(fig. 2.49–50)**.[48]

48 *Genus*, a central topological concept indexing connectivity, designates the maximum number of closed curves that can be drawn on an orientable (i.e., with consistent normal vector at every point), connected surface without splitting it into two disconnected parts. Its value is visually identifiable by the number of "handles" on the surface, being "0" for spherical surfaces, "1" for toroidal ones, and "2" or greater for those of a hyperbolical nature. These *phenotypes*–to which Burt added, without reference to genus, a fourth one called "primitive" for surfaces of a cyclic, stripe-like, columnar, or helicoidal nature–allude to families of topologically equivalent surfaces; in other words, they designate all surfaces or, more generally, "two-dimensional manifolds" that can be transformed into that giving a name to the family via a continuous sequence not involving cuts or holes in them. For example, a cube can be turned into a sphere through such a process, and therefore it belongs to the group of spherical surfaces, its genus being "0." Topologically equivalent two-dimensional manifolds are also called *homeomorphic*.

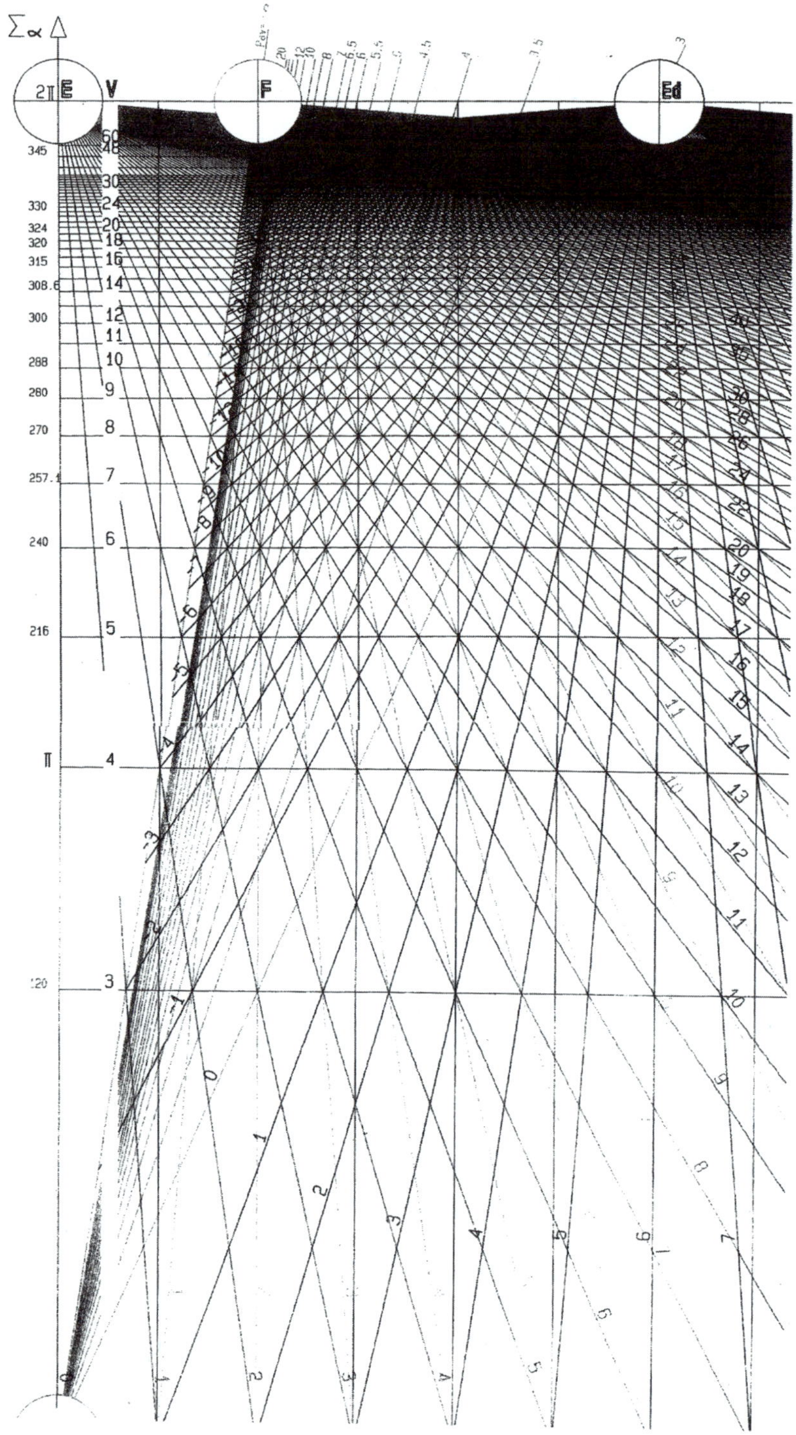


**2.49** Periodic table of the polyhedral universe for the genus = 0 domain.

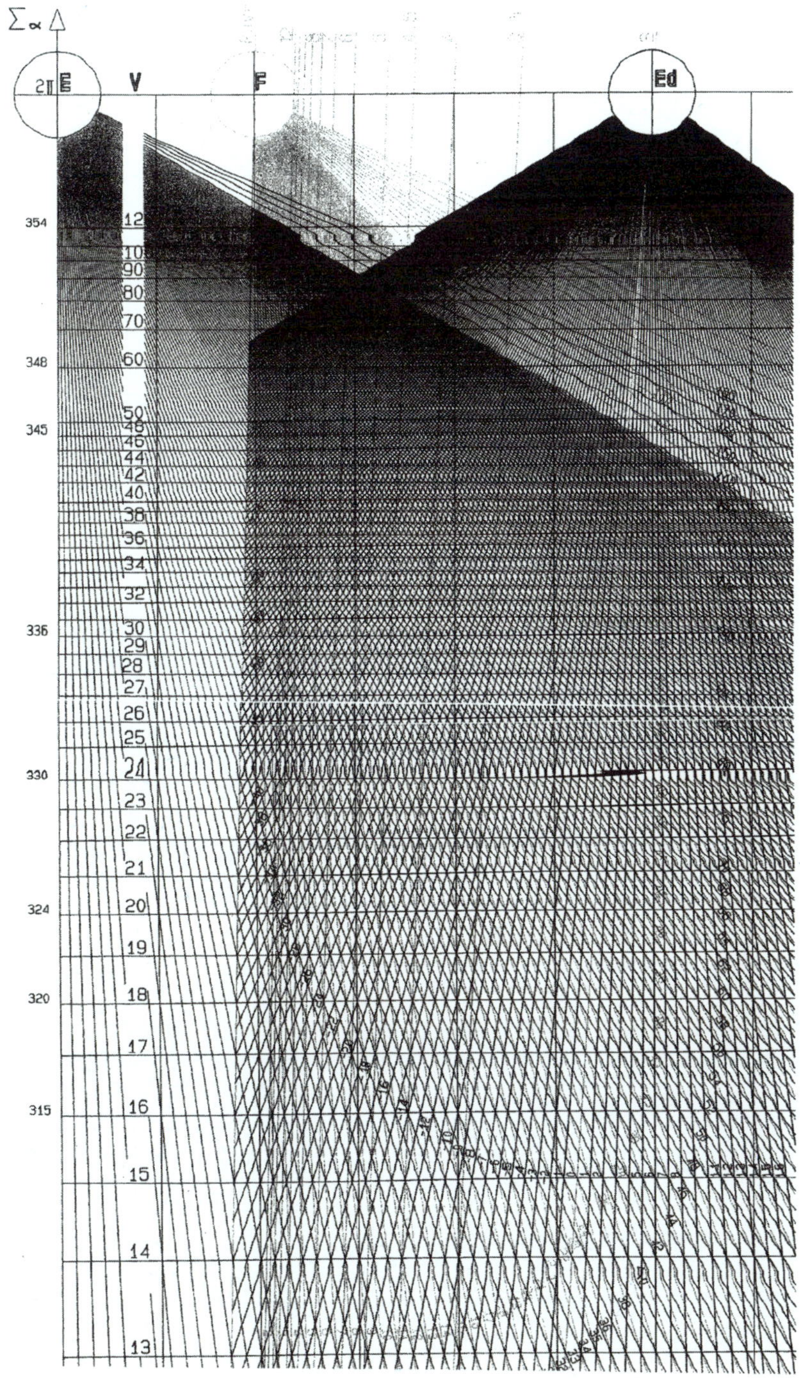


**2.50** Periodic table of the polyhedral universe. Range of Σα = 300° - 360°, within the genus = 0 domain.

**2.51** Limiting boundaries of polyhedral families within the table.

**2.52** Location pattern of polyhedral mechanisms.

Periodic table of the polyhedral universe - principal limiting boundaries: V=2; F=2 and $\Sigma\alpha=2\pi$.

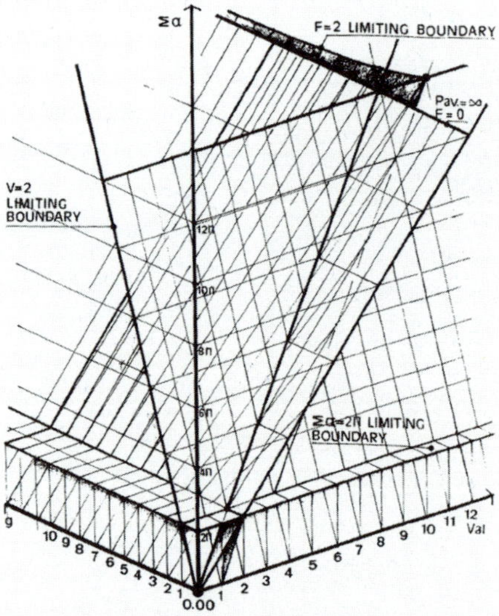


Location pattern of proper polyhedral mechanisms within the g-0 domain and isotops sharing V=6.

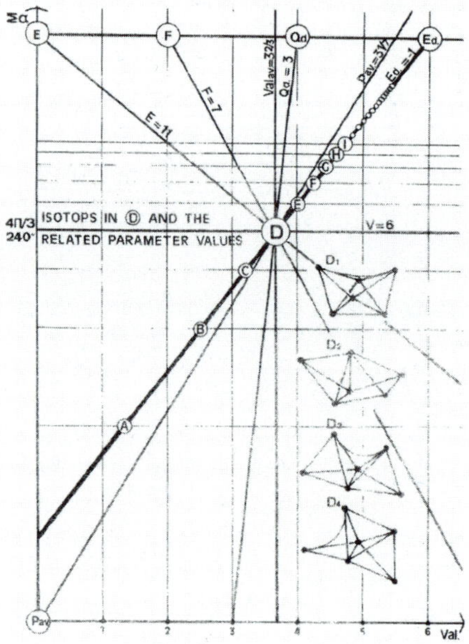

Burt emphasized the importance of adding genus to the traditional notation of polyhedra (otherwise defined by valency and sum of angles alone) so as to be able to account for the topological properties of the various polyhedral families. The three parameters constitute the coordinates of the Cartesian space of the table, wherein every three-dimensional polyhedron has a unique point representation. A significant effect of the table, Burt noted, is the bridging over the three main distinct topological domains—spherical, convex polyhedra (genus equal to zero), toroidal ones (genus equal to one), and hyperbolical, sponge ones, both finite and infinite (genus equal to or greater than two)—by way of offering a unifying perspective. The book also provides a comprehensive analysis of the limiting boundaries of the different polyhedral families within the table **(fig. 2.51)**, location patterns for these **(fig. 2.52)**, a notation for nonuniform polyhedral **(fig. 2.53)**, and a description of a particular family that Burt suggested calling "floral polyhedra" **(fig. 2.54)**, as well as other mathematical specifications such as the curvature of the polyhedral manifolds represented in the table. Noteworthy is his effort to signal the relations between the geometrical-topological properties of polyhedra and their engineering properties, with a chapter and two graphs devoted to the differences between polyhedral structures that may be non-stable, stable, or hyper-stable when rendered trusses or plate space frames **(fig. 2.55)**.[49]

In fact, Burt intended his table to be a research tool for designers dealing with structures of or akin to a polyhedral nature, one capable of aiding in their conception, analysis, and classification. This aim was rooted in the definition he had earlier provided of structural morphology—namely, the study of the structural performance of spatial configurations, and more precisely, the investigation of *the relationship between the structure of space and space structures*. Burt's theoretical explorations were based on the understanding that the key factor in structural performance is not the kind of construction material employed or its quantity, but rather the way in which it is distributed in space. He researched the latter through his geometric models and found several applications for them as space structures, several of which he patented in Germany, Israel, and the US. Thus, during the 1970s and 80s, he evolved a system for multilayer, bar-and-joint plate structures based on infinite polyhedral lattices **(fig. 2.56–60)** and was a chief researcher at two short-lived companies—Morphorit (1977–81) and Binot (1982–87)—involved in the development of lightweight structures (tensile membranes and shells) **(fig. 2.61–62)**. It was through these companies that Burt, along with his collaborators Eli Kent and Ami Glazman, erected a number of roof structures in Israel featuring modular, hyperbolic-saddle shape units for facilities of various kinds, such as swimming pools, malls, and university buildings **(fig. 2.63–64)**.

49 "It is the interaction of topological entities (number of vertices-joints, edges-bar elements), the Euler characteristic of the manifold and the associated curvature, which determine the level of structural performance; its stability, rigidity, stiffness, in relation to the amount of invested material and, in short, its resistance to deformation." Burt, *The Periodic Table of The Polyhedral Universe*, 72.

The extended notatio system of non-uniforr polyhedra applied to floral polyhedra.

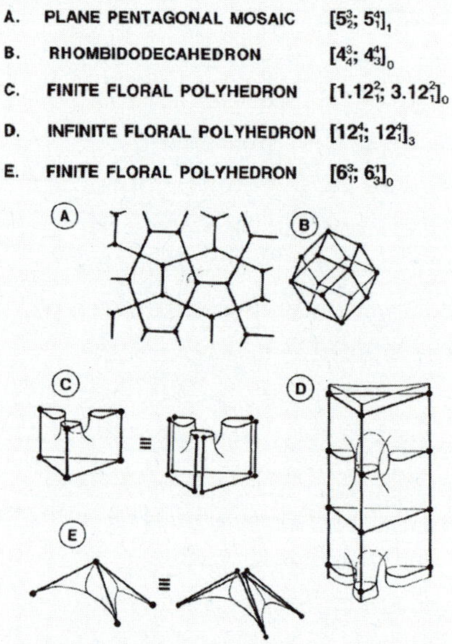


Floral polyhedra, families within the g=0 domain Aaranged according to their dual pairs.

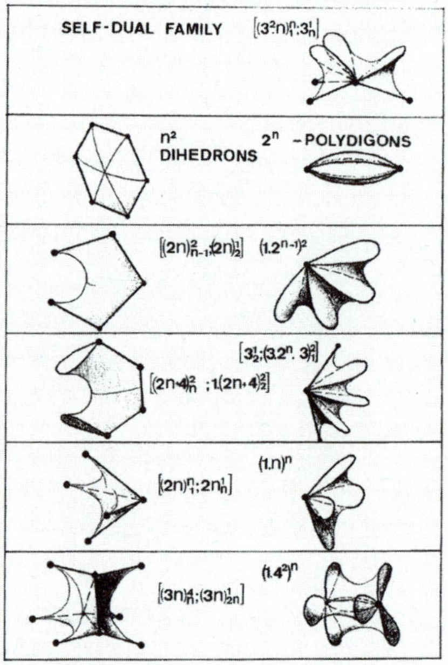


The grand divides of the polyhedral universe between labile and hyper-stable polyhedra.

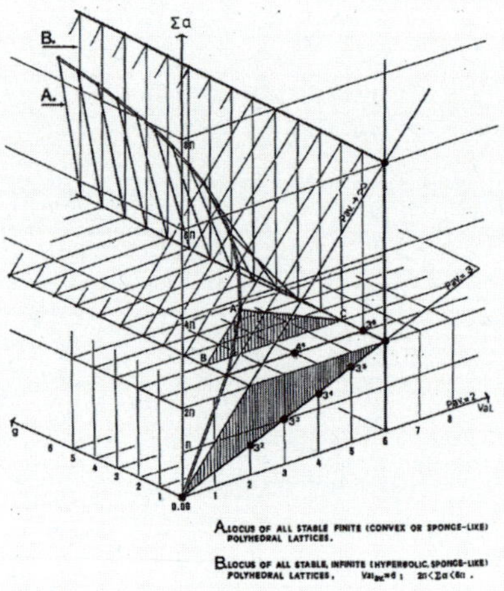


**2.53** Above, left: Notation for non-uniform polyhedra.
**2.54** Above, right: Floral polyhedra.
**2.55** Left: Stability of polyhedra when turned into trusses or plate space frames.

Opposite page:
**2.56–59** Patent for a system of multi-layer, bar-and-joint plate structures based on infinite polyhedral lattices (1986).

# I. P. L. – Plate Space Frames

by Dr. Michael Burt

A Presentation by R. J. Wimmer, Marketing Plus
127, Yigal Alon Road Tel-Aviv 67433 Israel Tel. 03-256252

Table of Contents



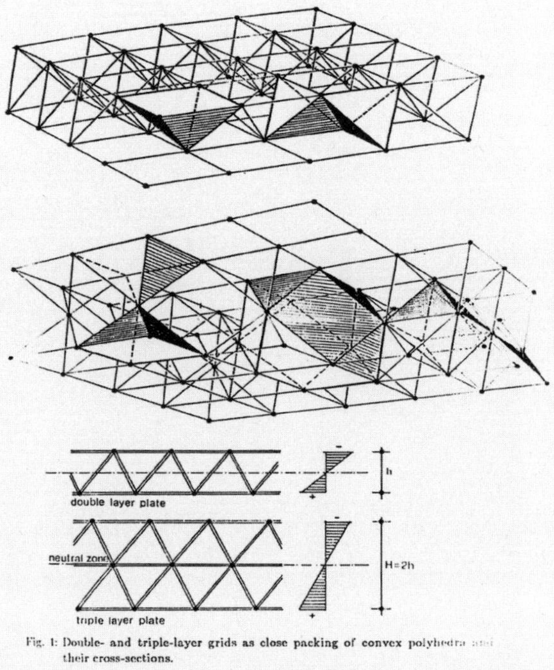


Fig. 1: Double- and triple-layer grids as close packing of convex polyhedra and their cross-sections.

-10-

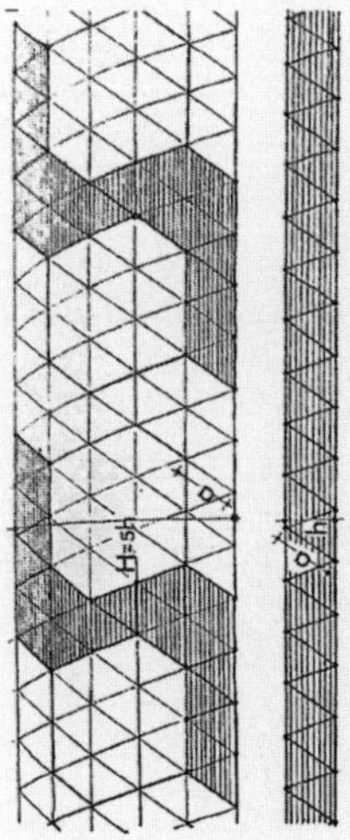


Fig. 7: A comparative cross-section of a T-334.3.4$_3$ I.P.L.–Plate and an octatruss.

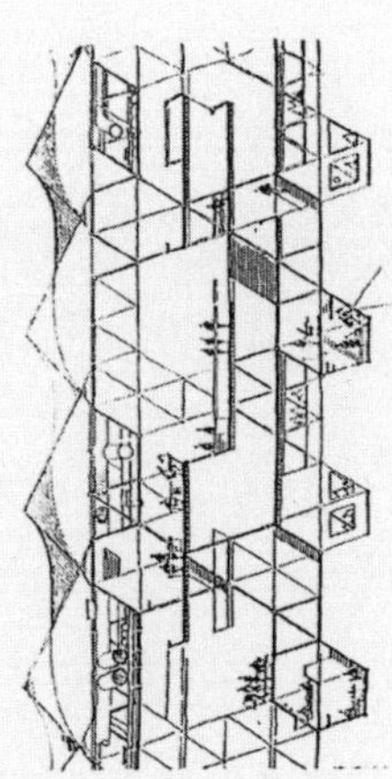

Fig. 8: Utilization of the inner space of the I.P.L.–Plate and the cladding solution by fabric membranes or lightweight, thin shell structures; a cross-section.

-21-

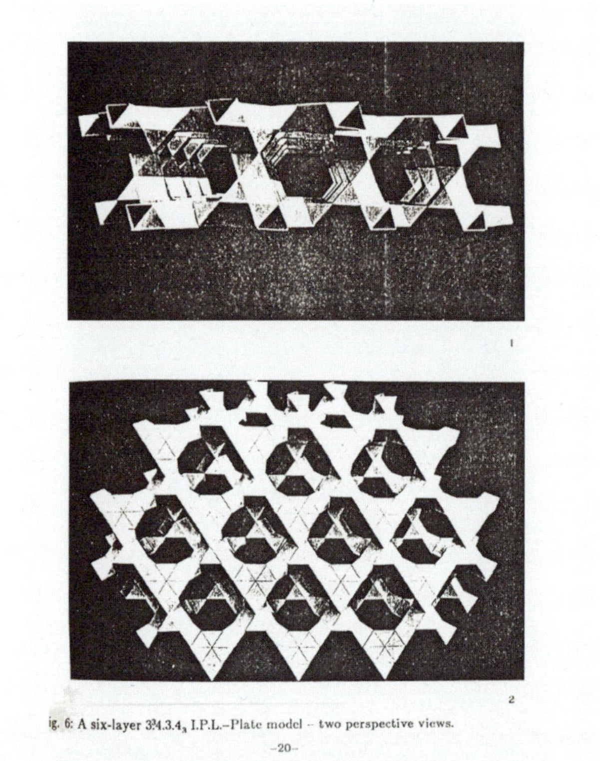


**2.60** Left: Patent for a system of multi-layer, bar-and-joint plate structures based on infinite polyhedral lattices (1986).

**2.61** Below, left: Light-weight structures built while a member of Morphorit (1977–81).

**2.62** Below: Light-weight structures built while a member of Binot (1982–87).

**2.63–64** Michaël Burt. Tensile membrane roof structure at Karmiel shopping mall (1987).

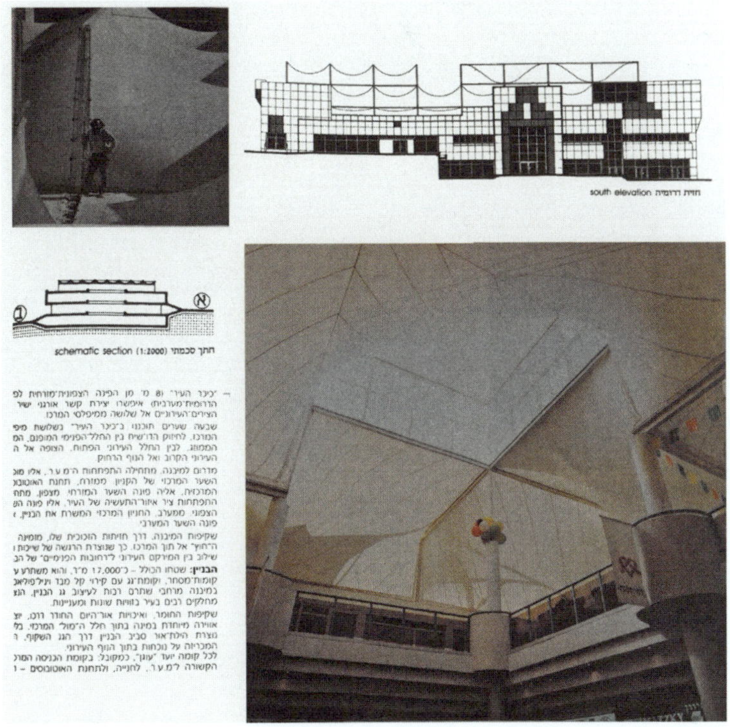

2.65 David Yitzhaki with Michaël Burt. Bridge structures in Israel, 1970s.

His engineering inclinations, however, had already found expression several years previously. In the summer of 1963, after graduating with his bachelor's degree, Burt was recruited by David Yitzhaki—then dean of structural engineering at the Technion, and subsequently the representative from that department on the second committee evaluating Burt's master's thesis—to participate in an international competition for the Bar-Yehuda bridge in Tel Aviv. With Burt's assistance, Yitzhaki won first prize, an accomplishment that triggered a period of twenty-one years during which the former was involved in a total of fifteen bridge projects, either as designer or consultant **(fig. 2.65)**.

## The Quintuplet Assembly

In a chart Burt drew a few years later, he tried to show that with *Infinite Polyhedra* and *The Periodic Table* he had progressively and substantially expanded the domain of polyhedra first initiated by the ancients (Plato, Euclid, Archimedes, etc.) and then crucially advanced by the mathematicians and chemists who started to think about the hyperbolic tessellations engendered by polyhedral sponges (Coxeter, Petrie, A.F. Wells, etc.) **(fig. 2.66)**.[50] More relevant here, however, is what had been emerging as the core of Burt's theory across his three publications, which he only began to formulate retrospectively around the turn of the century. Namely, seeking to define "the structure of space and the level of its order" by addressing the topology and ordering principles of the sponge spatial imaginary, he concluded that the essence of three-dimensional space was comprised of five constituents—that is, a pair of dual networks, two associated modes of polyhedral close packing, and a hyperbolical sponge surface. Burt referred to these as *3D Space Quintuplet Phenomena* or *the quintuplet assembly*, and characterized them as follows. Firstly, every three-dimensional network, whether periodic or not, comes with its dual, both determining each other uniquely. Secondly, every three-dimensional network gives rise to a close packing of polyhedral volumetric solids, and therefore every pair of dual networks yields two modes of polyhedral close-packing solutions (the shortest closed circuits of edges in a given network describe polygons, which in turn may be construed as faces of polyhedral solids; aggregation of these constitutes a compact packing that matches the original network). Lastly, every pair of dual networks is uniquely associated with an unbounded sponge surface unfolding in between the two, which features characteristic labyrinthine qualities of porosity and permeability, subdivides space into two subspaces or "tunnel systems" (one whose axes are, logically, the two interwoven dual space networks or *tunnel space lattices*), and is continuous throughout (it would only be perforated when transferring from one network to its dual) **(fig. 2.67)**. Four of the *quintuplet* components can be derived from the fifth, just as the repeating unit cell—which may be an *elementary periodic*

50 This achievement had partly been endorsed by Coxeter himself even before the publication of *The Periodic Table*, by acknowledging that Burt's *Infinite Polyhedra* had contributed a greater number of such polyhedra than A.F. Wells and another important figure in the domain of geometry, Italian physician and entomologist Alfredo Andreini. H.S.M Coxeter, "Three-Dimensional Nets and Polyhedra by A.F. Wells [book Review]," *Bulletin of the American Mathematical Society* 84, no. 3 (May 1978), 469.

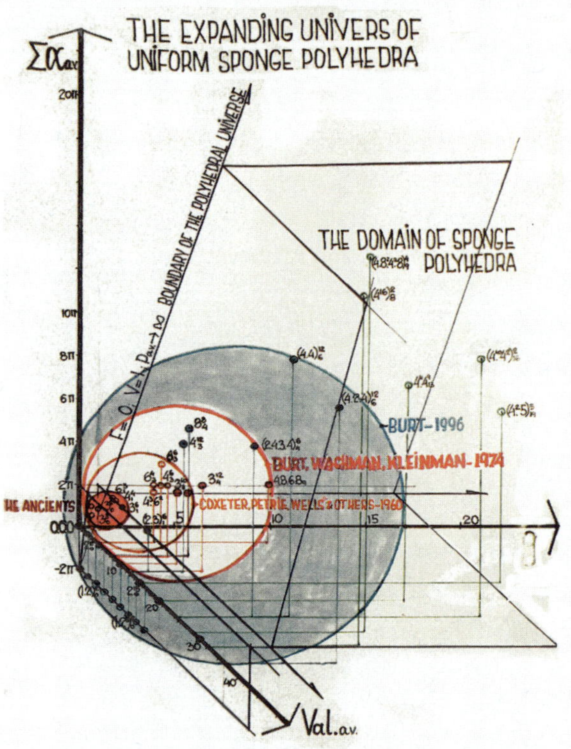
THE EXPANDING UNIVERS OF
UNIFORM SPONGE POLYHEDRA
BOUNDARY OF THE POLYHEDRAL UNIVERSE
THE DOMAIN OF SPONGE
POLYHEDRA
BURT-1996
BURT, WACHMAN, KLEINMAN-1974
COXETER, PETRIE, WELLS & OTHERS-1960
HE ANCIENTS
Val.av.

THE 'OCTET' QUINTET AND THE
ASSOCIATED DUAL NETWORK, THE SPONGE PARTITION AND PACKING SOLIDS.

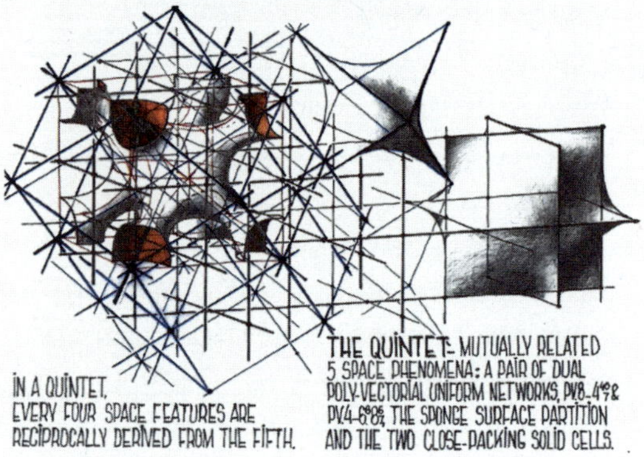
IN A QUINTET,
EVERY FOUR SPACE FEATURES ARE
RECIPROCALLY DERIVED FROM THE FIFTH.
THE QUINTET- MUTUALLY RELATED
5 SPACE PHENOMENA: A PAIR OF DUAL
POLY-VECTORIAL UNIFORM NETWORKS,
THE SPONGE SURFACE PARTITION
AND THE TWO CLOSE-PACKING SOLID CELLS.

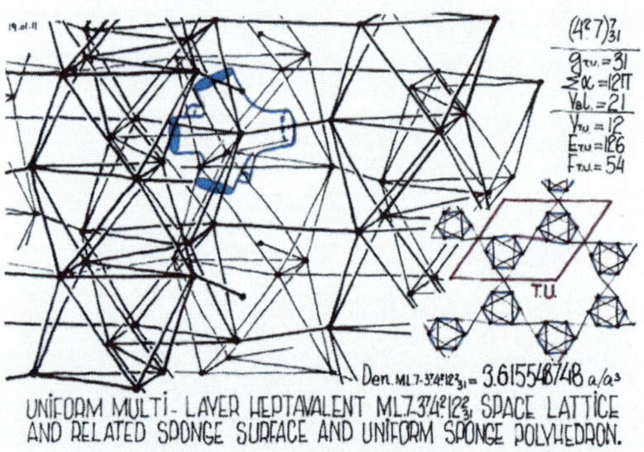
Val.=21
T.U.
Den. = 3.61555748 a/a³
UNIFORM MULTI- LAYER HEPTAVALENT SPACE LATTICE
AND RELATED SPONGE SURFACE AND UNIFORM SPONGE POLYHEDRON.

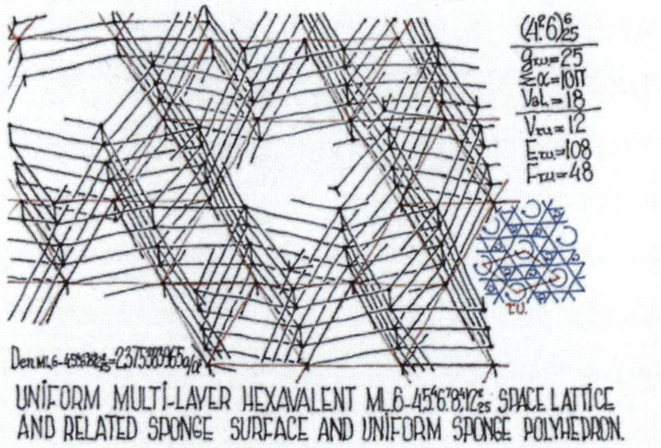
Val.=18
T.U.
UNIFORM MULTI-LAYER HEXAVALENT SPACE LATTICE
AND RELATED SPONGE SURFACE AND UNIFORM SPONGE POLYHEDRON.

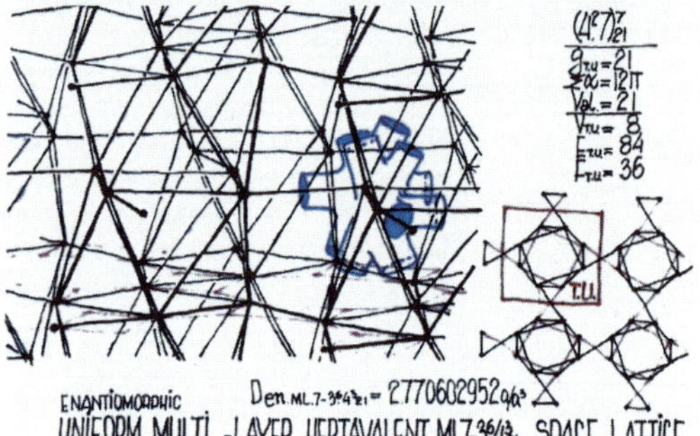
Val.=21
T.U.
ENANTIOMORPHIC
Den. = 2.770602952 a/a³
UNIFORM MULTI -LAYER HEPTAVALENT SPACE LATTICE
AND RELATED SPONGE SURFACE AND UNIFORM SPONGE POLYHEDRON.

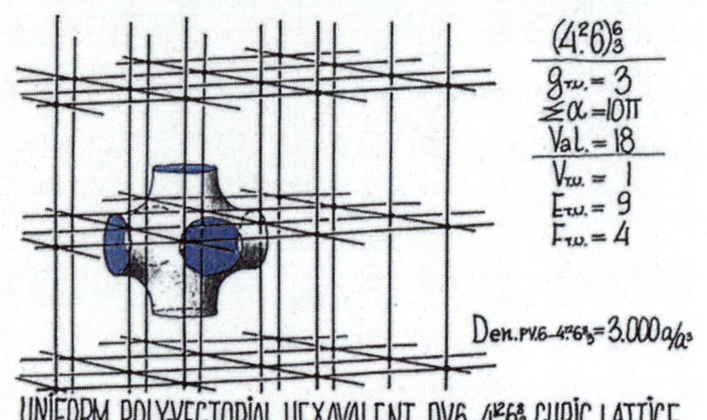
Val.=18
Den. = 3.000 a/a³
UNIFORM POLY-VECTORIAL HEXAVALENT CUBIC LATTICE
AND RELATED SPONGE SURFACE AND UNIFORM SPONGE POLYHEDRON.

*region* (if giving rise to the network by consecutive duplication and aggregation) or a *translation unit* (if generating it by sliding along the length of one of its edges)—encapsulates in itself the features of the entire configuration.[51] Other than by means of the two dual networks approach, Burt also generated sponge surfaces—those termed *double-layer*—through the so-called "genetic surface" method. Namely, a continuous, unbounded base (genetic) surface, whether spherical, toroidal, or hyperbolical, can be duplicated to produce a parallel one. The two resulting layers can then be perforated and connected in such a way that the double skin becomes a continuous, unpunctured surface. When performed across several genetic surfaces at once, the operation results in a *multilayer* sponge surface instead.[52]

## Space Network Theory

Based on these building blocks and the abovementioned three primary parameters, Burt sought to advance what he often referred to as *space network theory* by discovering as many uniform (i.e., periodic) space networks as might be theoretically possible. He produced literally hundreds of cards, each depicting a network, the related sponge surface and sponge polyhedron, and the corresponding notation, everything drawn by hand despite the overwhelming complexity **(fig. 2.68–72)**. This endeavor, which he pursued systematically from the late 1990s, might be perceived in his view "as an extension of graph theory dealing geometrically with a plurality that may exist in nature of focal entities and their inter-relations."[53]

Precedent page:
**2.66** Above, left: Burt's graph diagramming his contribution to the domain of polyhedra, 2000s.
**2.67** Above, right: Example of a quintuplet assembly.
**2.68–69** Below: Space networks, late 1990s–present.

51 Though formulations of this theory can be found in Burt's writings and manuscripts produced over a decade earlier, the most synthetic account of it is perhaps laid out in a later conference paper: Michaël Burt, "The Morphologically Associated Quintuplet Phenomena of 3D Space" (XIV Generative Art Conference, Rome, 2011), 321–31.

52 Michaël Burt, "Periodic Sponge Polyhedra–Expanding the Domain" (Form and Symmetry: Art and Science, Buenos Aires, 2007), 503.

53 Michaël Burt, "Toward a Theory of Space Networks and Space Subdivision" (manuscript, 2011), unpaged. Personal archive of Michaël Burt. In morphology, the terms "graph" and "network" or "net" are often used interchangeably, Schoen employing the former where Burt uses the latter. Strictly speaking, they mean different things, as will be touched on in the fourth chapter. According to Coxeter, it was A.F. Wells who, seeking to provide structural formulae for describing crystals, generalized the notion of infinite polyhedron to that of nets linked up to skew polygons in his 1977 *Three-Dimensional Nets and Polyhedra*. In a review of this book, he explained that Wells looked for nets that unfold in Euclidean space by translational symmetry in three independent directions. The similarities between this and Burt's search for networks are obvious enough, yet the latter only encountered Wells in the early 2000s, after having set out on his own path. It was, in fact, when first reading Wells's claim that "a theory of these nets does not appear to be known, and in fact no attempt to derive them systematically seems to have been made" (A.F. Wells, *Structural Inorganic Chemistry* (Oxford: Clarendon Press, 1962), 101) and further considering that subsequent efforts on the chemist's part–notably his *Three-Dimensional Nets and Polyhedra*–had not provided comprehensive enough an answer, that Burt envisioned the construction of his theoretical armature as a relentless search toward the possibility of such a theory. This would entail full comprehension and an exhaustive account of the domain of 3D networks, something Coxeter considered "out of the question" due to the unmanageable number of possibilities. Coxeter, "Three-Dimensional Nets and Polyhedra by A.F. Wells [book Review]," 470.

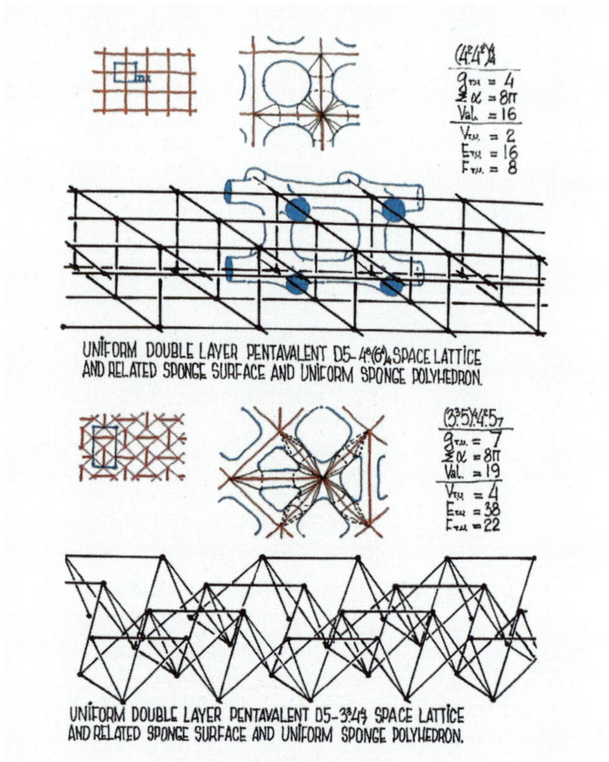


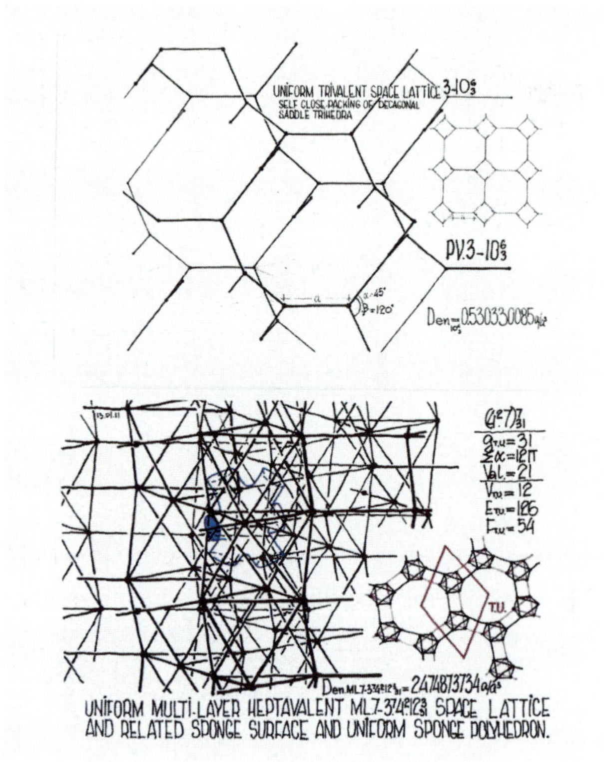


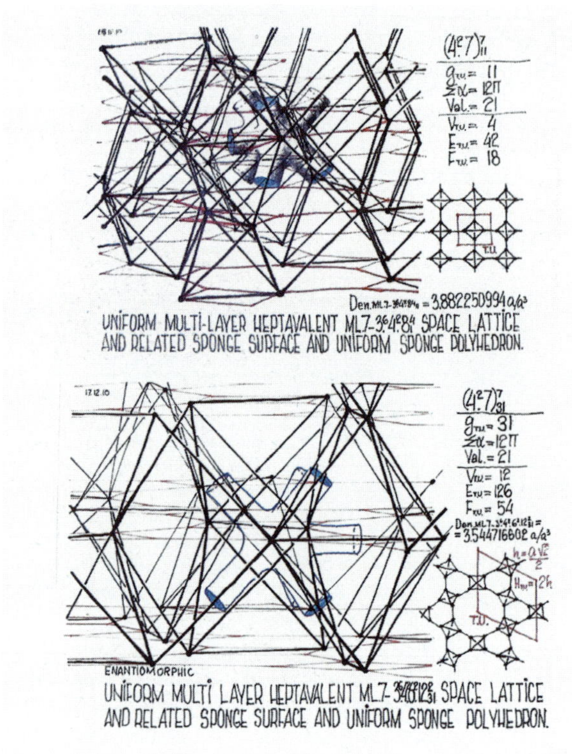


**2.70–72** Space networks, late 1990s–present.

## Quasicrystallinity

At the start of the new millennium Burt expanded his interest in crystallography further by engaging in quasicrystallinity. Up until the 1980s crystals had been thought to be always ordered and periodic. But in 1982 Dan Shechtman, Israeli material scientist and 2011 winner of the Nobel Prize in Chemistry, discovered that certain crystalline materials, such as rapidly solidifying aluminum-manganese alloys, feature a three-dimensional icosahedral symmetry—that is, one of a fivefold kind—which cannot exist in periodic structures. In other words, some crystals are ordered yet *not* periodic, hence they were named *quasiperiodic crystals*, or simply *quasicrystals*. A quasicrystalline pattern may unfold as close packing but will not present a repeating structure, since it will lack translational symmetry (i.e., at least one direction in which a pattern unit may be observed to be identically duplicated). On making the award to Shechtman, the Nobel Committee quite didactically observed the following:

> Aperiodic mosaics, such as those found in the medieval Islamic mosaics of the Alhambra palace in Spain and the Darb-i Imam shrine in Iran, have helped scientists understand what quasicrystals look like at the atomic level. In those mosaics, as in quasicrystals, the patterns are regular—they follow mathematical rules—but they never repeat themselves.[54]

Burt explored some of the geometric possibilities revealed by quasicrystals in a paper he gave in 2003 titled "The Quasi-Periodic Close Packings of Rhombic-Triacontahedra," where he showed a model for the construction of quasicrystalline patterns (i.e., pentagonal symmetry but not periodicity) based on the compact packing of two solids.[55]

54 Veronica Ek and Patrick Lannin, "Ridiculed Crystal Work Wins Nobel for Israeli," *Reuters* (blog), October 5, 2011, http://www.reuters.com/article/2011/10/05/nobel-chemistry-idUSL5E7L51U620111005. Accessed on January 28, 2015.

55 Burt's involvement in the domain of quasicrystals was triggered by his close friendship with Shechtman himself, with whom he had collaborated earlier in the organization of the 4th International Congress of the International Society for the Interdisciplinary Study of Symmetry, held at the Technion in 1998. Among Burt's other notable friendships were those with architect and engineer David Georges Emmerich and with Yona Friedman. Both were originally Hungarian, pursued studies together in Haifa after WWII, taught at the Technion at the time (Friedman partly as an assistant to Neumann), and ended up moving to Paris, Emmerich in 1953, Friedman four years later. When Burt was appointed dean in 1977, he invited Emmerich to teach at the Israeli school again for one semester, and generally stayed in touch with both men over the years, visiting Paris numerous times and residing in the French capital between 1994 and 1996. Neither Emmerich's nor Friedman's work, however, influenced his work in the way that Shechtman's did. The former's tensegrity structures, his more advanced contribution to structural morphology, were something that Burt never addressed. Meanwhile, he dismissed Friedman's engagement with geometry as merely "cartoonish" and "not real."

**2.73** Left: Michaël Burt, sculpture erected at Carbondale in 1971.

**2.74** Below, left: Michaël Burt. Penta Dome "Easy Camp" collapsible tent, 1969.

**2.75** Below, right: Michaël Burt. Hexahyp ("HEXAgonal HYperbolic Paraboloid") pavilion erected at the old Technion site in Haifa, Israel (1969).

# IDENTIFYING ARCHITECTURAL FORM IN BURT'S PRODUCTION

Before Burt devoted so much energy to minimal surfaces, especially at the beginning of his career, other mathematicians and geometers had already been studying them in depth.[56] Instead, the polyhedral domain, space network theory, and the general study of sponge surfaces emerge as the areas where he made his most significant contributions. Only certain outcomes of Burt's research, however, can be said to be directly relevant to form in an architectural sense. For not all of them describe spatial arrangements realistically capable of housing a set of human activities; in other words, not all of them incorporate the possibility of articulating a program. This partial relevance may be explained as follows.

## An Isolated Intuition

Early on, Burt declared himself committed to the architectural application of his research into surfaces and polyhedra. The applicability of continuous periodic surfaces is addressed in the closing chapter of his thesis, which suggested the use of surfaces and sponge polyhedra to organize architectural programs, as opposed to exclusively for structural and constructional reasons. He claimed that part of his goal was to transform minimal surfaces "into an *integral* part of architectural design," and to this end he supplied a number of hints as to how to turn his geometric configurations into the basis of actual buildings.[57] These included the option of installing linear utilities along the straight lines articulating the surfaces; the capacity of these to be partitioned into functional volumes following the logic of cells or cell groups; the possibility of suspending planar floor slabs so as to provide the necessary horizontal surfaces otherwise missing from the initial geometry; and the convenience of systems of internal communication unfolding along the axial trajectories of the lattice "tunnels."[58] Despite this ambition, however, the "architectural applications" turned out in practice to be sculptures **(fig. 2.73)**, small-scale collapsible tents **(fig. 2.74)**, and pavilions, the first of which was *Hexahyp* ("HEXAgonal HYperbolic Paraboloid"), completed in 1969 **(fig. 2.75)**. The one exception was *Aquaville*, a model for an underground habitat that a team of architects and students at the Technion led by Burt produced on the occasion of the 6th Paris Biennial for Young Artists.[59] This project was the only one in Burt's entire career wherein he envisaged

56 See for example Alan H. Schoen, *Infinite Periodic Minimal Surfaces Without Self-Intersections* (Cambridge, MA: NASA Electronics Research Center, May 1970), especially the references on 91–92.

57 Burt, *Spatial Arrangement and Polyhedra with Curved Surfaces and Their Architectural Applications - Doctoral Thesis*, 102. My emphasis.

58 See ibid., 131.

59 Founded by André Malraux ten years before, the 1969 installment of the Paris Biennial took place at the Musée d'Art Moderne and encompassed painting, sculpture, graphics, film, architecture, music, photography, literature, puppetry, dance, theatre, and stage design. Burt was invited to take part by Reuven Berman, a Tel Aviv art critic who had been appointed by the Ministry of Education and Culture to be commissioner for the Israeli participation at the Biennial.

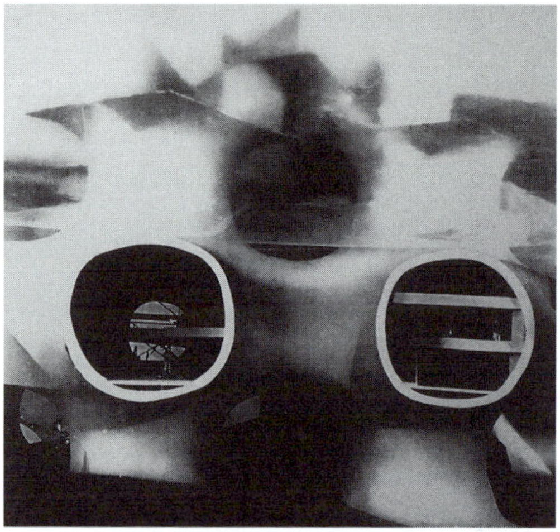

**2.76–77** Michaël Burt. *Aquaville* for the 6th Paris Biennial for Young Artists, 1969.

**2.78–79** Toyo Ito and Andrea Branzi. Forum for Music, Dance and Visual Culture in Ghent (Belgium). Competition entry, 2004.

the translation of one his spatial arrangements into a fully fledged building, featuring several floors inside the meandering surfaces, staircases at different levels, walkways, platforms, and entrances (fig. 2.76–77).

The design conception giving rise to *Aquaville*, along with the hints in his thesis concerning the architectural capabilities of his geometric configurations, clearly indicates that at some point Burt envisioned such capabilities to yield *buildings*. Nevertheless, when shown, nearly forty-five years later, the 2004 runner-up competition entry for the Forum for Music, Dance and Visual Culture in Ghent (Belgium) by Toyo Ito and former Archizoom founder Andrea Branzi—a scheme whose similarity to *Aquaville* is nothing short of striking (fig. 2.78–79)—he claimed to have never imagined it possible for a periodic minimal surface (the geometric basis of Ito and Branzi's project) itself to constitute a building.[60] Shocking though it may seem, given the attention both his thesis and *Aquaville* garnered at the time of their release, he may simply not have remembered. In fact, if that was the case, it makes sense that he did not, judging by the evolution of his production from the early 1970s onwards. For the architectural potential revealed through a series of clues in his thesis and later embodied in *Aquaville* appears, in retrospect, as an isolated intuition, with his subsequent work moving ever more decidedly into the science of geometry and its applications to engineering form. As regards geometry, many of his experiments exhibit a number of attributes, such an extreme complexity or an extraordinary density of units, which keep them from falling into the realm of possible programmatic configurations in architecture (fig. 2.80–81). In terms of applications, what Burt designed and built after his thesis and *Aquaville* were mostly large-span roof structures—either continuous periodic or single-span—for those swimming pools, shopping centers, and university buildings mentioned above. Indeed, the chief concern of structural morphology—namely, the study of the structural performance of spatial configurations—became a dominant driving force in his work. Since he conceived these configurations as roofs, rather than buildings themselves, they were not amenable to accommodating a set of human activities. Most were merely a variation on one-layer shell structures, thereby lacking the three-dimensional intricacy that is necessary to house architecture's programmatic elaborateness. Therefore, excessive complexity, on the one hand, or lack thereof on the other—as the result of materializing only one element within the whole of a building—are the reasons why many of the outcomes of Burt's body of research are not directly relevant to the problem of architectural form.

Conversely, those which are feature proportions and relational properties—that is, the way in which the different regions are connected to one another—that make them readily available to articulate function.

60 During the Q&A of a lecture delivered by this book's author at the Technion in Haifa on November 30, 2013.

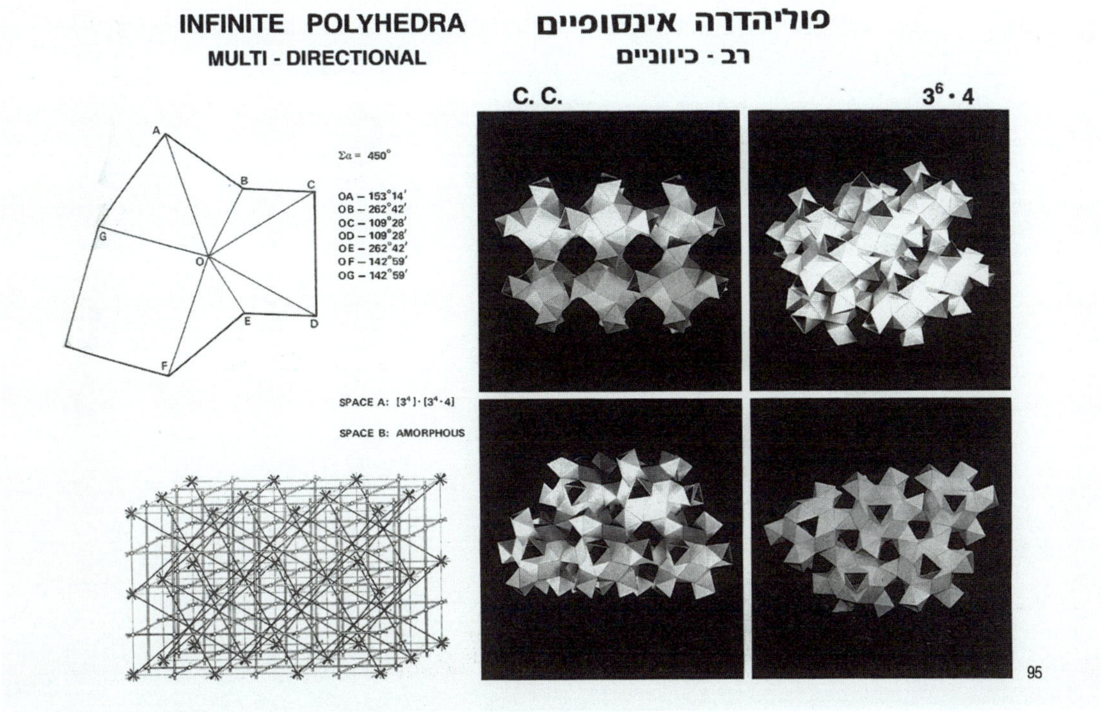


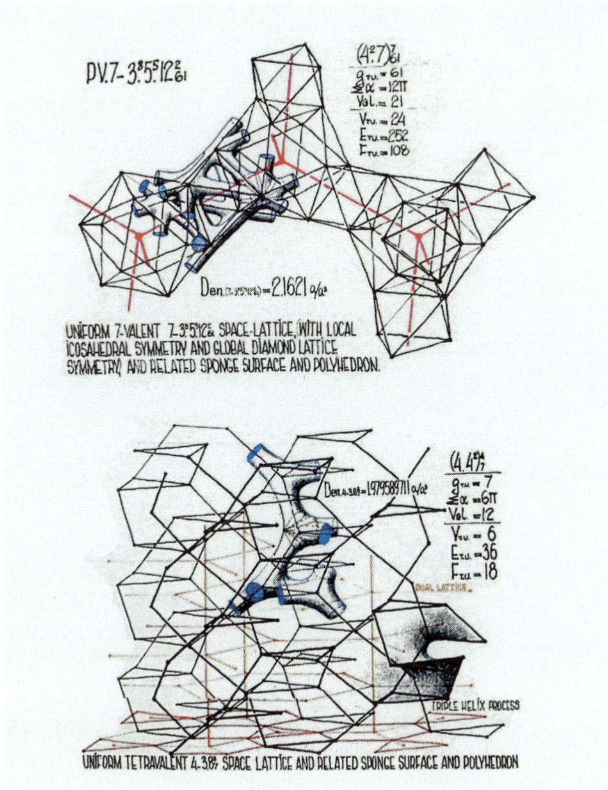


**2.80** Above: Overly complex multi-directional polyhedra.

**2.81** Left: Overly complex space networks.

SERIES OF CURVED SURFACES FORMING REGULAR "TWO DIMENSIONAL" LATTICES. (ANALOGOUS TO "REGULAR PLANE TESSELATIONS").

39

When discussing corrugated double layers it should be borne in mind spatial six-membered rings are not the only alternative for arranging spatial polygonsin two-dimensional space. To the same four and eight-membered rings, etc. are similarly feasible, combining to yield two-dimensional compact packings or what might (rather paradoxically) be termed "spatial two-dimensional lattices" or regular two-dimensional curved networks.

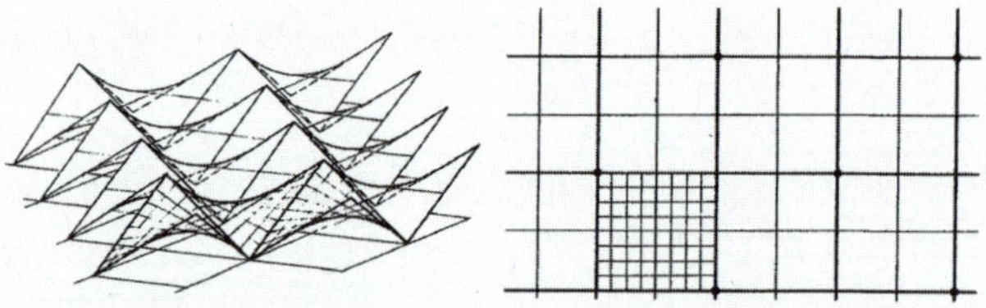

Series of curved surfaces whose vertices are in two parallel planes. The normal projection of the surfaces form a "regular tesselation".

1. 2. Lattice of spatial quadrants. Plan and axonometric drawing.

3. 4 Lattice of spatial hexagons. Plan and axonometric drawing.

מערכים של משטחים עקומים אשר קדקדיהם מסודרים בשני מישורים מקבילים. היטל ניצב של המשטחים נותן רשת מישורית רגולרית.

1.2. רשת של מרובעים מרחביים. תכנית ואקסונומטריה.

3.4. רשת של משושים מרחביים. תכנית ואקסונומטריה.

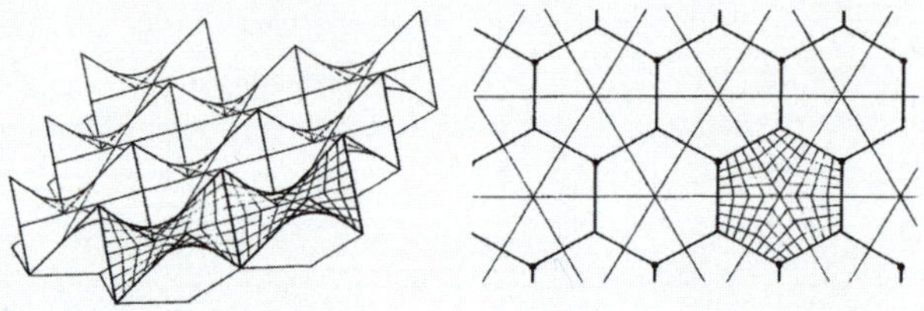

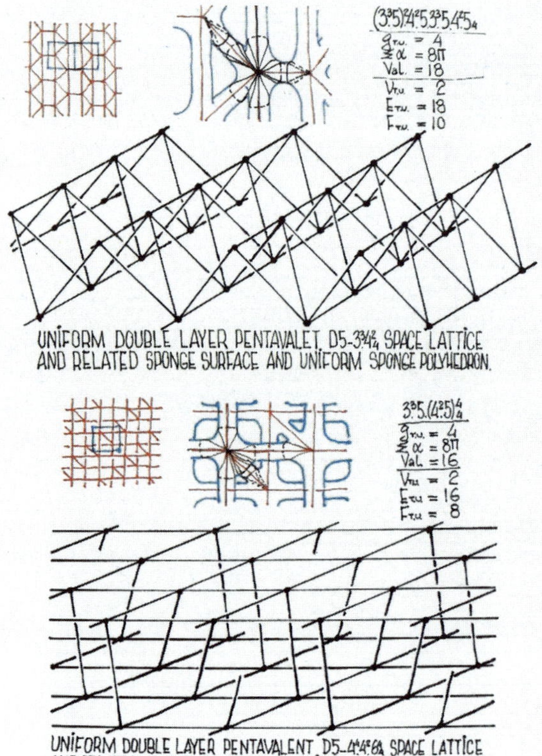


**2.82** Above: Two-dimensional lattices of marked architectural character.

**2.83** Left: Space networks of marked architectural character.

Though originated within a purely geometric regime or with a view to an engineering application, their specific characteristics nevertheless *happen to intersect* the domain of architectural form in a productive fashion. Instances falling into this category include, in addition to *Aquaville*, the regular two-dimensional lattices featured in this thesis **(fig. 2.82)**, some of the networks he relentlessly produced over the years **(fig. 2.83)**, a few of his minimal surfaces **(fig. 2.84)**, and several of the sponge polyhedra catalogued in his 1974 *Infinite Polyhedra* **(fig. 2.85)**. A distinction should be made, however, between the first three and the last.

## Distinction from the British Lineage

Although it could not be further from what Burt had in mind, it turns out that many of the sponge polyhedra in his *Infinite Polyhedra* can be taken to constitute form-program ensembles—indeed, buildings in embryo. It is thus possible to read into *Infinite Polyhedra* the scientization of the configurational kernel of buildings via an expanding geometric domain. This immediacy does not apply to his 2D-lattices, 3D-networks, and minimal surfaces, all of which, though embodying a programmatic potential, as will be discussed below, are yet several steps away from becoming something like a building.

It might seem that this outlook bears some similarity with that driving the various studies undertaken in architectural morphology elsewhere at the time, notably in the UK. In the 1970s and early 1980s, a number of figures coming out of the University of Cambridge, like Lionel March and Philip Steadman—both with a twofold background in mathematics and architecture—aimed to provide algebraic and geometric structures able to describe the spatial arrangements of buildings. Prompted by the newly available computer methods and supported first by the Martin Centre at the Cambridge School of Architecture, and then by the Centre for Configurational Studies at the Open University in Milton Keynes, these researchers declared themselves to be following in the footsteps of the pioneering contributions made by Christopher Alexander in the mid-1960s, generally known as "relational theory."[61] In their *The Geometry of the Environment* of 1971, however, they clarified that, in contradistinction to functional factors (which they ascribed to Alexander) and quantitative aspects involving measuring (such as area, volume, and angle, which they linked to the traditional role of geometry in architecture), their priority was to utilize the new mathematics of sets, groups, and graphs with a view to explaining logical patterns of entities or "structural relationships" *qualitatively*. Throughout their writings, they regarded these relationships, some of which were "adjacent to," "in the neighborhood of," or "contained by," as "topological."[62]

As his research progressed, Steadman in particular made it his goal to expand the domain of configurations at the architect's disposal.

61 See Christopher Alexander, *Notes on the Synthesis of Form* (Cambridge: Harvard University Press, 1964).

62 Lionel March and Philip Steadman, *The Geometry of Environment: An Introduction to Spatial Organization in Design* (London: RIBA Publications, 1971), 6–9.

**2.84** Model of minimal surfaces of marked architectural character.

**2.85** Opposite page: Multilayered polyhedra of marked architectural character.

The core of this theory—which he treated as falling into the realm of "architectural morphology" or "configurational studies"—concerned the consideration of the geometric and "topological" limits applicable to those configurations and the exhaustive production of all possible plans satisfying a specific scenario within those limits.[63] His tool for doing so included the available mathematical and computerized methods for automatically generating architectural plans, some of which he developed himself along with Robin Liggett and Cambridge-trained William Mitchell, fellow researchers based in the US. Steadman suggested the term "syntax" to designate the "possible architectural forms and arrangements," as opposed to "semantics," which would be the part of "architectural linguistics" dealing with "the systems of meaning" supported by "syntactic forms and structures."[64] This reference to "syntax" cannot be made without also mentioning the approach to configurational studies proposed around the same time by Bill Hillier and his team (notably Julienne Hanson) at The Bartlett in London. Under the heading of *Space Syntax* and building on the conceptual tools provided by graph theory, Hillier advanced a number of research methodologies, computer-based representations, and analytical techniques to examine the spatial configurations of buildings, neighborhoods, and cities. Through a body of work comprising an extensive number of case studies, he formulated several claims as to the social functioning of the built environment, useful mainly for diagnostic purposes

63 See preface to Philip Steadman, *Architectural Morphology: An Introduction to the Geometry of Building Plans* (London: Pion, 1983).

64 Ibid., 3.

## INFINITE POLYHEDRA פוליהדרה אינסופיים

### MULTI - LAYERED רב - שכבתיים

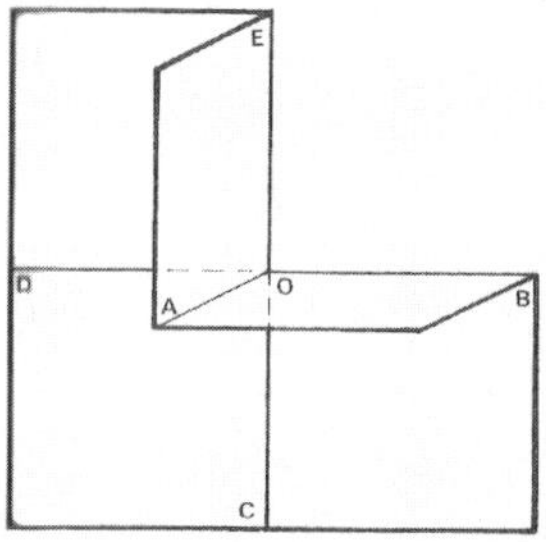


$\Sigma\alpha = 450°$

OA – 270°
OB – 90°
OC – 180°
OD – 180°
OE – 90°

PLANE TESSELLATION: $4^4$

SPACES A AND B CONGRUENT

SPACE A: $[4^3]^5$

SPACE B: $[4^3]^3$

C. (V) $4^5$ (3)

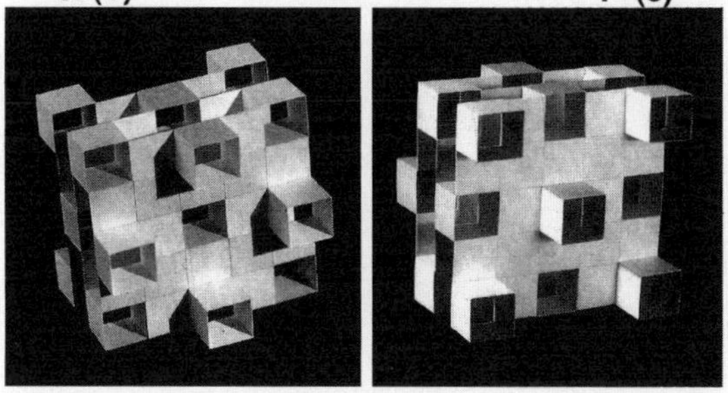

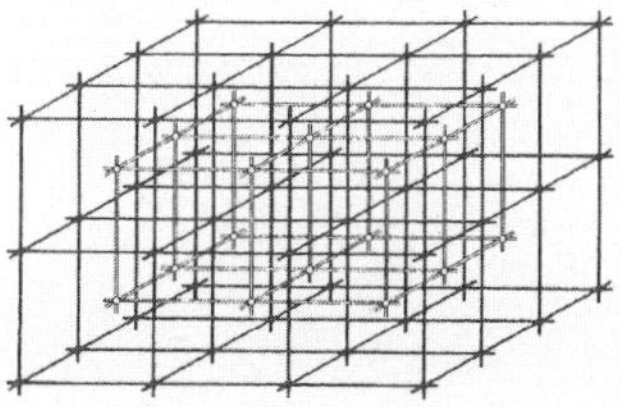

15

## INFINITE POLYHEDRA פוליהדרה אינסופיים

### MULTI - LAYERED רב - שכבתיים

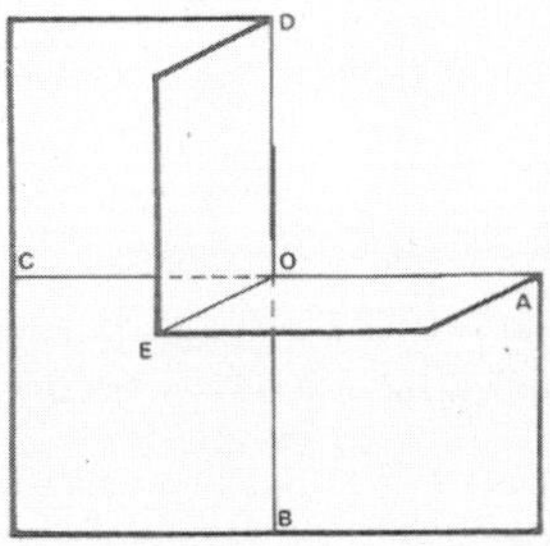


$\Sigma\alpha = 450°$

OA – 90°
OB – 180°
OC – 180°
OD – 90°
OE – 270°

PLANE TESSELLATION: $4^4$

SPACES A AND B CONGRUENT

SPACE A: $[4^3]^3$

SPACE B: $[4^3]^5$

$4^5$ (8)

concerning urban and housing layouts. Both the Cambridge and the Bartlett lineages were significantly imbricated.[65]

The conceptual relevance of both Hillier's and Steadman's theoretical apparatuses will be further considered in the fourth chapter. At this stage it will suffice to point out the differences with respect to Burt's work, which are as fundamental as the parallels. For one thing, Hillier and Steadman applied mathematical reasoning to architectural scenarios, specifically those captured by plan representations. Their investigations were therefore connected to architecture in principle. Burt, on the other hand, operated within geometry itself. He had in mind, somewhat loosely, that growing the formal vocabulary available would benefit any designer—and he found a few specific applications in engineering. But his focus was geometry *qua* geometry. Once again, it is only an *a posteriori* interpretation, not part of his original intent, that reveals the striking potential of his sponges for architecture, that is, vis-à-vis buildings as spatial arrangements. With respect to Steadman in particular, it is evident that his theory, being mainly analytical and interpretive, had a fairly limited generative power compared to Burt's. The former used simple geometric figures (essentially squares and rectangles) and provided multiple combinations within the boundaries of what they allow. The latter envisioned new ways of articulating space far beyond common pieces of geometry. Although justified on the basis of their convenience and flexibility in terms of design, the geometric language Steadman (and March, for that matter) utilized was largely constrained by the limitations of the computer, which was then too undeveloped to be able to deal with much more than squares and cubes. It was also conditioned by having to relate to architectural plans. Relying solely on his own brainpower and the laws of geometry, Burt's morphological field was drastically freer. Indeed, the use of a computer in the 1970s might have hindered rather than boosted such freedom. Further, Steadman's contribution was restricted to the two-dimensional domain, while Burt's was primarily three-dimensional. As for Hillier's theory, his target was the sociology of buildings. He supplied a code for identifying the social implications of existing architectural and urban configurations. The realm of his contribution was different from that of Burt and Steadman, both concerned with generating spatial configurations—albeitwith dissimilar intensity and approach.

65 Hillier and his group published their first piece on *Space Syntax*, "Space Syntax" (1976), in *Environment and Planning B*, a journal edited by Lionel March. Later Steadman included "Space Syntax," along with other publications by Hillier, as a bibliographic reference in his *Architectural Morphology* of 1983, where he also acknowledged "the intellectual stimulus and challenge" provided by the latter's morphological work. Some of the materials presented in this book had been discussed earlier in a seminar series held jointly by The Bartlett, Cambridge, and the Open University.

# A SCIENTIFIC EXPANSION OF BUILDING KERNELS: PROGRAMMATIC LINKAGES, VEILED FORMATION, AND DUAL NONREFERENTIALITY

Since *Infinite Polyhedra* registered an expansion of the domain of sponge polyhedra, and many of these can be construed as always-already-programmatic spatial arrangements—i.e., actual buildings in embryo—the book may be taken to feature a scientific expansion of the domain of architectural configurations. The type of building they may be made into is suggested by their configurational nature. The cylindrical types resemble tower envelopes **(fig. 2.42)**; the mono-layer ones can be read as single-story buildings with interior courtyards **(fig. 2.44)**; the multilayer and some of the multidirectional ones are assimilable to multistory buildings with open spaces at different heights **(fig. 2.85)**. Many of them showcase their own constitutive order very clearly, although several do not. The latter, mostly coinciding with the multidirectional subset, display the same quality as Giorgini's designs—namely, a whimsical arbitrariness that is only apparent, for in actuality it is the product of an underlying pattern **(fig. 2.86)**.

## Topologically Distinct versus Topologically Equivalent

Generally, the term "expansion" designates an extension of a previously known range that results from previously unknown (i.e., new) additions. Every one of these in *Infinite Polyhedra* is shown to be different by virtue of embodying a unique periodic construction (via a particular elementary periodic unit, along with the corresponding aggregational logic), and consequently, a unique notation. Insofar as they each actualize a singular spatial arrangement, irreducible to any other, they may be referred to as *topologically distinct*.[66] As discussed in the previous chapter, each topologically distinct primitive (e.g., plane, cylinder, Möbius strip, cube/sphere, torus, and hyperbolic surfaces) is characterized by a unique set of topological invariants (genus, orientability, number of edges, sides, and connections, flatness/nonflatness, etc.). All configurations are *topologically equivalent* which are reducible to the same primitive by means of a transformation process wherein all topological invariants are observed. Being irreducible, conversely, each primitive is topologically distinct.

66 Steadman used the phrase "topologically distinct" as well. However, he did so only to allude to different packings of rectangles filling a larger containing one. The packings were accomplished by simply moving those rectangles around within a given perimeter. The characterization of "topologically distinct" was thus restricted to known pieces of geometry and the two-dimensional domain. Philip Steadman, "Graph-Theoretic Representation of Architectural Arrangement," in *The Architecture of Form* (Cambridge [Eng.]: Cambridge University Press, 1976), 95–115, 107ff.

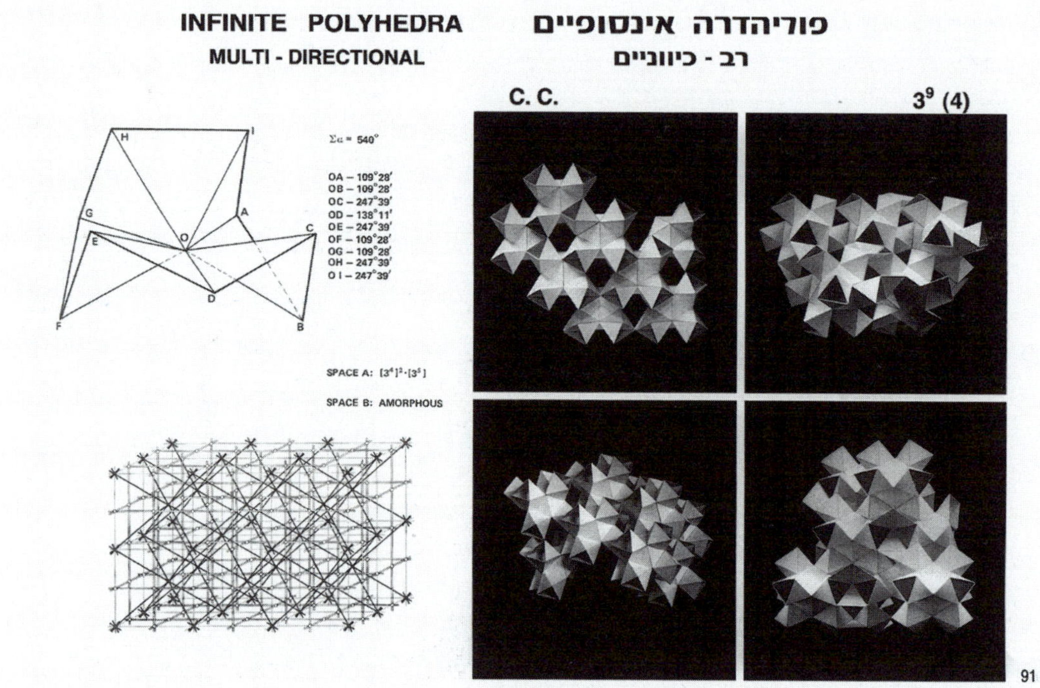


2.86 Multidirectional polyhedra. Apparent randomness, underlying order.

Insofar as the quality of connectedness defined by topological invariants is directly linked to the way in which space is bounded and articulated on a fundamental level, it can be said that each primitive, along with all of its derivatives, typifies a singular configurational kernel. At the core of topologically distinct primitives, therefore, is that which might be called *configurational irreducibility*. This property, inferred from within the realm of topology, is applicable to pieces of geometry in principle. However, some of these pieces, such as those in Burt's *Infinite Polyhedra*, may register as architectural forms in their own right, that is, when they are spatial arrangements that can readily and feasibly house a set of human activities. Their ontology straddling geometry and architecture, they can be viewed as the medium through which to transfer the concept of configurational irreducibility from one to the other. It thus follows that those singular spatial arrangements in *Infinite Polyhedra* that are always already programmatic embody irreducible configurations in an architectural sense, which is to say, they enable distinct programmatic relationships. Via a different route of argument, the same claim intimated in the previous chapter is arrived at here: that *topological equivalence* leads to formal sameness in an architectural sense, while *topological distinctness* yields formal singularity—form-program constituting an indissoluble construct.

## Fluctuating Programmatic Thresholds

The tunnel nets or "networks" can be taken to express the basis of these programmatic relationships, something Burt never envisioned. The nodes might represent *expansion areas*: sections—or rather, intersections—where the spatial continuum opens up in at least two directions that typically are not coplanar. The network lines might signal *transition regions*: zones connecting two expansion areas. Thus every expansion area is also the confluence of two or more transition regions. The materialization of these two types of elements varies depending on whether they are actualized in sponge surfaces or sponge polyhedra. The former are curved spatial fields where transition regions tend to be tunnel-like envelopes with a circular section, and clearly differentiated expansion areas. Most of the surfaces arising from the space networks that Burt pursued ceaselessly since the late 1990s can be read along the lines of this particular typology **(fig. 2.70)**. There is, however, a certain group of sponge surfaces—minimal surfaces and hypars—that, though a minority in respect of the entirety of his production, are nonetheless significantly dissimilar. In these, the transition regions are so short that their distinction from the expansion areas is not so obvious. As a result, the overall configuration reads as a more compact articulation **(fig. 2.39)**. Sponge polyhedra, on the other hand, are often comprised of planar faces and a limited number of angles—often just one: ninety degrees. Conversely here, most of the sponge polyhedra are compact articulations **(fig. 2.45)**, with only a relatively reduced number featuring clearly distinguishable transition regions and expansion areas **(fig. 2.44)**.

Based on this characterization, the programmatic potential of Burt's sponge surfaces and polyhedra differs. For one thing, transition regions that are sharply distinct are prone to be read as individual programmatic units. This turns expansion areas into *programmatic condensers*, that is, hybrid zones where several different programmatic units come together. The more compact articulations, on the other hand, lend themselves to be read as continuous fields where one navigates seamlessly through transition regions and expansion areas. In this case, multiple zoning possibilities appear available, as suggested by the manifold combinations of articulating elements and emerging openings comprising the surface or polyhedron. Alternatively, we might also speak of a progressive *programmatic unfolding*, that is, a sequencing of activities and functions that evolve into each other without a pre-established zoning. Derived from the nature of these surfaces and polyhedra, the concepts of *programmatic condenser* and *programmatic unfolding* are further examples of how program may inhere in form. Furthermore, this reading suggests that, rather than "rooms," Burt's networks can be taken to prompt "areas" and "regions," that is, zones in space whose identity is recognizable and yet whose limits are not fixed, there being no partitions. If rooms materialize a particular compartmentalization, it might be said that the three-dimensional tunnel nets engender a kind of *soft zoning*, where rather than empty, hard dividing lines, boundaries become fluctuating programmatic thresholds.

## From Geometric Manifold to Building

In the totality of Burt's production, there are a number of surfaces and polyhedra that would require a case-by-case interpretation to determine the programmatic nature of their three-dimensional continuity—whether because they have no accompanying tunnel net, or because their spatial characteristics of intricacy and connectivity cannot be analyzed in terms of transitional regions and expansion areas. The vast majority, however, can be understood on the basis of these two elements. In the latter group, it is mainly cylindrical, mono-layered, multilayered, and a few of the multidirectional sponge polyhedra featured in *Infinite Polyhedra* that can be viewed as buildings in embryo, that is, as instances where program inheres in form. The slenderness of the polyhedron itself, as well as its vertical segmentation coinciding with that of a sequence of stories, render cylindrical sponge polyhedra amenable to constituting the envelope of a tower **(fig. 2.42)**. The organization in horizontal layers—which would facilitate the supply of sufficient floor area, the proportions of those layers being akin to those of a series of floors—and the internal porosity—which would provide three-dimensional channels to introduce natural light into the volume—turn mono- and some multilayered polyhedra into direct bases for buildings, whether single-story or multistory as the case may be **(fig. 2.44, 2.87)**.

The immediacy with which these polyhedra can be interpreted as architectural structures is lacking in other geometric configurations of Burt's which, while also showing a programmatic potential, would necessitate at least one significant intermediate step to be able to register as buildings. The so-called "two-dimensional lattices," for example, might be taken as the seed of a topographical floor. For them to fully work as such, however, their slopes would have to be tamed considerably and their tessellation modified so that they could be inhabited in a realistic and efficient fashion. A further step would entail stacking them up to generate the various levels of a building **(fig. 2.29)**. Any space network, insofar as it can be interpreted as a set of programmatic relationships, might also be taken as a building's starting point. The basic moves here would involve ignoring the sponge surface associated with it whenever too complex (which is often the case) and deriving an equivalent three-dimensional envelope with a greater degree of architectural feasibility—e.g., one made up of flat surfaces only, or one featuring fewer and more gently curved surfaces while providing a sufficient habitable area **(fig. 2.88–89)**. Thirdly, there are several of the periodic minimal surfaces that might themselves be worked into buildings, as anticipated when discussing *Aquaville*'s and Ito and Branzi's project in Belgium. In

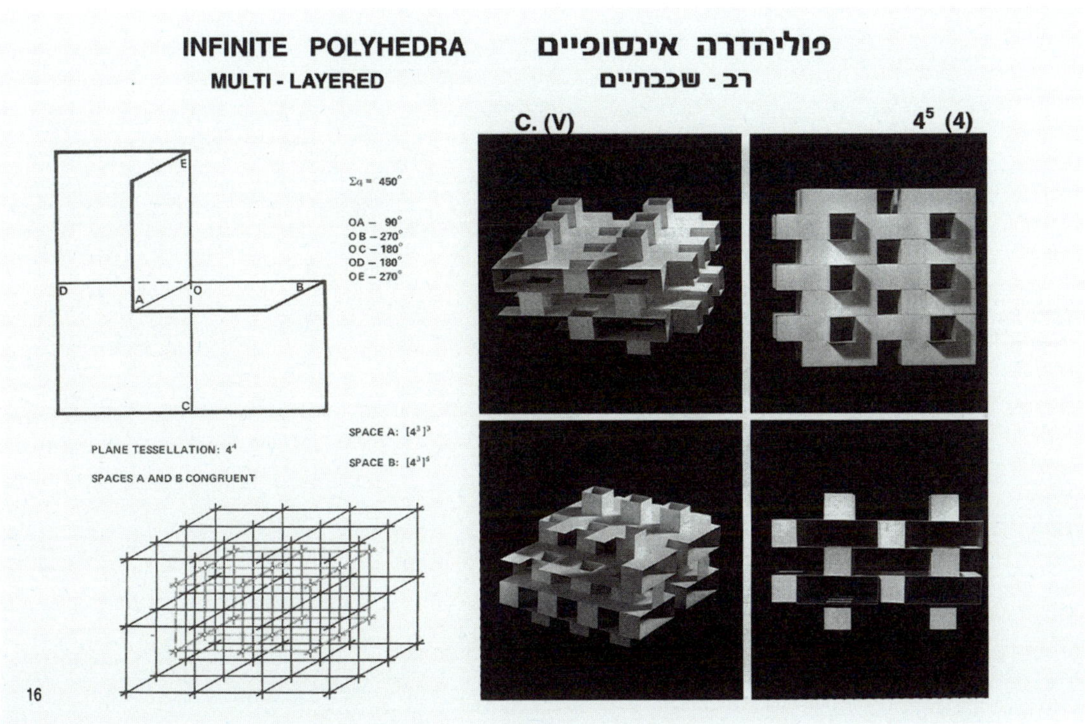


2.87 Horizontally arranged, internally porous multilayered polyhedra.

this case the main necessary step (especially if additional horizontal surfaces, absent in the original configuration, are to be avoided) would require expansion of the horizontal tangent regions so that they provide sufficient habitable floor area in between the vertical curved surfaces. A model for this particular alteration could be taken from some of the sponge surfaces that Burt developed toward the end of his career, which show a considerably expanded—if gently curved—area in between the tangent regions **(fig. 2.90)**.

There is therefore a sharp difference between geometric configurations whose spatial characteristics allow them to be construed directly as models for buildings (especially some of the sponge polyhedra in *Infinite Polyhedra*), and those which, while showing a particularly noteworthy architectural potential—whether in the form of an articulated, stackable floor; a three-dimensional cluster of intricate programmatic relationships; or a complex of curved surfaces that yields two sets of complementary spaces—nonetheless need substantial manipulation to accomplish the degrees of completeness and viability of the former. The way program inheres in form in the first cases is absolute, while only incipient in the rest.

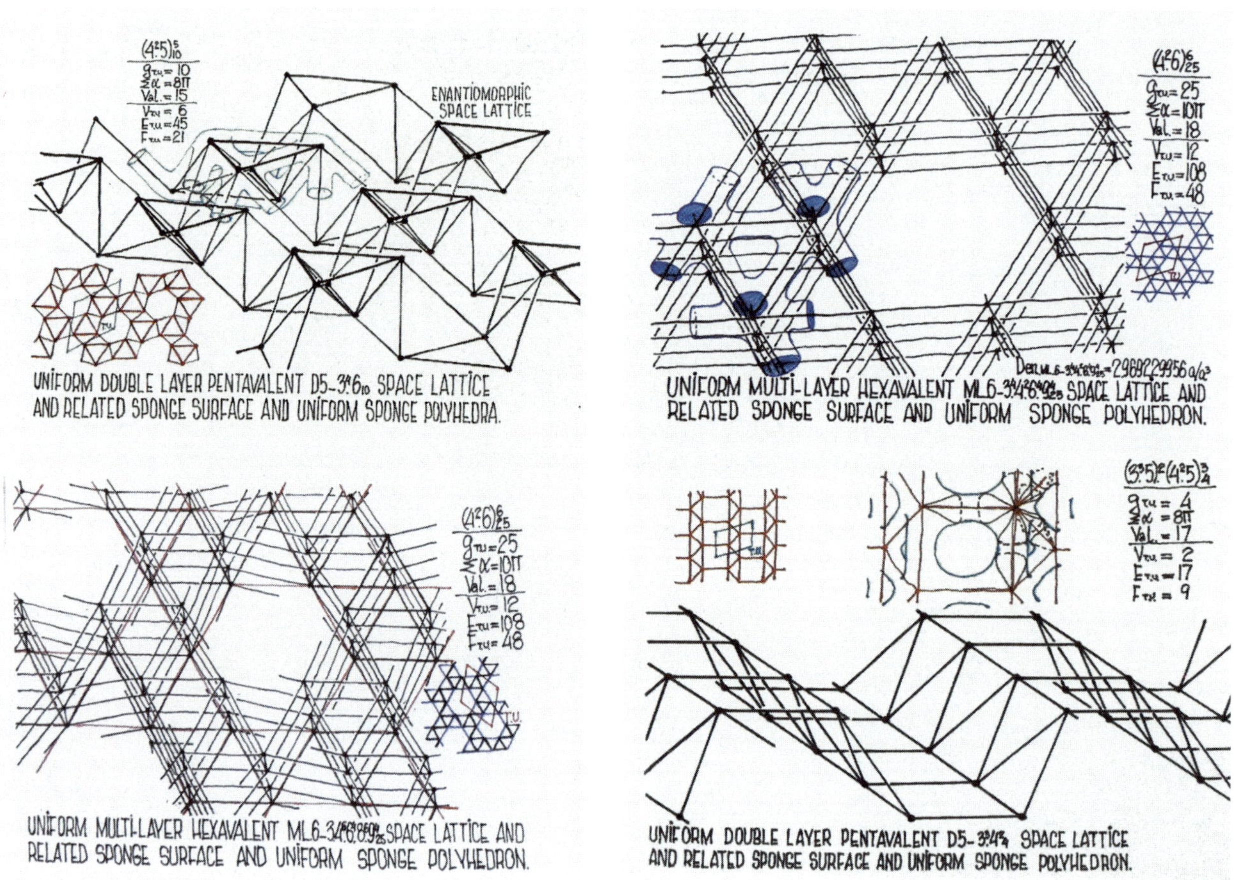


**2.88–89** Space networks that can be interpreted as starting points for architectural structures.

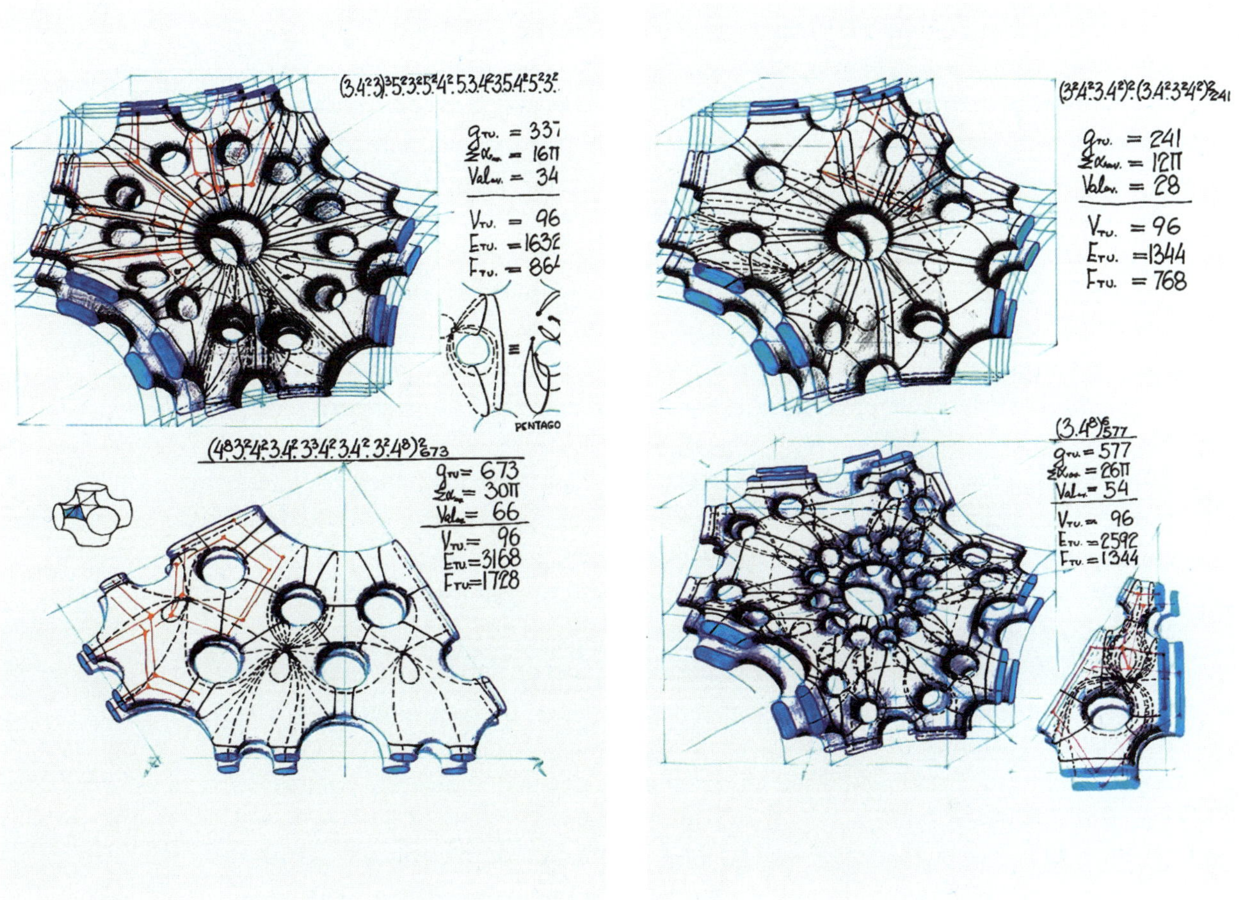


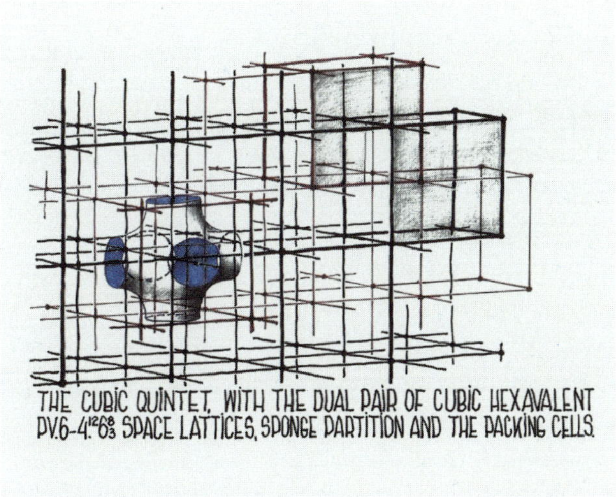


**2.90** Above: Hyperbolical sponge surfaces featuring considerable horizontal area.

**2.91** Left: Construal of networks as bearers of programmatic relationships provides an entry point into an architectural interpretation of the "quintuplet assembly."

## Simultaneity and Complementarity of Programmatic Orders

The construal of Burt's networks as bearers of programmatic relationships provides an entry point into the architectural interpretation of his so-called "quintuplet assembly": two dual networks, two polyhedral close packings, and a hyperbolical sponge surface **(fig. 2.91)**. The latter, dividing space into two complementary subsets, may embody the architectural structure itself, as is the case with the periodic minimal surfaces discussed above. At the same time, from a geometric standpoint, the sponge surfaces or "manifolds" constitute the references from which to derive the infinite sponge polyhedra and, by extension, the index of their genus. In the only passage in his entire production that directly addresses this question, Burt explained the rapport between the two types of geometric configurations thus: "[o]n each of these envelopes [i.e. hyperbolical sponge surfaces], topologically speaking, . . . different maps, composed of polygonal regions (faces), which are bounded by sets of edges and vertices, could be drawn, to represent what we call **polyhedra** or **polyhedral envelopes.**"[67] These polyhedral envelopes—otherwise called *tilings*, given how they come to be with respect to the sponge surfaces—will be sponge polyhedra, Burt clarified, only if they conform to Euler's theorem: V-E+F = 2 (1-g).

In many cases, however, it would seem that the sponge polyhedra might result directly from applying a topological transformation to a sponge surface in such a way that the outcome features only straight edges and flat surfaces, the genus value being maintained. Either way, infinite outcomes are possible since, even if genus is observed, different polyhedra—i.e., made up of different polygons and valencies—can be derived from the same sponge surface. Within the framework of the quintuplet assembly, therefore, it can be either the sponge surface (a configuration where typically program inheres in form only incipiently) or the sponge polyhedra (one where such an immanence can be absolute) that may constitute the seed for a building. If the first network expresses the programmatic relationships governing one of the two spatial subsets, its dual serves a similar purpose with respect to the other subset. Furthermore, the fact that the networks themselves constitute two modes of polyhedral close packing has implications on two counts. For one thing, it entails that, in addition to each network segment expressing a local programmatic link, there are programmatic units of a higher order that correspond to the close packing's repeating cell, each comprised of a number of segments. For another, since the packing is compact as opposed to loose, each individual programmatic link (i.e., network segment) always belongs to two of those units at once, which introduces another level of programmatic hybridity.[68] In short: if the networks are taken to represent a structure of programmatic relationships, then the packings would provide a code for understanding the two fundamental properties of those relationships, with the surface and range of polyhedra supplying options for

67 Burt, *The Periodic Table of The Polyhedral Universe*, 8.

68 Networks leaving spatial regions unaccounted for fall into the domain of *loose* packing, which is a form of three-dimensional open pattern.

materializing them in three dimensions. Therefore, in an architectural sense, the quintuplet assembly may be viewed as a particular kind of form-program ensemble; one comprising five constituents that are uniquely related to one another (insofar as four of them can be generated out of the fifth); one that features an underlying order that can be described independently of the specific way in which the configuration is materialized; one possessing special three-dimensional characteristics.

Two of these stand out conspicuously. Firstly, insofar as sponge surfaces and polyhedra are composite patterns of configurational continuity, they combine a compound character—by virtue of being comprised of repeating units—with a particular kind of continuity that is constantly folding upon itself to articulate space in an intricate manner. Secondly, multilayered and multidirectional polyhedra as well as periodic minimal and hyperbolical sponge surfaces bring forth two reciprocal subspaces. These, which in some cases may be congruent (i.e., identical), define each other three-dimensionally by means of sequential interpenetrations, even though they never intersect. In other words, they remain independent across the structure and yet form a series of interweaving regions that are adjacent to each other throughout, with the sponge surface or polyhedra serving as a separating "membrane" in between. Only if this membrane is perforated may a direct connection between the two sets of spaces occur. This particular condition gives rise to the concept of *spatial reciprocity*, whose architectural potential has barely been explored, despite its obvious resonances. Indeed, architectural design often operates on the basis of heuristic binaries, such as public versus private and open versus compartmentalized, that lend themselves to being articulated through reciprocal spaces in a particularly productive manner.

## Beyond Generic versus Specific

It is important to note that, in conceiving a building out of Burt's sponge surfaces and polyhedra, one would not be proceeding from the domain of geometry to that of architecture. By virtue of being always already programmatic, those configurations belong to the latter. They *are* architectural. This is not so in the modernist tradition around the duality of generic versus specific form, where the initial set of "forms" typically coincides with the group of Platonic solids.[69] For these are sheer pieces of geometry without the qualities of intricacy, and consequently, capacity for spatial articulation necessary for a "form" to be architectural. The transition here takes place from geometry to architecture, as would be the case if we were to imagine Terragni's Casa del Fascio deriving out of a cube. Put differently: Burt's sponge surfaces and polyhedra where program inheres in form are indeed "primitives," and in that regard they are conceptually close to a plane, a cylinder, or a Möbius strip.

69 For example, Le Corbusier's "Lesson of Rome" can be recalled here, where he famously claimed that all worthy architecture is reducible to the set of five elemental geometric solids.

The difference, however, is that the former are architectural primitives, whereas the latter are merely geometric ones.

The second aspect of Burt's *oeuvre* that contributes to overcoming the generic-versus-specific duality is the boundlessness of his sources of form, which contrasts with the finite character of the group of Platonic solids and their derivatives. The third and last aspect concerns the dynamic character built into his geometric configurations. The classical pieces of geometry comprising the domain of "generic forms" were commonly termed "absolute" and associated with a static, "ideal" domain of fixed instances. The kinds of geometric configuration Burt came up with, on the other hand, were always the result of generation methods. His networks are not just found and frozen in time and space: they are brought forth by a sequence of drawings and analytical steps. In other words, there is always a formation process involved. The starting point is an elementary repeating unit with a number of geometric characteristics that confer its periodic or translational qualities upon it, as the case may be. In order that an overall configuration may come into being, these units rely upon a self-iterative dynamic action performed in time that involves either aggregation or translation. In another example, the so-called "genetic surface" method describes an alternating sequence of surface duplications, perforations, and connections that gives rise to a particular type of sponge surface. Burt's sponges and polyhedra are therefore produced, although the formation process itself is not apparent in the outcome. Since any given geometric arrangement repeats the same pattern to infinity, there is no beginning or end to it. It can start anywhere. Furthermore, there are no irregularities indicating inflection points or boundaries between "steps" in the process; the repetition is relentless and homogeneous throughout. Thus, Burt's structures do not express their dynamic engine. Rather, this is disguised, concealed—masked as modular wholeness.

## Geometric Style versus Nonreferentiality

There has been a recurrent tendency, among players and commentators alike, to highlight the capacity of architectural morphology to engender new means of spatial expression—that is, new forms and spatial patterns. Neumann claimed that "the large array of space packing patterns, using the Platonic and Archimedean solids and their duals, prisms and antiprisms, has not yet found any architectural application"; critics like Keith Critchlow spoke about a "new spatial syntax";[70] Bottero stated her conviction about morphology's achievement in terms of novelty in language: "[i] t is instead a matter of a widespread feeling of dissatisfaction with the traditional modules of architecture and an attempt to create an original approach which, all things considered, implies a new definition of the architectonic language."[71] In this regard, while it is important to distinguish between Neumann's ambition to

70 Neumann, "Morphologic Architecture," 139, and Keith Critchlow, "New Geometrical Information," *Architectural Design* 40, no. 4 (April 1970), 164–66.

71 Maria Bottero, "Technological Research and Architecture," 231.

find architectural applications for known pieces of geometry (i.e., Platonic and Archimedean solids, and their duals) and Burt's contribution being about coming up with new, unknown pieces of geometry, the results from an aesthetic standpoint were similar on a fundamental level. Namely, their buildings and pavilions displayed a kind of geometric style where the polyhedric elements were apparent across the structure, and sometimes even emphasized. Segal rightly pointed out that those who considered Neumann's morphologic architecture to be mainly an aesthetic approach were missing the element of formal analysis that was so central to the nature of his work.[72] However, although that may be the case in terms of analysis, research, and design thinking, there is no question that, when it came to the buildings themselves, Neumann ended up developing a geometric style characterized by a strong literalness in terms of how the polyhedric configurations were materialized **(fig. 2.7, 9–10)**. This is also true of Burt's occasional architectural works—it suffices to look at designs such as Hexahyp (1969) **(fig. 2.75)** and Floris (1980) **(fig. 2.92)**. Therefore, those few works by Burt, just like those by Neumann, did not accomplish the stylistic nonreferentiality of those by Giorgini, for they featured elements that may be referenced to a style—i.e., elements belonging to codified formats of architectural expression ("morphological," "polyhedric," etc.) that a number of architects were working with at the time.

That said, many of the sponge polyhedra and surfaces that Burt discovered did show clear potential for such stylistic nonreferentiality. They lack the specific features which, when rendered architecture, would make the resulting building identifiable with a geometric style. In the case of the sponge polyhedra featured in *Infinite Polyhedra* **(fig. 2.42–45)**, the geometric literalness of Neumann's buildings is not a possibility because they are mostly comprised of straight edges, ninety-degree angles, and void-to-surface relations that result in a marked stylistic neutrality. Taken in isolation, some of these characteristics do certainly resonate with familiar architectural vocabularies. Yet taken together they do not amount to anything like a distinct style. Thus, here we might speak of a *neutral nonreferentiality*.

It is different with sponge surfaces. The curved continuity they display is equally alien to the specificities of Israeli geometric style, but its geometric characteristics do not echo familiar architectural vocabularies. On the contrary, they become a distinctive mode of expression when turned into architecture **(fig. 2.76–79)**. (Indeed, there is no precedent in the history of architecture for Ito and Branzi's Ghent competition entry.) In other words, when interpreted as architecture, sponge polyhedra embody a singularity that is comparable to that of Giorgini's designs, their elements enabling an expansion of the expressive imaginary of architecture. Accordingly, in this case we might speak of a *singular nonreferentiality*. Once again: while elements of style and expression unfold merely at the level of shape—and

72 See Segal, *Unit, Pattern, Site: The Space Packed Architecture of Alfred Neumann 1949–1968*, 105.

2.92 Floris pavilion in Haifa, Israel (1980).

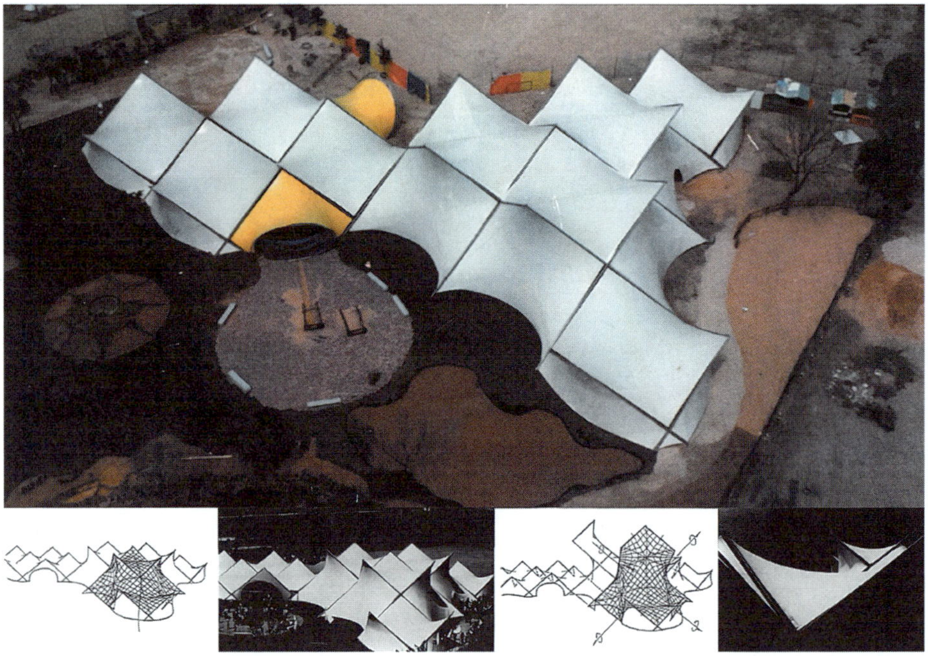

are therefore irrelevant in terms of the organizational properties of form—careful consideration of the relationship between shape and form allows us to identify that, on occasion, contributions to the domain of the latter may lead to contributions to that of the former.

## OPERATIVE UNAWARENESS

Several themes connected Burt's local context of influence in Israel with the shift toward an intense scientization of design taking place across the West over the course of the second half of the twentieth century. The possible applications of biological structuralism in design stand out as the most conspicuous of those themes. Neumann's own research not only stirred a curiosity about such applications, but also served Burt as a stimulus to find other relevant sources, such as Kepes's *The New Landscape in Art and Science* of 1956—itself a precedent to Neumann in terms of "pattern-seeing" becoming an attitude toward the discovery of nature's hidden imageries. Burt's interest in soap bubbles and crystallography, shared with many morphology researchers elsewhere, came as a result of this curiosity fueled by biological structuralism. The nonbiological, originally linguistic kind of structuralism is another theme palpably present in both Burt's direct context and international discourses of the 1960s and 1970s wherever some form of acute scientization of design was taking place. The figure working out of Israel at the time, through whom a structuralist interpretation of architecture appeared, was Al Mansfeld. Neumann's and Burt's morphologies did not figure in architectural structuralism internationally, although structuralism still appears as a valid lens through which to assess some of their core aspects, as discussed above. Moreover, Burt's ambition to industrialize building processes was linked to the larger field of environmental design, one with which architectural morphology has been generally associated.[73] Aside from studying the potential of geometry for standardization—with special emphasis on symmetry and close packing—architects involved in morphology strove to cause as small an impact as possible on the pre-existing setting. Hence, they favored the use of environmentally friendly materials and showed a bias toward lightweight construction.

Yet it is especially Neumann's impact on the young Burt that cannot be overstated. The Czech architect sought to instill in architecture a humanism implicitly judged as lacking in modernism by envisioning buildings whose three-

73 See for example Keith Critchlow, "Toward a New Philosophy of Structure," *Zodiac*, no. 22 (1972), 180–85.

dimensional composition, made up of small, repetitive spatial units, was meant to cater to the human scale. He turned morphology into a basis for design as a means to achieve this "humanization," the result being a series of projects that embodied an extension of that critique of modernism to a number of aspects relating to architectural thinking, such as functionalism, expressive language, and the possibility of transcending the notion of the building as an object. While organicism countered modernism by decrying rationalism, morphology—which originated as a science to begin with—did so through an intensification of rationalism, albeit in a different direction. Both organicism and morphology, however, shared the advocacy of an experimental rapport with nature via an engagement with biological structuralism.

Much less aware than Neumann about historical and discursive developments—indeed, exhibiting less of a general intellectual drive than his teacher—Burt focused on the means (morphology) as an end in itself and was oblivious to both the original motivation to exploit those means and the critique of modernism materialized in their outcomes. For, while maintaining a version of Neumann's biological structuralism, Burt was at heart moved primarily by the prospect of finding an ever more complex, underlying order in the abstract articulation of space, this being the main objective of theoretical morphology. The biological structuralism present in Burt's endeavors and that objective were linked, his interest in quasicrystallinity being a case in point. Quasicrystals provide models of organization that could have the capacity to arrange an architectural program three-dimensionally on the basis of a pattern that is ordered but not periodic. This characteristic turns them into sources for possibly extending the domain of architectural form while ensuring that the resulting piece of architecture would not display the kind of unforgiving repetition that often comes with periodicity and sometimes causes a palpable rejection. Burt ignored this architectural reading altogether. Instead, he was fascinated by the sophistication and novelty of quasicrystals solely in terms of geometric properties, that is, in terms of order in the abstract.

Whether the order Burt was seeking all along was found or constructed amounts to a metaphysical question to which only the beginning of an answer can be ventured here. The former presupposes that the existence of a particular order precedes the action itself that unveils it and thus, in a sense, that it is independent from such an action. The latter implies that the very contingencies of the action, in fact, *give rise to* that order, the two being inextricably connected. On assessing Burt's investigations, it could be speculated that the order he came to was proportionally more constructed than found. He manipulated the elements (periodic units, faces, vertices, etc.) and relations engendering the order embodied in a surface or polyhedron (translational symmetry, reciprocity, connectedness, etc.) in a way that was specific to him. Pearce, for example, either used fewer and sometimes different elements and relations, or handled many of them differently. As a result of these distinct approaches, the body of work they produced—i.e., the regimes of order they delineated—was significantly dissimilar.[74] Therefore, the fact that the "unveiled" order differed from researcher to researcher and was largely the product of the contingent set of procedures and elements they mobilized entails that, on some level, the order was primarily constructed. Burt's necessary use of generation methods to produce sponge surfaces—the so-called "genetic surface" and the dual network approach—further resonates with the idea of a constructed or created order.

### Science without Detriment to Specificity

In synthesis, Burt was a researcher whose central project involved the extension of the limits of morphology via geometry, and also, if secondarily, finding a number of applications for some of the spatial configurations he discovered. For his unremitting desire to expand the formal imaginary, while rendered with strong mathematical and geometrical significance, cannot be disengaged from a desire to address issues relevant to architectural construction, such as material distribution, membrane stresses, the possibility of minimum structural tension, and the modularity and prefabrication afforded by periodicity. This needs to be emphasized, since, while Burt's research represents the more extreme scientific approach within architectural morphology, characterizations of his project, such as that by Bottero as "an exclusively geometrical study aimed at demonstrating the multiple aggregational possibilities of complex polyhedra, unknown to present-day constructive practice based on the cube and the parallelepiped" are not entirely accurate, given the applicability driving and achieved by some of his geometric assemblages.[75] It is nonetheless true that questions concerning user, program, and phenomenological effects vis-à-vis architectural space were absent from the geometric processes yielding his formal structures. Indeed, his mindset was primarily that of an engineer-geometer, rarely that of an architect. Hence the aesthetic determinism he favored, which is typical of fields centered round science.[76]

The applications Burt found for his spatial configurations ended up falling mainly in the engineering domain (roof structures and patents) or else became small constructions (sculptures, tents, and pavilions). He never developed a comprehensive architectural interpretation of such configurations. In fact, he hardly even imagined this as a possibility, even though his early *Aquaville* scheme seemed to suggest it. Granted, many of the outcomes of his research fall outside the architecturally conceivable, although the analysis performed in this chapter reveals, among other things, that not only do some of those outcomes feature architectural properties, but more importantly, that these properties are directly relevant to the possibility of extending the realm of form in an architectural sense. In being inherently architectural, the sponge surfaces and polyhedra that are

74 For a wide range of different regimes of order produced through morphology see Haresh Lalvani, guest ed., "Special Issue on Morphology and Architecture," *International Journal of Space Structures*, vol. 11, no 1&2 (1996).

75 Bottero, "Editorial," 238.

76 One example of such aesthetic determinism is his belief that creativity gained in "objective validity" and became more "impersonal" when following his method of producing form, in reference to the external appearance of minimal surfaces being essentially the result of the forces acting within them.

always already programmatic allow Burt's production to bypass the criticism that a number of systematic design methodologies originating in the 1960s and often labeled "positivist" sought to "trade its [architecture's] specificity for a generalized scientism."[77] Here we get the scientism without losing the specificity, in spite of Burt's own blindness to it.

## Independence and Continuity

Burt's unwitting contribution to the architectural thinking around form is indissolubly connected to the singular nature of his career within the Israeli scene of the postwar decades. He appears as one of the most idiosyncratic figures within this idiosyncratic scene, and just like Giorgini's trajectory, Burt's presents at least two levels of idiosyncrasy, themselves related to one another. The first was anticipated above: while most of the architects inspired by Neumann to engage in architectural morphology did so mostly in the context of practice, Burt devoted himself primarily to research and teaching. Second, Israel's victory in the Six-Day War in 1967 led to a progressive shift in the national architectural landscape away from the modernist legacy in general and morphology in particular, and toward a historicized postmodernism of sorts, featuring vernacular elements in the tradition of the Old City of Jerusalem. With Neumann leaving for Canada in 1965, the Ramat Housing complex designed by Zvi Hecker in the early 1970s was, as Segal pointed out, the last attempt to maintain the project of morphology alive in opposition to growing postmodernism.[78] Operating from the somewhat withdrawn position of academia and his research workplace—albeit certainly aware of what was happening in practice—Burt has continued his commitment to morphology despite the changes taking place, up to this day. He was the only one to do so, as Wachman—the only other figure in Israel to start out on a similar research and teaching path in the early 1960s—did not dedicate nearly as much focused energy to morphology over the course of his career as Burt. Given the chronology, his graduate thesis being submitted in 1966 and published in 1967, it turns out that Burt's work was only in its initial stages when the prospects of morphology in Israel were already doomed. In other words, his production was the result of turning a rather short-lived experiment in architectural thinking and practice (Israeli morphology) into the platform for a life-long endeavor.

The combination of relative independence and continuity characterizing Burt's idiosyncratic trajectory was central to the possibility of his production taking morphology's critique of modernism to its logical conclusions. The intense and prolonged concentration on morphology facilitated by such independence and continuity allowed his project to acquire a scope, depth, and degree of ingenuity that was beyond the realm of possibility for those of other morphology colleagues, who were

77 K. Michael Hays, "The Oppositions of Autonomy and History," in *Oppositions Reader: Selected Essays 1973–1984*, 1st edition (New York: Princeton Architectural Press, 1998), x.

78 See Segal, *Unit, Pattern, Site: The Space Packed Architecture of Alfred Neumann 1949–1968*, 155–63.

driven in different directions by the ebbs and flows of practice and soon abandoned morphology. One other consideration to take into account here is that, though oblivious to the elements of morphology's critique of modernism, Burt's project was nevertheless grounded in the same foundations as that of Neumann as regards form and architectural thinking—foundations that contained the DNA of that critique.

### Modernist Critique at its Logical Conclusions

With these two conditions in place, the various ways in which Burt's work analyzed in this chapter revised a number of modernist themes can be discussed as follows. Firstly, if Neumann's spatial organizations were rather self-reliant—generated on the basis of a geometric rule system—Burt's were radically so. For, while Neumann took into account parameters of occupation and context that would eventually induce modifications in his morphological arrangements, Burt mostly ignored such parameters. In a sense, the radical autonomy of Burt's spatial organizations represents the ultimate alternative to functionalism, notwithstanding the fact that in some cases those organizations happen to be suitable for programmatic inhabitation. Secondly, while Neumann's buildings still retained a certain quality of objecthood, Burt never thought in terms of objects. Instead, it can be said that he exploited the possibilities of pattern thinking to the extreme, whether with regard to the complexity of the outcome, that of the elementary unit itself, or that of the relational properties governing the overall assemblage. Indeed, Burt's geometric configurations embody a replacement of contained objecthood by infinity, that is, its opposite from the point of view of figural definition. Thirdly, concerning language of expression, Neumann's morphological arrangements were restricted to a relatively limited set of formats assimilable to a geometric style. Burt's, on the other hand, even if occasionally overlapping with such a style, featured a much wider array of formats of expression overall—including double curvatures, faceted multisurfaces, and fields of various kinds—through which his work moved further away from the language of the Modern Movement.

Paradoxically, Burt's extreme geometric ambitions were not mirrored in other aspects of his persona. His initial projection seemed to presage a highly successful career, but he lacked the drive and competitiveness that would have been necessary to follow through. Every time an opportunity arose to grow internationally, he declined it. As a result, his impact overseas proved to be fairly limited and restricted almost exclusively to the field of morphology, where he took Neumann's initial excursions to a different territory. Even within Israel, his name did not resonate as much as those of others from his and the previous generations, especially outside academia. An unwavering commitment to his culture and family can largely explain what otherwise amounts to a somewhat puzzling career containment.

# Dispositional Intelligence in Architecture

CHAPTER 3

# Cecil Balmond: the Instabilities of Navigating Chance and Lawfulness

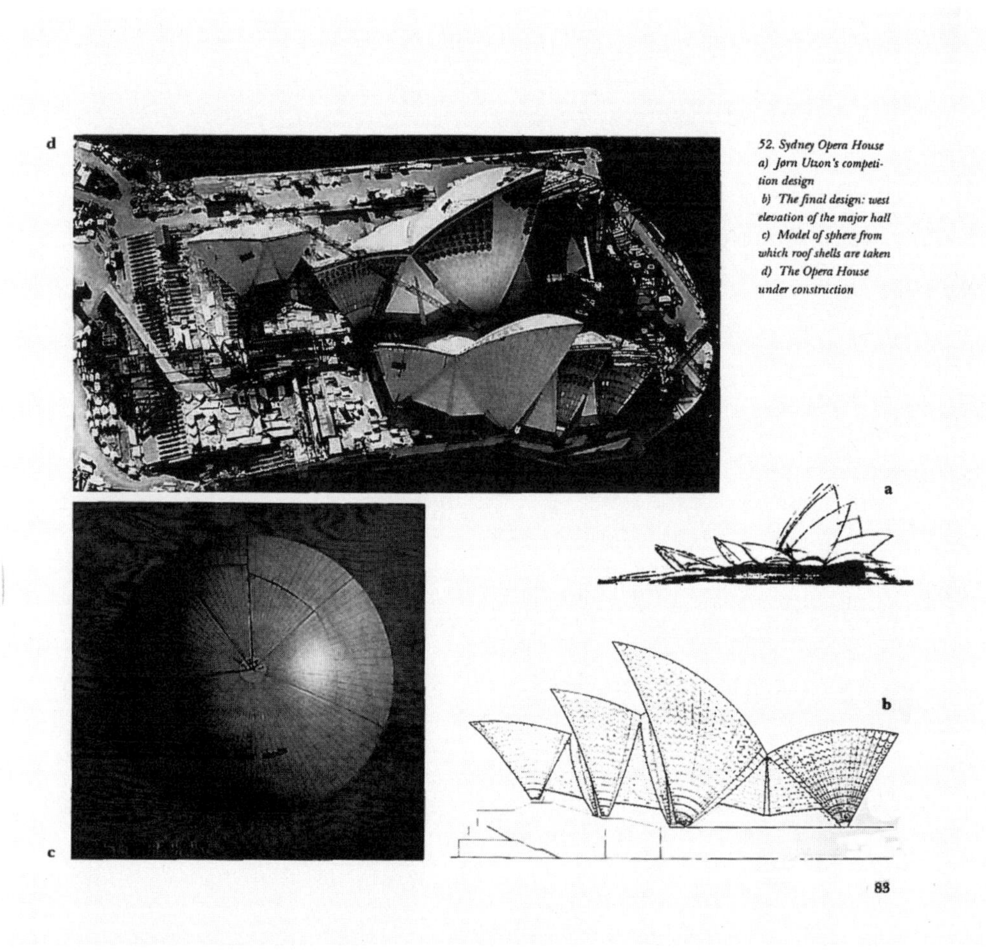


3.1 Left: Sydney Opera House. Jørn Utzon. Competition design, final design, spherical model for roof, and under construction.

3.2 Below: Gorilla House in London Zoo, 1933. Tecton architects.

# BALMOND'S AMBIVALENT RAPPORT WITH THE ARUP TRADITION

When Cecil Balmond (b. 1943) first arrived at ARUP London in 1968, the Sydney Opera House was still under construction. The accomplishment of its structural work, already completed by then, epitomized within the office the capacity of engineering to essentially reconceptualize the key elements of a major piece of architecture.[1] Experiencing the degree to which his profession could have an impact on architectural design was seminal for the young Balmond **(fig. 3.1)**.

During the years leading up to 1972, ARUP (founded in 1946) underwent a number of fundamental changes. In 1963 ARUP Associates, a fully operative architectural design firm, was established as a spin-off. In 1964 both the Computer Group and the Research and Development Group were formed within Ove Arup & Partners.[2] In 1970 the Ove Arup Partnership was born to become a parent firm of Ove Arup & Partners and ARUP Associates, thereby restructuring the nature of the whole company. In parallel, the firm's design ideology also started to transform. Up to that moment, it was known for the strong modernist inclinations with which Ove Arup had infused it through the influence of architects like Walter Gropius and Berthold Lubetkin, whom he had either met in London or worked with as far back as the early 1930s **(fig. 3.2)**.[3] But by the early 1970s, mirroring a more general trend that was animated by design developments in Britain from the 1960s (e.g., Archigram and Cedric Price), figures such as Jack Zunz—one of Arup's historic figures, then a senior partner—and notably Peter Rice had naturally evolved the modernist credo into a high-tech approach that became gospel within the company, if still maintaining a tendency to prioritize a certain structural purity and efficiency. These inclinations underpinned three of the four groups into which the company's building engineering section was divided when Zunz brought Balmond back to the office in 1972, after the completion of his postgraduate studies at Imperial College. The fourth group was a recently formed multidisciplinary unit whose creation had been nurtured by the general climate of transformation. Balmond benefited from it greatly, for Zunz—who may have sensed the young man's tendency toward unorthodox thinking—placed him in that unit.

From its origins, ARUP had specialized primarily in civil and structural engineering. Now the composition of the fourth group included mechanical,

1 Jørn Utzon's idiosyncratic curves, as expressed in his early competition sketches, proved too difficult to build at the time. They had to be rationalized. Although Utzon came up with the final solution–one in which all shells featured a uniform curvature as a result of being cut out of the same sphere–it was the ARUP consultants led by Jack Zunz who had previously argued in favor of regularizing the geometry and offered several ways to do so.

2 The Research and Development Group was comprised of engineers and scientists with various backgrounds who were to provide special consultancy to the various teams within the practice as well as pursuing their own independent projects and commissions.

3 See Jones, *Ove Arup*, 52. Let us recall that Ove Arup participated in a number of CIAM meetings. See ibid., 151. Ove Arup famously said that Lubetkin was his "first real teacher of architecture." See Peter Jones, *Ove Arup: Master Builder of the Twentieth Century* (New Haven, CT: Yale University Press, 2006), 55; and http://www.engineering-timelines.com/who/arup_O/arupOve5.asp (accessed February 4, 2018).

electrical, and plumbing engineers in addition to civil and structural. Cross-fertilization between the different domains of engineering cultivated an understanding of a building's architecture that grew at odds with the search for structural purity otherwise pervasive in the firm. At first, some of the big names, such as Peter Rice himself, were suspicious of what was perceived as a contamination of ARUP's traditional design values. But as they saw that some of the ideas engendered within the new group could be coupled productively with a high-tech approach—the importance of mechanical engineering for the design of Centre Pompidou being a paradigmatic example, with Rice in a prominent role along with Renzo Piano, Richard Rogers, and Gianfranco Franchini—they were eventually persuaded. In hindsight, it is evident that the fourth unit sowed the seed for what the company later became: a multidisciplinary firm with a considerable stylistic flexibility that offers consultancy in anything from public health, to fire safety, geotechnics, environmental services, and oil and gas extraction, to cite a few examples. Balmond took part in this process of diversification and cross-pollination from the outset.

More generally, there were a number of dynamics within the firm which contributed to the type of engineer Balmond later became. First: Ove Arup had established as two of his firm's core principles a close collaboration between architects and engineers and integration between the different disciplines involved in the conception of the built environment. He had been espousing these principles since the 1920s, even though such integration only started to take shape effectively within the company during the 1960s, with the formation of the Research & Development Group and the fourth building engineering group. These interdisciplinary ambitions—which may be read as an attempt to restore the generalist approach that had been dominant before architecture and engineering began to separate at the end of the eighteenth century—became written into Balmond's aspirations. Second: in 1966 Ove Arup first used the term "total design" to refer to the participation of the various engineering disciplines right from the start of a project and to their synthesis with architectural values such as "art" and "commodity."[4] The phrase was borrowed from Walter Gropius, and by 1970 Arup had replaced it with "total architecture." Within this ideal, however, there surfaced a slippage between *integration* and *invasion*. Just a few lines into Ove Arup's famous "Key Speech"—to this day required reading for every employee joining ARUP—total architecture "implies that all relevant design decisions have been considered together and have been integrated into a whole," while elsewhere it "means expanding our field of activity into adjoining fields," one of which is architecture.[5] Indeed, seven years earlier, ARUP Associates had been formed as an independent, full-service architecture office embedded in a larger engineering organization. Gradually, the possibility of engineering's sphere of action exceeding integrated design by becoming directly

4 Ove Arup, "Art and Architecture (1966)," in *Ove Arup, Philosophy of Design: Essays 1943–1981* (Munich; London: Prestel, 2012), 103.

5 Ove Arup, "The Key Speech (1970)," in *Ove Arup, Philosophy of Design: Essays 1943–1981* (Munich; London: Prestel, 2012), 162.

implicated in the design of architecture became one of Balmond's obsessions. Third: the company had a tradition of favoring the establishment of new ventures driven by individual motivation—whether foreign branches, subsidiaries, or the example of ARUP Associates itself, the creation of which had been prompted by architect Philip Dowson's interest in starting a practice of his own in the early 1960s. It is in light of this tradition that Balmond's foundation of the Advanced Geometry Unit (AGU) in 2000 ought to be seen.[6]

But while the context of ARUP shaped the figure of Balmond in a number of significant ways, other traits of the company appear fundamentally at odds with some of his inclinations. Ove Arup espoused a Western humanism of sorts through which he stressed the importance of honoring moral principles (like goodness, loyalty, and justice) among his employees. He believed human relations to be paramount to the prospect of a successful business organization, and consequently they had to be carefully cultivated. In his "Key Speech" Arup referred to the aims he promoted for his firm as implying "a humanitarian attitude, respect, and consideration for persons, fair dealings, and the rest."[7] In contrast, the implementation of these moral precepts in the professional domain was never a priority for Balmond. Moreover, on the basis of this humanist attitude, ARUP have historically attempted to occupy a middle ground between attracting gifted, strong-willed individuals and keeping as horizontal a hierarchy as possible, where authority was meant to extend far down the ranks. To that effect, even the financial structure was modified: between 1966 and 1977 the company went from a few partners owning most of it to their equity holding being transferred to charitable and employee trusts. As a result, all income started to be shared among employees based on length of service and degree of responsibility. With a preference for "teamwork rather than stardom," a certain element of self-driven initiative was encouraged, albeit always within certain limits.[8] Some notable ARUP engineers went so far as to claim that the tendency was to avoid promoting yourself and, in fact, to understate yourself.[9] In contradistinction to this, Balmond was driven by an unbridled ambition and relentlessly sought to single himself out—not only within ARUP, but also within the discipline of engineering at large. This attitude carried with it the kind of "arrogance" that Ove Arup associated with certain stereotypical artists and architects—one, he felt, prevented anyone from being a good team member.[10]

## Balmond vis-à-vis ARUP's Greats

To fully understand Balmond it is also necessary to place him in relation to a handful of engineers who had previously achieved great prominence within the company. Ove Arup himself was a very different kind of professional and personal specimen. He was certainly a fine engineer. But as a product of the Modern Movement, he gravitated

6 After his appointment as ARUP's deputy chairman in 2002, Balmond had far more politics and business to deal with than anything else. However, he kept in touch with design through the AGU (Advanced Geometry Unit), which he had founded in 2000 within a group led by ARUP director David Lewis, a long-time collaborator of Balmond since his early days. The AGU included mainly engineers and mathematicians, though also architects and programmers, and occasionally a musician, artist or scientist. Pursuing both research projects and their own architecture commissions in addition to collaborations with other architects and artists, the AGU epitomized Balmond's career-long attempt to boost a particular design ideology by bringing together specialists from different disciplines and apply it to architecture. Upon his retirement in 2008 he left the AGU–which only survived for two more years under Daniel Bosia–and in 2010, aged sixty-seven, he started his own firm, Balmond Studio.

7 Arup, "The Key Speech," 166.

8 Ibid., 165.

9 As described by ARUP Project Director Francis Archer–who worked with Balmond on a number of projects during the 1990s–in interview with the author conducted in London on October 14, 2013.

10 Arup, "Art and Architecture (1966)," 105.

3.3 At the Sydney Opera House site in 1966, Ove Arup gives instructions with Jack Zunz to his left and Mick Lewis to his right.

towards values such as functionality, beauty, simplicity, and spiritual quality which would have to be considered classical or, indeed, conservative from the perspective of Balmond's design ideology. Although Ove Arup's contributions—particularly in reinforced and pre-stressed concrete structures—should not be underestimated, his reputation stems far less from those than from the ethos around which he built his company, the enormous success that ensued, and the many brilliant engineers whom, over the years, he recruited, influenced, and inspired to carry out his ideas. In addition, he was a prolific theorist of the type of relationship between architect and engineer that, in his view, would be conducive to the integration of the two disciplines he so strongly advocated—even if in his professional experience (unlike in Balmond's after 1986, as shall be explored below) such integration never became the synergy that would qualify as an architecture-engineering hybrid. Indeed, Ove Arup mostly limited himself to providing engineering soundness to a design philosophy whose weight the architect in question carried almost entirely on his own. Although, to this day, he remains one of only three engineers to have received the RIBA Royal Gold Medal for Architecture (the other two being Pier Luigi Nervi and Peter Rice), he was fully aware that his stature within architecture was not of the highest.

In 1966, showing a modesty that would be completely alien to Balmond, he put it thus: "I have no doubt rendered some service to architecture of a rather ordinary kind—a little common sense here and there—but nothing spectacular like Nervi, Morandi or Maillart, and nothing to compare with the giants of architecture."[11]

Balmond got to interact with Ove Arup and in fact maintained that the company's founder was his mentor.[12] This is, however, not accurate. By the late 1960s and early 1970s it was extraordinarily difficult for any employee (with the exception of those he had closely worked with in the past) to come into frequent contact with "the Old Man," beyond occasionally being called to discuss details of some project or another.[13] Certainly, being but a young employee at the time, Balmond was even more of an exception in this regard. But while Ove Arup may have seen something distinct in Balmond's modus operandi—in addition to their shared passion for philosophy and mathematics—their intermittent rapport never developed into an actual mentorship.

If there was anybody close to being a mentor to Balmond at the beginning of his career, it was Jack Zunz. One of ARUP's historic figures—appointed Chairman of Ove Arup & Partners in 1977 and Co-Chairman of Ove Arup Partnership in 1984—Zunz had been hired by Ove Arup in 1950, only four years after the company was founded **(fig. 3.3)**. Known primarily for his essential role in rationalizing the shells of Jørn Utzon's Sydney Opera, his profile as an engineer was rather different than Balmond's. He leaned toward the same engineering values as Ove Arup himself, both of them coming from the modernist tradition. His preoccupations also included training, the overriding thrust of technology, the nature and evolution of the industry, the role of engineering within it, and by extension, the importance of the engineer in an industrial-technological society. Balmond also adopted another of Zunz's main concerns—namely, his resentment about the diminished presence he believed the engineer to have in the public eye, compared with the architect—to the point of obsession.[14] But beyond that—and in addition to bringing him back into the company after his postgraduate studies and placing him in the fourth building engineering group—Zunz was instrumental to Balmond's early professional advancement at a number of key moments. For example, when the latter was only in his late twenties, Zunz made him project manager on a sizeable brewery project for Carlsberg and gave him entire responsibility for a critical decision during construction of the cantilevered walls, thereby showing trust and support in the face of a rather challenging situation involving structural and budgetary risks. Later, Zunz had him meet and work with James Stirling on the competition for the Neue Staatsgalerie, which became a key turning point in his career, as shall be touched on below.

11 Ibid., 99.

12 In an interview with the author conducted in London on October 9, 2013.

13 Peter Rice pointed out that this difficulty was already the case even ten years earlier, around the time when he joined the company. See Peter Rice, An *Engineer Imagines* (London: Artemis, 1998), 67.

14 Jack Zunz, "Mirror Mirror on the Wall . . . How Fair Is the Engineer's Image?," *Arup Journal* 28, no. 2 (1993), 8–11.

**3.4** Peter Rice at La Villette, Paris. Undated.

It was around the time of this interaction with Stirling that a defining situation unfolded involving the third in this lineage of ARUP's greats: Peter Rice. By the mid-1970s, Rice was already becoming quite famous, and Balmond—only eight years his junior—admitted looking up to him. After winning the Neue Staatsgalerie, Rice was called to team up with Stirling for the construction of the building. But they never got along, and following an alleged episode in which the British architect characterized a sketch by Rice as depicting what "looked like a supermarket ceiling," the collaboration fell apart and Balmond, who was part of the team under Rice, took over.[15] After that, Balmond and Rice never spoke again, and the former acknowledged that he was quite sure the latter did not like him. This estrangement may seem paradoxical, since in many respects Rice was the closest precedent to Balmond within ARUP.

## Peter Rice as Balmond's Closest Precedent

In general terms, Rice pre-empted Balmond's success at addressing Ove Arup's bitter criticism of the secondary role of the engineer vis-à-vis the architect and ultimately overcoming it several times.[16] Specifically, Rice's main interests revolved around materials. He sought to develop a sophisticated grasp of their nature and physical properties as a path toward innovation and the production of spatial qualities: for example, he concluded that glass was "flexible" and could therefore be supported by a cable structure—glass and cables being the elements on which he tended to focus. Given his high-tech inclinations, he was also keen on experimenting with different assembly techniques and exposing them so that the manner in which the different pieces came together in a building was clearly readable. Balmond, as shall be discussed below, was a rather different kind of engineer. Yet there were a few revealing parallels between the two figures. In 1980, his creative side having recently been ignited after working on Centre Pompidou, an opportunity arose for Rice to work on a project in La Villette that ARUP did not want to do **(fig. 3.4)**. Having fallen in love with French culture and learned French, he set up a company in Paris to undertake it, along with industrial designer Martin Francis and architect

15 This episode was recounted by Balmond in an interview with the author conducted in London on October 9, 2013. Two other engineers in addition to Balmond appeared as co-authors of an article published in *The Arup Journal* on the recently completed project. See Cecil Balmond, David Atling, and Tom Barker, "Stuttgart Art Gallery," *The Arup Journal* 3, no. 19 (October 1984): 10–17. However, a slightly abridged version of the same piece that came out two years later in an issue of *Building Design* features Balmond alone, which seems to confirm his leading role in the team. See Cecil Balmond, "Stirling Style," *Building Design*, no. 807 (October 10, 1986): 34–35.

16 "[The architect] should have the engineer at his elbow as soon as he starts sketching. That, however, is rarely feasible. As a rule, the engineer is not even appointed then–which is wrong, of course. As a result it is often the architect who makes all the main structural dispositions, and the engineer is left the task of calculating the sizes of beams, columns, etc. Many architects, and still more clients, assume that to be the job of the structural engineer: even some structural engineers would accept this. But that is a degradation of the role of the structural engineer." Ove Arup, "The Architect and The Engineer (1959)," in *Ove Arup, Philosophy of Design: Essays 1943–1981* (Munich; London: Prestel, 2012): 60.

Ian Ritchie (RFR). His situation within ARUP became unique, as he remained an active director and a member of the group board while running another firm in another country. Years later, Zunz pointed out that Rice was "quite complicated in that way. And that was OK. We came to an accommodation."[17] This characterization might very well have applied to Balmond—indeed, Rice's independent enterprise resonates quite tellingly with the founding of the AGU twenty years later, even if not established within ARUP. For both engineers felt compelled to start a small, agile group with professional aspirations through which to pursue their agendas concerning the relationship between engineering and architectural design.

Nevertheless, their motivations differed. In contrast to Balmond, Rice stressed that innovation had to be of benefit to humankind and take into account a people's response, thereby echoing Ove Arup's moral overtones. But their partnerships were based on a similar principle, since Rice anticipated Balmond's strategy of crafting close collaborations with just a handful of renowned architects who welcomed an engineer having a substantial role in the design aspects of a building—Norman Foster, I. M. Pei, Rogers, and Piano being his most recurrent partners.[18] Piano described his creative relationship with Rice as one in which it was impossible to distinguish between architect and engineer because of the continuous "border-crossing," a description that echoed quite literally what Koolhaas once said of Balmond: "Is one of them the horse and the other the jockey? 'We swap around all the time'."[19] In this regard, Zunz portrayed Rice as a mathematics-oriented man who found in his mid-thirties that he was, in fact, a designer, thus becoming a "very rare" creature in engineering: someone with strong analytical capabilities but also imaginative conceptually.[20] Not only in the sense of this synergy between architecture and engineering, but also in their shared interest in other creative domains—such as art, music, and philosophy—did both Rice and Balmond attempt to bypass the notion that the engineer is but a specialist with a training in science, someone with a narrow disciplinary role. Along these lines, Rice suggested that, rather than arguing, refusing, or calculating, the engineer "imagines."[21] Another noteworthy similarity between the two figures is that they both carved out time to teach.[22]

## Common Ground, Radical Differences

Both Zunz and Rice expressed a marked resentment about the status of the engineer, either in relation to architects alone or in more general social and disciplinary terms. In his Institution of Structural Engineers Gold Medal acceptance speech, tellingly titled "Matters of Concern," Zunz asserted that "the work and worth of engineers is not properly understood and hence appreciated."[23] Elsewhere he wondered "[w]hy we can't have a Royal Institution of Engineers speaking on behalf of *all* professional engineers," complaining that "the role of the professional engineer is

17 12'24" in https://www.youtube.com/watch?v=v8ubOIkQCf4, accessed May 29, 2017.

18 Unlike Balmond, however—and despite having been awarded the RIBA Medal for Architecture—Rice saw himself exclusively as an engineer, not as an architectural designer in any way: ". . . people often call me an 'architectural engineer', but that's a load of rubbish—I am an engineer, plain and simple." Peter Rice, "RIBA Royal Gold Medal Speech," 1992, 23.

19 On Piano's description of his creative rapport with Rice, see 28'20" in https://www.youtube.com/watch?v=v8ubOIkQCf4, accessed May 29, 2017. Koolhaas's statement can be found in Graham Bizley, "The Rem & Cecil Show," *Building Design*, April 29, 2005, 21.

20 02'15" in https://www.youtube.com/watch?v=v8ubOIkQCf4, accessed May 29, 2017.

21 Toward the end of his life, Rice wrote *An Engineer Imagines*, his only book. In many ways, it can be understood as a plea for the engineering profession.

22 Rice taught at the Architectural Association, the Royal College of Art, and Cambridge University; Balmond at the Städelschule in Frankfurt, Yale, Harvard, the London School of Economics, and the University of Pennsylvania.

23 Jack Zunz, "Matters of Concern," *The Arup Journal*, no. 3 (1989), 22.

seldom if ever seen in documentaries, nor is it featured in light or serious drama," and adding that "[t]o raise the image of the engineer in the public's eye we have to strike a fairer balance between obsequious anonymity on the one hand, which is the general case at present, and unfair exploitation of the cult of personality and the 'I did it all' syndrome on the other."[24] For Rice, "the argument is that there are many engineering contributions that go unrecognized, or which are attributed to the architects or others with whom the engineer is working."[25] Justifying an unrelenting need to publish his work on the grounds that his collaborations with architects were often so intimate that he would not get the recognition he felt he deserved, the point of departure of Balmond's ambitions was identical to that of his predecessors.[26]

Despite sharing this common ground, Balmond's engineering and design thinking took a very different direction. Firstly, many of the core elements of his design ideology stood in opposition to the values of the modern tradition that ARUP had fostered over the years—values such as directness, honesty, appropriateness, unobtrusiveness, economy of means, and delight, in addition to those mentioned above. Secondly, Balmond was always critical of high-tech. He felt this approach entailed too great an investment of energy just to make the structure clear, and rejected its tendency to material explicitness, the fetishization of detail, and ultimately what he viewed as "excess." For him, all of these would satisfy the appetite of an engineering mindset, but not that of an architectural one, which would crave spatial narrative instead.[27] Promoting ideas that were vastly different from high-tech at a time when this design approach was showing signs of losing its hegemony in a sizeable sector of the British architecture and engineering scenes (late 1980s, early 1990s) was a way for the highly aspirational Balmond to single himself out within both the company and the wider engineering sphere. Thirdly, he distinguished himself in terms of the intellectual and scientific references motivating his design thinking, as shall be explored in a section below.

24 Zunz, "Mirror Mirror on the Wall . . . How Fair Is the Engineer's Image?," 11.

25 Rice, *An Engineer Imagines*, 75.

26 Balmond articulated such a need in an interview with the author conducted in London on October 9, 2013.

27 See also Bizley, "The Rem & Cecil Show," 20.

## THE OTTO EFFECT

During Balmond's first years at ARUP through the mid-1970s, the Structures 3 group led by Edmund Happold was immersed in a number of collaborations with Frei Otto.[28] Otto's influence through these collaborations became central to the origination and development of a high-tech sensibility not only at ARUP, but also in the British context at large, and beyond.[29] The German architect-engineer brought his consolidated experience with some of the key structural components of that sensibility—primarily lightweight tensile elements, like special cables, fabrics, and several kinds of attachable membranes.

Upon returning from work on the Sydney Opera House, Rice was assigned to Structures 3. The Arctic City competition in Berlin from 1970 was the first time Rice and Otto were part of the same design team. From that point on, Rice, enthused by Otto's expertise and range of experiments, tended to engage some form of high-tech in his design thinking. Such was Otto's impact at ARUP that in 1973 Happold founded the so-called Lightweight Structures Laboratory within the company, modeling it after Otto's own Institute for Lightweight Structures in Stuttgart, and persuading him to act as a co-director-in-charge. Fueled by Otto's input, ARUP's Lightweight Structures Laboratory busied itself with, among other things, the computer capabilities newly available at the time to generate formal complexity as well as software writing to analyze nonlinear behavior in lightweight structures.

In addition to his specific knowledge of lightweight structures, Otto came into the ARUP sphere with a reputation as an advanced researcher into questions concerning biological structuralism in relation to engineering thinking, such as the study of minimal surfaces via soap film experiments, and more generally the search for universal principles of optimal structure via examination of the world of nature. Otto's project combined the prospects of this biological structuralism with the anti-rationalist tradition of expressionist architecture, as his structures resulted from triggering autonomous form-finding processes analogous to those found in nature—an operative autonomy anticipated by Kepes—through the lens of his particular sculptural aesthetics.

Investigations involving autonomous processes of that kind were relatively widespread at the peak of the general shift toward a deep scientization of design

28 ARUP worked with Frei Otto on projects such as Grande Tende (1965), Arctic City (1970), and the Mannheim Multihalle (1975).

29 It was Otto himself who introduced Richard Rogers to the engineers comprising the Structures 3 group, one of whom was Rice, and recommended that he work with them. This introduction gave rise to the team that ended up winning the competition for the Pompidou Center in Paris.

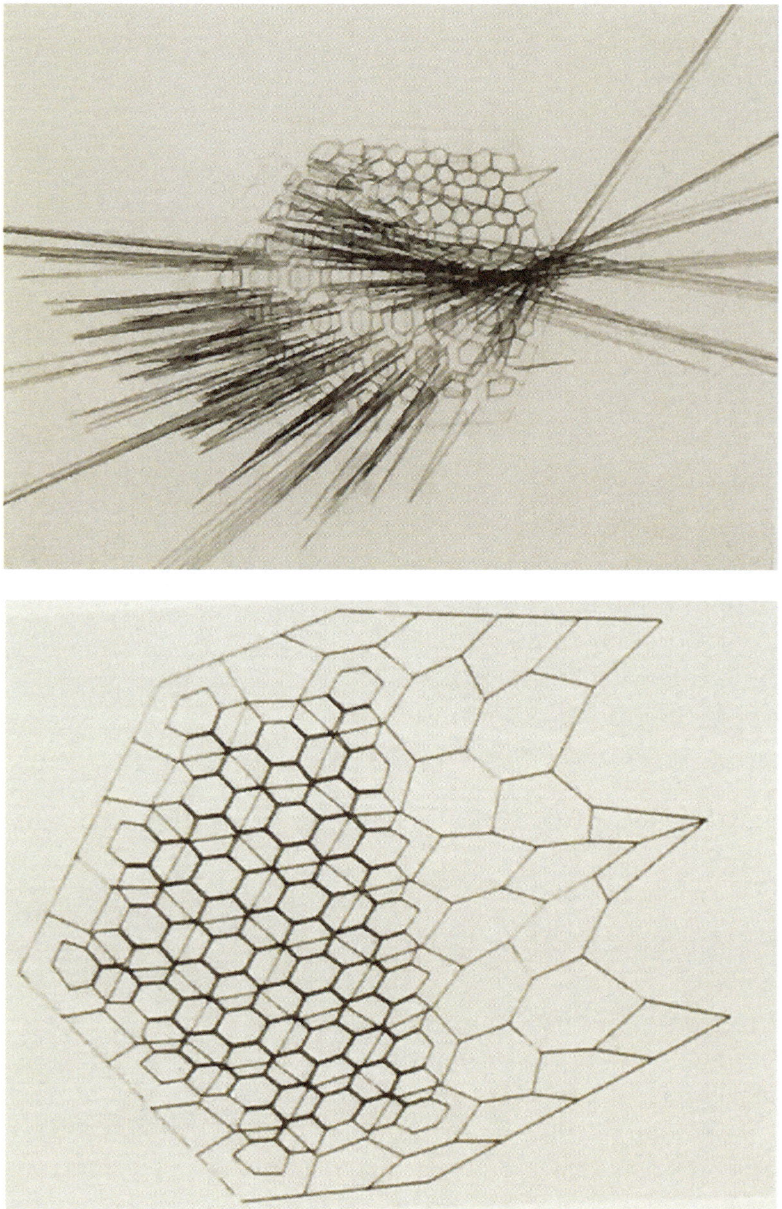

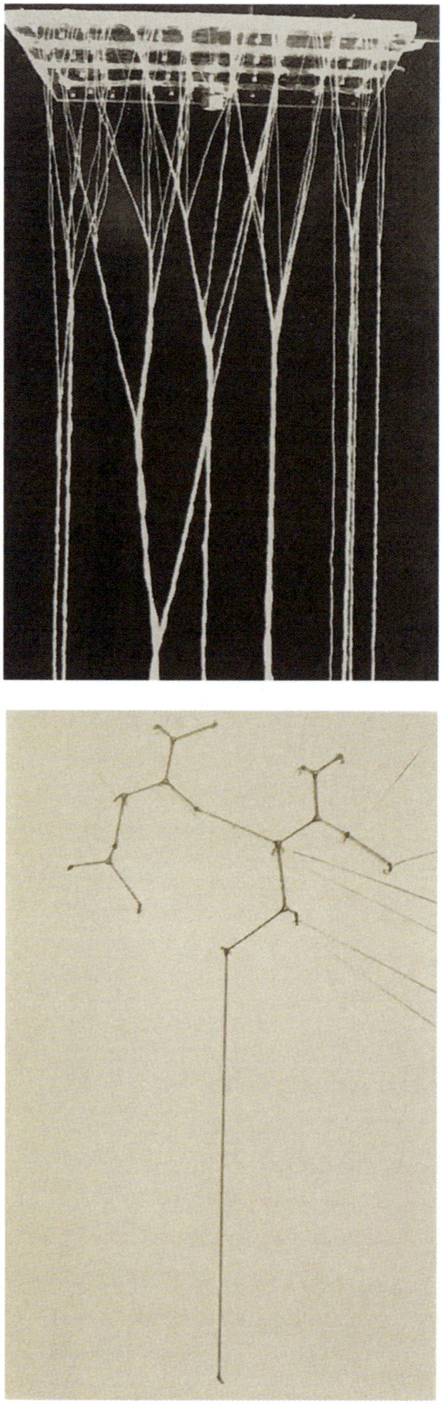

**3.5** Drawings for the KOCOMMAS government complex in Riyadh. Ove Arup & Partners with Frei Otto and Rolf Gutbrod.

**3.6** Otto's branching experiments.

taking place across the West during the 1960s. Like Otto, other researchers and designers found themselves experimenting with applications of automation, self-forming structures, intelligent machines, autopoiesis, and cybernetics in general—except in Otto's case such experiments were tied more to organic and inorganic matter than to computation. Furthermore, not unlike the organicist views flourishing elsewhere during the 1950s and 1960s, Otto's reverence for nature as a source of technical knowledge implied a direct condemnation of modernism. In the wake of World War II, the intelligence and goodness of nature were to be opposed to the potential atrocities that might be caused by excessive rationalism, in general, and the exclusive employment of human rationalism, in particular. The other side of this criticism was the challenge to the Modern Movement's set format of expression. As an alternative leading to an expansion of what is conceivable within architecture, Otto's "pneu" endeavor purported to put together an encyclopedia of possible structural arrangements reached through material experiments.

### A New Underlying Science

Whether through direct engagement with Otto or through some of the investigations he indirectly motivated, questions concerning nonlinearity, minimal surfaces, complex morphology, and biological structuralism became part of the regular lexicon at ARUP throughout the 1970s. Exposure to this lexicon significantly fed Balmond's design inclinations early on, to the point of much of it subsequently becoming central to his own design thinking. While Balmond was not in sympathy with the high-tech style and the engineering thinking that accompanied it, he did appreciate some of the underlying science, which he ended up co-opting mainly for generative rather than analytic purposes. It is therefore no coincidence that designs where Otto played a prominent role along with some ARUP engineers, such as the KOCOMMAS government complex in Riyadh, and a number of Otto's abstract experiments in form thinking, such as his study of branching patterns, resonate so strongly with some of Balmond's later work **(fig. 3.5–6)**.

The same exposure piqued Rice's curiosity about algorithms and the computer's capacity to enable complex modeling and analysis methods, these also being two of Balmond's main domains of concentration **(fig. 3.7)**. Yet while some of these domains relating to Otto's legacy certainly emerged earlier within the company, the degree to which Balmond honed in on them, expanded the references involved, and proceeded toward a theory of design based on their study differentiated him further from previous figures at ARUP.

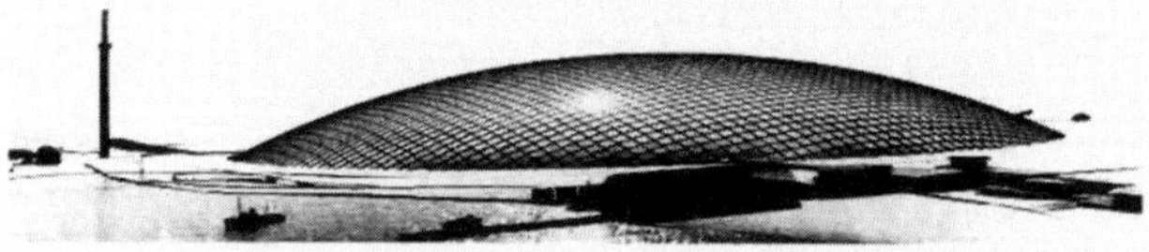

Study for 'Arctic City', architect, Frei Otto. An air-supported roof dome spanning 2km to enclose a town of 40,000 inhabitants in controlled climate.

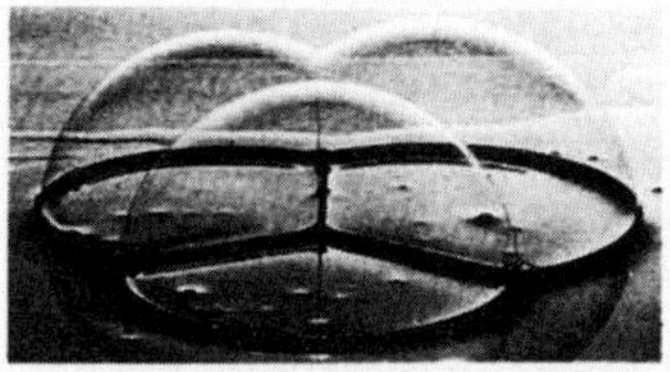

From a soap film surface study by Frei Otto at the Institute for Lightweight Structures, University of Stuttgart, Germany.

rience the vital relationship between stiffness, geometry or curvature and the stability of the surface under changing loads. The modelling is used to help generate surfaces which have a balanced relationship between curvature in one direction and curvature in the other and between curvature at different parts of the surface.

Fabric is a highly specialized subject. To design something in fabric, you have to guarantee that the shape has certain characteristics. The principal characteristic it must have is an anti-clastic curvature at all points in the surface. The term 'anti-clastic' means that if you take two cross-sections at right angles to each other, the curvature in one direction is the opposite to the curvature in the other direction, so that the fabric is tensioned against itself. This means that if you want to design something in fabric, you have to generate a form which has these characteristics, otherwise the fabric will flap in windy conditions or under other kinds of non-regular loading and it will tend to destroy itself.

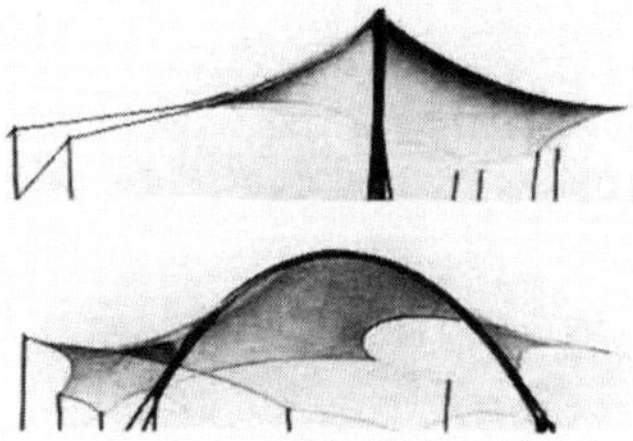

Soap film study by Frei Otto for Kuwait Sports City.

There are a whole variety of ways in which you can achieve this anti-clastic curvature in terms of the form. You can introduce simple tent-like structures, or you can introduce arches or other kinds of structural elements into the surface to create one particular line of curvature which is then used to offset the other curvatures. Certain areas of the fabric can be flat provided there is a sufficient amount of prestress in the surface. That's the second characteristic that you have to have. To prestress a fabric means that you have to be able to tension it up in such a way that under no-load the fabric has got tension in both directions throughout its surface. And this tension is such that one direction is pulling against the other direction of tension. It's possible to have flat areas of fabric provided they're not too extensive and provided they're bounded by areas of fabric which are not flat.

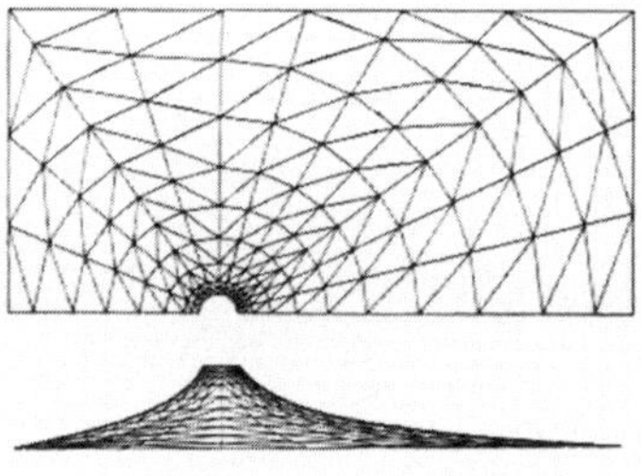

A 'finite element mesh' is the computer's version of the soap film. The membrane curvature can be altered by changing the balance of tension between one direction and another.

There are different kinds of fabric. But most of the kind of structures I have been designing use Teflon-coated glass fibre (polytetrafluoroethylene; PTFE), which is a relatively stiff fabric, permanent in nature. We are talking about a permanent building material because the Teflon is a non-deteriorating plastic and the glass fibre that is the load-carrying element within the fabric has the characteristics of glass so it is comparatively stiff. This means that high levels of accuracy and precision are needed when defining the fabric shape so that at no point in the surface is there any lack of prestress and at no point in the surface do you get creasing. But all of

Precedent page:
**3.7** Frei Otto's finite element studies of soap film solutions featured in Peter Rice's *An Engineer Imagines.*

## INTELLECTUAL BUILD-UP: A CHRONOLOGY

Balmond's interest in the humanities was first awakened through his family. His mother was a musician and his father a historian, in addition to being the president of Sri Lanka's only university at the time. During the 1950s, visitors to the family home were mostly scholars of classical studies and the arts, with people in science being the exception. This atmosphere stimulated in Balmond a fascination with the world of letters and the pursuit of universal truths in thinking, largely through the reading of Nietzsche and Spinoza. His training and the beginning of his professional career took him in a different direction. But in the mid-1970s he came across Bertrand Russell's classic from 1945, *A History of Western Philosophy*, which became a constant literary companion for the next ten years. This attachment to a philosophical source rekindled and further fueled his appeal to universals.

By 1983, the acquaintance he had gained with ancient philosophy through Russell's section on the pre-Socratics—with Empedocles becoming particularly influential, his four elements theory being a recurrent subtext throughout Balmond's later manuscripts—prompted another research path. He began to study Greek proportion theory, with a focus on *The Thirteen Books of Euclid's Elements*, and concluded that there was a dynamic component to the geometric reasoning featured in the various propositions, whether it be a line that gets progressively subdivided, multiplied, and redimensioned, or a polygon that varies in shape and proportion as a demonstration proceeds. From here he turned to source books of early mathematics: Euler became relevant in terms of prime numbers and the possibility of finding a structure of relations behind irrationals; the distinction between a sequence and a series—which shall be elaborated below—proved equally powerful.

### Chaos Theory

Also in 1983, Balmond encountered Goethe's theories concerning the formation and transformation of organic bodies. Based on principles like "unfolding" and "growth," such theories served to increase his awareness of the dynamic nature of form-thinking processes. Goethe led him first to look at late eighteenth- and early nineteenth-century German aesthetics, and eventually to Semper, who translated Goethe's genetic view of organic nature into an architectural code. Further to this developing interest in underlying dynamic patterns, in 1987 Balmond purchased

James Gleick's *Chaos: Making a New Science* upon publication. For the first time, chaos theory entered the picture of his intellectual imaginary. The new evolving geometries of nature resulting from Benoit Mandelbrot's concept of fractals and Mitchell Feigenbaum's calculation of a universal constant made a particularly strong impact. In parallel, he examined a number of studies on economic theory that had been undertaken at Princeton's Institute for Advanced Study during the 1970s, focusing on the fluctuation of market forces. Taken together, all of these references involved different approaches to the problem of complexity, which Balmond embraced wholeheartedly for decades to come. Specifically, he began to understand that structural, logical reasoning could help to unveil underlying patterns of complexity as well as their relationship to emerging forms.

The years 1986–87 turned out to be essential in Balmond's career. On the one hand, the nature of his collaborations with Rem Koolhaas, which started in 1986, fully set free his inner desire to practice a type of design thinking that was attuned to architecture, not only engineering. On the other, by 1987 he had acquainted himself with most of the domains that would serve as the basis of his philosophy of design: irrational numbers, fractals, the dynamic nature of form thinking, and chaos theory as the foundation of the nonlinear, all of which was to feed his ongoing interest in the universals of design thinking.[30]

Of those domains, chaos theory became the central one. For a large part of his production Balmond essentially turned its basic precepts into the pillars of his design approach. Chaos theory deals with *complex systems*, that is, those whose behavior is hard to model—and, therefore, understand—due to the great number of agents or parts as well as to the varied nature of their relationships, interactions, and dependencies. Examples of complex systems may be as diverse as cells, chemical reactions, tribes, corporations, animal species, the human brain, the marketplace—and an algorithm, as a particular concept of complexity describing a systematic way of performing a certain task that can be accounted for through purely mathematical reasoning and notation.[31] Complex systems, adaptive and dynamic, tend to self-organize into subgroups or subsystems, bound together for further cohesiveness of the whole.[32]

Chaos theory focuses on complex systems featuring an apparent randomness and unveils the underlying patterns driving their behavior. These particular systems are called *nonlinear*, which is why chaos theory is often referred to as "nonlinear science" or "nonlinear system analysis." In nonlinear systems—such as weather, the voltage and power in a resistor, and certain swarms, to mention a few—variations in the output cannot be explained through proportional variations in the input, even though the former remains dependent on the latter. The outcome is directly compatible with the initial conditions, but it cannot be univocally deduced from

30 In addition to his association with Koolhaas and the beginnings of his own theoretical framework, the second half of the 1980s marked the start of Balmond's teaching career in architecture at the Städelschule in Frankfurt, where he taught alongside Enric Miralles and Peter Cook.

31 See David Ruelle, *Chance and Chaos*, Princeton Science Library (Princeton, NJ: Princeton University Press, 1991), 137.

32 See, for instance, M. Mitchell Waldrop, *Complexity: The Emerging Science at the Edge of Order and Chaos* (New York, NY: Simon & Schuster, 1992), 11–12.

it, since the cause-and-effect relations linking the various variables are not stable and therefore cannot be diagrammed as straight lines. In other words, the outcome cannot be forecast: it possesses an *emergent* quality. Negligible changes to the starting point may bring huge alterations to the results—an occurrence commonly known as the "butterfly effect," or more technically, *sensitive dependence on initial conditions*, whose programming is one of chaos theory's preoccupations.

Such occurrence is due to the fact that nonlinear systems combine determinism and unpredictability: chaos theory shows that, under certain conditions, within a nonlinear system evolving along deterministic paths—where "determinism" stands for the lack of randomness involved in the future states of the system—certain processes of self-organization involving an element of chance may shatter the existing order and beget higher levels of organization and coherence. In other words, in some cases order may arise out of disorder and chaos. It is thus possible to speak about chance—a term synonymous with randomness within chaos theory—being embedded in an otherwise deterministic framework.[33] Jacques Monod, another author well-known to Balmond, put it another way when discussing the constitution of the biosphere in terms that recall those of Empedocles: chance and necessity, far from being mutually exclusive, can, and in fact, do coexist.[34]

Chaos theory presents itself in opposition to the classical science inherited from Newton, which viewed everything that exists as logically and causally connected, and attempted to systematically and comprehensively explain change and evolution on the basis of immutable, time-independent laws—with no room for spontaneous developments or randomness. Nonlinear processes are instead time-dependent, time-oriented, or more precisely, their characteristic temporality is *irreversible*. They cannot be re-enacted even if the initial conditions are replicated, unlike the processes described by classical or mechanistic science. Once in motion they cannot be traced backwards and forwards. Being concerned with "the global nature of systems" and making "strong claims about the universal nature of complexity," chaos theory is an inherently interdisciplinary endeavor.[35] It has also given rise to a very particular kind of imagery, featuring fractals, moving waves, swaying pendulums, and other structures underlying complexity, as well as a distinctive notional domain including terms such as "feedback loops" and "self-similarity." Balmond pioneered the in-depth study of chaos theory from within the domain of engineering, having encountered it just about a decade after its consolidation as a science.

33 I. Prigogine, *Order Out of Chaos: Man's New Dialogue with Nature* (Boulder, CO: New Science Library, 1984), xxi–xvi. On the synonym see Ruelle, *Chance and Chaos*, 5.

34 See Jacques Monod, *Chance and Necessity; an Essay on the Natural Philosophy of Modern Biology* (New York, NY: Knopf, 1971).

35 James Gleick, *Chaos: Making a New Science* (New York, NY: Viking Press, 1987), 5.

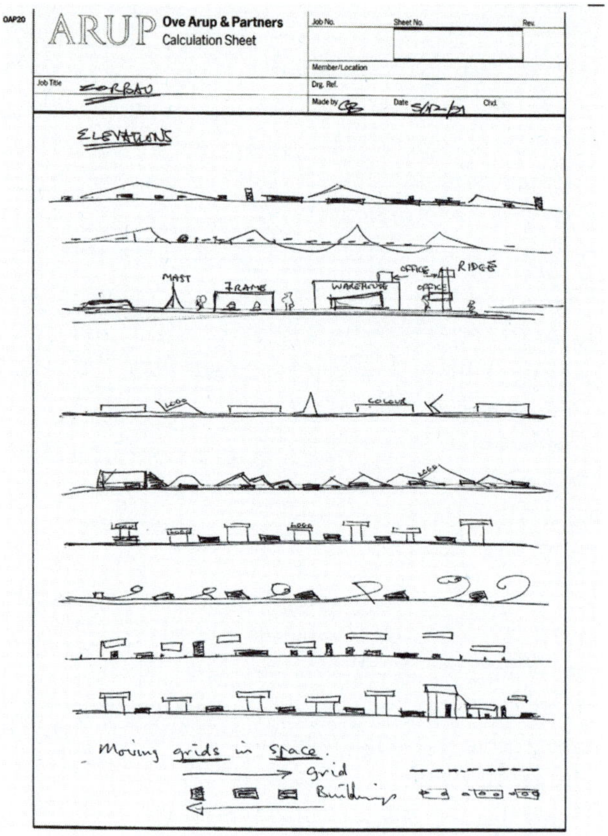


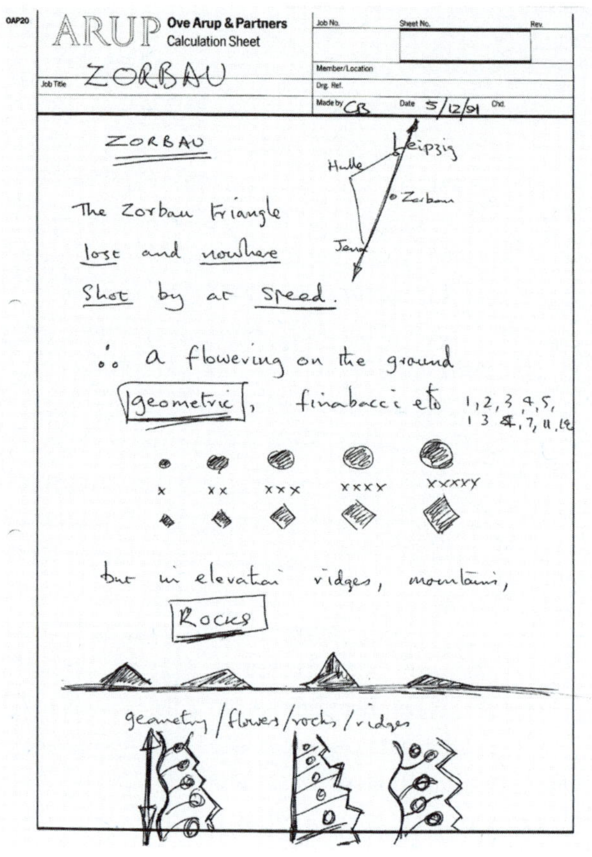


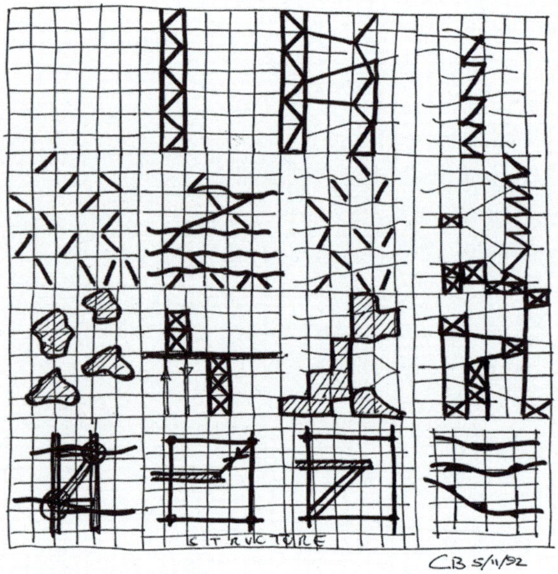


**3.8–9** Above: Sketches for a project in the German village of Zorbau, 1991.

**3.10** Left: Sketches for the Jussieu library project with Rem Koolhaas, 1992.

## From "Actions" to Nonlinear Systems

Once he had acquired the basis of this knowledge and his interest in architecture had matured through the various projects with Koolhaas, Balmond started to generate thoughts through abstract sketches and conceptual notes—the earliest of which date back to 1987—that ended up being relevant to his eventual theoretical project. Published in 2002 as *Informal*, the project as such was not conceived until 1996. In the meantime, he dug deeper into his intellectual references—primarily those around chaos theory—as he produced a vast amount of manuscripts comprising writings and abstract diagrams in nearly equal measure. Although the bulk of manuscripts directly germane to *Informal* date from 1995 and 1996, some key notions surfaced a few years earlier. The first to be found is *action*, which Balmond defined in 1988 as following "the idea" as its source, breaking down into "strategies" and "tactics," and necessarily unfolding "in small increments," rather than at once.[36] In 1991, the concept of *moving grids in space* emerged when he was working on a project in the German village of Zorbau. Here, the various programmatic elements would be distributed in plan according to a geometric pattern based on the Fibonacci sequence **(fig. 3.8–9)**.[37] In 1992, sketches made for the Jussieu library project with Koolhaas—depicting different structural systems sometimes cohabiting space, sometimes envisaged for separate sectors of the building—anticipated his notion of *episodic structure* **(fig. 3.10)**.[38]

In the March 1993 issue of the Spanish magazine *Quaderns d'arquitectura i urbanisme* the term "informal" appeared in print for the first time. Opposing an "active, dominant, overpowering" kind of technology that would reduce people's freedom, Balmond pointed out that, wherever possible, engineers would in fact favor passive systems, such as the use of natural light and ventilation regulated by intelligent envelopes. Invoking a rather common connotation of the term that has to do with tradition and idiosyncrasy, "informal" alluded to the character of these passive systems when seen in opposition to an overtly technologized environment. Insofar as the effect was to allow the user to exert control over an environment, Balmond further characterized this approach as "personal" and related it to the "micro, local and individual." By this point, chaos theory was starting to impact his views: "[t]he vertical form of decision making is being eroded. There is more simultaneity today. Aesthetics has a degree of randomness and chance, accidental interruption is allowed and seen as enhancing."[39]

In June that same year the term reappeared in an article in German for *Arch+*. By then it had acquired another dimension, the one which determined the basis of its definitive development. Anthropological undertones gave way to the question of a building's formal aspects. In Balmond's view, a widespread demand for regularity in architecture was conducive to a type of order that prioritized an

36 In a manuscript titled "Action and Ideas – Money," dated April 12, 1988, of which Balmond did not grant publication for this book.

37 Manuscript titled "Zorbau." Dated December 12, 1991. Courtesy of Balmond Studio.

38 Untitled manuscript, dated November 5, 1992. Courtesy of Balmond Studio.

39 Cecil Balmond, "Tecnologia: un forat negre? = Technology: the black hole," *Quaderns d'arquitectura i urbanisme*, no. 199 (March 1993), 90.

Zaragoza Bienale 3/94

The equation F + V − E = 2 generates all prismatic solid bodies. This expression is a minimum principle which instantly gives rise to a multiplicity of shapes.

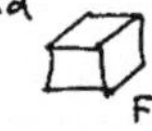

F+V−E=2

Like the horse (knight) move in chess if we take a right angled triangle with sides of value 1, and add to the hypotenuse $\sqrt{2}$ $(1^2+1^2=2)$ another value one but at right angles to the hypotenuse, and then keep doing this a few times we get the Archimedean spiral.

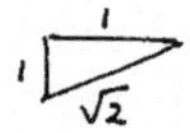


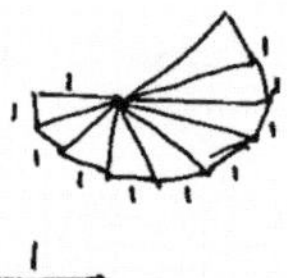

The minimum principle acts like an algorithm to generate the interesting and complex spiral.

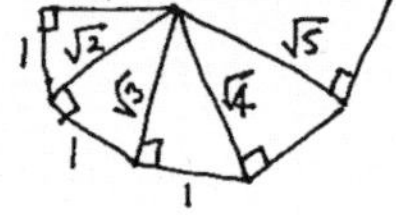


In mathematics consider the function of $\frac{1}{x}$. If x is 100, the value of $\frac{1}{x}$ is 0.01. If x is a 1000, the answer is 0.001, and getting smaller as x becomes ~~smaller~~ larger.

$\text{Lim}\ \frac{1}{x} \to 0$

$x \to \infty$

As x tends to infinity ($\infty$) the function tends to zero, but never gets there. This is because we do not know what infinity is, its a number bigger than imaginable. And as we get to infinity, the difference between plus and minus is not clear. It is a twilight zone and the function $\frac{1}{x}$ slips past, moving between and through the region of zero.

$\frac{1}{x} \to 0$
$x \to \infty$

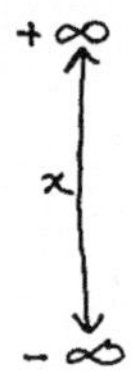


In this sense, zero is not a fixed point, but a succession of overlapping regions, all touching the concept of zero.

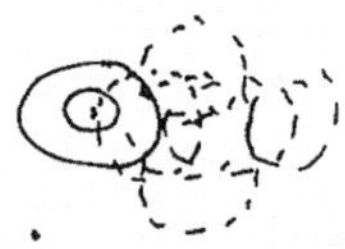

<u>Zero is fractal</u>, and <u>simultaneity represents movement</u>.

overarching repetition of elements and led to right-angled patterns. He regarded this order as "rigid" and labeled it "formal." Instead, the informal would involve "local individuality" in the treatment of the various elements—thereby echoing the same aspects he had anticipated in the previous text, if now used toward a different object. In the same piece, Balmond promoted a "certain randomness within the solution," and pointed out that "[f]or the Jussieu libraries different patterns for stability were studied, moving from the organized and traditional to an increased chaotic and random solution."[40] The influence of chaos theory was making itself felt more and more strongly.

The design ideology announced by these brief and somewhat vague thoughts began to grow the following year—if not yet consciously with a view to putting together a self-contained theoretical framework under the umbrella term of "informal." In fact, the term as such does not even feature in a lengthy manuscript written in March 1994 in preparation for an event at the II Zaragoza Biennial of Architecture and Urbanism, in which Balmond participated alongside David Chipperfield, Francesco Dal Co, and Luis Fernández-Galiano, among others. The manuscript did, however, contain a number of tenets and themes central to the 2002 book **(fig. 3.11)**. Threaded together under the heading of "limits," these included the coexistence of stability and instability; the dynamic relationship between large and small; the possibility of simplicity breeding complexity; the importance of hierarchies of complexity over repetitive monotony; the privileging of simultaneity; the exploration of regions of overlap; the notion of limits as passageways and areas of speculation, rather than barriers; the fractal quality of borders; and the transition from order to chaos through the grid: "as the grid gets smaller order tends to break down towards disorder, or a chaotic situation. More flexibility is possible as the Cartesian logic shrinks inwards on itself."[41] At this point, Balmond's interpretation of the attributes and potentialities of nonlinear systems involved both those he read into them himself for design purposes ("the exploration of regions of overlap") and those he simply paraphrased directly from chaos theory ("the coexistence of stability and instability"), the scientific domain at the peak of its impact on his thinking.

## Events of Order

In May that same year, in a précis of a lecture he delivered in Zurich titled "Aristotle Revisited," the term "algorithm" emerged for the first time in significant fashion—"informal" still remaining absent. Balmond used the notion of algorithm to discuss *sequence* and *growth*: "sequence is like an algorithm—a simple rule, that repeats and repeats . . . . Growth is an aggregation of sequence—in other words an algorithm. . . . . Sequence generates shape" **(fig. 3.12–13)**. He associated the term further with the universe of shapes of chaos theory, and illustrated the ways in which patterns of

Precedent page:
**3.11** Preparatory notes for an event at the II Zaragoza Biennial of Architecture and Urbanism, March 1994.

Following double-page spread:
**3.12–13** Precis of a lecture delivered in Zurich, May 1994.

40 Cecil Balmond, "Informelles Konstruieren," *Arch+*, no. 117 (June 1993), 59, 62.

41 Manuscript titled "Limits." Dated March 18, 1994. Courtesy of Balmond Studio.

## Fire and Energy.

The obvious sign of fire is the tongue of flame or the descending bolt of lightning. Both have the characteristic of branching.

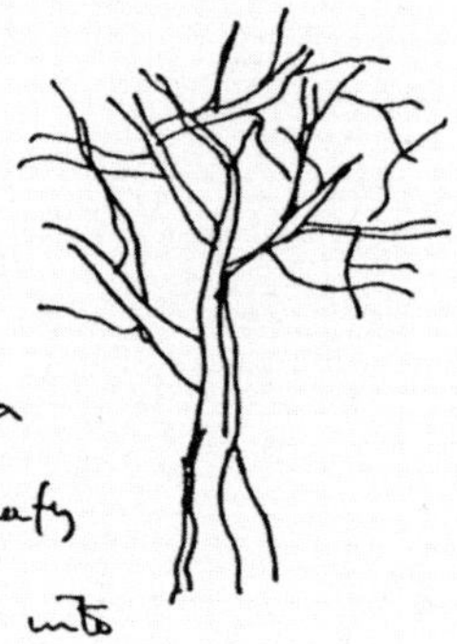

If we look at a tree we see the desire to branch, from trunk, to branch, from branch to twig, from twig to leaf. It is a network, open ended to the sun, as the leafy extremities look to convert chlorophyll into nourishing sugars. It is a network of communication. The lines are pathways of energy. And even in the leaves this sequence of branching occurs, taking nourishment through a fine tracery that covers the surface.

And sequence is like an algorithm – a simple rule, that repeats and repeats. The command to branch can be simple; go upwards or straight for some distance, and somewhere along this distance break off at an angle for a little.

If this is repeated many times over we get networks.

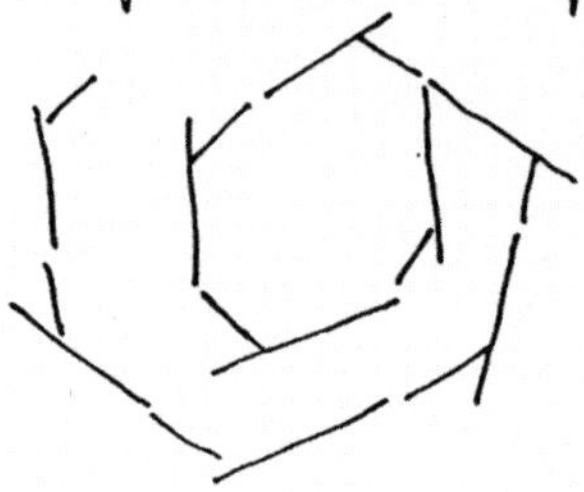

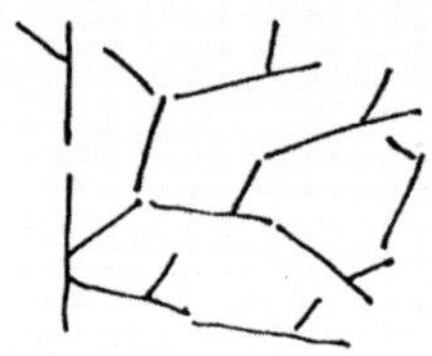

The symbol for branching is aptly a 'Y' shape therefore. There is an expectation in this open ended bifurcation, that begs another connection; and so we have growth, the inherent tendency of the "Y" shape.

Growth is an aggregation of sequence – in other words an algorithm.

Simple sequences of numbers generate shape.

To the fraction $\frac{2}{1}$ if 1 is added top & bottom, we get the sequence $\frac{2}{1}$ $\frac{3}{2}$ $\frac{4}{3}$ $\frac{5}{4}$ $\frac{6}{5}$ $\frac{7}{6}$ $\frac{8}{7}$ $\frac{9}{8}$ $\frac{10}{9}$ . . . etc.

If we start with $\frac{1}{2}$,

then we get $\frac{1}{2}$ $\frac{2}{3}$ $\frac{3}{4}$ $\frac{4}{5}$ $\frac{5}{6}$ $\frac{6}{7}$ $\frac{7}{8}$ $\frac{8}{9}$ $\frac{9}{10}$ . . . etc

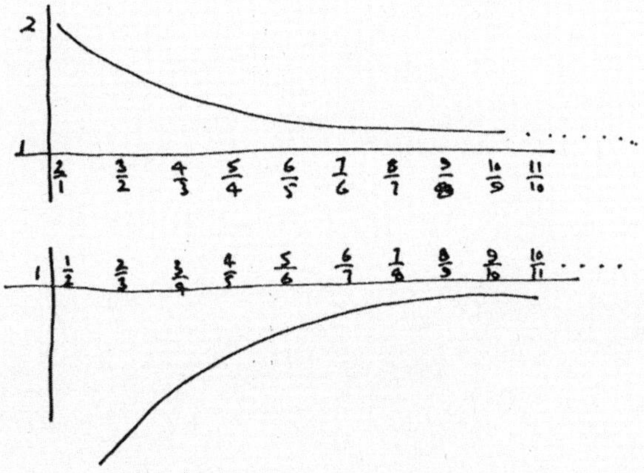


Sequence generates shape.

**Geometría de la cubierta**

El borde exterior de la forma oval se estableció a una altura fija. Como origen, se fijó un punto desviado respecto al centro como cota más baja de la cubierta.

Luego se trazaron una serie de contornos, desde el punto más bajo hacia afuera, hasta encontrar el borde exterior. El mapa de contornos resultante fue muy sugerente, semejante a uno de los extraños *atractores* que aparecen en la teoría del caos.

Para mantener los elementos de cubierta dentro de dimensiones estándar, se han agrupado las columnas; para responder a la falta de coincidencia dentro de la malla, se ha proyectado la malla de planta baja hacia arriba, hacia la cubierta inclinada.

**Cubierta de la Expo**

Lo más interesante de este edificio plagado de aspectos interesantes está en la cubierta. Se trata de una construcción híbrida de acero y madera, en la que se ha empleado ésta como elemento a tracción, algo poco habitual. El uso de la madera otorga calidez a los grandes espacios y su textura ofrece un agudo contraste con la atmósfera casi industrial del material de recubrimiento y de las brutales columnas de acero galvanizado.

El concepto de la cubierta proviene de las restricciones debidas a la protección contra incendios y a los requisitos de salida de humos. Para retener el humo dentro de compartimentos estancos, habría sido necesario instalar en la cubierta una serie de dispositivos verticales que habrían interrumpido la continuidad de la curva.

Y, así, la idea de concentrar de algún modo el humo dentro del vacío de la cubierta fue cobrando fuerza. Si la cubierta se mantenía *abierta* en un 50% ya no era necesario ningún tipo de dispositivo que sobresaliera por debajo de la curva inferior para retener el humo.

El material de cubierta iba a ser tablero metálico, por lo cual la elección evidente para

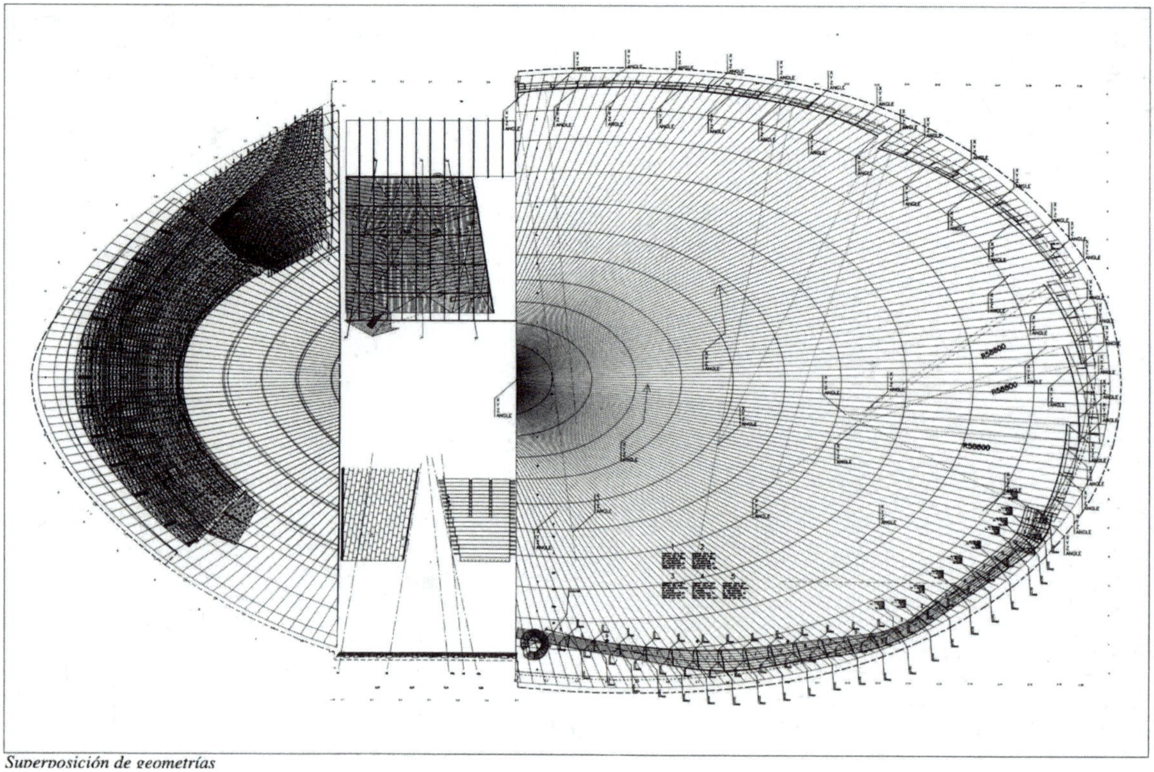

*Superposición de geometrías*

growth can be numerically controlled to generate branching logics. The piece ended with one of his favorite definitions: "chaos is a succession of events of order"—a definition to which he again alluded toward the end of 1994 in a piece on his collaboration with Koolhaas on the Congrexpo project, where he likened a drawing of the building's ceiling plan to the attractors of chaos theory **(fig. 3.14)**.[42]

By February 1995 the book on the horizon was not yet *Informal* but a more general one on "nature," tentatively titled *DNA* **(fig. 3.15)**. Here "the informal" resurfaced as a hypothesis:

> The idea for the book [DNA] comes from a series of lectures given to architecture schools over recent years. The subject matter of the lectures was on architectural themes but with a strong emphasis on abstraction, using modern concepts of science, mathematics and number theory to lay down a hypothesis of the informal. . . . The book explores the overlap between art and science. Between the world of man-made decision and the spontaneous action of Nature. . . . The subject matter explores the areas behind geometry, form and aesthetics. Therefore the book is a catalyst for anyone interested in how things happen or take shape. In addition to engineers and architects the book will appeal to the general reader interested in a fresh viewpoint on the natural sciences.[43]

The book's purpose was further developed in the following months. It was meant to address "those who want to delve into Nature and explore under that surface skin of apparent chaos and randomness. Underneath it all are powerful connections, archetypal patterns, and these advise us, not surprisingly, in our approach to design."[44] Elsewhere, "this book is about structure, the hidden and the obvious, the connections between things."[45]

In March 1995, interspersed in manuscripts which still mainly revolved around general topics in the natural sciences and mathematics (like energy, matter, biochemistry, entropy, prime numbers, and symmetry), Balmond produced a few paragraphs in which he elaborated the notion of informal for the first time. Presented in a public lecture in Berlin in June of that year—and very close to the version eventually published in the book—the manifesto-like piece added a few central aspects to those he had described earlier in scattered fashion, such as *opportunism* in the design process and *ambiguity* in the outcome as qualities sought out by the informal.[46] Another formulation of the "in-formal"—now hyphenated—followed just a month later. In this one, Balmond referred somewhat poetically to "the edge of chance" showing its face, and proposed the breaking of uniformity, the interruption of perfect balance, and the ignoring of order in the regimental sense,

Precedent page:
**3.14** Congrexpo project with Rem Koolhaas.

42 Cecil Balmond, "El Huevo Mecánico: Luces y Cubiertas En El Congrexpo de Lille," *Arquitectura Viva*, no. 39 (November 1994), 44; and Cecil Balmond, "Congrexpo - Oder 'Das Ei' in Lille," *Arch+*, no. 124/125 (December 1994), 32. The earlier definition can be found in a manuscript titled "Aristotle Revisited." Dated May 1994. Courtesy of Balmond Studio.

43 Manuscript titled "DNA." Dated February 2, 1995, revised February 26, 1995. Courtesy of Balmond Studio.

44 Manuscript titled "Nature – Book." Dated September 24, 1995. Courtesy of Balmond Studio.

45 Manuscript titled "Book Contents – Structure." Dated February 28, 1996. Courtesy of Balmond Studio.

46 Typed manuscript titled "Manifesto." Dated March 1995. Courtesy of Balmond Studio.

# DNA.

12/2/9
26/2/9

The idea for the book comes from a series of lectures given to architectural schools over the last years. The subject matter of the lectures were on architectural but with strong emphasis on abstraction, using modern concepts of science, mathematics & number theory to lay down a hypothesis of the informal.

The book explores the overlap between art and science between ~~man~~ the world of man made decision and the spontaneous action of Nature.

Engineering and architecture covers the built environment and offers insights into the morphology and connectivity of the world we live in. The pursuit of these insights lead to several abstractions. The aim is one of speculation, open ended, to invite the reader to enter the exciting possibilities of original hypothesis in the realm of ideas. It is therefore philosophical in outlook and is not a text book. But the subject matter explores the areas behind geometry, form and aesthetics. Therefore the book is a catalyst for anyone interested in how things happen or take shape. Apart from ~~student~~ engineers & architects the book will appeal to the general reader interested in a fresh viewpoint on the natural sciences.

Certain ideas are fundamental. They run through everything. Like a fractal, key ideas repeat, in a self similar way. ~~Unlike a normal text book written in linear form~~, The ~~book~~ will ~~have~~ be essays, shorter illustrated texts & 'windows' ideas. Different aspects of a similar idea will be treated in different ways. The idea is to reflect things in ~~intellectual~~ mirrors, so the book becomes an active meditation

26/2/95

~~[illegible] and looks at the genius of Nature from an unashamedly poetic viewpoint~~
~~[illegible] an unashamedly poetic viewpoint of wonder and [illegible]~~

defining it instead as "maybe only a special event of the transient."[47] Significantly, the three so-called "events" of the informal surfaced here for the first time. In addition to the originary "local," he put forward "hybrid" and "juxtaposition," noting that these would be given rise to by "overlap."[48]

## Architecture Enters the Picture

From this point on, Balmond focused on further clarifying the various aspects of the informal, rather than adding new ones in any substantial amount. In a manuscript dated January 14, 1996—at a time when he was intensifying his study of Thales, Plato, and Descartes on geometry and its relationship to numbers **(fig. 3.16)**—he replaced the term "events" with "characteristics" to designate the triad local, hybrid, and juxtaposition. As opposed to "categories," which in his mind would recall the stricter compartmentalization found in classical and early modern philosophy, these characteristics were meant to be fluid and influence one another. Thus, "juxtaposition" was to be viewed as a local concern and "hybrid" as an extreme juxtaposition, although no clear definition of each characteristic is as yet provided. Balmond did not hide the biological structuralism behind these characteristics. Quite the opposite, he offered a cell as an example and alluded to the final aggregated form in architecture as deriving from separate individual compositions unfolding simultaneously and influencing each other through "cooperation."[49]

At this juncture, with chaos theory's influence still in full force, statements punctuated his writings that at first glance appear oxymoronic, such as the fact that the informal "celebrates the irrational" while at the same time possessing a logical basis.[50] As if justifying it to himself, he indicates that it is precisely in discovering hidden order that the fun lies, for it stimulates speculation in the investigation. Gaining confidence as he thought it through further, Balmond became more and more ambitious about his informal ideology, now calling it a "new paradigm" for the first time in this manuscript.[51]

The most frantic period of manuscript production during the 1990s occurred in these prolific years of 1995 and 1996, when a shift occurred. Notwithstanding the abovementioned writings on the informal, work toward *DNA* was predominant in 1995 and carried over into 1996—albeit gradually giving way to disciplinary issues pertaining specifically to architecture and engineering. "Case studies" started to intersect his intellectual musings: the Kunsthal building with Koolhaas appeared in March 1996; the Chemnitz stadium project with Peter Kulka and Ulrich Königs in November the same year **(fig. 3.17)**. With this shift, the conception of *Informal* began to take shape as the abandonment of *DNA* neared. "The informal" stopped being a matter of scattered reflection and replaced "Nature" as the driving term of the project at hand. By mid-1996, the longest manuscript focusing on the notion

Precedent page:
**3.15** Notes on the DNA book project, February 1995.

Following pages:
**3.16** Notes on Thales, December 1995 (p. 238).
**3.17** Sketches for the Chemnitz stadium project with Peter Kulka and Ulrich Königs, November 1996 (p. 239).

47 The phrase "the edge of chance" echoes "the edge of chaos" rather faithfully. See Waldrop, *Complexity*, 12.

48 Typed manuscript titled "in-formal." Dated April 1995. Courtesy of Balmond Studio.

49 Typed manuscript titled "PARADIGM." Dated January 14, 1996. Courtesy of Balmond Studio.

50 The first statement appears in an untitled manuscript dated January 1, 1996; the latter in a typed manuscript titled "in-formal" and dated February 22, 1996. Courtesy of Balmond Studio.

51 Typed manuscript titled "PARADIGM." Dated January 14, 1996. Courtesy of Balmond Studio.

THALES

Element

23/12/95

Thales 640 or 624 BC – Still living in 548 BC.

Astute – clever. Inventor of deductive reasoning.

Cornered the oil presses & rented them the foll. yr. for profit – financed his teaching.

May 585 BC eclipse foretold by Thales. 28th May. Total eclipse.

A measure of coincidence | The Medes and Lydians were in 6th yr of war. Herodotus says they found themselves fighting a night battle. The eclipse scared them. They immediately concluded peace. They called him 'Sophos' – something he asked for.

Philosophy grasped Science until N & L.

|| Everything is Water: Take anything you like apart as far as you like/can & you will find nothing but water on your hands.
A summation of everything in space time & eternity.
Influenced by Babylonian frequent inundation.

57 The straight line of the senses suggested a wholly insubstantial str. line –
|| The str. line, a line without breadth does not exist in the material universe. It is a pure abstraction, an invention of the imagination. Idea in Eternal mind

(1) " Two str. lines have 1 pt in common – Thro 2 pts passes only 1 str line.
Not forbidden to think of point and straight line.
Str. line thro. centre of circle – then O^le is in two halves.

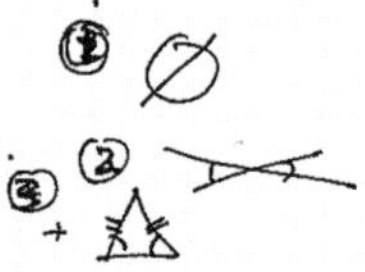

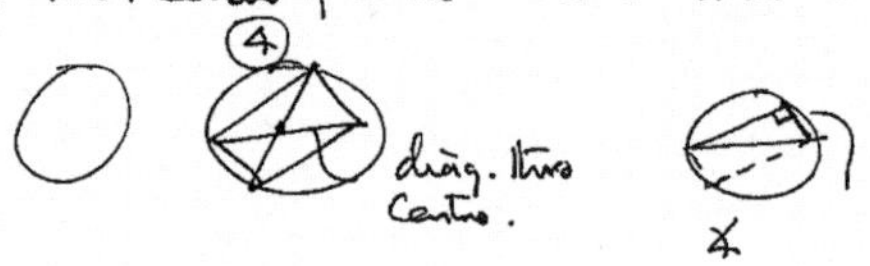


Invariance of N & L.

|| Thales took practical geometry & idealized it. From sensory experience to the abstractedness of ideal construction.

|| Secondly he imagined that some of the abstractions of geo facts of common observation might be deducible from abstractions of a simpler kind.

PATTERN

Chemnitz

3/11/96

// The serving steel ribs networking the roof in Chemnitz were originally put in by eye to help distribute the structural response.

// But would it be possible to have some sequence or algorithm to generate such patterns?

The method of sequencing would have to give irregularity and shallow arcs mixed in with those of sharper curvature

If a disc is rotated along a straight

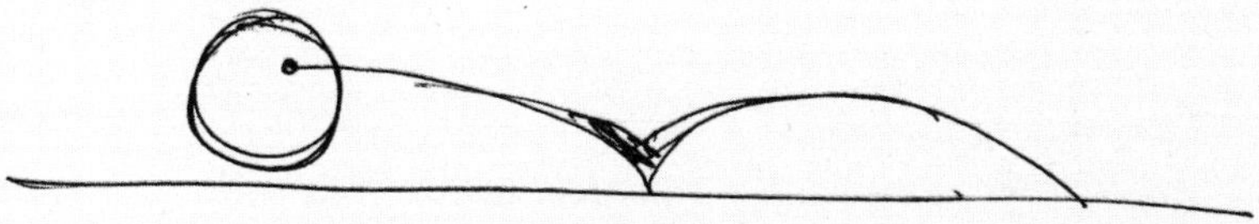

line and a dot painted on it – the path of that dot will follow the trajectory of a cycloid.

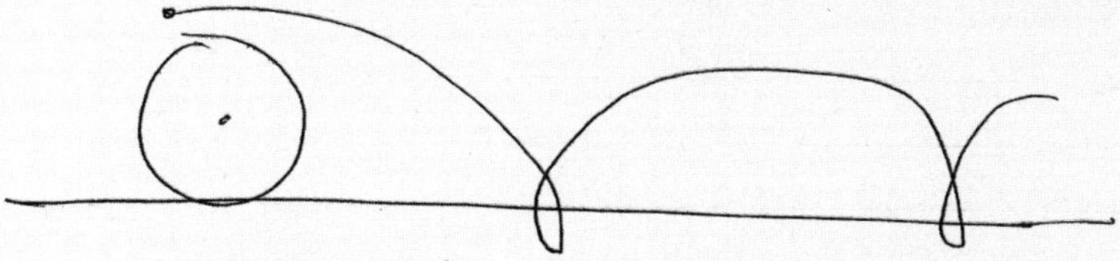

If the point is outside the disc then the path followed has an orbit that invades below the datum line.

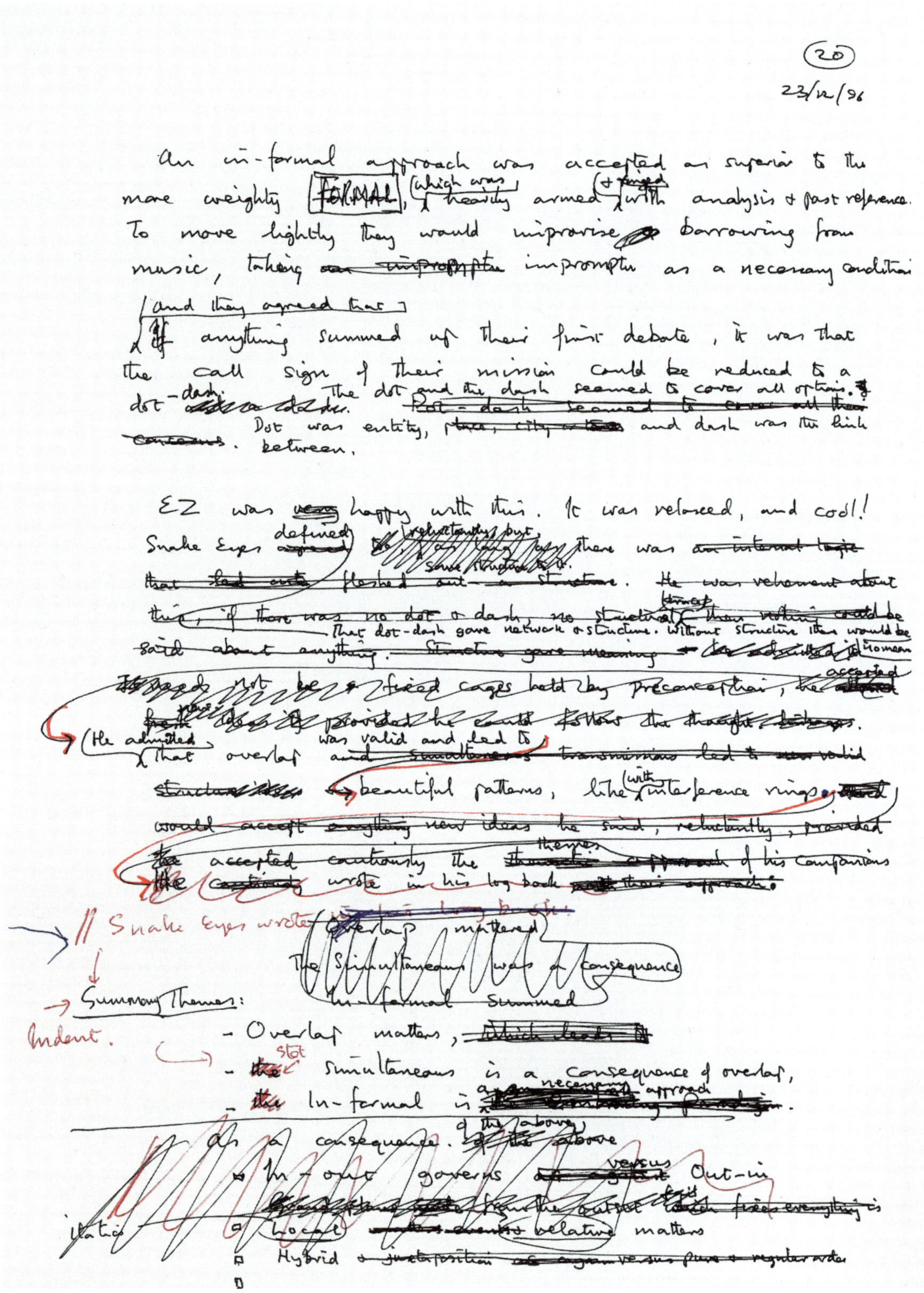

(20)
23/12/96

An in-formal approach was accepted as superior to the more weighty FORMAL, which was heavily armed + tinged with analysis + past reference. To move lightly they would improvise borrowing from music, taking impromptu as a necessary condition and they agreed that if anything summed up their first debate, it was that the call sign of their mission could be reduced to a dot-dash. The dot and the dash seemed to cover all options. Dot was entity, and dash was the link between.

EZ was happy with this. It was relaxed, and cool! Snake Eyes defined

That dot-dash gave network & structure. Without structure there would be

(He admitted that overlap was valid and led to beautiful patterns, like interference rings.

accepted

themes

of his companions

wrote in his log book

// Snake Eyes wrote

Overlap mattered

The Simultaneous was a consequence

In-formal summed

Summary Themes:

Indent.

- Overlap matters,

- Slot simultaneous is a consequence of overlap,

- In-formal is a necessary approach.

As a consequence of the above

In-out governs versus Out-in

from the outset

italics

Local relative matters

Hybrid

of the informal that Balmond ever produced discussed much of the theoretical substrate that was included in the book in nearly final form. Its themes included specific architectural gestures considered informal; further thoughts on the contrasts between order and chaos as well as between formal and informal; the importance of the "generic" and definitions of local, juxtaposition, and hybrid, all of which shall be analyzed below. Another manuscript dated December 23, 1996 broadened the range of central themes, listing "overlap matters," "the simultaneous is a consequence of overlap," and "in-out governs versus out-in" **(fig. 3.18)**.[52]

Precedent page:
**3.18** Notes on themes central to "the informal," December 1996.

## *DNA* versus *Informal*

In January 1997, Balmond relinquished his *DNA* project, "exhausted" and disappointed that, in his view, there were not many references to draw on regarding his approach and main theme.[53] As a therapeutic compromise to compensate for this failure, in 1998 he published *Number 9*. His first book, it was a somewhat esoteric fiction—indeed, a fairy tale of sorts—concerning the central position of the number nine within cyclic numbers. Though including a few drawn-up patterns, it excluded any explicit relationship to architectural thinking.[54] Previously, in August 1997, a piece for *Assemblage* titled "New Structure and The Informal"—the hyphen now gone for good—featured some of his final thoughts developed the previous year and incorporated the phrase "new structure" to signal that his inquiry into form and configuration was dynamic and carried out "from first principles."[55] A significantly expanded version appeared the following month in a special issue of AD titled *New Science = New Architecture* as well as the following year in *Lotus*. Noteworthy here is his elaboration on the notion of "structure as trace" as well as the first introduction of the problem of the nonlinear as such. The term "new structure" remained in this iteration, but was subsequently dropped.[56]

By 1998 all of the writings toward *Informal* had been produced. Publication was delayed until 2002 partly because of the actual book-design process—involving adjustments, cuts, edits, and minor rewriting—and partly due to alleged disagreements with the publishing house, mainly over printing specifications and paper choice.[57] The book on Nature was envisioned as broad in scope, philosophical in outlook, and centered round the written word. It was to comprise essays, shorter illustrated texts, and "windows" of ideas. *Informal*, on the other hand, targeted architecture and engineering more deliberately; was structured around design examples (i.e., several of the projects Balmond had worked on with architects); featured more image content than text; and relaxed the philosophical ambitions to favor accessible descriptions, narratives, and definitions—if still, for the most part, retaining a theoretical texture. In addition to the concept of the informal itself, a number of concerns from his research towards *DNA* wound up being central to *Informal*,

52 Untitled manuscript, dated December 23, 1996. Courtesy of Balmond Studio.

53 As explained in a soliloquy written nine years later, on January 1, 2006. Courtesy of Balmond Studio.

54 Hence it shall not be discussed in the context of this book. See Cecil Balmond, *Number 9: The Search for the Sigma Code: Nine Fixed Points in the Wind* (Munich: Prestel, 1998).

55 Cecil Balmond, "New Structure and the Informal," *Assemblage*, no. 33 (August 1997), 56.

56 Cecil Balmond, "New Structure and the Informal," *Lotus*, no. 98 (1998), 83.

57 The latter is according to Balmond himself in an interview with the author conducted in London on October 9, 2013.

notably ideas on patterns, irrational numbers, fractals, and geometric growth. In fact, regardless of the particularities of the project in question, Balmond's intellectual production as a whole is best described as a set of recurring terms, preoccupations, and theoretical statements expressed differently through a palimpsest of diagrams, sketches, definitions, metaphors, examples, allegories, mythical stories, and even soliloquies.

## THEORETICAL CONSOLIDATION INTO *INFORMAL*

In the introduction to *Informal*, Balmond manifested his discomfort at what he saw as a general trend in the architecture of the turn of the millennium: "cool new shapes and blobs are nothing more than mere façade if they are propped up by standard post and beam construction." Instead, he advocated for what he called "*integrity* in the establishing of a free shape," a term he never further substantiated.[58] As will become apparent below, what emerges across Balmond's whole design ideology is a somewhat idiosyncratic dialectic between control and freedom when handling the relational properties of form.

The first step of the informal approach was setting up a so-called "theoretical base" for the developmental character with which Balmond wished to infuse the form search process. Such a base comprised either an isolated element (say, a piece of geometry such as a particular tile shape) or a very basic disposition (for example, a grid of points). In either case, the base was activated by an initial action, one which might either become a built-in property (the tiles turn and flip over as they aggregate, thereby giving rise to a specific kind of network), or remain a single move generating a number of relational conditions (the same grid is duplicated and one of them is rotated over the other). This interest in the motion of elements and their recording was strongly influenced by previous, similar approaches in the visual arts of which Balmond was well aware, such as those advanced by Paul Klee nearly a century earlier concerning, in his case, *pictorial* form: "[g]enesis as formal movement is the essence of the work of art" **(fig. 3.19–21)**.[59] Indeed, Balmond believed that "as long as one is interested in the principles of organization, research on generative ideas on form making and form finding can go into architecture or any other media," which unavoidably recalls the notion that, in dealing with the complexity of systems—an abstract object of study—chaos theory cuts across disciplines.[60]

58 My emphasis. Cecil Balmond, *Informal* (Munich: Prestel, 2002), 14. Subsequently, some notable architects expressed their appreciation of this approach. Such was the case of Daniel Liberkind: "[Balmond is] exploring the whole issue of structure and pattern. It's not just using virtual reality and computers–there is a whole banalization of architecture where people are just playing games and inventing ludicrous shapes. But with Cecil it's not just a pretty façade with a different shape and traditional structure." In Jennifer Kabat, "Thinking Outside the Box," *BusinessWeek: Innovation*, February 7, 2007, http://www.businessweek.com/innovate/content/feb2007/id20070207_841153.htm. Accessed January 13, 2012.

59 Paul Klee, "Towards a Theory of Form Production," in *The Thinking Eye (The Notebooks of Paul Klee, v. 1)* (New York, NY: G. Wittenborn, 1961), 17. Klee's theories were compiled in two volumes under the general title of *The Notebooks of Paul Klee*, the German original dating from 1956 and the English translation from 1961. They are full of diagrams and sketches describing, for example, the ways in which different movements of a point might produce different kinds of lines; how a circle can be dynamically generated; the tension arising between lines when progressive motion acts upon them; and the interlocking of multidimensional growth. The Swiss painter tried to escape the fixedness of static conditions. Instead, he sought to capture intermediate states by translating them into visible form through pictorial language. His *Blühendes* (Blossoming) of 1934, depicting a particular moment within the process of a tree's blossoming in lieu of the tree itself, constitutes an instance of such an objective.

60 Cecil Balmond and Paul Makovsky, "Restructuring Plans: Cecil Balmond Talks to Us about His Recent Decision to Leave Arup for His Own Practice [Interview]," *Metropolis* 30, no. 6 (2011), 28.

## Local, Juxtaposition, Hybrid

Those activating actions can be instantiated through what in the terminology of *Informal* are called "templates:" "a series of provocations that animate the idea of geometry as nascent."[61] Templates included "starting grids (clusters of spatially related elements that are free to move in relation to one another) (fig. 3.22); "shifting boundaries" (a line whose topological condition is exploited, for example, by being now open, now folding over itself to create enclosed regions, or now making loops in sequence that in turn generate patterns) (fig. 3.23); systems of elements invading one another in order to favor the encounter of friction and order (fig. 3.24); and conventional tectonic assemblies used in extreme conditions, to mention the most recurrent ones.[62]

In a most didactic interpretation of chaos theory, Balmond mirrored the effect of *sensitive dependence on initial conditions* by utilizing "flexible starting points" as theoretical bases of form, due to the capacity he had observed in them to yield emergent conditions (fig. 3.25). Here the question of control versus freedom arises forcefully: initial rules are established which nevertheless aim to enable as many degrees of freedom as possible; in other words, potentiality engendered by constraint. Conventional starting points in engineering and design are "flexibilized" in Balmond's design theory through a number of conceptual shifts: "[i]nstead of line, surface; instead of equi-support, scatter; instead of fixed center, a moving locus; and instead of points, zones."[63] These transformations are unequivocally reminiscent of those theorized by Wassily Kandinsky in the 1920s, involving point, line, and plane—a body of work with which Balmond was also well acquainted.

The three main characteristics of the informal constitute a taxonomy of ways in which activating actions can relate to one another. *Local* designates an individual action that spreads its influence outwards. *Juxtaposition* alludes to two actions set forth side-by-side such that, by virtue of their proximity, a new formal event emerges. *Hybrid* refers to the overlap of two actions whose distinct natures become bound within each other.[64] Both juxtaposition and hybrid are therefore dependent on local, which turns the latter into the kernel of every form-generation process within Balmond's theoretical framework. Significantly, this convergence echoes the importance of individuality already present in his earliest writings on the informal. In addition—further to the control-versus-freedom dialectic—Balmond conceived local, hybrid, and juxtaposition so that opportunism, instinct, and the possibility of seizing the immediate could turn any one particular condition in the form-search process into another order. He enjoyed the idea that various kinds of order, which may have been born out of different relational logics, might be simultaneously embodied in the final outcome. If nonlinear systems may be seen as a succession

61 Balmond, *Informal*, 371.

62 The latter template was meant as a basis for the Bordeaux Villa designed with OMA, where a traditional table-like configuration is distorted by way of two skewed movements of columns both in plan and elevation.

63 Balmond, *Informal*, 14.

64 See Balmond, *Informal*, 116–17.

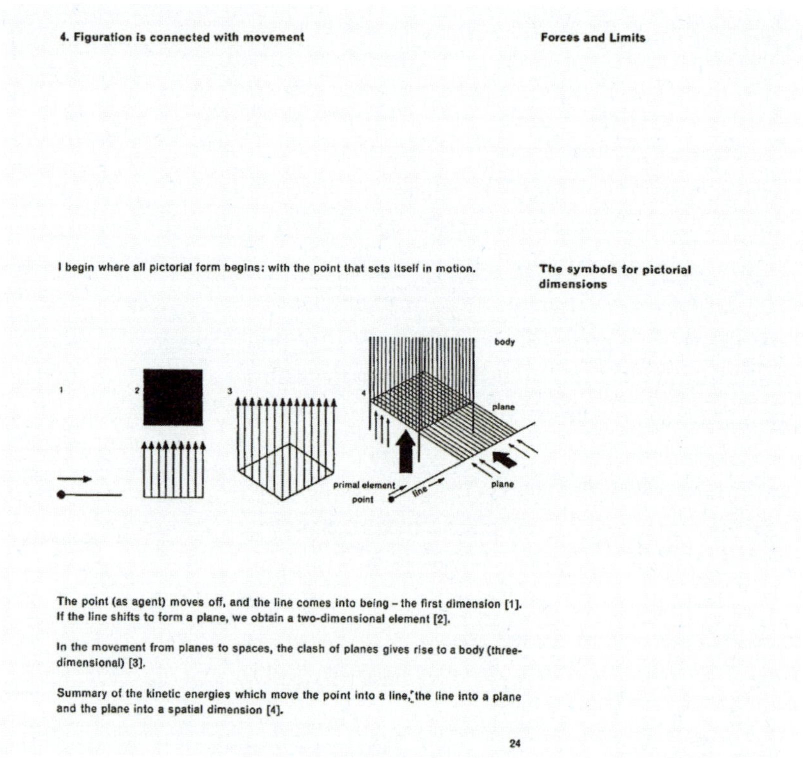

4. Figuration is connected with movement

Forces and Limits

I begin where all pictorial form begins: with the point that sets itself in motion.

The symbols for pictorial dimensions



The point (as agent) moves off, and the line comes into being – the first dimension [1]. If the line shifts to form a plane, we obtain a two-dimensional element [2].

In the movement from planes to spaces, the clash of planes gives rise to a body (three-dimensional) [3].

Summary of the kinetic energies which move the point into a line, the line into a plane and the plane into a spatial dimension [4].

24

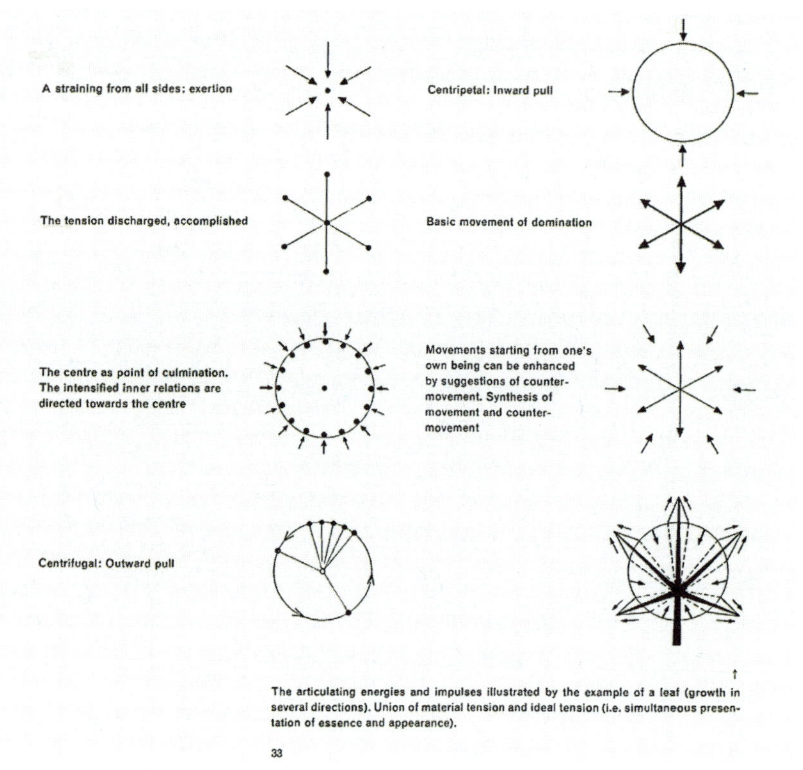

A straining from all sides: exertion

Centripetal: Inward pull

The tension discharged, accomplished

Basic movement of domination

The centre as point of culmination. The intensified inner relations are directed towards the centre

Movements starting from one's own being can be enhanced by suggestions of counter-movement. Synthesis of movement and counter-movement

Centrifugal: Outward pull

The articulating energies and impulses illustrated by the example of a leaf (growth in several directions). Union of material tension and ideal tension (i.e. simultaneous presentation of essence and appearance).

33

**3.19** Left: Paul Klee. The symbols for pictorial dimensions.

**3.20** Below: Paul Klee. The basic forms, their tensions and inner relations.

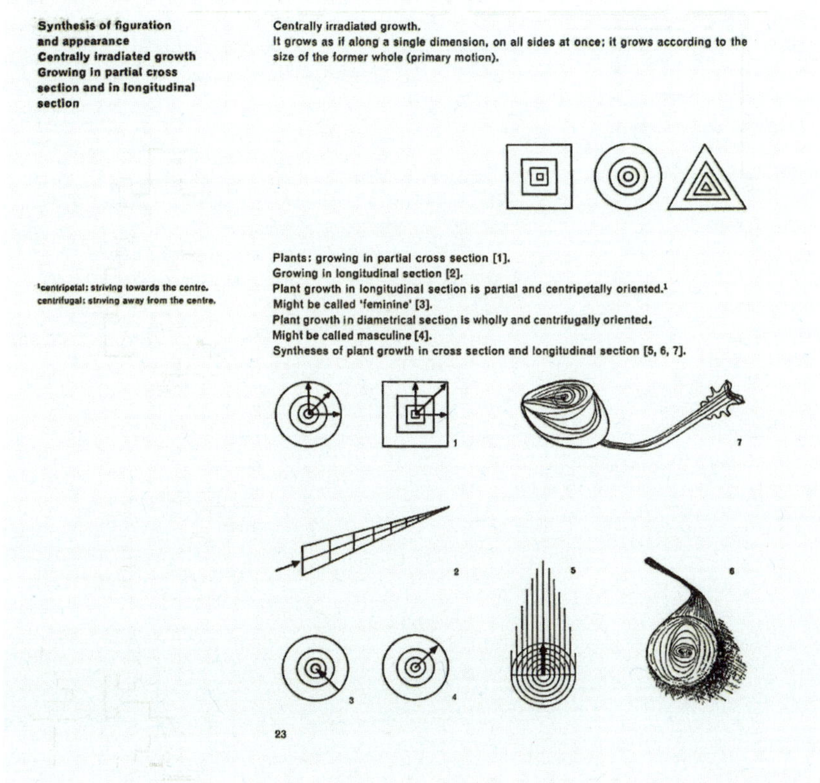


**3.21** Paul Klee. Synthesis of figuration and appearance, centrally irradiated growth growing in partial cross section and in longitudinal section.

of several orders, Balmond's simultaneity may be read as a collapse of an entire nonlinear sequence into one moment.

## Noncausal Adjacency

All in all, the consolidation of Balmond's theoretical framework in *Informal* favored the chaotic as a vehicle towards stabilities and coherence. Admitting feedback in the process, he searched for emergence while en route toward self-organization, with order resulting from the coming-together of a series of internal improvisations.[65] In applying nonlinearity to the domain of design, he argued that hierarchy imposed from above, in its inducing of predictability, was to be dismissed in favor of an in-to-out approach. Here the dialogue between control and freedom surfaces yet again: inner logic was to inform the whole along a path where rule and whim fed each other; where a self-defined rigor underlay the apparently capricious. Indeed, in Balmond's mind, what appeared so free was to be held together by internal strategies. Capitalizing on unpredictability as a generative factor, with evolution rooted in chance, his theoretical approach to design was grounded in the *noncausal adjacency* characteristic of nonlinearity; in other words, a move away from adjacency

65 "The capacity of recognizable order to arise from an initial state of apparent randomness" is Antoine Picon's didactic formulation of "emergence." Antoine Picon, *Digital Culture in Architecture* (Basel: Birkhäuser Architecture, 2010), 97.

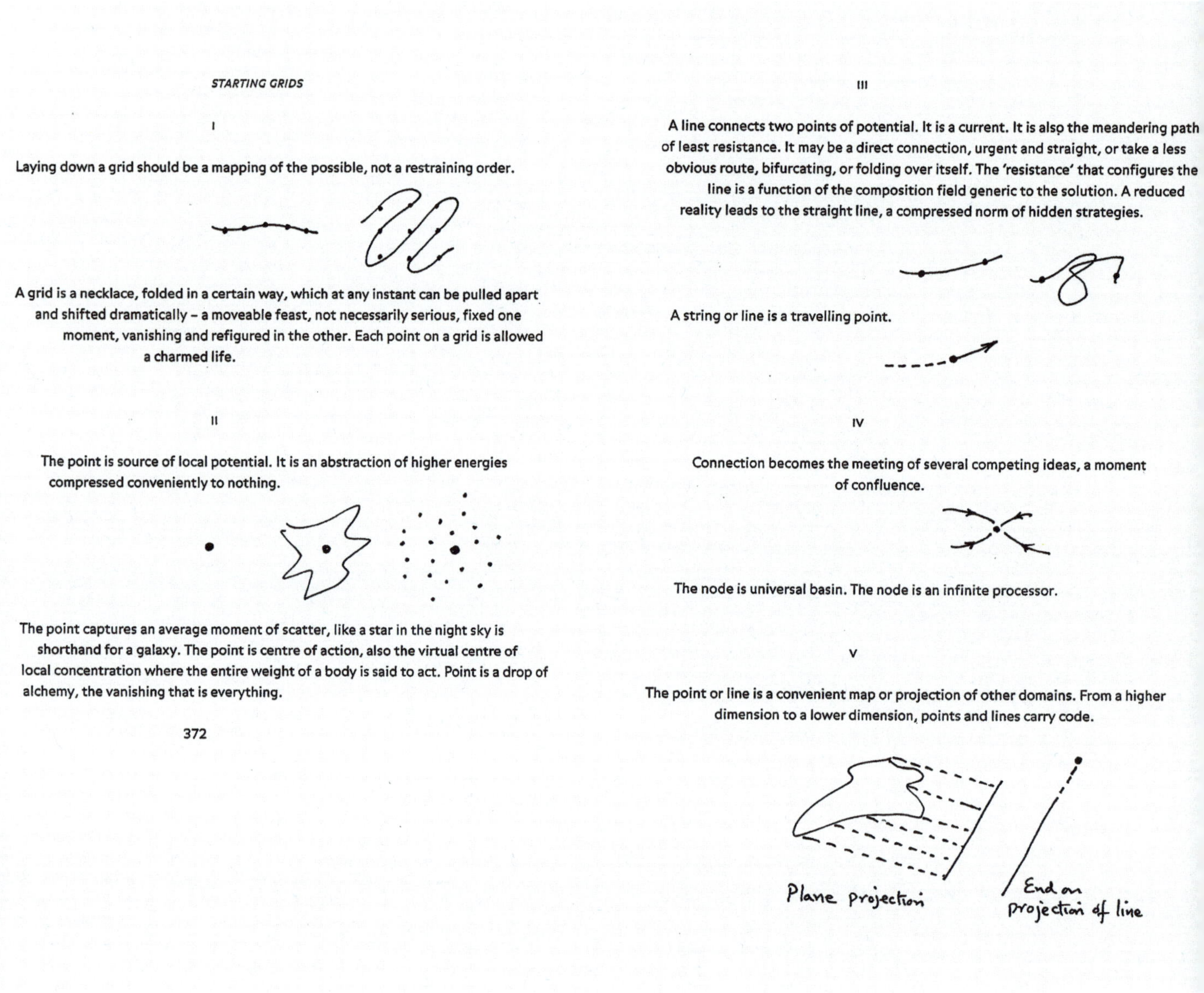

*STARTING GRIDS*

I

Laying down a grid should be a mapping of the possible, not a restraining order.

A grid is a necklace, folded in a certain way, which at any instant can be pulled apart and shifted dramatically – a moveable feast, not necessarily serious, fixed one moment, vanishing and refigured in the other. Each point on a grid is allowed a charmed life.

II

The point is source of local potential. It is an abstraction of higher energies compressed conveniently to nothing.

The point captures an average moment of scatter, like a star in the night sky is shorthand for a galaxy. The point is centre of action, also the virtual centre of local concentration where the entire weight of a body is said to act. Point is a drop of alchemy, the vanishing that is everything.

372

III

A line connects two points of potential. It is a current. It is also the meandering path of least resistance. It may be a direct connection, urgent and straight, or take a less obvious route, bifurcating, or folding over itself. The 'resistance' that configures the line is a function of the composition field generic to the solution. A reduced reality leads to the straight line, a compressed norm of hidden strategies.

A string or line is a travelling point.

IV

Connection becomes the meeting of several competing ideas, a moment of confluence.

The node is universal basin. The node is an infinite processor.

V

The point or line is a convenient map or projection of other domains. From a higher dimension to a lower dimension, points and lines carry code.



**3.22** Starting grids.

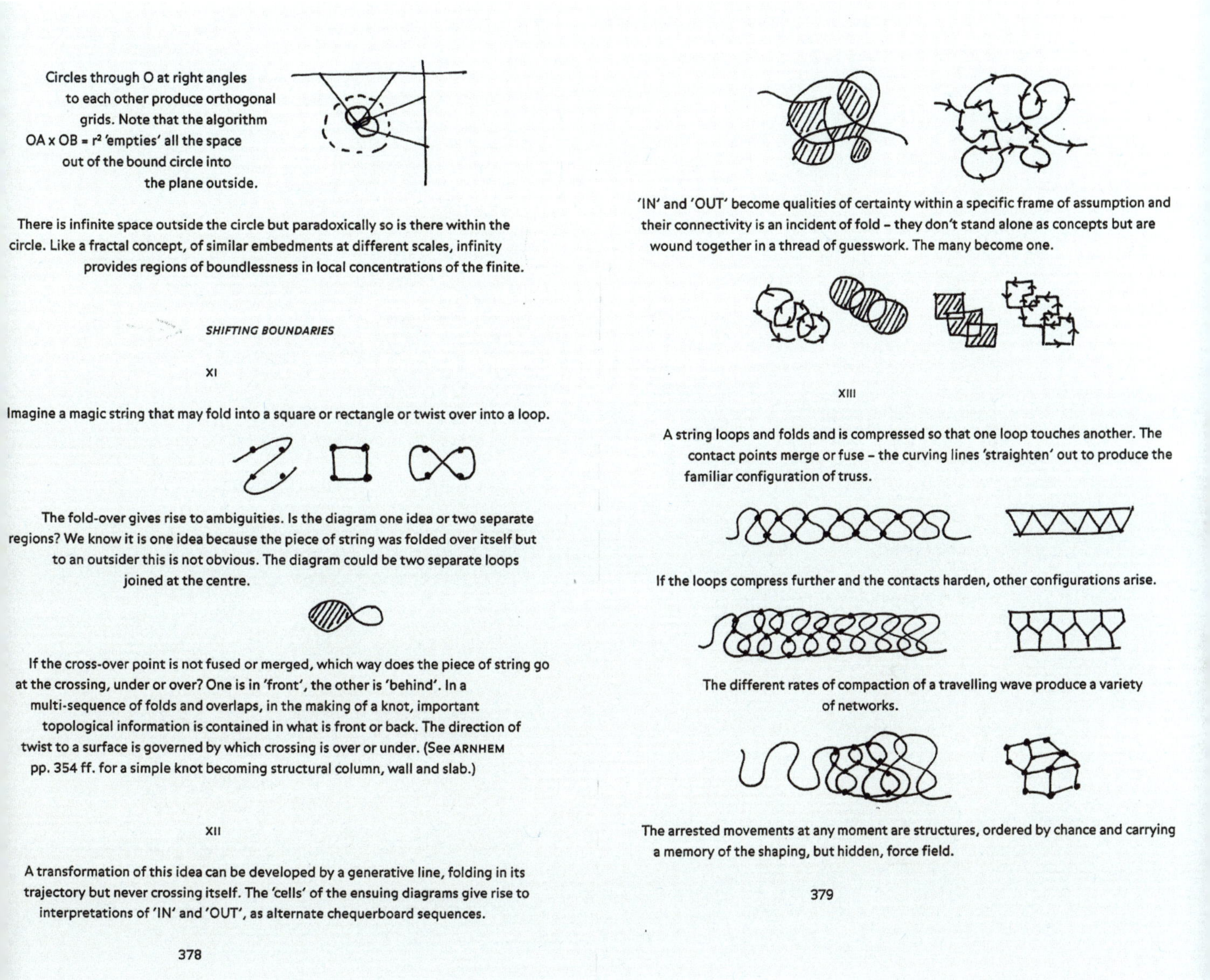

Circles through O at right angles to each other produce orthogonal grids. Note that the algorithm $OA \times OB = r^2$ 'empties' all the space out of the bound circle into the plane outside.

There is infinite space outside the circle but paradoxically so is there within the circle. Like a fractal concept, of similar embedments at different scales, infinity provides regions of boundlessness in local concentrations of the finite.

*SHIFTING BOUNDARIES*

XI

Imagine a magic string that may fold into a square or rectangle or twist over into a loop.

The fold-over gives rise to ambiguities. Is the diagram one idea or two separate regions? We know it is one idea because the piece of string was folded over itself but to an outsider this is not obvious. The diagram could be two separate loops joined at the centre.

If the cross-over point is not fused or merged, which way does the piece of string go at the crossing, under or over? One is in 'front', the other is 'behind'. In a multi-sequence of folds and overlaps, in the making of a knot, important topological information is contained in what is front or back. The direction of twist to a surface is governed by which crossing is over or under. (See ARNHEM pp. 354 ff. for a simple knot becoming structural column, wall and slab.)

XII

A transformation of this idea can be developed by a generative line, folding in its trajectory but never crossing itself. The 'cells' of the ensuing diagrams give rise to interpretations of 'IN' and 'OUT', as alternate chequerboard sequences.

378

'IN' and 'OUT' become qualities of certainty within a specific frame of assumption and their connectivity is an incident of fold – they don't stand alone as concepts but are wound together in a thread of guesswork. The many become one.

XIII

A string loops and folds and is compressed so that one loop touches another. The contact points merge or fuse – the curving lines 'straighten' out to produce the familiar configuration of truss.

If the loops compress further and the contacts harden, other configurations arise.

The different rates of compaction of a travelling wave produce a variety of networks.

The arrested movements at any moment are structures, ordered by chance and carrying a memory of the shaping, but hidden, force field.

379

**3.23** Shifting boundaries.

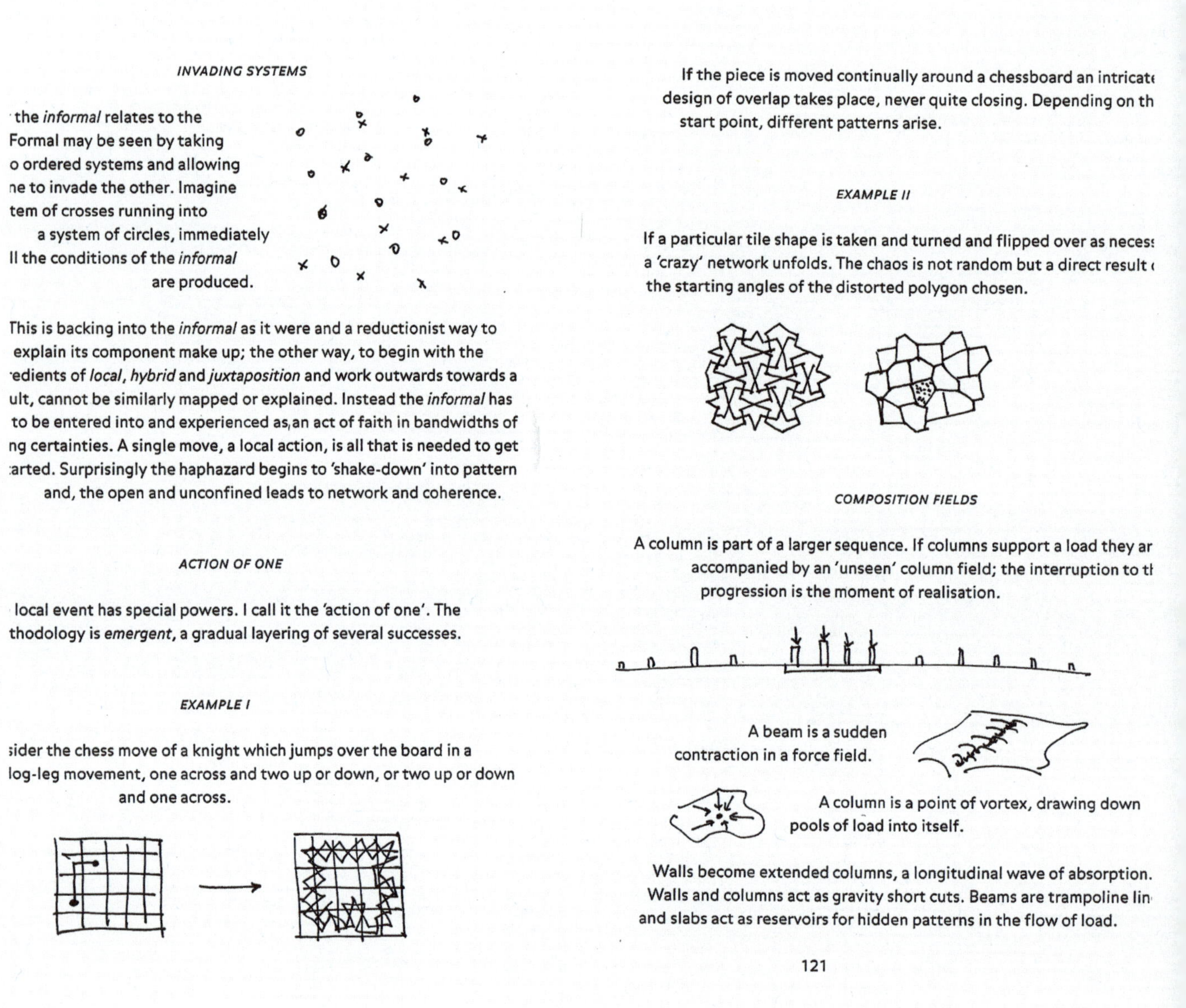

*INVADING SYSTEMS*

the *informal* relates to the Formal may be seen by taking o ordered systems and allowing ne to invade the other. Imagine tem of crosses running into a system of circles, immediately ll the conditions of the *informal* are produced.

This is backing into the *informal* as it were and a reductionist way to explain its component make up; the other way, to begin with the 'edients of *local*, *hybrid* and *juxtaposition* and work outwards towards a ult, cannot be similarly mapped or explained. Instead the *informal* has to be entered into and experienced as, an act of faith in bandwidths of ng certainties. A single move, a local action, is all that is needed to get :arted. Surprisingly the haphazard begins to 'shake-down' into pattern and, the open and unconfined leads to network and coherence.

*ACTION OF ONE*

local event has special powers. I call it the 'action of one'. The thodology is *emergent*, a gradual layering of several successes.

*EXAMPLE I*

sider the chess move of a knight which jumps over the board in a log-leg movement, one across and two up or down, or two up or down and one across.

If the piece is moved continually around a chessboard an intricat design of overlap takes place, never quite closing. Depending on th start point, different patterns arise.

*EXAMPLE II*

If a particular tile shape is taken and turned and flipped over as neces a 'crazy' network unfolds. The chaos is not random but a direct result the starting angles of the distorted polygon chosen.

*COMPOSITION FIELDS*

A column is part of a larger sequence. If columns support a load they ar accompanied by an 'unseen' column field; the interruption to th progression is the moment of realisation.

A beam is a sudden contraction in a force field.

A column is a point of vortex, drawing down pools of load into itself.

Walls become extended columns, a longitudinal wave of absorption. Walls and columns act as gravity short cuts. Beams are trampoline lin and slabs act as reservoirs for hidden patterns in the flow of load.

121

**3.24** Invading systems and composition fields.

XXIV

A generating line of structure, may crank, flex or branch.

This can happen in plan or elevation or both at the same time.

The motif may repeat in a regular rhythm or overlap.

Structural lines may bifurcate and come together again.

The zone created gives extra stiffness. If the diagram is an elevation, the structural cell may transmit load in a direction out of the plane of the paper. This direction may crank or flex or branch as required.

Moments of reverse curvature in elevation produce structure.

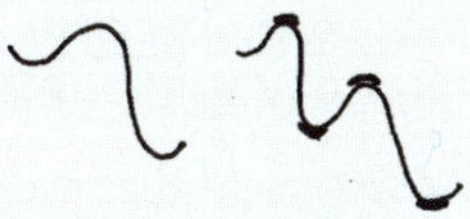

Peaks and troughs couple to produce 'beam' action out of the plane of the paper.

As the ideas overlap and the possibilities increase, the idea of 'line' disappears. Zones and surfaces take over. Column, beam and slab and wall become interpretations of a continuity. Ultimately plan and section lose their traditions.

XXV

If *local*, *hybrid* and *juxtaposition* are the interior characteristics of a design, the notation of their interdependencies may be assembled by a 3 x 3 matrix.

$$\begin{matrix} L_L & L_H & L_J \\ H_L & H_H & H_J \\ J_L & J_H & J_J \end{matrix}$$

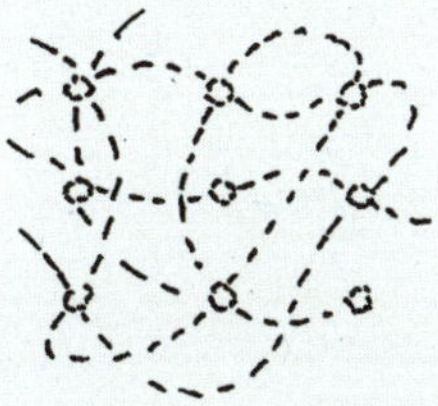

The leading diagonal $L_L - H_H - J_J$ denotes the pure nature of each characteristic. Entries off the diagonal describe mixed qualities, where $H_L$ is primarily hybridisation but having a local effect; whereas $L_J$ is a local action spreading the nature of a juxtaposition.

This informal matrix is equivalent to the 'stiffness' of a structure. It can lead to loose and flexible or narrow and rigid answers. External constraints may be viewed as forcing actions [P] and form as 'deflections' [D] arising from these actions. They are both collations of simultaneous activities and can be ascribed matrix notation. What negotiates between the two is I, the *informal*.

The equation is [P] = [I] [D]

To design, we engage the *informal* in a series of complex cross-multiplications. Like with structure, design is a series of adjacencies, of buried codes and local starts and aggregate resolutions; locked into it, at every level, are the characteristics $L_L - H_H - J_J$

XXVI

The ultimate matrix of simultaneous information is the DNA spiral. On its twisting threads lie the genetic codes that produce life.

Recent research shows that DNA winds around lumps called histones to make structure like a bead necklace, achieving a high density of compaction. The molecule itself is a twin thread of intertwining helices. Each thread is a backbone of phosphates and deoxyribose to which four bases, Thymine, Adenine, Cytosine and Guanine are attached in random arrays. The bases link up in pairs. Their specialised couplings bring a dynamic symmetry to the configuration.

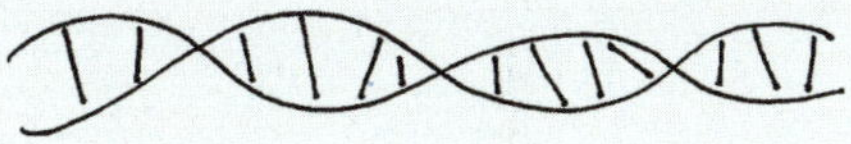

Cytosine with Guanine, and Thymine with Adenine.

The 'messages' from the base chain is read in adjacencies of three. Millions of such messages run to instruct the genes.

| C | A | C | T | G | T |
|---|---|---|---|---|---|
| G | T | G | A | C | A |

**3.25** Generating lines of structure and informal matrix.

as the causal route determining the course of the genesis of form. For the effect of the occurrence of chance is that the formal characteristics of one particular state within the process would not determine fully—or at all—those of the state immediately following.

After *Informal*, the next publication featuring a range of his work was a monograph that came out as a special issue of *A+U* in 2006. While *Informal* contained only ten projects, here the number of design examples was significantly increased, to include research being carried out at the AGU (at the time operating in full force), more buildings, pavilions, and bridges (some designed only with his ARUP team, others in collaboration with architects), and a whole master plan in London devised entirely at the AGU, which eventually came to nothing. On the other hand, his writings for the monograph did not add much to his theory of the informal. Many of the same notions published in the 2002 book reappeared again, and the new ones he either elaborated on through a somewhat loose poetic rhetoric (e.g., "deep structure"), or simply enunciated but did not articulate in depth (e.g., a distinction between form and shape).[66] The monograph served a purpose that became a near-obsession toward the latter part of his career, namely reasserting his designer role in projects otherwise attributed to architects, and beyond that, presenting him as a figure closer in discipline to the designer than the engineer.[67]

66 Cecil Balmond, *A+U Special Issue*, 114. On deep structure, see *Cecil Balmond, A+U Special Issue* (Tokyo: A + U Publishing Co., 2006), 17–19.

67 Despite the theoretical aspects of Balmond's project being most successfully encapsulated in *Informal*, he did not intend it as his most important discursive project. The design ideology around *Informal* encompasses only a fraction of his overall intellectual efforts. His true, yet unrealized career-long pursuit—at least ever since he started his theoretical production in the early 1980s—remains a book of philosophical texture dealing with the natural sciences at large. *DNA* was meant as such a book, but it never came to be. A version of it titled *Element* was published in 2007 as a collection of photographs of nature alongside a few sketches and computer drawings, but this one left out most of his theoretical texts, apart from a few scattered reflections here and there. At the time of this writing, another book project underway titled *Matrix*, incorporating many of the manuscript contents produced for *DNA*, would seem to be conceived as its reincarnation. But it is as yet unclear whether it will come to fruition.

# BALMOND VIS-À-VIS THE DIGITAL AVANT-GARDE IN ARCHITECTURE

Describing a series of abstract design moves, Balmond's informal can be seen as a conceptual tool instilled with an operational force. In this sense, an inescapable comparison to consider is that with the role that the "formless" played for Rosalind Krauss and Yve-Alain Bois—just at the time when Balmond was working on *Informal*—in their rethinking of some of the epistemological assumptions around modern art. That said, the domain of signification and, by extension, the formal implications of each conceptual tool differed substantially, with the art theorists' project being completely off Balmond's radar.[68]

## Algorithmic Thinking *Avant La Lettre*

One other domain of signification that uncannily anticipated that of Balmond's *Informal* was crafted nearly two decades earlier by Bill Hillier in *The Social Logic of Space* of 1984—a source of which Balmond was also unaware when working on his book. Elaborating on an example involving a cloud of midges that René Thom had given in his seminal *Structural Stability and Morphogenesis*—Thom being the founder of catastrophe theory, a field of mathematics featuring some overlap with chaos theory, though addressing a different set of problems—Hillier described a global form in terms that announced a key aspect of Balmond's thinking: the emergence of order out of randomness through an algorithmic logic.[69] In such a cloud it might be detected that every midge is moving randomly until its field of vision is clear of midges, at which point it will reorient itself in the direction of others. As a result of every midge following this rule, a structural stability of the cloud emerges, its global form recognizable. The rule is strictly local in that it applies to midges only in the vicinity of one another—midges that otherwise have no idea about what is happening elsewhere in the cloud. Hillier pointed out that for the cloud to emerge the rule has to be understood as a restriction on the midges' random movement. In other words, a pre-existing randomness is a background requirement for the operation of the rule, which in turn begets progressive gains within the overall organization. New levels of order appear within the system out of locally related entities deployed in a spatio-temporal medium—the emergent orders

68 Krauss and Bois's well-known exhibition and book *Formless*, dating from 1996 and 1997 respectively, set out to destabilize the categories of "form" and "content" by applying the *informe* entry in Bataille's *Dictionnaire Critique* of 1929–30 to the reading of a selection of modern art works from the late 1920s to the mid-1970s: from Arp, Duchamp and Picasso, all the way through to Fontana, Pollock, and Oldenburg. As with every other entry in the dictionary, Bataille intended not to provide a definition of the term, but rather to assign it a task, to turn it into a performative notion, to the point where the term itself became an operation: that of bringing things down in the world [*déclasser*]. Analogously, Krauss and Bois came up with four term-operations–"horizontality," "base materialism," "pulse," and "entropy"–through which to identify the workings of the formless in those works of modern art. In addition to a shared instrumentality, the parallels linking together the notions of informal and formless are significant, especially in methodological terms. Rather than being grounded in a definition easily accessible to conventional reason, both notions are better understood as an "ensemble of operations;" both pursued a displacement of the dichotomy of "form" and "content"–informal unwittingly, formless purposely; both rejected the presence of a clear hierarchy in the realizations they were connected to; both partook in a range of common themes, if interpreted differently (e.g., entropy and the dynamic nature of some of the operations);

occur in the manner of a ritual. This would be only a limiting case of such a system: one from which the random background process had been entirely removed. The operation of the rules within a spatio-temporal process which is otherwise operating only randomly gives rise to new levels of order in the system becaause there is a random background process. If there is no random background, then there is no gain in global order. In such a system the new levels of order are not necessarily conceived of at any stage by any individual participating in the system. At the same time both the rules and the higher-level emergent orders are objective realities independent of subjects.

In the light of this example, we may next consider a case where what is being arranged is not individuals, but space itself, namely a simple process by which a complex composite object can be generated from a collection of simple single objects, rather as a settlement can be generated by aggregating together a collection of houses. The elementary objects are square cells; the rule of addition of cells is a full facewise join (Fig. 1(a)), with all other joins, such as the vertex join (Fig. 1(b)), excluded; and the aggregation process is one in which objects are added randomly to whatever is already aggregated subject to only one restriction: each cell must retain at least one of its four 'walls' free from other cells. By the time a hundred cells have been aggregated, this generative process (which the reader may try for himself with paper and pencil) will look something like Fig. 2.

Fig. 1

Whatever the actual sequence of placing of objects, provided the process is properly randomised, the same generic global form will result: a dense and continuous aggregate of cells containing a number of void spaces – rather like courtyards – some of which are the same size as the cells, some twice the size, and some even larger. As the object grows larger 'holes' will appear.

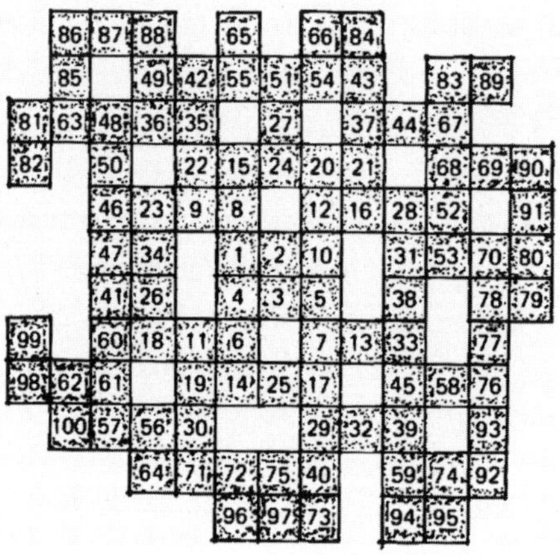

Fig. 2 A random full-face aggregation of square cells with one face per cell kept free, numbered in order of generation.

being independent from the individual entities. This was algorithmic thinking *avant la lettre*.

Hillier went on to extrapolate the analysis of the cloud of midges to another example involving a generative process. Here square cells representing houses are aggregated together randomly while remaining subject to the rule that one of the walls stay free from other cells. "Courtyards" thereby arise **(fig. 3.26)**. He stressed the fact that, for every iteration, the outcome's overall structure was the result of spatial laws independent of the human agency that had otherwise envisioned the process. Hillier transitioned effectively from algorithmic thinking to algorithmic design.[70] The similarities with Balmond's approach are striking indeed.

## Gap between Science and Architectural Thinking

About a decade after Hillier's premonitory writings, what Mario Carpo referred to as "the digital turn in architecture" became manifest, especially in the United States. Starting around 1992 and animated mainly by Greg Lynn's writings and his teachings at Columbia University, so-called "digital architecture" began to develop notably.[71] As presented in the influential, Lynn-edited issue of *Architectural Design* titled "Folding in Architecture" (1993), the particular kind of complexity driving the beginnings of digital design was characterized by a number of properties—such as "curvilinearity," "smoothness," "suppleness," and "pliancy"—that were meant as alternatives to deconstruction and ultimately led to an architecture of gentle splines. Along the lines of those properties, the complexity of digital design involved the possibility of introducing sequential differentiation within an otherwise continuous surface as well as singularities capable of being registered within such continuity. Interestingly enough, the main scientific reference behind these attributes was René Thom's catastrophe theory, as it had been for Hillier. The outcome, however, was sharply different, for there was no trace of nonlinearity, emergence, and algorithmic thinking either in Lynn's theoretical framework or in the works he sponsored.

As the chronology continues, the so-called "paperless studios"—seminal to the early advancement of digital architecture—were implemented by Bernard Tschumi in 1994 at Columbia University. That same year, a symposium titled *Architecture and Complexity* convened by Jeffrey Kipnis and Charles Jencks was held at the Architectural Association in London, featuring Lynn, Koolhaas, Peter Eisenman, and Sanford Kwinter, among others. Most of the relevant references concerning the sciences of complexity, including chaos theory, were in the air, but were not yet being translated into algorithmic design in architecture. The 1994 symposium—celebrated twenty-two years after another one on the same theme had taken place also at the AA **(fig. 3.27)**—brought the American developments in digital design to European audiences, which at the time did not number equivalent

Precedent page:
**3.26** Bill Hillier. Aggregate of square cells representing houses.

both staged their subcategories as fluid and porous, as opposed to airtight. Yet, on the other hand, there are two major differences that must be pointed out. While the role of formless is mainly interpretive, that of informal is primarily generative, being interpretive only indirectly. Secondly, the imagery associated with the formless–for instance, saliva, excrement, fried eggs, and spiders–had little to do with that produced by the informal.

69 While catastrophe theory focuses on abrupt changes causing discontinuities in an otherwise continuous function, chaos theory looks at systems that appear to be random but, in fact, are not, and can therefore be described deterministically. They both, however, study dynamic systems, and analyze the unpredictability of sudden yet significant shifts in behavior within them brought about by minor changes in circumstances.

70 Bill Hillier, *The Social Logic of Space* (New York, NY: Cambridge University Press, 1984), 33–36.

71 IIt was in 1992 when the first writings by Greg Lynn relating to digital design in architecture were published, in *Assemblage 19*. Lynn was twenty-eight years old at the time. Also, it was in 1992 that second-year graduate architecture students Gregg Pasquarelli and Ed Keller, along with Lynn himself–who was already a faculty member at Columbia GSAPP–"proposed the purchase of Silicon Graphics International (SGI) computers and animation software for the school's studios," under Tschumi's deanship. See Paul Makovsky, "Tschumi Steps Down," in *Metropolis Magazine*: http://www.metropolismag.com/cities/tschumi-steps-down/. Accessed August 11, 2017. The paperless studios as such, however, were not implemented until 1994.

# COMPLEXITY

Edited by Royston Landau

"It is one thing not to see the wood from the trees" Paul Weiss.

## COMPLEXITY AND COMPLEXING

Royston Landau

THE TWENTIETH century has been described as the age of complexity[1]. The idea of complexity does not always carry with it either popular or intellectual approval. It runs contrary to a long and respected tradition. Complexity is not an idea which is easy to conceptualize, for by definition it suggests a high degree of complication with the psychologically if not logically inferred likelihood of incomprehensibility or confusion.

A close connection between emerging present-day attitudes to the real world (especially among the post-World War II generation), and the newly developing theoretical understandings about complexity, is not coincidental. Both are part of the same emerging viewpoint and both have been gaining credibility under the aegis of each other.

In the theoretical world of the natural and applied sciences, the complexity topic has begun to change the whole structural balance between components and their relationships to their contexts. But in the much less clearly described social world of the condition of man, a similar but less well understood complexity view appears to be at the root of the changing balance between individuals, their institutions and their societies. Seen from this perspective, areas of specialization, such as the architectural and planning concerns of *AD* take on a radically new look.

In this short introductory essay I shall be looking at the emergence of the problem of complexity from the comparatively stable, relatively slow-moving world to the fast moving dynamics of the present day when even the term *complexity* itself, which belongs to a static, state-describing vocabulary, needs to be supplemented, if not yet supplanted, by a dynamic, process-describing equivalent as implied in the term *complexing.* Within the scope of these ideas, the implications of a shift in conceptual understanding from *state* to *process* is equally as important as that from *simple* to *complex.*

Approaches and attitudes to all forms of understanding and problem-solving have been dominated by the successes of science. Western science, through an impressive capacity to understand and explain the natural world, has brought widespread attention to the power of scientific investigation, although the similarities and differences between scientific problems and those of the applied sciences, and the appropriateness of applying the one programme to the other, has seldom been critically appraised. F.A. Hayek, however, has given detailed examination to, what he argues to be, the misinterpretations of science in the social realm, and has labelled the deceptive, thinking *scientism*[2]. While there is little doubt that *misunderstandings* of science have ironically been used to provide a powerful justification for certain applied activities (especially in computer-oriented realms), there have been recent changes which are making the scientism topic decreasingly important. These include:

1. Increasing approval to a shift-in-approach from *Atomism* to *Holism.*
2. The growing influence

**Royston Landau:** *b. 1927 Architect in private practice, UK. on the visiting faculty at the University of Pennsylvania. Consultant editor of AD.*

advances of their own. Other than Hillier's pioneering thinking, which remained somewhat on the sidelines, a notable exception was the work being done by John Frazer at the Architectural Association. Published in *An Evolutionary Architecture* (1995), Frazer's experiments stood out as the first to explore algorithmic design after the digital turn. That said, the formal organizations they yielded were so disjointed, complicated, and dismissive of any architectural parameters that Frazer's contribution fell into the domains of morphology and computer graphics rather than architecture proper, thereby signaling the same limitations observable in the vast majority of subsequent investigations into similar algorithmic processes **(fig. 3.28)**.

1995 also saw the publication of *The Architecture of the Jumping Universe.* This book, which Charles Jencks decided to write in the wake of the symposium at the AA, explores nearly all of the salient terms and concepts of the sciences of complexity: nonlinearity, emergence, self-organization, attractors, edge of chaos, etc. Europe had caught up with the US and possibly even overtaken it, at least in the theoretical realm. However, beyond formal and semantic metaphors, most of the buildings and design operations chosen by Jencks to illustrate such terms and concepts had not been generated by actual nonlinear processes or algorithmic design **(fig. 3.29)**. His phrase "nonlinear architecture" was thus utterly misleading. In 1997—the same year Brett Steele and Patrik Schumacher founded the DRL at the AA, which was to compete with Columbia in matters of digital design—Jencks guest-edited the special issue of *AD* mentioned earlier, titled "New Science = New Architecture." In addition to Balmond, who in the 1995 book had received only one mention in passing, the contributors featured here expanded significantly on some of the key concepts in the sciences of complexity. But aside from Balmond's design theories, the gap between scientific discussions involving chaos theory and nonlinearity, on the one hand, and architectural thinking, on the other, remained consistent across projects and texts. Here, too, algorithmic design was completely absent.

Precedent page:
**3.27** October 1972 issue of *Architectural Design* guest-edited by Royston Landau.

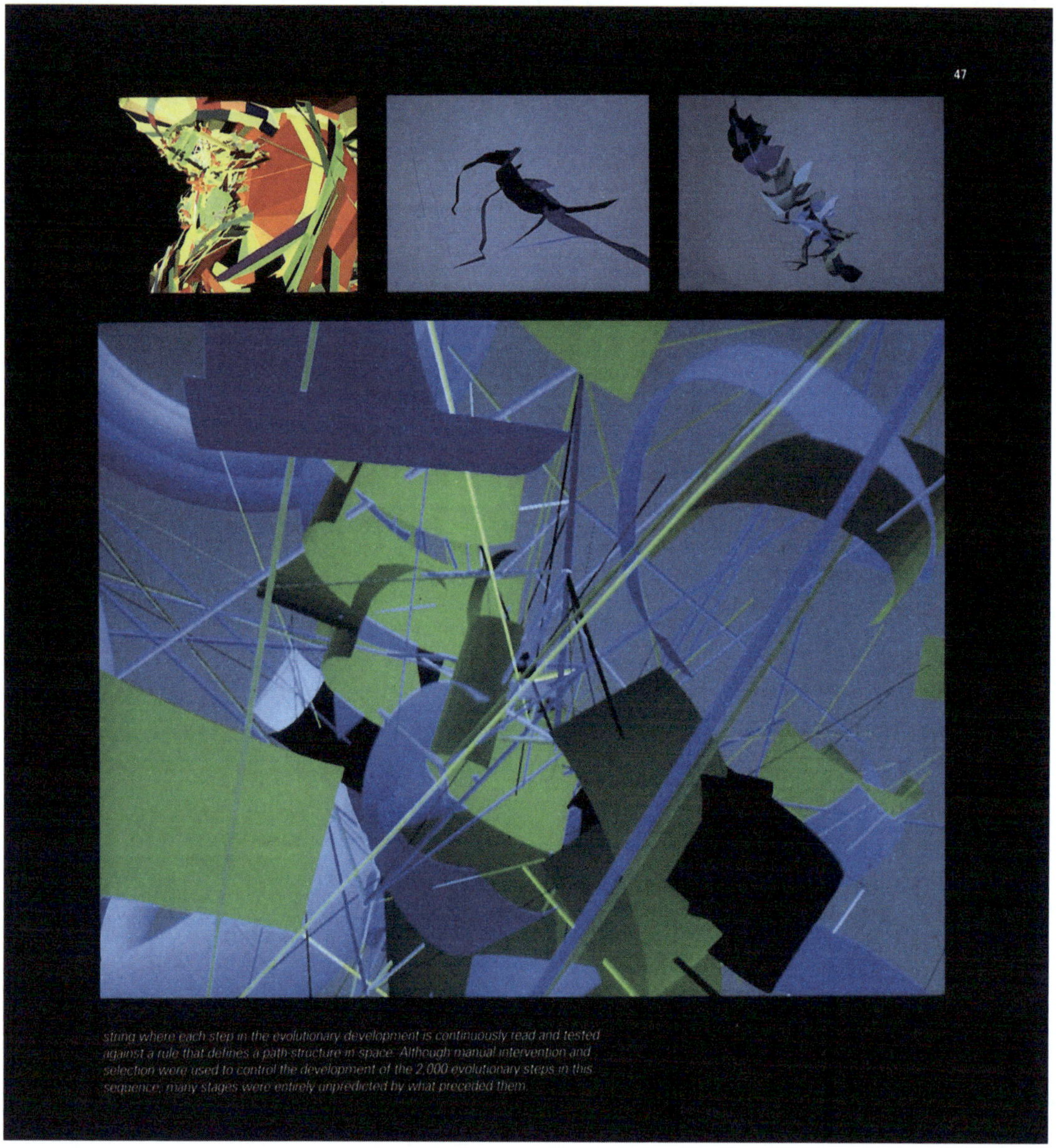


**3.28** An example of algorithmic design producing disjointed formal organizations in John Frazer's *An Evolutionary Architecture* (1995).

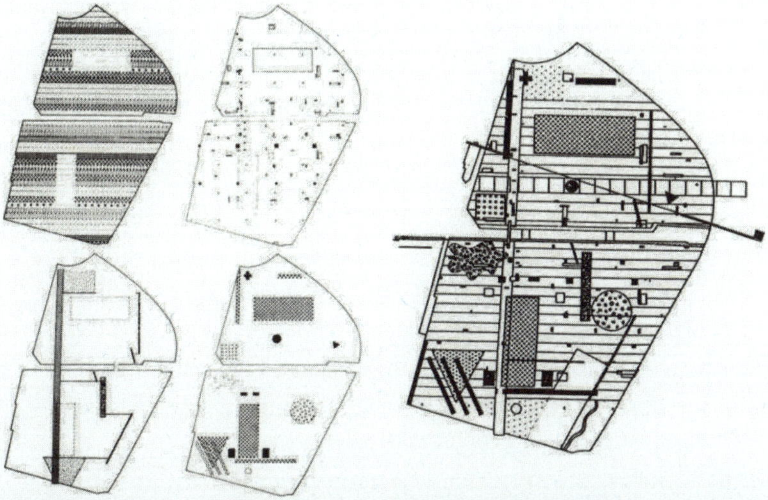

*Rem Koolhaas,* Pare de la Villette, *Paris, France 1982-3- Various organizational types — hands of planting, confetti of small furniture, circulation and existing buildings- are superposed in rich congestion.*

**78**

**3.29** OMA Rem Koolhaas, competition entry for the Parc de la Villette (1982–83).

## Hillier – Allen – Balmond

It was Stan Allen's theoretical endeavor that resonated closely with Hillier's and Balmond's—not only in terms of addressing algorithmic thinking, but also (in contradistinction to Frazer) in doing so while staying grounded in the specificities of architecture. Allen—who lent more toward the relationship between architecture and art than toward hardcore digital design *per se*, although he was still a central figure during the paperless studio years at Columbia—postulated the notion of "field conditions" around just the time when Balmond was busy at work on *Informal*: first in a studio syllabus of 1995, then fully articulated in his well-known "From Object to Field: Field Conditions in Architecture and Urbanism," published in a 1997 issue of *AD* titled "Architecture After Geometry." Expressing a preference for the post-minimalism of artists like Alan Saret, Eva Hesse, Bruce Nauman, and Barry Le Va, over the minimalism of an Andre or a Judd, Allen described post-minimalist production in terms of introducing "chance and contingency into the work of art," even using the word "informal" as a qualifier. Drawing on an art critic's quote from 1968, Allen termed these works "distributions": "whether 'random' or 'orderly' a 'distribution' is defined as 'relationships of points and configurations to each other' or concomitantly, 'sequences of events'."[72] Then he continued in his own words:

> local relationships are more important than overall form. The generation of form through "sequences of events" is somewhat related to the generative rules for flock behavior or algebraic combination. Le Va signals a key compositional principle emerging out of Post-Minimalism . . . the displacement of control to a series of intricate local rules for combination . ... not as an overall formal configuration.[73]

The similarities are such that it might have been Balmond himself writing. And yet, he was not aware of this Allen essay at the time, just as he was not of Hillier's book.

## Morphology and Computer Graphics versus Architectural Thinking

By 1999, *Animate Form* expanded Lynn's original project to deal more specifically with the relationship between computer-driven processes of form making and its shaping forces. Lynn, whose work was inseparable from the capabilities of Autodesk's Maya software at the time, proposed "animation" as a concept suggesting "animalism, animism, growth, actuation, vitality and virtuality," with nonlinearity and algorithmic thinking always absent.[74] Although, as Picon indicated, a few architecture schools such as MIT and Harvard had introduced the first courses in computer programming in the late 1980s and early 1990s, it was only around the mid-2000s that nonlinearity in algorithmic thinking entered the picture of

72 Stan Allen, "From Object to Field: Field Conditions in Architecture and Urbanism," *Architectural Design*, no. 67 (June 1997), 26.

73 Ibid.

74 Greg Lynn, *Animate Form* (New York: Princeton Architectural Press, 1999), 9.

digital design in architecture in a substantial fashion, hand in hand with a revival of the use of software scripting and coding.[75] At the heart of this wave was the possibility of using programming languages to transcend the stylistic inklings and limitations induced by pre-constituted software packages. There was John Frazer's significant precedent, mentioned above. Testa, O'Reilly, Weiser, and Ross's paper titled "Emergent Design: a crosscutting research program and design curriculum integrating architecture and artificial intelligence" (2001) discussed emergence, although once again the term "architecture" stands for a rather abstract domain. A 2002 issue of *AD* titled "Contemporary Techniques in Architecture," guest-edited by Ali Rahim, addressed nonlinearity to a certain extent and included some of Balmond's work at ARUP in addition to writings by Manuel de Landa, author of *A Thousand Years of Nonlinear History*. But it was not until the period between 2004 and 2006 that a number of important publications attested to algorithmic design being in full operation: namely, Leach, Turnbull, and Williams's *Digital Tectonics* (2004); Karl Chu's "Metaphysics of Genetic Architecture and Computation" (2004); another two issues of *AD*, "Emergence: Morphogenetic Design Strategies" (2004) and "Techniques and Technologies in Morphogenetic Design" (2006), the former including a review of Balmond's Advanced Geometry Unit; Kostas Terzidis's *Algorithmic Architecture* (2006); and *Tooling* (2006), co-authored by Benjamin Aranda and Chris Lasch. Following in the footsteps of Frazer, however, a considerable portion of these experiments and studies proved to be more relevant to morphology and computer graphics than to the architecture of buildings in any realistic sense.

## Anticipation

That Balmond did not participate in the 1994 symposium at the AA is symptomatic of the fact that at that point he was not part of the discussions taking place in the architectural avant-garde. He only started to gain access to those after 1995, as a result of his first public presentation of the *Informal* manifesto in Berlin that year coinciding with the increased awareness around questions concerning digital design that had been developing in the European scene since the year before. His presence in the 1997 Jencks-edited issue of *AD*—both in the acknowledgments to a piece by Mae-Wan Ho titled "The New Age of the Organism" and through his own separate contribution—indicates that Balmond was by then slowly becoming a player in the architectural conversations of the turn of the century. Granted, he had been collaborating with Koolhaas since 1986, but the Dutch architect was never a channel through which he was introduced to the new debates in architecture around digital design in the 1990s—among other reasons because Koolhaas himself never showed a strong interest in those.[76]

75 For more on the history and theory of digital design as regards scripting and coding see Malcolm McCullough, "20 Years of Scripted Space," *AD Profile*, no. 182 (August 2006): 12–15. On Picon's indication, see Picon, *Digital Culture in Architecture*, 95.

76 At the 1994 *Architecture and Complexity* symposium mentioned earlier, Koolhaas started his presentation by apologizing for not making explicit the connection between his presentation and the subject of complexity. He then criticized the visual aspects that, in his view, dominated discussions around complexity in architecture, in clear reference to the other speakers at the event. His lecture concerned urban issues around the city of Singapore, in particular those shedding light on why he believed it had been such a denigrated city up to that point. See https://www.youtube.com/watch?v=Ex1Cl3k3do8&t=665s Accessed August 12, 2017.

Where many architects were looking at catastrophe theory and Gilles Deleuze's theories of "the fold," Balmond—operating from an isolationism afforded by his being external to the discipline of architecture—was drawing on a primarily self-constructed body of references involving theories of chaos and Greek proportion. He started to examine these in the early 1980s—i.e., about a decade earlier than fellows in architecture came upon their references, with the notable exception of Kwinter.[77] As a result of this anticipation, Balmond had already produced manuscripts dealing with nonlinearity and algorithmic thinking by 1994, when knowledge of the sciences of complexity as well as theoretical production around it was only beginning to emerge in architecture. Furthermore, insofar as those manuscripts involved architectural design, Balmond pioneered the translation of the basis of some of those sciences into specific design moves of architectural consequence. In this regard, he turned out to be again about a decade ahead of developments in nonlinearity and algorithmic thinking reaching a significant presence within digital architecture. By 1999 he was rehearsing these design frameworks, not in the context of academia, or by utilizing them for small pavilions, furniture, or product design, but rather by applying them to the conception of fully fledged architectural projects, such as a tower scheme with Philip Johnson **(fig. 3.30–32)**. In this sense, he can also be considered a pioneer.

Opposite and following pages: **3.30–32** Correspondence with Philip Johnson on ideas for the Guang Zhou Tower scheme, 1999.

## COLLABORATIVE MALLEABILITY

The first large project that Balmond worked on was the Carlsberg brewery in Northampton (England), completed in 1973. Although formative in terms of experimenting with tectonic form, his role in that project remained squarely within the confines of structural engineering **(fig. 3.33)**. It did, however, turn out to be important to him for another reason. The building was designed by Danish architect Knud Munk. Ove Arup—then in his late seventies, when Balmond was in his late twenties—had already retired, but would come to his office every day to write and do some sporadic supervision. Being a compatriot of Munk's, he became involved in Carlsberg and thus reviewed Balmond's decisions on a number of occasions. These were the only direct interactions over a scheme between the two engineers.

In the years following, during his early to mid-thirties, Balmond busied himself with plenty of commercial work, primarily with a company called the London & Edinburgh Trust. This was when he sharpened his business acumen, proving successful at attracting substantial fees and being an effective negotiator all round.

77 See Sanford Kwinter, *Architectures of Time: Toward a Theory of the Event in Modernist Culture* (Cambridge, MA: MIT Press, 2001), 12–13. Kwinter started writing about related topics in 1984.

(4)

If 9 tubes and 45m dia.

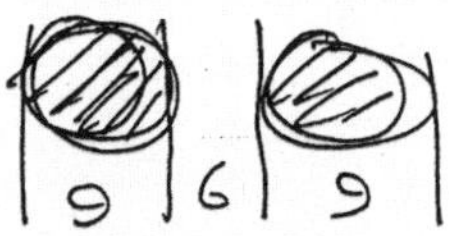


& 30m dia.
(less height).

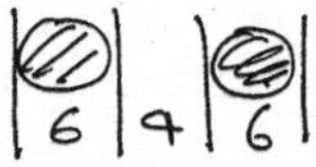


If 18 tubes, and 45m dia.

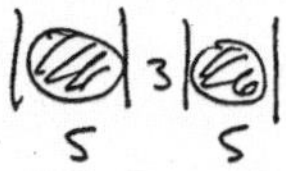


The nine point arrangement gives interesting algorithmic possibilities. Track the arrows.

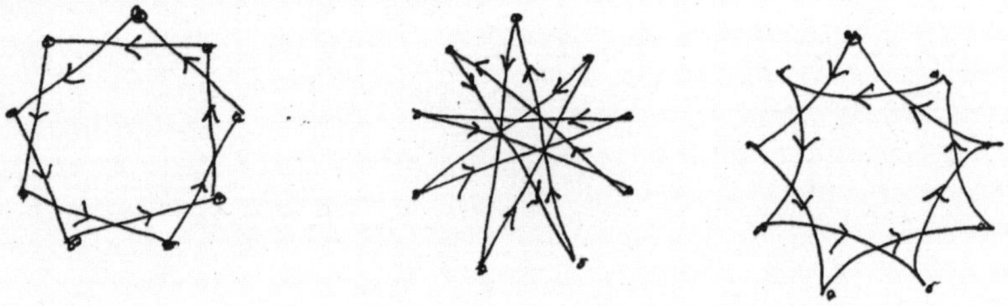

The patterns give interesting floor plates in plan but actually the patterns give rising spiral forms in elevation.

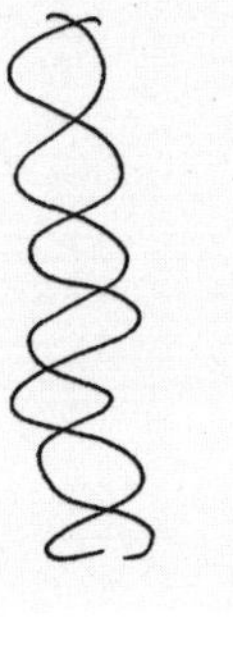

See fax sent last week.

Difficult to construct

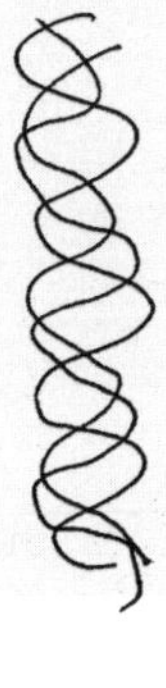

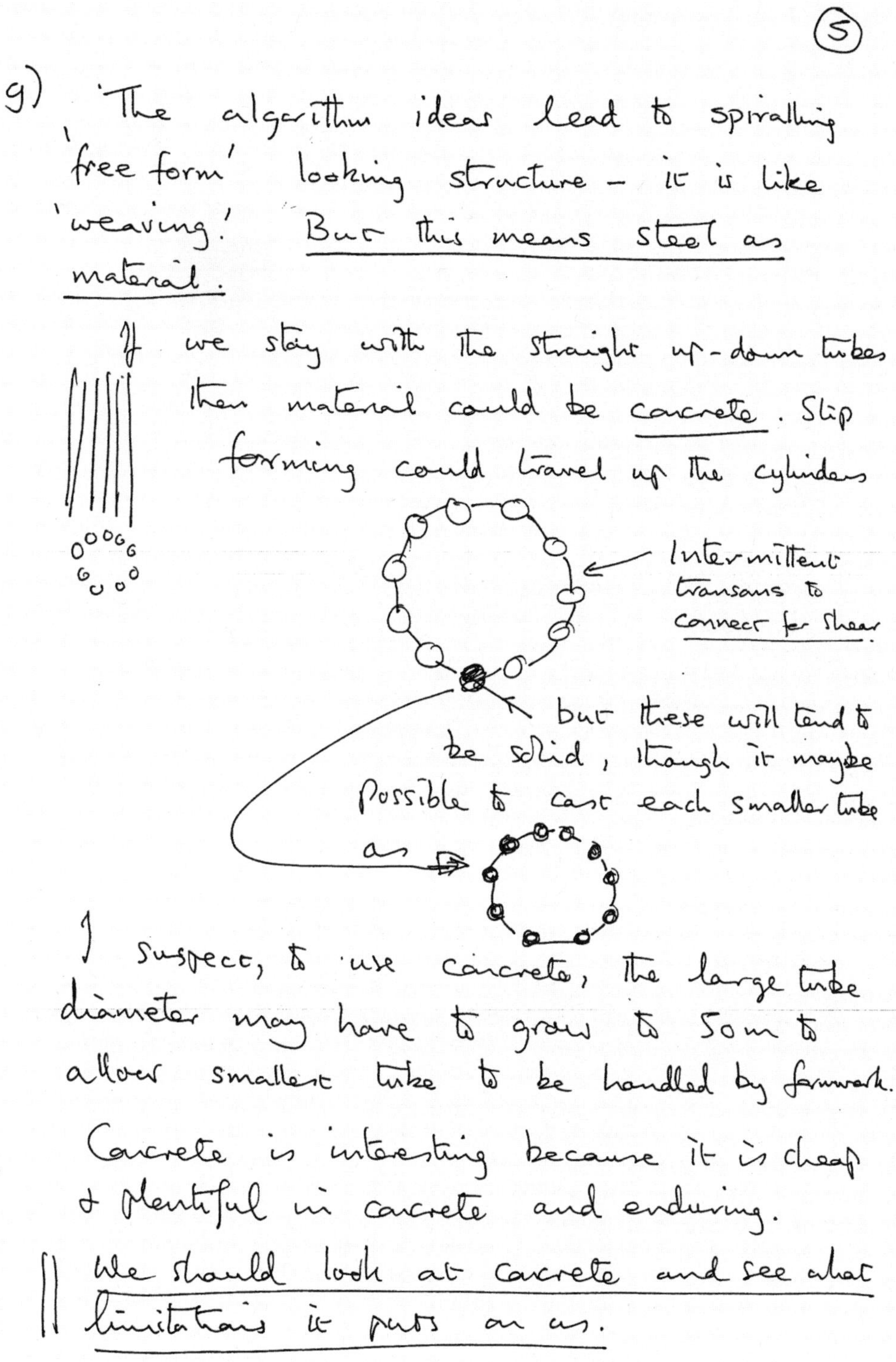

(5)

g) 'The algorithm ideas lead to spiralling 'free form' looking structure – it is like 'weaving'. <u>But this means steel as material.</u>

If we stay with the straight up-down tubes then material could be <u>concrete</u>. Slip forming could travel up the cylinders



but these will tend to be solid, though it maybe possible to cast each smaller tube as

I suspect, to use concrete, the large tube diameter may have to grow to 50m to allow smallest tube to be handled by formwork.

Concrete is interesting because it is cheap & plentiful in concrete and enduring.

|| <u>We should look at concrete and see what limitations it puts on us.</u>

h). (6)

Elevation

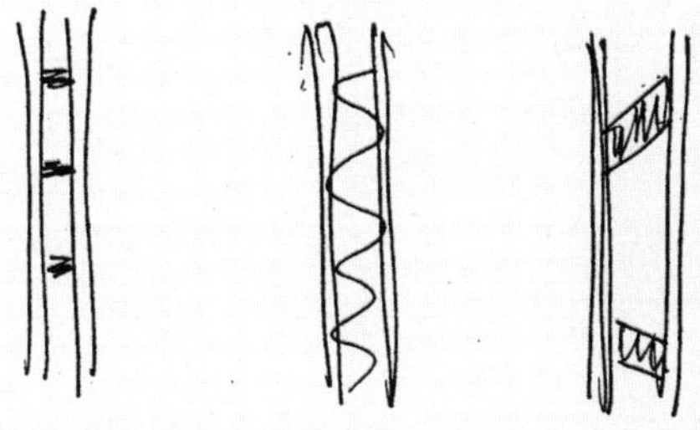

Each tube needs cross connection as discussed before. At various scales, the same idea should be used, straights / inclines / or webs.

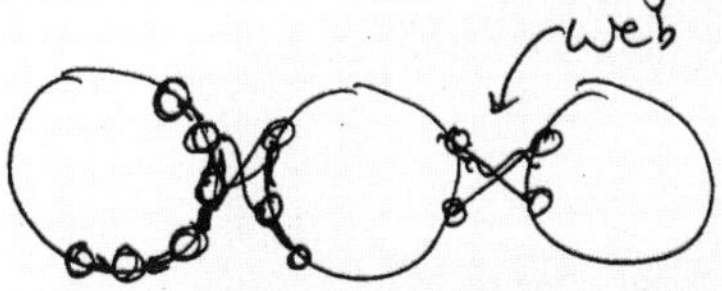


Each small tube can have one type and web like connections between each large dia. tube.

Other elevations.

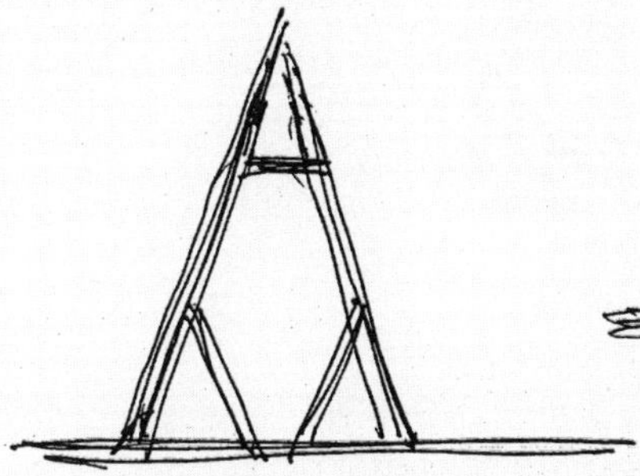

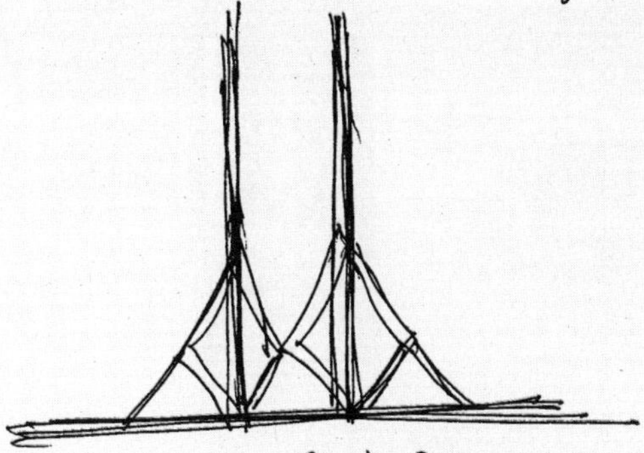

Quite Stray

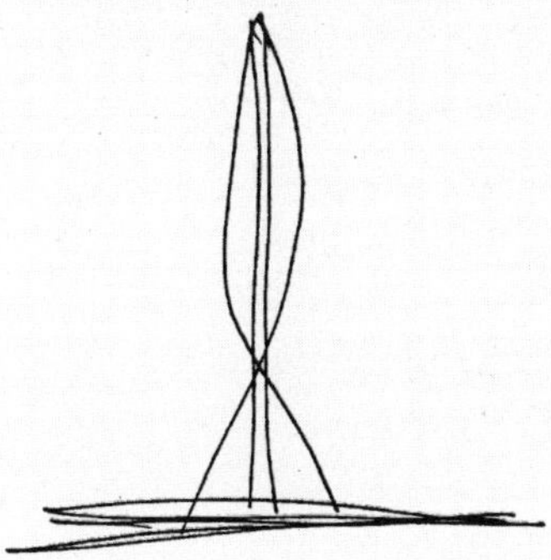

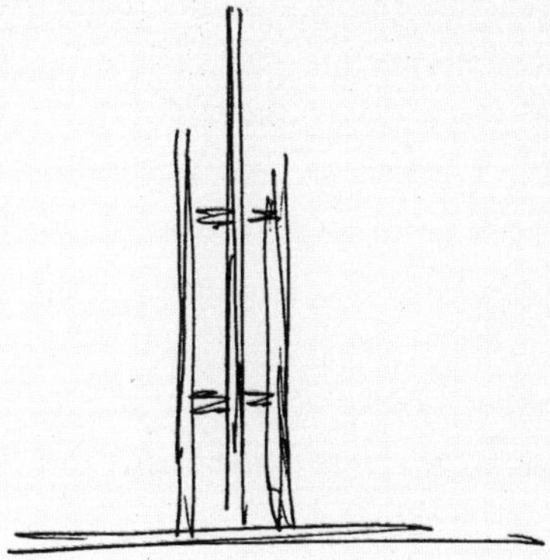

3.33 Architect: Knud Munk. Carlsberg brewery in Northampton (England). Under construction; completed in 1973.

The first noncommercial project that landed on his desk was James Stirling's Neue Staatsgalerie, won in competition in 1977 and built between 1979 and 1984. It was key in that it re-awakened his architectural curiosity and triggered a series of collaborations with some of the most respected architects worldwide, initiating a phase that lasted nearly thirty years (fig. 3.34). Neue Staatsgalerie was Balmond's apprenticeship in advanced design in architecture, to the point that, for the first time, he significantly intervened in a few of the decisions that were unmistakably architectural in nature. The design process as a whole, however, never developed along the lines of a fully fledged synergy between architecture and engineering—if only because Stirling, seventeen years Balmond's senior, was not particularly interested in the engineering being prominent or experimental. Rather, he was intent on rehearsing a certain kind of post-modernist stylistic code, with the engineering providing merely a basis for it. Stirling enjoyed Balmond's inputs and they continued to work together on a number of projects throughout the 1980s.

Such a synergy between architecture and engineering blossomed across his various partnerships with Koolhaas, whom he met in 1986 when the two were at similar career stages. Having formed his own group within ARUP (group #9) in the early 1980s, Balmond was already growing professionally by the time he crossed paths with the Dutch architect, even though presumably he was not yet particularly well known within the company.[78] From that point on, collaborations with Koolhaas included early competitions such as the Morgan Bank in Amsterdam and the City Hall in The Hague; all of the buildings that were devised during OMA's most creative years (ZKM, Zeebrugge, Très Grande Bibliothèque, Agadir, Congrexpo, Jussieu, Kunsthal, and Bordeaux House); and more recently, Seattle library, CCTV, Casa da Musica, and London's Serpentine Pavilion (fig. 3.35). Aside from Stirling and Koolhaas, other noteworthy alliances were those with Alvaro Siza, Daniel Libeskind, Philip Johnson, Shigeru Ban, UN Studio, Enric Miralles, and Toyo Ito, the last two being those with whom he had the greatest affinity. Concentrating on a few architects was the result of his business motto: "one architect, one developer and one contractor" at any one time wherever possible, which in a sense was an extension of Rice's earlier inclination to focus on Piano.[79]

## Episodic Structure

Balmond's collaboration with Koolhaas involved a rather Cartesian way of thinking about space, despite his repeated repudiation of such an approach. This design thinking was never heavily geometrical. Rather, it was about relatively subtle, somewhat counter-intuitive gestures embodied in a structure's specific moments. This is the notion of "episodes of structure" that Balmond first announced in 1993: in contrast to elements comprehensively distributed all across a building, there would be a juxtaposition of diverse structural systems and gestures driven by local considerations that would punctuate space in an array of varying distributions.[80] This is certainly the case at Kunsthal, for example, where one finds a delirious coexistence of inclined and horizontal slabs; tilted concrete supports and straight tree-trunk columns following different dispositions; ceiling trusses traversed by arching, semi-exposed braces; castellated beams turned ninety degrees; and X-shaped tension cables (fig. 3.36). Though Balmond typically claimed the idea of "episodic structure" as his, Koolhaas's influence here cannot be overstated. In fact, the chronology indicates that Balmond only came up with the phrase after the first, seminal projects with the Dutchman. The various structural "episodes" occurring at Kunsthal seem to derive directly from Koolhaas's well-known interest in envisioning a building as a narrative comprising a sequence of distinct, sometimes unexpected scenes, much like a movie script.

78 According to some of his colleagues at the time, such as Robert Lang, who worked with Balmond until the mid-1990s and was a director at ARUP at the time of an interview with the author in London, on October 15, 2013.

79 Balmond's business motto was articulated by David Lewis, a director at ARUP at the time of an interview with the author in London on October 7, 2013. By the early 1990s long-term relationships with particular architects were common practice at ARUP, with service engineer John Berry working closely with Michael Hopkins, and Tony Fitzpatrick with Norman Foster and Jean Nouvel. See Hugh Pearman, "Secrets of the Arup Archipelago," *World Architecture*, no. 18 (July 1992): 77.

80 Balmond, "Tecnologia," 88.

34 BUILDING DESIGN, October 10, 1986

## Golden years

The ramped approaches to the gallery form part of a public route.

The route winds around the outside of the central sculpture court.

Lighting and air-conditioning arrangeme

# STIRLING STYLE

**Cecil Balmond discusses Arup's joint involvement in the structures and services for James Stirling, Michael Wilford & Associates' hugely successful Stuttgart Staatsgalerie.**

STUTTGART's new art gallery opened in 1984 to much critical acclaim. The building has been hailed as a breakthrough for the new architecture; an original design that acknowledges the past while creating its own new style. Certainly, if the enthusiasm of the public is anything to go by, the building is a success.

The focus of the building complex is a large, open circular space called the sculpture court, around which the various exhibition spaces are planned, opening onto terrace and foyer levels, and linked by a series of curving zig-zag ramps. An imaginative feature of the scheme is the pedestrian route for the public, which winds up and round the central court, connecting Konrad Adenauer Strasse at the front of the site with Urbanstrasse at the rear. The public on this route may look into the sculpture court and view the activity of the podium and terrace areas without visiting the gallery.

Local marble and sandstone are used extensively for the external cladding to the building. Contrasting with this traditional look are the twisting glass walls of the foyer, the steel lattice canopy structures and the angular lines of the elevations themselves; it is a striking mix of high tech with classical form.

Ove Arup & Partners were invited to design the structure and services for the project, as part of a joint venture with Boll for structural engineering and Eser Dittman Nehring for the engineering services. It was agreed that Arups would lead the engineering design up to scheme stage and then transfer the lead to the German-based team for the production of the tender and working drawings.

The client was the local government of Baden-Wurttemburg.

The initial task for the design team was to work out a structural and services concept that would fit the tight planning of the various levels and yet not raise the building height above that of the existing gallery.

For the structure, downstanding beams were avoided where possible; floor slabs were designed to span directly onto columns or to be supported by walls serving as full storey-height beams. The layout of the services was planned to avoid large horizontal ducts. Consequently, the plantroom was stretched out along the whole length of the building with vertical service risers connected directly to strategic areas.

During the early concept stage the other matter for debate was whether an expansion joint was desirable. Wherever a joint line could be drawn in the structure the details became extremely contorted. The tight "layering" of the various levels did not lend itself to independent structural units; the walls located along all external sides of the building removed any "give" in the structure at the edges normally free for expansion and contraction, therefore it had to be a 90m by 100m structure without joints. It was agreed to deal with the problem by simple crack control procedures, based on the even distribution of strains induced by temperature and shrinkage.

In the detailed development of the structural design a series of finite element analyses was carried out on the main spanning wall/beam elements. Where stiffer wall elements framed into smaller and more slender elements local elastic stress distributions were calculated to satisfy the checking authority.

The competition brief required maximum use of natural light for viewing exhibits. Initially the upper gallery rooms were planned with fully glazed roofs. As the design progressed, however, areas of glazing were reduced to lower the air-condi-

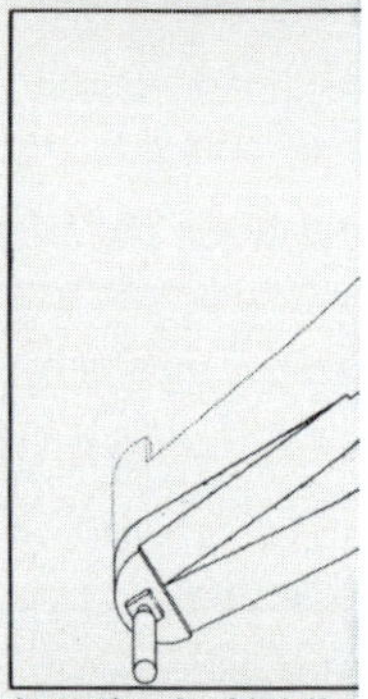

Axonometric up view of the double ra

Structure and mechanism of the lift

Architectural & Construction BOOKSHOP

The books listed below are available through the Architectural & Construction Bookshop. A special service for readers provided by Morgan-Grampian Construction Press.

**1. The Fireplace Book** by Roxana McDonald. A practical guide, encompassing both functional and aesthetic considerations, to fireplace design, maintenance and restoration. Price £10.95

**2. Building Regulations Explained and Illustrated** (Seventh edition) by Powell-Smith and Billington. Covers the new 1985 Regulations for all building types for England and Wales, with extensive illustrations and references to regulations and Approved Documents. Price £14.50 (paperback).

**3. Hotel Planning and Design: a guide for architects, interior designers and hotel executives** by Walter A Rutes and Richard H. Penner. Identifies the key opportunities in this field and analyses the planning and design criteria for nearly 30 different types. Specialised and up-to-date guidance unavailable elsewhere. Price £49.50.

**4. The Classical Orders of Architecture** by Robert Chitham. Immaculate line drawings and informative captions explaining the origins, development and practical usage of all the classical architectural elements. Invaluable to designers and fascinating for their clients. Price £16.45.

**5. The Architect's Guide to Fee Negotiations** by Ray Moxley. Competitive fee tendering has now become a reality of architectural practice. This book sets out all the items that have to be negotiated at each stage. Price £18.65.

**6. Construction Project Management using Small Computers** by Glen Peters. As well as explaining the principles of project management this book explains how they can be applied on small computers and which particular systems are most suitable. Price £15.35.

**7. Legal and Contractual Procedures for Architects** by Bob Greenstreet. New edition of this popular reference work which gives concise and simple guidance through the legal and contractual maze of everyday architectural practice. Price £9.85.

**8. Contractor's Claims: An Architect's Guide** by David Chappell. Explains how to avoid situations which give rise to contractor's claims for delays or expenses, and how to deal with them when they do arise. Price £15.35.

**9. Manual of Graphic Techniques 4** by Tom Porter and Sue Goodman. The latest volume in this series uses drawings to show every aspect of development and presentation of plans, from interiors to elevations, site sections to sectional perspectives. There are black and white photographs and line drawings throughout. Price £9.85.

**10. Specification 85** by David Martin. Eighty-second edition of this annual reference source for architects and specifiers in the construction industry. Volume 5 is a commissioned new volume devoted entirely to specification clauses. The six volumes set is supplied in a library box. Price £57.50.

**11. Standard Form of Building Contract** (Second edition) by John Parris. Probably the leading text on JCT 80, this has been revised to cover major changes in the law on professional liability, retention monies and interest on unpaid sums. Price £19.75.

**12. How Architects Get Work** by G. Golzen. Existing practices, as well as those thinking of taking the plunge into setting up on their own, will find this book stimulating and lively reading. Price £10.95 (paperback)

**13. The Interior Design Workbook: A Job Record and Diary** by David Fry FSIA RIBA. Fills a considerable gap in providing interior designers, with a working tool which sets out all the stages of an interior design project. Price £10.95.

**14. Design Liability in the Construction Industry** (Second edition) by D. L. Cornes. Includes extensive new material on the law of professional negligence including the latest cases after *Pirelli*. Price £19.00.

**15. AJ Introduction and Complete Index to the 1985 Building Regulations** Briefly explains what are the main changes: how to find all the references to any subject: a checklist of which British Standards are invoked by each section plus unique detailed subject index to every topic covered. Price £8.25.

**16. JCT Intermediate Form of Contract:** an architect's guide. By David Chappell and Vincent Powell-Smith. Practical advice for the architect, clearly set out in sample letters, flow-charts and tables. Studies the roles of each party involved and covers important topics such as claims and payment in depth. Price £19.80.

**17. Construction Law Reports.** A new series reporting decisions of the Official Referees Court which are binding on the whole industry. All members of the construction team must keep up to date with these decisions. Available as a subscription: 3 volumes a year £45.00.

**18. Archi-tetes Postcards 2 sets of 8 colour cartoons** by Louis Hellman. Set 1: Wright, Le Corbusier (twice), Aalto, Foster, Graves, Mies and Stirling. Set 2: Gaudi, Mackintosh, Ralph Erskine, Bruce Goff, Charles Moore, Leon Krier, Terry Farrell and Philip Johnson. Price: Set 1; £2.50: Set 2; £2.50.

**19. Architects' Data** by Ernst Neufert. Available for the first time in paperback, this well-known design guide offers over 400 pages of building types. Price £16.95.

**20. Handbook for Clerk of Works (Third Edition)** by GLC Department of Architecture and Civic Design. This Third Edition provides step-by-step guidance on the carrying out of all the duties of the Clerk of Works. Price £12.05.

**Space of Earth — Architecture: People and Buildings** by Charles Knevitt. The heavily illustrated book of the current Channel 4 series take a fresh look at some key issues of architecture and planning over the last 100 years: cities; skyscrapers; mass housing; conservation; and future trends, including community architecture. Price £9.85 (paperback) £16.45 (hardback). Inc P+P.

**LONDON ENERGY GROUP DATA BOOK AND DIARY 1987**
**A slim pocket diary — month to view with 32 pages of data on energy in buildings** compiled by Jack Peach ex Technical Secretary of CIBSE. A first edition in 1987 this could be your most valuable acquisition for it contains most of the U-values, degree days, appliance efficiences and other energy data you need from day to day. The project has financial support from RIBA and CIBSE. Order now to reserve your copy for November delivery. Price £4.60 inc VAT (Discounted prices available for multiples of ten copies or more with practice or company logo as an extra).

ORDER FORM

*To:* ARCHITECTURAL & CONSTRUCTION BOOKSHOP, MORGAN-GRAMPIAN (CONSTRUCTION PRESS) LTD.
30 CALDERWOOD STREET, LONDON SE18 6QH

Please send me the following books (print the full title)

Quantity Full title

☐ ____
☐ ____
☐ ____
☐ ____
☐ ____
☐ ____

NAME ____
COMPANY ____
ADDRESS ____

I enclose cheque/P.O. payable to Architectural & Construction Bookshop to the value of

BD 10/10/86

All prices include the postage and packing Please allow minimum 28 days for delivery

Such influence is consistent with the dynamic observed in the many faxes that the two men exchanged during their collaborations, especially from the early 1990s through the mid-2000s. There was a dominant unidirectionality whereby Koolhaas decided on concept and aesthetics, with Balmond offering structural solutions to go along with them. The acquiescent phrasing is rather telling: "[i]f you want this feel to [the] building, then . . .," wrote Balmond when working on a competition for a tower at La Défense in April 1991 **(fig. 3.37–38)**.[81] Later, in 1996, when busy with a commissioned study for a tower development in Seoul: "[o]nly detailed analysis will show whether we can match your aesthetic and proportions. As you said Rem . . . " **(fig. 3.39)**.[82] At times, the language reveals a Balmond bending over backwards to try and materialize Koolhaas's desires, as when addressing a defining moment for the Seattle library's envelope: "a light skin meeting a heavy box is an impossible condition," he concluded after teasing out up to three elaborate lines of engineering reasoning **(fig. 3.40)**.[83] With Koolhaas in particular, Balmond's most salient decisions often concerned materials, despite his belief that such aspects should be secondary to pattern and configuration.[84] The Kunsthal is one obvious instance. But also Congrexpo—where he was instrumental in the solution finally adopted for the roof of the exhibition area, involving a steel-timber hybrid section where the timber dropped ceiling works in tension—and the Zeebrugge Sea Terminal project—a phasing experiment in materials featuring a transition from concrete to steel to plastic. The driving force of Koolhaas's tendency to resort to materials used in idiosyncratic ways and combinations is strongly manifest here.

Precedent page:
**3.34** Cecil Balmond discusses ARUP's role in James Stirling's Neue Staatsgalerie (1977; 1979–84).

**3.35** Above: Cecil Balmond and Rem Koolhaas on one of their joint site visits and discussing CCTV at the latter's office in Rotterdam.

81 Fax dated April 16, 1991. Courtesy of Balmond Studio.

82 Fax dated April 6, 1996. Courtesy of Balmond Studio.

83 Fax dated December 18, 1999. Courtesy of Balmond Studio.

84 Cecil Balmond and Toyo Ito, "Conversation - Cecil Balmond and Toyo Ito: 'Concerning Fluid Spaces,'" *A + U: Architecture and Urbanism*, no. 5 (May 2004), 44.

**3.36** Left; OMA Rem Koolhaas. Views of the Kunsthal (1987–1992).

Opposite page:
**3.37–38** Fax correspondence with Rem Koolhaas over a competition for a tower scheme in Paris, 1991.

16/4/91

To Rem,

I think the scheme is great.

Here are my thoughts. Robert Pugh faxing more in 1 hours.

Services later pm.

I'm trying to get no horizontal zone for ducts.

Cecil.

Defense Competition

16/4/91

1) Basically offsets can be done. No inherent overturning stability problem but one of continuous transfer of offsets back into a defined structural core.

2) Two ways to look at it

2.1

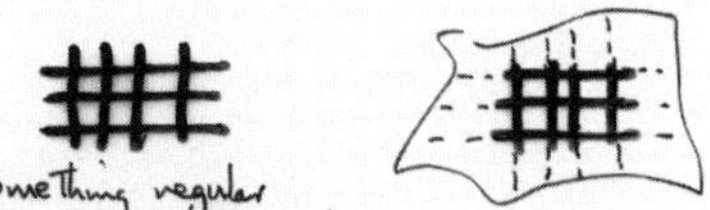

Something regular grows into offset shape

OR

2.2

Edge and offset complications bound onto and held by central interventions

This gives 'monolithic' nature to edge

3) One building on top of another means transfer at one level. Does not feel right.

If you want this feel to building then transfer zone should be defined over two storeys

≃ 6m – 7m articulation.

(5)

11) You began with a 25 m wide tower.

I said it should be wider – we looked at 30 m but it is too slender still.

With the rectangular shape & current height of roof 40 m is probably right.

To come under this, tuned mass dampers will be needed (equivalent to 4 or 5 storeys of weight at the top) and also probably hydraulic dampers at the levels of lean to & collar. Expensive!

12) Only detailed analysis will show whether we can match your aesthetic & proportions.

As you said Rem, the structure should dictate various architectural devices to cope with this staggering but exciting problem of a very tall building harnessed to other buildings.

13) If the sums show its possible then a wind tunnel test will need to be done to test movements & vibration.

Note 14) Inclined buildings will be structure on their outside. 

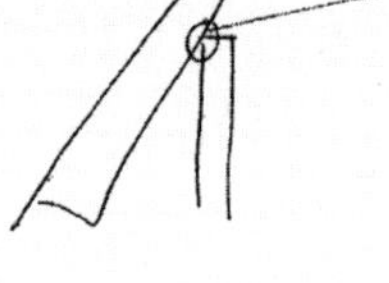

Points like this wont work.

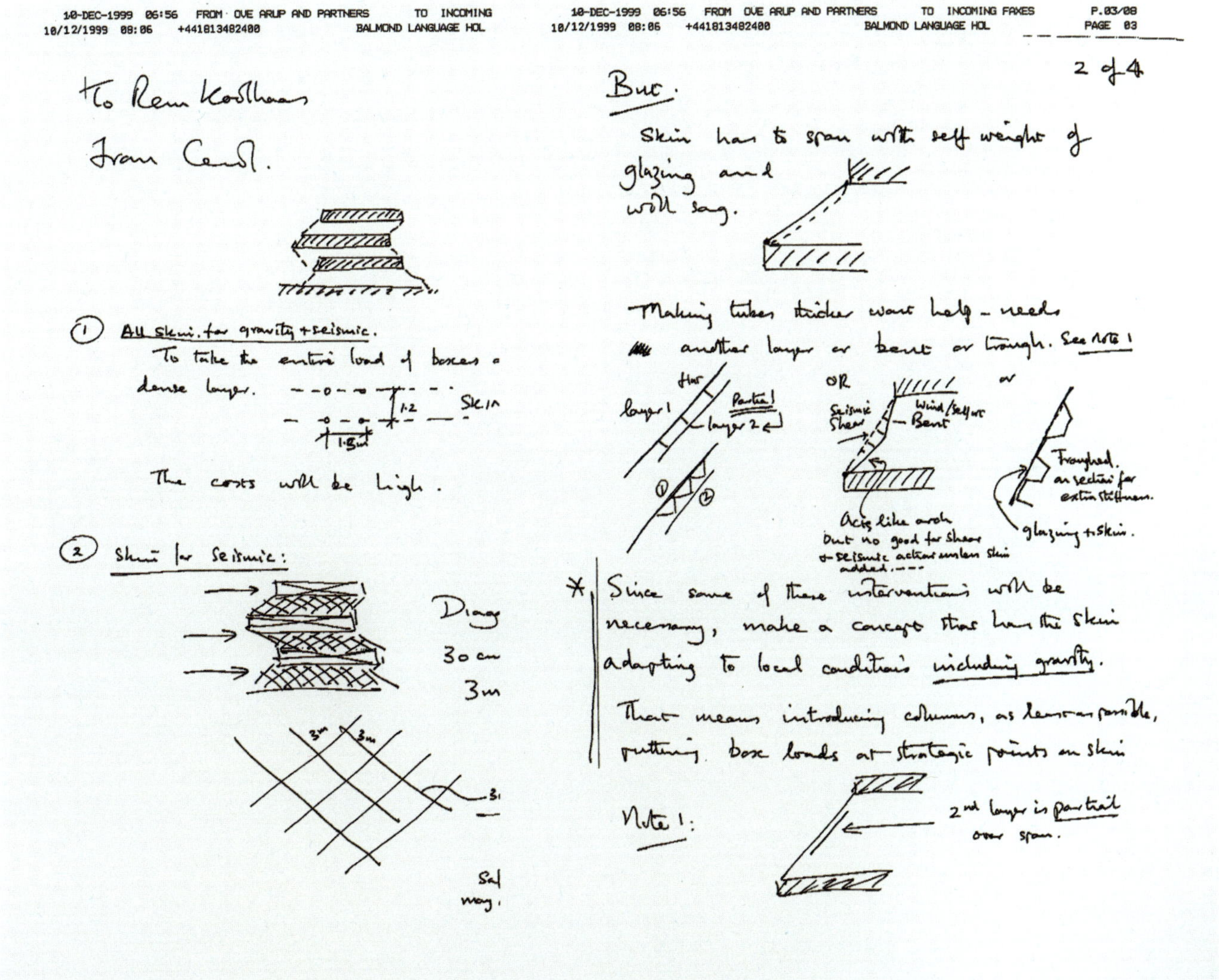

10-DEC-1999 06:56 FROM OVE ARUP AND PARTNERS TO INCOMING
10/12/1999 08:06 +441813482400 BALMOND LANGUAGE HOL

10-DEC-1999 06:56 FROM OVE ARUP AND PARTNERS TO INCOMING FAXES P.03/08
10/12/1999 08:06 +441813482400 BALMOND LANGUAGE HOL PAGE 03

2 of 4

To Rem Koolhaas
from Cecil.

(1) All skin for gravity + seismic.
To take the entire load of boxes a dense layer.

1.2
Skin
1.8m

The costs will be high.

(2) Skin for seismic:

Diag
30 cm
3m

3m
3m
3

Sel
may

But.

Skin has to span with self weight of glazing and will sag.

Making tubes thicker won't help – needs another layer or bent or trough. See note 1

layer 1
Partial layer 2
OR
Seismic Shear
Wind/Self wt
– Bent
or
Troughed. as section for extra stiffness.
glazing + skin.
Acts like arch but no good for shear + seismic action unless skin added....

* Since some of these interventions will be necessary, make a concept that has the skin adapting to local conditions including gravity.

That means introducing columns, as less as possible, putting box loads at strategic points on skin

Note 1:

2nd layer is partial over span.

Precedent page:
**3.39** Fax correspondence with Rem Koolhaas over a commissioned study for the Togok Towers scheme in Seoul, 1996.

Present page and following double-page spread:
**3.40** Fax correspondence with Rem Koolhaas over the development of the Seattle Library, 1999.

10-DEC-1999 06:56 FROM OVE ARUP AND PARTNERS TO INCOMING FAXES P.04/08
10/12/1999 08:06 +441813482400 BALMOND LANGUAGE HOL PAGE 04

3 of 4

Then we get cascade of flying box, minimum connection vertically + skin loaded.

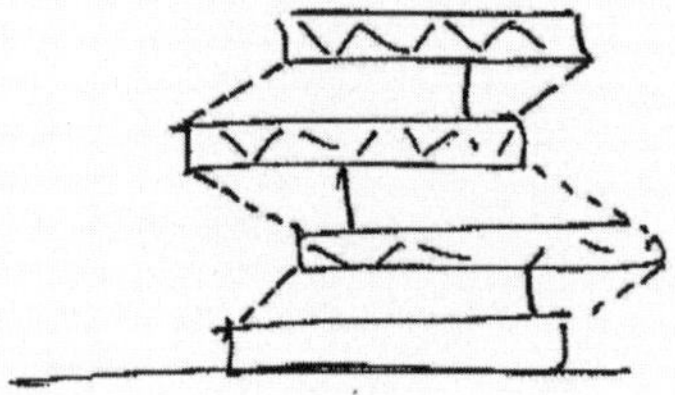

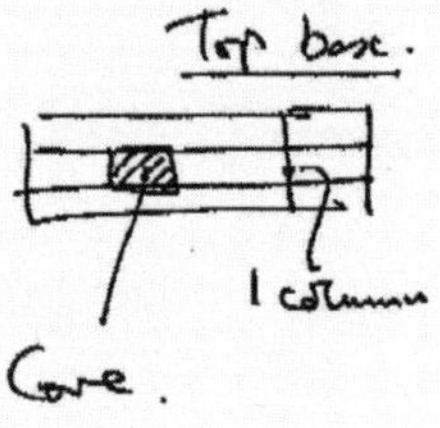


③ The core plays an important part now to keep skin light.

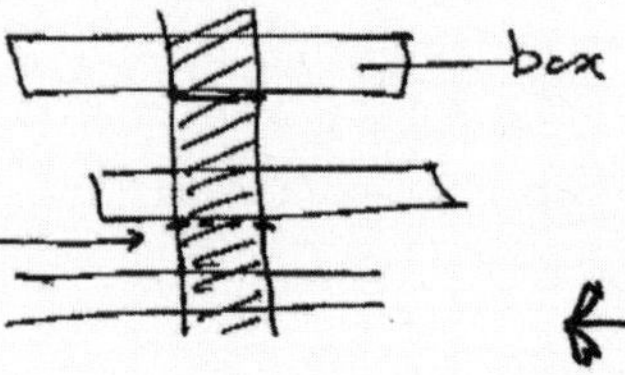


Put in viscous damper under ~~box~~ at core wall junction.

DOESN'T WORK IF BIG GRAVITY THRUSTS?

This is not expensive, absorbs energy, keeps skin light.

Summary

a light skin meeting a heavy box is an impossible condition.

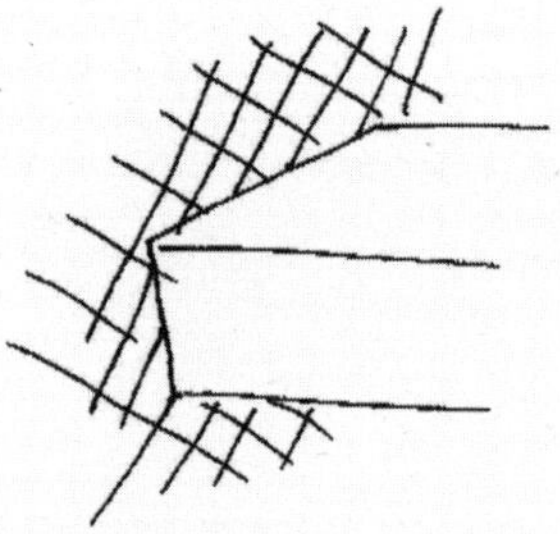

30 cm – 40 cm dia mass at 3 m c/c to 3.5 m c/c is light in relation to heavy box, edged with concrete bunker feeling.
(Concrete for perimeter OK – Fire protection –)

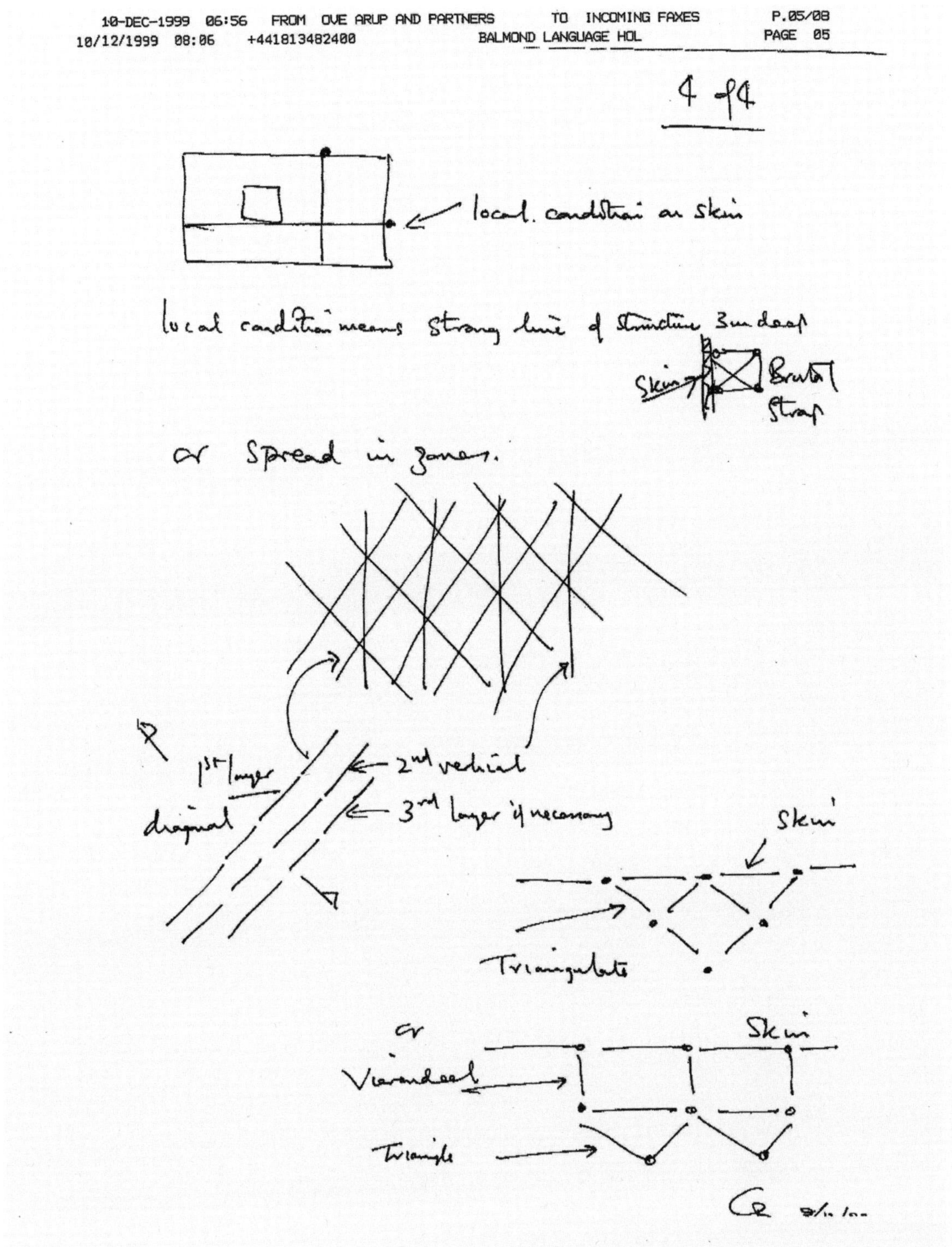
10-DEC-1999 06:56 FROM OVE ARUP AND PARTNERS TO INCOMING FAXES P.05/08
10/12/1999 08:06 +441813482400 BALMOND LANGUAGE HOL PAGE 05
4 of 4
local condition on skin
local condition means strong line of structure 3m deep
Skin
or spread in zones.
1st layer
diagonal
2nd vertical
3rd layer if necessary
Skin
Triangulate
or
Skin
Vierendeel
Triangle

Biennal 3/04

The limit of beam – Karlsruhe

As the span of a beam grows, so does its depth. There comes a point however when a truss is a more economical solution for large span rather than the solid section of a traditional beam.

But as the span grows further, the available headroom under a truss gets less. For long span then one answer is for the truss to occupy the whole space.

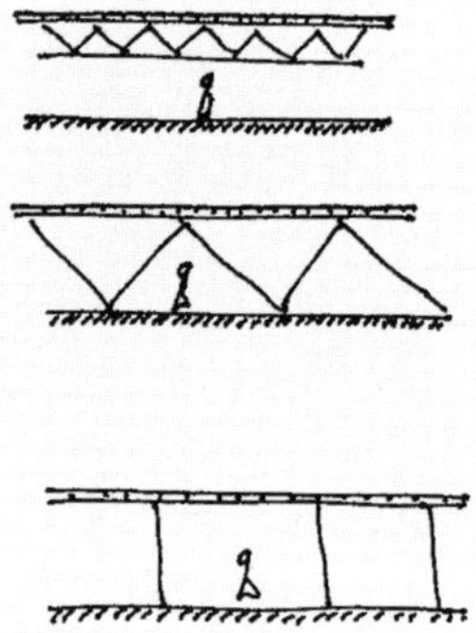

The problem here is that the diagonals limit the use of space. There is another solution that allows more freedom, that is when the diagonals straighten themselves as it were into vertical column elements, which then connect with horizontal boom members to form a network

or configuration of elements called a Vierendeel Girder.

The simple solid beam has transformed into open lattice truss and finally vanished as a constraint. The language of beam has disappeared at the limit, and a new liberation takes place.

A number of speculations are possible as the beam and column arrangement can be varied.

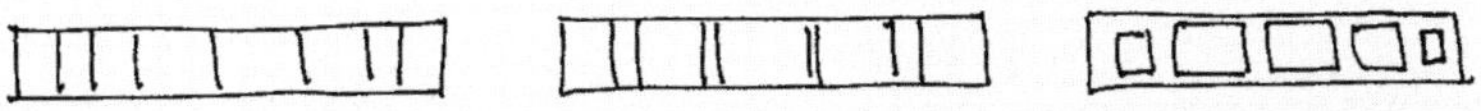

In the traditional beam of solid section, external forces are balanced by internal forces giving rise to shear and bending. In the truss, there is no bending or shear but only axial forces. But in the Vierendeel, all the elements have shear and bending in them to a significant degree – at the limit we have come full circle.

For the ZKM in Karlsruhe a series of Vierendeels was proposed, stacked up, allowing column free space on every alternate floor.

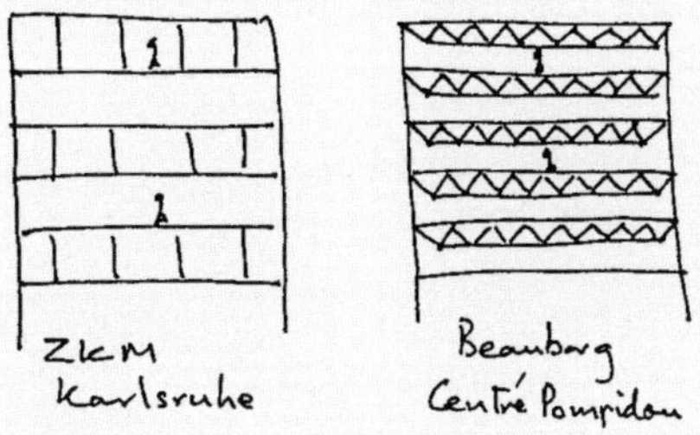


Compared to Beaubourg the section is a total liberation for freedom of movement.

Moreover the chords of the Vierendeel can be varied in position to suit program. The only thing to watch with the Vierendeel is to have a vertical chord near the support. This can be done in a variety of ways.

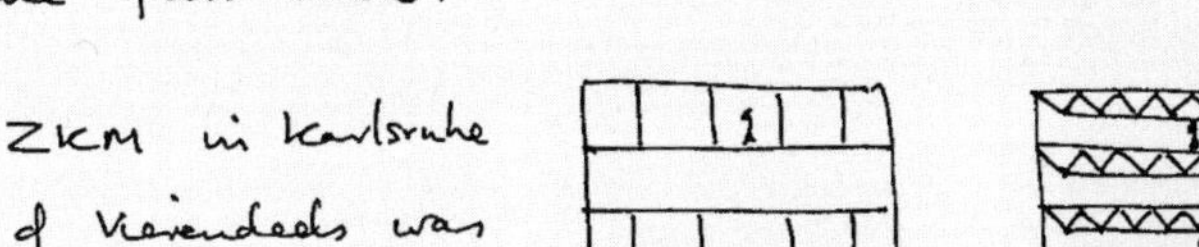


The chord nearest the support has the highest forces. A diagonal, borrowed from the language of truss, can alleviate the problem as well.

Precedent double-page spread:
**3.41–42** Balmond's notes on the possibilities of the Vierendeel beam as developed for the ZKM scheme in Karlsruhe (Germany) with OMA Rem Koolhaas, 1994.

**3.43** Left: Madelon Vriesendorp, Rem Koolhaaas, and Cecil Balmond during one of the last site visits at the Bordeaux House. Late 1990s.

## The Vierendeel

Koolhaas was constantly intrigued by and open to the structural systems proposed by Balmond. One such system was the Vierendeel beam, which the engineer suggested for the first time for the ZKM Center for Art and Media Technology. Balmond made Koolhaas see that the beam's vertical elements could be toyed with at will, whether in disposition, size, or proportions. To these compositional capabilities is added the fact that the floor underneath the beam can be columnless **(fig. 3.41–42)**.[85] Embracing the freedom it catalyzed—especially in terms of the huge voids it allowed him to carve out of a building's interior—Koolhaas embraced the Vierendeel full-on, employing it beyond ZKM in the Très Grande Bibliothèque project and the first version of Kunsthal. To Koolhaas's mind, the Vierendeel helped achieve a synthesis of sorts between sobriety and uncertainty: "[i]nstead of making unsober forms, we became interested in making unstable engineering behind sober forms."[86]

Koolhaas enjoyed working with Balmond to the extent that he asked him twice to go into business partnership with him during the 1990s, offering to share creative authorship on equal grounds **(fig. 3.43)**. But the engineer turned him down, arguing

85 For more on the possibilities of the Vierendeel as imagined by Balmond, see Rem Koolhaas and Bruce Mau, *S M L XL* (New York, NY: Monacelli Press, 1995), 672–85; and *Cecil Balmond, A+U Special Issue*, 241–45.

86 Quoted in Nicolai Ouroussoff, "An Engineer Magician, Then (Presto) He's an Architect," *The New York Times*, November 26, 2006, 25.

that he relished the independence of working at ARUP and needed the company's expertise to be able to realize his experiments. Be that as it may, Balmond might well have found it unbearable to be overshadowed by Koolhaas's towering figure within architecture circles.

### Quite Partially Informal

Balmond's informal ideology unfolded only partially across his collaborations with Koolhaas. At Jussieu (1992), the existence of two different structural arrangements—a regular grid of columns and a diverse sequence of sloping planes in varying dimensions and shapes—aspired to materialize his pursuit of simultaneity and regions of overlap **(fig. 3.44)**. At Kunsthal (1987–92), there is some of the dynamic quality he favored in the movement suggested by the arching brace semi-exposed in the ceiling of Hall 2 as well as the tree trunk-cladded rows of columns that slip past each other in Hall 1 **(fig. 3.45)**. The coexistence of stability and instability is certainly present at Bordeaux (1994–98), where the main concrete volume is supported partly on an eccentric steel cylinder that conceals a spiral staircase and partly on an L-shaped shelf beam, while also hung off a roof girder. This ensemble results in two of the vertical load paths diagonally across from each other running off the perimeter of the concrete volume **(fig. 3.46)**. Common to these and other works with Koolhaas was the emphasis on local action: the specific tilted plane in a particular sector of the building; the specific column arrangement on a particular level; the specific support system in one particular area of the house. There was, therefore, no overriding, homogeneous logic to the whole scheme—an unequivocal informal preference.

Yet other than that, there was never any algorithmic thinking at play. Local action never spread in a way remotely consistent with the characteristics of nonlinear systems. No self-organization; no systemic build-up over time that yielded emergent conditions. Granted, the examples of Jussieu, Kunsthal, and Bordeaux come relatively early in the development of Balmond's design ideology (even though he had been studying chaos theory since 1987). But the pattern remained throughout, as seen in later projects such as Casa da Musica, CCTV, and the Seattle library. Indeed, the vast majority of projects with Koolhaas—a post-modernist architect at heart—register as discrete aggregations of different moments, very much in tune with Koolhaas's interest in collage compositions in space. In essence, it was really Balmond's emphasis on local intensity and opportunism which, giving rise to the kinds of "accidents" for which the Dutch architect was always searching, enabled the two men to develop a fruitful creative rapport. For in other respects they could not have been further apart—Balmond interested in science, universal truths, and systems of complexity; Koolhaas in culture, fiction, and a sort of spatial adhocism.

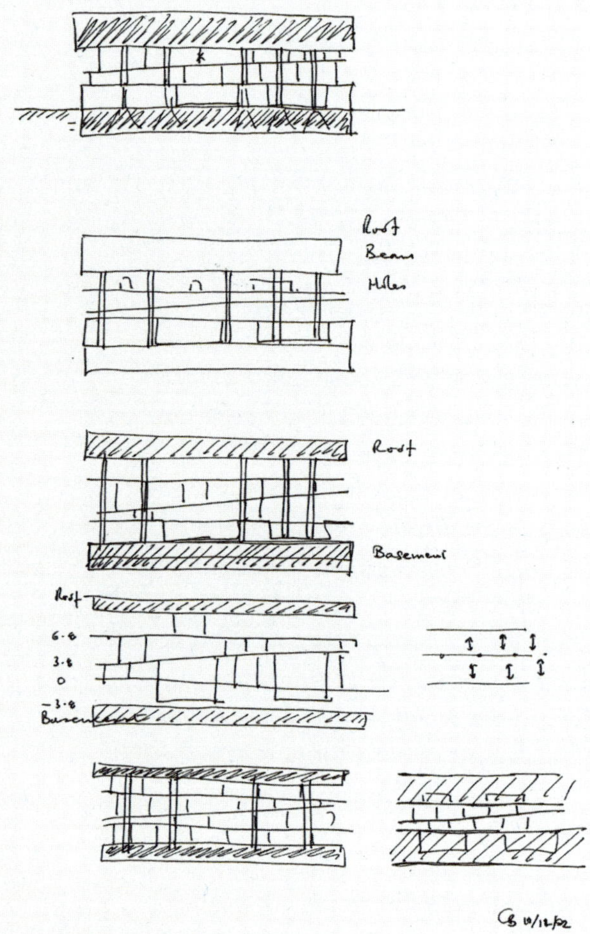


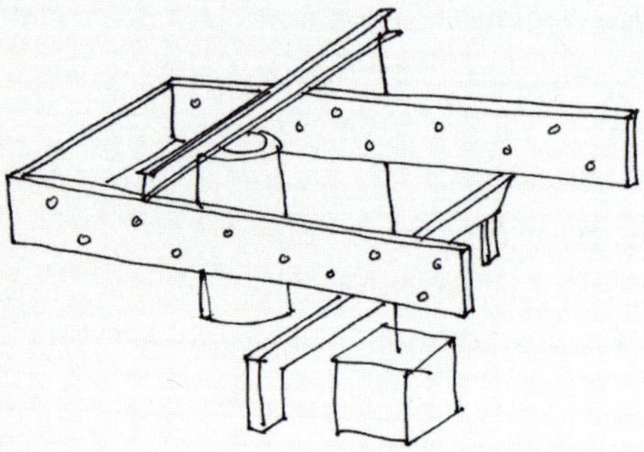

**3.44** Above: Balmond's sketches for the Jussieu Libraries scheme with OMA Rem Koolhaas, 1992.

**3.46** Left: Balmond's sketch of the structural concept for the Bordeaux House with OMA Rem Koolhaas (1994–98).

**3.45** OMA Rem Koolhaas. Views of the Kunsthal (1987–1992).

## Enric Miralles Stood Out

A similar collaborative dynamic to that with Koolhaas—one where the architect decided on the main spatial concepts and aesthetics, and Balmond supplied structural solutions—is observed with Enric Miralles. Working on a competition for a track-and-field stadium in Chemnitz (Germany) in 1995, internal correspondence within ARUP and external with Miralles shows the Catalan architect unilaterally establishing an idea—involving two hovering, asymmetric roof layers, one of which was to be hung on cranes—with Balmond and his team struggling to understand Miralles's sketches in order to be able to contribute their structural expertise **(fig. 3.47)**.[87] ARUP entered the same competition separately with two other German firms. Since it was the entry developed with one of these—a partnership between Peter Kulka and Ulrich Königs—that ended up winning, Balmond published it widely and frequently discussed it over the years in lectures and talks. Originally, however, he made it clear internally that he would have preferred Miralles's concept to be victorious: "[w]e must try to win this one—it would be a great structure to win for ARUP SA. (4 other Germans in competition—ARUP with 2 of them). So our chances are 3 out of 5—but I'd like Spain to win!!"[88] This is unsurprising given how much he cherished both the man himself and the nature of his working collaboration with Miralles. For Balmond counted Miralles as one of his best friends and indicated that with him he enjoyed his "first, really natural collaboration." By that he meant that, even though working with Koolhaas was, he felt, the most important part of his career—a feeling reciprocated by the Dutchman, judging from his recurrent, unusually laudatory remarks about the engineer—with him they would have to "reason up certain things," whereas with Miralles it was all "spontaneous."[89]

87 **Fig. 47** shows a series of annotated sketches through which Balmond tried to explain Miralles's idea to his ARUP team. Further correspondence concerning this stadium concept included faxes where Miralles addressed Balmond to provide additional clarifications about his idea. The latter did not grant permission to publish those faxes in this book.

88 Fax dated September 27, 1995. Courtesy of Balmond Studio.

89 In an interview with the author conducted in London on October 9, 2013. On Koolhaas's laudatory remarks on Balmond, see Jennifer Kabat, "The Informalist," *Wired*, no. 9.04 (April 1, 2001), 104; Balmond, *Informal*, 9; and *Cecil Balmond, A+U Special Issue*, 251.

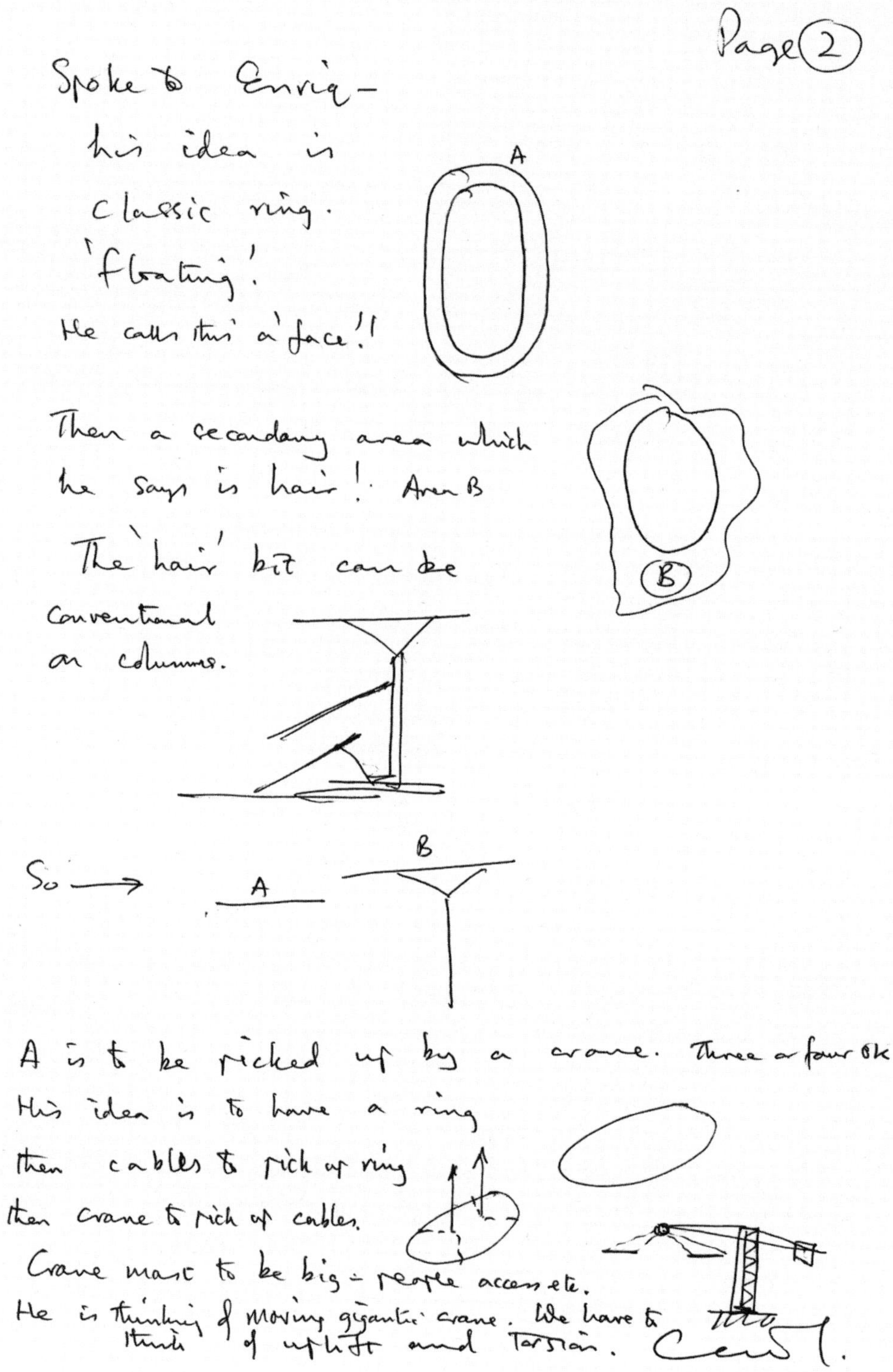

Page (2)

Spoke to Enriq –
his idea is
classic ring.
'floating'.
He calls this a 'face'!!

A

Then a secondary area which
he says is hair! Area B

B

The 'hair' bit can be
conventional
on columns.

So → A B

A is to be picked up by a crane. Three or four OK
His idea is to have a ring
then cables to pick up ring
then crane to pick up cables.
Crane mast to be big – people access etc.
He is thinking of moving gigantic crane. We have to think of uplift and torsion.
Cecil.

Not all of Balmond's partnerships with architects exhibited such an evident one-sidedness as those with Koolhaas and Miralles—two architects notorious for their relentless drive and strong character. For instance, exchanges over a project for the Cincinnati Art Gallery with Daniel Libeskind reveal a more bilateral language: "[a]s agreed we should keep the plan simple—a 'box'."[90] Moreover, Balmond took the initiative to express a number of rather architectural propositions involving the articulation of space and the building's internal atmosphere **(fig. 3.48–50)**. The same initiative was apparent when working with Philip Johnson on the tower project in China, mentioned above. "I thought a few notes from me would help you develop an idea for the Guang Zhou Tower. The first idea I proposed was for an undulation of tubes."[91] At times Balmond's phrasing would even become exhortatory, something that would never happen with Koolhaas or Miralles: "[s]pend the week building some models of different options + fax us. Let's agree next week on final idea to model."[92] Admittedly, some combination of Johnson (then aged ninety-three) having lost his earlier zeal, and his simply taking advantage of Balmond's input as much as he could—the project eventually being under his name anyway—may have allowed room for the engineer to have such a strong voice. Yet subsequent exchanges with Shigeru Ban over the Pompidou Metz building showed similar initiative and language on the part of Balmond, clearly keen to force his interest in algorithmic thinking into the project **(fig. 3.51–53)**:

> . . . the pattern I showed you on my computer. What I was looking for . . . What if a unit idea of weave were to grow the shape instead? . . . Small "spiral" square starts . . . Architecturally, we get a small square and a large square in the composition, being slowly distorted as the curvature sets in . . . I hope you like the idea.[93]

These and other conversations showcase Balmond's capacity to adjust his collaborative approach to the personality of the architect in question—a versatility that enabled him to work with so many diverse characters. They also prove that, in adjusting, he was constantly looking for the opportunity to advance his own ideas.

Precedent page:
**3.47** Fax correspondence with members of the ARUP team for a stadium competition, 1995. Architect: Enric Miralles.

Following pages:
**3.48–50** Fax correspondence with Daniel Libeskind over a project for the Cincinnati Art Gallery, 1998 (pp. 282–284).

90 Fax dated February 2, 1998. Courtesy of Balmond Studio.

91 Fax dated April 4, 1999. Courtesy of Balmond Studio.

92 Ibid.

93 In fax exchange with Shigeru Ban, early 2000s. Courtesy of Balmond Studio.

(1)

To Daniel Libeskind 18/2/98
from Cecil Balmond

Cincinnati Art Gallery.

(1) As agreed we should keep the plan simple – a 'box'.

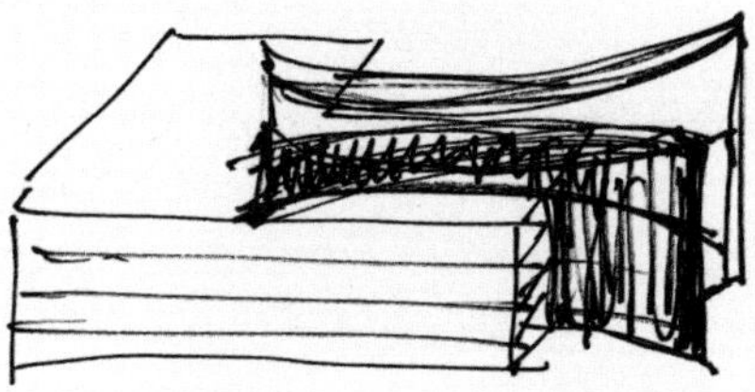

Elev.

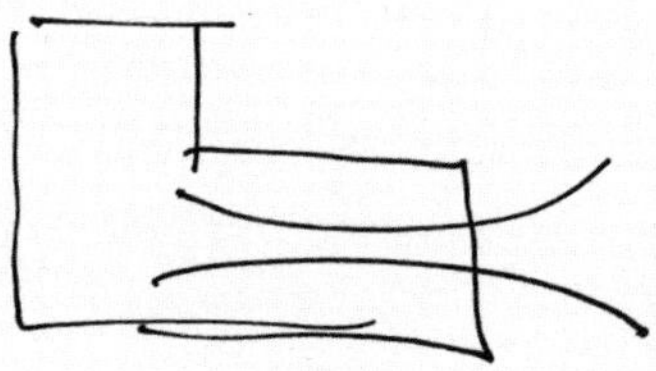

PLAN

But 'intercept' box with two curves.

These curves should give structural support and hence no columns in space. The edge of the building provides the other support.

PLAN

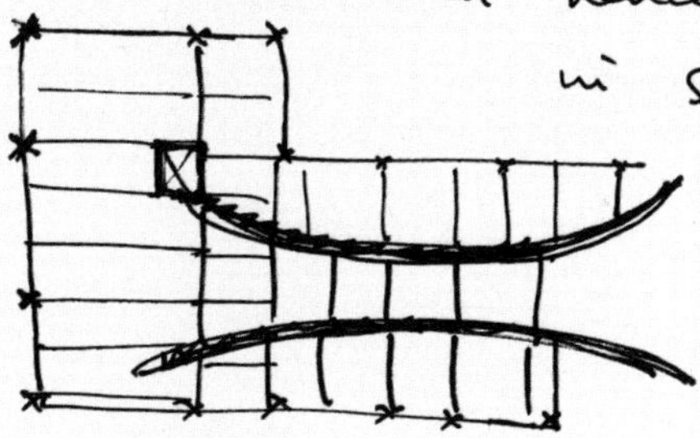

Steel solution, <u>no columns in space</u>, as a strategy!

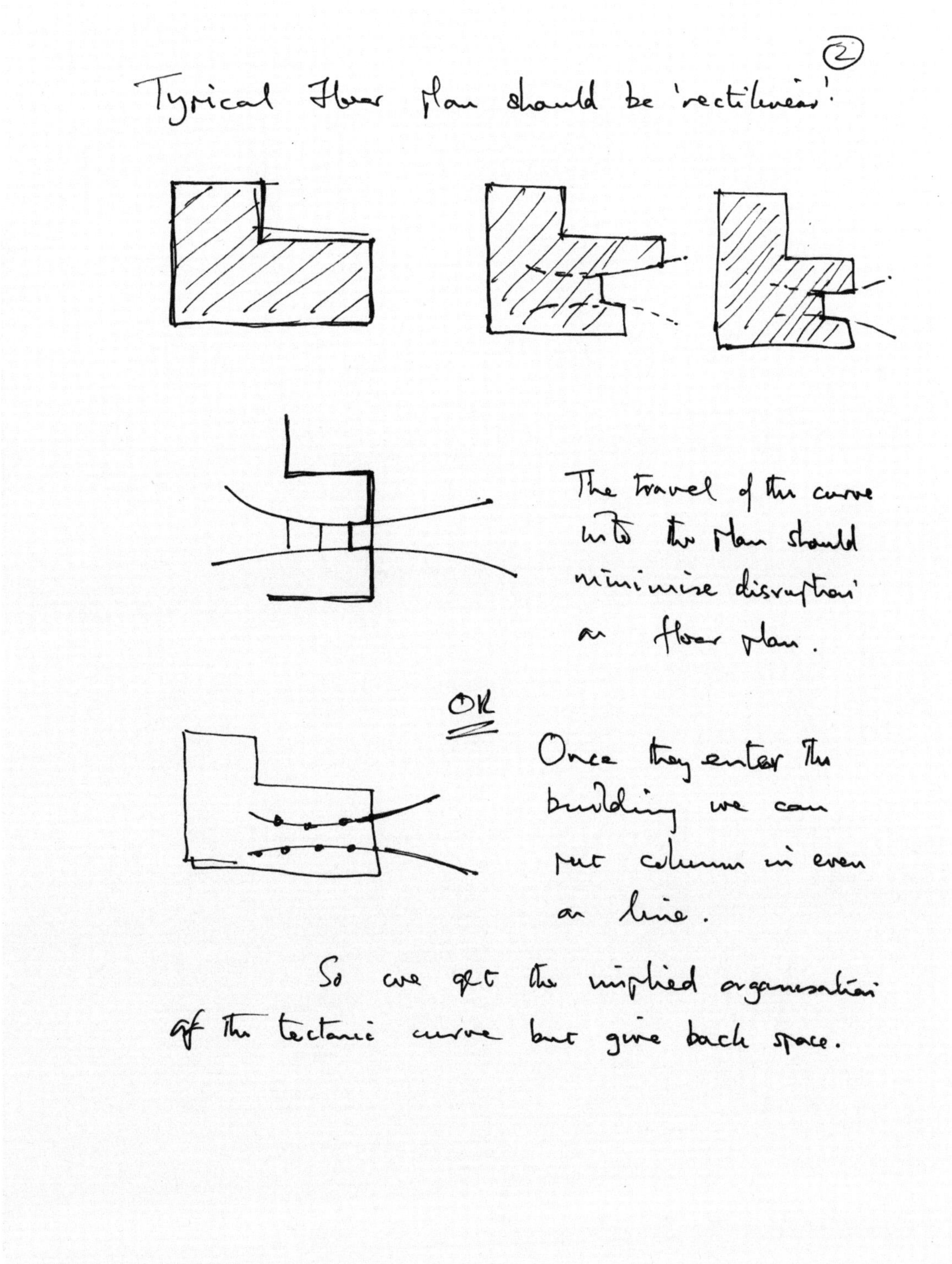
②
Typical Floor plan should be 'rectilinear'.
The travel of the curve into the plan should minimise disruption on floor plan.
OK
Once they enter the building we can put columns in even on line.
So we get the implied organisation of the tectonic curve but give back space.

③

Back Corner Feature.

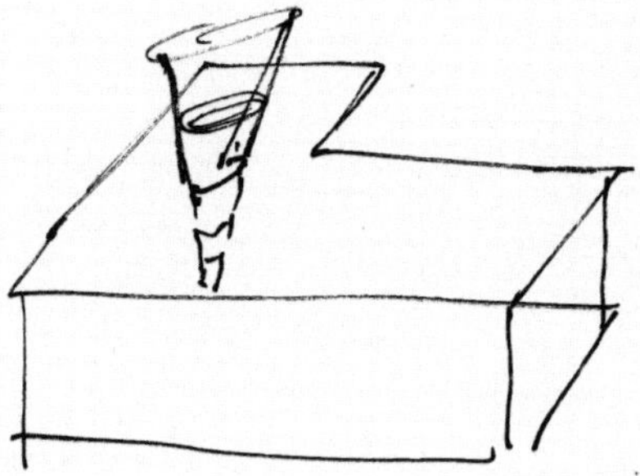

This feature can be at minimum a light shaft.

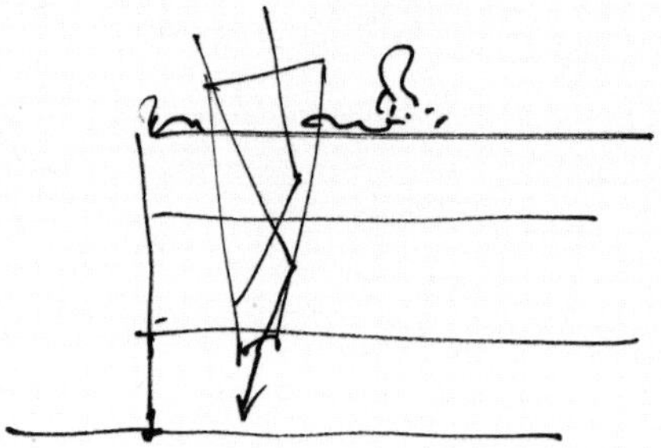

An organiser of light.
Surrounded by garden.

More ambitiously, we could convert the cone into a cooling tower.

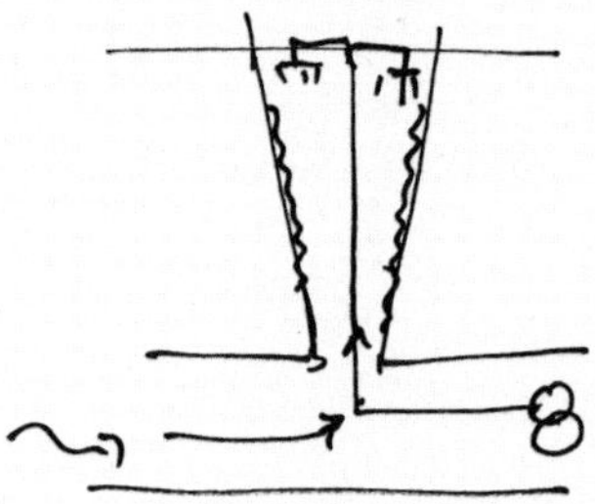


Chiller water is taken to the top + sprinkled down glass cone.
Fresh air taken from street blows up.
Water at bottom is cool + taken back into the chiller circuit is 'coolth.'

To SHIGERU BAN FAX 0081 3 3324 6789 (1)

cc Charles Walker.

LONDON
10th November.

Dear Shigeru

Apologies for not sending this earlier — I had trouble with the first idea of distorted Pentagons and a weave, the pattern I showed you on my computer.

What I was looking for was an undulation and reverse curvature ——— in elevation. If we have units of Pentagons (or any shape) as we put a curvature

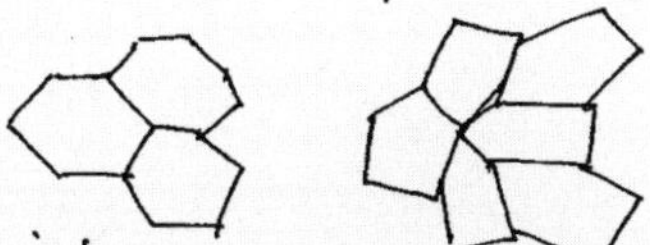

in elevation the units have to allow shape change on ~~their on~~ their boundaries.

This →
or →

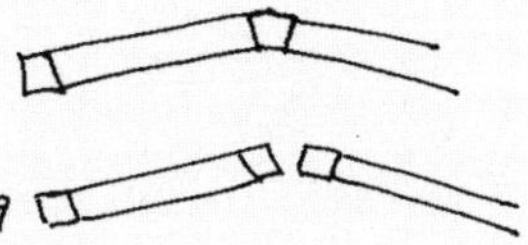

This can be done of course but to find a weave as

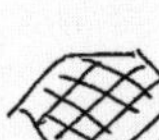

a secondary pattern to fill in left me with some problems on my first choice of pattern, the Pentagons. So we looked for a different answer, of having <u>only the weave</u> as changing or 'forcing' curvature. This is a new idea! Without sub frames.

As I said to you in Tokyo our first collaboration should break the convention.

(2)

We have the Mannheim roof as a net that is shaped but the shape is put in artificially, what if an unit idea of weave were to grow the shape instead?

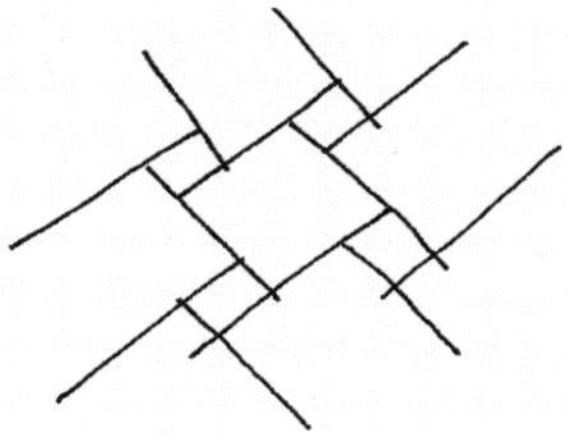

If each strip is placed over the other, a

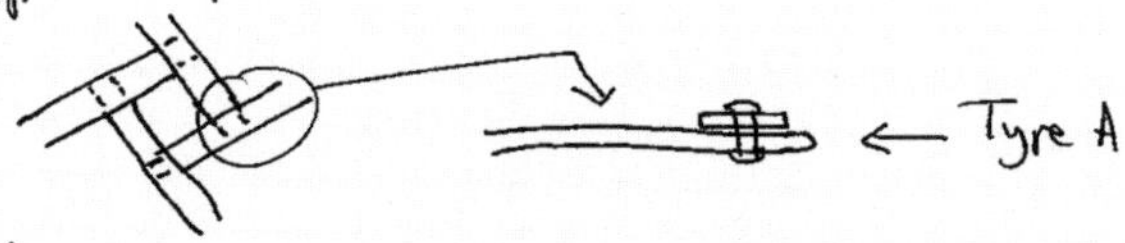


small 'spiral' square starts. As the lines grow a curvature grows. If the laps are changed, from under to over as in Type B, then a reverse effect to Type A is obtained. Charles built a test model.

This is a very interesting phenomenon. We are excited by it and thought it would be a good idea to build for your Pavilion project.

Architecturally we get a small square and a large square in the composition, being slowly distorted as the curvature sets in. But the

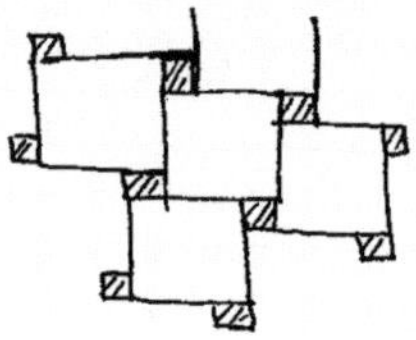

small against the large gives opportunity for scale effect.

(3)

The basic square is 1.2 m and the small square is 600 mm.

Another effect the pattern has for me is a curious flow or arrangement of local vortices.

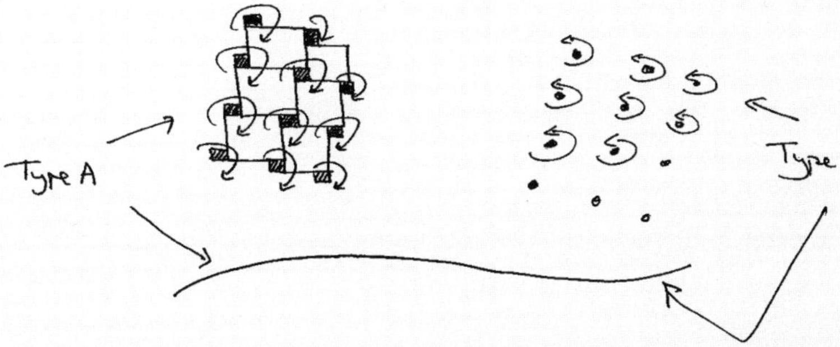


So the proposal we have is to think of a free-form plan

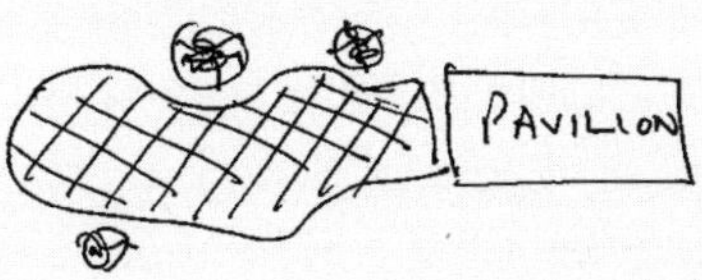


with a reverse curvature in elevation.

→ Drainage can be sorted out.

Edge is not closed like a boundary but can have edges like this on plan.

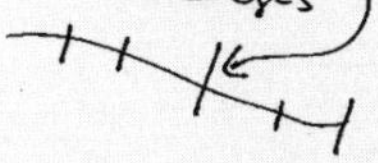

Supports positioned to suit.

Supports should have the same language as the roof in relation to pattern but can be more solid or duplicated in elevation.

## Structure as Trace Stayed Bidimensional

Notwithstanding his creative understanding with Miralles, it was really Toyo Ito's architectural inclinations that Balmond was the closest to. The bulk of their collaborations occurred during a period (first half of the 2000s) when the Japanese architect became particularly interested in spatial organizations that were at once systemic and differentiated—an approach well attuned to Balmond's sensibility. Just like Koolhaas, Ito regarded their collaboration as that of two equal partners working together on a project, rather than an architect and an engineer, and took every opportunity to enthuse about Balmond **(fig. 3.54)**.[94] While, with Koolhaas, Balmond explored the notion of episodic structure to counter what he termed "structure as skeleton"—a phrase describing "the padding out of a structure to fit form" typical, for example, of Frank Gehry's buildings—it was mainly with Ito that he promoted his other alternative: *structure as trace*. Appearing for the first time in a 1995 theoretical manuscript, the idea here was to envision structure as the result of having an element move sequentially in time along a differentiated path determined by an algorithm.[95] Attention to the local condition is common to both structure as episodes and structure as trace, albeit in a different fashion. In the former case "local" stands for the individuality of a site- or space-specific gesture that contingently changes the nature of the structural element or system relative to its adjacent ones. In the latter, "local" designates the individuality of an initial move that spreads outwards to generate a whole whose eventual characteristics—the unfolding of which is meant to mirror that of nonlinear organizations—are not known in advance. Referring to it as "in-to-out" (in contrast to "top-down" or "out-to-in"), Balmond turned this otherwise purely formal and algorithmic approach into a critique of what he saw as a dominant condition of contemporary architecture. Namely, he staged it as counter to the hierarchy implied in focusing on exterior appearances (cladding, surface treatments, etc.) and limiting the interior to enclosures of program residual to the outer skin—a hierarchy whose outcome he dismissed as "superficial."[96]

Precedent pages:
**3.51–53** Fax exchanges with Shigeru Ban over the project for the Pompidou Metz building, early 2000s (pp. 285–287).

94 See, for instance, Balmond and Ito, "Conversation - Cecil Balmond and Toyo Ito," 44.

95 Untitled manuscript, dated December 4, 1995. Courtesy of Balmond Studio.

96 Cecil Balmond, *A+U Special Issue*, 132.

**3.54** Cecil Balmond with Toyo Ito at the latter's office in Tokyo, early 2000s.

Following pages:
**3.55** Balmond's notes on the Serpentine Gallery pavilion with Toyo Ito, early 2000s (p. 290).
**3.56** Sketches for the Chemnitz stadium with architects Kulka and Königs (1995) (p. 291).

Despite this criticism, however, and unlike the previous instances involving the episodic structure, in the majority of the projects where Balmond rehearsed the notion of structure as trace, its impact was restricted to bidimensional elements. Such is the case on the landmark work with Ito, the Serpentine Gallery pavilion of 2002. An algorithm scripted by Daniel Bosia, whereby a vector moves consecutively from half to a third of a square's adjacent sides, ends up giving rise to a pattern of crisscrossing lines through a series of intermediary steps. Some of these lines become main structural components, others bracing, and the rest simply traces, completing the ordered randomness. Yet the structural pattern unfolds merely across the bounding planes of a box: the four facades and the roof. It is essentially an exterior envelope **(fig. 3.55)**. At the Chemnitz stadium with Kulka and Königs (1995)—the first example of Balmond's structure-as-trace approach—the engineer post-rationalized certain elements of the building after the competition and in one case he employed an algorithm. A dot on a rotating disc can generate a cycloid. Studying different locations for the dot and different starting points engendered an array of diverse patterns, some symmetrical and others more erratic. But the purpose of this geometric mechanism was only to control the lines articulating the roof structure, another bidimensional element **(fig. 3.56)**.

(2)

The $\frac{1}{2} \rightarrow \frac{1}{3}$ rule traces four lines in the original square that do not meet. If I had chosen

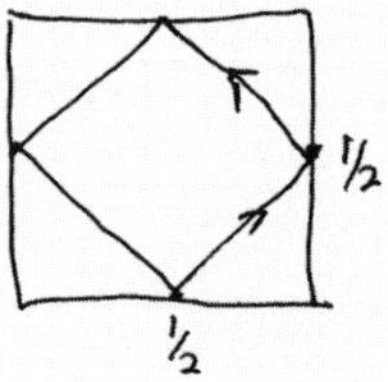


the half point instead, of each side, the trace $\frac{1}{2} \rightarrow \frac{1}{2}$ would close back on itself like a billiard ball bouncing perfectly around a square enclosure.

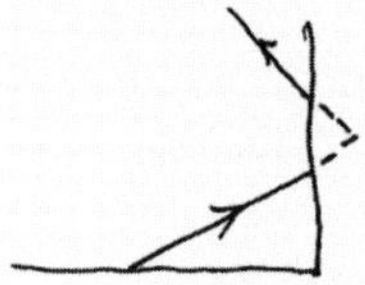

The half to a third rule, forces one to go out of the original square to create a new square so that the rule, or algorithm, may continue. If this is continued for six cycles, say, a primary structure is obtained. Then if these lines are all extended

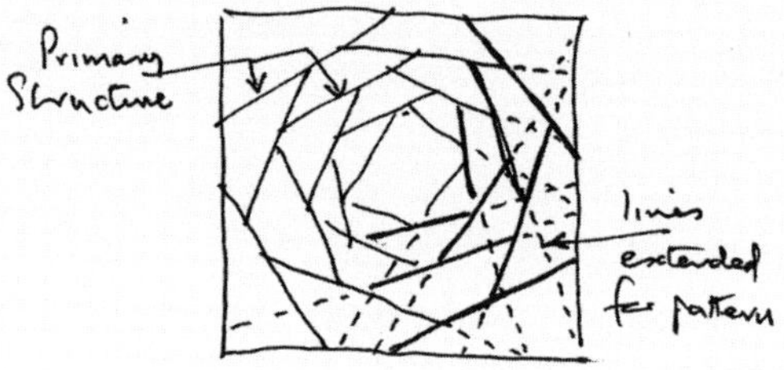


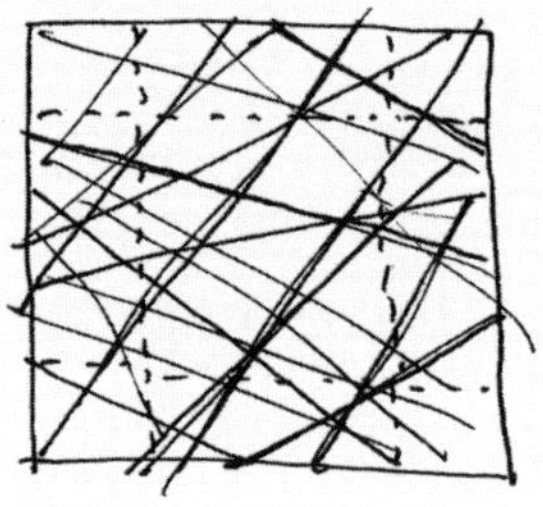

Pattern cut out at corners and folded into box shape.

a pattern of many crossings results. Some are primary for load carrying, some will serve as bracing as secondary, and the rest will be a binding motif of the random across the surfaces of the box typology.

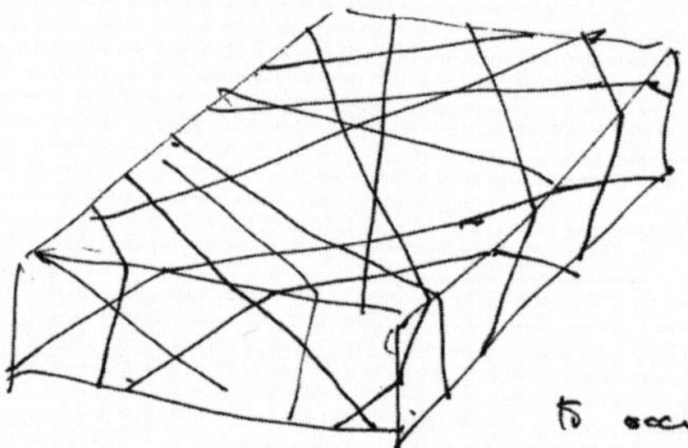

The aesthetic effect is to occupy a multiplex of web and as the eye traces the cells of engagement, the eye travels out and what is plane becomes limitless void. The box is no more.

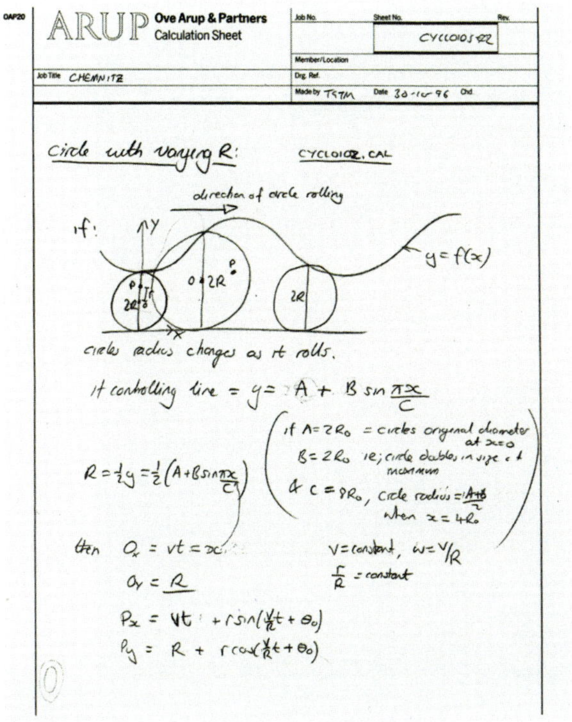
OAP20
ARUP Ove Arup & Partners
Calculation Sheet
Job No.
Sheet No.
Rev.
CYCLOIDS
Member/Location
Job Title CHEMNITZ
Drg. Ref.
Made by TSTM
Date 30-10-96
Chd.
circle with varying R:
CYCLOID.CAL
direction of circle rolling
if:
y
y = f(x)
P
2R
circles radius changes as it rolls.
if controlling line = y = A + B sin πx/C
if A = 2R₀ = circles original diameter at x=0
B = 2R₀ ie; circle doubles in size at maximum
& C = 8R₀, circle radius = (A+B)/2 when x = 4R₀
R = ½y = ½(A+B sin πx/C)
then Oₓ = vt = x
O_y = R
v = constant, ω = v/R
r/R = constant
Pₓ = vt + r sin(v/R t + θ₀)
P_y = R + r cos(v/R t + θ₀)

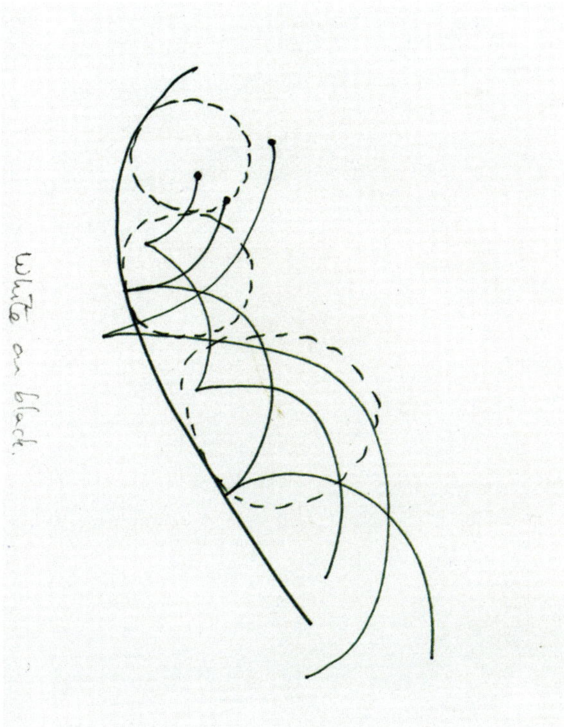
White on black.

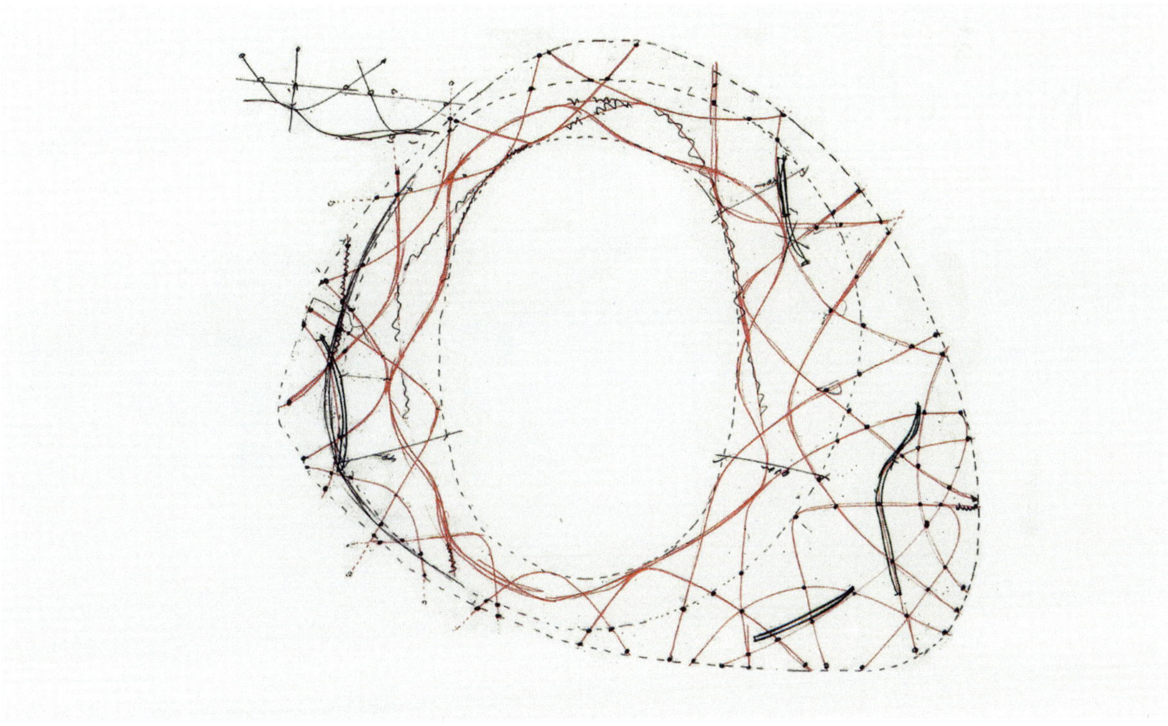

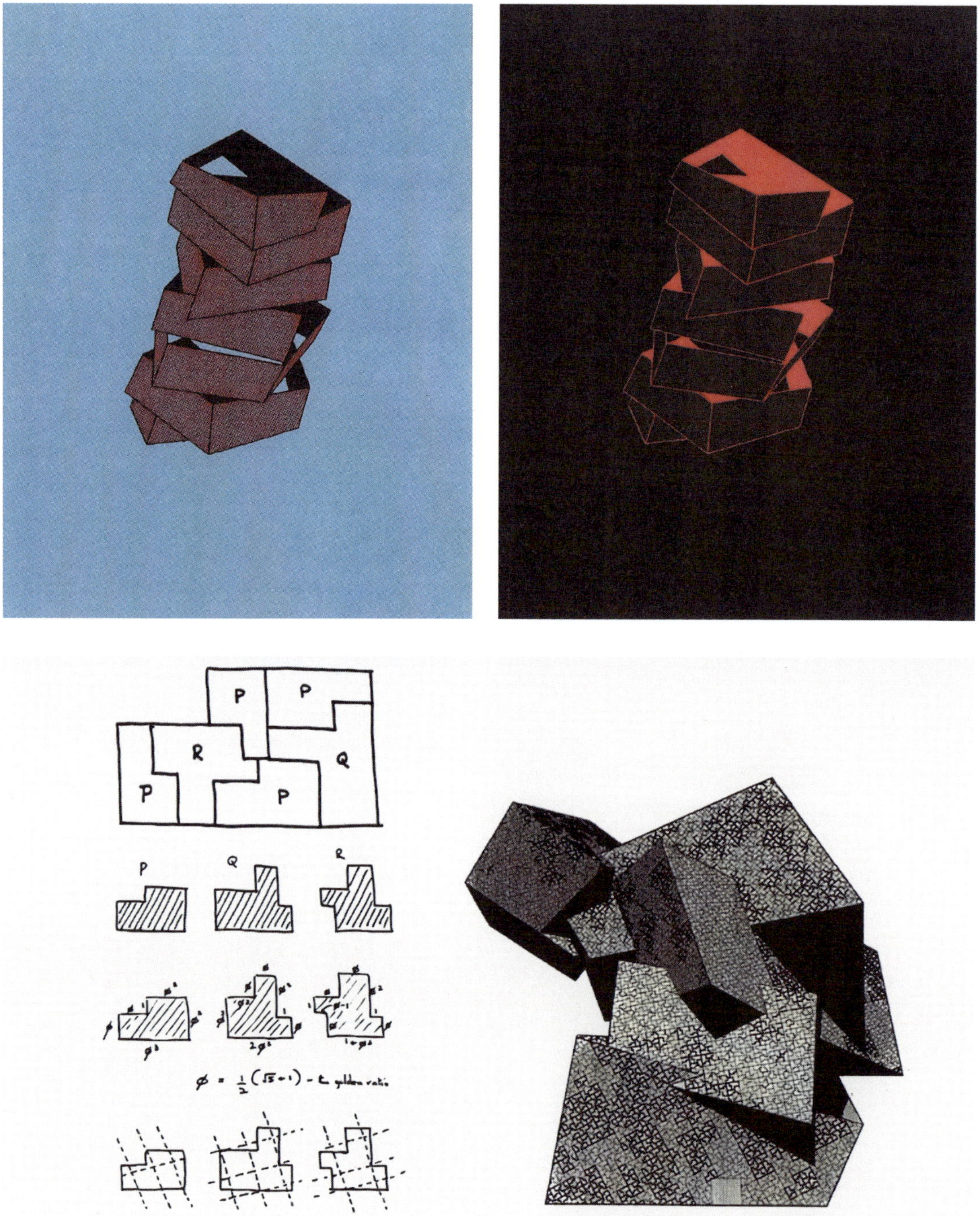


**3.57** Images and diagrams for the Victoria & Albert Museum scheme with Daniel Libeskind (designed 1996–2004; unbuilt).

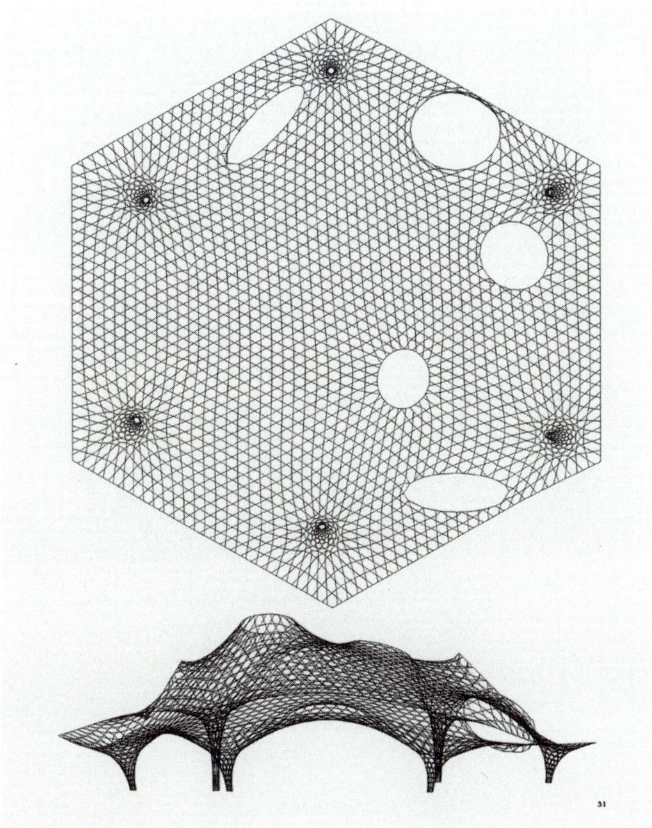

3.58 Computer-generated images for the roof structure of the Pompidou Metz building, early 2000s.

At the Victoria & Albert Museum scheme with Libeskind (designed 1996–2004; unbuilt), an irregular spiral comprised of straight segments resulted from having the spiral's center shift and its radius change as the segments transitioned from floor to floor. But the interlocking structural walls originated by this operation register once again as an envelope. Also in this project, Balmond and his team created an aperiodic fractal pattern through a recursive algorithm—only to turn it into the surface tiling of the spiraling walls **(fig. 3.57)**. Similarly, at the Pompidou Metz with Shigeru Ban (2004–9), another pattern—this time involving a unit idea of weaving wooden strips—was conceived solely to materialize the building's roof skin **(fig. 3.58)**. The one exception is the S-Project with Ito (2002). In this scheme for a department store in Glasgow, an algorithm based on a field array of numbers controls the seemingly random growth of a grid of columns leaning in different directions on each floor. These "dancing" columns, whose angles provide enough structural stability, articulate the interior of the building and extend their influence outward to determine the composition of the outer facades **(fig. 3.59-61)**.

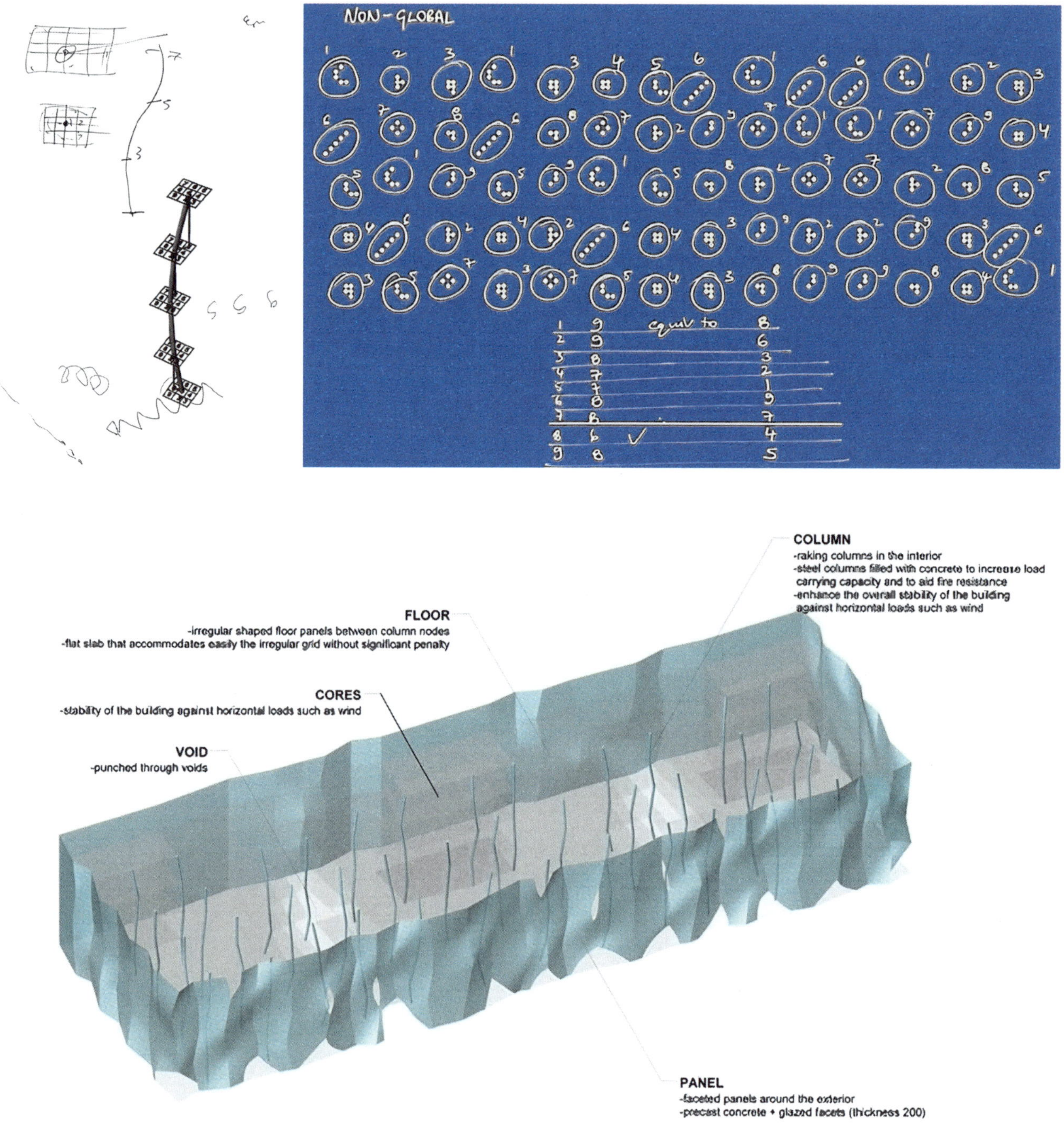


**3.59** Diagrams for the S-Project department store in Glasgow with Toyo Ito (2002).

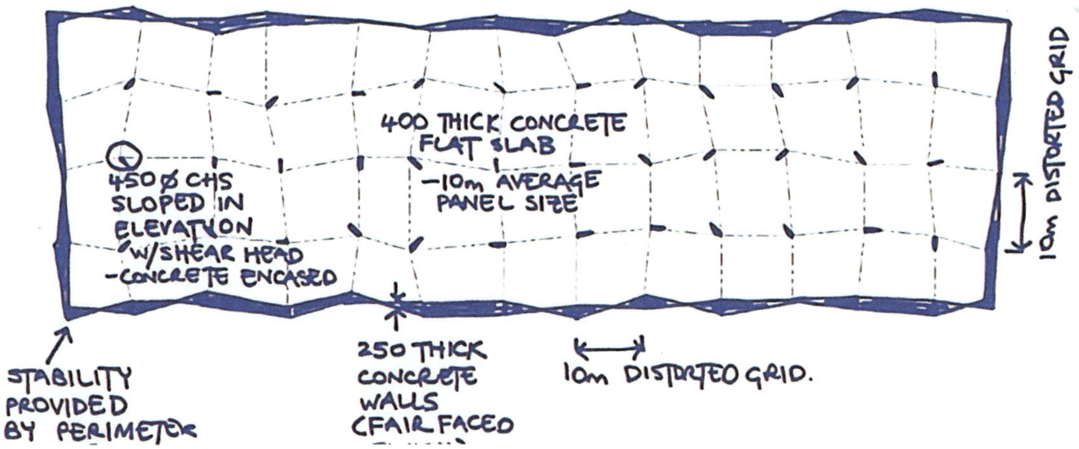


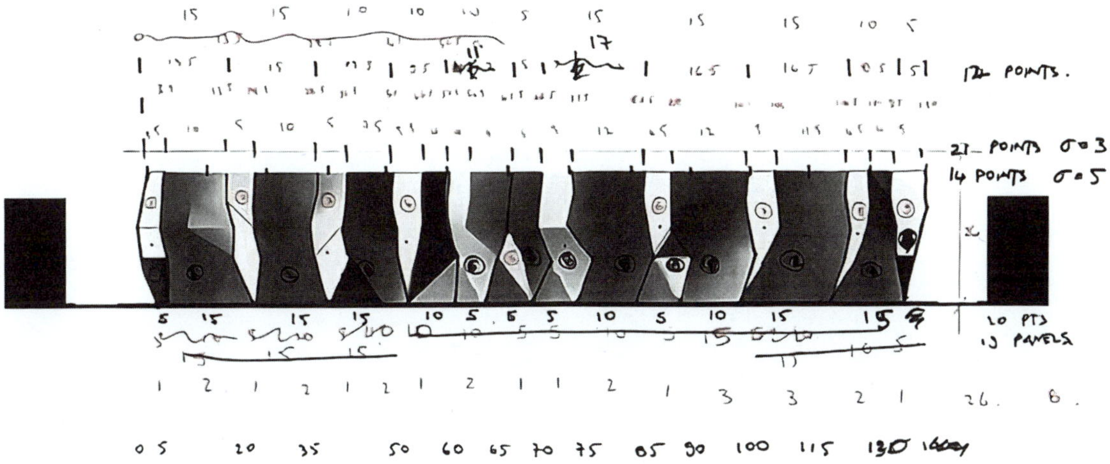


**3.60** Diagrams for the S-Project department store in Glasgow with Toyo Ito (2002).

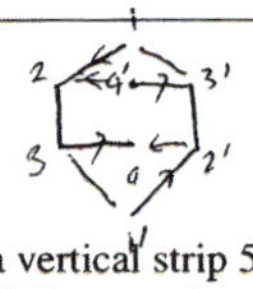

## 3. GEOMETRICAL STUDY

In order to achieve 6 panel types (a panel being defined as a vertical strip 5m wide over the full height of the building) we need to use a minimum of 4 different column lines to form the vertical panel edges. With the ability to flip the units 180° this results in 12 panels with 8 column lines.

We can give each of the 4 column lines the ID's 1, 2, 3 and 4. The 4 column lines generated by flipping the units can be given the ID's 1', 2', 3' and 4'. We then link the 8 column types together with panels in such a way to generate the 12 panel types required. The method of linking can be represented by a matrix as follows to give panel types A to F, and A' to F' respectively.

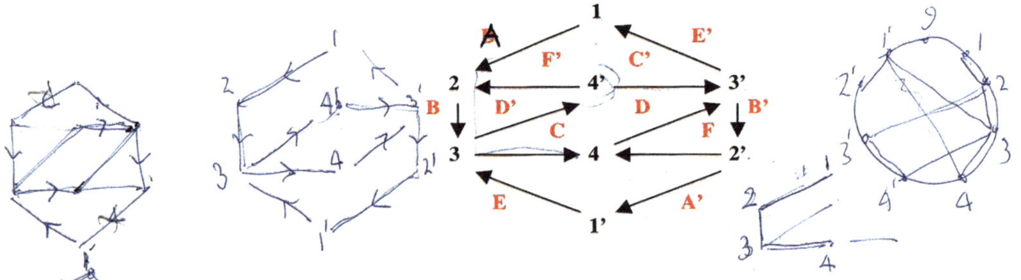


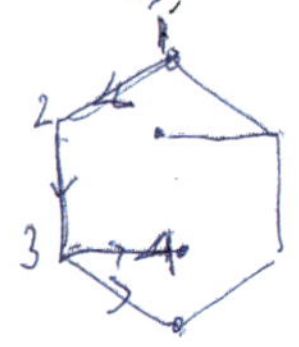

Therefore we can enter this sequence wherever we want in order to generate a completely random sequence of only 6 panels ie. if we start with a 2 type then we connect to a 3 type generating a B panel, then we can connect to either a 4 or 4' generating either a C or a D' panel and so on. This is analogous to how strands of the human DNA are generated.

Note that this is effectively what Toyo Ito and Associates have done to generate their current façade image (see below).

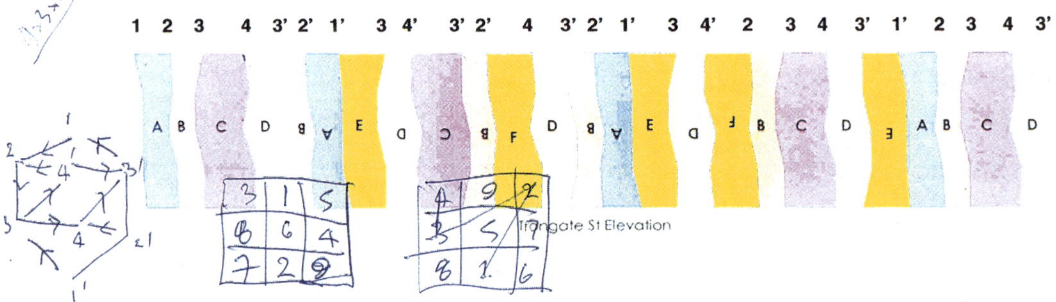


We must then take this rule set and apply it back to the original 9 point magic square rule which defines each individual column geometry.

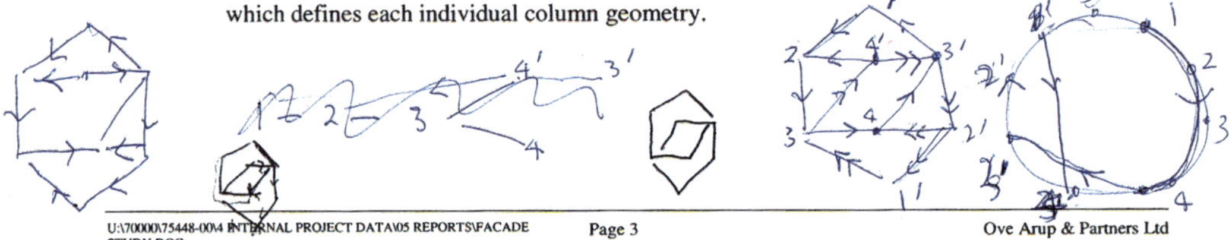

Precedent page:
**3.61** Numeric diagrams and notes for the S-Project department store in Glasgow with Toyo Ito (2002).

# TERMINOLOGICAL AND CONCEPTUAL STRUGGLES

The differences between the design methods of the Chemnitz stadium, with Kulka and Königs, and the Serpentine, with Ito, illustrate Balmond's shifting views on randomness vis-à-vis design process during the years around the turn of the century. In Chemnitz there was a transition from the early sketches, in which arches were simply placed by eye at random, to a rule-based procedure later on that calibrated such randomness. In contrast, at the Serpentine the trigger was an abstract, algorithm-generated diagram that was then turned into a series of architectural elements. In 2004 Balmond rejected the method followed at Chemnitz in favor of that at the Serpentine. Ito believed that "drawing lines at random results, not in the generation of new spaces, but the very opposite—that is, it is apt to lead to conventional spaces. One is more apt to achieve unexpected freedom using an algorithm." Responding to and agreeing with this observation, Balmond stated that human intuition alone cannot indeed match the "surprise" delivered by an algorithm, and therefore that algorithmic rules will always yield more "interesting" configurations than the designer's memory.[97] He never provided any grounds to substantiate these claims, though on some level there may be an element of truth to them. For the capabilities of algorithms—especially when coupled with computing power—to unleash and orchestrate complexity, catalyze leaps in logic and order, and generate enormous amounts of different outcomes are completely out of reach for the drafting hand. As a result, there is room to speculate that the degree of unpredictability afforded by such capabilities may be considerably higher—unpredictability being arguably a quality through which to measure surprise.

Earlier experiments involving the ambition to engender surprise through the trace of the human hand include, notably, those of *art informel*. Never part of Balmond's references despite the striking terminological similarity, there is little trace of *art informel* in the procedures and methods of his informal, although some of the sought-after qualities and goals can certainly be identified as being shared.[98]

97 Balmond and Ito, "Conversation - Cecil Balmond and Toyo Ito," 48–49.

98 *Art informel* was a pictorial movement that developed mainly in Europe during the generation after World War II. It is not to be confused with Krauss and Bois's formless, with which it bears a complicated relationship of both antagonism and occasional common operations. Both Balmond's informal and *art informel* shared a number of central inclinations, such as the search for freedom, spontaneity, chance, randomness, and the unforeseen; a preference to start creative processes from scratch (as opposed to via stylistic recycling) that was tied to their desire to rid themselves of preconceptions; and a certain emergent quality present in some *informel* paintings which, in subtly revealing a recognizable silhouette, such as that of a human figure, proceed from the nondifferentiated to the differentiated, as Krauss and Bois noted. On the other hand, *art informel*'s rejection of geometry and privileging of gestures and materials–in contrast to rules and form–stand at the antipodes of Balmond's design ideology. (Evidently enough, the use of algorithmic thinking, another core difference, was not available to *informel* artists as it was to the engineer.)

## Random versus Chance

Balmond's continued lack of clarity around the concept of randomness is worth pausing over. As mentioned above, in 1993 he claimed that randomness in a design solution was to be promoted. In 1996, randomness was described as a general condition synonymous with chance ("perhaps the nature of reality is chance and order may only be a particular small, local, steady state of the random"), which was now a bad thing: "[i]n the informal, chaos is not random; it is structured space of several degrees of order."[99] It continued to be undesirable in 1997: "[t]he informal is neither random nor arbitrary, it relies on overlap to bring forward a series of shifting certainties" and through the late 1990s: "[t]he random in its purest form is boring . . . In utter randomness there is the paradox of total uniformity. Chaos is much exciting."[100] Around the same time, he tried to clarify the relationship between "random" and "chance," without much success:

> Random and chance are misunderstood. Chance has to do with the probable ... The random begets chance. Chance is order nascent in chaos, hovering, embedded, in the fabric of the possible. Pure randomness is a concept like infinity ... it is the realm of ultimate dis-order. But randomness has its own laws.[101]

In 2004 he distanced the random from the informal yet again, writing that the latter "is not chaos in the sense of random and willful."[102]

## Adjacency versus Adhocism

Similar semantic instabilities emerge when examining his understanding of the "ad hoc." On one occasion he explained it in relation to two notions that appear recurrently in his writings, *spacing the gap* and *compiling the interval*. The former has to do with an *a priori* subdivision of a segment or a bounded region of space into repetitive or equal areas. Balmond associated this operation with what he saw as a conventional mode of architectural design, one rooted in the adhocism of each part relative to the next. In contrast, compiling the interval was meant to designate the rationale behind the unfolding of the informal. Two or more local design actions are allowed to play out in time. By adjacency—here to be distinguished from adhocism—the distances between elements and the various rhythms of growth may start to clash with one another, following a logic of accrual or resonance. Intervals are thus compiled in a sequence that leads from local to juxtaposition, and in extreme cases, where the two local dynamics wind up coalescing entirely, from juxtaposition to the unified condition Balmond referred to as hybrid.[103] This hybrid entity might then be projected as a new local design action yielding a new

99 Respectively, in a typed manuscript titled "the in-formal" and dated 1996, and an untitled one dated January 1, 1996. Courtesy of Balmond Studio.

100 Respectively, in Balmond, "New Structure and the Informal," August 1997, 55, and in a typed, untitled, undated manuscript, probably late 1990s. Courtesy of Balmond Studio.

101 Typed undated manuscript titled "The Art of the Probable," probably late 1990s. Courtesy of Balmond Studio.

102 Typed manuscript titled "The Matrix in My Mind." Dated November 11, 2004. Courtesy of Balmond Studio.

103 In an interview with the author conducted in New York City on April 10, 2015.

order, thereby consummating the chaotic behavior Balmond wished to build into his informal approach.

## Sequence versus Series

Within his theoretical framework, spacing the gap and compiling the interval partially hark back to the mathematical notions of series and sequence respectively.[104] A sequence is a list of numbers defined by a particular order. A series, on the other hand, is the addition of a subset of numbers within a sequence. The additive operation renders any particular order of numbers irrelevant, erasing the sequential structure. Balmond interpreted sequences as organizations (since the order is defining) that grow open-endedly (since they can continue to run into infinity). Further, he construed the uniqueness of each number in a sequence as an event, and by extension the whole sequence as a "compiling of events." This phrase becomes especially meaningful when referring to instances like the Fibonacci sequence, where each number is found by adding the previous two. Balmond enjoyed the evolving character of sequences—in contradistinction to the conclusive nature of series—as well as their multirelationality, whereby each number is determined at once by its unique, local position and the overall underlying order.

But revealing terminological inconsistencies appear here again. His structure-as-trace approach was clearly based around the notion of compiling the interval, and therefore around that of sequence. Indeed, it was meant to involve "the idea of algorithm, the idea of *sequential* movements." However, he referred to the outcome of such an approach as "*serial* structures," whereas a phrase like "sequential structures" would have seemed more accurate.[105] It was no different vis-à-vis the ad hoc. Just as he rejected the ad hoc at the end of his career, he did so, originally, in the 1995 manifesto by equating it with "collage."[106] Yet, only a little later in the 1990s, he welcomed it—both in general: "[c]haos is a more natural material to deal with. But we need a thinking method that deals with the spontaneous and ad-hoc," and in particular, when describing strategies to materialize structural members individually based on contingent circumstances: "[t]hey could be single beams or double beams, stronger nearer the supports where distortions are strongest. So here it is a do-it-yourself approach to design, and ad-hoc approach. There are no fixed rules or preconceptions. It is open territory, fashioned by local conditions."[107]

## Universals versus Absolutes

More contradictions surface around the question of "fixed rules." For someone who liked to think of himself as dealing with "universals"—going back to his interest in philosophy—and who states approvingly that "[a]rchitecture attempts universality, and in this sense it contains the seed of science," it seems odd to also reject fixed

104 Untitled manuscript, dated November 3, 2005. Courtesy of Balmond Studio.

105 Balmond and Ito, "Conversation - Cecil Balmond and Toyo Ito," 44. My emphasis.

106 Balmond, *Informal*, 212–13.

107 Typed, untitled, undated manuscript, probably late 1990s. Courtesy of Balmond Studio.

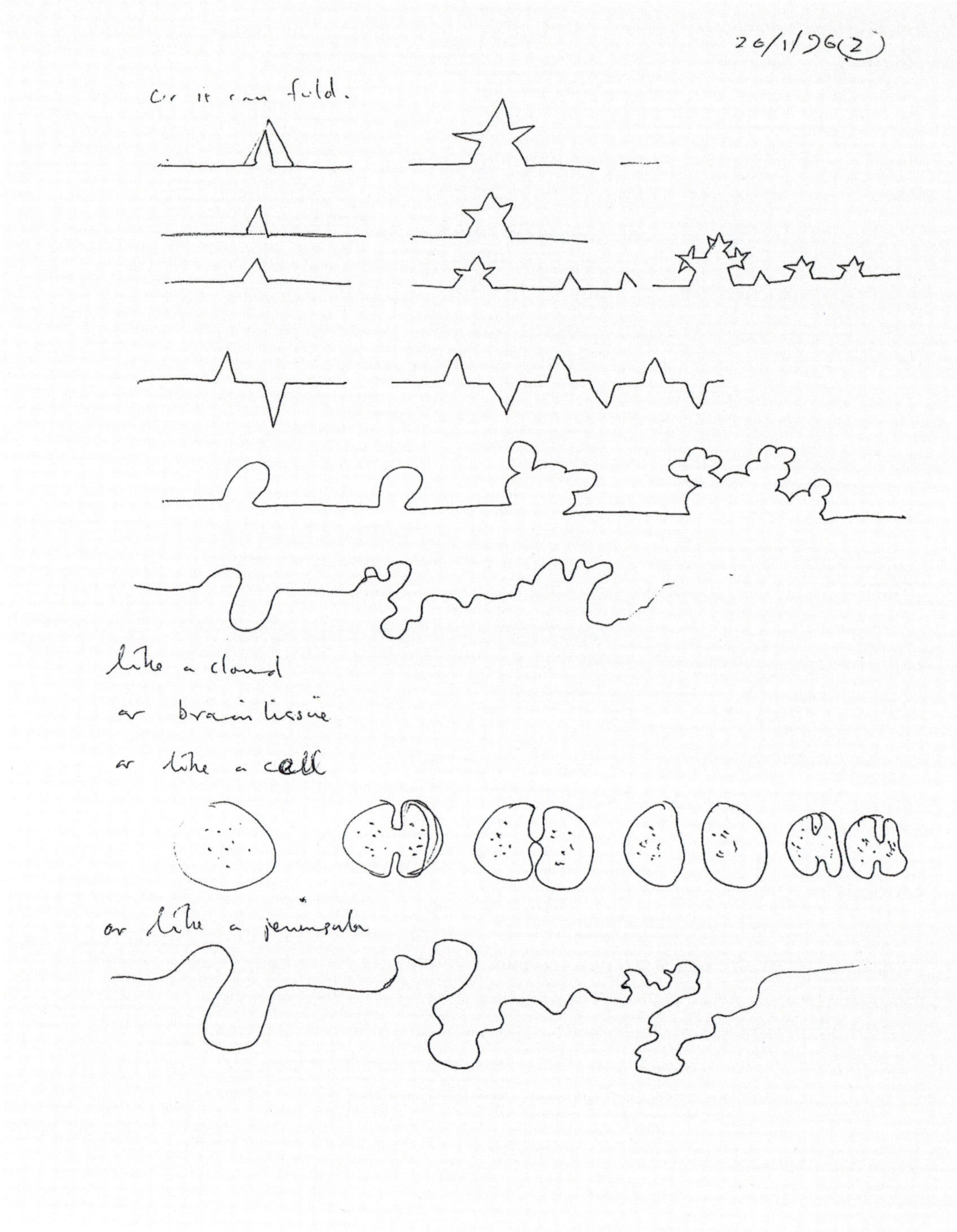


**3.62** Folding lines subdividing in a fractal manner, 1996.

rules and to claim elsewhere, when discussing the process of nurturing design ideas, that "[t]here will be no absolutes. Only humble relatives."[108] Certainly, to build a theoretical framework around notions that are counter-intuitive in relation to each other (such as random and order, local individuality and pattern, instability and equilibrium, certainties and shifts) without falling into contradictions and terminological inconsistencies requires an intellectual rigor that Balmond, otherwise quite intellectually acute, showed himself to lack to some significant degree. Some commentators of *Informal* went so far as to characterize it as whimsy in its attempt to rationalize the irrational.[109] While that is too extreme a judgment—insofar as Balmond's informal ideology does offer a coherent enough theoretical proposition, with recurrent notions and points of reference over the years—it is nonetheless true that, in epistemologically enacting some of the same principles he promoted across his conceptual musings (e.g., lack of hierarchy and opportunism), he constantly flirted with the operational hazards of caprice.

Following pages:
**3.63** Passageways between squares, 2005 (p. 302).
**3.64** Squares freeing up threshold areas, 2005 (p. 303).

## A TWOFOLD STRUCTURAL AWARENESS: PATTERN INTERACTIONS, NUMERIC BASIS FOR PROGRAM, ACCIDENT PROMPTS

Balmond's production focuses on organizational models and as such falls primarily within the domain of form, as distinct from shape. In fact, it features a tendency to resist the notion of shape, and it does so in two ways. On the one hand, it barely addresses it. It does not pay much attention to the figural conditions of objects, partly due to lack of interest and partly because it was the architect in question that would decide those aspects. On the other hand, Balmond repeatedly conjured up ways to turn the elements defining such figural characteristics—that is, borders and limits—themselves into regions of spatial speculation. In one instance, a line progressively opens up at intervals while maintaining its continuity. It loses its original status as a straight segment by giving rise to zones whose borders continue to subdivide ever so slightly in a fractal manner **(fig. 3.62)**. In another instance, by offsetting the squares in a nine-square grid inward, the original division lines become passageways between the squares **(fig. 3.63)**. Or the squares take on a life of their own as if pushed around by the lines, thus freeing up threshold areas **(fig. 3.64)**. In terms of form, the specific character of Balmond's configurational systems illustrates the ways in which a set of elements and relations may be open and yet retain a

108 Respectively, in Balmond, "Tecnologia," 88, and in an untitled manuscript, dated July 31, 1996. Courtesy of Balmond Studio.

109 Chris Wise, "Informal," *AA Files*, no. 49 (Spring 2003), 104.

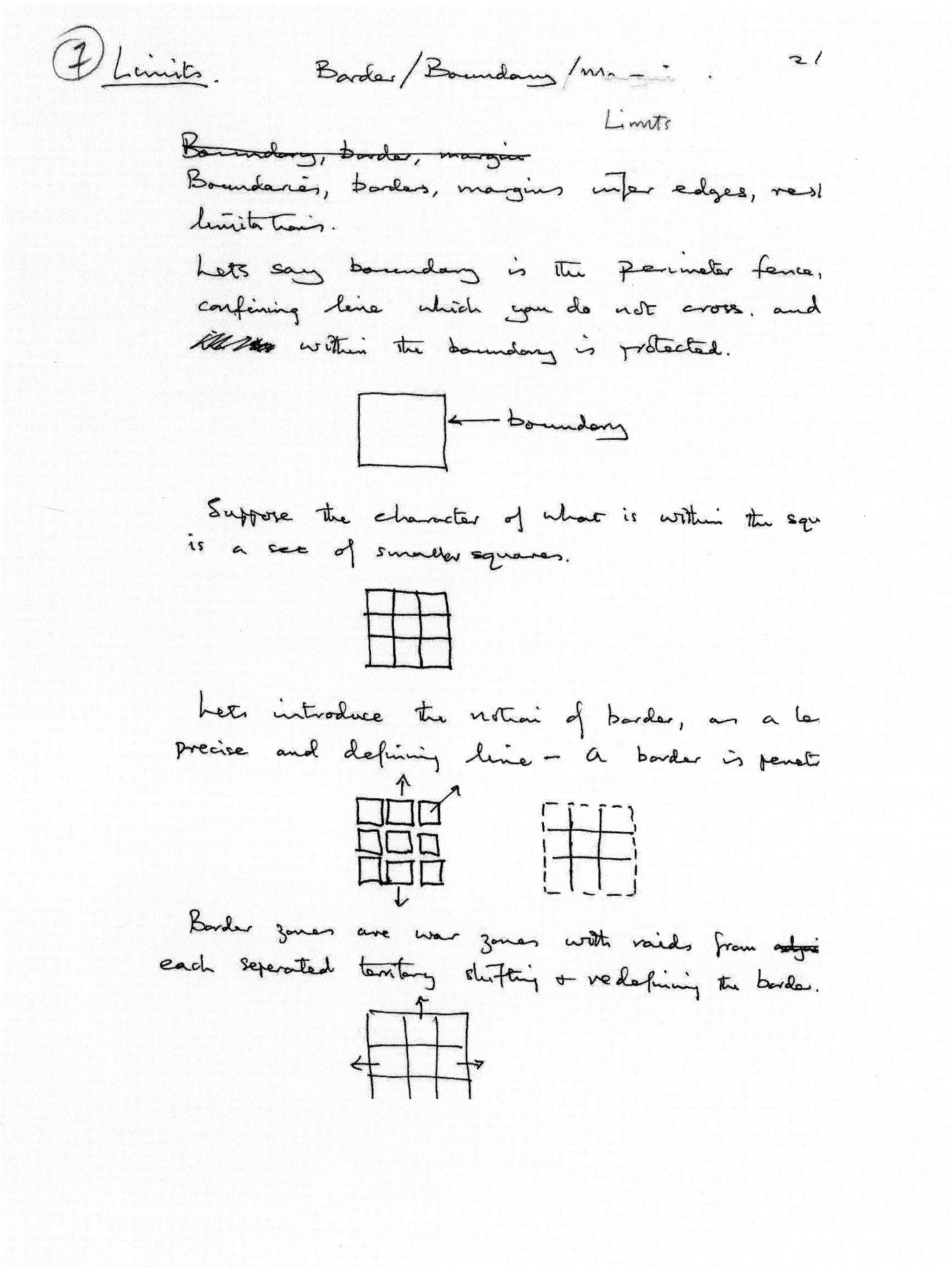

⑦ Limits. Border / Boundary / ma[illegible] . 21

Limits

~~Boundary, border, margin~~

Boundaries, borders, margins infer edges, resl limitations.

Lets say boundary is the perimeter fence, confining line which you do not cross. and ~~[illegible]~~ within the boundary is protected.



Suppose the character of what is within the squ is a set of smaller squares.

Lets introduce the notion of border, as a le precise and defining line – a border is penet

Border zones are war zones with raids from ~~edges~~ each seperated territory shifting + redefining the border.

2/10/05
②

<u>Limits</u>

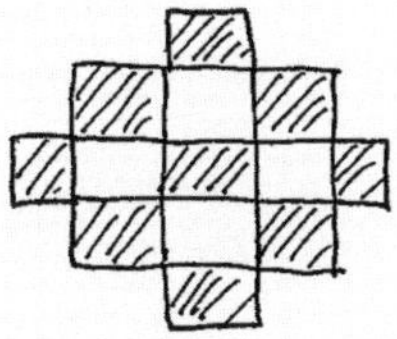

The figure has changed from simple square to a multifaceted shape.

The line that marks the shape is more akin to an extending or travelling margin. I use the word margin to allow a greater degree of ~~scope~~ freedom, & scope, for ~~[illegible]~~ the original to change, mutate.

There is another reason for ~~[illegible]~~ the word margin.

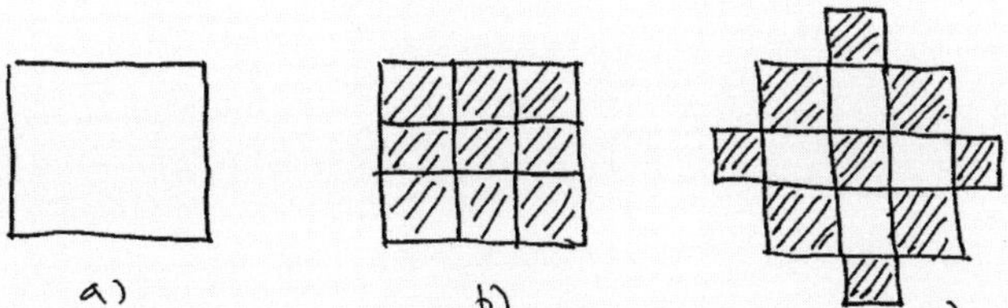

a) b) c)

Figure b) is a subdivision of a). Whereas figure c) is an extension of a) and can be traced by a single

line that comes back on ~~does not cross~~ itself. Figure b) cannot be drawn by a single line that does not cross itself.

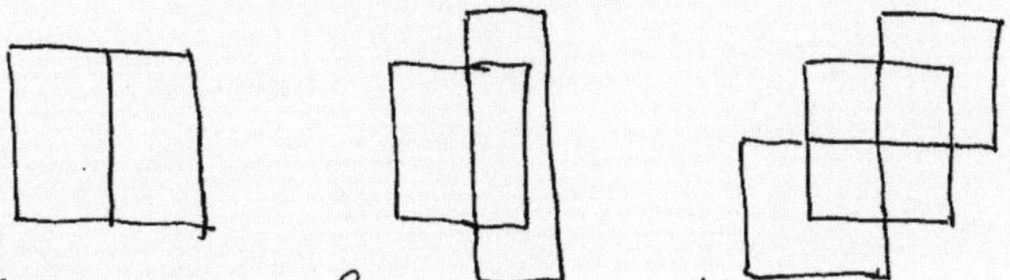

d e f

Figure d is subdivided. e & f are not.

(1)

To Philip Johnson
cc Elizabeth / Charles Walker
From Cecil Balmond.

Yorkshire
4/4/99

Dear Philip,

I am away for a few days in Yorkshire, walking the moors, but I thought a few notes from me would help you develop an idea for the Guang Zhou Tower.

a) The first idea I proposed was for an undulation of tubes. The key idea is that each tube is made up of other tubes.

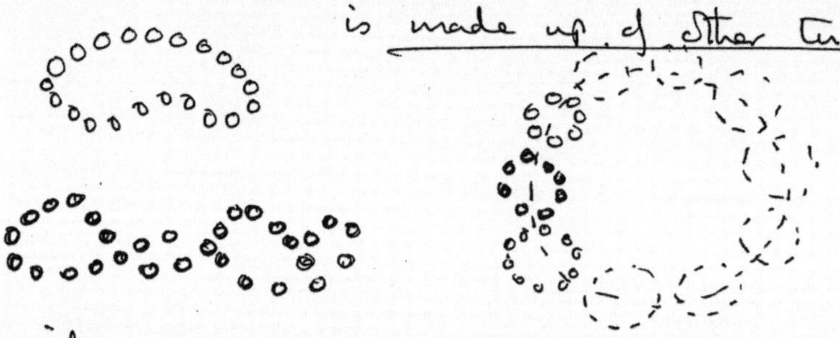

b) The idea can restrict itself to three tubes.

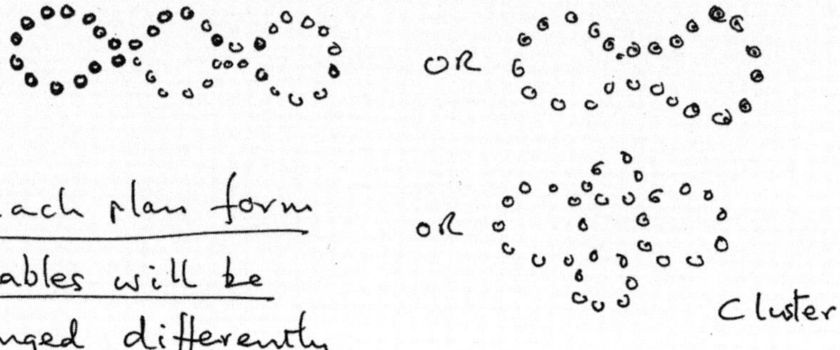


In each plan form tie cables will be arranged differently.

significant degree of specificity—rather than becoming something else altogether as such openness unfolds. The exchanges with Philip Johnson mentioned earlier exemplify this balance quite clearly. Balmond proposed a cluster of tubes in different configurations. They might form a bean-like perimeter to enclose a single area. They might become a sequence of circles tangential to one another. The circles can unfold along a larger circumference to give rise to another space inside. They might overlap. Or they might be drawn together to create a secondary cluster of regions in-between. The openness—that is, the degree of maneuverability—exhibited by this set of instantiations does not sacrifice its identity as a cluster of tubes **(fig. 3.65)**.

Precedent page:
**3.65** Openness and identity in clusters of circles. Correspondence with Philip Johnson on ideas for the Guang Zhou Tower scheme, 1999.

Following double-page spread:
**3.66** Ammann tiling for a facade texture. Victoria & Albert Museum scheme with Daniel Libeskind (p. 306).
**3.67** Inscription of a triangular pattern within a hexagonal one through a branching operation, early 1990s (p. 307).

## Interdependence through Nesting

One of these instantiations demonstrates the first of two ways in which various orders can simultaneously coalesce in a design concept by Balmond. Little tubes are arranged along small circumferences to form small circles. This is the first order. The second one organizes these small circles along a larger circumference. The relationship between the two orders here is one of interdependence—more specifically, one of *nesting*. One pattern is contained within another: the small circumferences of little tubes are subsumed under the larger circumference. Further, the two nested patterns have a fractal quality, since they are identical and occur at different scales. Another such instance is the aperiodic tiling developed for the V&A project that was introduced by team member Francis Archer on the basis of the one discovered by mathematician Robert Ammann in the early 1970s. A tile delineated by an inflected contour comprising ten straight segments subdivides into smaller, self-similar tiles within it. The sequence, generated by coding a subdivision algorithm, may be taken to infinity **(fig. 3.66)**. Three different tiles with the same intrinsic property of modularity make up the overall tiling, which in this case is aperiodic because the patterns within it engendered by the composition of the three tiles are never identical—unlike in the more common, periodic tiling.

A relationship of nesting between two orders does not need, however, to be fractal. For example, when studying the construction of Platonic solids in the early 1990s, Balmond sketched out a procedure to arrive at a triangular pattern inscribed within a hexagonal one through a branching operation **(fig. 3.67)**. Also, in the instance above involving the little tubes, it would suffice to consider the small circles following one another along a square trajectory, rather than a circumferential one.

## Independence through Superimposition

In one exception, the interdependence between orders is not one of nesting. A series of sketches drawn up by Balmond in 1994 shows a number of simple line patterns—triangular, zigzagging, spiraling, square, etc.—on which straight or

# 2D Tiling

**Ammann Tiling**

**2次元タイリング**
**アマン・タイリング**

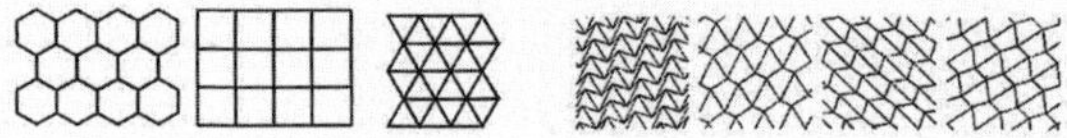

*Periodic tiling.*

The research of the AGU into aperiodic tiling started with the study of a two-dimensional tiling system called Ammann tiling, by the name of the mathematician Robert Ammann who discovered it in the early 1970s. The tiling is a two-dimensional fractal aperiodic system consisting of three different tiles, subdividing into self-similar tiles, whose dimensions relate to the parent tiles by the golden ratio. Through the vertices of this tiling system run four sets of parallel lines in orthogonal pairs. These sets of lines are spaced at two different intervals following harmonic sequences. The aperiodic tiling was automatically generated by coding of subdivision algorithms in CAD environments. The AGU also discovered ways of making the fractal nature of the pattern emerge graphically by stopping the subdivision of certain tiles. Ammann tiling was selected for its fractal properties and intrinsic modularity as the decorative facade pattern for the Victoria and Albert Museum Spiral. Running along the 600 m-long strip of wall surfaces, the pattern demonstrated the sequential nature of the spiral as well as displaying the incredible richness of the fractal pattern.

非周期的なタイリングについてのAGUの研究は、アマン・タイリングと呼ばれる2次元のタイリング・システムの研究に始まった。アマンは数学者で、1970年代初頭にこのシステムを発見した人物である。タイリングは2次元のフラクタルな非周期的システムで、3種類のタイルで構成される。それらのタイルは、その元となるタイルに対して黄金比となる大きさの異なる自己相似形に細分化される。このタイリング・システムの交点からは、それぞれ2本組で直交する4セットの平行線が走行している。これらの線のセットは、あるリズムをもって2つの間隔を保っている。

CADを用いることで、この非周期的なパターンは、細分化のアルゴリズムをコーディングすることによってコンピュータによって自動的に生成される。AGUはまた、特定のタイルの細分化を停止することで、このパターンのフラクタルな特性をグラフィカルに生成させる方法を発見した。

アマン・タイリングは、そのフラクタルな特性と元来備えていたモデュール性によって、ヴィクトリア・アンド・アルバート・ミュージアムの装飾的なファサードのパターンに採用されている。長く連続するスパイラルの壁面に600mにわたって続くパターンは、螺旋の連続的な特性を示しているのみならず、浮き彫りと彫り込みとを組み合わせたフラクタルなパターンがもち得る驚くほどの多様性を示している。

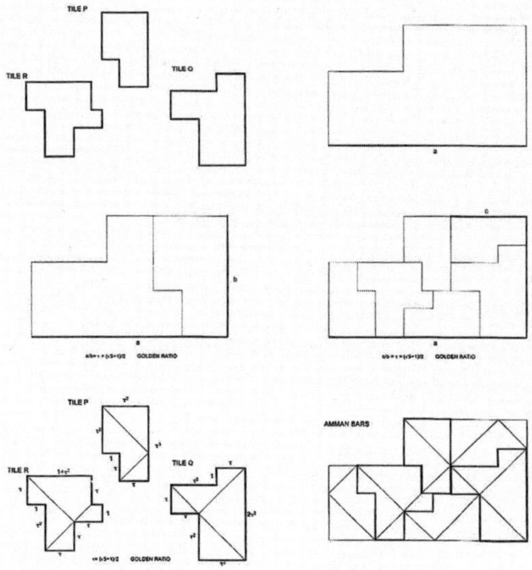


*Aperiodic tiling. Ammann tiling.*

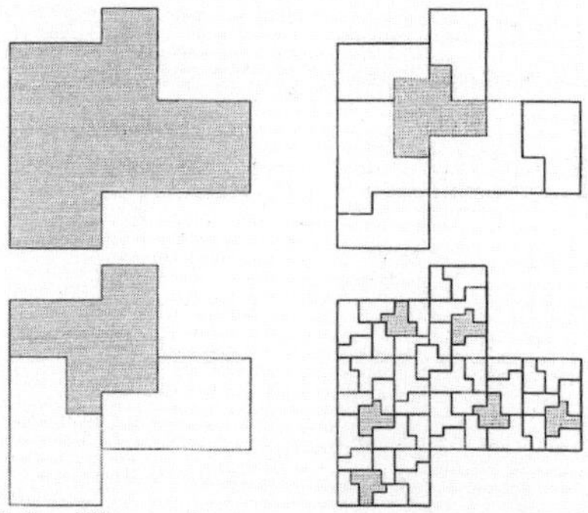

*Tile R at different scales.*

*Below: V&A Spiral; the pattern emerged from stopping the subdivision of the Tile R.*

下：V&Aスパイラル；タイルRの細分化の停止によって生成されたパターン。

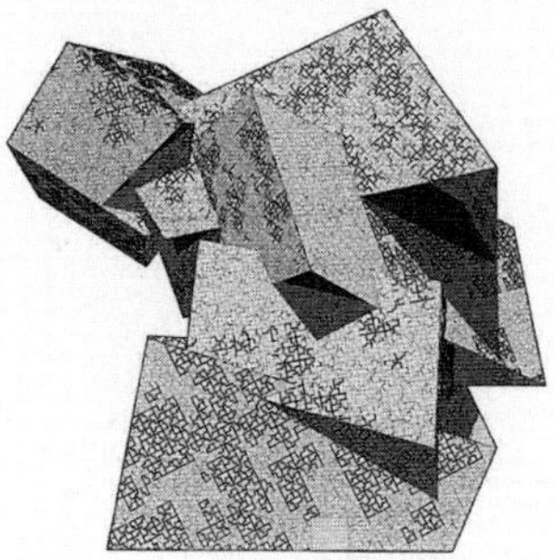

FRACTAL

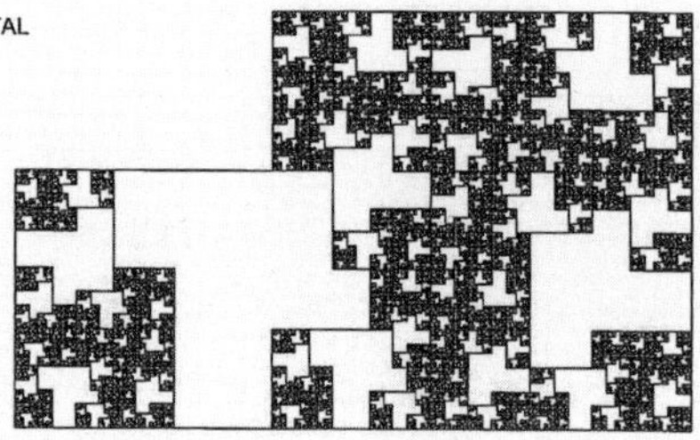

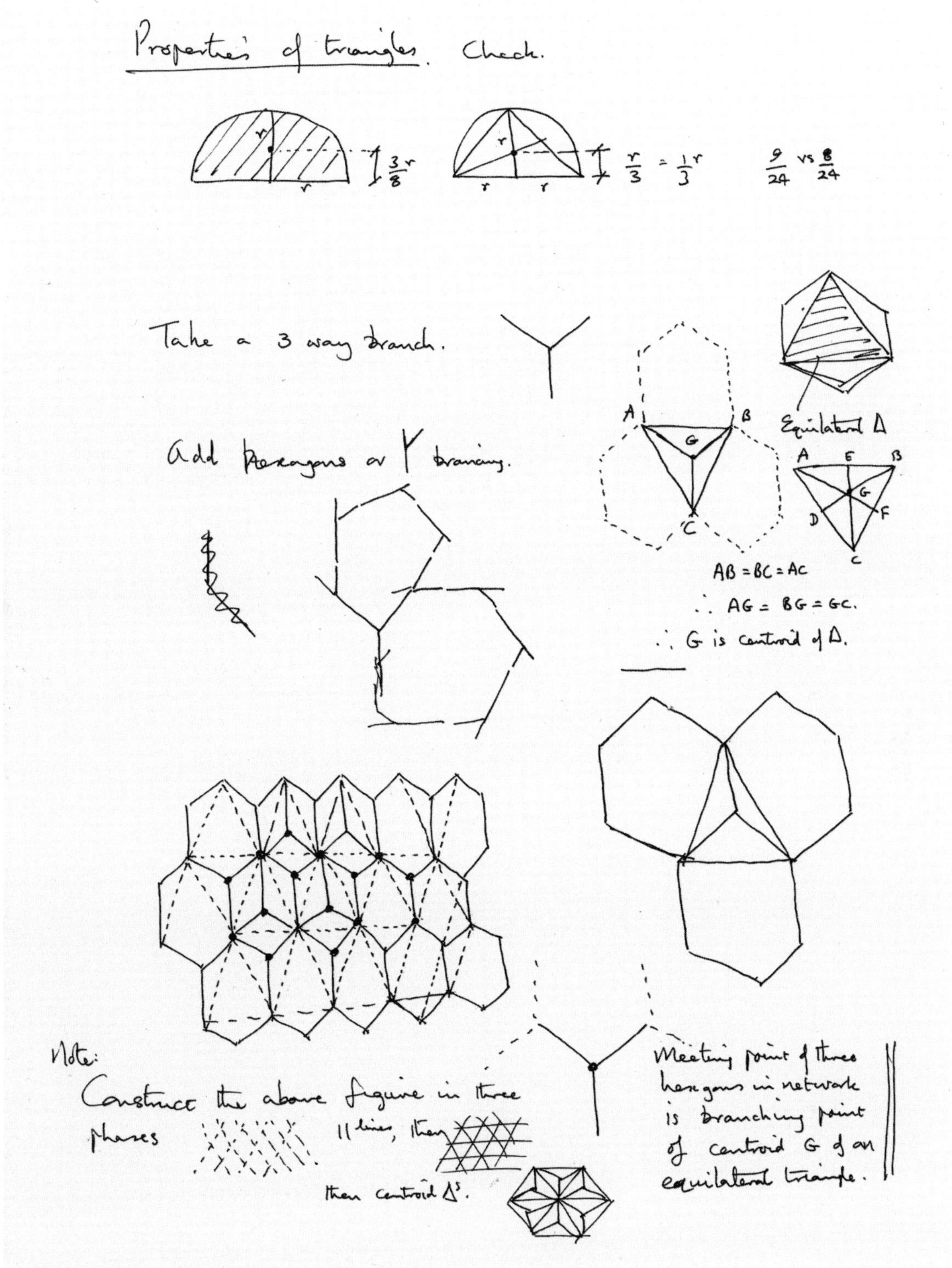
Properties of triangles. Check.
3/8 r
r/3 = 1/3 r
9/24 vs 8/24
Take a 3 way branch.
Add hexagons or ⅄ branching.
Equilateral Δ
A E B G D F C
AB = BC = AC
∴ AG = BG = GC.
∴ G is centroid of Δ.
Note:
Construct the above figure in three phases
|| lines, then
then centroid Δs.
Meeting point of three hexagons in network is branching point of centroid G of an equilateral triangle.

Implied in growth is asymmetry. This is another way of saying branching. My own investigation shows this.

This can be readily seen by writing out a series of numbers to define a shape.

If the shape is static, symmetrical, certain numbers we choose lie near to each other in straight line association, either vertical or horizontal.

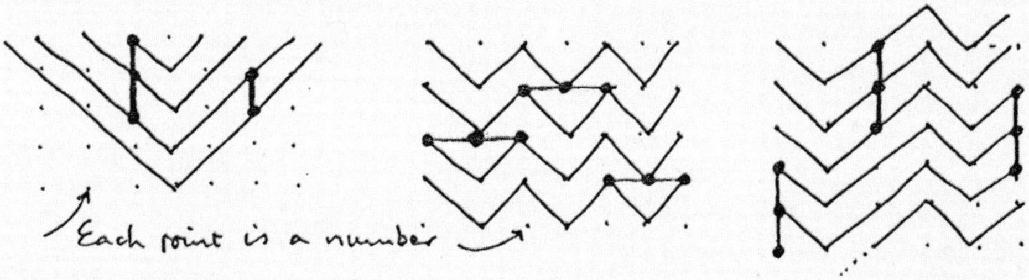


If however the patterns generated are open ended or reflecting a natural form, then the same chosen numbers that stood in lines now show a tendency to branch.

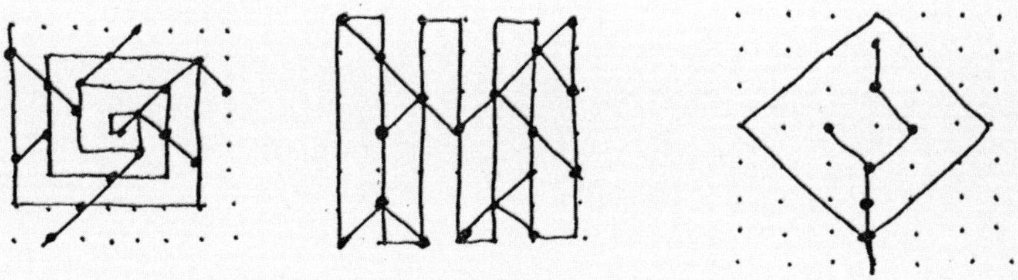

Each point on the grid is a number.

branching networks unfold, their nodes lying on the lines. Here the network's logic and size are not entirely circumscribed within those of the pattern, albeit partially dependent upon it **(fig. 3.68)**. This exception can, in fact, be seen as a midpoint between design concepts where the relationship between orders is one of interdependence and those where it is one of independence. More specifically, such a relationship of independence tends to be one of *superimposition*: two orders grounded in different logics cohabit within the same region of space.

Precedent page:
**3.68** Line patterns and branching networks.

It would seem that many of Balmond's collaborations with Koolhaas rely on this strategy, but on closer inspection this is not the case. To take Kunsthal as a paradigmatic example, the various "episodes" of structure coexisting in the building never become a pattern. They stay at the level of the "local action" without spreading to grow into a fully-fledged order. As a result, such actions—in the form of diverse structural systems and the relatively limited range of their spatial arrangement—stand adjacent to each other, whether vertically or horizontally. They do not overlap **(fig. 3.69)**. The most representative exception is Jussieu, which illustrates the strategy of superimposition quite clearly. A spiraling sequence of slanting floor elements unfolds from the bottom to the top of the building while intersecting a regular grid of columns that equally takes up the entirety of the interior volume **(fig. 3.10)**.

### Missing Three-Dimensionalization

Notably, the number of orders coalescing is typically restricted to just two. Also, in the vast majority of design concepts where interdependent orders are found, these are expressed bidimensionally, whether in sketch form or as a surface component of a building. This is, however, no surprise, since many such concepts bear the traces of the structure-as-trace approach, whose limited realm of application is primarily bidimensional. For a designer where shape plays barely any role in defining form, it is paradoxical that many of his formal organizations end up unfolding within the bidimensional regime of shape. And it is here that there would be room for exploring novel three-dimensional arrangements. For example, it is relatively simple to imagine a fractal pattern turned into a three-dimensional articulation of space. Its intrinsic modularity resonates productively with a demand commonly placed on architectural design for the cohabitation of different scales within a building. In a fractal arrangement with, say, three self-similar units, the small one could cater to the individual scale, the medium one to that of small groups, and the big one to that of larger concentrations of people. The type and number of units could be varied at will within each region of the building, while remaining part of a cohesive whole that is easy to manage and understand. Similar architectural readings might be made of three-dimensionalizations of the patterns used in the Chemnitz Stadium or the Pompidou Metz, to cite two of the aforementioned projects—as well as

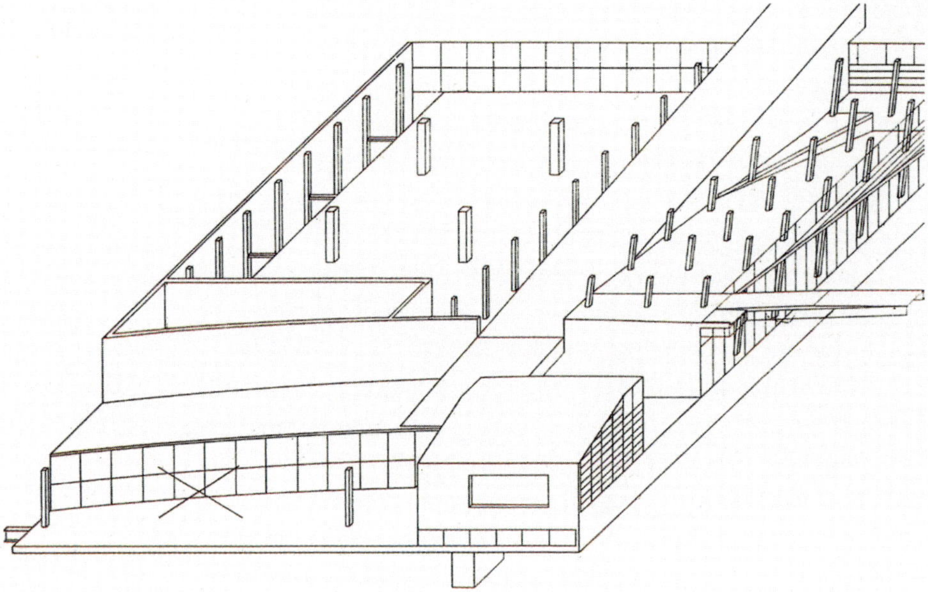

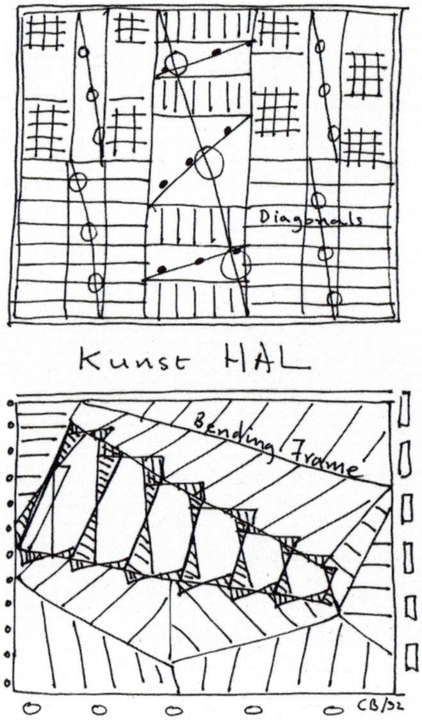


**3.69** Above: Adjacent structural systems at the Kunsthal.

**3.70** Left: Balmond's sketches for the Kunsthal. Tilted columns in relation to the moment frame provided by the ensemble they form along with the inclined structural slabs.

many of Balmond's bidimensional sketches that were never developed into a fully fledged scheme. In short, some of the fundamental rules, patterns, and strategies for contributions of this kind to the domain of spatial organizations in architecture can be found scattered throughout Balmond's production involving structure-as-trace and interdependent orders—albeit often not fleshed out into three-dimensional models; that is, albeit often merely at the level of a potentiality.

Following pages:
**3.71–74** Single surface folding upon itself to engender an alternating sequence of positive and negative spaces based on their structural rationale (1996) (pp. 312–15).

## Abstract Scenarios

In Balmond's design procedures, the definition of patterns—the first abstract deployment of elements and relations—and configurations—a second step in which the pattern becomes a more recognizable architectural arrangement—precedes any consideration concerning dimensioning or materials. And yet, such patterns and configurations tend to possess a certain structural intelligence from the outset by virtue of embodying a *twofold structural awareness*: for one thing, in the traditional sense of the building's physical support (load-bearing structure); for another, in that of the organizational traits of form. One of the most paradigmatic examples of this fusion in a developed scheme is the S-Project with Ito mentioned above. In certain instances, it was the manipulation of the properties of structural members that generated a spatial code orchestrating their spatial disposition. Such is the case with Kunsthal's lecture theater, where the specific placement and angle of the tilted columns relate directly to the moment frame provided by the self-stabilizing ensemble that they form along with the inclined structural slabs **(fig. 3.70)**. This subversive disciplinarity, determined by Balmond's capacity to translate aspects of his own discipline into architectural terms, differentiated him from other practitioners of digital design. For unlike the work of many of those, the outcomes of his formal experimentation were, in fact, buildable at an architectural scale. In this regard, in addition to the cases previously analyzed, it is worth calling attention to a series of abstract diagrams in which he explored the possibilities of a single surface that folds upon itself to engender an alternating sequence of positive and negative spaces based upon their structural rationale **(fig. 3.71–82)**.

Furthermore, Balmond's tendency to set up starting points as abstract situations—common in an engineer's *modus operandi*, although here they yield architectural outcomes—does away with typological and representational references at the beginning of form-generation processes. An approach grounded in abstraction along with a lack of concern for the domain of shape—wherein the set of figural traits defining a style unfolds—catalyze the stylistic nonreferentiality embedded in his design thinking. In turn, this stylistic nonreferentiality is to be seen as a tool to enable collaboration with architects of many diverse stylistic inclinations.

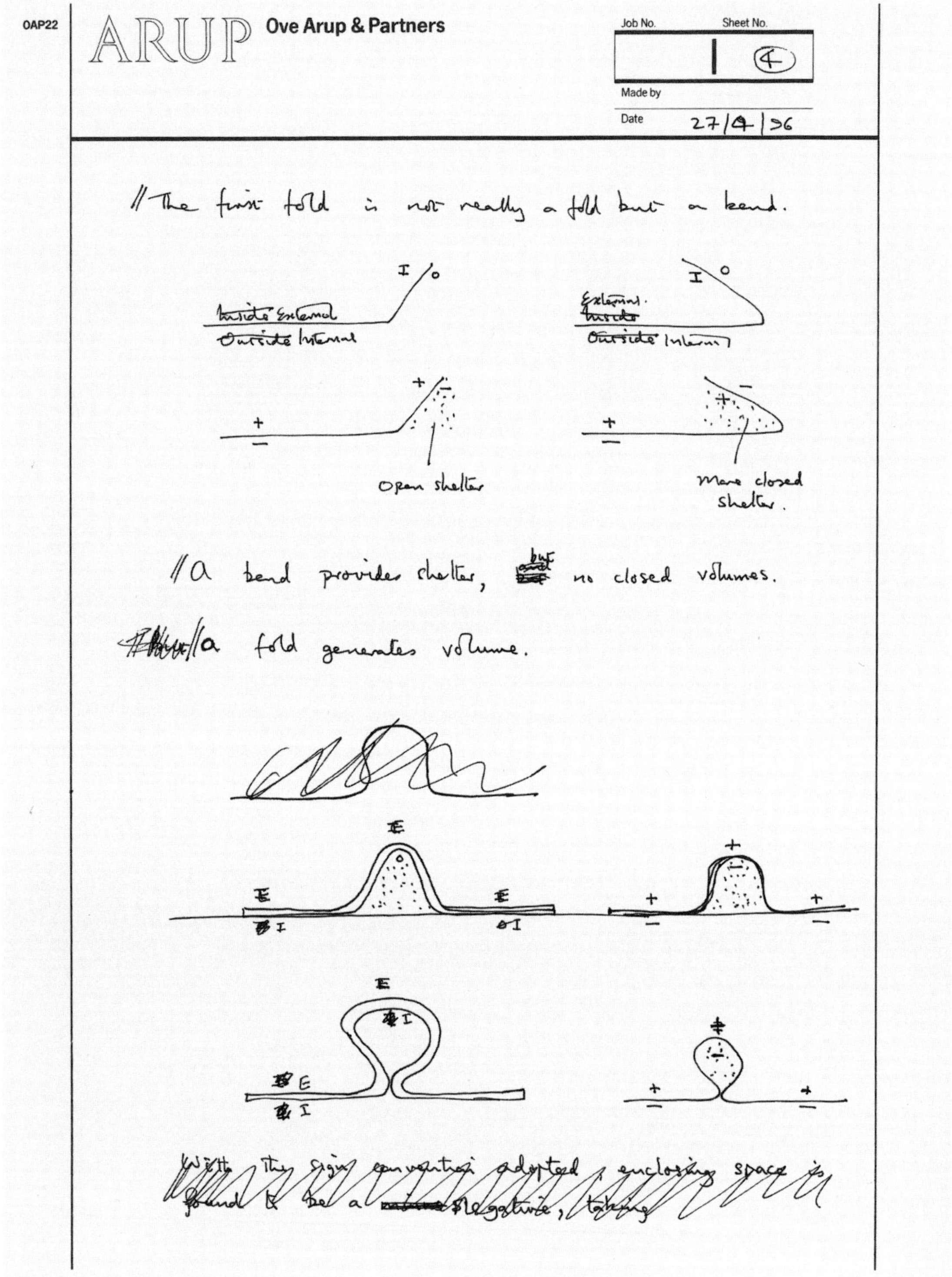
OAP22
ARUP Ove Arup & Partners
Job No.
Sheet No.
4
Made by
Date 27/4/96
// The first fold is not really a fold but a bend.
External
Internal
Open shelter
More closed shelter.
// a bend provides shelter, but no closed volumes.
// a fold generates volume.
With the sign convention adopted enclosing space is found to be a negative, taking

OAP22

ARUP Ove Arup & Partners

Job No. | Sheet No. 1 (5)

Made by

Date 27/4/96

The first reversal is in the customary notion we have of enclosure. Folding takes the contact surface and warps it creating enclosed volume. That which was outside, the contact surface, becomes an internal boundary condition for the volume.

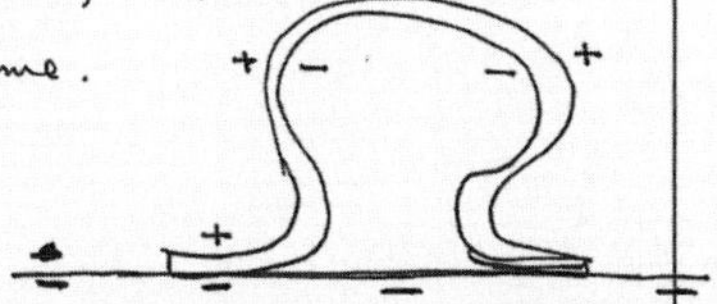

The space contained is negative. This sounds like a ridiculous notion. But it has some sense to it. Open, undivided space, is undifferentiated. It has a maximum resting entropy – a maximum loose fit. an accumulation of void in every direction. To create something is to raise entropy, which is opposite to the direction space wants to be.

To create containment there has to be a form which absorbs energy That The action of the fold generates energy. And a positive impetus has its reaction, as a negative. So the action of fold takes up energy, leaving the trapped enclosure as a negative.

wants to run free. Something has to give.

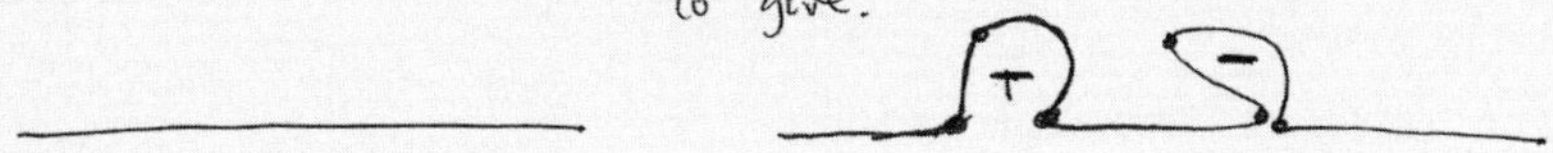

Another way of seeing this is to say that to create something is to spend energy to give form. Maintaining that form is against nature. It reduces entropy. It goes against the direction of disorder. Enclosure is therefore a negative concept.

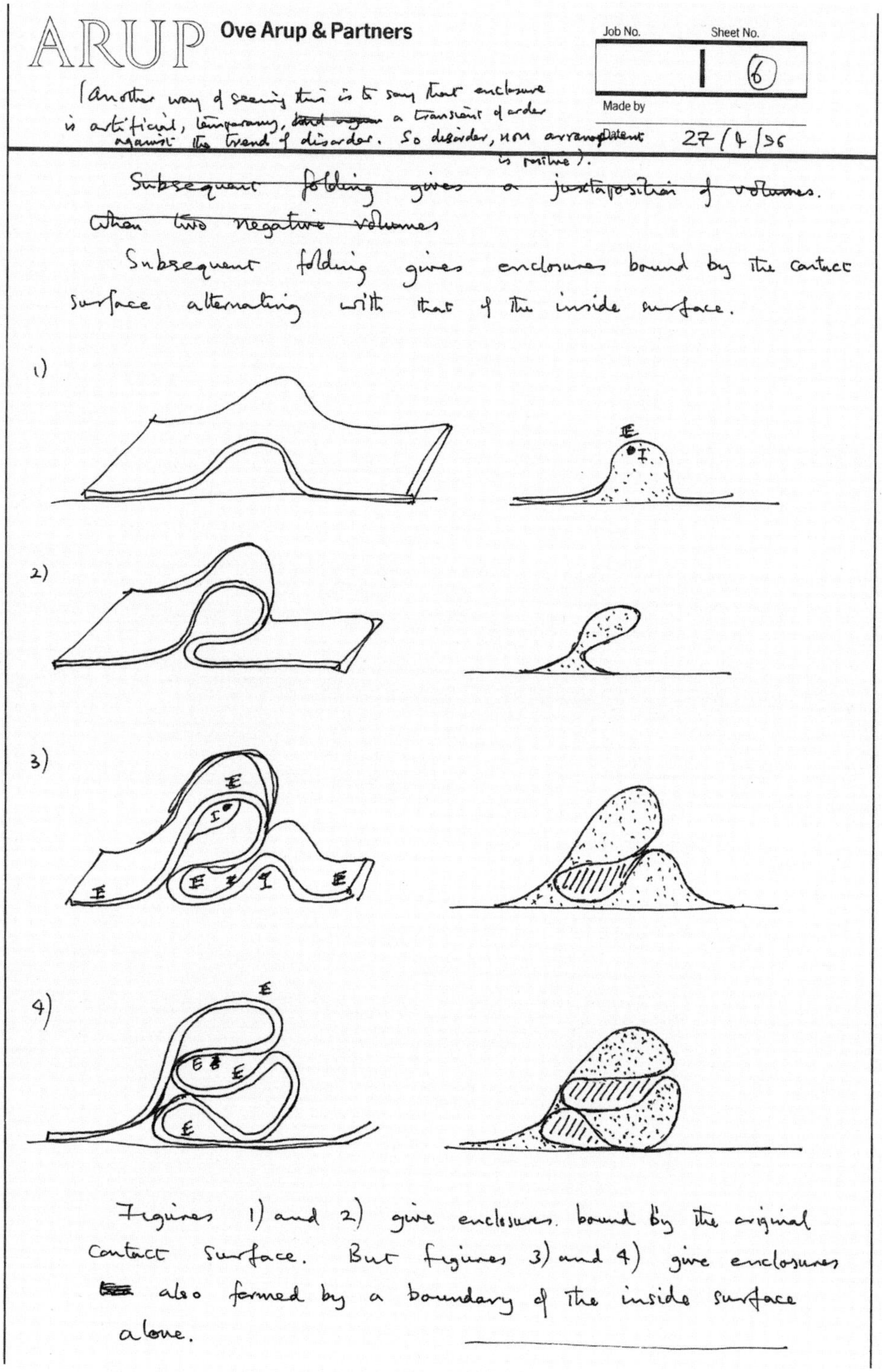

OAP22

ARUP Ove Arup & Partners

Job No. Sheet No. 1 6

Made by

Date 27/4/96

[Another way of seeing this is to say that enclosure is artificial, temporary, ~~and again~~ a transient of order against the trend of disorder. So disorder, non arrangement is positive).

~~Subsequent folding gives a juxtaposition of volumes. When two negative volumes~~

Subsequent folding gives enclosures bound by the contact surface alternating with that of the inside surface.

1)

2)

3)

4)

Figures 1) and 2) give enclosures bound by the original contact surface. But figures 3) and 4) give enclosures also formed by a boundary of the inside surface alone.

OAP22 ARUP **Ove Arup & Partners**

Job No. Sheet No. (7)

Made by

Date 27/4/96

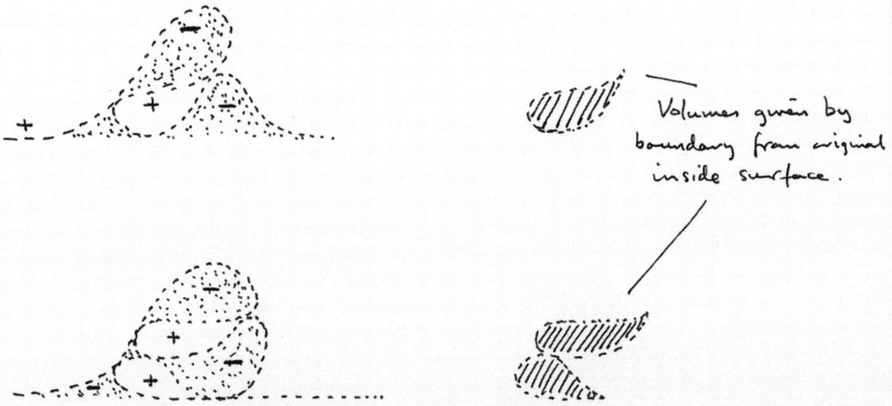


The way to generate a positive volume according to the sign convention adopted would be to take the original surface and fold it back on itself.

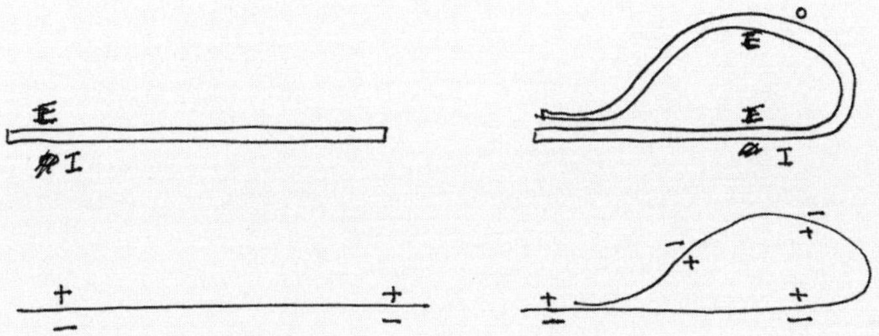

Continuing to generate a fold means reversing direction again.

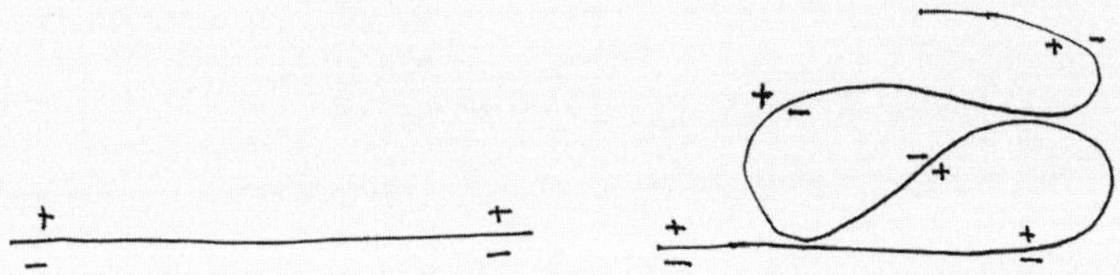

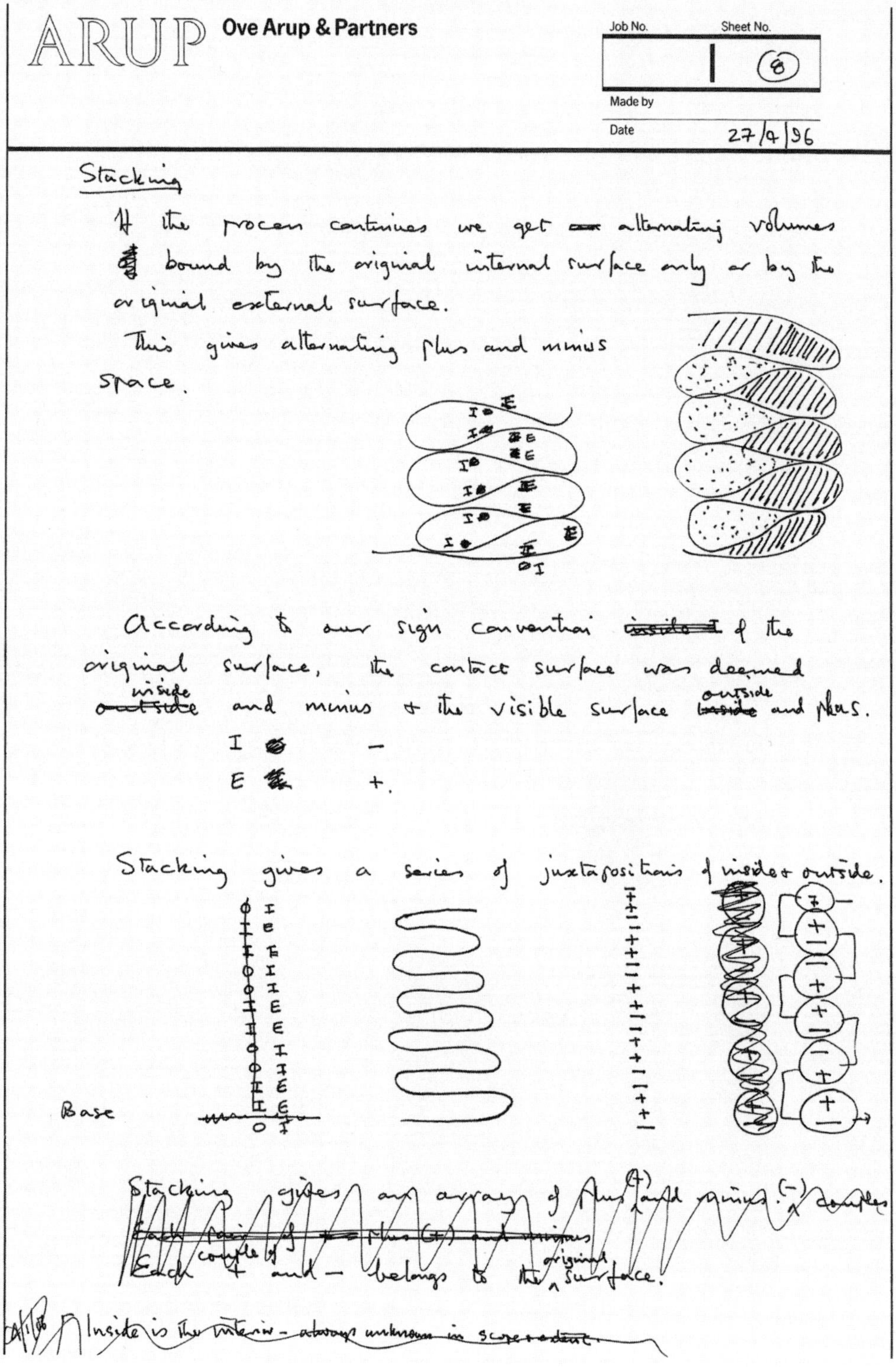

OAP22 ARUP Ove Arup & Partners

Job No. | Sheet No. (8)

Made by

Date 27/4/96

Stacking

If the process continues we get alternating volumes bound by the original internal surface only or by the original external surface.

This gives alternating plus and minus space.

According to our sign convention ~~inside~~ of the original surface, the contact surface was deemed inside ~~outside~~ and minus & the visible surface outside ~~inside~~ and plus.

I –

E +.

Stacking gives a series of juxtapositions of inside + outside.

Base

Stacking gives an array of plus (+) and minus (–) couples

~~Each pair of plus (+) and minus~~

Each couple of + and – belongs to the original surface.

~~Inside is the interior – always unknown in scope and extent.~~

OAP22

ARUP Ove Arup & Partners

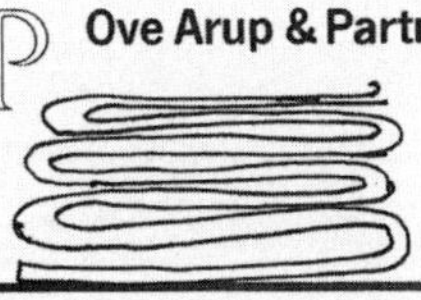

Job No. | Sheet No. 9

Made by

Date 27/4/96

Stacking or tight folding gives an intricate array of pluses and minuses.

— + + — — + + — — + + — — + + —

~~Each the minus couples with the plus for each surface.~~

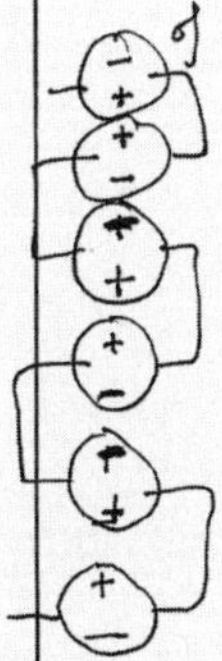

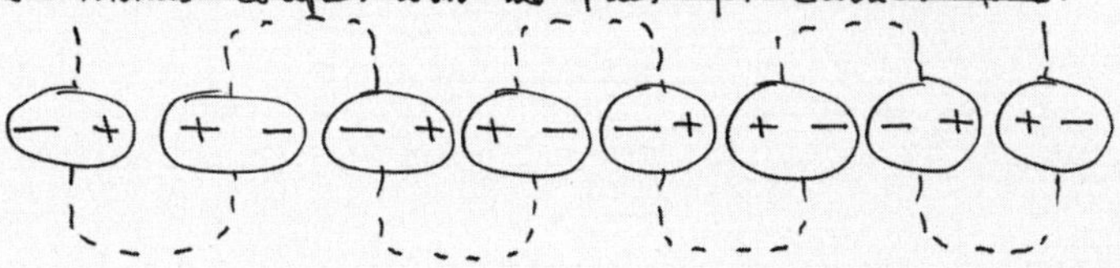

// This series of + and – gives an insight into nature. ~~Nothing quite touches in Nature~~ There are scenarios of tight folding as in brain tissue or in labyrinthine highly compacted strands of DNA molecule.

// But nothing quite touches in Nature. That is easy to see from the above diagram. Each fold brings together like minded values, plus against plus, minus against minus.

~~Though the repels like.~~

// The tighter the fold for maximum compaction, the more sure we can be that things won't touch!

// Across the interface like repels like.

+ against +

— against —

OAP22 ARUP **Ove Arup & Partners**

| Job No. | Sheet No. |
| --- | --- |
| | 1 |

Made by

Date 28/4/96.

Structural Configuration and Folding

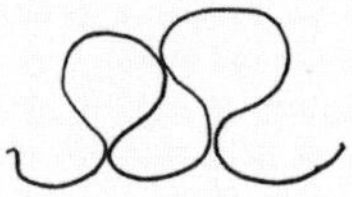

Consider three complete folds which have one enclosure bound by the original external surface only; (according to the convention we have adopted at the beginning).

Let us say that enclosures formed by the contact surface have an innate characteristic of support. as if an imprint of that first steady equilibrium is imparted to the contact surface. And say structural lines can only go through these support enclosures.

Then the interior zone formed by the original external surface becomes special – a void that is positive according to the sign convention we have adopted – nothing ideally should cut through this space. If something did it would have a special impact & should be seen as such.

To plot a structure, there has to be nodes. The contact point of the folds provide such nodes. Firstly we plot these nodes, above a structural datum the original contact surface.

OAP22

ARUP **Ove Arup & Partners**

Job No. | Sheet No. (2)

Made by

Date 28/4/96

Various structural configurations are possible:

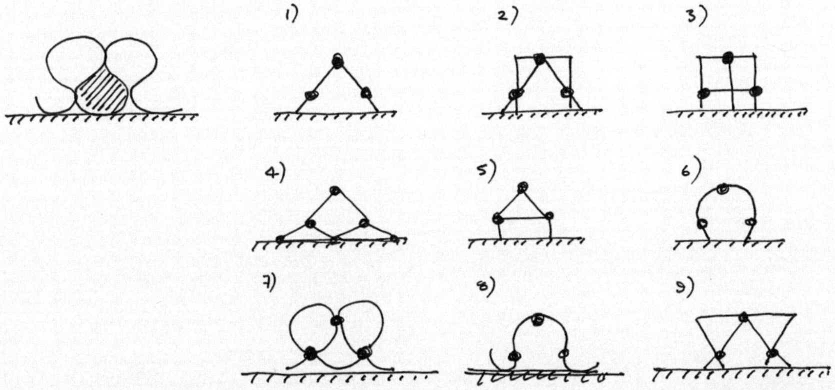

Just 3 points, 3 nodes, but a wealth of possibility arises. Some are utilitarian and connect the nodes with minimum fuss. fig 1.

Others stay faithful to the original loops as in 7).

Solutions 3) and 5) have elements that pass straight through the interior zone, something according to our ~~idealistic~~ convention we do not desire. But structure is a pragmatic art and if these elements were used in the solution, they should be seen as ~~contrary~~ elements impacting with a contrary nature to the space they travel through.

OAP22 ARUP Ove Arup & Partners

Job No. | Sheet No. 3

Made by

Date 28/4/96

Folding and Structural Configuration.

What if an architectural program gave a series of loops and a structural solution was sought?

Consider five complete loops.
~~Let us take a simple example to begin with.~~

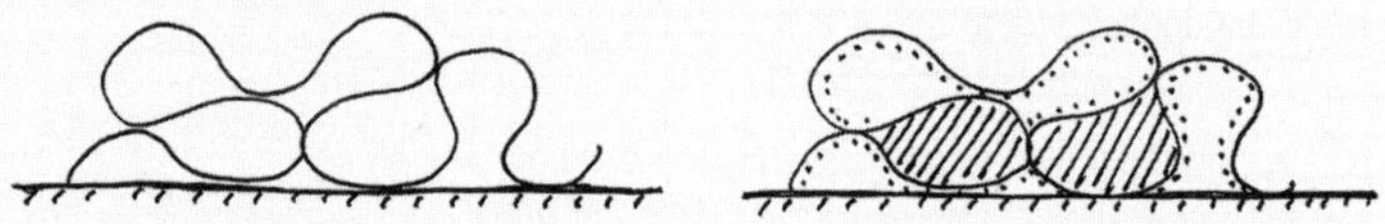

A series of five complete loops define the problem. Using the sign convention for the contact surface and inside surface two enclosures bound by the inside surface are given, sheltering within other zones formed by the boundaries of the contact surface.

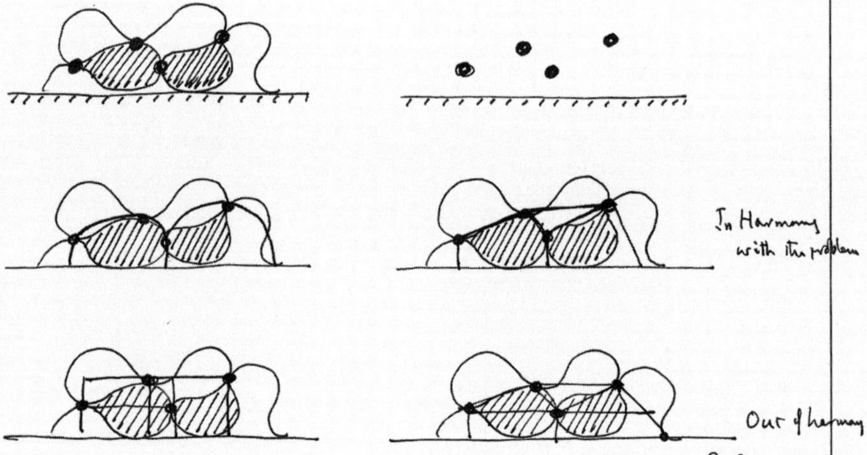

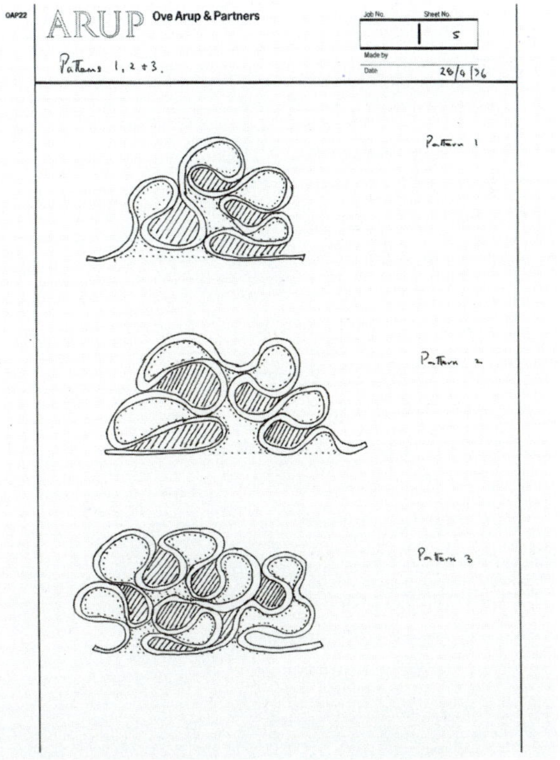


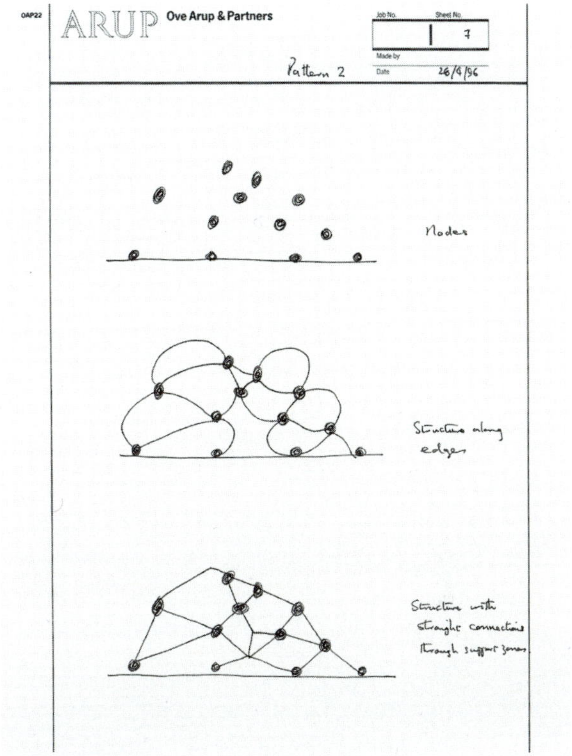


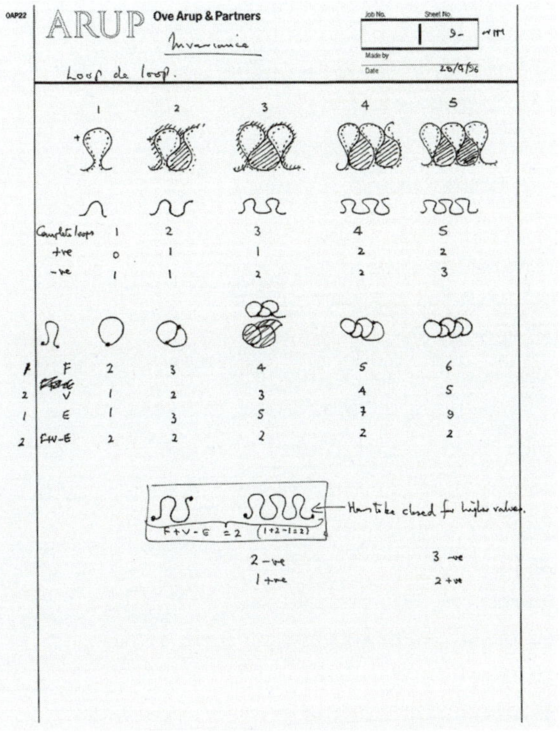


Preccedent pages

**3.75–82** Single surface folding upon itself to engender an alternating sequence of positive and negative spaces based on their structural rationale (1996). (pp. 316–21)

## Bypassing Formalism

Commentators were divided around Balmond's attitude toward form. Where one used the phrase "authentic formalism" to characterize his work, another recommended it "for critics in search of approaches to architecture that evade formalism."[110] He himself claimed to understand "function and form as interwrapped, not slavishly following one upon the other but a feedback loop of one educating the other."[111] Upon close examination, that turns out to be an overstatement. Questions of function or program are for the most part absent throughout his sequences of graphic explorations, his chief preoccupation remaining the production of organizational models in the abstract. That said, many such organizational models do incorporate the idea of a program—that is to say, the possibility of a set of human activities realistically taking place within them—even if it not explicitly taken into account. For example, in a sketch exploring the notion of "invariance," a single line gives rise to a pattern in which a number of interlocking spaces become entangled with those defined by the adjacent line. The pattern's proportions and relational properties are such that it is easy to read a building plan directly into it—one comprising a series of spatial regions now interpenetrating, now flowing into one another (fig. 3.83). Another series of drawings seems to suggest the inhabiting of several kinds of vertical trusses (fig. 3.84). In yet another pair of sketches, one depicts a four-by-four matrix with niches hatched in two different ways, while the other features two mirrored sets of numbered L-shapes forming a rectangle. Their dimensions, proportions, and degree of intricacy are so realistically architectural that the sketches might very well stand for building sections, with hatches and numbers indicating different programmatic areas. Far from what Balmond had in mind at the time, however, the two drawings simply represent numeric relationships involving symmetry (fig. 3.85).

Indeed, engineers have historically made use of a numeric basis to generate *engineering forms*—that is, material organizations attuned to serving an engineering purpose (bridges, dams, etc.). Alternatively, much of Balmond's production shows, often unwittingly, some of the ways in which it is possible to embed the possibility of program inhering in form in such a numeric basis. In other words, many of Balmond's sketches can be readily interpreted as architectural form even if their origin was a numeric basis, typically an engineering starting point. Certainly, practitioners of digital design in architecture during the 1990s and 2000s used a numeric basis to generate form. Yet frequently the resulting spatial arrangements failed to be architectural. For most of the forms conceived through algorithmic and parametric design were so complex, dense, and entangled—featuring proportional relations of such a disjunctive nature—that they could not house a set of human activities in any realistic sense.

110 See, respectively, Kester Rattembury, "Drowning by Numbers," *Building Design*, no. 1397 (May 28, 1999), 32, and Piet Vollaard, "Informal [by] Cecil Balmond [Book Review]," *Archis*, no. 3 (2003), 117.

111 Cecil Balmond, *A+U Special Issue*, 133.

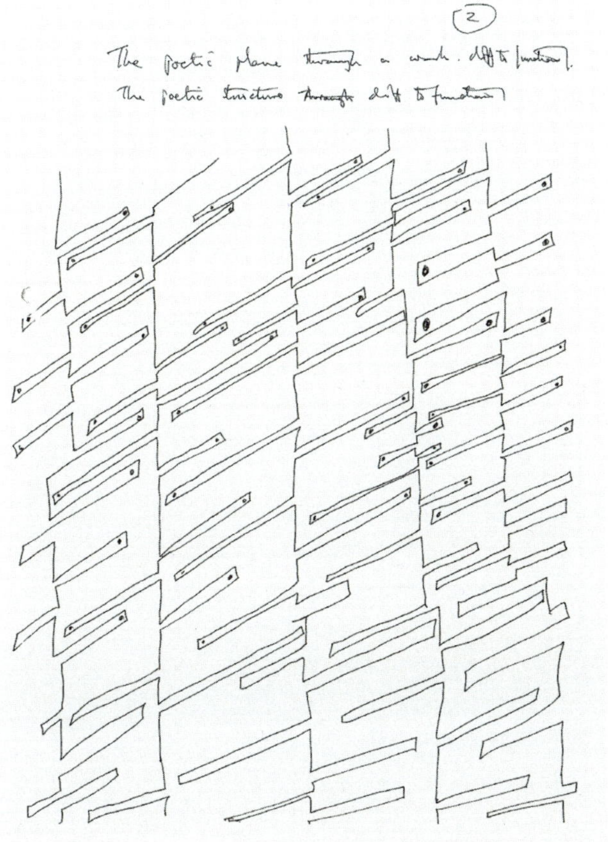

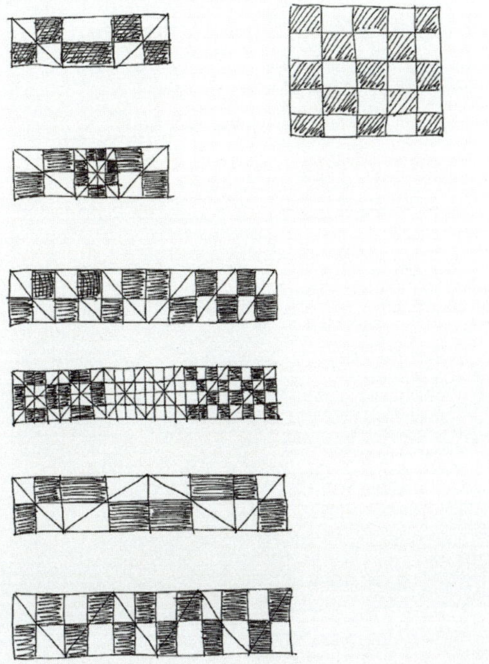

Hence they fell within the domains of computer graphics or morphology, rather than architecture. Working as a structural engineer with architects for decades—therefore having to respond to designs that were architectural in nature—coupled with a strong drive to play a role in decisions impacting a building's design, cultivated in Balmond a certain sense of proportions and spatial relations that naturally surfaced in many of his abstract sketches. Be that as it may, the lack of three-dimensional interiority in the final application of his organizational models—notably those resulting from the structure-as-trace approach—is accompanied by another insufficiency—namely, an incapacity to measure up to the standards of his architectural peers when it came to proposing an overall architectural scheme himself, which will be discussed in greater depth below.

**3.83** Above, left: Single line giving rise to interlocking spaces.

**3.84** Above, right: Typology of vertical trusses.

Following page:
**3.85** Two mirrored sets of numbered L-shapes forming a rectangle.

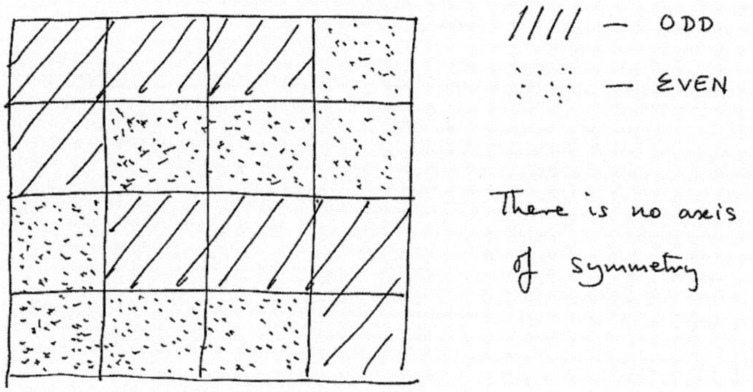


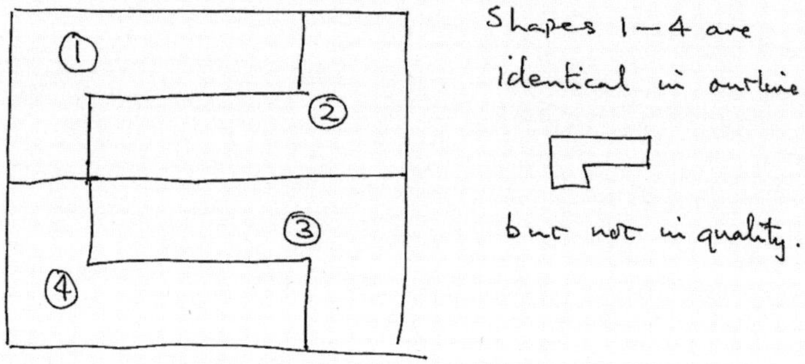


Shapes 1 and 3 are odd numbers –
Shape 1 has to be lifted out of the paper (into another dimension) and then turned over to fit over 3.

Similarly 2 – 4 have the same relationship.

To get 1 overlap 2, shape 1 has to be rotated 180° in the same plane.

180° same plane rotation gives upside down
180° out of plane rotation gives reversal.

## The Dynamic Bringing About the Anomaly

The dynamic character of Balmond's formal procedures establishes the conditions for accidents to occur. For it is the way in which their evolutionary nature is directed and manipulated that brings about the anomaly within an otherwise dominant pattern. There are two ways in which such accidents are prompted, loosely corresponding to the two methods analyzed above: structure as episodes and structure as trace. In the former case, there is an abstract step-by-step series of idiosyncratic decisions that relate to the logic of the pattern at hand only to displace it. In turn, this displacement has direct engineering implications and, by extension, architectural implications too. This approach is evident at Bordeaux, where the conceptual design process may be interpreted as follows. The starting point is an ideal grid in which each point represents a vertical structural element. All vertical supports are confined within two parallel horizontal planes, which means that the bases of all vertical supports are coplanar and so are all of their ends. Next, four points are extracted and induce a different logic. Two points are shifted in plan in such a way that they establish a diagonal relationship with the other two points. Then one point pertaining to each pair—the shifted one and the untouched one—is moved up in elevation. Since each point represents a vertical structural element, the otherwise purely abstract, diagrammatic moves have real consequences. Two of the elements form a structural hanger and the other two a cradle support; a counterweight becomes necessary to keep the whole structure in balance (fig. 3.86–87). This formal procedure illustrates how its dynamic, step-by-step character allows the designer to intervene in it with decisions that create accidents within an ideal grid, to which the scheme remains nonetheless tied.

The second approach involves the so-called "emergent" effects typically associated with nonlinearity. The facade of the CCTV building in Beijing exemplifies it didactically. A generic diagrid pattern with six-story units is agreed upon at the outset. Then, through a number of numerically controlled operations responding to structural parameters, local deformations occur that yield the appearance of accidents across the pattern. These accidents are, in fact, different orders that end up coexisting with the parent one, whose make-up has in turn been slightly adjusted to negotiate the emergence of new ones within it (fig. 3.88).

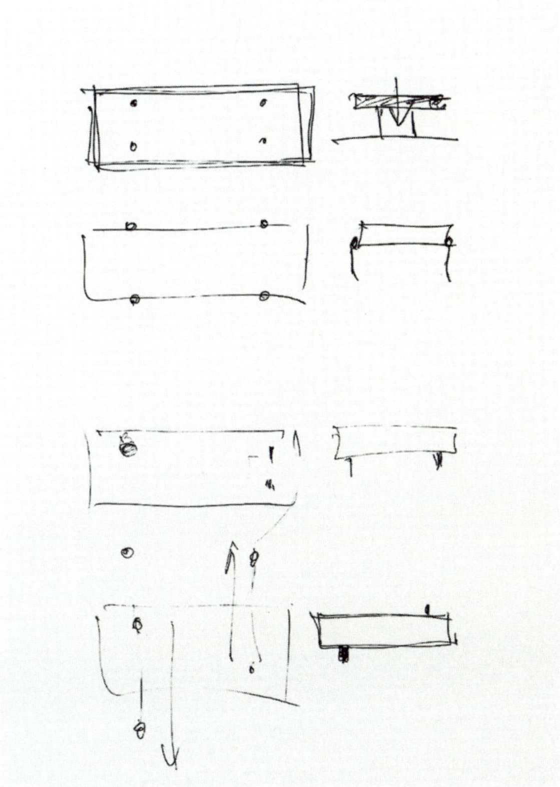

**3.86** Basic diagrams of structural concept for the Bordeaux House.

Following double-page spread:
**3.87** Drawings of structural elements for the Bordeaux House (p. 326).
**3.88** Numerically controlled operations to generate the facade pattern of the CCTV building in Beijing, designed with OMA Rem Koolhaas (p. 327).

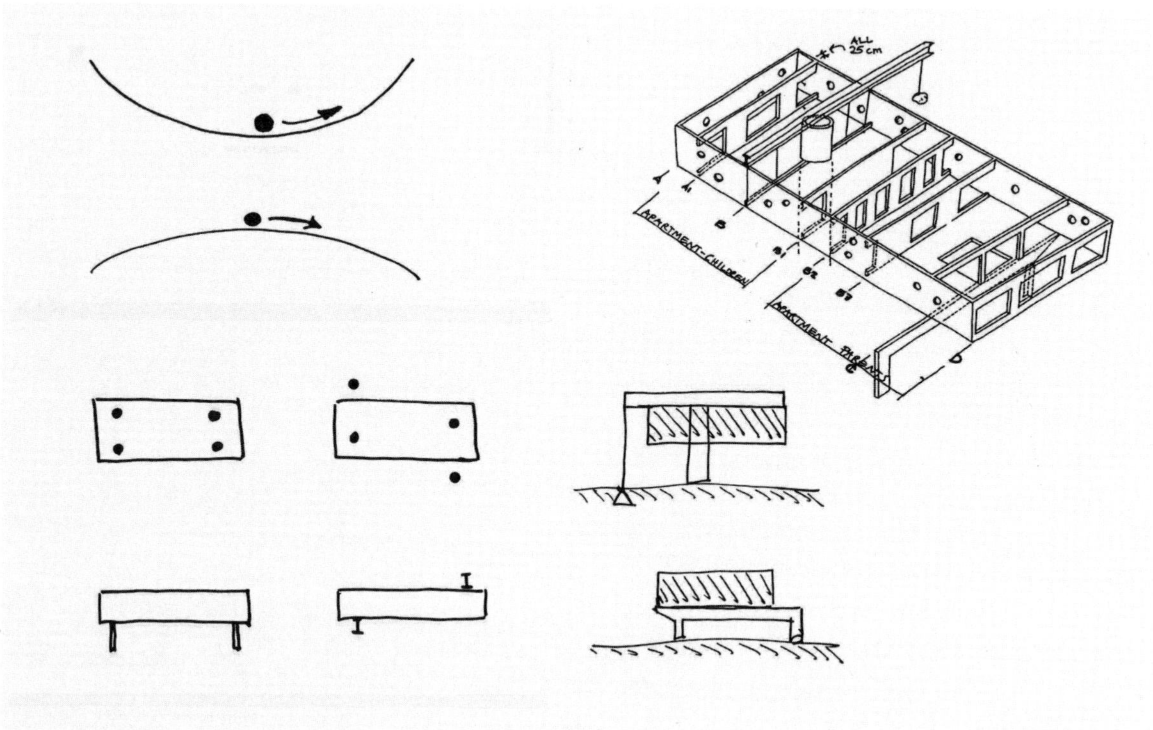
ALL 25 cm
APARTMENT-CHILDREN
APARTMENT PARENTS

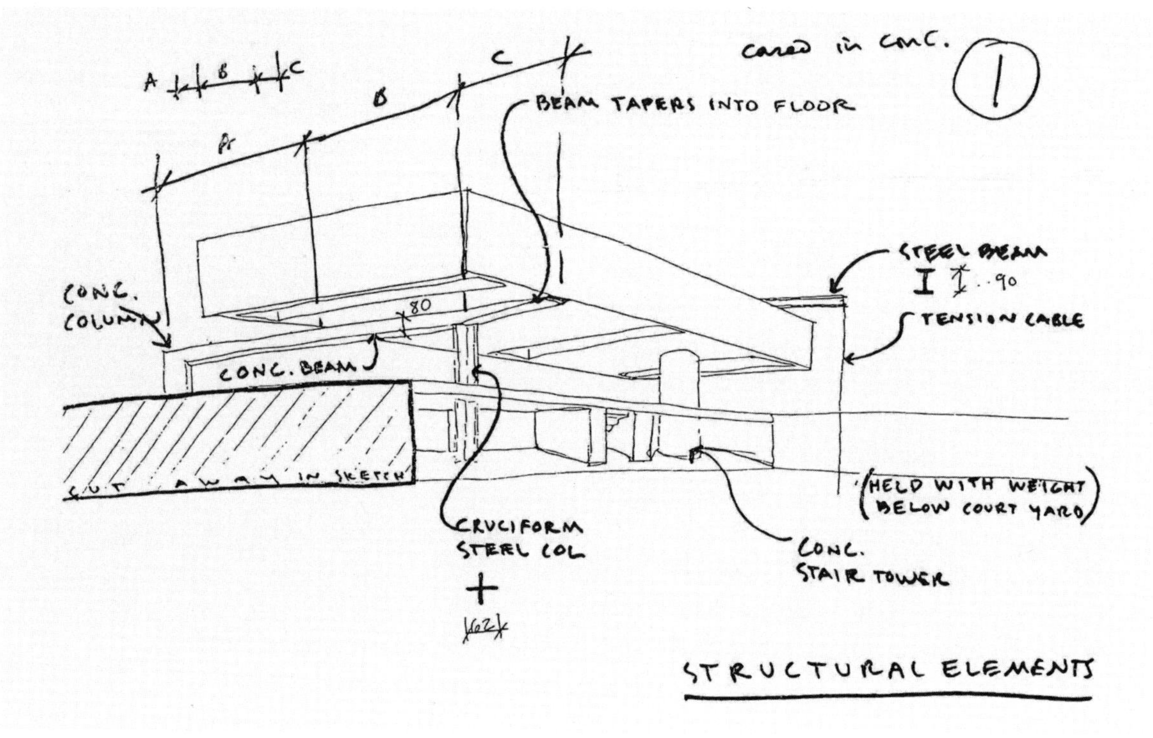
CASED IN CONC.
BEAM TAPERS INTO FLOOR
CONC. COLUMN
80
CONC. BEAM
STEEL BEAM
TENSION CABLE
CUT AWAY IN SKETCH
HELD WITH WEIGHT BELOW COURT YARD
CRUCIFORM STEEL COL
CONC. STAIR TOWER
STRUCTURAL ELEMENTS

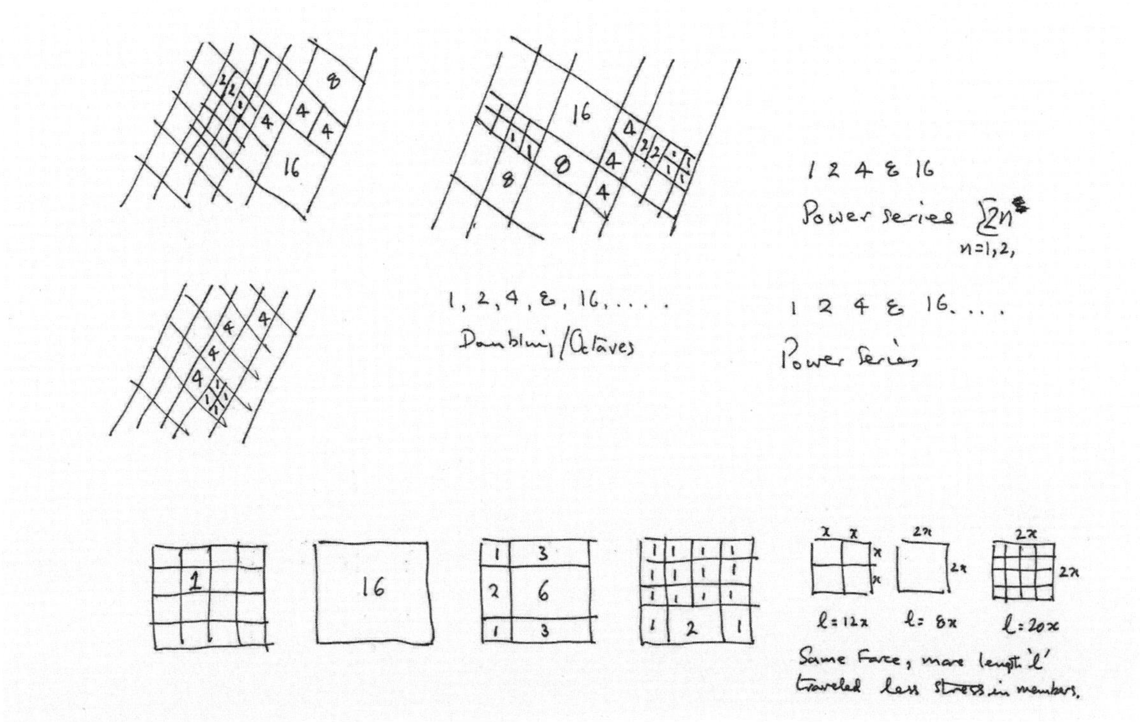
1 2 4 8 16
Power series
1, 2, 4, 8, 16, . . . .
Doubling/Octaves
1 2 4 8 16. . . .
Power Series
l=12x
l=8x
l=20x
Same Force, more length 'l' traveled less stress in members.

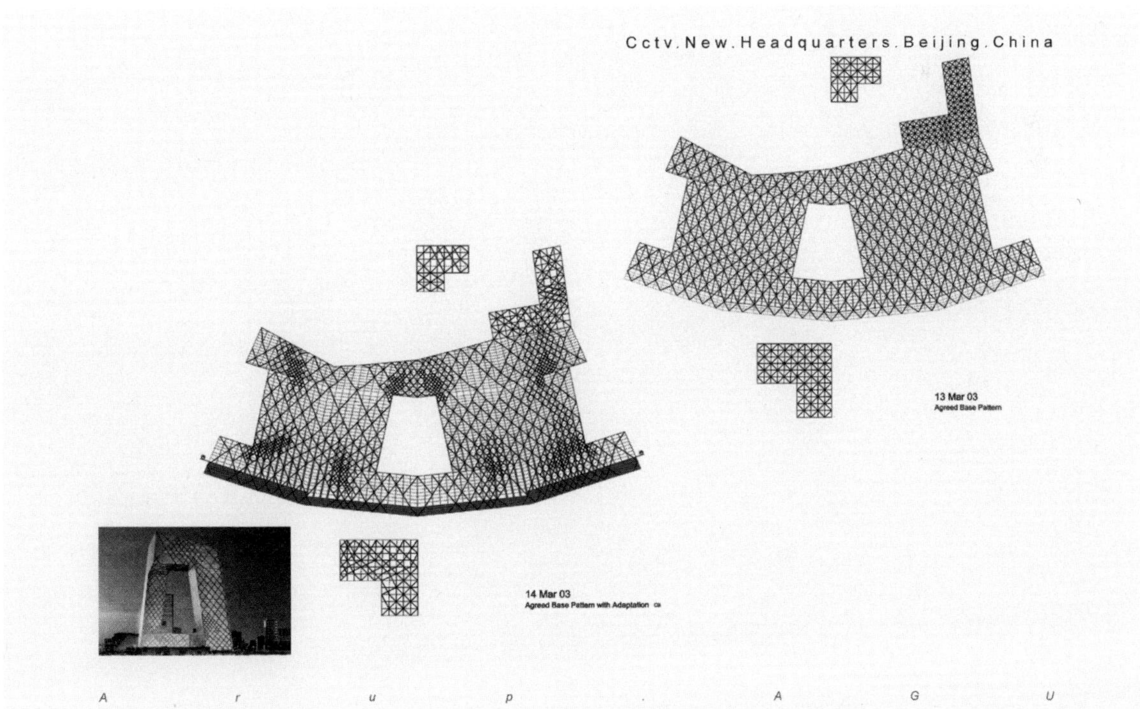
Cctv.New.Headquarters.Beijing.China
13 Mar 03
Agreed Base Pattern
14 Mar 03
Agreed Base Pattern with Adaptation
A r u p . A G U

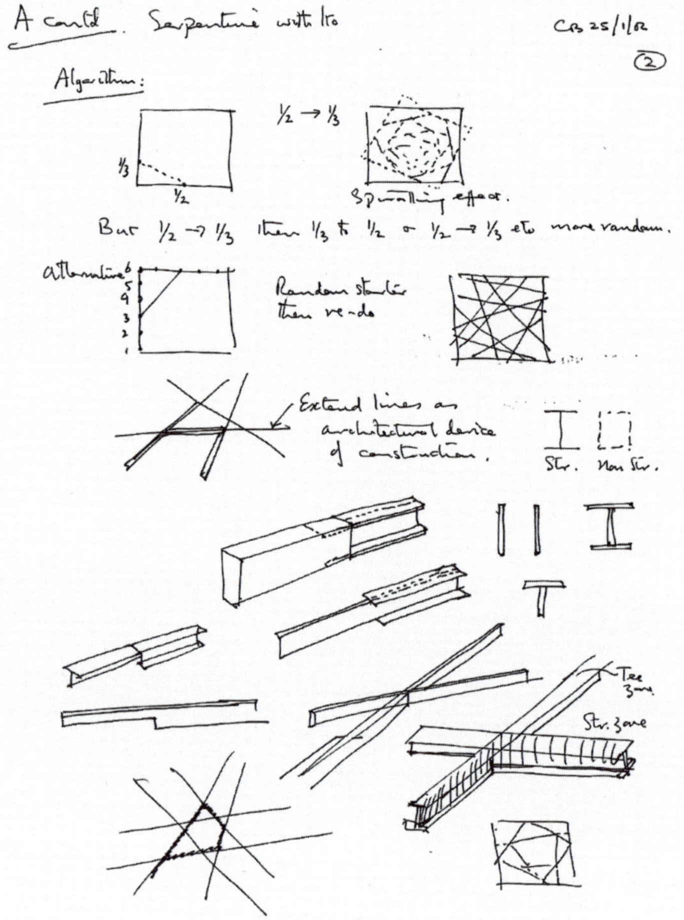


**3.89** Left: Correspondence of structural elements to outcome of algorithm scripted by Daniel Bosia for the Serpentine Gallery pavilion with Ito, 2002.

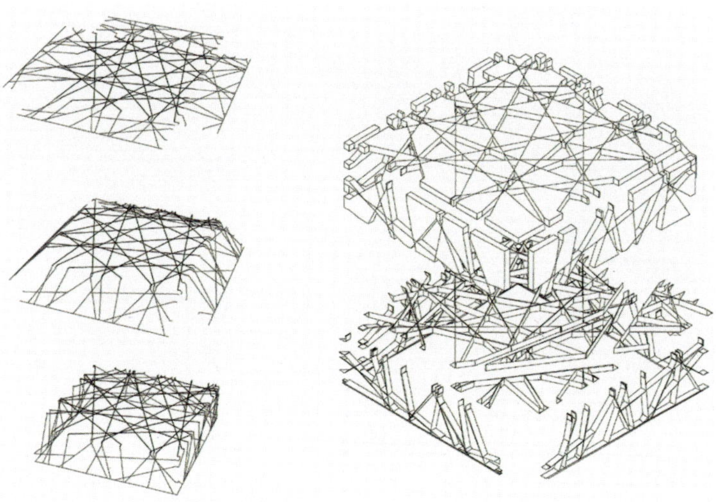

**3.90** Below: Adaptation of geometry to bounding box serving as a basis for the enclosure of the Serpentine Gallery pavilion, 2002.

Disjunctions, singularities, disharmony, redundancies—these and other features distance the final outcome from the completeness and homogeneity of the original diagrid without compromising the overall perception of an ordered yet differentiated arrangement.

## Outcome versus Process Design

It is important to stress that, where nonlinearity and algorithms were involved, there were usually a few independent design moves that either ensured the architectural feasibility of the outcome, or, in the more extreme cases, went all the way through to transforming an abstract pattern into a building. In the Serpentine Pavilion with Ito, a square was deliberately selected as a planar bounding box for the primary algorithm. Then, after running six cycles of it, the lines obtained were extended so that their crossings would supply the structure with enough stiffness. Last, four sections running along the edges of the bounding box were turned inward by ninety degrees so that they could function as the pavilion's wall elements **(fig. 3.89–90)**. Another paradigmatic example is the V&A project. Initially a shifting spiral was numerically generated which was limited to two dimensions. But there was a long stretch between that and the final building. A series of design decisions bridged the gap, involving the calibration of the right turning angle; the unraveling of the spiral in three dimensions; their conversion to wall axes and, eventually, structural panels; the intersection of the spiraling walls so that the enclosure became self-stabilizing without the need for extra columns, etc. **(Fig. 3.91–93)**

If an analysis of the dynamic character of Balmond's formal thinking is key to unpacking the ways in which it negotiates logic and accident, it also points to its weaker aspects. Indeed, while the overall realistic nature of his spatial conceptions—in terms both of buildability and programmatic inhabitability—singled out his production within that of the digital avant-garde from the 1990s and early 2000s, they still shared a marked emphasis on process that bordered on fetishization. In deliberately displacing such an emphasis from outcome *qua* work of architecture onto process, digital practitioners wound up operating in the realm of *process design* rather than architecture. The former's validating purpose does not coincide with the latter's: in the case of algorithmic processes in particular, such purpose is grounded in motivations like the search for morphological novelty, the embrace of errors and anomalies, and a spontaneity in decision making that was meant to counter design frameworks where image and form preceded process. These motivations, relating mostly to pure logic, processual complexity, and computer graphics, were often favored, irrespective of any architectural judgment of the outcome—an outcome whose importance was secondary to begin with.[112] Lack of attention to outcome implied lack of attention to its appearance, the main focus being the nature of the

112 As clearly stated by Charles Walker, one of Balmond's closest collaborators during the AGU years: "[t]ypically in design the author is critically engaged in the result, the solution, but in a divergent process where there are hundreds of potential solutions the author becomes more critically engaged in the process, making value judgments at a number of points along the way." Charles Walker, "A Research Based Model as an Alternative to the Design Based Model of Architectural Invention" (Research symposium 2005: Design as research, RIBA, 2005), 6.

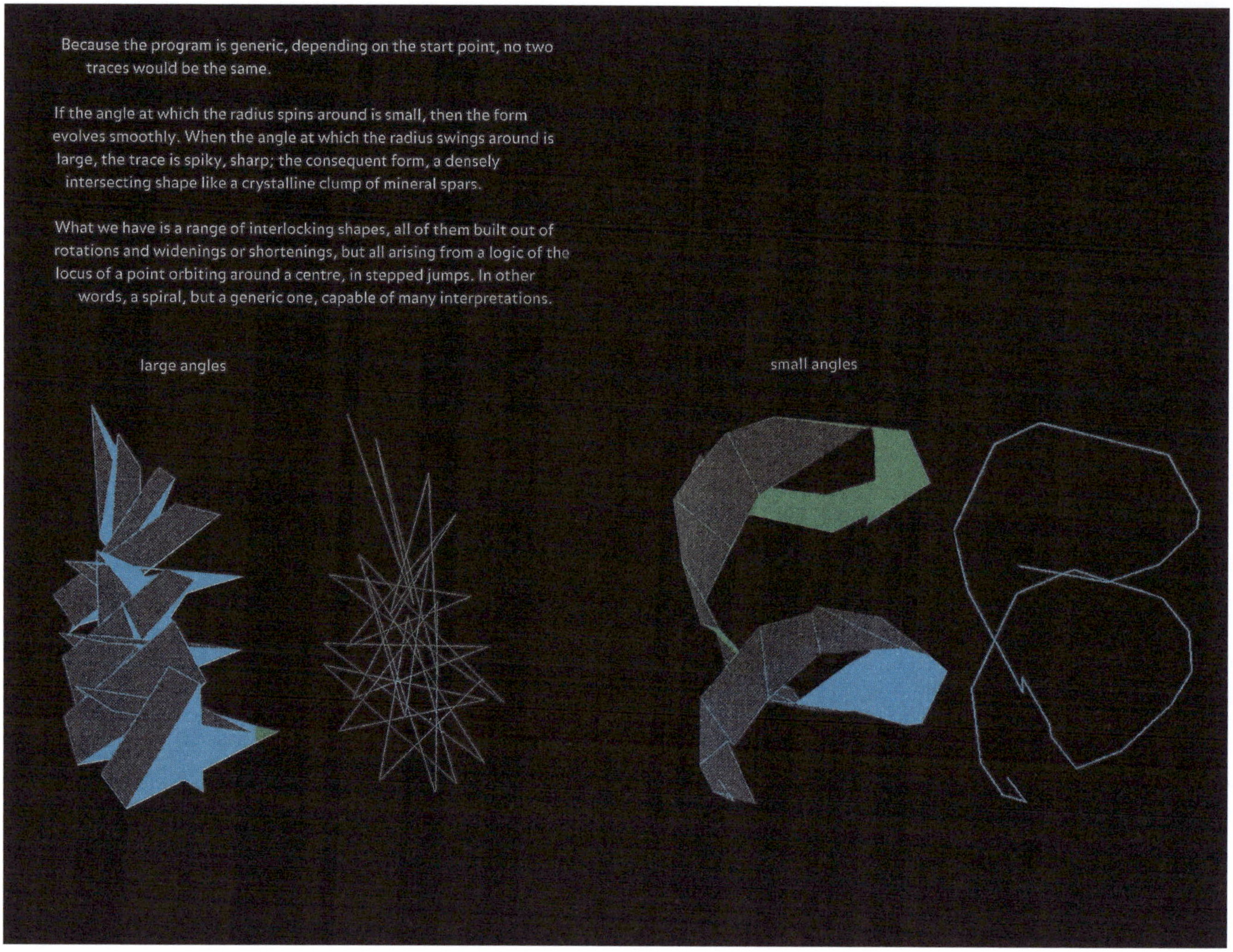


**3.91** Angle calibration of spiral for the V&A museum with Libeskind.

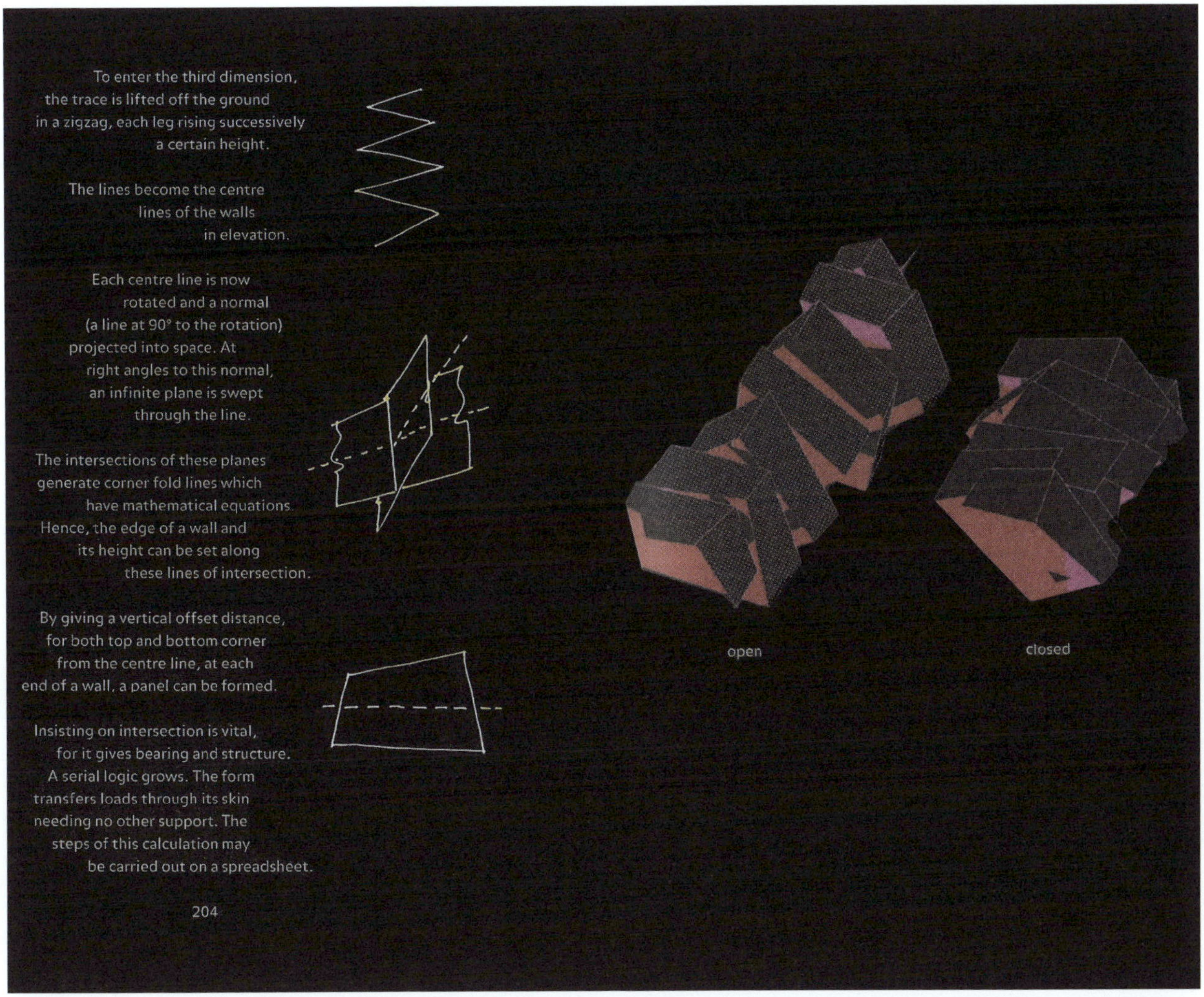

To enter the third dimension, the trace is lifted off the ground in a zigzag, each leg rising successively a certain height.

The lines become the centre lines of the walls in elevation.

Each centre line is now rotated and a normal (a line at 90° to the rotation) projected into space. At right angles to this normal, an infinite plane is swept through the line.

The intersections of these planes generate corner fold lines which have mathematical equations. Hence, the edge of a wall and its height can be set along these lines of intersection.

By giving a vertical offset distance, for both top and bottom corner from the centre line, at each end of a wall, a panel can be formed.

Insisting on intersection is vital, for it gives bearing and structure. A serial logic grows. The form transfers loads through its skin needing no other support. The steps of this calculation may be carried out on a spreadsheet.

open

closed

204

**3.92** Progression from line to closed wall spiral. V&A museum with Libeskind.

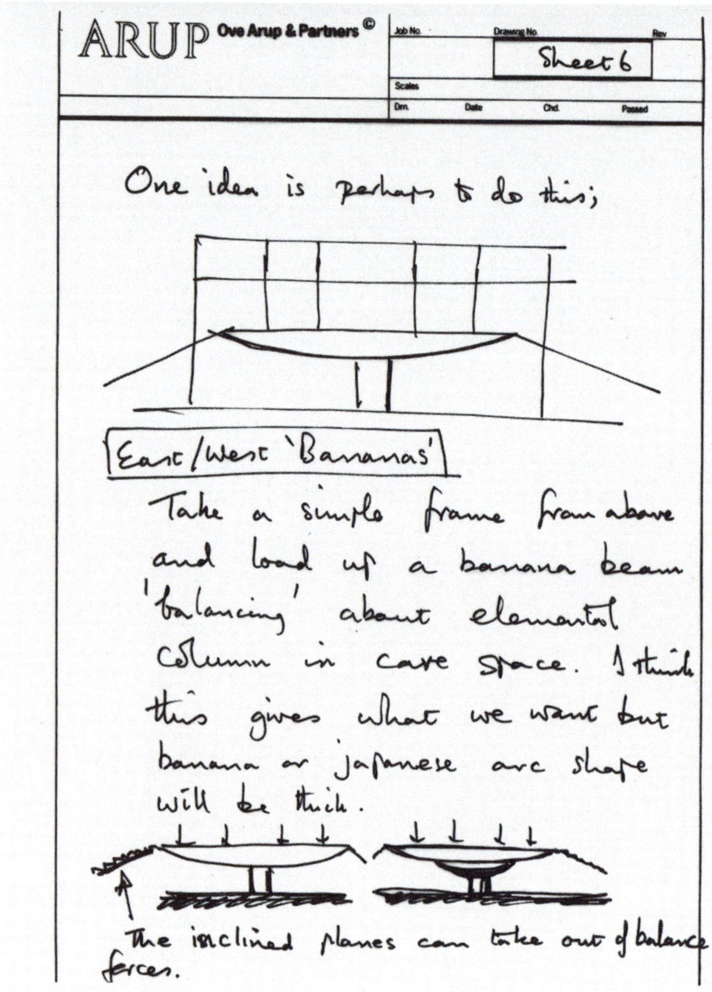


**3.93** Left: Model for the V&A museum with Libeskind.

**3.94** Below: Concept for Congrexpo as proposed by Balmond to Koolhaas in fax correspondence, 1992.

algorithm itself and how its rules are ordered, rather than what the results look like. In other words, *processual aesthetics* subsumed those of the architectural object, a shift in which Balmond partook wholly: "[m]y exploration focuses on the concept of beauty not as a property of objecthood but in the evolutionary process of creating a work."[113]

If most consideration and energy are devoted to process in lieu of result, it is no wonder that such a result may not be that successful. Further, in order to conduct experiments in architecture, it is necessary to have an acute speculative sensibility grounded in knowledge of the discipline in addition to expertise in a certain set of techniques. Such a sensibility cannot be built into any algorithm, which invalidates some people's belief that design choices can be left to them.[114] And if the designer himself does not possess it to the desirable degree—as was the case with Balmond, an engineer by training and, in spite of his design thinking tapping into architecture in significant ways, still a figure practicing for decades in the domain of engineering—then it is no surprise that, whenever he had a chance to propose a fully fledged architectural scheme, this scheme was not particularly strong. Even a cursory look at the few times Balmond had such a chance suffices to determine that his proposals were not outstanding. They turned out to be either somewhat clunky **(fig. 3.94)**, too narrowly focused on a specific sculptural gesture **(fig. 3.95)**, or missing the main concept that the architect in question wished to pursue **(fig. 3.96)**.

## "I AM A PROFESSIONAL PRACTICING ARCHITECT"

The formative years of Balmond's career at ARUP took place at a moment in the late 1960s and early 1970s when a number of central aspects pertaining to the company's modernist tradition were being significantly questioned, whether implicitly or explicitly. For one thing, the emergence and subsequent sustained importance of high-tech engendered a favorable territory for alternative modalities to emerge, although high-tech itself still privileged structural qualities such as purity and efficiency that were directly wired into a modernist sensibility. On a different level, these qualities were themselves also being challenged through the creation of the fourth engineering section in which Balmond was placed, which replaced what was seen as a productive fusion of several of the engineering disciplines with the former concentration on civil and structural engineering alone.

113 Cecil Balmond and Pablo Lazo, "Why Cecil Balmond Never Says No [Interview]," *Log*, no. 4 (2005), 70.

114 Walker, "A Research Based Model as an Alternative to the Design Based Model of Architectural Invention," 7.

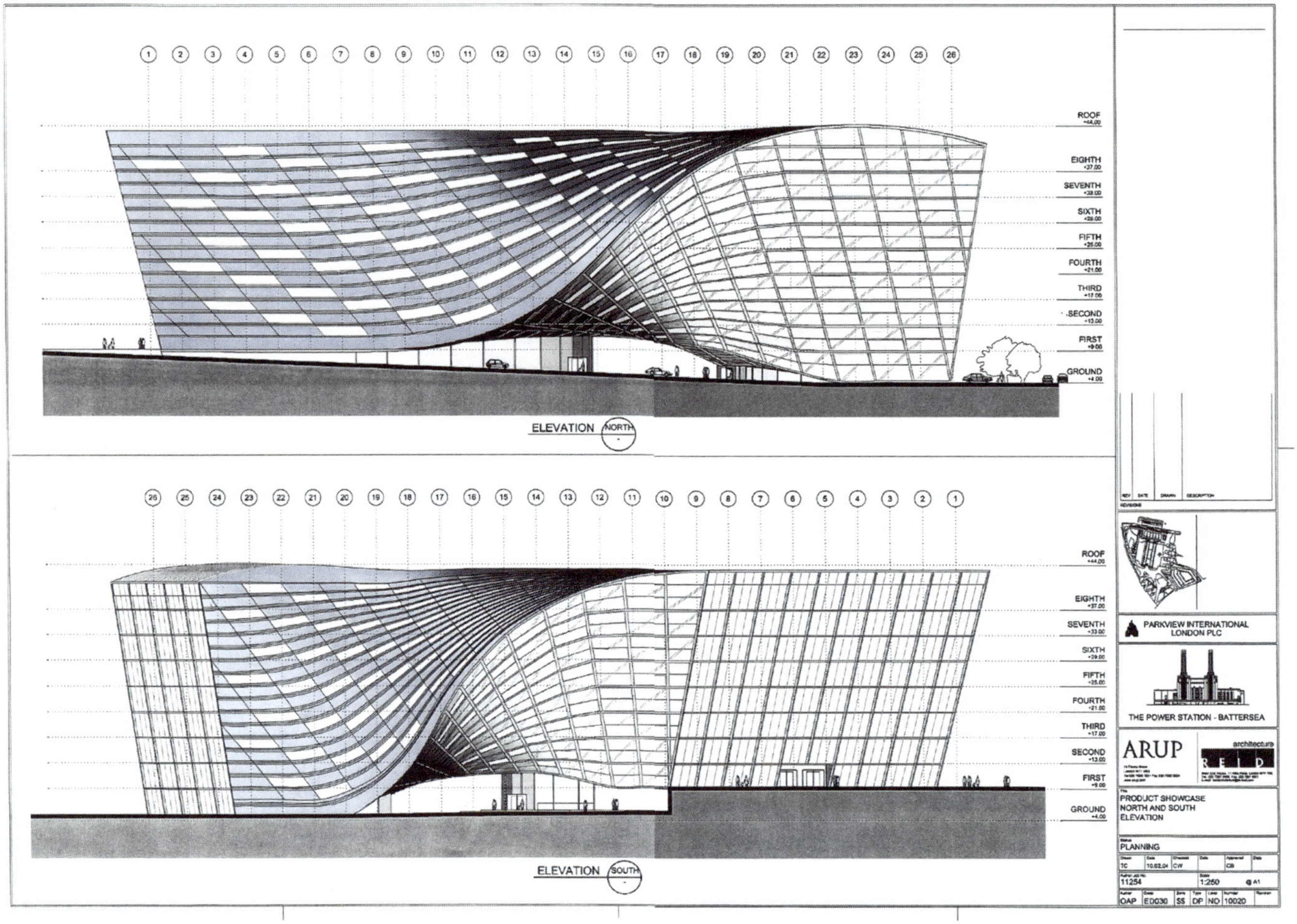


**3.95** "Twist" building as part of the Battersea Power Station Redevelopment commissioned from the ARUP AGU run by Balmond. First concept phase, 2003.

Opposite page:
**3.96** Concept for the Togok Towers scheme in Seoul as proposed by Balmond to Koolhaas in fax correspondence, 1996.

(2)

No obvious way to reduce this effect.
The lower half of the building needs to be torsionally
Strong ← strong skin.

Complex interaction of collar with strong vertical towers will help. Don't know till we do sums.

The beauty & asymmetry & daring of the concept is striking. But my nervousness returns everytime I consider the scale & local effects being so great.

One idea that may help (though it's not as nice I suspect) is to form more of an A frame with lean to & tower (not the tall one)

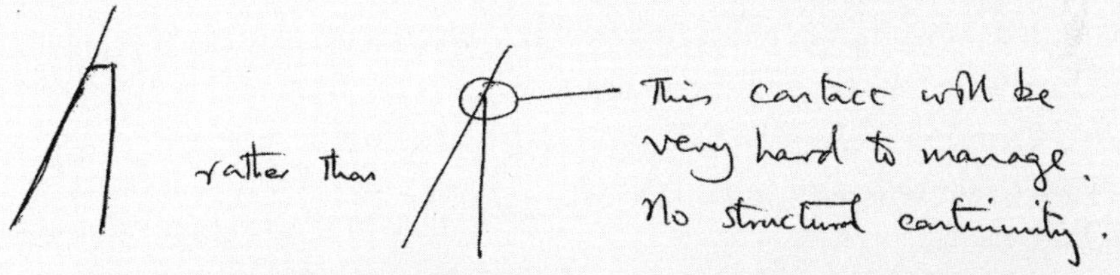


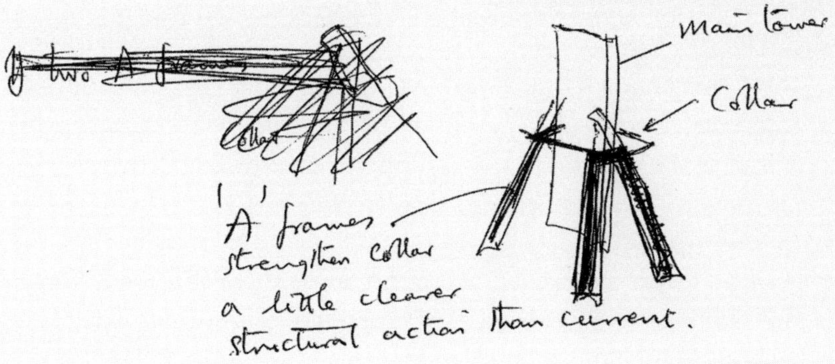

And then there was Otto. His irruption into the company's design and research landscape brought an emphasis on nature as a scientific source for universal principles in engineering; inspired an expressionist, anti-rationalist attitude about design aesthetics; and ultimately ignited an interest in questions concerning nonlinearity, minimal surfaces, and complex morphology through the harnessing of computer capabilities. In addition to avowedly embracing interdisciplinarity and rejecting the specificities of the high-tech approach, here it has been shown that, out of the entire climate of reaction against modernism to which Balmond was exposed early on at ARUP, it was Otto's domains of interest and underlying scientific themes—if not the expressionism of his aesthetics—that appeared to be closest to some of the core specific methodologies and subject matters constitutive of the Sri Lankan engineer's later work and design ideology. It is therefore no coincidence, for instance, that the same criticism of such typical modernist attributes as Cartesianism, symmetry, and fixity that Balmond recurrently voiced are everywhere to be found in Otto's *oeuvre*, even if he never mentioned anything about its particularly defining role.

High-tech was a universalizing design approach that capitalized on the technological expression of construction systems and engineering components. Otto's research into autonomous, form-finding processes and his anti-modernist biological structuralism found multiple parallels in other discursive and cultural contexts. Indeed, the emphasis on the science of these changing sensibilities and preoccupations was characteristic of the shift toward an intense scientization of design taking place at the time across the West. Insofar as this was the case, such sensibilities and preoccupations connected Balmond's specific context to larger disciplinary dynamics unfolding elsewhere. Yet, with respect to the immediate context that provided the boundary conditions for his design thinking to originate and evolve, Balmond—just like Giorgini and Burt—presented two levels of idiosyncrasy. For contrary to how Charles Jencks saw it, his subversiveness did not exactly fit with ARUP's ethos.[115]

## At Odds with ARUP's Ethos

For one thing, Ove Arup's moral dispositions were completely alien to Balmond. He never acted as though he particularly cared about loyalty to the company's aims, which was a priority to the founder.[116] In addition, his unremitting drive to single himself out ran counter to their explicit emphasis on collectivity and flat hierarchy. Balmond's acute sense of politics enabled him to artfully manage himself within the organization in such a way as to advance, and to become a successful businessman in the profession, skillful at establishing and maintaining relationships with both architects and clients. Meticulous in keeping a record of all his sketches—to the extent of, on occasion, rescuing them from the trash—and constantly considering

115 Jencks held that the type of engineer Balmond became sprang naturally from ARUP's organizational framework. See Balmond, *Informal*, 5.

116 Arup, "The Key Speech (1970)", 168.

what might get published, his PR abilities were renowned. Many of his colleagues over the years had trouble with Balmond's tendency for self-promotion, both within the company and with a view to making a name for himself within the discipline at large. Just how much such a tendency clashed with Ove Arup's ethics of keeping singularity in check—"[w]hat we must aim at is to make 'we' include as many as possible as often as possible"—cannot be overstressed.[117]

The second level of Balmond's idiosyncrasy vis-à-vis his direct context involves the stark contrasts between many of the elements of his design ideology—notably, though not exclusively, those derived from chaos theory—and those of the Newtonian convention generally favored at ARUP. Disagreements regarding style and design ideas did but add to Balmond's status as a controversial figure within ARUP, especially toward the latter part of his career. Deemed as lacking integrity, honesty, and consistency when pitted against the ARUP tradition, his engineering approach bewildered a fair number of his colleagues. Moreover, having progressively lost touch with calculations as he rose through the ranks of the company, he was even criticized for often being technically wrong, whether in practice or in some of his publications.[118] But architects did not care. They appreciated the boldness and unconventionality of his engineering proposals as well as the form-making creativity he brought to the table. Ironically, while Balmond did not find it easy to deal with the conservative engineers prevalent in the UK throughout his career, it was that same type of conservative engineer that he would have to call upon in order to have his daring proposals checked.

## Advantageous Externality

Essentially, Balmond interpreted a number of scientific themes in terms of architectural thinking before and independently of architects, and this was mainly because, as shown above, his influences came through the traces that the Otto legacy left in ARUP, rather than through architecture circles. The biological structuralism relating to some of those themes can be found in two guises. On the one hand, it is implicit in chaos theory, since the purpose of this domain of science is to identify underlying levels of order, and the kinds of complex systems with which it concerns itself are living forms. On the other hand, some of these living forms, such as cells, natural tissues, and landscape formations, often served a more direct purpose for Balmond, by way of graphically or behaviorally illustrating some of the characteristics of his informal design framework. The latter kind of biological structuralism stems directly from Otto's methodologies, though it is worth noting that, for all its influence, Otto's body of work comprised mostly roof structures and membranes, whereas Balmond's involved largely three-dimensionally intricate spatial organizations.

117 Ibid.

118 Francis Archer pointed this out specifically about *Number 9* in interview with the author conducted in London on October 14, 2013.

Balmond's subversive disciplinarity enabled his anticipation. Indeed, it only makes sense that engineering, a more intensely scientifically based domain than architecture, seized upon complexity theories, nonlinearity, and algorithms well before architecture did. The externality of his point of departure being engineering also allowed him to single himself out within the digital avant-garde of the 1990s and 2000s, and by extension within the larger shift toward an intense scientization of design in architecture of which the digital avant-garde was in many ways the culmination. For it was Balmond's engineering mindset that endowed his spatial organizations with the twofold structural awareness necessary for their realistic, architectural conception as a building's primary spatial matrix, and this combination of feasibility and domain of applicability stands in stark contrast to remaining within the confines of academia, or limiting design outcomes to product and furniture design, computer graphics, facades and 2D surfaces, and small pavilions—these being the two most pervasive tendencies characterizing the digital avant-garde. That said, the majority of Balmond's spatial organizations resulting from the structure-as-trace approach (i.e., those most specifically involving nonlinearity and algorithmic logic) primarily found a bidimensional application despite their inherent or easily derivable three-dimensionality. In other words, Balmond ended up falling short when it came to the development of such spatial organizations into fully fledged designs and realized projects—spatial organizations otherwise featuring a constitutive twofold structural awareness that distinguished them within the overall production of "digital" designers. It is suggested here that this and other shortcomings as regards outcome have to do with a certain fetishization of process design that Balmond shared with the digital avant-garde.

### Absolute Newness

Balmond's terminological inconsistencies, especially around the notion of randomness—acceptable if relating to chance, not acceptable if synonymous with arbitrariness—as well as the conflict between the pursuit of universals and the rejection of absolutes, ought to be seen as the natural discursive manifestations of his attempts to orchestrate chance and lawfulness of form in design at the same time. As Jean Petitot explained, the neo-Darwinian paradigm—the one into which Balmond believed himself to be tapping—is characterized precisely by an obscuring of the intelligibility of morphological processes owing to its denial of any lawfulness of form in favor of such processes being solely the "by-product of evolutionary chance."[119] A structuralist approach, on the other hand, would posit the prevalence of an organized system whose internal relations satisfy some formal lawfulness. Contrary to what he thought, what Balmond was seeking all along was not a neo-Darwinian approach, but rather what Petitot called *dynamical structuralism*,

119 Jean Petitot, *Morphogenesis of Meaning; Trans. by Franson Manjali* (Bern; New York, NY: PLang, 2004), 31.

whereby the positional information of every element comprising a formal structure embodies a synthesis of both evolutionary emergence in time and a pattern of internal relations describable *a priori*.[120] That said, only a relatively reduced segment of his work in design materialized this dynamical structuralism comprehensively enough. The Serpentine Pavilion with Ito—featuring both components generated through a time-based procedure and an ascertainable organization of underlying, rotating squares—constitutes perhaps the most successful example.

The discrepancies found in Balmond's conceptual terminology make it problematic to transfer his ideal of integrity from the domain of design to that of the discursive foundations underpinning his theoretical constructions. However, the combination of this semantic instability with the stability lent by the notions and arguments that consistently reappeared across such constructions may also be seen as the result of rehearsing, across his intellectual production, the same qualities with which he tried to endow his structures, even if he never claimed to be doing so.[121] His near-obsession with obtaining formal emergence out of the unforeseeable appears partly as a by-product of an ability to operate with a fuzzy logic involving both certainties and uncertainties—though in the light of his considerable ambition, it is hard not to also see it as a relentless search for what Jacques Monod called *absolute newness*.[122]

## An Acute Attention to the Local Condition

The scientific basis Balmond used to generate and qualify this fuzzy logic received criticism from all sides. For some, much of it was "a repetition of classical maths rather than offering moments of great insight."[123] For others, it was too complicated for the general public.[124] There is certainly some truth to these views. However, it would be wrong to pass judgment on Balmond only on the basis of scientific innovation and comprehensibility. For, as attempted in this chapter, to fully understand his contribution it is indispensable that it be assessed from the standpoint of design thinking, that is to say, in terms of how he embedded a careful selection of scientific themes within a larger design framework in order to catalyze ideas relevant to both architecture and engineering.

Rather than venturing himself into the conception of fully fledged architectural schemes, Balmond's strength lay in his theoretical contribution, which allowed him to collaborate productively with many diverse prominent architects. Stemming from a *mélange* of certain rules and patterns as well as room for improvisation within them, the instabilities of Balmond's theoretical framework bestowed upon it an operative suppleness that enabled a significant collaborative pliability capable of adjusting to a variety of design approaches. While the recurrence of terms and concepts lent a recognizable specificity to his theoretical framework,

120 Ibid., 32.

121 Both Koolhaas and Jeremy Melvin hinted at the fact that handling such ambiguities may have been particularly natural to a non-European whose background in colonial Ceylon and subsequent trajectory went a long way toward preventing an assimilation of clear-cut cultural boundaries. See Balmond, *Informal*, 9, and Jeremy Melvin, "Engineering by Numbers [Cecil Balmond]," *Architects' Journal* 207, no. 10 (March 1998), 35.

122 "According to modern theory, the idea of 'revelation' applies to epigenetic development, but not of course to evolutionary emergence, which, owing precisely to the fact that it arises from the essentially unforeseeable, is the creator of *absolute newness*." Monod, *Chance and Necessity; an Essay on the Natural Philosophy of Modern Biology*, 116.

123 Wise, "Informal," 104.

124 See Rattembury, "Drowning by Numbers."

the collaborative pliability it facilitated was such that the Balmond who worked with Koolhaas and Miralles seemed rather a different engineer-designer than the one who teamed up with Ito or Ban. Indeed, there was an evolution throughout his career towards a more geometric, algorithm-driven design mindset that ran parallel to, and took advantage of, the development of digital design through the 1990s and early 2000s—the culmination being the AGU, where, under the "research" label, most of the efforts were devoted to experiments in morphology, morphogenesis, and computer graphics carried out without an architectural application in mind.[125] Still, to upset this otherwise evident tendency, projects with Koolhaas not relying on that mindset stretched through the mid-2000s (e.g., the 2006 Serpentine Pavilion in London).

These two Balmonds only shared one of his many attitudes addressing just a subset of the attributes he explicitly criticized: namely, an acute attention to the local condition—whether treated as an exception or as a trigger of an unfolding pattern—as a way to avoid repetition, homogeneity, neutrality, and predictability. Here the notion of "integrity" ought to be read as an ideal through which Balmond attempted to further validate such an attitude—an ideal he pursued on two fronts. On the one hand, it involved the possibility of a meaningful relationship between load-bearing structure and architectural form—with form understood as an organizational model or configuration. This "meaningful relationship" entailed the possibility of having engineering arguments yield formal decisions, however unconventional. On the other hand, it concerned a certain systematicity underlying the processes of form generation, even if such systematicity might not be readily apparent or implemented comprehensively. This approach was meant to accommodate opportunistic breaks and exceptions within rule sets—though also, significantly, it allowed for the inverse. For in some cases an otherwise idiosyncratic gesture is circumscribed within a larger pattern that at first appears absent. The reading of the Bordeaux Villa offered above exemplifies how an external interpretation may at times be required to unveil such a pattern and thus divest the gesture of its purely willful character.

## Architecture-Engineering Hybrid versus Invasion Model

A design thinker at heart, Balmond saw himself occasionally as a natural philosopher.[126] But he was obviously no proper philosopher or scientist, and in fact, at times he admitted as much, regarding himself rather as just a practitioner.[127] Here it becomes evident that the same ambiguity, the same condition on the edge that applied both to his design approach and to some methodological aspects of his epistemology surfaces yet again in the form of contradictory impulses when pinpointing his disciplinary nature as an intellectual. Beyond these contradictions, those who knew him well largely agreed on his profile: a troubleshooter in the early

125 Some of these experiments included 2D Tiling, 3D Packing, Voronoi/Delaunay, Branching, and Knotting, to mention a few. See *Cecil Balmond, A+U Special Issue*, 136–49.

126 Balmond and Ito, "Conversation - Cecil Balmond and Toyo Ito", 49.

127 In an interview with the author conducted in New York City on April 10, 2015.

days, willing to take on the difficult challenges, genuinely interested in design, inspirational though better critic than designer *per se*, and possessing an ability to gather talent around him as well as a great capacity to push things over the limit.

Indeed, Balmond's contributions to the company are not to be ignored. Engineering is often treated as a commodity. Clients feel that engineers are typically competent, and therefore they go with whoever is cheapest. In architecture, on the contrary, clients are more frequently willing to spend more in office X than Y due to the special things the former can offer. Owing to his particular engineering approach, Balmond became a distinguishable choice within his profession and thereby implicitly fought engineering's commodification. This is one of the ways in which he was capable of bringing engineering closer to architecture. The other way, discussed throughout this chapter, was by producing formal organizations attuned to architecture yet conceived on an engineering basis.

Finding procedures to mobilize general rules in order to generate particular outcomes endowed with a three-dimensional potential in architecture qualified Balmond's work to fall squarely into the domain of *the architecture-engineering hybrid*. But this approach is to be distinguished from those few times when Balmond attempted to conjure up fully fledged architectural or even urban schemes, such as the three cases mentioned above or the redevelopment of the Battersea Power Station in London, commissioned in 2003 from the AGU as design principal and master planner. This overstepping all the way into architecture leaves the architecture-engineering hybrid and becomes an invasion of a different discipline—that is to say, one with its own set of specificities stemming from cultural, social, historical, aesthetic, and typological considerations. The architecture-engineering hybrid straddles the two disciplines by producing a spatial intricacy that qualifies as a building kernel while remaining rooted in engineering thinking. In the invasion model, the engineer attempts to go beyond the prototypical phase by defining a piece of architecture to a level of comprehensiveness that requires deep-seated architectural expertise.

Yet this was precisely Balmond's ultimate aspiration. When asked in 2001 why he did not switch to architecture altogether—especially when Koolhaas offered to partner up with him—he answered that, being in his mid-forties, it was too late when he found out what he wanted to be.[128] He kept trying nonetheless: by proposing architectural ideas to architects every time he had the chance; by founding the AGU so that he could enjoy the freedom of doing architecture without entering into conflict with his client-architects; by starting up his own design company upon retiring in 2010. In a moment of self-convincing assertion toward the end of his career, he even awarded himself the definition of "a professional practicing architect."[129]

128 Jennifer Kabat, "The Informalist," *Wired*, no. 9.04 (April 1, 2001): 104.

129 In an interview with the author conducted in New York City on April 10, 2015.

CHAPTER 4

# On Dispositional Intelligence in Architectural Form[1]

The bodies of work of Giorgini, Burt, and Balmond were born out of the contingencies of certain historical developments: the anti-modernist organicism of the post-war Florentine school in Giorgini's case; the Israeli architectural morphology inaugurated by Neumann, in Burt's; a number of aspects central to the ARUP tradition and the emergence of chaos theory, in Balmond's. Driven by a strong individualism, they each turned some of those contingencies into the basis of a design ideology, which they pursued for a period of time that far exceeded that of its original context. In other words, they turned historical contingency into permanent project.

The currency of the more particular elements differentiating each project proved uneven over the years that each designer spent perfecting them, especially in the cases of Giorgini and Burt: the former's organicism did not retain the same interest after the mid-1960s; polyhedral studies of space in architecture lost their grip as countercultural movements faded. Regardless, their projects continued to rest on the same foundations throughout. Their more general elements, on the other hand, constitute the common ground found here that connects the work of all three designers. The shared attributes making up this common ground are typically engineering and yet are attuned to generating architectural configurations, with their characteristic intricacy and relational properties. To enumerate them once again, such attributes include a reliance on an objective basis of knowledge, a reduction of the contextual sphere to that of form itself, an interpretation of nature as a source of patterns and configurational laws, a profuse enactment of procedural thinking, and a lack of emphasis on the experiential dimension.

Giorgini, Burt, and Balmond developed and materialized these attributes in a way that distinguished their work within the entire architecture-engineering hybrid tradition of the second half of the twentieth century and, by extension, within the overarching shift toward an intense scientization of design taking place across the West during the same time period. One central characteristic of their hybrid approach is the twofold structural awareness mentioned in the chapter on Balmond. In synthesizing elements pertaining to the logic of a building's physical support and the organizational traits of form, such twofold structural awareness catalyzes a productive link between the feasibility of a three-dimensional physical frame and its capacity to house a set of human activities. It is this link that was discussed in association with the term "integrity" in said chapter.

1 In psychology "dispositional intelligence" refers to the subject's capacity to discern how dispositions relate to actions; in other words, how personality relates to behavior. For example, if a subject has a tendency to foresight versus not predicting outcome, is he or she fully aware of how that disposition compels him or her to act in certain ways and not others? Attention versus distraction, skepticism versus gullibility, deep logical reasoning versus spontaneous decision-making—does the subject have an accurate understanding of how his or her set of dispositions explain his or her conduct? The use of the term in this book, however, has nothing to do with its meaning in psychology, since "disposition" means different things in this field and in architecture. In psychology "disposition" alludes variously to personality traits and mental ability, while in architecture it involves a rationale for distributing material elements, objects, and activities in three-dimensional space. The term dispositional intelligence, therefore, is employed here to designate the greater or lesser sophistication of that rationale as embodied in an architectural artifact.

Two things are meant by "productive link." Firstly, wherever there is one chief logic governing both aspects of an architectural configuration, an efficiency of design thinking results that would be absent if two separate logics were required—efficiency that is usually favored from an engineering standpoint. Secondly, turning properties and laws typically associated with the engineering control of a three-dimensional physical frame into a generative spatial code in certain ways may push the bounds of possibility of the domain of architectural configurations. Two instances in which this procedure may be accomplished are the veiled coextension of force and spatial organization found in some of Giorgini's schemes (which stood in contrast to either the total neglect of force, on the one hand, or the characteristic determinism of form-finding processes, on the other), and the systematicity of Burt's and Balmond's patterns of form-generation, whether or not readily apparent.

Since the production of these three figures amounts to a rather reduced segment of design thinking and research within the architecture-engineering hybrid tradition, it can by no means be taken as representative of any disciplinary tendencies occurring in the second half of the twentieth century. Indeed, this book does not seek to unearth any such tendencies. Rather, it aims to discuss the basis of a specific kind of design thinking which, rooted in the hybrid condition mentioned above, illustrates an important twenty-first-century phenomenon: an ever-closer rapport between architecture and engineering, and the ever-growing presence of scientifically-minded designers in architecture that comes with it—which in many ways represents a logical evolution of the shift toward an acute scientization of design that had been unfolding over the previous decades.

The historical substrate of this hybrid design thinking has been examined in the preceding chapters. Among other things, it helped address the question posed at the outset, namely, whether it was not until the second half of the twentieth century that the hybrid design approach explored here could have produced three-dimensional organizations in architecture whose genesis and configurational nature were inextricably tied to it. The answer is in the affirmative, for this approach is unequivocally determined by the sources from which Giorgini, Burt, and Balmond drew, and those appeared only in the second half of the twentieth century (or else became known in the design disciplines during that period): topology started to enter architecture in the mid-1950s, with Giorgini encountering it later in the early 1970s; Neumann's architectural morphology emerged only in the mid-1950s; chaos theory began to constitute itself as a science in the late 1970s.

These differences in terms of sources were mirrored by differences concerning the biological structuralism driving each body of work. Giorgini's was a biological structuralism in reverse. He was first attracted to the expressive language of curves and asymmetry he associated with the living world, and then—via cymatics and a number of references in the sciences and engineering—developed organizational logics of formation *a posteriori*. Burt's interest in nature concerned the lawfulness of certain intricate spatial forms—primarily the periodicity of crystals and the structural efficiency of soap bubbles, which he translated into various geometric codes. Balmond looked at the interaction of cells and its intrinsic dynamic characteristics (growth, cooperation, etc.) as well as at the hidden patterns found and rationalized by chaos theory.

Each biological structuralism has to be seen in the light of larger developments taking place when each figure's design ideology was taking its first steps. These developments were indissolubly connected to the larger shift toward a deep scientization of design: the imagery involving hidden structures of nature à la Kepes enabled by the new technologies of visualization from the 1950s; a fascination with modularity typical of practices which, often animated by links to countercultural movements, engaged with morphology during the 1960s and 1970s; the significant growth of the sciences of complexity in the late 1970s and 1980s running parallel to advances made in computation and digitality. In turn, these diverse versions of biological structuralism underwrite the differences singling out each figure's design production, many of which were discussed above. To point out one more at this juncture: in the tradition of Gaudí and Ronchamp, Giorgini was not keen on using polyhedra, even if there was a strong geometric rationale behind his curved designs. Balmond, on the other hand, would employ them, but the potential he found in their organization differed substantially from that focused on by Burt. Rather than repetition, the Sri-Lankan engineer was interested in growth and change; rather than the periodic unit and its univocal determination, he was attracted to the undecidability of the peripheral areas and the zones in between.

It is important to note that the specific architecture-engineering hybrid embodied in the work of Giorgini, Burt, and Balmond stands in stark contrast to the modernist tradition bringing the two disciplines into relationship with one another. Engineers invented forms by enforcing "the rationalist principle," to use John Summerson's phrase in his famous "The Case for a Theory of Modern Architecture" of 1957.[2] Many of those structural forms—such as frames, girders, trusses, arches, cantilevers, and other components comprising a building's structural carcass—were then assimilated into the architect's vocabulary of expression, as noted by Ove Arup and Summerson himself around the same time.[3] The architecture-engineering hybrid here delineated is rooted in the same general rules pertaining to the rationalist principle and yet produces architectural forms, as opposed to structural ones. No assimilation or absorption is possible *a posteriori* with regard to those forms, since they are architectural to begin with. It is for this reason that, as a result of enforcing the rationalist principle through a particular hybrid approach,

2 John Summerson, "The Case for a Theory of Modern Architecture (1957)," in *Architecture Culture 1943-1968: A Documentary Anthology* (New York, NY: Rizzoli, 1993), 234.

3 See Ove Arup, "Modern Architecture: The Structural Fallacy (1955)," in *Ove Arup, Philosophy of Design: Essays 1942-1981* (Munich; London: Prestel, 2012), 47.

designers like Giorgini, Burt, and Balmond accomplished a scientific expansion of the domain of architectural configurations.

Analysis of the historical substrate of their practices yielded an essential understanding of their fundamental differences. In what follows, it is primarily the aspects shared by the work of all three that will allow the consolidation of the theoretical grounds of the architecture-engineering hybrid to which such work corresponds, and through it, a contribution to the epistemology of architectural form.

## THE BASIS OF ARCHITECTURAL FORM

In disciplines like logic, mathematics, linguistics, and computer science the notion of "form" refers variously to organization, structure, syntax, and related terms surrounding a single, distinct domain of signification: that of a certain rationale of internal relations along with a set of descriptors underpinning it.[4] The term "shape," on the other hand, is typically of no use within those fields, which seems hardly a coincidence, since there are no visual aspects fundamentally involved in them. It is different in architecture and the visual arts, where the two terms, "form" and "shape," are often conflated, and therefore where form is commonly taken to encompass the surface elements of an artwork or a building, those the subject apprehends through the senses. As is well known, the tradition of Western philosophical thought considers formal knowledge as that which is not derived from perception but from mental processes alone, as is the case with logic and mathematics. But even if the distinction between form and shape holds in architecture, would it be possible to establish that knowledge of architectural form can only occur independently of perception? In other words, is architectural form, strictly speaking, nonrepresentational? Furthermore, what are the gains of distinguishing between form and shape in architecture to begin with?

The conceptual framework suggested here is centered around form designating the spatial organization of a piece of architecture—the configuration of its internal relations—and shape alluding to surface properties such as volumetric outline, mass, and figural conditions. As anticipated in the introduction, there were several authors writing in the second half of the twentieth century who identified a distinction between form and shape: chronologically, Louis Kahn (1960), Christopher Alexander (1964), Maurizio Sabini (1985), Kent Bloomer (1986), Antonio Juárez (2000), and Adrian Forty (2000). Balmond himself also touched on it briefly in

4 To offer a didactic reference in that regard: philosopher Rom Harré suggested the terms "structural" and "organizational" as alternative qualifiers for what he called "formal" concepts in science. See Rom Harré, *The Philosophies of Science* (Oxford: Oxford University Press, 1965), 28.

a short paragraph in 2006.[5] None of these figures, however, elaborated on such a distinction or the realm of form *per se*.

The first consequence of focusing on form as posited here is the turning of the piece of architecture into an object of knowledge made up of a set of internal relations in space. This approach was already brilliantly and singularly set up by Bill Hillier in the introduction of *The Social Logic of Space* (1984), although he still used the term "form" to mean "shape," and his goal was ultimately the sociology of buildings, rather than the expansion of the bounds of possibility of architectural form *qua* relational systems in three-dimensional space.[6]

### Form as Organization of *What*?

If architectural form is organization, what exactly is being *organized*? Form involves organization in a twofold sense. On the one hand, it comprises a number of material elements deployed three-dimensionally in a particular way. Form, therefore, *embodies* the very organization of those elements. On the other hand, the resulting three-dimensional ensemble gives rise to a sequence of spaces ordered in a manner linked to—but not coincidental with—that of its material elements. Form *begets* a specific organization of space.

And what about those elements comprising form? Two different sets of elements jointly determine the way the overall volume of space bounded by a building's external envelope is organized internally. ("A building" can be substituted here as the quintessential piece of architecture.) Historically, they often converged into one. But in modern and contemporary architecture, the two sets of elements are usually discernible on the basis of hierarchy and permanence.

There is, on the one hand, a three-dimensional material set of elements providing the primary articulation of space, prior to the introduction of partitions. This ensemble, which generates a first series of subvolumes of programmed space, is here termed *spatial infrastructure*.[7] The load-bearing framework plays an essential role in the materialization of a spatial infrastructure, but is not coextensive with it *a priori*.[8] The greatest number of buildings today are articulated around the quintessential spatial infrastructure of the twentieth century as propounded in Le Corbusier's Maison Dom-Ino: a stack of parallel floor slabs held apart by vertical supports.

On the other hand, the second set of elements that contributes to the compartmentalization of interior space is the collection of partition walls. Partitions are subordinate to the spatial infrastructure, since their placement and arrangement can only be decided in relation to it. Further, the spatial infrastructure remains generally unaltered throughout the life of a building, whereas partitions can be changed relatively easily, as needed. In other words, a given spatial infrastructure

5 *Cecil Balmond, A+U Special Issue* (Tokyo: A + U Publishing Co., 2006), 114.

6 Bill Hillier, *The Social Logic of Space* (New York, NY: Cambridge University Press, 1984), 1–3.

7 An extended discussion of this concept was published in *Spatial Infrastructure: Essays on Architectural Thinking as a Form of Knowledge* (New York and Barcelona: Actar, 2022), 129–149.

8 This distinction is not clear in Pezo von Ellrichshausen's related notion of "spatial structure," even though the very word "structure" partakes in the term. In fact, just exactly in what register spatial structure falls is not clear to begin with. Unlike spatial infrastructure, which is a material ensemble, spatial structure seems to be primarily an abstract, representational construct, since Pezo von Ellrichshausen refers to it variously as a "system of relations" and a "mental image." See Pezo von Ellrichshausen, Spatial Structure (Copenhagen, Denmark: Arkitektur B, 2016), 139–40, 218–19. To be sure, sometimes load-bearing framework and spatial infrastructure are one and the same. At Mansilla + Tuñón's Castilla and León Museum of Contemporary Art in León, Spain, selected vertical extrusions within a pattern of adjacent stripes made up of alternating squares and rhombi provide the main spatial organization for the building and constitute the load-bearing walls. Yet structure and spatial infrastructure do not always necessarily coincide. At FOA's Yokohama Terminal, for example, the material construct engendering the building's spatial organization is a continuous, nondirectional surface—encompassing bifurcating paths, flat open areas, and smooth transitions between levels—which is not itself the primary load-bearing structure. Rather, this surface is held in place by a discrete, bi-directional assemblage of transversal ribs and longitudinal girders.

allows for multiple distributions within an envelope while retaining its three-dimensional specificity. Owing to its hierarchical primacy and degree of permanence, therefore, the spatial infrastructure—and not the partitions—fundamentally defines a building's internal three-dimensional identity.

## Buildability and Inhabitability

Referring to the elements of form as "material" inevitably raises the question of whether form can be considered architectural only when built. Certainly, architectural form can be observed, studied, and analyzed on a computer screen, and to the extent that this is the case, it can indeed exist as an object of knowledge in a digital realm, to pick one not involving actual building. In fact, in the vast majority of instances architectural form originates in mediums other than the building process itself—such as paper blueprints, computer drawings, images, or models—which do not (cannot) replicate the conditions of an actual construction site. However, architectural form is meant to be occupied by a collection of human or a human-related activities, for which it has to be built. Therefore, when dealing with architectural form in a situation other than the erection of the built artifact itself, it must be presupposed that it could be built, which will inflect its conception in a particular way.[9] Concurrently, as suggested above, the load-bearing structure is central to architectural form *qua* spatial infrastructure. For these two reasons combined, the incorporation of engineering in the study of architectural form emerges as a matter of course.

Yet, will *any* conceivable spatial organization of material elements that can be built qualify as architectural form? Certainly not, since the number of these is greater than that of those that can actually be inhabited. For example, due to impossible proportions, excessive complexity, or lack of horizontal surface, many spatial organizations can be materialized which could nevertheless not be occupiable in any practical sense. In other words, the material elements of architectural form ought to be spatially arranged in such a way that the resulting three-dimensional ensemble provides a realistic basis for accommodating a set of human or human-related activities. Therefore, *inhabitability* is a more restrictive condition than *buildability* when it comes to architectural form; inhabitable forms constitute a subset of all possible buildable forms. By the same token, all three-dimensional forms that can be occupied can be built which is true intuitively anyway—which means it suffices to consider inhabitability and not buildability when discussing the grounds of architectural form.

9 At this juncture it may seem that the concept of spatial infrastructure is very close to Kenneth Frampton's "structural unit as the irreducible essence of architectural form," which in turn echoes Karl Bötticher's notion of Kernform. See Kenneth Frampton, "Rappel à L'Ordre, the Case for the Tectonic (1990)," in *Theorizing a New Agenda for Architecture, an Anthology of Architectural Theory 1965–1995* (New York, NY: Princeton Architectural Press, 1995), 516–28. Indeed, spatial infrastructure and Frampton's "structural unit" are related, but they are not the same. First, Frampton's formulation designates the structural framework per se–as an assemblage of constructional elements–whereas the thrust of spatial infrastructure lies in the organization of space it begets. Second, spatial infrastructure does not prioritize "the tectonic," unlike Frampton's structural unit. Third, as suggested above, the primary load-bearing framework plays an essential role in the materialization of a spatial infrastructure, but is not *a priori* coextensive with it.

## FORM-PROGRAM

To claim that architectural form is *always already* endowed with the capacity to hold a collection of human or human-related activities is to suggest that *program*—a term that can be used in its contemporary sense to refer to such activities—necessarily inheres in form insofar as it is architectural. That is, architectural form is necessarily inflected with a programmatic potential and as such it incorporates program as an immanent constituent.[10] Along these lines, the notion of *form-program* can be proposed to further emphasize the synthesis of, on the one hand, the organizational aspect of form, and on the other, program as its inherent content, as opposed to an *a posteriori* infill.

A look at the literature addressing the nature of spatial relationships in a work of architecture further substantiates that synthesis. For example, Summerson referred to those relationships in connection with "the physical conditions required for the convenient performance of specific functions" and called them "program."[11] Hillier, on the other hand, associated the organization of space catalyzing the relations between people with the "form of buildings."[12] In other words, some authors accessed the realm concerning spatial relations via form while others did so via program. This is an unmistakable indication that focusing on spatial relations paves the way for dissolving the duality of form versus program. By becoming a unitary construct encapsulating the fundamental aspects bringing the two poles together—those defining the arrangement of material elements making up architectural form in conjunction with the ways in which such an arrangement is effectively attuned to accommodating human occupancy—form-program captures such a dissolution.

### Program versus Function

The preference here for the term "program" over "function" is deliberate. Attempting a thorough discussion of both these domains of signification would require another book, but there is room for at least a few necessary clarifications. Over the last four decades, it is apparent that "program" has evolved towards a narrower meaning than "function." As Alan Colquhoun put it in 1988, architecture's "set of functions" may be taken to designate "what is external to architecture," that is, architecture's role in the civic, cultural, and public spheres, to mention just a few.[13]

10 It is worth comparing this set of propositions to those Andrew Benjamin offered in 2000 regarding what he termed variously as the "interarticulation," "indissolubility," and "homology" between what he sometimes regarded as "function" and at others as "program," on the one hand, and either form, design, or architecture, on the other. Having diverse goals, his epistemological framework differs greatly from the one articulated here; also, it is at times unclear what he meant exactly by "function" or "program." See Andrew Benjamin, *Architectural Philosophy* (London; New Brunswick, NJ: The Athlone Press, 2000), 2–4, 9–10, 72, 74–75.

11 Summerson, "The Case for a Theory of Modern Architecture (1957)," 233.

12 Hillier, *The Social Logic of Space*, 2.

13 Alan Colquhoun, "Postmodernism and Structuralism: A Retrospective Glance," *Assemblage*, no. 5 (February 1988), 15.

Therefore, while it is difficult to maintain a sharp distinction between the two terms, since they are sometimes utilized interchangeably, it still seems appropriate to adopt "program" in its typical contemporary sense—that is to say, as a description of the set of activities internal to the piece of architecture—and thus prevent possible misunderstandings concerning the externalization to other spheres that has come to be linked to "function" more often than "program." In addition, employing "program" helps bypass the problems that, as Forty poignantly indicated, have come to be associated with the so-called "form-function" paradigm since the Modern Movement—problems involving, among other things, behavioral determinism.[14] In this regard, suggesting that form-program ought to be understood as a unitary construct entails that neither side is more important than the other.

It should be emphasized that "program" here is not meant to allude to a particular programmatic package—say, a "library," a "house," or a "museum." Rather, it refers to the basic aspects of human occupancy involved in the performance of any number of activities, prior to their grouping into such pre-established packages.[15] Also, while the study of programmatically inflected three-dimensional organizations belongs in the domain of architecture, research into spatial configurations without any programmatic immanence pertains variously to computer graphics and morphology. The majority of the forms generated through algorithmic and parametric design over the past twenty-five years fell into those two domains. As a result, many of them were so complex, dense, and entangled—featuring proportional relations of such a disjunctive nature—that they overshot the realm of possible programmatic configurations in architecture. By further nuancing its character as a programmatically inflected three-dimensional organization, the form-program qualifier critically distinguishes a given spatial infrastructure from the outcomes of the merely morphological operations to which digital practices have largely limited themselves.

## Gradients of Programmatic Resolution

As a consequence of the above, form, architectural form, and building may be seen as three moments in a gradient of programmatic resolution, from lowest to highest. A form (the moment of zero resolution) that acquires programmatic immanence becomes architectural; an architectural form that is further refined and completed with a number of necessary additional elements (facade, partitions, etc.) becomes a building. Other terms can also be positioned along this gradient. For instance, Balmond's "patterns" (abstract deployments of elements and relations) straddle form and architectural form, whereas his "configurations" (more recognizable buildings in embryo) fall decidedly in the latter's camp—sometimes even further along the gradient. This term, "building in embryo," proposed in relation to Burt's

14 Adrian Forty, "Form," in *Words and Buildings: A Vocabulary of Modern Architecture* (New York, NY: Thames & Hudson, 2000), 172.

15 Cf. "generic function" in Bill Hillier, *Space Is the Machine* (New York, NY: Cambridge University Press, 1996), 223.

production, is but an analogous interpretation of the spatial infrastructure making up architectural form. In its determination, a building in embryo involves a distinct, realistic potential for human occupancy, while a building *per se* results from the realization of that potential into a fully fledged navigation device that houses a particular program—a device including partitions, facades, all-around accessibility, intelligibility of spatial sequences, climatic and environmental conditioning, etc.

The classificatory operativity of the concept of "type" bifurcates into two categories in relation to the gradient of programmatic resolution. Architectural forms can be studied as spatial types: generic organizations preceding programmatic specificity, from a traditional courtyard configuration to Burt's polyhedra and sponge surfaces featuring spatial reciprocity.[16] Buildings, on the other hand, lend themselves to being taxonomized on the basis of programmatic types: models conceived on the grounds of an identity between a fully realized architectural artifact—including its symbolic and representational dimensions—and the package of activities that are meant to unfold inside: from Durand's "examination of the principal kinds of buildings" (e.g., colleges, libraries, observatories, and museums) to the typical suburban American house of the second half of the twentieth century.

When discussing Burt's work, it was suggested that, in some of his pieces of geometry, program inheres directly whereas in others it does so only in incipient fashion. Those pieces where program inheres directly tend to fall in between architectural form and building and therefore show the same degree of programmatic resolution as Balmond's "configurations." Those where program is incipient sit somewhere between form and architectural form and consequently feature the same lack of resolution as Balmond's "patterns"—albeit still embodying a distinct programmatic potential. The design steps that are necessary to push any of these spatial organizations further down the gradient of programmatic resolution may be of a different nature. As a result, they may leave the outcome at a number of diverse stages along such a gradient. In the case of the project for the Victoria & Albert Museum, the decisions discussed in chapter three—involving the unfolding of the spiral in three dimensions, the calibration of the turning angle, the conversion of the spiral stretches into wall axes, and the study of their intersection so that the enclosure became self-stabilizing—took the original spiral from the level of being an abstract pattern to the vicinity of architectural form; somewhat past it, in fact, already on its way to becoming a building. With the Serpentine pavilion, the strategic design moves to pick a square as a bounding box, thicken the crisscrossing lines, extend them to attain enough stiffness for the whole structure, and turn four sections of the bounding box ninety degrees to obtain vertical walls brought an algorithmic pattern nearly all the way to its full materialization as the final piece of architecture.

16 On spatial types, cf. Greg Lynn, "Multiplicitous and Inorganic Bodies (1992)," in *Folds, Bodies & Blobs: Collected Essays* (Brussels: La Lettre Volée, 1998), 36.

It is worth pointing out the difference between these kinds of decisions, containing a certain degree of design specificity, and the steps that would be required to evolve Burt's geometric organizations where program inheres only incipiently to the level of architectural form. Examples examined earlier included his two-dimensional lattices, space networks, and periodic minimal surfaces. In all cases the operations suggested were generic enough for the outcome to be left at a point where it could be read as a building in embryo; a considerable number of specific design steps would still be necessary to turn such an outcome into a building.

The following sequence could therefore be established: form incorporating program only incipiently combines the need for substantial three-dimensional manipulation with a basic yet distinct potential for programmatic immanence; architectural form features a full programmatic immanence owing to its realistic relational properties, organizational structure, and proportions, along with a distinct potential for zoning and enclosure strategies suggested by these attributes; a building actualizes this potential by organizing human activities into subsets through a worked-out system of zoning or compartmentalization, thereby embodying the finest grain of programmatic resolution.

A fundamental consequence of approaching the discussion of architectural form through engineering thinking is the possibility that program inhering in form can be embedded in a numeric basis. In Giorgini's case, numbers control the operations involving rotation, bending forces, and triangular symmetry driving the various topological transformations in such a way that the resulting geometric outlines describe programmatically realistic spatial configurations. The periodicity, symmetry, porosity, permeability, and proportionality of Burt's sponge polyhedra—characteristics that confer them with the condition of inhabitability—all rest on the grounds of the numeric foundations giving rise to such polyhedra. The parameters of the numeric algorithm behind the S-Project—discussed in the context of Balmond's work—are calibrated so that the column pattern and growth they generate materialize a spatial disposition capable of housing the program of a department store, as well as varying angles for the vertical elements that ensure structural stability for the whole scheme. Once again, it is important to stress that this is the very opposite of the dominant tendency observed within the production of the digital avant-garde since the early 1990s, where numeric bases served as platforms to either engender shapes—which, when applied in a building's scenario, resulted primarily in a sculptural envelope detached from an otherwise trite logic of parallel floor slabs—or yield spatial organizations without any programmatic immanence.

## TOPOLOGICAL THINKING AND CONFIGURATIONAL IRREDUCIBILITY

As anticipated in the chapter on Giorgini, the proposition here is that topological analysis can be made instrumental to determining formal singularity in architecture. In other words, it can help identify what it means for an architectural form to organize a bounded section of space differently, which is a necessary epistemological operation if an extension of the bounds of architectural form is at stake. This understanding of topology differs from that in Banham's "The New Brutalism" of 1955, which was primarily metaphorical, and that of Norberg-Schulz in his *Intentions in Architecture* of 1963, where the term "topological" was used to mean little more than "loose" when describing spatial relations. It was only Maurizio Sabini who, in 1985—via Kahn, D'Arcy Thompson, and Le Ricolais—first hinted at a productive link between a more rigorous, accurate grasp of topology and form as "the very ultimate elements of an architecture, regardless of dimensions, defining relationships from a qualitative point of view."[17] He did not, however, provide any further grounds for such a link.

The aspects of topology most pertinent to the subject matter of this book were introduced in the preceding chapters—both in terms of the general theoretical basis (so-called "point-set topology"), through notions such as orientability and connectedness, and also in regard to some of their applications in the realm of geometry ("geometric topology"). Singularity is a quality that can only be identified by contrast with a set of entities that are equal in some fashion. By extension, formal singularity can only be recognized in contradistinction to a set of entities that have the same form.

### Topology in Architectural versus Geometric Terms

In his *Structural Stability and Morphogenesis* of 1972, mathematician René Thom provided a clue for employing topology with a view to establishing formal sameness. It involved homeomorphism, which he considered "the fundamental idea of topology." In his answer to the question "what is form?" he put it thus: "two spaces *A* and *B* have the same form, or are *homeomorphic*, if there is a bijective, bicontinuous map of *A* onto *B*."[18] Expressed in the language of three-dimensional manifolds, a homeomorphism would describe a one-to-one correspondence or

17 Maurizio Sabini, "Between Order and Form. Fragments of an Idea of Architecture," *Rassegna*, no. 21 (March 1985), 24.

18 René Thom, *Structural Stability and Morphogenesis; an Outline of a General Theory of Models* (Reading, MA: W. A. Benjamin, 1975), 152. See also 12.

equivalence relation between points in two manifolds that is continuous in both directions. Put differently, if two manifolds are homeomorphic, then it would be possible to arrive at one through transformations of the other and vice versa. Such transformations may include stretching, bending, rotating, and crumpling, but not tearing, perforating, or gluing the manifold's surfaces, since the characteristics of connectedness and compactness, among others, ought to remain constant.

Homeomorphism being a topological notion, topology being a subset of mathematics, and form being typically understood in mathematics as organization or structure of relations—indeed Thom himself referred elsewhere to homeomorphism as applicable to organisms having the same *organization*—the suggestion presents itself that homeomorphism may be used as a conceptual device to assess spatial organizations in relation to each other.[19] From all of this it follows that, if two manifolds are homeomorphic—that is, if they have the same form—then the two of them will provide equivalent spatial organizations at some fundamental level. That would be the case, for example, with cube and sphere, the two being homeomorphic pieces of geometry. Furthermore, since operations involving stretching, bending, rotating, and crumpling modify the outlines of a manifold without altering its topological nature, the specificities of such contours are irrelevant when it comes to identifying formal sameness in a topological sense. Two manifolds may feature vastly different volumetric outlines and yet have the same form, that is, they may look surprisingly different and yet embody the same spatial organization. Perception of shape, therefore, is of little use when analyzing form.

That said, notions of point-set topology applied within the domain of geometry cannot exactly be rendered the same way when viewed in relation to architecture. Since the conditions of buildability and inhabitability hold in architecture but not in geometry, the two domains rest on different epistemological grounds, and therefore geometric form cannot simply be equated with architectural form, if subsets of the former may intersect the latter. Although only at the level of brief commentary, a few noteworthy clues concerning an architectural interpretation of topology were provided by Juan Antonio Cortés in his "Architectural Topology: An Inquiry into the Nature of Contemporary space" of 2008. By way of examining a number of projects by SANAA, Cortés suggested, for example, that an outline remaining a single line across a series of transformations might be viewed as a marker of topological equivalence (the term he uses for homeomorphism) between two buildings.[20] He also called attention to one of the main factors distinguishing architectural from topological space, namely the directionality imposed by the existence of a gravitational vector which, present in the former and absent in the latter, prevents all sectional cuts of a piece of architecture from being tantamount

19 On homeomorphism in Thom, see René Thom, *Semio Physics: A Sketch* (Redwood City, Calif.: Addison-Wesley Pub. Co., Advanced Book Program, 1990), 105.

20 Juan Antonio Cortés, "Architectural Topology: An Inquiry into the Nature of Contemporary Space," *El Croquis*, no. 139 (2008), 41.

to one another based on the specific relationship that each has with the horizontal ground.[21]

## Formal Sameness

Insofar as two topologically equivalent (or homeomorphic) forms feature the same spatial organization at a fundamental level, it could be said that *topological equivalence reveals formal sameness*. In order for there to be any homeomorphism between two forms, there can be no topological alteration throughout the series of operations transforming one into the other. In turn, for there to be no topological alteration, the so-called topological invariants (e.g., genus, orientability, connectedness, compactness, and the possibility of being mapped flat) ought to remain constant as those formal operations are effected. All of the forms sharing the same topological invariants are—regardless of external appearance—reducible to the same primitive, even though the processes of transformation involved in this reduction process may differ based upon the elements defining the initial state of the form in question. Put differently, a given family of topologically equivalent forms, arranging a bounded section of space identically in essence, is characterized by a specific set of topological invariants. This set of invariants is embodied most clearly in the primitive to which all such forms are reducible.

When interpreted architecturally, those invariants embody the "intrinsic qualitative properties" of a building's spatial organization, to use Cortés's formulation. Yet, again, in the passage from topology into architecture, those invariants ought to be interpreted in the latter's key. For example, orientability—the topological notion indicating whether there is a consistent normal vector at every point of a manifold—can be seen as a marker for the occupiability of either side of the same surface. The vast majority of horizontal surfaces built in architecture are orientable: they have two clearly distinguishable sides, one of which users can step on, the other functioning as a ceiling. Conversely, if a surface is non-orientable, there will be no distinction between a positive, occupiable side (floor) and a negative, non-occupiable one (ceiling) holding throughout its extension. Rather, the opposition between positive and negative side at a given sector will flip at another—without compromising the integrity of the surface—based on how the normal vectors vary. The Möbius strip is a quintessential non-orientable surface, but more complex configurations unfolding three-dimensionally, such as many of Giorgini's geometric manifolds as well as Burt's sponge surfaces, also possess the same property.

Genus, on the other hand, is the topological invariant designating the maximum number of closed curves that can be drawn on an orientable, connected surface without splitting it into two disconnected parts. As explained in the chapter on Burt, the genus value is visually recognizable by the number of "handles" on a

21 "Changes to the horizontal floor, a basic reference point in architecture, affects the nature of an architectural space much more than the shape of the perimeter of that space, or even whether the surrounding walls are vertical or not." Ibid.

given surface: "0" for spherical surfaces, "1" for toroidal ones, and "2" or greater for those of a hyperbolical nature. The architectural equivalent of these genus-related handles are the volumetric absences detectable in relation to a greater volume of enclosed space. Courtyards and patios, for instance, would qualify as absences of that sort. Here, from the standpoint of intrinsic qualitative properties, an architectural form with no courtyards at all is fundamentally different from another with one vertical courtyard, several vertical courtyards, or multiple ones interconnected three-dimensionally.

Thirdly, the property of an outline remaining a single line, as suggested by Cortés, might be read architecturally as another invariant of a topological nature, albeit primarily a bidimensional one. Topologically, a single line is such if it features one edge only, itself. It is undivided; it has only two nodes, one at each end. Lines divided by extra nodes into more edges are topologically different. Architecturally, a building whose perimeter is a continuous line can be said to fall into the category of the single line, while those either delimited by a broken line with sharp corners, or dissolving into a discontinuous perimeter may each be seen as traceable to diverse primitives.

To offer a fourth example, the quadrangular units attaching to one another on any or all of their four sides to house a field of diverse activities in Mansilla + Tuñón's Castilla and León Museum of Contemporary Art in León, Spain (2001–2004) can be interpreted as another topological invariant.

Insofar as topological equivalence concerns itself with essential structures it ignores the fine details that are superfluous to such structures. Thom didactically expressed this precept through examples in biology: two cats may be homeomorphic even if they "do not necessarily have the same number of hairs."[22] French naturalist Étienne Geoffroy Saint-Hilaire took into account little more than the skeleton in order to demonstrate transcendental principles across species and their morphologies. In this regard, earlier in the twentieth century D'Arcy Thompson had employed the term "principle of negligibility." He argued it was mathematicians and physicists who made use of it, rather than biologists—the former concerned with general forms, the latter with particulars.[23]

The analogy in architectural terms presents itself rather easily. Two buildings may feature, for example, cantilevers in different positions, diverse colors here and there, light wells laid out in dissimilar configurations; one may be rather tall, the other low-rise. Yet, if they both share the same essential spatial infrastructure—for instance, a common pile of floor slabs held up by linear, vertical supports—they will be topologically equivalent and will therefore revolve around the same form at a fundamental level.

22 Thom, *Semio Physics*, 106.

23 See D'Arcy Wentworth Thompson, *On Growth and Form* (New York, NY: Dover Publications, 1992), 1029–32.

To be sure, some of those architectural elements and design gestures, though insignificant with regard to a possible homeomorphism, may alter the nature of the spatial organization in question if only a topological frame of judgment applied to geometry were to be considered. The appearance of windows is the clearest example: in topology, cuts and holes would change the nature of a manifold, thereby preventing topological equivalence. But once again, a piece of geometry does not have to be occupied and inhabited, while a piece of architecture has to be, with windows and doors (openings, in general) being some of the elements that are necessary to render a spatial organization inhabitable. Generalizing, it can be said that, where topological equivalence is to be observed, a number of formal elements must be allowed in architecture that would not hold in geometric topology, owing to the conditions of buildability and inhabitability distinguishing the former from the latter.

It must be emphasized that this necessary epistemological adjustment leaves intact the validity of topological thinking as far as architectural form is concerned. It simply requires that proper formal judgment be made when it comes to disregarding any number of elements inessential to the configurative nature of a piece of architecture. Thus, two square buildings with a patio inside will be topologically equivalent even if one has a window on the north facade and the other does not.

## Formal Singularity

If topological equivalence reveals formal sameness, *topological distinctness yields formal singularity*. Every primitive is defined by a unique set of topological invariants; every primitive articulates space differently in essence—plane, cylinder, sphere, and torus being some of the most easily recognizable in geometric topology. Throughout the processes of reduction to these, all invariants as established in topology must be observed. Architectural primitives, on the other hand, share the same property of irreducibility yet incorporate a programmatic potential. For this reason, they tend to display a certain quality of intricacy that is characteristic of spatial organizations attuned to housing a set of human activities—especially as the architectural form at stake moves away from the neutral container.

It can be said, in other words, that architectural primitives are *irreducible spatial infrastructures*. As discussed above, in shifting from a strictly topological frame of assessment to an architectural one inflected by topology, the set of applicable invariants ought to adjust accordingly. The ultimate principle remains, however, unaltered: namely, that each architectural primitive embodies a unique configurational kernel distinguishing it from all others. Insofar as some of Burt's sponge polyhedra featured in *Infinite Polyhedra* constitute buildings in embryo, and every one of these is shown to be unique through a distinct notation describing the elements of its periodic construction (an elementary periodic unit and a corresponding aggregational logic), this subset of polyhedra provides a useful example as to how to demonstrate the irreducibility of an architectural primitive.

## Expansion of the Realm of Spatial Organization

Thom suggested a coextension of form and what he termed "topological type" that conceptually resonates with the framework proposed here in a productive fashion.[24] However, that terminology is somewhat misleading when attempting an architectural interpretation of topological thinking vis-à-vis form. For *any* architectural form does not "typify" in a topological sense. The vast majority of architectural forms, while embodying a transcendental topological type, do not represent it. Only an irreducible form or architectural primitive actualizes a singular configurational kernel—that to which all other forms in its family may be reduced through topological transformations—with the characteristic purity written into the concept of type.[25]

Indeed, only buildings in embryo featuring a property of *configurational irreducibility* may be regarded as topological types in an architectural sense. Further, there is another sense in which the notion of topological type is deceptive here, and it becomes apparent through that of genus. Genus determines the three topological domains most easily recognizable in three dimensions—spherical (genus equal to zero), toroidal (genus equal to one), and hyperbolical (genus equal to two). It may seem that these domains coincide with the number of topological types. Yet, the number of topological types is greater than that of topological domains, since several configurationally irreducible forms may share the same genus value.[26] This clarification also unveils that genus is of limited use vis-à-vis configurational irreducibility.

Any primary spatial infrastructure embodying a previously unavailable primitive expands the domain of architectural form. In other words, configurational irreducibility can be employed as a marker for the extension of the realm of form in an architectural sense. This extension can be deemed to be of a scientific kind if the configurational irreducibility of the manifold constituting the spatial infrastructure in question has been scientifically proven. This is the case for those of Burt's sponge surfaces and polyhedra that are always already programmatic. And so would it be for Balmond's fractal patterns were they turned into three-dimensional articulations of space (as opposed to being merely two-dimensional), for fractals are also known to have a describable, unique generation method.

Addressing formal singularity as a domain of research in its own right enables historically significant contributions to the domain of spatial organizations inflected with a programmatic potential, which otherwise tend to restrain themselves to those traceable to the groups of Platonic and Archimedean solids.

24 Thom, *Structural Stability and Morphogenesis; an Outline of a General Theory of Models*, 6.

25 Greg Lynn employed the related term "topological geometric type" vis-à-vis the nature of the blob, but he did so in a contradictory way. On the one hand, he claimed that "there is no essential difference between a more or less spherical formation and a blob." On the other, he referred to blobs as being "of all different sizes and shapes and irreducible essences." If blobs were irreducible essences, then they would not be reducible to spheres. At stake here is whether the notion of "topological geometric type" in Lynn's sense may have paved the way for an extension of the domain of spatial organizations, or simply provided a label for a set of diverse appearances reducible to known primitives. Beyond the contradiction, Lynn did not address the question of topological types on the grounds of spatial organization, let alone regard program as an immanent constituent of form. Therefore, his topological geometric types were not architectural in principle. See Greg Lynn, "Blobs (1995)," in *Folds, Bodies & Blobs: Collected Essays* (Brussels: La Lettre Volée, 1998), 166, and Greg Lynn, "Blob Tectonics, or Why Tectonics Is Square and Topology Is Groovy (1996)," in *Folds, Bodies & Blobs: Collected Essays* (Brussels: La Lettre Volée, 1998), 169.

26 See Michaël Burt, *Spatial Arrangement and Polyhedra with Curved Surfaces and Their Architectural Applications - Doctoral Thesis* (Haifa, Israel: Technion, Israel Institute of Technology, 1966), 21; and Michaël Burt, *The Periodic Table of The Polyhedral Universe* (Haifa, Israel: Technion, Israel Institute of Technology, 1996), 28.

## THE PROGRAMMATIC REGIME OF GRAPHS, NETWORKS, AND SPECIAL ORGANIZATIONAL ENSEMBLES

Jean Cousin's *Topological Organization of Architectural Spaces*, published in 1970—one year before Lionel March and Philip Steadman's *The Geometry of the Environment*—stands out as a pioneering study centered around the relationship between topology and a mathematical device used prolifically during the second half of the twentieth century to address the question concerning the structure of space: the graph. In fact, this publication reads primarily as a basic treatise on graph theory that ends up delivering a number of architectural applications for graphs.

In general terms, a graph comprises a number of segments representing relations between points which, in turn, represent objects, elements, entities, or domains of some sort. The dominant architectural interpretation—suggested by Cousin as well as subsequent researchers working primarily during the 1970s and early 1980s—involves establishing that the points represent spaces and the segments a possibility of communication or proximity between them. What results from reading architecture into graph theory, in Hillier's later words, is the notion that a graph can capture "the spatial structure of a building."[27] Some topological properties are built into a graph thus construed, insofar as variations to its shape, dimensions, and angles will not affect that which it essentially defines: the system's number of elements as well as the type and number of relations between them (hence some authors, like Ranko Bon, referred to a graph as a "topologic structure").[28]

Such was Cousin's understanding of topology—an accurate basis indeed which, though rather unsophisticated given the number of topological aspects he left unaddressed, contributed substantially to casting graph language as a notation facilitating an understanding of topology in an architectural sense. In addition to this basic understanding, Cousin posited a number of "topological constraints" of an architectural nature, namely direct access, direct views, and as much or as little distance as possible between two spaces.[29] These, however, were built around the notion of "room" as the medium introducing a set of relations, rather than the primary spatial infrastructure.

27 Hillier, *The Social Logic of Space*, 16.

28 Ranko Bon, "Allometry in the Topologic Structure of Architectural Spatial Systems," *Ekistics* 36, no. 215 (1973), 272.

29 Jean Cousin, *Topological Organization of Architectural Spaces* (Montreal, Canada: Les Presses de l'Université de Montréal, 1970), 116.

## Generative Capabilities

In the tradition of the 1970s and early 1980s, a graph whose points represent spaces and whose segments represent connections between was described as an *adjacency graph*. Its dual was termed *plan graph*: here the segments represent the limits or partitions between spaces, the points being the intersection between those limits or partitions. Since plan graph and adjacency graph mutually define each other—with the latter representing relationships between activities making up a program and the former the physical frame in which they occur—their identification is but a marker of the immanence of program to form introduced above. By extension, they can also be read as analytical devices arising naturally out of the twofold organizational sense written into the concept of architectural form: as organization of elements (plan graph) and as organization of spaces hosting human activities (adjacency graph).

Topology is also inherently built into the relationship between a graph and the spatial configuration it represents, since the same graph is valid for many a configuration featuring different angles, proportions, shapes, and dimensions, provided their fundamental relational properties correspond to those of the graph. For the most part, Hillier made analytical use of graphs; he used them primarily to examine sets of spatial relations embodied in existing pieces of architecture. Cousin, on the other hand, employed them to develop a generative approach, that is, to produce architectural configurations out of the planar interactions to which graphs give rise. The procedure he proposed firstly involved drawing up an adjacency graph diagramming a distribution of rooms and connections based upon needs and function, and then a corresponding plan graph representing the rooms themselves—albeit not yet with their final dimension and shape, which would have to be defined eventually by the designer (hence Cousin called the plan graph *topological plan of a building*).[30] The possibility of optimizing the layout of the various areas and rooms in a building according to a given set of requirements implies a functional determinism that has been a typical tenet of building science since the late 1960s. In this regard, Steadman—whose work, however, remained mostly within the limits of the analytical approach—rather didactically used the term *requirement graph* to designate an adjacency graph conceived the way Cousin anticipated.

Suggesting that Burt's tunnel nets or "networks" can be interpreted as the basis of programmatic relationships requires further assessment of the comparison introduced in chapter two concerning the production of Steadman and Hillier—a comparison that now ought to include Cousin's work as well. All three used bidimensional graphs to represent links between the various activities housed in a building. Therefore, these links were comparable to those read into Burt's networks, involving the connective programmatic tissue. Additionally, all three rooted their approaches, whether implicitly or explicitly, in a qualitative organizational sense that

30 Ibid., 128.

the British researchers, in particular, expressed through phrases like "adjacent to," "contained by," etc.

But that is about the extent of the analogy. As a special kind of graph, a network is made up of a repetitive unit, such as a square, a hexagon, or a triangle. In other words, a network is a patterned graph. In the vast majority of his production, Burt dealt with networks, not graphs, since he was primarily interested in underlying order. Further dissimilarities mentioned earlier include the fact that Steadman and Hillier, just like Cousin, operated with architectural scenarios from the outset, while Burt focused on geometry itself; the former's limitation to two dimensions (plan layouts), with the later working exclusively in three dimensions; and the use of computers on the part of Steadman and Hillier—mentioned in Cousin's text as well—which contrasts to Burt's complete neglect of computational technologies throughout his career.

Leaving Hillier aside—since the domain of his contribution was distinctly the sociology of buildings, even if the core aspects of his analytical apparatus were shared—it could be said that, insofar as Burt's networks can be interpreted as expressive of programmatic relationship, their generative character may be assimilable to those Cousin advanced for graphs and those that Steadman rehearsed in the very few sections of his theories concerned with the production of spatial arrangements. However, as discussed in chapter two, there is a second sense in which Burt's networks are generative, namely with regard to the possibility of scientifically expanding the range of available spatial organizations. This second generative ambition is absent from both Cousin's and Steadman's work, which—like that of others figures with similar interests during the 1970s and early 1980s—limited itself to a range of known pieces of geometry (squares and rectangles) and therefore did not offer any fundamental additions to the overall domain of spatial organizations. In general terms, all of these figures focused on the average as a model: average architectures, average pieces of geometry. Burt, on the other hand, was constantly seeking the singular, and through it, to push the boundaries of the average, one exception at a time.

Operating solely from a geometric standpoint, Burt himself never envisaged his networks as bearers of programmatic relationships. Thus, there was no desire on his part to build into them any optimization vis-à-vis functional requirements and needs. Indeed, those networks were not derived out of the application of functional constraints. Rather, it is proposed here that they be taken as suggestive of links between the various activities taking place in a building—which, given the properties of the network in question, may offer alternatives to received ways of articulating programmatic packages.

## Quintuplet Assembly versus Dual Graphs

Burt's quintuplet assembly exemplifies this possibility quite clearly. Essentially, the quintuplet assembly is but a particular type of form-program construct: it is one where a spatial configuration that lends itself to being materialized (i.e., the sponge surface) and a set of programmatic relationships intrinsically determine one another in such a way that the whole features a number of specific attributes, for example, configurational continuity, periodicity, and spatial reciprocity. When interpreted as programmatic links, the quintuplet assembly's two dual networks yield unitary clusters of activities embodied in the close packing's repeating cells as well as a degree of hybridity written into every individual link which results from the fact that each one of them simultaneously belongs to two of those clusters. Thus, an alternate entry point to the organization of activities housed in a piece of architecture presents itself.

It is necessary to clarify that, although the quintuplet assembly as a whole quintessentially exhibits program's immanence to form, its two networks are not to be mistaken as equivalent to adjacency graph and plan graph, despite both pairs being dual. For while the adjacency graph could be taken as analogous to one of the networks—difference in dimensionality notwithstanding—the plan graph is meant to represent the architectural structure itself, rather than a reciprocal set of programmatic links, as the second network does. Differently put, neither of the two networks is the thing itself; it is the surface or sponge polyhedra unfolding in between them that would constitute the architectural structure.

One other important aspect to point out here is the conflict between sameness and singularity underwriting the relationship between a given network and the programmatic regime it brings about. Steadman showed that in some cases a single adjacency graph may be shared by a number of topologically unique plan graphs, which he represented as mosaics of rectangles he termed "dissections." In other words, an adjacency graph is not a sufficient condition for topological uniqueness. Analogously, there are many cases where one single network in Burt's work corresponds to a series of topologically unique manifolds. Since, by virtue of being topologically unique, each one of these manifolds ultimately embodies a different programmatic configuration, it follows that any given network may not be sufficiently specific to encapsulate by itself all of the configurational aspects of a programmatic regime. It will certainly capture a set of core configurational properties common to all of the spatial organizations it may be made to correspond to. But these will possess additional properties conferring on them their topological uniqueness, as the case may be.

This argument can also be illustrated in reverse. When attempting to express the basic programmatic tissue of a topologically unique spatial arrangement, it is possible to do so through a network that may also happen to be the outcome of said abstraction process applied to a different topologically unique arrangement. Architecturally, therefore, the programmatic links suggested in a network inspire a set of possible spatial organizations whose ultimate definition nonetheless requires additional configurational decisions. As regards Burt's production, it is relevant to note in passing that a similar conflict between sameness and singularity also holds for the rapport between sponge surfaces and polyhedra, since it is the case that multiple sponge polyhedra may have the same sponge surface as a referent.

### Discounting Partitions: Rooms versus Regions

The last significant difference to account for between the production of researchers like Steadman and the analyses offered in this book concerns whether or not partitions are to be regarded as the elements establishing a building's spatial organization. Just like Cousin, both Steadman and Hillier understood buildings primarily as cellular dissections or aggregations of rooms, which they signaled by means of the graph medium. By contrast, the epistemological framework proposed here intimates that the organizational nature of a piece of architecture is only traceable to a material ensemble preceding the definition of rooms: the spatial infrastructure.

What appeared as a result of enacting this framework upon an interpretation of Giorgini's and Burt's production was a distributional approach termed soft zoning. Although the spatial configurations they envisioned showed a great number of distinctive particularities, implicit in many of them is a common regime of inhabitability involving two components: the main programmatic areas—naturally with a certain purpose of destination and static character—and a connective tissue comprising a number of transition thresholds. Therefore, rather than building elements that clearly differentiate themselves from the surrounding field (such as walls), in this regime's framework the definition of the main programmatic areas is dependent on those thresholds—spaces which, being more dynamic in nature, can themselves sometimes incorporate program in addition to their connective role. These thresholds and main programmatic areas come closer to the character of regions than rooms: their identity is recognizable, but their limits can fluctuate.

Based on the particularities of each configuration, main areas and transition regions may take on different characters. For example, these various areas in Giorgini's structures featured shifting, often interchangeable characteristics. The main programmatic areas present in a significant number of Burt's sponge surfaces are expansive in character, opening up in at least two directions that tend not to be coplanar, and acting as programmatic condensers as a result of being the confluence of several, clearly differentiated transition regions. Dissimilarities notwithstanding, common to all of these three-dimensional configurations is that the identity of the spatial zones into which they can be broken down is recognizable and yet their limits are not fixed, partitions not being assumed *de facto*.

In the more extreme cases, the notion of fluctuating programmatic thresholds written into the soft zoning approach yields the possibility of *latent arrangements*, anticipated vis-à-vis Giorgini's work. Here the various components of an architectural configuration do not determine a specific compartmentalization unequivocally, but rather give rise to a range of possible interior arrangements among which only one is actualized at any one time, based on how the various areas are merged or separated, organized, and dimensioned. Essentially, the soft zoning approach decodifies the ways in which a programmatic tissue inheres in a given spatial infrastructure by unveiling the dispositional and enclosure strategies intrinsic to its attributes.

In its diverse manifestations and potentialities, the soft-zoning approach favors the possibility of occupying a given architectural form differently over time by avoiding the constraints that come with the relative rigidity of partitions. In so doing, it enables a certain level of hybridization of activities that may ultimately lead to the reconfiguration of received programmatic packages.

## Three Open Territories for Experimentation

Some form-program ensembles ought to be regarded as special types in their own right, due to the particular kinds of characteristics that single them out. Such is the case, for instance, of those featuring spatial reciprocity. Two three-dimensionally interwoven sets of spaces that mutually define each other without ever intersecting may function as an alternative heuristic device for rethinking typical binaries relating to inhabitability—such as public versus private or open versus enclosed—and ultimately materializing them through a number of distinctive spatial qualities.

Another example is the aperiodic property of the quasicrystals in which both Burt and Balmond took an interest (albeit never envisioned in relation to programmatic questions). An aperiodic tessellation is patterned but not periodic. Therefore, if turned three-dimensional, it would provide an organizational model for articulating program that ensures order and avoids repetition, the pattern sections never being self-identical. As a result, the various activities comprising a programmatic package could be combined into different zoning assemblies based on location within the whole arrangement while benefitting from remaining tied to the underlying pattern.

Fractals, more generally, could be mentioned as a third example. As stated in the chapter on Balmond, their self-similar modularity lends itself to addressing a common demand in architectural design for the productive coexistence of various programmatic scales within a single building.

## FORMATION

Throughout the analysis of how these and other form-program ensembles envisioned by Giorgini, Burt, and Balmond came into being, an approach to their origination emerged that featured a number of common aspects. These involve a certain dynamic character embedded in the formation process as well as the grounding of this process in a series of ascertainable patterns. In Giorgini's case, sequences of step-by-step topological transformations driven by geometric and load-bearing considerations gave rise to his vocabulary of curved spatial infrastructures. Burt's networks arose out of the exploitation of the self-iterative, periodic, and translational qualities built into the make-up of an elementary unit. A specific spatial move applied iteratively or recursively to a basic piece of geometry generated many of Balmond's configurations. All of these procedures share a principle of spatial connection between parts which, enacted over time, produces a larger whole. This spatiotemporal unfolding can be interpreted as driven by an internal organizing force, one that takes on different manifestations in each case. It appears most literally in Giorgini's work, playing a few distinct roles (those implicit in geometric schemes, diagrams of forces, etc.). But it can also be read into the translational vector catalyzing the aggregation of Burt's elementary units as well as Balmond's activating actions, to mention the most significant instantiations.

### Beyond Traditional Structuralism

An approach synthesizing sets of internal relations capable of lawful description with evolutionary development over time is best framed in the context of Jean Petitot's dynamic structuralism, as anticipated in the previous chapter for the case of Balmond. In a nutshell, structuralism was a twentieth-century mode of thought invested in the identification of systems of order underlying existing realities. Structuralist thinkers would generally privilege the relationships between the elements constituting those systems of order or *structures* over the elements themselves. These elements were deemed interchangeable yet retained their meaning in their dependence upon the whole, which in turn was independent of its relationship to the elements. Taking his cue from the Goethean tradition, Petitot put forward a dynamic interpretation of the structuralist categories, which he suggested involve "topological intuitions (position, junction, paradigmatic categorization, connection, etc.)."[31] Transformations bound to time imply a diachronic view of the development of form that is fundamentally incompatible with the synchronic, static, ahistorical character of the structuralist notion of structure.[32] Petitot's dynamic structuralism aimed to address such a diachronic view while retaining the positional intelligibility typically afforded by structuralist frameworks.

Aside from being epistemologically closer to dynamic than traditional structuralism, there are a few other differences between the formation approach explored here and traditional structuralism that are worth pointing out. Many attributes are found throughout the production of Giorgini, Burt, and Balmond that resonate with what Stan Allen famously theorized as "field configurations." One is particularly conspicuous, namely the emphasis on the local connectivity of elements—on part-to-part relationships or "local syntax"—instead of the establishment of an overarching geometric scaffolding *a priori*.[33] Somewhat analogously, Thom referred to the multiplicity of "local determinisms" integrated into a coherent, global structure.[34] In Giorgini, an essential local determinism involved the so-called "beam shell;" in Burt it was the elementary periodic unit; in Balmond, the individuated action. As a result of this emphasis on the local, *element* is not necessarily construed as hierarchically inferior to *structure*—a precept that fundamentally opposes structuralist stances. On the other hand, since in most cases the element or action contains all the specific information that yields a particular whole, changing it would result in a different outcome. This local nonreplaceability with regard to overall structure also clashes fundamentally with structuralist views.

Furthermore, structuralist projects aimed to lay bare systems of order which, insofar as they were embedded into pre-existing realities, predated the project's action itself. These systems of order were, in a sense, waiting there to be unveiled, given the appropriate epistemological approach. In contrast to *found* order, the body of work scrutinized here dealt primarily with *constructed* order, for it was the very particularities of their design actions that gave rise to systems of order, these not preceding such actions.

And it was constructed in the more ambitious sense. Some designers driven by a strong contextualism operate within the confines of found order; for example, those unearthing a certain pattern present on their site of intervention which is then turned into the basis for their design's spatial organization. In that regard, found order has a bottom-up quality. Others install a system of order alien to the project's circumstances—hence top-down—but traceable to previous solutions known within the history of architecture or geometry. This is true for the vast majority of cases: invoking Platonic solids and their derivatives, these designers also construct order—insofar as it is not found in a pre-existing situation—but this order is reused or recycled. Instead, common to much of the production of Giorgini, Burt, and

31 Jean Petitot, *Morphogenesis of Meaning*, trans. Franson Manjali (Bern; New York, NY: PLang, 2004), 54.

32 A similar point started to be made in the late 1960s with regard to the problem of signification in Western philosophy and literary theory. See, for example, a 1968 interview of Jacques Derrida with Julia Kristeva titled "Semiology and Grammatology," in Jacques Derrida, *Positions* (Chicago: University of Chicago Press, 1981): 27–28. This interview was first published in *Information sur les Sciences Sociales* 7, June 3, 1968.

33 See Stan Allen, "From Object to Field: Field Conditions in Architecture and Urbanism," *Architectural Design*, no. 67 (June 1997), 25.

34 Thom, *Structural Stability and Morphogenesis; an Outline of a General Theory of Models*, 151.

Balmond, is the setting up of methods for generating organizational patterns many of which, *if interpreted architecturally*, can be claimed to be novel—that is to say, understood as contributions to the general domain of organizational models in architecture. To the extent that this is the case, their engagement in constructed order was of a more ambitious kind, for they largely bypassed the implementation of received formats.

In some instances, especially in Giorgini's and Burt's production, the system of order in question is brought forth through one single framework: topological manipulation of one growing, double-curved surface in the case of the former; incremental aggregation of one polyhedron, in that of the latter. In Balmond's procedures, on the other hand, several frameworks of order are often made to coalesce in the origination of an organizational model, whether their rapport is one of interdependence or one of independence, as discussed in the previous chapter.

## Unfitness of Systems Theory

While the work of Giorgini, Burt, and Balmond does not quite fit with the tradition of structuralist thinking—in spite of the obvious resonances—the same is true for that of systems theory. The intimate link between systems theory and structuralism is well known, the former being a mathematical field closely linked with computer science, the latter a philosophical outlook relevant to a host of different fields in the humanities and the social sciences, albeit born specifically out of Saussurean linguistics.[35]

Certainly, Bertalanffy's concept of "organized complexity" appears pertinent to the epistemology crafted in this book as a basis for architecturally rationalizing the combination of parallel, overlapping, and penetrating spatial systems—as do other concepts playing a central role in systems theory such as causality and teleology.[36] More specifically, insofar as it deals with the "scientific exploration of 'wholes' and 'wholeness'," systems theory seems to be particularly attuned to Burt's production, this being largely about how to generate structured wholes.[37] However, systems theory is also fundamentally about interacting components; indeed about wholes consisting of parts "in interaction." Hence the emphasis it places on the notions of self-regulation and feedback as well as on questions concerning control mechanisms—the latter quite relevant, in turn, within cybernetics. From the perspective of systems theory, these dynamic aspects are constitutive of systems as finalized, fully operational realities, while the dynamic quality found in the work of Giorgini, Burt, and Balmond applies to the ways in which their forms were generated. It is not one they feature once they have come into being, for there is nothing interactive, self-regulatory, or capable of change through feedback loops either in the structures they built or the patterns they generated—nor was any of

35 See, for example, Ludwig von Bertalanffy, *General System Theory; Foundations, Development, Applications* (New York, NY: G. Braziller, 1969), xviii–xix.

36 On organized complexity, see ibid., 34, 93.

37 On wholes and wholeness, see ibid., xx.

that part of their agenda. In this other sense, therefore, the basis of systems theory is completely at odds with the design ideology behind the bodies of work examined in this book.

## Intelligibility and Flexibility

In addition to an emphasis on the local action or element, the other basic characteristic determining the dynamic quality of the generation processes studied here is the relative openness they afforded to the systems they produced—which is another attribute shared with Allen's "field conditions," while being in conflict with what Petitot called "non-compositional totalities."[38] Cases in point include the ability of Giorgini's spatial arrangements to integrate extensions and distortions in size in order to incorporate extraneous entities, whether internal or external to the system; the possibility of adding or subtracting elementary units at will from any number of Burt's geometric configurations—for example, to create programmatic protrusions or voids within the system—without altering their intrinsic nature; and the various ways in which Balmond's formal procedures create the conditions for accidents to occur.

A dynamic quality grounded at once in the generative role of the local condition and the holistic openness enabled by this type of generativity lends a formation process a distinctive combination of intelligibility and flexibility. For the logic underwriting the resulting spatial organization is traceable to an individuated element or action, while remaining flexible enough as it emerges to incorporate differentiation within it.[39] Insofar as this dynamic quality is meant to produce wholes of a specific nature—coherent yet differentiated—it ultimately itself establishes the framework according to which such outcomes are to be assessed. In other words, it turns the formation process into a critical tool. The outcome will be successful to the extent that it embodies a delicate balance between variation and repetition; the individual and the collective; figure and field; diversity and consistency—and in the most sophisticated instances (found notably in Balmond's work), between indeterminacy and order; chance and laws. Moreover, in establishing this framework, such a dynamic quality places a specific demand on architectural epistemology; namely, that it theorize the middle ground, and in doing so, that it collapse those dichotomies.

38 In noncompositional totalities, parts are not construed as independent or detachable from the whole. See Petitot, *Morphogenesis of Meaning*, 34.

39 Cf. Allen, "From Object to Field: Field Conditions in Architecture and Urbanism," 25.

## THE POSSIBILITY AND CONSEQUENCES OF STYLISTIC NONREFERENTIALITY

Once the outcome of the formation process becomes available, the question of style is inescapable. Does the obtained architectural form embody a set of aesthetic elements pertaining to a codified framework that has been established by the discipline's tradition? Is there an alternative to this?

### Style is Irrelevant to Form

These aesthetic elements, typically including decoration, ornament, color palettes, textures, materials, embellishments, and more generally, surface components and details of various kinds, unfold primarily at the level of volumetric envelope and figural conditions: that is, at the level of shape.[40] Therefore, if topological analysis is essential to formal characterization, while perceptions of shape, as stated above, are of virtually no importance to topological analysis, it follows—contrary to much of conventional knowledge—that stylistic questions are of little use when judging form. In other words, the introduction of topology as central to the determination of architectural form makes style irrelevant. Hence it is perfectly conceivable that two spatial organizations identified as formally singular through topological reasoning may be rendered in the same style. The paradox that has emerged in this book is that, while style is practically inconsequential to the problem of architectural form, extending the bounds of architectural form may afford significant contributions to the realm of style.

### Neutral versus Singular Nonreferentiality

Common to most of Giorgini's, Burt's, and Balmond's generation methods is a process-based approach in which stylistic elements are absent from the beginning. Instead, abstract scenarios are submitted to laws made immanent to them, whether they are adapted or taken directly from physics, mathematics, topology, geometry, and some form of pure logic. The resulting expressive singularity characterizing many of the architectural forms they produced cannot be but tied to this search for processual consistency grounded in a scientific rationale and devoid of stylistic motifs. The outcome is therefore doubly self-referential: on the one hand, it is univocally bound to the immanent laws underwriting the formation process giving

40 Cf. Hillier, *The Social Logic of Space*, 1; and Forty, "Form," 161. Hillier specified that the purpose of style has traditionally been that of endowing an artifact with cultural identity or meaning. An element of pleasurable contemplation might be added as well. In a historically situated statement made in regard to modernism, Forty, on the other hand, did not mean form as spatial organization *per se*, but rather something closer to enduring structure, if still to be contrasted with ornament. Granted, certain recurrent formal arrangements and relationships can also be referred to under the label of style, such as in "the modern style" (see Summerson, "The Case for a Theory of Modern Architecture (1957)," 227.) But this conception has been far less common in disciplinary usage.

rise to it; on the other, the format of architectural expression it embodies tends to refer to no codified linguistic framework, only to itself. In this regard, the latter type of self-referentiality engenders what might be called nonreferentiality—that is, a marked absence of stylistic references, which, while not explicitly pursued by any of the three figures studied here, can nonetheless be read into their work *a posteriori*.

Giorgini's curved schemes and Burt's sponge surfaces possess a *singular nonreferentiality*: whether taken individually or as a whole, their characteristics do not echo any given, familiar architectural vocabulary. In contrast, the notion of *neutral nonreferentiality* would be more accurate to designate most of Burt's sponge polyhedra. Considered individually, some of their features do resonate with known formats of architectural expression—for example, a certain kind of conventional abstraction. But assessed as a whole, they do not amount to anything like a recognizable style.

Architectural forms that are singularly nonreferential (versus those merely neutrally so) are capable of contributions to the aesthetic repository of architecture, since their high degree of singularity prevents them from being describable with respect to any received stylistic framework, and this outsideness enables an expansion of the expressive imaginary of architecture. This is then a case where contributions to the domain of form—via processual self-consistency yielding novel organizational models—allows for contributions to the subdomain of shape wherein style unfolds. And the reverse can also be true. In constantly avoiding fixing any aspects of that particular subdomain of shape, Balmond turned many such aspects—like contours, borders, and limits—into themselves regions for spatial speculation. In doing so, it can be said that he turned the kinds of elements that make up the aesthetic repository of architecture into catalysts for contributions to the domain of architectural form.

## Aesthetic Concerns

Balmond's neglect of questions concerning shape along with the abstraction in which his formal procedures were rooted enabled a stylistic nonreferentiality that largely bypassed the kinds of typological and representational references commonly associated with specific styles. However, it is important to emphasize, more generally, that focusing on form (as opposed to shape) throughout generation methods does not mean not caring about aesthetics—a realm traditionally linked with style. For one may well be preoccupied with aesthetic perception on some level even if the main concern remains the production of organizational models.

As illustrated in chapter one, Giorgini's idiosyncratic geometric vocabulary fulfilled a primarily aesthetic drive. Though it is fair to say that his interest lay mainly in spatial organizations, the elements of shape inflecting the sequences of his formation processes—that is, the curve in its various manifestations—were there, consciously or unconsciously, to satisfy a specific aesthetic preference. Burt did not introduce any shape components unessential to the forms he devised, but he did favor a marked aesthetic determinism in abiding by the "beauty is truth, truth beauty" axiom predominant in the scientific disciplines. Here the objective validity of the generation method is made to condition the aesthetic judgment of the outcome. Balmond's processual aesthetics constitute a third instance. He conferred aesthetic value on a number of qualities embodied in his form-thinking processes, such as complexity, pattern overlaps, and a combination of randomness and order.

An emphasis on form as spatial organization can therefore coexist with aesthetic concerns: sometimes they will come through a secondary interest in certain shape-related questions that will be interwoven with the generation methods giving rise to those spatial organizations; others will find a different path. In sum, while style is, strictly speaking, irrelevant to form, nevertheless a realm typically associated with style, aesthetics, still can play a role in the definition of form—which, in turn, when involving singular nonreferentiality, may allow for significant stylistic contributions.

## FROM OXYMORON TO NECESSITY

Answers to the opening questions now present themselves clearly. For one thing, "formal" designates a particular kind of knowledge whereas "form" represents an object of knowledge in the phrase "knowledge of form." Thus, formal knowledge is not the same as knowledge of form. And it just so happens that knowledge of architectural form cannot be purely formal—that is to say, merely analytic, entirely derived from logic. In other words, architectural form cannot be nonrepresentational.

The key to this question is provided by the earlier discussion regarding inhabitability and buildability. If these are necessary conditions for form to be architectural, there is no way to determine them other than through representations in the empirical world. Configurational and relational properties, proportional bases, ratio of horizontal surface per volume—these and other attributes defining the conditions of inhabitability and buildability can only be ascertained via representational mediums, which implies that such conditions are inherently representational to begin with. Typically, these mediums comprise drawings, images, and models of various kinds, although it is also possible to use words instead. If this is the case, however, a description of attributes pertaining to inhabitability and buildability by means of words alone could not rest on a purely discursive process of logical reasoning, but rather on a representational utilization of meaning of the kind to which descriptive passages in literature or journalism often resort, to offer two common examples.

Just like the conditions of inhabitability and buildability, other aspects fundamental to acquiring an intimate knowledge of architectural form—such as those relating to the principle of negligibility, the visualization of spatial graphs, or stylistic issues—cannot be wholly deduced from logical reasoning either. No wonder all of the publications cited here included graphic materials. To borrow an appropriately convenient terminology from the Western philosophical tradition (in particular, Kantian): insofar as observation in the empirical world is required, both essential and supplementary knowledge of architectural form must be obtained through synthetic (rather than analytic) propositions, even if arguments about the concept of architectural form can be made analytically, as demonstrated throughout this chapter. The apparent paradox here is that, while given its representational nature a purely formal knowledge of architectural form is impossible, the concept of form in an architectural sense nevertheless retains the semantic grounds of "formal" from the expression "formal knowledge." These semantic grounds imply a sense of the ruled structure of relations capable of organizing content in a meaningful way, whether that content be mathematical symbols or human activities.

As regards the gains from the distinction between form and shape, the first comes as a contribution to architectural epistemology, introducing a greater degree of accuracy in the understanding of the architectural artifact as well as the thinking that goes along with it. The second has to do with an implicit claim maintained throughout this book, namely, that contrary to popular belief, architectural thinking has not engaged historically with very many forms, but rather with few forms and many variations of shape. This being the case, those few forms have simply been accepted *de facto*—consciously or unconsciously; implicitly or explicitly—while emphasis has by and large been placed on shape. Here the emphasis is shifted to form, which catalyzes an increase in the variety of formal culture as a matter of course, while still allowing for the same richness of aspects involving shape. In other words, a shift in emphasis towards form enables an extension of the bounds of possibility of spatial organizations in architecture, which, given how the formal domain has been delineated in this book, would also have an impact on central questions concerning program.

As anticipated in chapter two, pursuing a boundlessness of architectural forms (as opposed to shapes) contrasts with the tradition rooted in the duality of generic versus specific form, which gravitated around just a few architectural forms (typically Platonic solids and their derivatives). This tradition—at the heart of the historical tendency of architectural thinking to engage with few forms and many variations of shape—yields apparent versus real variability in terms of spatial organization in architecture, provided this notion is understood in a fundamental sense. Indeed, the qualifier "generic" naturally designates a limited number: in contrast, wherever many are to be described, much specificity is required to account for the differences, specificity being the opposite of genericness. The range of buildings in embryo in Burt's *Infinite Polyhedra* is a case in point.[41]

In order to put together the conceptual framework with respect to which these conclusions can be offered, a number of common aspects found across the production of Giorgini, Burt, and Balmond have been taken into consideration. The contributions to this conceptual framework stemming from each body of work can nonetheless be sequentially singled out. Via Giorgini, the liberation of form from shape accomplished through topological thinking releases the possibility of identifying spatial kernels featuring configurational irreducibility. Via Burt, several different rationales and terms are separately described that extend the

41 The dynamic sense written into the concept of form as proposed here also contrasts with the static character typical of generic form. This is, in principle, not connected to the distinction between form and shape. However, in most instances where glimpses of form as spatial organization appeared is a tendency to construe form as dynamic, as evident in the Goethean-Semperian tradition, later adopted by Kwinter.

boundaries of architecture's organizational registers by expanding the number of available spatial kernels and their qualities. Via Balmond, a philosophy of order is incorporated which, taking some of its central cues from the counterintuitive logics of nonlinearity, pushes this formal thinking toward the productive concomitance of some of those rationales and terms within the same architectural configuration. Thus, distinctness, expansion, and concomitance underlie the contribution to the epistemology of architecture made here, one where the oxymoronic nature of form's patterned idiosyncrasy has been turned into a necessary condition for rethinking its bounds of possibility.

## ACKNOWLEDGMENTS

This book is based on doctoral research conducted at Princeton University's School of Architecture. My deep appreciation goes first and foremost to my advisor, Sylvia Lavin, for her generosity in guiding the original project, and for offering her tremendous, singular intellectual acuity. I am also enormously grateful to my additional PhD committee members: Axel Kilian, who has been a constant source of learning on all matters concerning design, computation, construction, engineering, and science in general ever since I was fortunate enough to teach with him at Princeton SoA in 2014; Stan Allen, for not only serving as a key reference point in terms of the theory of architectural thinking, but also for supporting *The Building*, my first significant endeavor in architectural discourse; and Sanford Kwinter, whose work exhibits such true humanism across disciplines and such a level of nuance, depth, and novelty that it has always been a constant model of excellence.

I am particularly thankful to Mary Mcleod, who first inspired an interest in intellectual production when I was a student at Columbia back in 2008; to Beatriz Colomina, for always encouraging ambitious, independent thinking; and to Alejandro Zaera-Polo, for creating a stimulating conversational arena at a key moment in the research behind this work during the 2013/14 academic year. Taking part in discussions about architects such as Kersten Geers, Jun'ya Ishigami, and Momoyo Kaijima right next door to our PhD room fueled an impetus to utilize the discursive power of history and theory with a view to advancing architectural thinking. The Graduate School of Architecture, Planning and Preservation at Columbia, where I started my teaching career in 2013, and later the College of Architecture, Art, and Planning at Cornell University, the College of Architecture at Texas Tech University, and the School of Architecture at Yale University have been equally invigorating environments for the growth and development of relevant ideas.

A number of conversations with Peter Eisenman, Kenneth Frampton, Francisco González de Canales, Juan Herreros, Antoine Picon, Bernard Tschumi, Enrique Walker, and Mark Wigley proved critical to the development of this project. I am also indebted to numerous PhD colleagues at Princeton, Columbia, Harvard, and several other schools in Europe for the exchanges we have had over the years about the rapport between architectural thinking and discursive knowledge—especially Joseph Bedford, Marta Caldeira, Gabriela García de Cortázar, Francisco García Triviño,

María González Pendás, Costandis Kizis, Bryan Norwood, Etien Santiago, Federica Vannucchi, and Aaron White.

Hal Foster and Claudia Brodsky were perhaps the most inspiring professors I had at Princeton outside the School of Architecture. The ambition and sophistication of Brodsky's intellectual reach were not only incredibly enriching in themselves, but crucially also directed my attention toward the deep workings of philosophical thought. In this regard, I should also mention the central role played in shaping my analytical approach by the faculty members whose courses I repeatedly enjoyed in the Philosophy departments at Princeton and Columbia, notably Taylor Carman, Desmond Hogan, and Philip and Patricia Kitcher.

Marco del Francia (who holds Vittorio Giorgini's personal archive), Michaël Burt, and Cecil Balmond were gracious enough to allow access to sizeable collections of materials, and to speak with me extensively concerning the matters in this book. Among the many interviews I conducted, I particularly appreciated those with Giuliano Fiorenzoli, Haresh Lalvani, Caroline Gallois, Rafi Segal, Julia Grinkrug, Robert Lang, David Lewis, and Francis Archer. The continued discussions with Daniel Bosia—a recurrent teaching collaborator and one of Cecil Balmond's right hands during the 2000s—were deeply informative for sections of chapter three. At different points in time, the CCA in Montreal and ARUP London provided helpful assistance in carrying out research, as did Avery library at Columbia and the library at Princeton SoA on an ongoing basis.

I would like to thank Ricardo Devesa for taking on this project and for his wisdom throughout, as well as our outstanding team at Actar—Marga Gibert for her talent and care with the text and design, and Gloria Schönburg and Gabriel Sastre for their commitment, rigor, and reliability. Sonia Hill's brilliant editorial acumen has been essential in navigating the complications of writing in a foreign language.

Most significantly, I thank my parents, José Antonio and Marcela, and my sister Marcela, who, as she herself grows as an intellectual, has become one of my main interlocutors and challengers. For their unwavering encouragement, support, and love, this work is dedicated to them.

**José Aragüez**
Paris, June 2024

## AUTHOR'S BIOGRAPHY

**José Aragüez, PhD**, is a licensed practicing architect heading José Aragüez Architects, a Paris-based office for architecture and urbanism that maintains substantial connections with New York and Spain. Also a writer and an educator, he teaches at Yale University, having previously led graduate studios and seminars at Columbia University from 2013–20 and held the 2020–21 H. Deane Pearce Endowed Chair at Texas Tech. Aragüez obtained a PhD in the History and Theory of Architecture from Princeton University. Earlier he graduated with a Master of Architecture and Urbanism from the University of Granada, Spain (Honorable Mention, University Graduation Extraordinary Award, and 1st National Prize in Architecture) and, from Columbia GSAPP, with a post-professional Master's degree (Honor Award for Excellence in Design) and a Graduate Certificate in Advanced Architectural Research. Aragüez has lectured extensively across Europe and North America—including most of the top schools—in addition to the Middle East and Japan. Besides Columbia and Texas Tech, he has taught at Cornell, Princeton, Penn, Rice University in Paris, and University of Granada. His six-year project, involving the publication of *The Building* (Lars Müller Pub., 2016), is widely regarded in international circles as one of the most significant contributions to architectural discourse in the 2010s. His writings have also appeared in *Domus*, *e-flux*, *Flat Out*, *The Routledge Companion to Criticality in Art, Architecture and Design* (Routledge, 2018), *Radical Pedagogies* (MIT Press, 2022), and *TECNOSCAPE: The Architecture of Engineers* (Fondazione MAXXI, 2022), among other media. His second book, titled *Spatial Infrastructure*, was published by Actar in fall 2022.

## INDEX OF TERMS

## SELECTED BIBLIOGRAPHY


### Introduction

Alberti, Leon Battista. *On the Art of Building in Ten Books.* Translated by Joseph Rykwert, Neal Leach, and Robert Tavernor. Cambridge, MA: MIT Press, 1988.

Alexander, Christopher. *Notes on the Synthesis of Form.* Cambridge, MA: Harvard University Press, 1964.

Angerer, Fred. *Surface Structures in Building: Structure and Form.* Lecture/Essays Series 6. London: A. Tiranti, 1961.

Aragüez, José, ed. *The Building.* Zürich: Lars Müller Publishers, 2016.

Arnheim, Rudolf. *The Dynamics of Architectural Form: Based on the 1975 Mary Duke Biddle Lectures at the Cooper Union.* 30th anniversary ed. Berkeley, CA: University of California Press, 2009.

Arup, O. N. *Ove Arup, Philosophy of Design: Essays 1942–1981.* Munich; London: Prestel, 2012.

Balmond, Cecil. *Informal.* Munich: Prestel, 2002.

Banham, Reyner. "The New Brutalism." *Architectural Review,* no. 118 (December 1955): 354–61.

Bayazit, Nigan. "Investigating Design: A Review of Forty Years of Design Research." *Design Issues* 20, no. 1 (January 1, 2004): 16–29.

Benjamin, Andrew. *Architectural Projections.* Melbourne: RMIT University Press, 2012.

Bergdoll, Barry. *European Architecture, 1750–1890.* Oxford History of Art. Oxford; New York, NY: Oxford University Press, 2000.

Bergson, Henri. *Creative Evolution.* New York, NY: H. Holt and Company, 1911.

Billington, David P. *Robert Maillart and the Art of Reinforced Concrete.* New York, NY: Cambridge, MA: Architectural History Foundation; MIT Press, 1990.

———. *Robert Maillart: Builder, Designer, and Artist.* Cambridge; New York, NY: Cambridge University Press, 1997.

———. *Thin Shell Concrete Structures.* New York, NY: McGraw-Hill, 1982.

Bloomer, Kent. "Form, Shape, and Order in the Work of Charles Moore." In *Charles Moore: Buildings and Projects 1949-1986,* 21–28. New York, NY: Rizzoli, 1986.

Brodsky, Claudia. "Architecture and Architectonics: 'The Art of Reason' in Kant's Critique." *Canon, Vol. 3 of The Princeton Journal: Thematic Studies in Architecture,* 1988, 103–17.

———. "Architecture in the Discourse of Modern Philosophy: From Descartes to Nietzsche." In *Nietzsche and an "Architecture of Our Minds."* Los Angeles, CA: Getty Center for the History of Art and the Humanities, 1999.

———. *Lines of Thought: Discourse, Architectonics, and the Origin of Modern Philosophy.* Durham, NC: Duke University Press, 1996.

Bürger, Peter. *Theory of the Avant-Garde.* Theory and History of Literature, v. 4. Minneapolis, MN: University of Minnesota Press, 1984.

Bryan, James, and Rolf Sauber, eds. "Interviews with Robert Le Ricolais." In *Structures Implicit and Explicit,* 88–91. Philadelphia: Graduate School of Fine Arts, University of Pennsylvania; distributed by Wittenborn, New York, 1973.

Buchanan, Robert Angus. *The Engineers: A History of the Engineering Profession in Britain, 1750–1914.* London: Jessica Kingsley, 1989.

Cache, Bernard. *Earth Moves: The Furnishing of Territories.* Cambridge, MA: MIT Press, 1995.

Cahoone, Lawrence. *From Modernism to Postmodernism: An Anthology.* Expanded 2nd ed. Malden, MA: Blackwell Publishers, 2003.

Chilton, John. "Heinz Isler's Infinite Spectrum: Form-Finding in Design." *Architectural Design* 80, no. 4 (2010): 64–71.

Chu, Karl. "Metaphysics of Genetic Architecture and Computation." *Perspecta* 35 (January 1, 2004): 74–97.

———. "The Turing Dimension." In *ArchiLab: Radical Experiments in Global Architecture,* 490–94. London: Thames & Hudson, 2001.

———. "X Phylum." *Domus,* no. 822 (January 2000): 42–45.

Deswarte-Rosa, Sylvie, and Bertrand Lemoine. *L'Architecture et les Ingénieurs: Deux Siècles de Construction.* Paris: Éditions du Moniteur, 1980.

Dunster, David. "Architectural Form." *The Architectural Review* 221, no. 1320 (February 2007): 36–39.

Durand, Jean-Nicolas-Louis. *Précis of the Lectures on Architecture; with, Graphic Portion of the Lectures on Architecture.* Los Angeles, CA: Getty Research Institute, 2000.

Dutta, Arindam, with Stephanie Tuerk, Michael Kubo, Jennifer Yeesue Chuong, and Irina Chernyakova, eds. *A Second Modernism: MIT, Architecture, and the "Techno-Social" Moment.* Cambridge, MA: MIT Press, 2013.

Eisenman, Peter. "Foreword: [Bracketing History]." In *Histories of the Immediate Present: Inventing Architectural Modernism,* vii–xii. Cambridge, MA: MIT Press, 2008.

———. *The Formal Basis of Modern Architecture.* Baden: Lars Müller, 2006.

———. "Toward an Understanding of Form in Architecture." In *Eisenman Inside Out: Selected Writings, 1963–1988,* 2–9. New Haven, CT: Yale University Press, 2004.

Evans, Robin. *The Projective Cast: Architecture and Its Three Geometries.* Cambridge, MA: MIT Press, 2000.

Finch, Elizabeth. "Languages of Vision: Gyorgy Kepes and the New Landscape of Art and Science." PhD Dissertation, City University of New York, 2005.

Foreign Office Architects. *Phylogenesis: Foa's Ark.* Barcelona: Actar, 2003.

Forty, Adrian. "Form." In *Words and Buildings: A Vocabulary of Modern Architecture,* 149–72.

New York, NY: Thames & Hudson, 2000.

Fraser, Murray, and Joe Kerr. *Architecture and the "Special Relationship": The American Influence on Post-War British Architecture*. London; New York, NY: Routledge, 2008.

Fried, Michael. "Art and Objecthood." In *Art in Theory 1900--1990: An Anthology of Changing Ideas*, 822–34. Oxford, UK; Cambridge, MA: Blackwell, 1992.

Galison, Peter, and Emily Thompson, eds. *The Architecture of Science*. Cambridge, MA: MIT Press, 1999.

Gelernter, Mark. *Sources of Architectural Form: A Critical History of Western Design Theory*. Manchester: Manchester University Press, 1995.

Gerbino, Anthony. *François Blondel: Architecture, Erudition, and the Scientific Revolution*. The Classical Tradition in Architecture. London: Routledge, 2010.

Giedion, S. *Building in France, Building in Iron, Building in Ferroconcrete*. Texts & Documents. Santa Monica, CA: Getty Center for the History of Art and the Humanities, 1995.

Gould, Stephen Jay. *The Hedgehog, the Fox, and the Magister's Pox: Mending the Gap between Science and the Humanities*. New York, NY: Harmony Books, 2003.

Greenberg, Clement. *Clement Greenberg: The Collected Essays and Criticism*. Chicago, IL: University of Chicago Press, 1986.

———. "Toward a Newer Laocoön." In *Art in Theory 1900–1990: An Anthology of Changing Ideas*, 554–60. Oxford, UK; Cambridge, MA: Blackwell, 1992.

Greenough, Horatio. *Form and Function: Remarks on Art, Design, and Architecture*. Berkeley, CA: University of California Press, 1947.

Habermas, Jürgen. *The Philosophical Discourse of Modernity: Twelve Lectures*. Studies in Contemporary German Social Thought. Cambridge, MA: MIT Press, 1987.

Häring, Hugo. "Approaches to Form." *Architectural Association Quarterly* 10, no. 1 (1978): 21.

Hays, K. Michael. *Architecture's Desire: Reading the Late Avant-Garde*. Writing Architecture Series. Cambridge, MA: MIT Press, 2010.

———, ed. *Architecture Theory since 1968*. Cambridge, MA: MIT Press, 2000.

———, ed. *Oppositions Reader: Selected Readings from a Journal for Ideas and Criticism in Architecture, 1973–1984*. New York, NY: Princeton Architectural Press, 1998.

Hegel, Georg Wilhelm Friedrich. *Aesthetics: Lectures on Fine Art*. Oxford; New York, NY: Clarendon Press, 1998.

Herrmann, Wolfgang. *Gottfried Semper: In Search of Architecture*. Cambridge, MA: MIT Press, 1984.

———. *The Theory of Claude Perrault*. Studies in Architecture, v. 12. London: A. Zwemmer, 1973.

Hilberseimer, Ludwig. "Construction and Form." In *The Tradition of Constructivism*, 122–23. New York, NY: Da Capo Press, 1974.

Ingraham, Catherine. *Architecture and the Burdens of Linearity*. Theoretical Perspectives in Architectural History and Criticism. New Haven, CT: Yale University Press, 1998.

Jameson, Fredric. *Postmodernism, or, The Cultural Logic of Late Capitalism*. Post-Contemporary Interventions. Durham, NC: Duke University Press, 1991.

———. *The Cultural Turn: Selected Writings on the Postmodern, 1983–1998*. London; New York, NY: Verso, 1998.

Jencks, Charles, ed. *The Post-Modern Reader*. London: New York: Academy Editions; St. Martin' Press, 1992.

Jones, Caroline A. "Artist/System." In *A Second Modernism: MIT, Architecture, and the "Techno-Social" Moment*, 507–49. Cambridge, MA: MIT Press, 2013.

Juárez, Antonio. "Topology and Organicism in the Work of Louis I. Kahn. Notes on the City Tower." *Perspecta* 31 (January 1, 2000): 70–80.

Kahn, Louis. "Form and Design." In *Louis Kahn: Essential Texts*, 62–74. New York, NY: W. W. Norton, 2003.

Kaufmann, Emil. "Claude-Nicolas Ledoux, Inaugurator of a New Architectural System." *The Journal of the American Society of Architectural Historians* 3, no. 3 (July 1, 1943): 12–20.

Kepes, Gyorgy. *Structure in Art and in Science*. Vision + Value Series. New York, NY: George Braziller, 1965.

Kuhn, Nicola, Helmut Jahn, Werner Sobek, and Susanne Anna. *Archi-Neering: Helmut Jahn - Werner Sobek*. Berlin: Hatje Cantz Publishers, 2000.

Kwinter, Sanford. "Confessions of an Organicist." *Log*, no. 5 (Spring/Summer 2005): 71–75.

———. "Who's Afraid of Formalism?" In *Phylogenesis: Foa's Ark*. Barcelona: Actar, 2004.

Lang, S. "De Lineamentis: L. B. Alberti's Use of a Technical Term." *Journal of the Warburg and Courtauld Institutes* 28 (January 1, 1965): 331–35.

Laugier, Marc Antoine. *An Essay on Architecture*. Los Angeles, CA: Hennessey & Ingalls, 1977.

Lavin, Sylvia. *Quatremère De Quincy and the Invention of a Modern Language of Architecture*. Cambridge, MA: MIT Press, 1992.

Le Corbusier. "On Discovering Gaudi's Architecture." In *Gaudi*. Barcelona: RM, 1958.

———. *Œuvre Complète*. Basel; Boston: Birkhäuser, 2006.

———. *Toward an Architecture*. Texts & Documents. Los Angeles, CA: Getty Research Institute, 2007.

Ledoux, Claude Nicolas. *Architecture de C.N. Ledoux*. Princeton, NJ: Princeton Architectural Press, in association with the Avery Architectural and Fine Arts Library of Columbia Universiy, 1983.

Le Ricolais, Robert. "1935–1969, Etudes et Recherches." *Zodiac*, no. 22 (1973): 17–19.

———. "Introduction to the Notion of Form (1966)." In *Data: Directions in Art, Theory and Aesthetics*. Greenwich, Connecticut: New York Graphic Society Ltd., 1968.

———. "Topology and Architecture." *Student Publications of the School of Design, North Carolina State College* 5, no. 2 (Spring 1955): 10–16.

Leach, Neil, David Turnbull, and Chris Williams, eds. *Digital Tectonics*. Chichester, West Sussex, UK; Hoboken, NJ: Academy Press, 2004.

Leslie, Stuart. *The Cold War and American Science: The Military-Industrial-Academic Complex at MIT and Stanford*. Reprint edition. New York, NY: Columbia University Press, 1994.

Lobsinger, Marie Louise. "Two Cambridges: Models, Methods, Systems, and Expertise." In *A Second Modernism: MIT, Architecture, and the "Techno-Social" Moment*, 653–85. Cambridge, MA: MIT Press, 2013.

Lynn, Greg. *Animate Form*. New York: Princeton Architectural Press, 1999.

———, ed. *Folding in Architecture*. Rev. ed. Architectural Design. Chichester, West Sussex, UK; Hoboken, NJ: Wiley-Academy, 2004.

———. *Folds, Bodies & Blobs: Collected Essays*. Brussels: La Lettre Volée, 1998.

Lyotard, Jean-François. *The Postmodern Condition: A Report on Knowledge*. Theory and History of Literature, v. 10. Minneapolis, MN: University of Minnesota Press, 1984.

Mallgrave, Harry Francis. "Introduction." In *Style in the Technical and Tectonic Arts; or, Practical Aesthetics*. Los Angeles, CA: Getty Research Institute, 2004.

Mallgrave, Harry Francis, and David Goodman. *Introduction to Architectural Theory: 1968 to the Present / Harry Francis Mallgrave and David Goodman*. Malden, MA: Wiley-Blackwell, 2011.

Margolius, Ivan. *Architects + Engineers = Structures*. Chichester, UK: Wiley, 2002.

Middleton, Robin, and M. N. Baudouin-Matuszek. *Jean Rondelet: The Architect as Technician*. New Haven, CT; London: Yale University Press, 2007.

Museum of Modern Art (New York, NY). *Seven Structural Engineers: The Felix Candela Lectures*. New York, NY: Museum of Modern Art: Distributed in the United States and Canada by D.A.P./Distributed Art Publishers, 2008.

Nesbitt, Kate, ed. *Theorizing a New Agenda for Architecture: An Anthology of Architectural Theory 1965–1995*. New York, NY: Princeton Architectural Press, 1996.

Neumann, Alfred. "Architecture as Ornament." *Zodiac*, no. 19 (1969): 90–98.

———. "Morphologic Architecture." *Zodiac*, no. 16 (1966): 136–39.

Neumeyer, Fritz. *The Artless Word: Mies Van Der Rohe on the Building Art*. Cambridge, MA: MIT Press, 1991.

Norberg-Schulz, Christian. *Intentions in Architecture*. Cambridge, MA: MIT Press, 1968.

Nordenson, Guy. *Patterns and Structure: Selected Writings 1972–2008*. Baden: Lars Müller, 2010.

Ockman, Joan, and Edward Eigen, eds. *Architecture Culture, 1943–1968: A Documentary Anthology*. Columbia Books of Architecture. New York, NY: Rizzoli, 1993.

Palladio, Andrea. *The Four Books on Architecture*. Cambridge, MA: MIT Press, 1997.

Pérez Gómez, Alberto. *Architecture and the Crisis of Modern Science*. Cambridge, MA: MIT Press, 1983.

Perrault, Claude. *Ordonnance for the Five Kinds of Columns After the Method of the Ancients*. Texts & D. Santa Monica, CA: Getty Center for the History of Art and the Humanities, 1992.

Petit, Emmanuel J. *Irony; or, The Self-Critical Opacity of Postmodern Architecture*. New Haven, CT: Yale University Press, 2013.

Pfammatter, Ulrich. *The Making of the Modern Architect and Engineer: The Origins and Development of a Scientific and Industrially Oriented Education*. Basel; Boston: Birkhauser-Publishers for Architecture, 2000.

Picon, Antoine. *Claude Perrault, 1613–1688, Ou, La Curiosité D'un Classique*. Paris: Picard Éditeur, Caisse nationale des monuments historiques et des sites; Délégation à l'action artistique de la ville de Paris, 1988.

———. *French Architects and Engineers in the Age of Enlightenment*. Cambridge Studies in the History of Architecture. Cambridge, UK; New York, NY: Cambridge University Press, 1992.

———. "La Notion Moderne de Structure." *Les Cahiers de La Recherche Architecturales*, no. 29 (1992): 101–10.

———. *L'Art de l'Ingénieur: Constructeur, Entrepreneur, Inventeur*. Paris: Centre Georges Pompidou: Le Moniteur, 1997.

———. *Marc Mimram: Hybride Architecte Ingénieur = Hybrid Architect Engineer*. Gollion: In folio, 2007.

———. "Santiago Calatrava: Tettonica o Architettura?" *Casabella*, no. 615 (September 1994): 24–25.

———. "Technological Traditions and National Identities: A Comparison Between France and Great Britain during the 19th Century." In *Science, Technology and the 19th Century State*, 13–21. Athens: Institut de Recherches Nohelleniques, 2000.

Picon, Antoine, and Ecole nationale des ponts et chaussées (France). *L'invention de l'ingénieur Moderne: L'Ecole Des Ponts et Chaussées, 1747–1851*. Paris: Presses de l'Ecole nationale des ponts et chaussées, 1992.

Porter, Theodore M. *Trust in Numbers*. Princeton, NJ:

Princeton University Press, 1996.

Pugin, Augustus Welby Northmore, and Bard Graduate Center for Studies in the Decorative Arts. *A. W. N. Pugin: Master of Gothic Revival*. New Haven, CT: Yale University Press for The Bard Graduate Center for Studies in the Decorative Arts, New York, 1995.

Pugin, Augustus Welby Northmore, and Victoria and Albert Museum. *Pugin: A Gothic Passion*. New Haven, CT: Yale University Press, 1994.

Quatremère de Quincy. *The True, the Fictive, and the Real: The Historical Dictionary of Architecture of Quatremère De Quincy*. London: Andreas Papadakis, 1999.

———. "Type, (Introduction by Anthony Vidler)." *Oppositions*, no. 8 (Spring 1977): 147.

Rappaport, Nina. "Deep Decoration." *30/60/90*, no. 10 (2006): 95–103.

———. *Support and Resist: Structural Engineers and Design Innovation*. New York, NY: Monacelli Press, 2007.

Reas, Casey. *Form+code in Design, Art, and Architecture*. New York, NY: Princeton Architectural Press, 2010.

Rice, Peter. *An Engineer Imagines*. London: Artemis, 1998.

Riegl, Alois. *Late Roman Art Industry*. Archaeologica 36. Rome: Giorgio Bretschneider, 1985.

———. *Problems of Style: Foundations for a History of Ornament*. Princeton, NJ: Princeton University Press, 1992.

Robertson, Howard Morley. *The Principles of Architectural Composition*. London: The Architectural Press, 1924.

Rocha, Altino João Magalhães. "Architecture Theory, 1960–1980: Emergence of a Computational Perspective." PhD Dissertation, Massachusetts Institute of Technology, 2004.

Rohe, Mies Van Der. "Building." In *The Artless Word*, 242–43. Cambridge, MA: MIT Press, 1991.

———. "On Form in Architecture." In *The Artless Word*, 257. Cambridge, MA: MIT Press, 1991.

———. "Regarding the New Volume." In *The Artless Word*, 257. Cambridge, MA: MIT Press, 1991.

Romba, Katherine. "Aesthetics and the Professional Identity of the Modern German Engineer." In *Proceedings of the Second International Congress on Construction History*, 2727–41. Cambridge, UK: Construction History Society, 2006.

———. *Iron Construction and Cultural Discourse: German Architectural Theory, 1890–1918*. Saarbrücken, Germany: VDM Verlag Dr. Müller, 2008.

Rowe, Colin. *The Mathematics of the Ideal Villa and Other Essays*. Cambridge, MA: MIT Press, 1982.

Saarinen, Eliel. *The Search for Form in Art and Architecture*. New York, NY: Dover Publications, 1985.

Saint, Andrew. *Architect and Engineer: A Study in Sibling Rivalry*. New Haven, CT; London: Yale University Press, 2007.

Sasaki, Mutsurō. Flux Structure. Tokyo: Tōtōshuppan, 2005.

Scott, Geoffrey. *The Architecture of Humanism: A Study in the History of Taste*. The Classical America Series in Art and Architecture. New York, NY: W.W. Norton & Company, 1999.

Semper, Gottfried. *The Four Elements of Architecture and Other Writings*. Cambridge, MA: Cambridge University Press, 2010.

Schmarsow, August. "The Essence of Architectural Creation." In *Empathy, Form, and Space: Problems in German Aesthetics, 1873–1893*. Santa Monica, CA: Getty Center for the History of Art and the Humanities, 1994.

Schopenhauer, Arthur. *The World as Will and Representation*. Indian Hills, CO: Falcon's Wing Press, 1958.

Schwarzer, Mitchel. "Ontology and Representation in Karl Bötticher's Theory of Tectonics." *Journal of the Society of Architectural Historians*, no. 52 (September 1993): 267–80.

Soane, John. *Sir John Soane: The Royal Academy Lectures*. New York, NY: Cambridge University Press, 1999.

Somol, Robert. "12 Reasons to Get Back in Shape." In *Content*, 86–87. Cologne: Taschen, 2004.

Straub, Hans. *A History of Civil Engineering; an Outline from Ancient to Modern Times*. London: L. Hill, 1952.

Sykes, Krista, ed. *Constructing a New Agenda: Architectural Theory 1993–2009*. New York, NY: Princeton Architectural Press, 2010.

Terzidis, Kostas. *Expressive Form: A Conceptual Approach to Computational Design*. London: Spon Press, 2003.

Timošenko, Stephen. *History of Strength of Materials with a Brief Account of the History of Theory of Elasticity and Theory of Structures*. New York, NY: Dover Publ., 1983.

Tyng, Anne. "Geometric Extensions of Consciousness." *Zodiac*, no. 19 (1969): 130–62.

———. *Simultaneous Randomness and Order: The Fibonacci-Divine Proportion as a Universal Forming Principle*. PhD Dissertation, University of Pennsylvania, 1975.

Upitis, Alise. "Nature Normative: The Design Methods Movement, 1944–1967." PhD Dissertation, Massachusetts Institute of Technology, 2008.

Vallye, Anna. "The Middleman: Kepes's Instruments." In *A Second Modernism: MIT, Architecture, and the "Techno-Social" Moment*, 145–85. Cambridge, MA: MIT Press, 2013.

Vidler, Anthony. "Neoclassical Modernism: Emil Kaufmann." In *Histories of the Immediate Present: Inventing Architectural Modernism*, 17–59. Cambridge, MA: MIT Press, 2008.

———. "The Idea of Type: The Transformation of the Academic Ideal, 1750–1830." *Oppositions*, no. 8 (1977): 95–115.

———. "The Third Typology." *Oppositions*, no. 7 (Winter 1977): 293–94.

Viollet-le-Duc, Eugène-Emmanuel. *Lectures on Architecture*. New York, NY: Dover Publications, 1987.

———. *The Foundations of Architecture: Selections from the Dictionnaire Raisonné*. New York, NY: George Braziller, 1990.

Vitruvius Pollio, Marcus. *On Architecture*. Translated by Richard Schofield. London: Penguin Books, 2009.

Wittkower, Rudolf. *Architectural Principles in the Age of Humanism*. Chichester, West Sussex, UK: Academy Editions, 1998.

Zevi, Bruno. *Architecture as Space; How to Look at Architecture*. New York, NY: Horizon Press, 1957.

———. *The Modern Language of Architecture*. Seattle, WA: University of Washington Press, 1978.

## CHAPTER 1

### Giorgini's own production and publications

Giorgini, Vittorio. "Comunicazione Personale." In *Utopia E Crisi Dell'antinatura: Momenti Delle Intenzioni Architettoniche in Italia: Topologia E Morfogenesi*, 128–31. Venice: La Biennale di Venezia, 1978.

———. "Early Experiments in Design Derived from Study of Nature's Morphologies." *International Journal of Space Structures* 11, no. 1 & 2 (1996): 57–68.

———. "Genesi Del Tipo Di Ricerca." In *Prima Triennale Itinerante d'Architettura Italiana Contemporanea*, 102–6. Florence: Edizioni Centro Proposte, 1965.

———. "Gli Sviluppi Contemporanei Della Scienza Del Progetto = Buckminster Fuller Centennial Exhibition [Exhibition Review]." *Arca*, no. 103 (April 1996): 92.

———. "Osservazione al ponte di Messina." *Arca*, no. 137 (May 1999): 92.

———. "Spatiology and Thin Shell Structures." In *LSA86: Proceedings of the First International Conference on Lightweight Structures in Architecture, Sydney, Australia, 24–29 August 1986.*, 224–31. Kensington, NSW, Australia: Unisearch Limited, University of New South Wales, 1986.

———. *Spatiology: The Morphology of the Natural Sciences in Architecture and Design = Spaziologia: La Morfologia Delle Scienze Naturali Nella Progettazione*. Milan: L'arca, 1995.

———. *Strutture Soniche - Ipotesi per Un Habitat Più Naturale, Catalogo Della Personale Tenuta a Ferrara Nel Palazzo Dei Diamanti*. Ferrara, 1968.

———. "USA e Getta = USE and Throw." *Arca*, no. 82 (May 1994): 100.

Giorgini, Vittorio, Gérald Gassiot-Talabot, Lara Vinca Masini, and Giovanni Michelucci. "Les Architectes de Florence." *Aujourd'hui*, no. 53 (June 1966): 68–77.

### Other sources

Abercrombie, Stanley. *Ferrocement: Building with Cement, Sand, and Wire Mesh*. New York, NY: Schocken Books, 1977.

Aragüez, José. "Towards a Critique of 'The Organic' in Architectural Thinking." *Pidgin*, no. 12 (2011): 246–63.

Arnaboldi, Mario Antonio. "Sperimentazione e Ricerca = Experimentation and Research." *Arca*, no. 73 (August 1993): 44–47.

Baldassini, Niccolò. "Logica e Aggregazione: River Crane Center, New York." *Arca*, no. 92 (April 1995): 28–31.

*Baratti-Arch. Vittorio Giorgini-Casa Saldarini*, 2010. http://www.youtube.com/watch?v=ln-r_Ek_Deo&feature=youtube_gdata_player.

Bardeschi, Marco Dezzi, and Lara Vinca Masini. *Prima Triennale Itinerante d'Architettura Italiana Contemporanea*. Edizioni Centro Proposte, 1965.

Barr, Stephen. *Experiments in Topology*. New York, NY: Crowell, 1964.

Bois, Yve-Alain, and Rosalind E Krauss. *Formless: A User's Guide*. New York, NY: Zone Books, 1997.

Bottero, Maria, and Frederick Kiesler. "Frederick Kiesler's Shrine of the Book Revisited." *Zodiac*, no. 19 (1969): 6–18.

Cantella, Claudio. "Struttura: Anacronismo o Realtà? = Structure: Anachronism or Reality?" *Arca*, no. 26 (April 1989): 44–51.

Casciato, Maristella. "The Promise of Organic Architecture." In *Frank Lloyd Wright: Europe and Beyond*, 76–99. Berkeley, CA: University of California Press, 1999.

Castellano, Aldo. "Il walking tall per New York = The walking tall for New York." *Arca*, no. 4 (March 1987): 76–81.

———. "La città sull'acqua: Hydropolis e genesis = A city on the water: Hydropolis and genesis." *Arca*, no. 5 (April 1987): 76–81.

Cattaneo, Renato. "Il territorio progettuale = Territorial planning." *Arca*, no. 52 (September 1991): 6–11.

Del Francia, Marco, and Anna Guerriero. *Vittorio Giorgini: La Natura Come Modello*. Florence: A. Pontecorboli, 2000.

Dezzi Bardeschi, Marco. "Kiesler, La Scuola Fiorentina e La Curvatura Del Mondo." *ANATKH*, no. 14 (June 1996): 70–81.

———. "L'influenza Della Personalità Nell'insegnamento Dell'architettura." *Casabella*, no. 287 (May 1964): 16–18.

Gregotti, Vittorio. *New Directions in Italian Architecture*. New York, NY: George Braziller, 1968.

Jenny, Hans. *Cymatics: A Study of Wave Phenomena and Vibration*. Newmarket, NH: MACROmedia, 2001.

Kiesler, Frederick, and Virgil Thompson. "Frederick Kiesler

1923–1964." *Zodiac*, no. 19 (1969): 19–49.

Koenig, G. K. "L'esperienza Organica in Italia e La 'Scuola Fiorentina.'" *Casabella*, no. 337 (June 1969): 8–19.

Kraus, Eva. "Plaidoyer Pour Une Archisculpture = Plea for Archisculpture." *Architecture d'aujourd'hui*, no. 349 (2003): 58–63.

Kull, Ulrich. "Frei Otto and Biology." In *Frei Otto, Complete Works: Lightweight Construction, Natural Design*, 45–54. Basel; Boston: Birkhäuser, 2005.

Pevsner, Nikolaus. *An Outline of European Architecture.* Harmondsworth, Middlesex, UK: Penguin Books, 1963.

Phillips, Stephen John. *Elastic Architecture: Frederick Kiesler and His Research Practice – A Study of Continuity in the Age of Modern Production.* PhD Dissertation, Princeton School of Architecture, 2008.

"Pratt Institute School of Architecture Faculty and Student Projects." *Pratt Journal of Architecture* 2 (1988): 181–209.

Rawes, Peg. *Space, Geometry and Aesthetics: Through Kant and Towards Deleuze.* Renewing Philosophy. Basingstoke, UK: Palgrave Macmillan, 2008.

Riani, Paolo. "Case immaginarie: abitazioni per la citta' futura." *Ville giardini*, no. 258 (April 1991): 38–41.

Riani, Paolo. "Case imaginaire: Vittorio Giorgini, lo spazio dell'anima." *Ville giardini*, no. 257 (March 1991): 38–41.

Sonzogni, Valentina. "Casa Saldarini, Baratti, Italie: Vittorio Giorgini Architecte = Vittorio Giorgini: Casa Saldarini, Baratti, Italy." *Architecture d'aujourd'hui* 2003, no. 349 (2003): 64–67.

———. "Frederick Kiesler et La Maison Sin Fin." *Architecture d'aujourd'hui*, no. 349 (2003): 48–57.

Stirling, James. "Ronchamp: Le Corbusier's Chapel and the Crisis of Rationalism." *Architectural Review*, no. 119 (March 1956): 155–61.

Thompson, D'Arcy Wentworth. *On Growth and Form.* Cambridge, UK: Cambridge University Press, 1917.

Unknown author. "Houses: The Sculptural Turn." *House Beautiful* 108 (September 1966): 162–63.

Unknown author. "Villa à Populonia, Italie." *Aujourd'hui* 7, no. 41 (May 1963): 80–81.

*Utopia E Crisi Dell'antinatura: Momenti Delle Intenzioni Architettoniche in Italia: Topologia E Morfogenesi.* Venice: La Biennale di Venezia, 1978.

Vitta, Maurizio. "Agora – Dreams and Visions: Vittorio Giorgini." *Arca*, no. 214 (n.d.): 34–41.

Zevi, Bruno. *Towards an Organic Architecture.* London: Faber & Faber, 1950.

## CHAPTER 2

### Burt's own production and publications

Burt, Michaël. "Extrait d'une Thèse de Diplôme Présentée Au Technion de Haïfa, Faculté d'Architecture." *L'Architecture d'Aujourd'hui* 40, no. 143 (May 1969): 89–96.

———. "New Forms and Conceptual Architecture." In *Conceptual Architecture*, Exhibition catalog, 20–44. Haifa, Israel: Haifa Museum, Museum of Art, 1998.

———. "Periodic Sponge Polyhedra—Expanding the Domain," 500–504. Buenos Aires, 2007.

———. "Saddle Polyhedra & Close-Packing." *Zodiac*, no. 22 (1972): 162–71.

———. *Spatial Arrangement and Polyhedra with Curved Surfaces and Their Architectural Applications – Doctoral Thesis.* Haifa, Israel: Technion, Israel Institute of Technology, 1966.

———. "The Morphologically Associated Quintuplet Phenomena of 3D Space," 321–31. Rome, 2011.

———. *The Periodic Table of The Polyhedral Universe.* Haifa, Israel: Technion, Israel Institute of Technology, 1996.

———. "The Quasi–Periodic Close Packings of Rhombic-Triacontahedra." Budapest, Hungary, 2003.

———. "Toward a Theory of Space Networks and Space Subdivision." manuscript, 2011. Personal archive of Michaël Burt.

Burt, Michaël, Menachem Kleinmann, and Avraham Wachman. *Infinite Polyhedra.* Haifa, Israel: Faculty of Architecture and Town Planning of the Technion, Israel Institute of Technology, 2005.

Burt, Michaël, and Ami Korren. "Rigid Edge, Building Attached Membrane Structures. Case Study: Amado Roof Structure, Technion - Israel." IASS Symposia. Beijing, China, 2006.

### Other sources

Aldo van Eyck. *Forum.* Vol. 7. Amsterdam: G. van Saanen, 1959.

Alexander, Christopher. "Systems Generating Systems." *Architecture Canada* 45, no. 11 (November 1968): 39–44.

Alpert, Carl. *Technion: The Story of Israel's Institute of Technology.* New York, NY: American Technion Society, 1982.

Andrew Rabeneck. "Whatever Happened to the Systems Approach?" *Architectural Design* 46, no. 5 (May 1976): 298–303.

Berman, Reuven. "Art Is What Artists Make." *The Jerusalem Post Magazine*, November 7, 1969, unpaged.

Bertalanffy, Ludwig von. *General System Theory; Foundations, Development, Applications.* New York, NY: George Braziller, 1969.

Boness, Stefan. *Tel Aviv: The White City.* Berlin: Jovis, 2012.

Bottero, Maria. "Editorial." *Zodiac*, no. 22 (1972): 238–39.

———. "Scientific Abstraction and Concrete Thought in Buckminster Fuller's Utopia." *Zodiac*, no. 19 (1969): 224–30.

Burt, Michaël, Menachem Kleinmann, and Avraham Wachman. *Infinite Polyhedra.* 2nd ed. 1974; Haifa, Israel: Faculty of Architecture and Town

Planning of the Technion, Israel Institute of Technology, 2005.

Coxeter, H. S. M. *Projective Geometry*. Toronto: University of Toronto Press, 1974.

———. "Regular Skew Polyhedra in Three and Four Dimensions, and Their Topological Analogues." *Proceedings of the London Mathematical Society* 43, no. 2 (1937): 33–62.

———. "The Regular Sponges, or Skew Polyhedra." *Scripta Mathematica*, no. 6 (1939): 240–44.

———. "Three-Dimensional Nets and Polyhedra by A.F. Wells [Book Review]." *Bulletin of the American Mathematical Society* 84, no. 3 (May 1978): 466–70.

Critchlow, Keith. *Order in Space; a Design Source Book*. New York, NY: Viking Press, 1970.

Daitz, Sonia. "Michael Burt: Profile of a Maverick Architect." *Technion* VI, no. 2 (Summer 1970): 9–13.

Deleuze, Gilles. *Difference and Repetition*. Translated by Paul Patton. New York, NY: Columbia University Press, 1994.

Derrida, Jacques. *Positions*. Chicago, IL: University of Chicago Press, 1981.

———. *Speech and Phenomena, and Other Essays on Husserl's Theory of Signs*. Northwestern University Studies in Phenomenology & Existential Philosophy. Evanston, IL: Northwestern University Press, 1973.

Efrat, Zvi. "The Object of Zionism: Architecture and Statehood in Israel 1948–73." Basel, Swiss Architecture Museum, 2012.

———. "The Object of Zionism: Architecture of Statehood in Israel, 1948–1973." PhD Dissertation, Princeton School of Architecture, 2013.

Ek, Veronica, and Patrick Lannin. "Ridiculed Crystal Work Wins Nobel for Israeli." *Reuters* (blog), October 5, 2011. http://www.reuters.com/article/2011/10/05/nobel-chemistry-idUSL5E7L51U620111005.

Emmerich, David Georges. *Course in Constructive Geometry; Morphology*. Seattle, WA: Dept. of Architecture, University of Washington, 1970.

Gabriel, J. François. *Beyond the Cube: The Architecture of Space Frames and Polyhedra*. New York, NY: Wiley, 1997.

Goethe, Johann Wolfgang von. "Morphology." In *Scientific Studies*, edited by Douglas Miller. 1790–1808; Princeton, NJ: Princeton University Press, 1995.

Goodovitch, Israel. *Architecturology: An Interim Report by I.M. Goodovitch*. New South Wales: George Allen & Unwin Ltd, 2014.

Gross, Jonathan, and Thomas Tucker. *Topological Graph Theory*. New York, NY: Dover Publications, 2012.

Heuvel, Wim J. van. *Structuralism in Dutch Architecture*. Rotterdam: Uitgeverij 010 Publishers, 1992.

Hoenich, P. K. "An Op Art Picture on Contiguous Double-Curved Minimal Surfaces." *Leonardo* 4, no. 1 (Winter 1971): 23–26.

Janot, Christian. *Quasicrystals: A Primer*. Oxford: Oxford University Press, 2012.

Keith Critchlow. "Closepacking." *Zodiac*, no. 22 (1972): 172–78.

———. "New Geometrical Information." *Architectural Design* 40, no. 4 (April 1970): 164–66.

———. "Toward a New Philosophy of Structure." *Zodiac*, no. 22 (1972): 180–85.

Levin, Michael. *White City: International Style Architecture in Israel, a Portrait of an Era*. Tel Aviv: Tel Aviv Museum, 1984.

Lüchinger, Arnul. *Structuralism in Architecture and Urban Planning*. Dokumente Der Modernen Architekt. Stuttgart: K. Krämer, 1981.

Maniaque-Benton, Caroline. *French Encounters with the American Counterculture 1960–1980*. Burlington, VT: Routledge, 2011.

Mansfeld, Alfred. *Al. Mansfeld, Private & Public Structures: Models, Drawings, Photographs, Etc.* Israel: Israeli Museum, 1994.

———. "On Structuralism: Designing for Growth, Change, Uncertainty." In *Al Mansfeld, Architekt in Israel = Al Mansfeld, an Architect in Israel*, edited by Anna Teut, 131–43. Berlin: Ernst & Sohn, 1999.

———. *Structuralism in Architecture: Selected Works of Al Mansfeld and His Team*. Montréal: Z. Drucker, 1987.

March, Lionel, and Philip Steadman. *The Geometry of Environment: An Introduction to Spatial Organization in Design*. London: RIBA Publications, 1971.

Maria Bottero. "Editorial." *Zodiac*, no. 16 (1966): 237.

———. "Technological Research and Architecture." *Zodiac*, no. 21 (1971): 229–32.

Neumann, Alfred. "Architecture as Ornament." *Zodiac*, no. 19 (1969): 90–98.

———. "Irrational Factors in Building Industrialization." *Architecture Canada* 45, no. 11 (November 1968): 37–38.

———. *L'humanisation de l'espace: Le Système M Ph.* Boulogne-sur-Seine: Éditions A.A., 1956.

———. "Morphologic Architecture." *Zodiac*, no. 16 (1966): 136–39.

Oriol, Miguel, and Antonio Carrillo. "Investigaciones Sobre Ordenacion Del Espacio." *Revista Nacional de Arquitectura*, no. 55 (July 1963): 28–38.

———. "Recherches Pour La Comprehension et l'Ordonnancement de l'Espace." *L'Architecture d'Aujourd'hui* 34, no. 117 (November 1964): 102–5.

Pearce, Peter. *Structure in Nature Is a Strategy for Design*. Cambridge, MA: MIT Press, 1978.

Safdie, Moshe. "Finding a Genetic Code." *Architecture Canada* 45, no. 11 (November 1968): 55–56.

———. "Industrialized Buildings." *Architecture Canada* 45, no. 11 (November 1968): 35–36.

———. "New Environmental Requirements for Urban Building." *Zodiac*, no. 19 (1969): 180–82.

———. "Systems and Evolutions." *Architecture Canada* 45, no. 11 (November 1968): 50–54.

———. "Variety within Repetition." *Architecture Canada* 45, no. 11 (November 1968): 49.

Saussure, Ferdinand de. *Course in General Linguistics*. LaSalle, IL: Open Court, 1986.

Schoen, Alan H. "Infinite Periodic Minimal Surfaces Without Self-Intersections." Cambridge, MA: NASA Electronics Research Center, May 1970.

———. "Reflections Concerning Triply-Periodic Minimal Surfaces." *Interface Focus*, May 30, 2012. http://rsfs.royalsocietypublishing.org/content/early/2012/05/28/rsfs.2012.0023.

Segal, Rafael. "Unit, Pattern, Site: The Space Packed Architecture of Alfred Neumann 1949-1968." PhD Dissertation, Princeton School of Architecture, 2011.

Sieden, Lloyd Steven. *Buckminster Fuller's Universe*. Cambridge, MA: Perseus Publishing, 1989.

Smithson, Alison Margaret, and Team 10. *Team 10 Primer*. Cambridge, MA: MIT Press, 1968.

Steadman, Philip. "Graph-Theoretic Representation of Architectural Arrangement." In *The Architecture of Form*, 95–115. Cambridge, UK: Cambridge University Press, 1976.

Stewart, Bonnie Madison. *Adventures Among the Toroids; a Study of Quasi-Convex, Aplanar, Tunneled Orientable Polyhedra of Positive Genus Having Regular Faces with Disjoint Interiors*. Tall Search Book, no. 1. Okemos, Michigan, 1970.

Thompson, D'Arcy Wentworth. *On Growth and Form*. 1917; New York, NY: Dover Publications, 1992.

Trudeau, Richard. *Introduction to Graph Theory*. 2nd edition. New York, NY: Dover Publications, 1994.

Tyng, Anne. "Geometric Extensions of Consciousness." *Zodiac*, no. 19 (1969): 130–62.

———. "Urban Space Systems as Living Form, Part I." *Architecture Canada* 45, no. 11 (November 1968): 45–48.

Wells, A. F. *Structural Inorganic Chemistry*. Oxford: Clarendon Press, 1962.

———. *Three-Dimensional Nets and Polyhedra*. New York, NY: Wiley, 1977.

## CHAPTER 3

### Balmond's own production and publications

Balmond, Cecil. *Cecil Balmond: Frontiers of Architecture I*. Humlebaek, Denmark: Louisiana Museum of Modern Art, 2007.

———. "Congrexpo - Oder 'Das Ei' in Lille." *Arch+*, no. 124/125 (December 1994): 30–33.

———. *Crossover*. Munich; London; New York, NY: Prestel, 2013.

———. "El Huevo Mecánico: Luces y Cubiertas En El Congrexpo de Lille." *Arquitectura Viva*, no. 39 (November 1994): 42–45.

———. *Element*. Munich: Prestel, 2007.

———. "Forming the Informal: A Conversation with Cecil Balmond." *Dialogue*, no. 67 (2003): 19–27.

———. *Informal*. Munich: Prestel, 2002.

———. "Informelles Konstruieren." *Arch+*, no. 117 (June 1993): 59–63.

———. "My Kind of Town." *Architecture Today* 2007, no. 183 (2007): 104.

———. "New Structure and the Informal." *Assemblage*, no. 33 (August 1997): 46–57.

———. "New Structure and the Informal." *Lotus*, no. 98 (1998): 70–83.

———. *Number 9: The Search for the Sigma Code: Nine Fixed Points in the Wind*. Munich: Prestel, 1998.

———. "Stirling Style." *Building Design*, no. 807 (October 10, 1986): 34–35.

———. "Tecnologia: un forat negre? = Technology: the black hole." *Quaderns d'arquitectura i urbanisme*, no. 199 (March 1993): 87–91.

———. "The Arup Archipelago." *World Architecture*, no. 57 (June 1997).

Balmond, Cecil, David Atling, and Tom Barker. "Stuttgart Art Gallery." *The Arup Journal* 3, no. 19 (October 1984): 10–17.

Balmond, Cecil, and Christian Brensing. "Music as the Fount of Inspiration: An Interview with Cecil Balmond." *Detail, English Ed.* (2006), 14–19.

Balmond, Cecil, and Toyo Ito. "Conversation - Cecil Balmond and Toyo Ito: 'Concerning Fluid Spaces.'" *A + U: Architecture and Urbanism*, no. 5 (May 2004): 44–53.

Balmond, Cecil, and Pablo Lazo. "Explorando la complejidad: una conversación con Cecil Balmond [interview]." *Arquine: revista internacional de arquitectura y diseño = International architecture and design magazine*, no. 30 (2004): 66–77.

———. "Why Cecil Balmond Never Says No [Interview]." *Log*, no. 4 (2005): 65–77.

Balmond, Cecil, and Paul Makovsky. "Restructuring Plans: Cecil Balmond Talks to Us about His Recent Decision to Leave Arup for His Own Practice [Interview]." *Metropolis* 30, no. 6 (2011): 28.

Balmond, Cecil, and Shonquis Moreno."... Q + A: Cecil Balmond [Interview]." *I.D.* 56, no. 1 (2009): 24–25.

Balmond, Cecil, and Philip Nobel. "Rencontre Avec Cecil Balmond, Ingénieur [Interview]." *Architecture d'aujourd'hui*, no. 329 (August 2000): 44–49.

Balmond, Cecil, and Axel Sowa. "Entretien Avec Cecil Balmond: Tresser, Tisser, Entrelacer = Weave, Braid, Entwine [Interview]." *Architecture d'aujourd'hui*, no. 369 (April 2007): 56–61.

Balmond, Cecil, and Michael Weinstock. "The Digital and the Material: Cecil Balmond in Conversation with Michael Weinstock." *Architectural Design* 72, no. 1 (2002): 46–51.

Yoshida, Nobuyuki, ed. *Cecil Balmond, A+U Special Issue.* Tokyo: A + U Publishing, 2006.

### Other sources

Allen, Stan. "From Object to Field: Field Conditions in Architecture and Urbanism." *Architectural Design*, no. 67 (June 1997): 24–31.

Arup, Ove. *Ove Arup, Philosophy of Design: Essays 1942–1981.* Munich; London: Prestel, 2012.

———. "Art and Architecture (1966)." In *Ove Arup, Philosophy of Design: Essays 1943-1981*, 99–107. Munich; London: Prestel, 2012.

———. "Structure in Relation to Architecture (1957)." In *Ove Arup, Philosophy of Design: Essays 1943–1981*, 50–52. Munich; London: Prestel, 2012.

———. "The Architect and The Engineer (1959)." In *Ove Arup, Philosophy of Design: Essays 1943–1981*, 58–63. Munich; London: Prestel, 2012.

———. "The Key Speech (1970)." In *Ove Arup, Philosophy of Design: Essays 1943-1981*, 161–68. Munich; London: Prestel, 2012.

Barthel, Rainer. "Natural Forms – Architectural Forms." In *Frei Otto, Complete Works: Lightweight Construction, Natural Design*, 17–30. Basel; Boston: Birkhäuser, 2005.

Bizley, Graham. "The Rem & Cecil Show." *Building Design*, April 29, 2005, 20–21.

Bois, Yve-Alain, and Rosalind Krauss. *Formless: A User's Guide.* New York, NY: Zone Books, 1997.

Brensing, Christian. "Frei Otto and Ove Arup: A case of Mutual Inspiration." In *Frei Otto, Complete Works: Lightweight Construction, Natural Design*, 103–108. Basel; Boston: Birkhäuser, 2005.

Brown, André. *Peter Rice.* London: Thomas Telford, 2001.

Frazer, John. *An Evolutionary Architecture.* London: Architectural Association Publications, 1995.

Gleick, James. *Chaos: Making a New Science.* New York, NY: Viking Press, 1987.

Gropius, Walter. *Scope of Total Architecture.* New York, NY: Harper, 1955.

Janot, Christian. *Quasicrystals: A Primer.* Oxford: Oxford University Press, 2012.

Jencks, Charles. *The Architecture of the Jumping Universe.* London: Wiley, 1995.

Jones, Peter. *Ove Arup: Master Builder of the Twentieth Century.* New Haven, CT: Yale University Press, 2006.

Kabat, Jennifer. "The Informalist." *Wired*, no. 9.04 (April 1, 2001): 104.

Koolhaas, Rem, and Bruce Mau. *S M L XL.* New York, NY: Monacelli Press, 1995.

Kwinter, Sanford. *Architectures of Time: Toward a Theory of the Event in Modernist Culture.* Cambridge, MA: MIT Press, 2001.

Landau, Royston, ed. "Complexity." *Architectural Design* (October 1972).

McCullough, Malcolm. "20 Years of Scripted Space." *AD Profile*, no. 182 (August 2006): 12–15.

Ouroussoff, Nicolai. "An Engineer Magician, Then (Presto) He's an Architect." *The New York Times.* November 26, 2006.

*Ove Arup 1895–1988.* London: The Institution of Civil Engineers, 1995.

Ove Arup & Partners. *Arups on Engineering.* London: Ernst & Sohn, 1996.

Pearman, Hugh. "Secrets of the Arup Archipelago." *World Architecture*, no. 18 (July 1992): 76–81.

Picon, Antoine. *Digital Culture in Architecture.* Basel: Birkhäuser Architecture, 2010.

Rattembury, Kester. "Drowning by Numbers." *Building Design*, no. 1397 (May 28, 1999): 32.

Rice, Peter. "A Celebration of the Life and Work of Ove Arup." *RSA Journal* 137, no. 5395 (June 1989): 425–37.

———. *An Engineer Imagines.* London: Artemis, 1998.

———. "RIBA Royal Gold Medal Speech." *The Arup Journal*, vol. 27 no. 4 (Winter 1992-93): 20–23.

———. "Unstable Structures." *Columbia Documents of Architecture and Theory* (1992): 71–89.

Sommer, Degenhard, Herbert Stöcher, and Lutz Weisser. *Ove Arup and Partners: Engineering the Built Environment.* Basel: Birkhauser, 1994.

Vollaard, Piet. "Informal." *Archis*, no. 3 (2003): 115–17.

Walker, Charles. "A Research Based Model as an Alternative to the Design Based Model of Architectural Invention." RIBA, 2005.

Wise, Chris. "Informal." *AA Files*, no. 49 (Spring 2003): 103–5.

Zunz, Jack. "Matters of Concern." *The Arup Journal*, no. 3 (1989): 20–24.

———. "Mirror Mirror on the Wall . . . How Fair Is the Engineer's Image?" *Arup Journal* 28, no. 2 (1993): 8–11.

———. "My Life and Times with Ove." In *Ove Arup 1895–1988*, 54–61. London: The Institution of Civil Engineers, 1995.

### CHAPTER 4

Arup, Ove. "Modern Architecture: The Structural Fallacy (1955)." In *Ove Arup, Philosophy of Design: Essays 1942–1981*, 45–49. Munich; London: Prestel, 2012.

Benjamin, Andrew. *Architectural Philosophy.* London; New Brunswick, NJ: The Athlone Press, 2000.

Bergson, Henri. *Creative Evolution.* New York, NY: H. Holt and Company, 1911.

Bon, Ranko. "Allometry in the Topologic Structure of

Architectural Spatial Systems." *Ekistics* 36, no. 215 (1973): 270–76.

Caniggia, Gianfranco. *Architectural Composition and Building Typology: Interpreting Basic Building*. Florence: Alinea, 2001.

Colquhoun, Alan. "Postmodernism and Structuralism: A Retrospective Glance." *Assemblage*, no. 5 (February 1988): 6–15.

Cortés, Juan Antonio. "Architectural Topology: An Inquiry into the Nature of Contemporary Space." *El Croquis*, no. 139 (2008): 33–57.

Cousin, Jean. *Topological Organization of Architectural Spaces*. Montréal: Les Presses de l'Université de Montréal, 1970.

Derrida, Jacques. *Edmund Husserl's Origin of Geometry: An Introduction*. Lincoln, OR: University of Nebraska Press, 1989.

Forty, Adrian. "Form." In *Words and Buildings: A Vocabulary of Modern Architecture*, 149–72. New York, NY: Thames & Hudson, 2000.

Frampton, Kenneth. "Rappel à L'Ordre, the Case for the Tectonic (1990)." In *Theorizing a New Agenda for Architecture, an Anthology of Architectural Theory 1965–1995*, 516–28. New York, NY: Princeton Architectural Press, 1995.

Goethe, Johann Wolfgang. *Schriften zur Morphologie*. CreateSpace Independent Publishing Platform, 2014.

Goethe, Johann Wolfgang von. *Scientific Studies*. Edited by Douglas Miller. Princeton, NJ: Princeton University Press, 1995.

———. *The Metamorphosis of Plants*. Cambridge, MA: MIT Press, 2009.

Hillier, Bill. *Space Is the Machine*. New York, NY: Cambridge University Press, 1996.

———. *The Social Logic of Space*. New York, NY: Cambridge University Press, 1984.

Kuhn, Thomas S. *The Structure of Scientific Revolutions*. Chicago, IL: University of Chicago Press, 1996.

Le Ricolais, Robert. "1935–1969, Etudes et Recherches." *Zodiac*, no. 22 (1973): 17–19.

———. "Introduction to the Notion of Form (1966)." In *Data: Directions in Art, Theory and Aesthetics*. Greenwich, CT: New York Graphic Society Ltd., 1968.

———. *Robert Le Ricolais. Visiones y Paradojas / Visions and Paradox*. Madrid: Fundación Cultural COAM, 1997.

———. "Topology and Architecture." *Student Publications of the School of Design, North Carolina State College* 5, no. 2 (Spring 1955): 10–16.

Lynn, Greg. *Animate Form*. New York, NY: Princeton Architectural Press, 1999.

———. "Blob Tectonics, or Why Tectonics Is Square and Topology Is Groovy (1996)." In *Folds, Bodies & Blobs: Collected Essays*, 169–82. Brussels: La Lettre Volée, 1998.

———. "Blobs (1995)." In *Folds, Bodies & Blobs: Collected Essays*, 157–68. Brussels: La Lettre Volée, 1998.

———. *Folds, Bodies & Blobs: Collected Essays*. Brussels: La Lettre Volée, 1998.

———. "Multiplicitous and Inorganic Bodies (1992)." In *Folds, Bodies & Blobs: Collected Essays*, 33–61. Brussels: La Lettre Volée, 1998.

March, Lionel, ed. *The Architecture of Form*. New York, NY: Cambridge University Press, 1976.

Petitot, Jean. *Morphogenesis of Meaning; Trans. by Franson Manjali*. Bern; New York, NY: PLang, 2004.

Plato. *The Collected Dialogues of Plato, Including the Letters*. Princeton, NJ: Princeton University Press, 1969.

Popper, Karl R. *Conjectures and Refutations: The Growth of Scientific Knowledge*. New York, NY: Routledge, 1989.

Sabini, Maurizio. "Between Order and Form. Fragments of an Idea of Architecture." *Rassegna*, no. 21 (March 1985): 14–25.

Schumacher, Patrik. *The Autopoiesis of Architecture, Volume I: A New Framework for Architecture*. Chichester: Wiley, 2011.

———. *The Autopoiesis of Architecture, Volume II: A New Agenda for Architecture*. Chichester: Wiley, 2012.

Steadman, Philip. *Architectural Morphology: An Introduction to the Geometry of Building Plans*. London: Pion, 1983.

———. "Graph-Theoretic Representation of Architectural Arrangement." In *The Architecture of Form*, 94–115. New York, NY: Cambridge University Press, 1976.

Steigerwald, Joan. "Goethe's Morphology: Urphänomene and Aesthetic Appraisal." *Journal of the History of Biology* 35, no. 2 (2002): 291–328.

Summerson, John. "The Case for a Theory of Modern Architecture (1957)." In *Architecture Culture 1943–1968: A Documentary Anthology*, 227–36. New York, NY: Rizzoli, 1993.

Thom, René. *Semio Physics: A Sketch*. Redwood City, CA: Addison-Wesley Pub. Co., Advanced Book Program, 1990.

———. *Structural Stability and Morphogenesis; an Outline of a General Theory of Models*. Reading, MA: W. A. Benjamin, 1975.

Thompson, D'Arcy Wentworth. *On Growth and Form*. 1917; New York, NY: Dover Publications, 1992.

Vidler, Anthony. "Toward a Theory of the Architecture Program." *October*, no. 106 (Fall 2003): 59–74.

# ILLUSTRATION CREDITS

## CHAPTER 1

**1.1**_Vittorio Giorgini Archive in Follonica.

**1.2**_Vittorio Giorgini Archive in Follonica.

**1.3**_Vittorio Giorgini Archive in Follonica.

**1.4**_Vittorio Giorgini Archive in Follonica.

**1.5**_Vittorio Giorgini, Gérald Gassiot-Talabot, Lara Vinca Masini, and Giovanni Michelucci. "Les Architectes de Florence," *Aujourd'hui*, no. 53 (June 1966): 72.

**1.6**_Marco Del Francia and Anna Guerriero, *Vittorio Giorgini: La Natura Come Modello* (Florence: A. Pontecorboli, 2000), 130.

**1.7**_Vittorio Giorgini Archive in Follonica.

**1.8**_Vittorio Giorgini Archive in Follonica.

**1.9**_Vittorio Giorgini Archive in Follonica.

**1.10**_Vittorio Giorgini Archive in Follonica.

**1.11**_Vittorio Giorgini Archive in Follonica.

**1.12**_Vittorio Giorgini Archive in Follonica.

**1.13**_Vittorio Giorgini Archive in Follonica.

**1.14**_Vittorio Giorgini Archive in Follonica.

**1.15**_Eva Kraus, "Plaidoyer pour une Archisculpture = Plea for Archisculpture," *Architecture d'aujourd'hui*, no. 349 (2003): 61.

**1.16_1**_Vittorio Giorgini Archive in Follonica.

**1.16_2**_© 2024 Artists Rights Society (ARS), New York / VG Bild-Kunst, Bonn

**1.17**_© 2024 Austrian Frederick and Lillian Kiesler Private Foundation, Vienna

**1.18**_Vittorio Giorgini Archive in Follonica.

**1.19**_Vittorio Giorgini Archive in Follonica.

**1.20**_Aldo Castellano, "La città sull'acqua: Hydropolis e genesis = A city on the water: Hydropolis and genesis," *Arca*, no. 5 (April 1987): 80.

**1.21**_Mario Antonio Arnaboldi, "Sperimentazione e ricerca = Experimentation and research," *Arca*, no. 73 (August 1993): 45.

**1.22**_Vittorio Giorgini Archive in Follonica.

**1.23**_Vittorio Giorgini Archive in Follonica.

**1.24**_Vittorio Giorgini Archive in Follonica.

**1.25**_Vittorio Giorgini Archive in Follonica.

**1.26**_A selection of water samples animated by various audible sound frequencies. From Cymatics: A Study of Wave Phenomena and Vibration, by Hans Jenny. Revised Edition ©2024 MACROmedia Publishing, www.CymatiSource.com. Used by permission

**1.27_1 and _2**_Vittorio Giorgini, *Spatiology: The Morphology of the Natural Sciences in Architecture and Design = Spaziologia: La Morfologia Delle Scienze Naturali Nella Progettazione* (Milan: L'arca, 1995), 36 (top), 62 (bottom).

**1.27_3**_D'Arcy Wentworth Thompson, *On Growth and Form* (Cambridge: University Press; 1917), 744.

**1.28**_© The Museum of Modern Art/Licensed by SCALA / Art Resource, NY

**1.29**_© The Museum of Modern Art/Licensed by SCALA / Art Resource, NY

**1.30**_© The Museum of Modern Art/Licensed by SCALA / Art Resource, NY

**1.31**_© The Museum of Modern Art/Licensed by SCALA / Art Resource, NY

**1.32**_© The Museum of Modern Art/Licensed by SCALA / Art Resource, NY

**1.33**_Vittorio Giorgini Archive in Follonica.

**1.34**_Vittorio Giorgini Archive in Follonica.

**1.35**_*Utopia E Crisi Dell'antinatura: Momenti Delle Intenzioni Architettoniche in Italia: Topologia E Morfogenesi* (Venice: La Biennale di Venezia, 1978), 130.

**1.36**_Vittorio Giorgini, *Spatiology: The Morphology of the Natural Sciences in Architecture and Design = Spaziologia: La Morfologia Delle Scienze Naturali Nella Progettazione* (Milan: L'arca, 1995), 41.

**1.37**_Vittorio Giorgini, *Spatiology: The Morphology of the Natural Sciences in Architecture and Design = Spaziologia: La Morfologia Delle Scienze Naturali Nella Progettazione* (Milan: L'arca, 1995), 45 (left), 46 (top right), 47 (bottom right).

**1.38**_Vittorio Giorgini Archive in Follonica.

**1.39**_Vittorio Giorgini, *Spatiology: The Morphology of the Natural Sciences in Architecture and Design = Spaziologia: La Morfologia Delle Scienze Naturali Nella Progettazione* (Milan: L'arca, 1995), 30 (left), 31 (top right), 33 (bottom right).

**1.40**_Vittorio Giorgini, *Spatiology: The Morphology of the Natural Sciences in Architecture and Design = Spaziologia: La Morfologia Delle Scienze Naturali Nella Progettazione* (Milan: L'arca, 1995), 64 (left), 65 (right).

**1.41**_Vittorio Giorgini, *Spatiology: The Morphology of the Natural Sciences in Architecture and Design = Spaziologia: La Morfologia Delle Scienze Naturali Nella Progettazione* (Milan: L'arca, 1995), 52 (top left), 54 (left), 53 (top right).

**1.42**_Vittorio Giorgini Archive in Follonica.

**1.43**_Vittorio Giorgini Archive in Follonica.

**1.44**_Vittorio Giorgini Archive in Follonica.

**1.45**_Vittorio Giorgini Archive in Follonica.

**1.46**_Vittorio Giorgini Archive in Follonica.

**1.47**_Vittorio Giorgini Archive in Follonica.

**1.48**_Vittorio Giorgini, *Spatiology: The Morphology of the Natural Sciences in Architecture and Design = Spaziologia: La Morfologia Delle Scienze Naturali Nella Progettazione* (Milan: L'arca, 1995), 54.

**1.49**_Vittorio Giorgini, *Spatiology: The Morphology of the Natural Sciences in Architecture and Design = Spaziologia: La Morfologia Delle Scienze Naturali Nella Progettazione* (Milan: L'arca, 1995), 52.

**1.50**_Vittorio Giorgini, *Spatiology: The Morphology of the Natural Sciences in Architecture and Design = Spaziologia: La Morfologia Delle Scienze Naturali Nella Progettazione* (Milan: L'arca, 1995), 170.

**1.51**_Vittorio Giorgini Archive in Follonica.

**1.52**_Vittorio Giorgini Archive in Follonica.

**1.53**_Vittorio Giorgini Archive in Follonica.

**1.54**_Vittorio Giorgini Archive in Follonica.

**1.55**_Vittorio Giorgini Archive in Follonica.

**1.56**_Vittorio Giorgini Archive in Follonica.

**1.57**_Vittorio Giorgini Archive in Follonica.

**1.58**_Vittorio Giorgini Archive in Follonica.

**1.59**_Vittorio Giorgini Archive in Follonica.

**1.60**_Vittorio Giorgini Archive in Follonica.

**1.61**_Vittorio Giorgini Archive in Follonica.

**1.62**_Vittorio Giorgini Archive in Follonica.

**1.63**_Vittorio Giorgini Archive in Follonica.

**1.64**_Vittorio Giorgini Archive in Follonica.

**1.65**_Vittorio Giorgini Archive in Follonica.

**1.66**_Vittorio Giorgini Archive in Follonica.

**1.67**_Vittorio Giorgini Archive in Follonica.

**1.68**_Vittorio Giorgini Archive in Follonica.

**1.69**_Vittorio Giorgini Archive in Follonica.

**1.70**_Vittorio Giorgini Archive in Follonica.

**1.71**_Photos by the author.

**1.72**_Vittorio Giorgini Archive in Follonica.

**1.73**_Vittorio Giorgini Archive in Follonica.

**1.74**_Vittorio Giorgini Archive in Follonica.

**1.75**_Vittorio Giorgini Archive in Follonica.

**1.76**_Vittorio Giorgini Archive in Follonica.

**1.77**_Vittorio Giorgini Archive in Follonica.

**1.78**_Vittorio Giorgini Archive in Follonica.

**1.79**_Vittorio Giorgini Archive in Follonica.

**1.80**_Photo by the author.

**1.81**_Vittorio Giorgini Archive in Follonica.

## CHAPTER 2

**2.1**_Courtesy of the Rechter Center of Architecture.

**2.2**_Anna Teut, ed., *Al Mansfeld: An Architect in Israel* (Berlin: Ernst & Sohn, 1998), 141.

**2.3**_The National Library of Israel, Jerusalem. Used with the architect's permission.

**2.4**_I.M. Goodovitch, *Architecturology: An Interim Report by I.M. Goodovitch* (London: George Allen & Unwin, 1968), 20, 22.

**2.5**_*Technion* 6, no. 2 (Summer 1970): 11.

**2.6**_As published in *Zodiac*, no. 19 (1969): 130–31.

**2.7**_As published in *Zodiac*, no. 19 (1969): 127.

**2.8**_As published in *Zodiac*, no. 19 (1969): 116–18.

**2.9**_As published in *Zodiac*, no. 16 (1966): 141.

**2.10**_As published in *Zodiac*, no. 16 (1966): 142.

**2.11**_Rafael Segal, *Unit, Pattern, Site: The Space Packed Architecture of Alfred Neumann 1949–1968* (PhD Dissertation, Princeton School of Architecture, 2011), 374. Images courtesy of Rafi Segal

**2.12**_Rafael Segal, *Unit, Pattern, Site: The Space Packed Architecture of Alfred Neumann 1949–1968* (PhD Dissertation, Princeton School of Architecture, 2011), 376. Images courtesy of Rafi Segal

**2.13**_Rafael Segal, *Unit, Pattern, Site: The Space Packed Architecture of Alfred Neumann 1949–1968* (PhD Dissertation, Princeton School of Architecture, 2011), 378. Images courtesy of Rafi Segal

**2.14**_Rafael Segal, *Unit, Pattern, Site: The Space Packed Architecture of Alfred Neumann 1949–1968* (PhD Dissertation, Princeton School of Architecture, 2011), 380. Images courtesy of Rafi Segal

**2.15**_Michaël Burt, *Spatial Arrangement and Polyhedra*

*with Curved Surfaces and Their Architectural Applications - Doctoral Thesis* (Haifa, Israel: Technion, Israel Institute of Technology, 1966), 23, 30. ©Michaël Burt's personal archive in Haifa. Retrieved from Faculty of Architecture & Town Planning Technion I.I.T Haifa 32000 Israel

**2.16**_Michaël Burt's personal archive in Haifa.

**2.17**_Michaël Burt's personal archive in Haifa.

**2.18**_*Technion* 4, no. 4 (October 1968): 27.

**2.19**_*L'Architecture d'Aujourd'hui* 34, no. 117 (November 1964): 100.

**2.20**_Peter Pearce, *Structure in Nature is a Strategy for Design* (Cambridge, MA: MIT Press, 1978), 163, © 1978 Peter Pearce, by permission of The MIT Press.

**2.21**_Peter Pearce, *Structure in Nature is a Strategy for Design* (Cambridge, MA: MIT Press, 1978), 124, © 1978 Peter Pearce, by permission of The MIT Press.

**2.22**_Alan H. Schoen, *Infinite Periodic Minimal Surfaces Without Self-Intersections* (Cambridge, MA: NASA Electronics Research Center, May 1970).

**2.23**_Alan H. Schoen, *Infinite Periodic Minimal Surfaces Without Self-Intersections* (Cambridge, MA: NASA Electronics Research Center, May 1970), 17.

**2.24**_Alan H. Schoen, *Infinite Periodic Minimal Surfaces Without Self-Intersections* (Cambridge, MA: NASA Electronics Research Center, May 1970), 7.

**2.25**_Alan H. Schoen, *Infinite Periodic Minimal Surfaces Without Self-Intersections* (Cambridge, MA: NASA Electronics Research Center, May 1970), 87.

**2.26**_Michaël Burt, *Spatial Arrangement and Polyhedra with Curved Surfaces and Their Architectural Applications - Doctoral Thesis* (Haifa, Israel: Technion, Israel Institute of Technology, 1966), 8–9. ©Michaël Burt's personal archive in Haifa. Retrieved from Faculty of Architecture & Town Planning Technion I.I.T Haifa 32000 Israel

**2.27**_Michaël Burt, *Spatial Arrangement and Polyhedra with Curved Surfaces and Their Architectural Applications - Doctoral Thesis* (Haifa, Israel: Technion, Israel Institute of Technology, 1966), 27, 34. ©Michaël Burt's personal archive in Haifa. Retrieved from Faculty of Architecture & Town Planning Technion I.I.T Haifa 32000 Israel

**2.28**_Michaël Burt, *Spatial Arrangement and Polyhedra with Curved Surfaces and Their Architectural Applications - Doctoral Thesis* (Haifa, Israel: Technion, Israel Institute of Technology, 1966), 37–38. ©Michaël Burt's personal archive in Haifa. Retrieved from Faculty of Architecture & Town Planning Technion I.I.T Haifa 32000 Israel

**2.29**_Michaël Burt, *Spatial Arrangement and Polyhedra with Curved Surfaces and Their Architectural Applications - Doctoral Thesis* (Haifa, Israel: Technion, Israel Institute of Technology, 1966), 39–40. ©Michaël Burt's personal archive in Haifa. Retrieved from Faculty of Architecture & Town Planning Technion I.I.T Haifa 32000 Israel

**2.30**_Michaël Burt, *Spatial Arrangement and Polyhedra with Curved Surfaces and Their Architectural Applications - Doctoral Thesis* (Haifa, Israel: Technion, Israel Institute of Technology, 1966), 42, 78. ©Michaël Burt's personal archive in Haifa. Retrieved from Faculty of Architecture & Town Planning Technion I.I.T Haifa 32000 Israel

**2.31**_Michaël Burt, *Spatial Arrangement and Polyhedra with Curved Surfaces and Their Architectural Applications - Doctoral Thesis* (Haifa, Israel: Technion, Israel Institute of Technology, 1966), 123, 125. ©Michaël Burt's personal archive in Haifa. Retrieved from Faculty of Architecture & Town Planning Technion I.I.T Haifa 32000 Israel

**2.32**_Michaël Burt, *Spatial Arrangement and Polyhedra with Curved Surfaces and Their Architectural Applications - Doctoral Thesis* (Haifa, Israel: Technion, Israel Institute of Technology, 1966), 98, 101. ©Michaël Burt's personal archive in Haifa. Retrieved from Faculty of Architecture & Town Planning Technion I.I.T Haifa 32000 Israel

**2.33**_Michaël Burt, *Spatial Arrangement and Polyhedra with Curved Surfaces and Their Architectural Applications - Doctoral Thesis* (Haifa, Israel: Technion, Israel Institute of Technology, 1966), 122. ©Michaël Burt's personal archive in Haifa. Retrieved from Faculty of Architecture & Town Planning Technion I.I.T Haifa 32000 Israel

**2.34**_Michaël Burt, *Spatial Arrangement and Polyhedra with Curved Surfaces and Their Architectural Applications - Doctoral Thesis* (Haifa, Israel: Technion, Israel Institute of Technology, 1966), 6, 12. ©Michaël Burt's personal archive in Haifa. Retrieved from Faculty of Architecture & Town Planning Technion I.I.T Haifa 32000 Israel

**2.35**_Michaël Burt, *Spatial Arrangement and Polyhedra with Curved Surfaces and Their Architectural Applications - Doctoral Thesis* (Haifa, Israel: Technion, Israel Institute of Technology, 1966), 11, 13. ©Michaël Burt's personal archive in Haifa. Retrieved from Faculty of Architecture & Town Planning Technion I.I.T Haifa 32000 Israel

**2.36**_Michaël Burt, *Spatial Arrangement and Polyhedra with Curved Surfaces and Their Architectural Applications - Doctoral Thesis* (Haifa, Israel: Technion, Israel Institute of Technology, 1966), 14. ©Michaël Burt's personal archive in Haifa. Retrieved from Faculty of Architecture & Town Planning Technion I.I.T Haifa 32000 Israel

**2.37**_*Zodiac*, no. 22 (1972): 163.

**2.38**_Michaël Burt, *Spatial Arrangement and Polyhedra with Curved Surfaces and Their Architectural Applications - Doctoral Thesis* (Haifa, Israel: Technion, Israel Institute of Technology, 1966), 18–19. ©Michaël Burt's personal archive in Haifa. Retrieved from Faculty of Architecture & Town Planning Technion I.I.T Haifa 32000 Israel

**2.39**_Michaël Burt, *Spatial Arrangement and Polyhedra with Curved Surfaces and Their Architectural Applications - Doctoral Thesis* (Haifa, Israel: Technion, Israel Institute of Technology, 1966), 15–16. ©Michaël Burt's personal archive in Haifa. Retrieved from Faculty of Architecture & Town Planning Technion I.I.T Haifa 32000 Israel

**2.40**_*Zodiac*, no. 22 (1972): 169.

**2.41**_Michaël Burt, Menachem Kleinmann, and Avraham Wachman, *Infinite Polyhedra*, 2nd ed. (1974; Haifa, Israel: Faculty of Architecture and Town Planning of the Technion, Israel Institute of Technology, 2005), III. ©Michaël Burt's personal archive in Haifa. Retrieved from Faculty of Architecture & Town Planning Technion I.I.T Haifa 32000 Israel

**2.42**_Michaël Burt, Menachem Kleinmann, and Avraham Wachman, *Infinite Polyhedra*, 2nd ed. (1974; Haifa, Israel: Faculty of Architecture and Town Planning of the Technion, Israel Institute of Technology, 2005), VIII. ©Michaël Burt's personal archive in Haifa. Retrieved from Faculty of Architecture & Town Planning Technion I.I.T Haifa 32000 Israel

**2.43**_Michaël Burt, Menachem Kleinmann, and Avraham Wachman, *Infinite Polyhedra*, 2nd ed. (1974; Haifa, Israel: Faculty of Architecture and Town Planning of the Technion, Israel Institute of Technology, 2005), IX. ©Michaël Burt's personal archive in Haifa. Retrieved from Faculty of Architecture & Town Planning Technion I.I.T Haifa 32000 Israel

**2.44**_Michaël Burt, Menachem Kleinmann, and Avraham Wachman, *Infinite Polyhedra*, 2nd ed. (1974; Haifa, Israel: Faculty of Architecture and Town Planning of the Technion, Israel Institute of Technology, 2005), 2, 12. ©Michaël Burt's personal archive in Haifa. Retrieved from Faculty of Architecture & Town Planning Technion I.I.T Haifa 32000 Israel

**2.45**_Michaël Burt, Menachem Kleinmann, and Avraham Wachman, *Infinite Polyhedra*, 2nd ed. (1974; Haifa, Israel: Faculty of Architecture and Town Planning of the Technion, Israel Institute of Technology, 2005), 17, 22. ©Michaël Burt's personal archive in Haifa. Retrieved from Faculty of Architecture & Town Planning Technion I.I.T Haifa 32000 Israel

**2.46**_Michaël Burt, Menachem Kleinmann, and Avraham Wachman, *Infinite Polyhedra*, 2nd ed. (1974; Haifa, Israel: Faculty of Architecture and Town Planning of the Technion, Israel Institute of Technology, 2005), 85, 87. ©Michaël Burt's personal archive in Haifa. Retrieved from Faculty of Architecture & Town Planning Technion I.I.T Haifa 32000 Israel

**2.47**_Michaël Burt, Menachem Kleinmann, and Avraham Wachman, *Infinite Polyhedra*, 2nd ed. (1974; Haifa, Israel: Faculty of Architecture and Town Planning of the Technion, Israel Institute of Technology, 2005), XV, XIX. ©Michaël Burt's personal archive in Haifa. Retrieved from Faculty of Architecture & Town Planning Technion I.I.T Haifa 32000 Israel

**2.48**_Michaël Burt, Menachem Kleinmann, and Avraham Wachman, *Infinite Polyhedra*, 2nd ed. (1974; Haifa, Israel: Faculty of Architecture and Town Planning of the Technion, Israel Institute of Technology, 2005), 15. ©Michaël Burt's personal archive in Haifa. Retrieved from Faculty of Architecture & Town Planning Technion I.I.T Haifa 32000 Israel

**2.49**_Michaël Burt, *The Periodic Table of The Polyhedral Universe* (Haifa, Israel: Technion, Israel Institute of Technology, 1996), 146–146a. ©Michaël Burt's personal archive in Haifa. Retrieved from Faculty of Architecture & Town Planning Technion I.I.T Haifa 32000 Israel

**2.50**_Michaël Burt, *The Periodic Table of The Polyhedral Universe* (Haifa, Israel: Technion, Israel Institute of Technology, 1996), 147–147a. ©Michaël Burt's personal archive in Haifa. Retrieved from Faculty of Architecture & Town Planning Technion I.I.T Haifa 32000 Israel

**2.51**_Michaël Burt, *The Periodic Table of The Polyhedral Universe* (Haifa, Israel: Technion, Israel Institute of Technology, 1996), 63. ©Michaël Burt's personal archive in Haifa. Retrieved from Faculty of Architecture & Town Planning Technion I.I.T Haifa 32000 Israel

**2.52**_Michaël Burt, *The Periodic Table of The Polyhedral Universe* (Haifa, Israel: Technion, Israel Institute of Technology, 1996), 63. ©Michaël Burt's personal archive in Haifa. Retrieved from Faculty of Architecture & Town Planning Technion I.I.T Haifa 32000 Israel

**2.53**_Michaël Burt, *The Periodic Table of The Polyhedral Universe* (Haifa, Israel: Technion, Israel Institute of Technology, 1996), 113. ©Michaël Burt's personal archive in Haifa. Retrieved from Faculty of Architecture & Town Planning Technion I.I.T Haifa 32000 Israel

**2.54**_Michaël Burt, *The Periodic Table of The Polyhedral Universe* (Haifa, Israel: Technion, Israel Institute of Technology, 1996), 67. ©Michaël Burt's personal archive in Haifa. Retrieved from Faculty of Architecture & Town Planning Technion I.I.T Haifa 32000 Israel

**2.55**_Michaël Burt, *The Periodic Table of The Polyhedral Universe* (Haifa, Israel: Technion, Israel Institute of Technology, 1996), 77. ©Michaël Burt's personal archive in Haifa. Retrieved from Faculty of Architecture & Town Planning Technion I.I.T Haifa 32000 Israel

**2.56**_Michaël Burt's personal archive in Haifa.

**2.57**_Michaël Burt's personal archive in Haifa.

**2.58**_Michaël Burt's personal archive in Haifa.

**2.59**_Michaël Burt's personal archive in Haifa.

**2.60**_Michaël Burt's personal archive in Haifa.

**2.61**_Michaël Burt's personal archive in Haifa.

**2.62**_Michaël Burt's personal archive in Haifa.

**2.63**_Michaël Burt's personal archive in Haifa.

**2.64**_Michaël Burt's personal archive in Haifa.

**2.65**_Michaël Burt's personal archive in Haifa.

**2.66**_Michaël Burt's personal archive in Haifa.

**2.67**_Michaël Burt's personal archive in Haifa.

**2.68**_Michaël Burt's personal archive in Haifa.

**2.69**_Michaël Burt's personal archive in Haifa.

**2.70**_Michaël Burt's personal archive in Haifa.

**2.71**_Michaël Burt's personal archive in Haifa.

**2.72**_Michaël Burt's personal archive in Haifa.

**2.73**_Michaël Burt's personal archive in Haifa.

**2.74**_Michaël Burt's personal archive in Haifa.

**2.75**_Michaël Burt's personal archive in Haifa.

**2.76**_Michaël Burt's personal archive in Haifa.

**2.77**_Michaël Burt's personal archive in Haifa.

**2.78**_Photo by Hiroshi Ueda.

**2.79**_Photo by Hiroshi Ueda.

**2.80_**Michaël Burt, Menachem Kleinmann, and Avraham Wachman, *Infinite Polyhedra*, 2nd ed. (1974; Haifa, Israel: Faculty of Architecture and Town Planning of the Technion, Israel Institute of Technology, 2005), 95. ©Michaël Burt's personal archive in Haifa. Retrieved from Faculty of Architecture & Town Planning Technion I.I.T Haifa 32000 Israel

**2.81_**Michaël Burt's personal archive in Haifa.

**2.82_**Michaël Burt, *Spatial Arrangement and Polyhedra with Curved Surfaces and Their Architectural Applications - Doctoral Thesis* (Haifa, Israel: Technion, Israel Institute of Technology, 1966), 39. ©Michaël Burt's personal archive in Haifa. Retrieved from Faculty of Architecture & Town Planning Technion I.I.T Haifa 32000 Israel

**2.83_**Michaël Burt's personal archive in Haifa.

**2.84_**Michaël Burt's personal archive in Haifa.

**2.85_**Michaël Burt, Menachem Kleinmann, and Avraham Wachman, *Infinite Polyhedra*, 2nd ed. (1974; Haifa, Israel: Faculty of Architecture and Town Planning of the Technion, Israel Institute of Technology, 2005), 50, 15. ©Michaël Burt's personal archive in Haifa. Retrieved from Faculty of Architecture & Town Planning Technion I.I.T Haifa 32000 Israel

**2.86_**Michaël Burt, Menachem Kleinmann, and Avraham Wachman, *Infinite Polyhedra*, 2nd ed. (1974; Haifa, Israel: Faculty of Architecture and Town Planning of the Technion, Israel Institute of Technology, 2005), 91. ©Michaël Burt's personal archive in Haifa. Retrieved from Faculty of Architecture & Town Planning Technion I.I.T Haifa 32000 Israel

**2.87_**Michaël Burt, Menachem Kleinmann, and Avraham Wachman, *Infinite Polyhedra*, 2nd ed. (1974; Haifa, Israel: Faculty of Architecture and Town Planning of the Technion, Israel Institute of Technology, 2005), 16. ©Michaël Burt's personal archive in Haifa. Retrieved from Faculty of Architecture & Town Planning Technion I.I.T Haifa 32000 Israel

**2.88_**Michaël Burt's personal archive in Haifa.

**2.89_**Michaël Burt's personal archive in Haifa.

**2.90_**Michaël Burt's personal archive in Haifa.

**2.91_**Michaël Burt's personal archive in Haifa.

**2.92_**Michaël Burt's personal archive in Haifa.

## CHAPTER 3

**3.1_***Ove Arup 1895–1988*, 83. Photo of the spherical model ©ARUP. Photo of Sydney Opera House under construction, unknown photographer.

**3.2_**©Riba Collections

**3.3_**©Max Dupain/Arup. Retrieved from: Mitchell Library, State Library of New South Wales

**3.4_**Peter Rice, *An Engineer Imagines* (London: Artemis, 1998), 113. @Batsford Books

**3.5_**Christian Brensing, "Frei Otto and Ove Arup: A case of Mutual Inspiration." In *Frei Otto, Complete Works: Lightweight Construction, Natural Design* (Basel: Birkhäuser, 2005), 106.

**3.6_1_**Rainer Barthel, "Natural Forms – Architectural Forms." In *Frei Otto, Complete Works: Lightweight Construction, Natural Design* (Basel: Birkhäuser, 2005), 28–29. Illustration by Gabriele Möck/ Holger Schmidt: "Verzweigungen mit Fäden," IL-Student work Nr. 04/82.

**3.6_2_**Rainer Barthel, "Natural Forms – Architectural Forms." In *Frei Otto, Complete Works: Lightweight Construction, Natural Design* (Basel: Birkhäuser, 2005), 28–29. ©ILEK, Institut für Leichtbau Entwerfen und Konstruieren, Stuttgart University Archive

**3.7_**Peter Rice, *An Engineer Imagines* (London: Artemis, 1998), 96. @Batsford Books

**3.8_**Balmond Studio archive in London.

**3.9_**Balmond Studio archive in London.

**3.10_**Balmond Studio archive in London.

**3.11_**Balmond Studio archive, London.

**3.12_**Balmond Studio archive in London.

**3.13_**Balmond Studio archive in London.

**3.14_**Cecil Balmond, "El Huevo Mecánico: Luces y Cubiertas En El Congrexpo de Lille," *Arquitectura Viva*, no. 39 (November 1994): 44.

**3.15_**Balmond Studio archive in London.

**3.16_**Balmond Studio archive in London.

**3.17_**Balmond Studio archive in London.

**3.18_**Balmond Studio archive in London.

**3.19_**Paul Klee, "Towards a Theory of Form Production," in *The Thinking Eye (The Notebooks of Paul Klee, v. 1)* (NY/Lund Humphries, London: G. Wittenborn, 1961), 24. Edited by Jürg Spiller.

**3.20_**Paul Klee, "Towards a Theory of Form Production," in *The Thinking Eye (The Notebooks of Paul Klee, v. 1)* (NY/Lund Humphries, London: G. Wittenborn, 1961), 32. Edited by Jürg Spiller.

**3.21_**Paul Klee, "Towards a Theory of Form Production," in *The Thinking Eye (The Notebooks of Paul Klee, v. 1)* (NY/Lund Humphries, London: G. Wittenborn, 1961), 23. Edited by Jürg Spiller.

**3.22_**Cecil Balmond, *Informal* (London: Prestel, 2002), 372–73.

**3.23_**Cecil Balmond, *Informal* (London: Prestel, 2002), 378–79.

**3.24_**Cecil Balmond, *Informal* (London: Prestel, 2002), 120–21.

**3.25_**Cecil Balmond, *Informal* (London: Prestel, 2002), 388–89.

**3.26_**Bill Hillier, *The Social Logic of Space* (Cambridge: Cambridge University Press, 1984), 35. ©Cambridge University Press Reproduced with permission of the Licensor through PLSclear.

**3.27_**October 1972 issue of *Architectural Design* guest-edited by Royston Landau.

**3.28_**John Frazer, *An Evolutionary Architecture* (London: Architectural Association Publications, 1995), 47. ©AA Publications.

**3.29**_Charles Jencks, *The Architecture of the Jumping Universe* (Hoboken, NJ: Wiley, 1995), 78.

**3.30**_Balmond Studio archive in London.

**3.31**_Balmond Studio archive in London.

**3.32**_Balmond Studio archive in London.

**3.33**_Balmond Studio archive in London.

**3.34**_Cecil Balmond, "Stirling Style," *Building Design*, no. 807 (October 1986): 34.

**3.35**_Balmond Studio archive in London.

**3.36**_Balmond Studio archive in London.

**3.37**_Balmond Studio archive in London.

**3.38**_Balmond Studio archive in London.

**3.39**_Balmond Studio archive in London.

**3.40**_Balmond Studio archive in London.

**3.41**_Balmond Studio archive in London.

**3.42**_Balmond Studio archive in London.

**3.43**_Balmond Studio archive in London.

**3.44**_Balmond Studio archive in London.

**3.45**_Balmond Studio archive in London.

**3.46**_Balmond Studio archive in London.

**3.47**_Balmond Studio archive in London.

**3.48**_Balmond Studio archive in London.

**3.49**_Balmond Studio archive in London.

**3.50**_Balmond Studio archive in London.

**3.51**_Balmond Studio archive in London.

**3.52**_Balmond Studio archive in London.

**3.53**_Balmond Studio archive in London.

**3.54**_Balmond Studio archive in London.

**3.55**_Balmond Studio archive in London.

**3.56**_Balmond Studio archive in London.

**3.57**_Balmond Studio archive in London.

**3.58**_Balmond Studio archive in London.

**3.59**_Balmond Studio archive in London.

**3.60**_Balmond Studio archive in London.

**3.61**_Balmond Studio archive in London.

**3.62**_Balmond Studio archive in London.

**3.63**_Balmond Studio archive in London.

**3.64**_Balmond Studio archive in London.

**3.65**_Balmond Studio archive in London.

**3.66**_Nobuyuki Yoshida, ed., *Cecil Balmond, A+U Special Issue* (2006): 138.

**3.67**_Balmond Studio archive in London

**3.68**_Balmond Studio archive in London

**3.69**_Balmond Studio archive in London

**3.70**_Balmond Studio archive in London

**3.71**_Balmond Studio archive in London

**3.72**_Balmond Studio archive in London

**3.73**_Balmond Studio archive in London

**3.74**_Balmond Studio archive in London

**3.75**_Balmond Studio archive in London

**3.76**_Balmond Studio archive in London

**3.77**_Balmond Studio archive in London

**3.78**_Balmond Studio archive in London

**3.79**_Balmond Studio archive in London

**3.80**_Balmond Studio archive in London

**3.81**_Balmond Studio archive in London

**3.82**_Balmond Studio archive in London

**3.83**_Balmond Studio archive in London

**3.84**_Balmond Studio archive in London

**3.85**_Balmond Studio archive in London

**3.86**_Balmond Studio archive in London

**3.87**_Balmond Studio archive in London

**3.88**_Balmond Studio archive in London

**3.89**_Balmond Studio archive in London

**3.90**_Balmond Studio archive in London

**3.91**_Cecil Balmond, *Informal* (London: Prestel, 2002), 206–7.

**3.92**_Cecil Balmond, *Informal* (London: Prestel, 2002), 204–5.

**3.93**_Balmond Studio archive in London

**3.94**_Balmond Studio archive in London

**3.95**_Balmond Studio archive in London

**3.96**_Balmond Studio archive in London

**Dispositional Intelligence in Architecture**

Published by
Actar Publishers, New York, Barcelona
www.actar.com

Author
José Aragüez

Graphic Design
Marga Gibert, Actar Pro

Copy editing and proofreading
Sonia Hill

Printing and binding
Arlequin SL

All rights reserved
© edition: Actar Publishers, editors
© texts: their author
© design, drawings, illustrations, and photographs: their authors

Distribution
Actar D, Inc. New York, Barcelona.

New York
440 Park Avenue South, 17th Floor
New York, NY 10016, USA
T +1 2129662207
salesnewyork@actar-d.com

Barcelona
Roca i Batlle 2
08023 Barcelona, Spain
T +34 933 282 183
eurosales@actar-d.com

Indexing
English ISBN: 978-1-63840-132-2
Library of Congress Control Number: 2024941248
Printed in Spain
Publication date: September 2024

This work is subject to copyright. All rights are reserved, on all or part of the material, specifically translation rights, reprinting, re-use of illustrations, recitation, broadcasting, reproduction on microfilm or other media, and storage in databases. For use of any kind, permission of the copyright owner must be obtained.

Every effort has been made to supply complete and correct illustration credits. In the event of errors or omissions, please contact the publisher so that corrections can be made in any subsequent edition.

This publication is made possible in part by a grant from the Barr Ferree Foundation Fund for Publication, Department of Art and Archaeology, Princeton University.